HOW TO PLAN, CONTRACT, AND BUILD YOUR OWN HOME

Richard M. Scutella
Dave Heberle

Illustrations by
Jay Marcinowski

Fourth Edition

McGraw-Hill

New York   Chicago   San Francisco
Lisbon   London   Madrid   Mexico City
Milan   New Delhi   San Juan   Seoul
Singapore   Sydney   Toronto

The McGraw-Hill Companies

Cataloging-in Publication data is on file with the Library of Congress.

2 3 4 5 6 7 8 9 0   DOC/DOC   0 1 0 9 8 7 6

ISBN 0-07-144885-3

The sponsoring editor for this book was Cary Sullivan and the production supervisor was Pamela A. Pelton. The art director for the cover was Handel Low. It was set in Melior by Patricia Wallenburg.

Printed and bound by RR Donnelley.

 This book is printed on recycled, acid-free paper containing a minimum of 50% recycled de-inked fiber.

McGraw-Hill books are available at special quantity discounts to use as premiums and sales promotions, or for use in corporate training programs. For more information, please write to the Director of Special Sales, McGraw-Hill, Two Penn Plaza, New York, NY 10121. Or contact your local bookstore.

CONTENTS

Over twenty years have passed since the editors at McGraw-Hill received the manuscript for the first edition of this book. Back then, they measured it up and declared it was more than they had bargained for—both in words and illustrations. So everyone looked at it, hoping to find chapters, or parts of chapters, that could be cut. After a while, it became evident that the book would be more helpful to its readers as it stood. So nothing was cut and the publisher kindly agreed to put out a longer and more profusely illustrated version than originally planned.

In a sense, the same thing happened with the second edition, which came out in 1991. Except for a few minor changes, little of the original material was deleted, because almost everything still held true. At that time, additional information was included in many chapters. The book became thicker, packed with new material.

The third edition, published in 1999, received a general overhaul, with numerous chapter upgrades and many new sections. Manufacturers continued to get better at what they do—designing and making innovative home products. Outdated information was stricken from the previous edition, replaced by discussions about better components and construction techniques that gave homebuilders more options than ever before.

That leads us to this, the fourth edition. Like the others, this edition also contains more information than the publisher expected. But we couldn't help it. Current conditions demanded a concentrated focus on energy conservation. Why? Have you fueled up your car, van or truck lately? If so, remember when paying $1.50 per gallon unleaded seemed like robbery? Today that would be a bargain. The sad truth is that fuel costs—including home heating and cooling prices—are likely to keep rising. They may back down a bit, for a while, but competition for raw materials and energy is heating up as countries such as China, India, and others industrialize to supply modern living conditions and goods to their citizens. To help ease the pain of rising energy prices, the fourth edition of this book features practical information on construction details that will save homeowners energy and money. Lots of energy and money. Realistic, cost-effective ways of including energy-saving components in your new home are discussed in practically every chapter of this edition.

But saving energy and money are not the only reasons to take charge of your homebuilding process. We live—now, more so than ever—in an age of information. We know more about practically everything. Motion pictures and television, supported by the print media, bring video and audio segments of war, ethnic atrocities, natural disasters, and political unrest into our very living rooms. Cable and satellite television carry 24-hour programming on nearly every imaginable subject. You want round the clock coverage of the financial markets worldwide? How about an unending succession of cooking shows? You'd like health, medicine, and wellness? Or fishing, golf, professional wrestling, country western music, rock videos? Do you like romance movies? Science fiction? Home shopping networks? Travel channels? Court TV? News headlines? History? Cartoons? Science? Weather? You name it. There are channels that focus on nothing but home and garden. Watch a side-to-side split-level from planning stage to move-in condition. The Internet, which has literally come of age since the first edition of this book, can quickly tap what seems to be an endless supply of details about any topic. Personal computers, ever more powerful and accessible, run CD-ROMs containing enormous amounts of information, which will help you select from various products to consider for your home. The Internet will also supply information on products available from numerous manufacturers. In short, there's an incredible amount of information out there, which can be had for the asking.

To acquire such a cosmopolitan array of information, we've had to trade off much of the basic knowledge that our fathers and their fathers and grandfathers had once known. Granted, they had learned such knowledge not by choice, but by necessity. A few hundred years ago, for example, people grew their own food, doctored their own sick, and built their own homes—with their own hands. They took care of all their basic needs by themselves.

Thanks to the collective progress realized over the past few centuries, much of that all-around knowledge has become of little use to the average person. How many people must still be able to shoe a plowhorse, dig their own well, deliver their own babies, or even teach their own children how to read and write?

Today, if you're an accountant, you're an accountant. You have to keep up with an avalanche of changing accounting information to service your clients. If you're a farmer, you're a farmer, and you have to subscribe to the latest agricultural techniques to be a success. Or, if you're a builder of houses, you're a builder of houses.

If you can't perform in whatever business you're in, and if you don't really know the ins and outs of the trade, you'll be supplanted by other professionals who do. Specialists who keep up-to-date with the evolving nature of their business will acquire the competitive edge needed to stay ahead of their peers. Consequently, people no longer have the time, need, or inclination to acquire many of the basic skills our forefathers found unavoidable.

Take the subject of houses, for example. Because the public has largely turned the job of housebuilding over to a group of professional builders, not many people really understand exactly what a house consists of, or how all the parts must mesh together to make a satisfactory dwelling.

And that's the reason for this book. The idea is simple enough: by understanding houses, you can better arrive at an understanding house—one that suits you perfectly, one that is constructed to give maximum enjoyment and value with minimum investment.

Everybody has to live somewhere, that's a fact. You can live at someone else's place for free, with parents or benevolent friends. Or you can make do at a place provided by an accommodating employer. You can reside at someone else's place and pay rent. Then again, you can choose to live in something you own. And at some point in their lives, most people prefer the latter option. This book has been written for people in search of a modern home situated in either a subdivision down the street or on five acres out in the boondocks. Although it focuses on new construction, it also proposes what to look for in existing houses, new or old.

Without knowing better, people considering the purchase of a new house will approach one or more builders with a sketch and floor plan ripped out of a magazine. Then they'll ask the builder how much he'll charge to complete that same house for them. Depending on the amounts and quality of materials used, or rather, depending on what specifications or "specs" are followed, the cost of a 2000-square-foot two-story house can vary by tens of thousands of dollars. By providing only a simple generic floor plan as a building guide, eager buyers overlook important pre-construction choices that should, in fact, be made by the buyers themselves. Instead of exercising their own wishes in the planning and construction of their new house, these trusting buyers leave consequential decisions completely up to the builder.

Another irony is that, when faced with such a complex and expensive task as the purchase of a new house, most people remain interested merely in the basic floor plan, the amount of square footage of living space, the appearance of the exterior sheathing, and other incidentals such as the color of the flooring and carpeting and the style and stain of kitchen cabinets. Rarely do they care what thickness the outer walls will be, or on which side of the house the garage should be located. They leave detail after detail to the builder's discretion.

Naturally, in this competitive business, the builder provides what the buyer wants in a manner most advantageous to the builder himself. He tends to use materials that he's been using on other houses he's built, and he probably gets them in bulk, at a discount. Unless otherwise requested, this usually means he'll provide the absolute minimum specs needed to satisfy local building codes, even when, for a few dollars more, substantial long-range savings and additional conveniences can be enjoyed by the buyers.

Most minimum building codes can be satisfied with economy-grade materials. "Economy grade" is a misleading term at best, because materials in that class actually end up costing *more* than materials of high quality, due to frequent maintenance and repairs needed and shorter life spans. That can mean early replacements, all at extra cost and inconvenience to the homeowner. And marginal products, because they're less durable, can lead to a very annoying and even uncomfortable house. Unfortunately, marginal quality materials are found not only in low-priced houses, but in many high-priced dwellings as well.

High-quality flooring, paneling, wiring, heating, and many other products cost only a little more, by and large, than the same products of marginal quality. Certainly, the installation costs are about the same in either case; an identical amount of labor is required to put down a new floor of the best or worst vinyl. All things considered, studies indicate that the initial price of a house built with high-quality materials will run only about 8 to 10 percent more than an identical economygrade dwelling.

The argument to go with quality materials is a persuasive one. But even before that comes the question: do you want to build a new house or move into an existing one?

It's entirely possible to find an older or recently built house that meets most of your needs, and is constructed similar to the guidelines described in the following chapters. Such houses can be difficult to locate, but in many cases, due to circumstances of the present owners, you can get more house for the money, but not without certain trade-offs: the house might be in a location you don't like, or it might have everything you asked for *except* a basement, a den, or a two-car garage.

With new construction you have the opportunity to custom design your own house. With new construction you'll end up with more built-in conveniences, with better insulation and more energy efficient appliances and heating/cooling systems. There are also less repairs to worry about and less time spent maintaining things, especially with many of today's maintenance-free items. New homes generally require lower down payments, with better financing terms available to owners. Kitchens can be loaded with modern appliances and built-ins. There are better roofing materials, flooring, easy-care carpeting, windows, and exterior sheathings. And it's also a nice feeling to move into a house knowing that you and your family will be the first to live there. It has that wonderful sweet new-house smell of sawdust, plaster, and carpeting.

New homes are clean to the eye and touch, and hold their value well when soundly constructed. Everything is under warranty. You know exactly what went into the place, having periodically inspected its erection. You know that it's a structurally sound dwelling, built with the latest high-quality, energy-efficient materials.

No matter what you decide to go with—new construction or an existing home—buying any house is a major investment. Let's face it, finding or arriving at the right house for you can be a tough (though enjoyable) process. It's not like buying a stereo, for example, where you can walk into a stereo store and listen to different brands and different models, turn them on, one after another. You can pick up a *Consumer Reports* and read reviews on them. You can shop for the same models all over town.

But a house? The two biggest words in real estate have always been "buyer beware," and for no small reason. There are endless possibilities open to house buyers and endless pitfalls.

A house is a lot more than a "hedge against inflation" or a pleasant alternative to paying rent. And sure, owning property will probably give you the urge to become involved with the community, and will probably encourage you to send out roots. But most of all, a house is a dwelling in which human drama unfolds. Children grow up in houses.

Marriages and other relationships flourish or flounder in them, in unique environments created within the home's outer shell. In homes we grow up, learn things, spend time together, eat, play, party, laugh, fight, cry, make love, pray, and entertain one another. Homes reflect our personalities and uniqueness, and they deserve to be acquired as the result of careful deliberation instead of happenstance.

Everybody has to live somewhere. If you have a say in the matter, then exercise it. Get involved with selecting what you're going to live in. It only makes sense. Why settle for less? Why put up with a building that doesn't meet your and your family's basic requirements?

Especially if within those same means you have the ability to attain a dwelling far superior, with an optimal plan custom tailored to your needs.

Talking new construction, you have to familiarize yourself with building jargon (it's not tough) and prepare yourself for entering into a close and beneficial relationship with a general contractor who builds houses for a living. You must understand the advantages and disadvantages of the various types of homes available in order to make an educated choice: ranch, Cape Cod, two-story, split foyer, or split-level.

You should know how to arrange the rooms you choose for the greatest convenience of both initial construction and everyday living. Beyond that, you should figure out if you might want to enlarge the house at a later date. If so, a few relatively minor modifications up front can mean a lot of savings later. You need to know how to match the home you want to a building site. And you need to know additional do's and don'ts along the way. In fact, in many cases, just knowing what *not* to do will lead you to a correct choice. It's a complex mix of qualities and factors that can make a difference between ending up with an extremely pleasant and valuable home, or a disaster.

But don't worry. Again, it's not that hard to acquire a lot more house than you ever thought you could afford—one built with conveniences and quality not usually included with your neighbor's house. And it will be a lot of fun.

To get the most out of this book, first read the table of contents for a general idea of what's covered. Then take it a chapter at a time, section by section, at a leisurely pace. Make notes on the numerous ideas that will result in energy savings.

After you've read the entire book, you can proceed with confidence that you are sufficiently prepared. Arrive at the house you want—in your mind and on paper. Use the checklists and summary points throughout the book so you don't ignore any important considerations.

Determine what construction costs are running by going to open houses and by asking builders and real estate agents at those open houses. Realtors can provide valuable and free financial information, perhaps a helpful summary of mortgage rates in your area. And they can be instrumental in putting together packages requiring creative financing (especially when a sale hinges upon you getting the loan).

Although no one person could possibly use every shred of information contained in this book, together the details provide a comprehensive backdrop from which readers can draw whatever is needed to help illuminate their own specific situations.

Okay. Enough talk. Now let's get into it. Let's begin with some style.

What to Build

To arrive at the best-possible home for yourself, first take a step back—away from houses and house construction in general—and review some basic concepts about what a home can and should contain. You need to think about the pros and cons of the various house styles and types available, and how you can arrive at floor plans that will most favorably suit your present and future needs. You should realize that features can be built into a new house, at minor cost, that will permit efficient and convenient expansion of living space years later. And you should also be mildly familiar with typical house construction plans, prints, and drawings.

It's best to arrive at your "ideal" house on your own, with the help of books or articles, before approaching builders who will naturally, even with good intentions, lead you toward house types they prefer or think that you should prefer. But if you already have a building site picked out, and your brother-in-law happens to be a builder, so be it. Still, read the chapters about what to build. If your initial plans (or those of your brother-in-law) are correct, then you'll be able to proceed full of confidence. On the other hand, if you discover that a different type of house would be better for you, don't let anyone tell you otherwise.

Don't be one of the thousands of home buyers who are just on the receiving end of a new house, passively accepting whatever happens along. Let there be conscious reasons for everything you end up with.

A House Divided

The modern house consists of at least six main types of areas:

- Living and Recreation Space. In any one dwelling, this can include a living room, family room, den, library, music room, sunroom, or other rooms and niches planned for entertainment, relaxation, hobbies, or study.

- Food Preparation Space. The kitchen ranks number one here, followed by additional food storage areas such as nearby walk-in pantries and "satellite" serving platforms, bars, and grills conveniently located in family rooms and other living and recreational spaces.

- Dining Space. Depending on the floor plan, this can be a separate formal dining room adjacent to the kitchen, or an open dining area having the kitchen on one side and the living room or family room on another. Or, when economy is desired, a portion of the actual kitchen itself can be reserved for a dining table or booth.

- Bathing and Washing Space. This means bathrooms, both full and half, plus toilets, hand sinks, showers, saunas, and indoor hot tubs.

- Sleeping and Dressing Space. Bedrooms, dressing nooks, and related storage areas.

- Service and Storage Space. Everything else in a house fits in here: basement, attic, stairs, hallways, laundry rooms, and garages.

LIVING AND RECREATION SPACE

We've come a long way since our primitive ancestors stalked through forests in search of daily sustenance. Indeed, prehistoric life was tough. There were no plumbers, no cable televisions, no supermarkets, doctors, or economists. Instead you had one continuous struggle against the elements, with little time to do anything but attempt to satisfy the most basic of needs. And even if the typical primitive *had* the time, he or she still wouldn't have known how to put a formal living room to good use.

Okay, so they did have dens—in the strictest sense of the word (Fig. 1.1). Back then a shelter was just that—a few walls against which to huddle. There was a roof for protection from rain, sleet, and snow, under which early humans could hunker down, relatively safe from predators.

Even though our primitive forerunners had the protection of rough shelters, they were still lucky just to make it through their teens in one piece. In fact, as late as the early 1900s, the expected American life span was only 46 years for men and 49 for women. That didn't leave much free time for recreation.

FIGURE 1.1

A primitive den.

Thanks to revolutionary medical and pharmaceutical advances, look how long people are living today. Consider also, especially during the latter half of this century, how work weeks have grown shorter and family sizes smaller. Automobiles, trucks, and aircraft have given us mobility, and sped up the delivery of time-saving conveniences to our doors. New leisure time has created a demand that greater attention be paid to the living and recreational space in modern dwellings.

Simply put, a house's living and recreation rooms should contain enough space to satisfy the needs of its occupants. It means enough space for general and specific leisure activities such as entertaining friends, watching television, listening to music, practicing musical instruments, gaming, reading, studying, writing, bookkeeping, children's play, and plain old relaxing . . . all in comfort, and, if need be, privacy.

Living and recreation rooms must also be adequate in size to hold sufficient furniture for comfortable seating. At the same time they should be large enough to permit the rearrangement of major pieces of furniture into a variety of positions while still maintaining good traffic circulation within the room.

Depending on a dwelling's size and floor plan, living and recreational space may be planned as a number of individual rooms, or may be distilled into a single, all-purpose area.

The Living Room

If one all-purpose room is all you desire, or all you can afford at the outset, that room should probably be the living room. At one time referred to as a parlor, the living room was originally designed to entertain guests in a formal fashion. The living room should be at a quiet place for reading and conversation. It should be close to the front door, next to dining space, and away from sleeping areas. There should also be a closet outside the living room, near the front door, for coats, hats, boots and other items. There are two main types of living rooms: traditional and open.

A traditional living room is a room placed away from the kitchen and other work or recreational rooms in the house. This out-of-the-way placement allows at least two separate entertainment centers (including the kitchen in a smaller house) so that more than one family member can plan activities with outside friends at the same time, without infringing on each other's privacy. The traditional living room is usually situated at a dead-end location to minimize unwanted interruptions and through traffic. Doors can be considered for additional privacy.

As mentioned earlier, if the house you plan will not accommodate other recreation rooms beyond a living room, then consider that your living room will have to be used for whatever leisure-time activities you enjoy. When a single room must serve a variety of functions, a more open type of room is often the most practical choice. In fact, due to the overall reduction of square footage in recent years for cost reasons, open planning is becoming increasingly important because it lends the impression of maximum space for the money. In fact, it does give you more square footage of usable space, because there are less walls to take up space. Open planning serves well in the more contemporary and expensive plans, and in households having few or no children, where privacy is not as important as it would be to a large family. However, a danger in open-type rooms is that spaces must be carefully planned so they don't appear jumbled and haphazardly thrown together.

The Family Room

A second recreational room that has grown popular in the past few decades is the family room. Instead of wearing out the living room furnishings, informal activities such as children's play, listening to music, and lounging on sofas while watching television can be comfortably pursued in a more casual environment.

A home that contains both a living room and a family room will typically have the main television set placed in the family room. And like it or not, television has become a mainstay in most modern households. On average, the tube is on for over seven hours per day, 365 days per year in every household that has one. Videocassette players are practically as common as toasters.

Because people want the television where groups of family members and guests can watch it comfortably, it has a definite impact on interior decoration. This means a wall or corner is effectively removed from the placement of seating and other furniture. Thus, when the room is originally sized and laid out, the television placement should be taken into account: preferably some spot where the glaring sun will not interfere with viewing.

If you plan to have a separate family room in addition to a living room, consider locating it next to the kitchen, where only a few steps will separate food and drink from leisure-time activities, and where a parent can still work in the kitchen while supervising children at play.

Another desirable feature for a family room is an outdoors access, commonly provided by sliding glass doors that lead to a patio, terrace, or deck. Although some people add doors to the family room to seclude it from the rest of the house, most active families prefer an open-type plan allowing easy movement to and from the kitchen and fostering efficient communications between the two areas.

Fireplaces

Whether you decide upon one living room/family room combination, or multiple living and recreation rooms, one feature to consider—even in the warmer climates—is a fireplace.

When planned from the beginning, one or more fireplaces can be integrated in the house in such a manner as to save space, materials, and money. For instance, if the back of a fireplace is located inside the garage, you can reduce the number of expensive finishing bricks or stones normally needed to construct an outside wall chimney. Not only that, but instead of dissipating heat outside through an outer chimney wall, some heat will radiate into the garage, where it will do some good. The ash cleanout door can be built so it opens at a convenient height within the garage, where messy ashes and grits can be removed and disposed of in one efficient step. No more trudging across carpets, or climbing stairs.

If you plan to put a fireplace in a first-floor living or family room, consider two other points: First, if your house will have a basement, do you plan on doing much socializing there? If so, you might want to include a second fireplace. Then an economical way would be to align both fireplaces one right over another.

Second, due to their very nature, fireplaces demand comfortable seating around them, and require freedom from internal traffic and other interference. Therefore a door next to a fireplace is poor design. Anyone entering or exiting the room through such an access becomes an immediate intruder, an interruption to the conversation group. A door near a fireplace also prevents the placement of furniture on that side of the hearth, creating wasted space that in turn will effectively shrink the amount of usable space in a large living or family room down to that of a much smaller area.

Windows and Glass Doors

An important feature common to all living and recreation rooms are windows and glass sliding doors. While you should make sure that living and recreation rooms are bright and cheerful from natural light, and plenty of ventilation is provided, too much glass—especially sliding glass doors and floor-to-ceiling windows—can pose a number of irritating problems:

1. If too much wall space consists of glass there might be no place to arrange furniture unless you decide to block off some of the glass with a piece of furniture such as a sofa or plush chair.

2. If you deliberately decide to place furniture in front of glass, consider how the furniture will look from outside, too.

3. Remember that too many glass walls will severely restrict possibilities for hanging pictures and other decorative works of art.

4. When you entertain in glass-lined living or recreation rooms, large panes of glass can be distracting. During the day, people find themselves gazing out the windows instead of paying attention to the conversation, and at night huge panes of blackened glass make certain individuals uncomfortable: they feel that they're being watched from the outside.

The inclination to overuse glass is especially strong on sites having dramatic views, when the owners are naturally moved toward taking full advantage of those views. In this situation you must be careful not to get carried away. Instead, strike a happy balance between beautiful views and functional rooms.

Along the same lines, in most settings (except in rural locations where a house is tucked back from the main road), avoid an oversized picture window in the front of the house. Such a window invariably gets covered with drapes or blinds anyway, for privacy. When it's not covered, the residents feel like goldfish in a bowl. And typically, all that can be seen through the front window is passing traffic. The larger picture windows are far more productive when placed at the side or back of the house, facing a private patio, terrace, yard, or other more intimate and less "public" views.

Built-Ins

To make for a more aesthetically pleasing appearance, it's wise to include sufficient built-ins for living and recreation rooms, especially to accommodate the items you want to store there. Books, records, mementos, knickknacks, card tables, and even fireplace wood are a few common objects to keep in mind.

Built-in bookcases and shelves are installed most efficiently when the carpenters and woodwork stainers are putting up the rest of the house trim.

Patios

Another recreation space to consider when planning a new house is a patio. Because it can easily become an important part of your home living experience, a patio deserves the same careful thought that goes into the arrangement of your interior living and recreation areas.

When pinching dollars, settle first for the foundation and concrete slab, and plan to add a roof, privacy screen, and other conveniences later. Location is a major factor for enjoyment of an open or screened-in patio or deck. Remember that an open concrete patio can get as hot as a city street when it bakes in the sun.

Other Living and Recreation Rooms

Rooms sometimes built into a house are a library, den or study, and a music or other hobby room. There are darkrooms for amateur photographers, billiard rooms for would-be Mosconis, sewing rooms, trophy rooms, and rooms designed specifically for personal computers and video games. These are special areas in a house which, depending on the interests of you and your family, can greatly enhance the total living experience.

FOOD PREPARATION SPACE

For the bachelor who scratches his head in bewilderment while attempting to boil water for instant coffee, a kitchen complete with the appliances of his dreams might consist of a frost-free refrigerator, a microwave oven, a double-slotted toaster, and the plainest of sinks. Others, individuals who fancy themselves a step or two below award-winning French chefs, need wide expanses of counter space, double ovens, microwaves, electric grills and barbecues, three-tubbed stainless steel sinks, boxes of hand appliances, and piles of pots, pans, and multipurpose utensils.

Food is always being highlighted by the media. Sales of cookbooks and culinary magazines have reached best-selling proportions. Talk shows serve up celebrity cooks. Medical studies stress how a healthy diet can ward off heart disease, stress, and even cancer. And there's no denying that everyone has to eat. It's not something we can elect to pass up.

In any household, the primary food preparation area is the kitchen.

Kitchen Size

The overall size of your kitchen should depend on the following points:

1. The size of your family and the number of individuals in your family who like to cook. Usually, the bigger the family, the bigger the kitchen. And don't exclude the children. Psychologists say that youngsters, especially teenagers, should be encouraged to learn how to cook, and that culinary creativity helps a child's overall development.

2. Do family members and many friends and guests tend to congregate in the kitchen? Then make the kitchen large enough to accommodate plenty of seating space.

3. Do you approve of or insist upon having meals other than breakfast in the kitchen? If you prefer nightly suppers in the kitchen, then you'd better plan an eat-in kitchen arrangement, with space for a table and chairs. If only breakfast will be served there, then a bar at which three or four people can comfortably sit is likely to be all the eating space you'll need.

4. What are your shopping habits? If you prefer to go long periods of time between shopping, you'll need ample storage space for canned or packaged goods, as well as a roomy refrigerator and probably a separate freezer. Additional base and wall cabinets might be necessary, and an extra-large food pantry is a must. On the other hand, if

your total food and beverage inventory at any one time is likely to consist of a six-pack of beer, a quart of buttermilk, and a few frozen TV dinners, you can get by with a lot less kitchen.

5. You might want to install a small built-in desk in the kitchen, for making out shopping lists, menus, recipes, phone call messages, and financial records. Or taking this a step further, consider an equipment desk with a computer, printer, and storage files for keeping in touch with children and your cooking while "working" on the Internet and accomplishing desk work. Many dandy recipes are available via the Internet, which will work out handily from this location. A broom closet keeps long and bulky brooms, mops, sweepers, and ironing boards out of sight in case your house doesn't include a first-floor laundry or utility room.

6. While it's true that a family's kitchen should be a direct reflection of how much that family likes to cook (Why have a big kitchen if you spend most of your time in fast food restaurants?), it should also be an indication of what kinds of cooking are preferred. A lot of baking encourages the installation of double ovens. In fact, if you have the room, consider leaving space in the form of cupboards for a second oven just in case a future potential buyer of your house finds the ability to have a double oven an attractive feature. If you do a lot of entertaining, plan for an indoor grill or barbecue. If fancy presentations are important to you, select any of the other truly marvelous food preparation aids available. Even simple items such as brackets and shelves for condiments and spices, and bookshelves for cookbooks should be carefully planned in advance so enough space is allowed. These built-ins might seem minor, but if you just ignore their placement until everything else is completed, you'll be hard-pressed to neatly accommodate them. Finishing touches are often what separates the attractive, efficient kitchen from one that's awkward to work in and always appears cluttered.

Kitchen Functions

No matter what overall size your kitchen is, it still should:

1. Provide adequate working space. Any kitchen can be thought of as a combination of three work areas (Fig. 1.2). The first is food

FIGURE 1.2

A kitchen work area.

preparation, which includes counter space, utensil storage drawers and cabinets, places to store cutters, knives, food processors, chopping boards, glassware, cups, and plates. The second is food cooking, which includes the range, oven, counter space, and storage areas for pots, pans, cooking utensils, seasonings, ingredients, and other cooking supplies. The third is food cleaning, which includes single or dual basin sinks, counter space, dishwasher, trash facilities, and perhaps a garbage disposal.

Even the smallest kitchens should be set up so that the items stored at each work area are used for corresponding activities. For instance, the groceries should be stored near the refrigerator, so the sandwich maker has easy access to the peanut butter, jelly, bread, and milk without walking all over the kitchen. Likewise, cooking utensils and aids are best kept by the stove. Cleaning supplies and pot scrubbers should be stored within reach of the sink.

2. Provide sufficient counter space. Counter space at both sides of the sink is crucial. At least three linear feet of counter should be installed between the sink and refrigerator so that you can remove food from storage and put it away with ease, and can cut and chop foods or roll out dough. The counter space between the sink and refrigerator is often called the *mix center*. Near the sink, you need one place to stage dirty cookware and dishes before you rinse and wash them, and another to let them dry off after washing. Sink counter space is still a requirement even if you plan to have an automatic dishwasher.

The range or cooking center should also have counter space on both sides so you can place prepared foods in one place before cooking and afterwards in another while cooked foods are cooling. People frequently don't allow enough counter space here, and family cooks are sorry later on.

Beyond these areas, there should be enough additional counter space to accommodate all your favorite items and appliances such as a mixer, blender, food processor, toaster, crockpot, microwave oven, electric sharpener, can opener, bread box, and even a telephone.

3. Provide ample storage space. In the kitchen, enough storage space can mean the difference between a food preparation area that's easy to organize, easy to work in, and easy to keep clean—or an area that's difficult to work in and always a mess. Neatness and cleanliness count heavily toward a cook's efficiency and enjoyment of his or her work. And it's a proven fact that substantial psychological stress occurs to people who occupy cluttered, disheveled areas.

Here are a few points to keep in mind when planning your kitchen storage:

- All kitchens should contain cabinets beneath the sink to hold items such as soaps, cleaning utensils, washcloths, and drying towels. If you desire, a garbage disposal can make short work of most food waste and scraps, and an automatic dishwasher can be installed under one side of the sink counter to take care of dirty dishes, pots, pans, glasses, and utensils.

- There should be a good supply of cabinets and drawers around the food preparation area for utensils, cutters, chopping boards, and glassware. The range and cooking center also requires cabinet space on both sides for pots, pans, dishes, trays, casserole dishes, strainers, and dozens of miscellaneous objects.

- A pantry is a helpful addition for storing food, beverages, liquors, a stool, and even a small sweeper for quick cleanup (Fig. 1.3).

- After making sure you have sufficient base and wall cabinets, drawers, and pantry space, give careful consideration to the size of your refrigerator and freezer units. Analyze your shopping habits again, and plan to purchase large enough refrigerators

FIGURE 1.3

A pantry.

and freezers so you won't find yourself short of storage space for cold and frozen foods. Do you like to hunt and fish? Is one of your hobbies picking farm-fresh fruits and vegetables? Do you raise your own bumper crops, or prefer to buy meats in bulk?

■ Have an efficient layout. There are four widely accepted arrangements of the three kitchen work centers: the U-shape, the L-shape, the parallel wall, and the one-wall.

THE U-SHAPE

With this plan the sink is usually placed in the center leg of a U-shaped counter, between the food storage and cooking centers. The work triangle consists of three relatively short and equal-length distances. This, plus the fact that no through traffic interferes with the triangle, is what makes the U-shape plan the most efficient and desirable arrangement for many kitchens. It's compact, step-saving, and keeps the cooks out of the limelight (Fig. 1.4).

REF.

SINK

EAT

RANGE

FIGURE 1.4

A U-shaped kitchen.

FIGURE 1.5

An L-shaped kitchen.

THE L-SHAPE

This arrangement fits well on two adjacent walls and provides a good location for dining or laundry space on the opposite side of the room. It's not as convenient as the U-shape, but it's the next best thing. This plan can be converted into a U-shape by the addition of an island or peninsula section of counter and cabinet to work with (Fig. 1.5).

THE PARALLEL WALL

This arrangement has one work center on one wall and the others along an opposite wall. If your house seems to demand a parallel wall or "corridor" style of kitchen, take precautions to prevent kitchen traffic from interfering with the work triangle. Try to locate doors so people won't naturally cut through the kitchen when entering or departing through a back or side door. For the sake of whatever traffic you end up with, this corridor between the two walls should be a minimum of 4 feet wide between facing appliances and equipment. This lets two people easily pass each other while working. Avoid placing the refrigerator or oven where their open doors will block off a frequently used passageway. Otherwise, a work triangle arrangement almost as efficient as that of a U-shape can be constructed using this plan (Fig. 1.6).

A parallel kitchen.

THE ONE-WALL

One-wall kitchens are best suited to small houses where space is extremely tight. At best, cabinet and counter space is minimal, and you have no choice but to live with relatively long kitchen traffic patterns. However, if the distance from one end of the cabinetry to the other is close to 10 feet, some degree of efficiency can be realized through carefully laid out appliances, even when a true work triangle is lacking (Fig. 1.7).

A sidewall kitchen.

The same traffic precautions that apply to the parallel wall kitchen also pertain to the one-wall plan.

Any kitchen arrangement can be further improved upon or detracted from by placement of windows and doors. Effective lighting over the sink and main work surfaces is essential. Whenever possible, place a window that opens easily over the sink, for light, ventilation, keeping an eye on children, and even to provide a view to make washing dishes more palatable. Naturally, an electric light is still needed for night work at the sink.

Doors should encourage traffic to go around the kitchen work area instead of through it. This minimizes interruption of the cooks and the possibility of spilling hot foods on innocent bystanders. The work area should also be out of the way to individuals who enter and exit the house from the rear or side, and should not be directly adjacent to kitchen tables and chairs.

Other points to think about when planning the kitchen include:

1. Someone will be spending a lot of time in the kitchen. Try to arrange the nicest views available through the windows or sliding doors.

2. There should be an exhaust fan or range hood with a built-in fan directly over the range. You need a way to expel cooking smoke, fumes, and odors to keep your kitchen fresh.

3. Plan for plenty of electrical outlets along the kitchen walls and counters. It's frustrating not to have enough outlets for the standard complement of kitchen appliances.

4. Be aware that because a kitchen is considered the heart of any household, it's best situated in a central location, close to dining areas and family entrances near the garage so groceries can be easily carried into the house. If you plan a family room, consider having it adjoin the kitchen along one wall to facilitate traffic, communications, and even the ability to spread out if ever you throw a sizeable party.

DINING SPACE

People have all kinds of theories on what dining should be. Some individuals prefer to dine on the run, and aren't particular about what they eat, where they eat, or even how the food tastes. To them, eating is merely a necessary fact of life, a biological requirement.

Others enjoy taking the time and effort either to prepare or seek out gourmet-style meals. Good meals to them are to be slowly savored in the company of others, in carefully structured atmospheres at home or in fine restaurants.

A typical household leans toward a happy median between the "fast-food" meal and a candlelit dinner. That's why there are often two dining areas in a typical home—one for quick breakfasts, lunches, and children's meals, and another for more formal dining, which, though less frequently, still plays an important role in holiday celebrations and special family events. In any event, a dining room should have direct access to the kitchen.

In many households, a third dining area consists of an outdoor patio or deck with a gas grill. All three areas, however, should be located near the kitchen food preparation site for greatest convenience.

You have several basic choices to make when deciding upon informal and formal dining space: quick, easy meals and snacks can be served either at an attractive utilitarian bar, which is simply an extension of the kitchen work counter, an overhanging portion of counter that can accommodate three or four bar stools (Fig. 1.8), or a table/chairs or booth/bench arrangement included as part of an extension of the kitchen—often referred to as a breakfast room or nook.

If you don't want a formal dining room, you should probably opt for a table/chairs set that's placed right into the heart of the kitchen, yet out of the cook's way. This arrangement is referred to as an eat-in kitchen. Formal meals can still be served in an eat-in kitchen when special attention is given to items such as appropriate lighting, ventilation, and mood music.

The kind of kitchen dining space you prefer also depends on if you plan to use the table, booth, or bar for other purposes. Certainly, you can hardly play cards at a breakfast bar.

If you want more than a breakfast bar and eat-in kitchen, and you have the space and resources, then go with a formal dining room too. This can be footage borrowed from a living or family room, often delineated by special interior decorations or furnishings such as vinyl flooring, wallcoverings, or a chair rail. Or it could be a separate room of its own.

For ultimate privacy, doors can be installed to completely close off the dining room from the kitchen and living or family room. This

FIGURE 1.8

An eating bar, or breakfast bar.

can come in handy for special events such as birthday or graduation celebrations.

A dining room implies both enclosed space and service at the table. For this you'll need plenty of table space, chair space, access and serving space, plus room for any china hutch or side table server you want. When laying out your dining room, consider space for extra furniture and guest seating. One way to achieve this is to have the dining room connected to the living room (or family room) area. This will make the home seem larger and allow for relaxed seating before and after dinner. Also, in case you need to expand the dining room table for extra seating, furniture could be arranged for temporary dining-table expansion. A chandelier or other suspended lighting fixture, preferably one controlled by a dimmer switch, makes a lot of sense. The ability to lower the lighting level, at little cost, will provide a relaxing and classy atmosphere.

While a separate formal dining room is more traditional, an open-style dining room can fit nicely into an active family's lifestyle. Without the walls of a formal dining room, communications between the kitchen and living or family room are greatly improved. And due to the additional cost of a separate dining room, plus the overall reduction of square footage in many of today's modern houses, the open-style dining room situated directly between the kitchen and living or family room is becoming increasingly popular.

BATHING AND WASHING SPACE

Three questions must be addressed when you consider the bathing, washing, and comfort facilities you want in your new house: Are there enough bathrooms planned? Are the bathrooms large enough? And are the bathrooms conveniently located?

Are There Enough Bathrooms?

We've come a long way since the days of an outhouse behind every barn. Today, even a house having one complete bathroom is considered old-fashioned.

It's tempting to trade away the relatively high cost of bathroom construction and the space bathrooms require for more living and work space. But as it is, to ensure a good market value for your house, you should seriously consider at least two bathrooms, and possibly more if you have a large family.

Bathrooms come in both full and half sizes. A full bath includes a toilet, hand sink, bathtub, and/or shower (Fig. 1.9). Most modern pre-molded units combine a bathtub and shower in the same piece. A half bath consists of a toilet and hand sink (Fig. 1.10).

To begin with, one full bathroom should be designated for general use, close to the bedrooms. It should be accessible from most areas of the house and should not be reached by traveling through other rooms. A second bath, often directly adjacent to or back-to-back with the main

FIGURE 1.9

A full bath.

bath so plumbing fixtures can be shared, is usually located next to a master bedroom. A third bath, or at least a half bath, can be a great convenience, especially when positioned near the living room, family room, and kitchen.

With the exception of single-level ranch houses, it is definitely a plus to locate a bathroom on each living level. This results in time and energy savings over the short and long runs. If there's one thing that can make a house feel too small, it's standing in line in the morning, waiting to use the only bathroom.

Are the Bathrooms Large Enough?

All bathrooms should be large enough for ease of movement, proper traffic flow, and plenty of storage. Individuals who frequently get dirty at work or at play need roomy bathrooms with easy-to-clean surfaces. So do families with lots of children. People who depend on their appearances, such as models, airline attendants, politicians, salespeople, businesspeople, and others, might also prefer more spacious personal care areas with generous vanities, wide mirrors, and plusher appointments.

No matter what size full and half bathrooms you decide upon, all the required fixtures and accessories should be provided and sensibly located:

FIGURE 1.10

A half bath.

- Built-in storage for towels, soap, toilet paper and tissues, shampoo, and other personal aids should be included.

- A roomy vanity and medicine cabinet rounds out the basic storage.

- Many clever and attractive shelving arrangements consisting of materials from woven reeds to glass and chrome can be custom installed into otherwise unusable space.

- A laundry hamper or built-in laundry chute will save many steps and will help keep bathrooms neat and uncluttered.

- When no window space is available, a ventilation fan unit can be installed to ensure a turnover of fresh air and prevent stuffiness. If a window is used, though, the bathtub should not be placed beneath it. Sufficient lighting is important, and so is a heat vent.

Are the Bathrooms Conveniently Located?

In addition to being located near the bedrooms, bathrooms should also be planned near the main floor living and working areas. If your family often engages in outdoor activities, at least one half bathroom should be placed near the outside access. That same half bath can then be used by guests and family members who congregate in the living or family room, and by individuals coming from the kitchen and dining areas. This half bath is a real step-saver, especially in a sprawling single-story ranch home. And remember, people—especially guests—should be able to use the bathrooms without being seen by everyone else.

The nearer to other plumbing lines you can locate the bathrooms, the better. Placing two baths back-to-back saves on the installation labor and material costs and takes up a minimum of space. So does situating rooms containing plumbing fixtures as close as possible and practical to where the sewer and water lines enter the house—this effectively reduces the length of indoor service piping and allows for fixtures to be drained and vented with a single stack.

SLEEPING AND DRESSING SPACE

We spend practically a third of our lives in bedrooms. When examining how bedrooms will fit into your new house, six factors should be given careful attention: size, layout, windows, closets, noise, and the importance of having a master bedroom.

Size

There should be a rhyme and reason for bedroom sizes. Look at each one separately. Will it be for children or adults? Do you want bunk beds or queen- and king-size versions? Will a spare bedroom also serve as a sewing room? Are you planning a master bedroom complete with its own bath? In addition to providing space for beds, bedrooms should be able to comfortably accommodate a small desk, a dresser, and other clothes storage areas. Children's bedrooms should have suitable space for doing homework, for a desk, computer, computer stand, and printer. They should also contain storage shelves and sufficient closet space. There should also be enough room for dressing and personal care, and ample window space to provide sufficient air and natural lighting.

Layout

There are no tricks to designing functional bedrooms, but a frequent mistake is to have a poor bed location in relation to the bedroom's traffic pattern. Because bedrooms usually have at least several doors—the entrance door from a hallway, closet doors in various arrangements, and possibly a door to a private bathroom, dressing room, or even to an adjoining child's nursery—these entranceways make continuous wall space for furniture, including the bed, hard to find.

Typical bedroom traffic patterns are from the main bedroom door to the bathroom, clothes closet, or dresser, in that order of frequency. If you have to walk around the end of the bed to reach any of these places, you'll have an awkward traffic pattern. When laying out each bedroom make sure there's a place to locate the bed or beds that won't result in the creation of obstacle courses.

An unused "secondary" bedroom is ideal for guests. If you expect frequent visitors, consider equipping such a bedroom with an attached bath for privacy. Try to have the heating and cooling for this bedroom zoned for energy savings.

Windows

Bedroom windows, like most other windows, have two primary functions: to provide light and ventilation. Windows are helpful both in cool climates where they let the sun in to illuminate and heat bedrooms (although windows can also be mediums of rapid heat loss when the sun is absent), and in warm climates, where windows on opposite walls provide refreshing cross ventilation breezes. At the same time, heavy-duty window shades or coverings can be used during the day to keep out hot sunrays. In unusual circumstances, when only inside walls enclose a bedroom, the need for cross ventilation can be negated by the installation of central air-conditioning.

When considering the style, efficiency, and placement of bedroom windows, think about the possibility of drafts during cold weather, especially at the head of a bed placed near a window. On the other hand, such drafts can become cooling breezes welcome on hot summer evenings. Weigh the pros and cons and remember that certain types of windows positioned over the head of a bed might be difficult to open or even reach.

After deciding on the types of windows you want, make sure they'll provide adequate safety, including an escape route in case of a fire. In a child's bedroom, you won't want windows so low that you'll have to worry about children falling out of them. But if the windows are too high off the floor, or too small, then the kids can't reach or escape from them during an emergency. All sleeping areas should have at least one easy-to-open window with an opening of not less than 7 square feet. Check local building code requirements for window opening width and height, as well as the sill height above the floor. All window locks should be able to be unlatched quickly so a child or adult needing to exit for a fire is not delayed.

Closets

Closet space is vital to any bedroom. Without closets, orderly clothes storage becomes impossible. In fact, even individuals living in houses with an abundance of storage space always seem to want more closet room as the years go by and possessions keep accumulating.

To head off what could be an eventual problem, plan generous closets that make the most of their space. Consider going with a split-design version: half of it open all the way up so dresses, raincoats, and other long garments can be hung, and the other half consisting of two double-decked pole and shelf arrangements, for shorter garments. Small items can be placed on shelves installed in what otherwise would have been wasted space within conventional closets. Many people are surprised when they learn how much a scientifically designed closet can neatly hold (Figs. 1.11 and 1.12).

For sheer convenience, there should be an inside light in every closet; not one operated by a pull string. Install an electrical switch either inside or outside the closet doors. Pull strings and chains have a way of getting tucked up on a shelf as something is being put away, then they become difficult to find in the dark. Don't use a bare lightbulb without some kind of glass cover. There's a danger of fire if the bulb is not at least 18 inches from the edge of the nearest shelf or from the closest item of clothing. A better alternative is to install recessed lighting in all closets.

Last, if you choose not to store extra replacement linens in a bedroom closet, see that storage for them is available in a different closet located close to the bedrooms, perhaps in a hallway.

FIGURE 1.11

An example of an efficiently laid out closet.

Noise

As a rule, bedrooms should be placed together in a part of the house that's protected from outside vehicle noise from nearby streets. As much as possible, they should also be secluded from living, entertainment, and working space noise inside the house. Some dwellings lend themselves to a clear-cut separation of sleeping

FIGURE 1.12

Another example of an efficiently laid out closet.

space: two-story homes, for example, usually reserve the second floor for bedrooms. This clustering of bedrooms, generally near bathroom facilities, makes parental supervision easier and ensures a quiet sleeping area.

The Master Bedroom

The term "master bedroom" sounds like a throwback to medieval times, when the master and mistress of the house lived out their lives in luxury, catered to hand and foot by indentured servants. Today, a master bedroom is one common luxury item that most homeowners still enjoy. A master bedroom offers the utmost in convenience and privacy; it should at the very least include a half bath (a full bath is much preferred), and should be large enough to permit several alternative furniture arrangements. Include enough uninterrupted wall space for a queen- (or king-) size bed.

As mentioned before, the clothes closet should be roomy. Two separate closets—"hers" and "his"—are ideal. The closets should have a minimum depth of 24 inches. The poles should have a height of between 5 and 6 feet and be at least 12 inches from the closet rear wall. If hanging poles are to be double stacked, the top pole should be installed at least 6 feet high. It's also a good idea to soundproof the wall between the master bath and master bedroom for the late-sleeping/early-rising couple.

SERVICE AND STORAGE SPACE

There's nothing glamorous about service and storage space. You can have spectacular living rooms for talk-of-the-town entertaining, modern kitchens that grace the covers of architectural magazines, luxurious master bedrooms, and spacious whirlpool and sauna bathrooms for pampering yourself. But who can get excited about hallways or stairs? Or laundry and utility rooms? Usually the homeowners who have ill-planned ones.

Certainly these behind-the-scene features cannot be excluded from the typical house. Storage areas are also necessary accompaniments to the more popular parts of every dwelling. They include closets, small storage nooks and crannies, plus garages, basements, and attics.

Hallways

There's something disconcerting about a main entrance that opens directly into your living room. Instead, look for a center hallway plan that offers access to any part of the house without leading you conspicuously through living and entertainment areas. On the other hand, excessive hallway footage, along with its special walls, means costly wasted space. To limit the space used by an entrance hall, make the entry a part of a corner of your living room, but still keep it "separate" by installing a different flooring and by breaking up the ceiling line directly above the change of flooring.

Instead of completely writing off necessary hallway space as practically useless except as a pathway between rooms, consider the wall surfaces as potential showcases for artwork and photos. Strategically located lighting fixtures will also help support an individual decorating effort. Where needed, specify 42-inch-wide hallways when possible. They make carrying large pieces of furniture safer and easier.

Stairways

This kind of house space has had its ups and downs over the years. Wrongly positioned, stairways—like hallways—can rob otherwise useful living and working space from any floor plan. To avoid this wasted effort, stairways should be constructed one on top of another whenever possible.

Even though you've probably heard a lot of nice things about the spiral stairway, don't believe all of them. Although this setup, which takes approximately 4 by 4 feet of floor space, is the most compact arrangement you can have, it's also the most expensive, inconvenient, and dangerous. The novelty quickly wears off. Ask anyone who has had to raise children around a spiral.

The most economical and convenient choice is a standard straight stairway taking up about 8 by 3 feet of floor space. An altered version of the straight stairway that can be very acceptable is the landing stairway, consisting of a half flight of stairs that leads to a rectangular landing and then another half flight to the next floor level. The landing stairway takes up about 7 by 7 feet of floor space. It adds an extra touch to a room at a cost higher than that of a straight stairway, but without the hazards of the spiral.

When planning a basement, consider the practical advantages gained by an outside stairway. Bulky items can be carried from the back or side yard to the basement, and vice versa. This also increases the likelihood that you'll use your basement for storage instead of just dropping everything in the garage.

Laundry and Utility Rooms

Mention "laundry room" as a topic of conversation to anyone and you'll likely receive a polite nod and a yawn. Most home buyers tend to overlook the importance of both laundry and utility rooms because these areas simply don't have the pizzazz potential of other parts of a house. That's unfortunate. Laundry and utility rooms haphazardly planned are usually tucked somewhere out of the way, with little consideration for convenience.

There are two kinds of utility rooms: those with laundry facilities and those without. Utility rooms without laundry facilities can be located practically anywhere toward the outer reaches of the central living and work areas of the house. Utility rooms having laundry facilities must be positioned more carefully and can be located successfully in a number of places within a house.

A basement is one locale. This can be an economical place, although over the years you'll have to contend with constant stair climbing. If you decide on the basement as your laundry/utility area, give serious thought to a direct outside basement access (Fig. 1.13). A door to the yard lets you hang clothes outside during nice weather. It also lets you enter from the outdoors in wet or dirty clothes that can be changed right in the laundry area. Then you simply wash up at the laundry tub and proceed through the house. A clothes chute from the upstairs levels to the basement laundry basket can be another step-saver.

A garage or carport is another locale. In warm-climate locations people often choose to put their utility room either in the garage/carport or in an adjoining space called a "mud" room—so named because of its outdoors accessibility. There are no steps to climb (or very few), and with a laundry tub you can enjoy all of the conveniences found in a basement utility room having direct access to the outside. If there's a second story in the house, a laundry chute can be arranged to drop clothes straight into a garage or carport or mud room hamper.

The first floor of the house is yet another alternative. There are two types of in-house laundry rooms that can be positioned on the first floor of any house. First, there's a laundry room that's a full-size room a little smaller than the average bedroom but large enough to hold a washer, dryer, stationary tub, ironing board, soap, bleach, cleansers, a sewing machine and supplies, and, if enough space is available, a working surface for sorting clothes before and after washing, drying, and ironing (Fig. 1.14). There should also be a clothes closet with floor space for storing dirty laundry out of sight. The closet should have shelves for laundry sprays, softeners, measuring cups, and scrub

FIGURE 1.13

Outside basement stairs.

brushes. Consider having the clothes rod go only three-quarters across the closet, so one-quarter of the vertical space can be reserved for shelves affixed from top to bottom.

The second type of first-floor in-house laundry room is a laundry center that's installed entirely within a closet (Fig. 1.15). This is a more economical route than the full-size room. Although you don't have as much space or versatility, you do have the basic necessities for washing clothes in a first-floor location. The closet in question need be only as deep and as wide as required to accommodate a washer, dryer, and stationary tub. A shelf across the top of the appliances can hold laundry baskets, soap, and other items. You might have room to stand up an ironing board, too. If not, just place it in a kitchen broom closet. A screen or folding louvered door should be installed to conceal the laundry center when no one is using it. This setup is clean, simple, and convenient.

FIGURE 1.14

A full laundry room.

When possible, try to have one of the first-floor laundry arrangements. They're usually the best alternatives and have the most conveniences.

Once you decide on the size and type of first-floor laundry you want, a number of other things must be considered when you're planning its location:

1. If it's situated near an outside door, you'll save wear and tear on carpeting. Someone walking into the house after playing football in the rain, jogging, or fishing can easily change clothes and clean up before trooping through the rest of the house. An outside access also makes it easier to hang clothes in the yard.

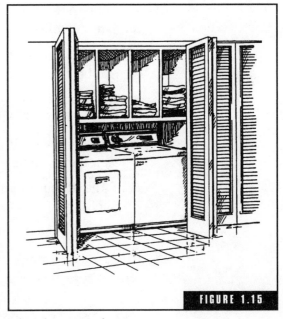

FIGURE 1.15

A laundry center closet.

2. The nearer the kitchen, the better. Clothes washing can be made much more palatable when done in between other tasks. If the laundry is close to the kitchen, you can move from one area to another with ease and accomplish more work in a shorter timespan.

3. If you plan your house so the main bath and bedrooms are on the same floor as the kitchen, consider locating the laundry between the main bath/bedrooms and kitchen. Again, being near the kitchen will allow you to move easily between those work areas. Being near the main bathroom will save steps when collecting soiled clothing. And being near the bedrooms will make it simpler to put away clean clothes. If you plan a two-story house with the main bath and bedrooms on the second floor, try to include a clothes chute that will usher soiled clothes straight into the laundry room collection hamper.

4. It's nice to have a window in the laundry for the daytime sun. If you can't arrange one due to your layout (for instance, if you have room for only a hallway closet–type laundry center) then make sure you plan for adequate lighting. Working in the dark causes eyestrain and general fatigue.

5. The ideal laundry room should provide storage space to accommodate the following:

   ■ Soiled clothes. Preferably more than one container so clothes can be sorted as they accumulate.

   ■ Detergents, bleach, sprays, iron, and related supplies. Be sure they are out of children's reach.

   ■ Space/shelves for folded clean clothes. Preferably a section for each family member.

   ■ If the room is large enough, an ironing board and sewing machine.

   ■ A place to hang clothes, especially permanent press items.

6. If you have enough room a conventional standup ironing board will do fine. However, even if space isn't a factor, one arrangement to consider is a built-in ironing board (Fig. 1.16) that hides or folds into a wall when not in use. These ironing boards are usually strong and durable, and between 40 and 48 inches in length. The

STORAGE

INDICATOR
LIGHT

SAFETY
SWITCH

CLOTHES HOOK

TIMER

WORK LIGHT

SLEEVE BOARD

ADJUSTABLE
IRONING BOARD

FIGURE 1.16

Built-in ironing center.

units can be recessed into a wall or simply attached to it. The fold-out ironing board is especially handy when you have to press one or two garments in a hurry. Ironing centers can be purchased with a variety of features, including:

■ Unfinished wood cabinet doors, allowing you to stain, paint, or paper them to match a room's decor. A fully mirrored door is another alternative.

■ Storage shelves. In some there's a special shelf for an iron to rest on, and it's constructed so you can put the iron away immediately after use, with no cooling required. Other shelves are arranged to hold spray starch, water bottles, hangers, and similar items.

■ Automatic iron shutoffs. They'll turn off your iron if you forget. A timer is set when you begin to iron, for up to 60 minutes. If you're called away and cannot return before the 60 minutes are up, a red light will come on and the iron is automatically turned off. You simply reset the timer when you return. Look for a unit with a safety switch that turns off the electricity to the ironing center when the ironing board is put into its storage position.

■ Adjustable work lights. A built-in work light that swivels up, down, and sideways to provide illumination exactly where you need it.

■ Hanger hooks. For just-ironed garments. The hook folds flat against the door when not in use.

■ Swivel units. Some ironing centers have ironing boards that can swivel a full 180° to face whatever direction you wish. This adds greater installation flexibility. An unusual room design or the location of furniture in the room can usually be accommodated by swiveling the board one way or another.

■ Optional sleeve boards. This affords about a 4-inch clearance between the board and base, allowing room for maneuvering and arranging garments while ironing. They're great for ironing sleeves, pant legs, pleated garments, and baby clothes.

7. Double-stacked clothes washer/dryer arrangements can be used when space is at a premium. Improved design has resulted in narrower units that can be located in places previous models could not. A variety of excellent 24-by-24-inch stackable washers and dryers are available. If you can live with the smaller capacities, they can be placed in a closet 30 inches wide by 30 inches deep. Necessary sprays, spot cleaners, and detergents can be kept in the same closet or in a nearby cabinet. One company makes a standard-capacity washer/dryer unit that can be placed side by side separately or doublestacked. This is an ideal option if you need large-capacity washing but still want to save space by stacking.

The nice thing about double-stacking is that the clothes washing and drying machines can actually be located in a space comparable in size to an entrance hall closet.

8. A stationary sink located near the clothes washer will save a lot of steps. It's handy for a variety of tasks:

- Pre-machine washing

- Spraying spot remover on garments

- Soaking items

- Drying items

- Filling pails with water

- Cleaning and spraying houseplants

- Cleaning and rinsing off large items such as boots

Stationary sinks come in a variety of materials, including plastic, fiberglass, steel, and stainless steel. You'll find the plastic models to be extremely efficient and economical.

9. Clothes chutes and hampers can be an important part of the laundry center. The use of a clothes chute will save labor and time in getting the dirty clothes to the washer. Simplifying this task will encourage everyone to properly dispose of the items to be washed instead of leaving them all over the house.

    In addition to keeping the dirty clothes out of sight, hampers can be an attractive addition to the hallway or bathroom decor. Their style and shape can vary from a rectangular floor model to a bookcase-style stand-up model with adjustable shelves, an overhead cabinet, and a tip-out hamper on the bottom.

    The most popular hampers are made of machine-washable fabrics such as cotton and polyester, supported by a hardwood or brass-plated steel frame. Hand-woven rattan or willow strips are also very serviceable. If space permits, two separate hampers can be used, one for whites, and one for colors.

10. One drawback to laundry centers can be the tangle of hoses and electrical cords that surround washing machines and dryers. A washing machine outlet box groups together all of the water connections, drains, and electrical outlets for both machines into one neat, compact unit that can be almost hidden from view, recessed into a wall. Made of molded ABS plastic, the device meets safety standards and is available in a cream color that blends with any laundry decor. The unit should also have a contoured bottom for overflow drainage.

11. To prevent mold and mildew from forming inside closets, make sure clothes are dry before storing them. To help this happen, closets can be outfitted with louvered doors to provide air circulation.

As you can see, a variety of arrangements are available to accommodate your laundry center. Some are more convenient than others. No matter where you locate it, here are a few additional considerations:

■ Make sure there is an outside dryer vent. Otherwise moisture from the clothes dryer will cause an uncomfortable environment that's tough on laundry machines and other appliances, tough on the house (moisture causes mold and mildew, will soften plasterboard, and will rust metal), and even tough on people (it's hard on the lungs).

■ If you're concerned with the possibility of overflowing wash or rinse water, have a drain installed beneath the washer. With a first-floor laundry not set up over concrete, consider vinyl flooring so spills can be efficiently mopped up without leaving a mess.

Garages

People who have never had a garage don't realize what they're missing. They say that their cars have always been out in the weather, and if not for a little inconvenience during winter, who needs a garage anyway? But once they move to a place that has a garage—even a small detached garage—they'll never go without one again. It's nice to get into a dry car after an all-evening snowstorm. It's nice to be able to pull out of the garage in the morning and drive past the neighbors who are stamping their feet and swearing while they scrape sheets of ice from their windshields. And by the same token, in the South or Southwest, it's nice to climb into a car that hasn't been roasting all day in the sun. Persistent sunlight fades paint, rots fabric, and cracks vinyl.

It's also nice to have storage space outside the house for seasonal items that can go six months of the year out of sight secured on garage rafters. It's nice to be able to lock up your cars, bicycles, golf clubs, tools, and spare tires in a garage.

When determining the size of your garage, consider how many vehicles you have (or plan to acquire), as well as the quantity of other items you want to store there. A roomy garage can serve many purposes other than being a car barn. Will you need additional room for workshop or hobby areas? You'll find a garage useful for storing canned foods, holding garage sales, and even as a handy play area for children when it's raining. When designing your garage:

1. Insist on at least one floor drain. If the garage will be connected to the house, there should be a drain under each car space. Contour the concrete floor to the drains so the surface can be easily cleaned. Without the drains, dirt, mud, and slush will inevitably get tracked into the house.

2. If the garage is built under the same roofline as the rest of the house it will simplify construction efforts and costs. The property assessment will also likely be lower with that kind of arrangement, which will in turn minimize real estate taxes.

3. A garage should conform to the slope of the lot. If necessary, side-sloping lots can be accommodated by lowering the garage to meet the natural lot line, but this increases the number of steps needed from garage to living area, and by doing so takes away from some of the garage's usable space. On the other hand, if the garage is located higher on the same side-sloping lot, the driveway and garage floor will have to be built up substantially. This will be discussed further in chapter 15, on garages.

4. In warm-climate locations the garage is sometimes used to house the furnace, air conditioner, water heater, and laundry equipment. Whatever items you plan on installing, make sure your garage will be large enough to carry out your designs. If you place any equipment having natural gas pilot lights in a garage, precautions must be taken, especially if flammable liquids are stored there.

5. If the back of your fireplace will protrude into the garage, that must be taken into account. As mentioned earlier, such a setup will save on chimney finishing bricks, and excess heat will be radiated into the garage instead of being lost directly outside.

6. If there's enough room on the lot, consider having a 3-car garage. After all, the garage is one of the least expensive parts of a house. In addition to the parent's vehicles, a son or daughter will often use the third space.

Basements

The decision to have or not have a basement is often influenced by the regional custom of the area you're building in. Most houses in cold-climate locations will have basements. But in areas having exceptionally high groundwater tables (swampy places, for instance) or not experiencing freezing temperatures during winter, houses do not need and sometimes should not have basements. In general, though, there are a number of advantages to a basement:

1. A basement will provide handy storage space for household materials and outdoors equipment, especially when an outside access door is installed.

2. It's an ideal out-of-the-way place to put your water heater and furnace. Both of these appliances are simple to service and repair in a basement.

3. A house with a basement is usually easier to protect from wood-destroying insects such as carpenter ants and termites.

4. In a basement, water pipes are less likely to freeze, and wiring and all piping installed beneath the house are easy to get at for repairs and modifications.

5. A basement offers economical potential for future living expansion. A family room, bedroom, sauna, bathroom, workshop, darkroom, or other hobby and game room can be neatly situated within a basement. Consider a 9-foot-high basement for easier finishing later.

Some people, even though they live in areas where a basement is traditionally included with the typical house, have strong feelings that such a feature is a waste of both money and space. They consider basements as dark, dank areas suitable for merely storage and the housing of a furnace and water heater. Here are some frequently mentioned drawbacks to having a basement:

1. The necessary stairway encroaches on usable space both in the basement and on the floor above.

2. There's no doubt that basements *can* be dark, gloomy, wet, and clammy.

3. There's an expense for waterproofing and establishing proper draining around the foundation.

4. There's also the cost of basement flooring, finished walls if desired—plus heat, wiring, and lighting.

5. If the money spent on the basement could be used elsewhere, you could substantially add on to your upstairs living levels.

6. Unlike the rest of the house, the typical basement has little natural light or ventilation.

Attics

Here's a house feature that appears to be nearing extinction, going the same way as the covered sitdown front porch. Years ago, when two- and three-story houses were crammed together along big city streets like upright dominoes, attics were included with every dwelling.

They held (and still do) old chests and cardboard boxes loaded with Christmas decorations, clothes, toys, school papers, books, antiques, and other mementos. Attics have always been cluttered, dusty repositories of family memorabilia—mostly because there was little other space built anywhere else into the house for storage. If you happen to decide on an attic, remember:

1. Although the attic opening should be located in a concealed, out-of-the-way area, it should be easily accessible when you have to use it. A good place to put a pull-down stairway unit is inside a utility room or spare bedroom closet.

2. The attic opening should at least be 23 × 54 inches. Don't settle for anything less than a drop-down staircase or ladder arrangement, especially when the attic opening is situated in the garage.

3. If possible, allow for ample attic height and headroom to enable you to move around without constantly stooping over.

4. Some individuals believe they can store items across the attic floor joints without laying down flooring. Don't fall for that trap. Never settle for a completely unfloored attic. The more you lay down, the better.

5. Provide lighting and an electric outlet in the attic. Attics are generally dark inside. It's an inconvenience having to always carry a flashlight up there, or to string an extension cord every time you want to use a vacuum cleaner, light, or power tool.

6. Provide ventilation in the attic to alleviate harmful heat and moisture buildup during summer.

7. If a pull-down stairway is not selected, don't settle for a flimsy piece of wood pulled over the attic access doorway. Instead, consider specifying a custom-made steel access door with frame, built on hinges for ease of use. This type of door will not warp, has an excellent fire rating, can be purchased with recessed hinges and catches, and is fully insulated.

Storage Space

A sufficient amount of storage space will make a home a much more pleasant place to live in. While some individuals catalog everything they own and are able to find the most obscure item at a moment's notice, others are so disorganized that they routinely lose anything from their Christmas decorations to last year's swimsuits.

The relatively recent reduction in the overall square footage of houses has wreaked havoc with storage space and has thus increased the importance properly designed storage space can mean to you. Efficient storage in bedrooms and kitchens is especially critical. Here are a few points to consider when planning your overall storage space:

1. Place a clothes closet near the main entrance.

2. Have a linen closet near the bedrooms and main bathroom to hold sheets, pillow cases, towels, washcloths, comforters, and other bulky whites.

3. Try to place a clothes closet near the garage or side entrance.

4. Locate a pantry closet in the kitchen for holding canned foods, beverages, liquor, and lots of other kitchen items.

5. Make sure that your "live" storage—for items used day-in and day-out—is very accessible. Live storage requires drawers, shelves, closets, and at times, chests. Each storage area should be thought out in advance for particular needs and sized accordingly. And each should be located in the proper place.

6. Your "dead" storage—for things you use only infrequently during the year, such as lawn furniture and snow tires—can be put in out-of-the-way locations. Find dead storage in the most inaccessible spots, in places such as attics, basements, and garages. Use boxes and chests to store smaller items in.

It only stands to reason that as far as possible, your house should provide you with whatever you need for safety, comfort, enjoyment, and privacy. For individuals having particular interests requiring special adaptations, facilities such as the following may be desired: a sauna, steam bath, hot tub, greenhouse, elaborate garden, fountain, swimming pool, place for animals, patio/garden living room, or various outdoor work and hobby areas.

No matter which areas are most important to you, make sure you at least consider each of the six main types of spaces under roof. That way you can make intelligent decisions when custom designing your house, realizing the trade-off effects that having too much or too little of any particular space are likely to have once you move in.

A house ultimately expresses the unique personalities, goals, and lifestyles of its inhabitants. Thus, a totally satisfying residence will provide you with deep-seated feelings of personal achievement and will remain a source of continuous pride.

▶▶▶▶▶ POINTS TO PONDER

1. Consider that a modern house consists of six main types of space: living and recreation, food preparation, dining, bathing and washing, sleeping and dressing, and service and storage space.
2. Carefully review and question your need for *both* a living room and a family room. Having both is no longer as necessary or traditional as it was in past years.
3. To make for a more aesthetically pleasing appearance, it's wise to include sufficient built-ins for living and recreation rooms, such as bookcases and shelves to exactly match the wood trim that's being installed throughout the home.

4. Plan in advance for special needs such as photo darkrooms, a library, den, billiard room, exercise room, or home office. They can be special areas that, depending on your interests, can greatly enhance the total living experience.

5. If you've ever heard the saying, "I hardly ever cook, so that's why I like such a small kitchen," don't believe it. The importance of counter space and storage space in a kitchen cannot be stressed enough. Consider the value of an open connection between the kitchen and family room. You can visit with family members, relatives, and guests while preparing or cleaning up food and refreshments.

6. To keep extremely messy teenagers and other so-inclined family members out of the nice bathrooms, consider a "knockaround" bathroom installed in the basement for those individuals to shower in, put makeup on, and toss their dirty clothes (if there's a basement laundry) directly near the washing machine.

7. Many homebuilders never understand how important closets are to bedrooms. Make them larger than you think they should be. And put lights and sturdy shelves in them.

8. Go for a larger garage than you think you'll need. If you've got enough room on the lot, and you can make it fit with the overall house plan, a three-car garage may not cost much more, proportionally, than a two-car garage.

9. A well-planned attic can add inexpensive storage (and sometimes expandable) space to certain types of homes, especially when properly insulated, floored, and wired.

10. Keep in mind the value of a first-floor laundry. It will save you time and energy when conveniently located.

House Styles and Types

Your ideal house, a dwelling that's both handsome and practical, is much more than simply a collection of great rooms. Certainly, a well-designed house that offers plenty of living security, enjoyment, and pride of ownership should feature memorable individual rooms. But that's not enough.

To work as a single unit, rooms should be arranged to match your living requirements and lifestyle as closely as possible. Your home should contain the correct amount of space to suit yourself and your family or future family. It shouldn't be too small, nor too large.

The best way to go about putting a house together in your mind is also the most logical. First, decide on the amount of space you want roofed over. Once that's established you can go on to the style and type of house that will best lend itself to your objectively arrived at space requirements and your subjectively arrived at preferences for appearance and setting. Naturally, both advantages and disadvantages exist for all the various types of houses, and these characteristics will be pointed out later in the chapter.

Somewhere in the back of your thoughts, while considering space requirements and house types, keep in tune with your financial parameters. If money or income is a major problem, pay particular attention to the chapter on planning for future expansion.

When deciding how much space will be roofed over:

1. Arrive at the number of rooms you want. The six types of space were discussed in the previous chapter. Figure out your ideal number of rooms: what they are, their sizes, and then, just to be safe, also determine the minimum number of rooms you can get along with (keeping in mind you can add more at a later date).

2. Determine a dollar-per-square-foot cost and decide how much you can afford or wish to spend. Consider how much of a down payment you can come up with, plus the cost of current mortgage rates in your area. To arrive at how much you can expect to pay per square foot of house space, attend new construction open houses that are built with similar materials and workmanship to what you'd consider acceptable. When at an open house, ask what the going price for the house is, *excluding* the lot, then divide those total dollars by the amount of square feet the house has. Square footage means the livable area of the house. It doesn't include the garage, basement, or attic. What you can spend on a home mortgage is usually governed by ratios of indebtedness to income that are conservatively set by banks and savings and loans.

3. Decide on the style of architecture you'd prefer. Some styles are innately larger than others. Some styles are low key, while others literally exude a certain social status. Your choice is likely to be influenced by climate, geographic location, personal tastes, finances, and also by the dwellings already built in the area or neighborhood you decide upon.

4. The last consideration, and a consideration more important than style, is the *type* of house you want: a single-story, a one and one-half-story, a two-story, split foyer, or multilevel.

HOUSE STYLES

Style is a broad concern that will ultimately affect your choice of house. It most commonly indicates the decorative features of the exterior and to some degree the interior. An overview of the various house architectural styles reveals that individual styles are best suited to their own particular climates and locations. They're frequently constructed of local or native materials, with exteriors and even appropriate colors that complement their surroundings.

When looking at particular styles you will find that Early American, Cape Cod, Colonial, Georgian Colonial, and Southern Colonial are all styles that have withstood the whims of change. The first two are compact, informal houses well suited to the northern sectors of the United States. The Georgian and Southern Colonial are larger and more formal. The Georgian is adaptable to both the northern climates and the milder climates, and the Southern Colonial—actually a form of the Georgian—is especially suited to the warm and humid climate of southeastern regions. Meanwhile, the Mission or Adobe style is particularly good in the hot, dry climate of the Southwest; in the warm, wet areas of the Southeast, adobe would not withstand a single rainy season. The Adobe is a prime example of how house styles often incorporate local materials of a particular region.

A popular and far-reaching style that has been evolving over recent years is the Contemporary. This style is suited to the theory "anything goes" and has few rules to follow or break. Contemporary houses can be simple, basic, and inexpensive. Or they can be extremely liberal in their composition, consisting of any of a variety of singularly dominant characteristics, from long, sweeping rooflines, to a half-dozen levels juxtaposed over one another. Contemporaries can be full of big open spaces, constructed with huge panes of glass, hand-hewn stones, posts and beams, and modern brightly colored manufactured materials. Innovative features such as passive solar heating, central courtyards or greenhouses, interior balconies, and spacious wood decks are frequently part of the Contemporary plan.

But Contemporaries are not for everyone. They can mean skilled engineering, expensive plans and drawings, tricky construction, costly materials, and high utility bills from heating cathedral ceilings and similar extravagant spaces.

Although individual construction styles may vary greatly from one another, they all must answer to certain design guidelines. No matter which style you lean toward, consider the following points in regard to your own house plans:

1. Think about the design of your house in relation to the complexity of construction. If the house makes a turn anywhere, for example—

L-shaped or U-shaped rather than running in a straight line—you introduce construction complications. A gable roof, which is simply two sloped surfaces meeting at a high point called a ridge, is economical and comparatively easy to build, *until* you choose to turn a corner with it; then the junction forms a V-shaped indentation and the affected rafters require compound angle fitting, a construction technique that takes much more time and skill. Instead of laying down simple angles where all the rafters are positioned in the same fashion, boards must be individually measured and cut to multiple lengths and angles.

Another suggestion that will keep construction costs lower is to build the outside walls free from a lot of ins, outs, jigs, and jogs (Fig. 2.1). Most houses look better anyway if they don't have a sizeable amount of rooflines joined together. Otherwise a house will appear cluttered and haphazardly designed. In general, a simple square or rectangular plan gives you more house for the money.

2. A few additional comments about the roof and roofline can be made here: a continuous roofline gives an impression of greater size than a roofline broken up into several different planes. A roof should extend or overhang past the outer walls 2 to 4 feet. This not only lends a handsome and distinctive appearance to the house,

FIGURE 2.1

A house cluttered with many ins, outs, jigs, and jogs.

but it also helps protect windows and outer walls from snow, rain, and sun. Another plus is that it keeps water away from the foundation and basement. A substantial overhang is a feature largely ignored by many builders. It shouldn't be excluded. For the relatively small cost of an overhanging roof, there are too many benefits to go without one.

A roof over the main entranceway will shield you from the elements while you're fumbling for your house key, or will keep visitors out of the rain while they're waiting for you to answer the door. It also provides a nice spot for you to sit on a patio or lawn chair in comfortable shade during the summer.

3. Remember that good proportions are one of the first rules of a good-looking house. The exterior of your house should not have more than two (at the *most*, four) sizes of matching windows, apart from glass sliding doors. At the same time, the doors should not be of abnormal size or located in odd places. To arrive at a satisfactory scale and proportion of doors and windows, compare what's already been installed on existing houses in neighborhoods you'd feel comfortable in. Get a feeling for the styles of windows and doors you prefer.

The tops and bottoms of all equal-size windows should line up, conforming to one long horizontal line across the house. Smaller windows should line up with the tops or bottoms of larger windows. When the tops of exterior doors also line up with window tops, things will look even better.

The exterior should not consist of more than two, or at the very most three, kinds of siding materials, so that the whole appearance works toward a single theme. If a wide variety of materials are present, the house will not be pleasing to the eye, plus the exterior will likely end up costing more than necessary and will be difficult to maintain properly. Never mix more than three materials such as aluminum siding, wood siding, bricks and stone, or glass. Each will compete with the others, resulting in an extremely "busy" and disconcerting effect.

Just as too many different building materials will clutter up the exterior of a house, so will too many colors. You've probably heard of Hollywood entertainers who paint their mansions a bright orange or obscene purple. If you merely want a practical, handsome exterior that won't draw curiosity seekers and will help ensure a good resale value, then the exterior of your house should be consistent with the exteriors on the rest of the neighborhood dwellings.

4. It makes sense to select a house style that will closely match the living pattern of your family. Consider your entertainment activities, hobbies, children's pastimes, gardening interests, maintenance desires, and even the amount of time you like to spend away from home on vacation.

5. If you might want to add another room or section later on, when designing for expandability remember that building up or down is always cheaper than building out. Also remember that building out, if the only alternative, at a later date will be more cost efficient if you plan for it at the outset.

HOUSE TYPES

House "type" denotes the number and arrangement of a dwelling's living levels. The basic types of houses are the single-story ranch, the Cape Cod or one and one-half-story, the two-story, the split foyer, and the multilevel.

Again, an important consideration that will affect your choice of house type is your lifestyle. You want the house that best fits your needs and meets your ideas of personal acceptance and preference, as well as something that fits the setting you desire.

Some family activities that will affect the type of house you want are:

■ Entertaining—card playing, informal and formal dinners, outdoor barbecues, large cocktail parties, teenage parties, and other pursuits all present different requirements.

■ Privacy—families and individual members differ in their desire and needs for privacy.

■ Hobbies—these can present special problems related to space, storage, and noise levels. For example, a drummer needs a different kind of space than a stamp collector. The woodworker needs room for bulky tools and materials and will be a major generator of noise.

The Single-Story Ranch

This type of house (Fig. 2.2) can be constructed in a wide variety of sizes, shapes, and designs. It can be built over a full or partial basement, a crawl space, or a concrete slab foundation (Fig. 2.3).

Before the advantages and disadvantages of the ranch are discussed, here are some general guidelines applicable to all single-story plans:

- The single-story plan should provide access from both the front main entrance and a rear or side entrance into the house without routing people directly through the center of the living room or kitchen work area.

- The living room should not be used as a corridor at the expense of carpeting and furnishings, but should instead provide the privacy for which it was intended. An entry foyer should distribute traffic so visitors don't have to step directly into the living room. This prevents congested cross-traffic and interruptions.

- The kitchen, laundry, family room, and any busy work center of the house should be accessible from an outdoor patio or deck, if one is included with your plan.

FIGURE 2.2

A ranch home.

FIGURE 2.3

A ranch home cutaway.

- The master bedroom suite should be assured of privacy by its remoteness from the family room, kitchen area, and outdoor living space.

- If you choose to go with a ranch house, don't try to match it to a lot with a substantial forward slope. Ranches look best if they appear to be hugging the ground; a forward-sloping lot requires an exposed foundation in the front, which detracts from the low look of a ranch (Fig. 2.4). Single-story houses are ideally suited to flat lots or sites that gently slope to the sides or rear, particularly if the plans call for a walkout from a basement or lower living area. This is also a way of economically increasing the amount of living space since the lower level is an extension of the foundation.

Advantages

1. Single-stories offer the greatest liveability for all members of the household regardless of age. Major rooms are located on a single level (unless a basement has been expanded into living space). The overwhelming advantage of this house is its suitability to families having senior citizens or young children. There are no second-story stairs to climb up or tumble down.

FIGURE 2.4

A ranch home on a forward-sloping lot.

2. Single-stories can be made very relaxing and informal through the use of outdoor space. They offer the most convenience for indoor/outdoor living, with plenty of possibilities for porches, patios, terraces, planters, and gardens that can be built adjacent to and integral with any room.

3. Single-story houses can have spacious basements. You might be one of those persons who thinks if you're going to have a cellar, it might as well be a large one. After all, basements are good for storage, workshops, heating appliances, billiards, ping-pong and other sports and hobbies, for future expansion of living space, and for laundry facilities if you can't have your laundry on the first floor.

4. As a rule, ranch houses are easy to build. They're close to the ground. You needn't resort to double-length ladders and scaffolding to reach much of the structure, as you have to with two-stories and Cape Cods, for instance.

5. Because there are fewer living levels, heating and cooling systems don't have to negotiate additional floors and ceilings once the main living level is taken care of. The same is true with the plumbing

system. There is much less maneuvering of ducts, pipes, and electrical wiring in a single-story.

6. A single-story plan is the easiest house to keep clean after it's built. Not having to climb stairs is a big time-saver. In a ranch you don't have to worry about keeping cleaning equipment on more than one floor.

7. A single-story is easy to expand even if no preparations were made at the time of original construction. You can simply convert part of the basement into living area, or you can add on an exterior wing. Of course, if you know in advance that you want additional space later (as discussed in chapter 4), you can then make provisions in the walls where the expansion will be.

8. With a single-story house, you can consider a contemporary-looking sloped ceiling that follows the pitch of the roof so ceiling joists are not required and a feeling of spaciousness is created. Insulation and ceiling materials are applied directly to the rafters. This is a common building practice in the South, but it can also be used—with today's energy efficient insulation—in the North as well.

9. When designed with trussed rafters, a ranch can benefit from the popular open planning in which living, dining, kitchen, and family alcove sections are designed as part of one interconnected space. Because structural partitions are not needed except for privacy, areas can be arranged by furniture placements, room dividers, folding partitions, and even projecting or freestanding fireplaces.

10. A one-story house is much easier to inspect and maintain due to its proximity to the ground. The roof pitch is usually very low, so it's not difficult to climb onto, walk on, or repair. The outside walls, if constructed of painted materials, are simple to touch up or repaint, and it's easy to perform other routine housekeeping tasks such as washing windows and cleaning out gutters.

Disadvantages

1. Single-stories have been described as being typically informal due to the reduced amount of privacy found between their walls. The

single-floor layout increases the importance of effective interior zoning—for the careful placement of physical buffers between the living, working, and sleeping areas. The need for such buffers (along with an aversion to stair climbing) may be greater in a family that includes very old or very young members who need more rest than other family members.

2. Some people just don't feel comfortable sleeping on a first-floor level, for reasons of privacy and security.

3. Ranch houses cost more to build per square foot than other house types, because of their high ratio of foundation and roof to living space.

4. It's difficult and expensive to build upward on a ranch.

5. Single-level houses usually require relatively wide lots and might be difficult to locate on smaller size parcels found in many neighborhoods.

6. Heating and cooling costs tend to be higher per square foot in ranches because all the ceilings and floors are essentially exterior surfaces. Exterior surfaces allow heat to leak out during the winter and coolness to escape during summer. On multilevel houses, at least some ceilings and floors are interior surfaces.

7. Although it's easy enough when you have room to spread out on a building site, expanding a single-story house can be expensive and difficult on smaller parcels where the house has already been situated on the lot according to zoning restrictions. Local restrictions might prohibit expanding any closer to lot sides and setbacks.

The Cape Cod

This traditional design (Fig. 2.5) derived its nickname from the place where it was first built. Originally a testament to pure function, it resembled a simple Monopoly-style square house capped with a broad low-slung roof all constructed around and over a massive stone chimney that stood erect through the dead center of the house.

Such a monumental chimney served several purposes. First, since the entire house had been built up around the chimney, each room had its own fireplace—either for cooking and/or warmth, and all fireplaces

FIGURE 2.5

A one and one-half-story home.

conveniently shared the same chimney. Second, the chimney also helped give the house stability against fierce Atlantic gales and shifting seacoast sands.

Most of the original Cape Cods were 38 by 29 feet or smaller. They had low ceilings, rarely over 7 feet high. That was about the largest space that could be heated with wood. The entrance was centered at the front of the house, directly opposite a central stairway that led to the second floor. The second floor started at the roofline and was often supplemented with "eye" dormers for additional room, light, and ventilation. Its resulting dormitory-style rooms were popular for storage and for children's bedrooms.

On the first floor, the front of the house consisted of two large rooms, one on each side of the central stairway. A large "Colonial" kitchen took up the entire rear of the dwelling and was flush against the massive all-purpose fireplace hearth. The bathroom was out back. Way out back.

The Cape Cod's windows were small and shuttered to keep out windblown sand, hail, and driving January snows. The small panes or "lites" making up each window were used due to the limitations of the glass-blowing industry in those days. Large panes were difficult to make true and clear.

The entire house usually faced squarely south to take advantage of every available ray of winter sunshine, plus, cleverly enough, to enable occupants to tell time: when the sun's rays came straight through the front window, hitting a marker on the floor in such a way, the people inside knew it was high noon.

As decades passed, and long after the original reasons for the Cape Cod design had ceased to exist, the one and one-half-story house again found supporters during the Depression days of the 1930s. Home-builders liked them because Cape Cods were compact, thrifty houses to construct, especially when the huge fireplaces were left out. Cape Cods had another resurgence after the World Wars when builders mass-produced row after row of them. And the houses are still popular today, in larger more luxurious versions.

Here are a few general guidelines for the one and one-half-story house:

- It can be built over a full or partial basement, a crawl space, or a concrete slab foundation.

- Although the Cape Cod typically still has a front center entrance, it's also a good idea to have a rear access as well.

- As with the ranch, an entrance foyer should distribute traffic so visitors don't step directly into the living room from the outside.

- In a Cape Cod, the master bedroom is often located on the first floor, with the other bedrooms upstairs. Whether on the first or second floor, the master bedroom should be assured of privacy.

- Even if the second story will not be finished off initially, make provisions for future expansion (Fig. 2.6). Have the ceiling/roof area insulated instead of the second floor (more on this in chapter 4).

Advantages

1. It's an economical house to build, with a low cost per square foot of living area. It requires proportionally less materials and labor to construct than other types, and because of its relatively small basement foundation and roof, a larger amount of living space can be had for a smaller financial outlay.

FIGURE 2.6

A one and one-half-story home cutaway.

2. Its two living levels allow distinct zoning for privacy.

3. The Cape Cod is known for its low heating and energy costs, due to its efficient shape.

4. It can be constructed on a small lot.

5. The completed Cape Cod needs fewer furnishings, less interior decoration, and takes less time to clean and maintain than other types.

6. Its low roofline makes it fairly simple to build and maintain, but not so simple as a ranch.

7. The second story can be left unfinished and initially used for attic storage. Later, if more living space is needed, the area can then be employed for practical expansion. This is an economical approach to the problem of insufficient funds. You can initially run heat and air-conditioning pipes and ducts, plumbing pipes, and electrical lines to the second floor and then cap them off there. For air circulation you can install louvered ventilators at each end of the attic from the start. In short, a design like the Cape Cod offers a great "finish it later" potential. This is good for young starters or newly-weds who at first need only a minimum of space but want more later on, as the family grows. Then, when the children eventually leave home, the second floor can be converted into an income unit or merely sealed off and used for storage.

8. Here, one person's advantage can be another's disadvantage. Many people contend that climbing stairs in a Cape Cod or other house having stairs is good exercise to help keep a person fit.

Disadvantages

1. Upstairs rooms beneath the roof tend to be hot during summer and cold during winter unless special care is taken when insulating and installing heating and air-conditioning.

2. When poor planning is followed, the second floor can be cut up into odd-size rooms, with sloping ceilings and dormer windows—causing awkward room layouts.

3. There's the need to provide space for a stairway leading to the second floor. This is space taken away from the first level. And stairs have to be ascended every time you want to visit the second floor.

4. If there's a basement beneath the house, the opening used by the downstairs stairwell takes up more space wreaking havoc with the compact first floor, where every square foot counts.

The Two-Story House

All things considered, the two-story house is one of the best, most efficient designs available (Fig. 2.7). It has become increasingly popular for families looking for a spacious yet economical and private dwelling. A two-story can be built over a full or partial basement, a crawl space, or a concrete slab foundation (Fig. 2.8). Some general guidelines to consider are:

- Once again, through the use of an entry foyer, access should be provided to all parts of the house from the main entrance. The entry foyer is usually the best place to start the upstairs stairway, so those entering the house can go straight to the second floor if they choose.

FIGURE 2.7

A two-story home.

2ND FLOOR

1ST FLOOR

BASEMENT

FIGURE 2.8

A two-story cutaway.

■ As in the other house types, the living room should not be a traffic runway.

■ A rear entrance should be provided (or a side entrance), with direct access to the kitchen, laundry, family room, and all other working and living areas of the house.

■ The upstairs bedrooms should be planned so you don't have to walk through one bedroom to reach another.

Advantages

1. There's natural zoning between the upstairs and downstairs. The upstairs serves as an effective buffer between the sleeping areas and the downstairs living and work spaces.

2. Certain individuals prefer the feelings of privacy, security, and comfort brought about when the bedrooms are located on a second story, well above ground level.

3. Building up as opposed to out is cheaper per square foot. A two-level square house with a given amount of floor space requires only half as much foundation and roof as it would if constructed as a single-level dwelling. Building down means a basement. One justification for a basement is its value as living area. But here the term "living area" is broadly used to cover basement recreation rooms, workshops, hobby areas, and similar spaces planned for special activities. If the basement will likely become a depository for junk, then it shouldn't be considered as possible living space.

4. Size being equal, it's cheaper to heat and cool a two-story than a ranch. Cool air falls, and heat rises. At least one level in a two-story reaps certain benefits, no matter what the outside temperature is.

5. The two-story is adaptable to small lots. In fact, no other common type can match it for getting the most house on the least lot. It's a good choice on either high-priced land or on a tight little parcel. And a simple way to gain more space on the second level without affecting the foundation space requirements is to have the second-story walls overhang the first-story walls, Garrison style. This also aesthetically breaks up the highwall appearance you might otherwise find unappealing.

6. A two-story can be successfully expanded without much advance planning. A family room or wing on the side can be added, but at substantial cost. Due to its compactness on a lot, there's usually plenty of room to build an attached garage. Naturally, if you decide at the time of original construction that someday you will need more space, by building expandable features into the house, you'll save money in the long run.

7. Physical fitness buffs will swear that a two-story improves the cardiovascular system because occupants are forced to exercise by climbing up and down stairs.

Disadvantages

1. Having to frequently go up and down stairs makes housekeeping tougher and puts a strain on parents of young children and on the elderly.

2. It puts restrictions on a family that likes to spend a lot of time outdoors. Although the downstairs can be designed for easy access to the backyard, you might find the times needed to trudge upstairs to retrieve something from a bedroom will amount to a noticeable inconvenience.

3. Unless the attic of a two-story is properly ventilated, the upstairs bedrooms will get uncomfortably hot during summer.

4. Without an elaborate network of wood decks and patios, the upstairs bedrooms are usually shut off from direct access to the outdoors and are not easy to escape from in case of fire or other emergencies.

5. Although the per-square-foot cost of a two-story is much lower than that of a single-story, extra footage must be provided in the two-story to compensate for the space lost to the second-floor stairway. Plus the upstairs stairway limits the flexibility of the overall design.

6. Long ladders are needed to reach the roof, gutters, and second-story windows.

The Split Foyer

A split foyer (Fig. 2.9) is essentially a raised single-story house with the basement or lower level lifted halfway out of the ground and joined to an entry foyer. The lower level is usually finished off into part of the house's living quarters. An identifying characteristic of the split foyer is that the entry foyer is always located about halfway between the two living levels. In other words, once you step into a split foyer you have to go either up or down (usually a half flight of stairs) to reach a living level (Fig. 2.10). Split foyers have also been called, rightly and wrongly, mid-levels, raised-levels, and raised ranches. As with the other house types, there are general points to keep in mind when designing a split foyer:

FIGURE 2.9

A split-foyer home.

FIGURE 2.10

A split-foyer home cutaway.

- Split foyers are meant to be constructed on lots having front-to-back or back-to-front slopes. It's silly to place them on dead level ground. Take a drive through practically any middle-class suburb. You'll notice that the worst-looking split foyers—the "no design" kind, have all been erected on flat lots. Built so, they appear ungainly and awkward. Instead, they should be closely fitted onto sloping parcels, so a natural marriage between the house and land results.

- The two levels of a split foyer provide distinct zoning to help separate working and living activities. Further, room functions can be planned in a variety of ways. On a front-to-back downward sloping lot, the rear entrance is likely to be located in the upper living area, even if it means the construction of an outside wood deck or concrete patio with steps to the ground.

- A split foyer's entry, like the other entry setups, must direct traffic through a hall or foyer arrangement to upstairs and downstairs rooms without marching visitors through the center of other rooms along the way. The rear entrance should also permit easy travel to the kitchen, laundry, and remaining areas.

- The arrangement of living areas can vary greatly in split foyers. Some plans have all the bedrooms on one floor, with the working and living space on the other level. Some plans combine living and sleeping areas on both floors. The garage can be included in the lower level, or attached to the side of the house with its own entry. In any layout, the bedrooms—especially the master bedroom—should be assured privacy from the rest of the house.

Advantages

1. This design offers easy entry from the outside to either interior level.

2. The entrance foyer midway between the upper and lower levels has direct access to at least one bath, thus reducing traffic near the main living areas.

3. Properly designed, a split foyer can look handsome and large, with only a short stairway from either level to the outdoors.

4. The split foyer can provide automatic interior zoning with the sleeping area on one level and the working and living areas on the other.

5. Greater window depth is allowed in the lower level, which yields improved lighting and ventilation. In turn, this helps the area normally referred to as the basement become more desirable for recreation rooms, baths, and bedrooms.

6. The split foyer uses its floor area to the maximum. It has a lower per-square-foot cost compared to a single-story ranch.

7. The simple floor plan and relatively compact design of this house results in construction convenience and savings.

8. With proper attention to correct insulation and careful positioning of heating and cooling appliances, the split foyer is easier to make energy efficient than a dwelling that has many projections and corners, or one that is spread out.

9. Most split foyers are suitable for small lots.

10. The minimal foundation and roof areas help reduce construction costs.

11. When the upper living area faces downhill, you enjoy the full advantage of a view with height.

12. Again, with this design, a physical fitness buff will proclaim that exercise on the stairs helps strengthen the heart.

Disadvantages

1. There's the inconvenience of frequent stair climbing.

2. Even though this dwelling can be energy efficient, because the stairway is more open than that of a two-story, for instance, heat quickly rises to the upper level. If proper insulation, heating, and cooling steps are not taken, the lower level tends to be cold during winter. Special wall insulation below ground level is necessary, and a well-designed heating/cooling system is a must. Rooms over the garage can also be chilly if not well insulated. And during summer, without enough insulation, rooms on the upper level will tend to be on the warm side.

3. The open stairway also reduces the effect of the zoning. Not visually, but because it allows odors and noise to freely move from floor to floor.

4. The split foyer, due to its structure and design, is not easily expandable at a later date.

5. Because the lower level of a split foyer is usually designed for living areas, there's not much room to have a basement workshop or storage facilities.

The Split- or Multilevel

These houses (Figs. 2.11 and 2.12) are essentially split in half vertically with two or more levels so the upper level is only half as high as the ground level floor. A typical layout for this design has the kitchen,

FIGURE 2.11

A multilevel home.

FIGURE 2.12

A split-level home.

dining room, and living room on one level (the ground level), with the bedrooms on another level a half story higher. The ground level may be over a full basement, or constructed on a crawl space in warm-climate regions, with the upper half story over a garage that's on a grade. Here are some general guidelines to keep in mind when planning a multilevel house, or split-level:

- Split-levels are ideally suited for side-sloping lots on hilly terrain where the bottom level faces and opens toward the downhill side and the upstairs level opens toward the uphill side (Fig. 2.13). A split-level house placed on a flat lot will look awkward and will not be a very functional dwelling.

- Arrangements of living areas vary in split-levels. It's best to have the living facilities on one of the upper levels with the sleeping rooms on another for noise breakup and privacy zoning. As with other types of homes, the bedrooms, especially the master bedroom, should be carefully located for privacy.

FIGURE 2.13

A split-level home cutaway.

- The main entrance may be either on the upper or lower grade, as determined by the slope of the building site relative to the street.

- Matching a split-level to a side-sloping lot allows close to a full height exposure on both sides of the dwelling, making each side fully accessible to the outdoors.

- As with other house types, it's a good idea to have a front and rear entrance in a split-level, even though these entrances may be located on different levels. In any event, the living and working centers of the home, including the kitchen and laundry, should be easily accessible from either entrance.

- An entry foyer should distribute traffic via a hallway to the rooms on its own level, and to the stairs leading to other levels.

- Consider that the basement is usually the best place to put the heating unit, storage space, and perhaps a workshop if desired.

Advantages

1. It adapts well to lots with side slopes.

2. A split-level has many of the same advantages a split foyer has. It produces automatic interior zoning. The sleeping area can be on one level, and the working and living areas on other levels.

3. A split-level can offer easy entry from the outdoors to any interior level. On a side-sloping lot you will have at least two main floors with access straight to the outside.

4. When properly designed, a good split-level will look handsome and large, with only a short stairway from one level to another.

5. There can be greater window depths in the lower level, which will gain improved lighting and ventilation for possible expansion of the lower level into a recreation room, bedrooms, or any other living and working space that you may desire.

6. If the areas beneath the upper level are being used for living space, or even for a garage, that means at least three-quarters of the floor area is actively put to good use, thus making the price per square foot reasonably low.

7. Frequent short bursts of stair climbing are considered a plus by the health conscious.

8. When the upper level faces downhill, there's the scenic advantage of a view with height.

9. With the ability to have access from the outside on at least two levels, there should be no problem locating a bathroom near each entrance.

Disadvantages

1. Split-level room arrangements can be jumbled and disjointed if care is not taken during the initial planning stage. You could end up with a house that requires you to climb steps no matter where you want to go, or what you want to do.

2. The heating and cooling requirements of split-levels can be very demanding. The lowest level tends to be cold during winter and needs special wall insulation for any area below ground. A well-designed heating/cooling system is a must. Rooms constructed over a garage tend to be chilly, and the rooms in the upper level are frequently too warm in summer unless proper precautions are taken. This is largely due to the number of open stairways present, similar to those in a split foyer.

3. The open stairways reduce the zoning effect by letting odors and sounds travel freely from one level to another.

4. Because the split-level house has so many different levels, it can be tough to build. This runs up the cost per square foot, especially if substantial bulldozing of the lot is needed for the foundation and landscaping, or if retaining walls must be constructed.

5. Another drawback to split-levels is that they're often difficult to expand due to limitations of the lot and also because tampering with the original plan can easily harm the dwelling's appearance. Too many jogs and angles in the rooflines or exterior walls make them look cluttered and unplanned, as if put together piecemeal.

6. The split-level is a poor choice for individuals who prefer large basements for woodworking shops or want surplus storage space and footage to eventually turn into a basement recreation room.

7. With the two sections of the side-to-side split-level framed under two distinct rooflines, the builder must skillfully integrate the two sections in an artistic manner to avoid the appearance of two separate houses joined together to make a single dwelling.

ALTERNATE HOUSING

In this discussion, alternate housing refers to homes that are constructed differently from typical modern dwellings found in standard subdivisions across the country. Some dwellings, though, due to local building materials and climates, can be considered "alternate" in one location, but not in another (an adobe home in Michigan, for example, would be neither normal nor serviceable).

Special care is needed when planning alternate housing:

1. Allow plenty of time for the construction. Special materials must be obtained. Financing and building permits must be secured from institutions that may not be familiar with "different" methods of construction.

2. A builder experienced in the kind of construction techniques needed for you might be difficult to find.

3. You'll need good, complete budget estimates.

4. Site selection is usually crucial to the overall success of the completed home. Little things can mean a lot. Water tables, prevailing winds, orientation, and topography are all very important.

Steel-Framed Construction

Although steel-framed construction is not really a "type" of housing, the use of steel instead of wood framing members varies far enough from traditional construction methods to be mentioned here. Indeed, to some individuals, steel-framed dwellings sound just as "alternative" as the term "underground" housing. To others, they're a logical extension of modern architecture. After all, steel framing has been employed successfully with industrial and commercial buildings for decades.

Advantages

1. Steel is strong and relatively light for its weight. Steel studs and other framing components with outer dimensions equal to wood members are considerably lower in bulk and greater in strength. Steel members provide increased protection against high winds, hailstorms, heavy snows, hurricanes, earthquakes, and other weather extremes. Due to steel's positive methods of attachment to the foundation, it's less likely that the home will separate from the foundation during an earthquake, hurricane, or other cataclysmic event.

Because of steel's high strength-to-weight ratio, and depending on the design, studs can be placed farther apart instead of using standard 16-inch wood stud centers (Fig. 2.14). This permits greater lengths of uninterrupted wall insulation, with fewer thermal breaks in between. Other advantages to steel's high strength-to-weight ratio include successful home design and construction on soils that have poor bearing capacities, without using expensive oversize footings.

2. Steel framing allows for more flexible design with larger open spaces, including longer floor spans and higher walls. Light steel-framed walls can be used with dwellings of almost any shape.

3. Uniform manufacturing tolerances maintain a consistent, dimensionally correct steel product. That translates to level floors, flat

Twenty-four-inch steel stud centers.

walls, and straight rooflines. Wood members are more likely to contain natural imperfections such as knots or weak spots.

Cheaper wood studs may arrive at the building site twisted and can continue to warp even after being nailed in place. Unstable lumber can add to building costs and create unsightly drywall stress cracks and nail "pop outs" that are frustrating to repair. Steel is available in cut-to-length pieces to reduce in-field cutting and minimize waste.

4. Steel won't rot, splinter, crack, or readily warp, buckle, or twist. It's not as affected by moisture. Other building products, including paper, gypsum, and wood components, are affected by humidity, groundwater, and additional sources of moisture.

5. Steel framing members can be ordered to exact lengths and speci-fications, plus they're on the market in a wide variety of precut standard shapes and sizes. Custom shapes are also available. No high premiums must be paid for extra-long steel framing members, as must be paid for wood, because steel is, of course, manufac-tured to length, while not all logs can be sawn into extra-long boards and beams.

6. Steel resists termites and other wood-destroying insects that can cause wood roofs to sag, floors to slope, and main beams and posts to crumble.

7. Steel is not combustible. Although it can be ruined in a hot fire, it will not burn like wood and does not help fuel a home fire. That can result in lower fire insurance premiums for some policy holders.

8. Screw-attached metal framing members eliminate squeaks and "nail pops," which frequently occur with wood. Screws and bolts won't loosen or pull out under stress like nails can. Steel framing can be manufactured with openings and punch-outs spaced at reg-ular intervals, allowing utility components such as electrical and plumbing lines to be roughed-in easily, instead of drilling holes through wooden framing members. Grommets or conduits can protect the wiring from sharp edges of the punch-outs (Fig. 2.15).

9. Steel framing provides square walls and doors that aren't affected by moisture and don't stick. Such strongly built houses are also much less likely to settle over the years.

WALL STUD
(C-MEMBER)

PREPUNCHED
HOLES FOR
UTILITIES

FIGURE 2.15

Steel framing with punch-outs.

10. Steel framing components, and especially studs, are resilient. That means they help the walls absorb sound. When combined with sound-attenuating insulation, they provide quiet bedrooms and other living spaces.

11. Steel framing also helps achieve good indoor air quality because no pesticides or other chemical treatments are used, nor are resin adhesives present, as they may be with wood.

12. Because steel framing allows for larger open spans (up to about 60 feet without interior support walls), a home can be designed with very few interior load-bearing partitions. Later on, additional nonbearing walls can be added, removed, altered, or even relocated without major disruptions to the home's structure.

13. What about lightning? Wouldn't a steel-framed home attract direct hits, like a lightning rod? The steel, if struck, would actually provide many conductive paths directly to ground, where electrical energy would disperse with no greater chance of explosions, fires, or personal injury than with a dwelling made from wood framing.

14. What about radio-wave interference? The steel framing shouldn't interfere with radio, TV, phone reception, or garage door openers because the waves can still pass through the spaces between the studs.

15. What about fastening pictures on walls or other fixtures onto wall studs? No problem. Simply use metal screws instead of nails.

Disadvantages

There aren't many drawbacks to the steel framing members and panels themselves, but what has been perceived as limiting factors to construction with steel framing are as follows:

1. Availability of steel framing members at building supply centers is somewhat limited, but is improving as various contractors are becoming familiar with using steel in residential dwellings. More and more lumberyards and commercial building supply warehouses are adding steel framing product lines as alternatives to wood.

2. Numerous builders are reluctant to switch from wood to steel simply because that would be a departure from long-standing building techniques they have been using throughout their entire careers.

3. There can be relatively high cost to ship steel framing members from out-of-state manufacturers, while wood is much more likely to be "manufactured" locally—and subject to lower transportation costs.

4. A perception exists with many individuals that wood is a warm, natural, renewable resource and steel is "cold" and manufactured mainly for commercial use.

5. Some people fear that steel will rust, be an electrical hazard, and result in dwellings that look like commercial buildings.

STEEL-FRAMED CONSTRUCTIONS BASICS

Entire books are available on steel-framed construction, and manufacturers offer videos, plans, written instructions, courses, and guidebooks on their products. Some basic points and characteristics of steel construction offered by the various steel kit, component, and package manufacturers include the following:

■ Steel frame houses appear, inside and out, like wood frame construction. Once they're finished, the steel framing is not apparent.

■ Steel component manufacture is typically cold-formed steel in shape, size, and function that mirrors dimensional lumber. The framing components are essentially used in four types of "sections": floor joist systems, exterior and load-bearing walls, non-load-bearing partition walls, and roof rafter and support systems.

FLANGE

NOMINAL
DIMENSION
OUTSIDE

WEB

LIP

FIGURE 2.16

C-member.

■ Steel components such as studs, joists, and rafters are stamped into a squared C shape, called structural-C, C-members, or simply C. The C configuration is made of the cross-sectional configuration consisting of a web, flange, and lip. The web is the part of a C-section that connects the two flanges (Fig. 2.16). Web stiffeners are additional pieces attached to the web to strengthen the web against buckling or crimping (Fig. 2.17). A flange is the part that is perpendicular to the web, and the lip is the part of the C-section that extends from the flange at the open end.

The lip increases the strength characteristics of the member and acts as a stiffener to the flange (Fig. 2.16). C-studs, precut or site cut, are used in structural and nonstructural walls. Channel type wall studs are designed so facing materials can be screw-attached quickly (Fig. 2.18). Those made for load-bearing walls are heavier, typically 20- to 16-gauge steel (gauge is a unit of measurement to describe the nominal thickness of steel—the lower the gauge, the greater the thickness). The studs can be ordered in sizes up to 8 inches in depth. Deeper studs are used in plumbing walls and other special situations. Larger C-members such as 2 × 6s, 8s, and 10s are also made of heavier steel and are used as floor joists, headers, and in some cases, rafters. When extra strength is needed, C-members are joined together to form heavier components. Studs are paired or assembled with tracks to create support posts and jack-stud assemblies. Deeper C-members are joined back-to-back, or flange to flange where heavier beams and headers are required (see Fig. 2.18).

■ U-shaped channels, or tracks, are used for rim joists and wall plates, and built-up assemblies of C-members (Fig. 2.19). The track has a web and flanges, but no lip. When used as wall plates, vertical studs fit inside the tracks and the flanges are fastened together (Fig. 2.19). Clip-angles are L-shaped short pieces of metal, usually with a 90-degree bend, used for connections (Fig. 2.20).

A web stiffener.

Channel type wall studs.

TOP PLATE (TRACK)

WALL STUD

BOTTOM PLATE (TRACK)

FIGURE 2.19

U-shaped channel.

FIGURE 2.20

Clip angle.

■ The zinc-coated galvanized steel protects against rust, as does the "red iron" with its red oxide coating.

■ A homebuilder can purchase the steel framing components or a complete house package with windows, doors, roof, utilities, and more. All the steel framing members are predrilled, color coded, and numbered according to the purchase plans so they bolt together almost like a life-size erector set. Most builders use screw guns and self-tapping screws and sometimes glue to fasten just about any material to steel framing.

■ A steel-framed house is typically built over a conventional poured concrete slab, foundation, or block basement featuring anchor bolts poured in concrete and sticking up for anchoring (Fig. 2.21). Subsequently, each I beam framing assembly is securely bolted in place.

■ Manufacturer kits often include flexible floor plans with clear span interiors and options such as raised or vaulted ceilings and decks.

■ Steel framing members are usually numbered and marked for specific kits and plans. Framing assemblies bolt together then can be tilted up onto the foundation, each bolted to the anchor plates. For ranch homes, the assemblies are often light enough to be handled by several workers without special lifting equipment. Some designs use individual roof trusses, and others combine the roof framing members with the wall framing sections.

■ To help compensate for thermal conductivity of steel, builders include a nonconducting buffer between the exterior siding and the steel studs—most generally a high-density foam board instead of plywood or fiberboard.

■ It's possible to erect insulation vertically and hold it in place with z-furring channels. The channels typically hold insulation blankets, polystyrene insulation, gypsum panels, or other rigid insulation (Fig. 2.22).

■ A typical steel framing roof system is a purloin system which bolts to the top of the main frame rafters. They provide excellent strength and will not sag or weaken over standard lifetimes.

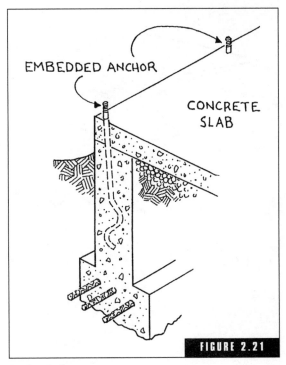

FIGURE 2.21

Anchor bolts.

■ An excellent option when selecting steel framing is the use of prebuilt panels or assemblies—walls, floors, and other components that have been prefabricated. Panels come in handy especially when there is a repetition of panel types and dimensions. Panels can be erected quickly on site and can even be put into place during freezing weather. Because the assemblies are constructed by experienced crews and preinspected, they greatly reduce on-site wasted materials.

■ Steel can't do it all. Even when a home is framed with steel, floor decking and roof sheathing are likely to be plywood or oriented-strand board. The wood backing, sheathing, and decking are also screwed into place, as are wood window and door frames. Casings and trim can then be nailed to these wood components in traditional fashion.

■ If you decide to help engineer your own steel framing, consider that most steel suppliers offer in-house engineering at reduced rates.

INSULATION

DRYWALL

FIGURE 2.22

Z-furring channels.

■ Screws should be about ⅜ to ½ inch longer than the thickness of the connected materials. At least three exposed threads should extend through the steel to ensure a good connection.

■ Insulation should be placed between all studs in exterior walls, between structural members and door and window frames on all four sides, in small spaces between window and door framing members, behind outlet boxes in exterior walls, against second-floor header joists and edge joists, between the top plate and subfloor of two-story and split-level dwellings, between ceiling joists of unheated garages or porches when the rooms above are used for living areas, between ceiling joists below unheated attics, below stairways to unheated attic spaces, in knee walls of heated attics, on basement walls when those spaces are used for living areas, around the inside perimeter of a concrete slab floor in heated spaces, and other logical spaces that, due to the building's design, would need insulation.

■ Check that the places where framing members meet are flat or square as they should be, with no uneven surfaces, odd projections, or extra-wide seams or gaps.

Solar Houses

If anything was ever thought to be the answer to the heating fuel crisis, it has been (and continues to be) the sun. Just the thought of all that free energy has sent environmentalists scurrying to the bookstores and libraries for information and plans on how to construct solar devices. Located just a tad over 90 million miles away from our planet, the sun is ultimately the single source of practically all energy we've ever used.

There are two main types of solar heat and energy producing systems: passive and active. *Passive systems* include design features such as windows, skylights, and greenhouses coupled with materials that will absorb or collect and store heat so the heat can be gradually returned to the home's living areas. *Active systems* feature more advanced methods of storing and distributing the sun's heat and energy.

In a nutshell, solar systems include about five variations, the first two being passive, and the latter three, active:

1. Solar Windows. Even in the coldest climates the south side of a building is warmed by the sun, especially on clear, cloudless days. Windows positioned on the south side of a home are the collectors that let the inside surfaces absorb heat. Depending on the heat-absorbing materials (floors, furniture, air, and so on), the heat is radiated back into the living spaces quickly or slowly.

2. Building Materials/Components Designed for Heat Collection and Storage. These could be a masonry or stone wall or floor, or a water container of some type. Something that would hold heat for a long time and radiate it back into the living spaces at a slow rate, even after the sun has set.

3. Active Collector with Storage and Distribution. These are what you'd probably recognize as solar panels positioned on the roof or side of a building. Heat is drawn from the collector by circulating air or liquid through the collector and is transferred to a storage device. The stored heat is then sent throughout the building through air ducts or piping and radiators.

4. Active Systems that Power Other Heating and Cooling Equipment. The only difference from the previous system is that the collected heat is here used to power a secondary heating or cooling system, rather than directly distributing the collected heat throughout the dwelling.

5. Photovoltaic Cells. These devices convert the sun's energy to electricity, which in turn can provide heat as well as plain old electric energy for a variety of other uses.

Almost every home possesses some sort of passive energy features. Many can be designed into the building plans at surprisingly little cost. Full-fledged, active solar heating, though, is another story. It can be quite expensive, especially when the services of a knowledgeable architect are required.

Naturally, site planning is also a critical consideration when arranging for solar heating.

Wind-Powered Houses

Rarely are wind-powered homes entirely powered by wind. Instead, the available wind machines or "windmills" are designed to supplement energy usages.

Underground Houses

In the mid-nineteenth century, settlers throughout the midwestern prairies had little selection of building materials. Due to the lack of forests, little else was available but the sod of the earth. Early sod homes offered poor protection from the elements. They were dark, damp, and drafty. By itself, soil is an inadequate insulator. The walls of a typical sod dwelling possessed an R-factor between 1 and 2, about the equivalent of a thin piece of plywood.

Today, what we know as underground dwellings also use soil and sod in their construction. The main difference is that they're finely engineered to give their occupants the following benefits:

- They conserve a site's surface space. They're no longer built *upon* the surface of the ground. Instead, they're tucked into the site, beneath part of the surface.

- They provide the owner with low energy consumption. At least several sides, often three, are heavily banked with soil. This cave-like effect more easily maintains a constant temperature, summer or winter.

- They offer excellent privacy and quiet acoustics. Not much sound can penetrate from outside in, or vice versa.

- Modern designs provide stable, durable construction, unlike the old sod homes that easily eroded in the face of prairie storms and winds.

- They're constructed needing low maintenance.

On the other hand, underground homes do not enjoy good reputations by individuals unfamiliar with their construction. People recall the cramped underground bomb shelters popular in the 1950s, or imagine themselves emerging in a bright sunny morning from a dark cellarlike space, eyes squinting like a mole's.

Legitimate concerns are for an underground dwelling's ventilation, waterproofing, and roof construction. In poorly engineered underground homes, those could pose major problems.

Log Houses

This easily recognized home can be built in practically any size, style, and floor plan. It's fairly inexpensive because it uses less framing in its construction than is required of more typically modern dwellings. They can be either custom-built or of the kit type. A kit log house is usually the lowest cost option because the manufacturer supplies only what is necessary, with everything cut to size and little waste. Directions are simple and the construction time quick, although inclement weather can be a major factor here, as in most construction schedules.

One limiting factor, however, is where the log home can be built. It looks out of place in a modern subdivision. Much of its charm comes from it being located on an agricultural or wooded site.

Pole Frame Houses

Frequently featured in architectural magazines, pole frame homes feature a rather strong, easy, cost-effective technique of construction, that of pressure-treated poles embedded in the earth 4 to 6 feet deep instead of the standard concrete foundation. When firmly anchored in the subsoil, pole frame homes can be safely constructed in areas unsuitable for standard foundations, including extremely swampy, rocky, uneven, or even potentially seismic terrains. This can be so because the wood pole foundation for a pole frame house also serves as the major framing members of the dwelling.

Pole frame dwellings also fit nicely into the most modern, exclusive neighborhoods and subdivisions. Their exteriors can be clad with modern sidings and frequently feature passive solar components because fewer load-bearing walls are required with pole/beam construction.

Some building codes, however, have not caught up with pole frame construction, and in certain places it could be difficult to talk savings and loans and building inspectors into rubber stamping the plans.

Also, fewer contractors are familiar with this type of construction, so accurate cost and time estimates may be more difficult to come by in your location.

Prefabricated or Manufactured Houses

Prefabricated houses include all factory-built dwellings. For our purposes, we'll exclude the motor homes and the mobile homes, and move on to the three remaining "prefabs": the shell home, the modular or sectional home, and the panelized home. Each type is available in a mind-boggling range of plans, cost, and quality.

SHELL HOUSES

These homes consist of little but the exterior shell: walls, rough flooring, and a roof. The idea is to put up a weather-tight outside shell of the home, so the inside can be finished off at leisure by the owner, who frequently, for better or for worse, chooses to do much of the work him- or herself.

MODULAR OR SECTIONAL HOUSES

These homes are completely built in the factory and are simply placed or assembled on a waiting foundation. Wiring and plumbing are already included in the sections or walls. These kinds of homes can be ready to be occupied within a few days of delivery.

PRECUT AND PANELIZED HOUSES

Precut homes are assembled on the building site out of materials that have been precisely cut and packaged at the factory. There's very little waste, but there's also a need for strict security at the building site to prevent theft of parts, of boards or key framing members that might disappear as they sometimes do from conventional stick-built sites, where they aren't missed as much. Panelized homes consist of wall sections built on a factory assembly line. Unlike the walls for modular or sectional houses, these walls must be finished off at the building site, frequently by a contractor who must be hired to erect them.

Considerations when comparing prefabricated houses include:

- Will the finished product be what you expect? Take a look at several homes that have already been erected, and speak with their occupants. Prefab manufacturers, at least some of them, have wooed customers with all sorts of free giveaway gimmicks, extras, and other high-pressure sales tactics. Remember that reputable outfits will offer sound value and reliable customer follow-up services.

■ Supposedly, the cost of prefabs should be less than the cost of stick-built houses because the factories use large quantities of the same materials, with less-expensive labor and less waste. Depending on the distance from the factory, those savings could be offset by transportation costs to get the finished product to your site.

■ Popular designs include the A-frame, ski-chalet, and to a lesser extent, the geodesic and other multisided dwellings. These designs are frequently built as second homes, with their uniquely "different" floor plans affording their owners dramatic relief from everyday conventional dwellings.

Plenty of literature is available on prefabricated housing. Manufacturers offer brochures, reports, and sales materials, and many annual publications and monthly magazines are devoted to listing, discussing, and rating the various prefabs currently on the market.

▷▷▷▷▷ POINTS TO PONDER

1. Think about your lifestyle and how you presently live it, or how you want to change it. Then decide on the amount of space you'll need under roof.
2. Review and weigh the advantages and disadvantages of various home types found in this chapter.
3. Decide on the type and style of house that will best lend itself to your objectively arrived at space requirements and your subjectively arrived at preferences for appearance and setting.
4. Seek additional advice from real estate professionals who may urge you to plan more than you need to guarantee increased value or sales prospects if the home must eventually be sold.
5. All things considered, the two-story house is one of the best, most efficient designs available. But it does have stairs from one living space to another.

6. Single-story ranch homes offer the greatest liveability for all members of a household regardless of age.

7. Cape Cods or story-and-a-half homes are economical to build, heat, cool, and expand their living space from an unfinished second floor at a later date.

8. Split foyers and split- or multilevel dwellings are best constructed on lots having front-to-back or back-to-front or side-to-side slopes.

9. Don't be afraid to consider alternate construction methods and materials, including steel framing, solar-power assistance, kit homes, pole framing, log homes, and prefabricated or manufactured homes. There could even be a manufacturer's incentive available for you to be the first in your area to showcase certain dwelling models.

10. If alternate housing is elected, pay particular attention to choosing a contractor who has had experience with building the type of home with the type of construction materials and methods required by your plans.

Traffic Planning and Zoning

After you've reviewed the first two chapters, you should be ready to begin sketching the general layout and design of your house. As you do this, give careful consideration to the overall traffic plan and interior zoning best suited to your own particular situation.

First let's look at the space in a typical house from another angle. What about the place you're living in now? Chances are, you can (or you wish you could) identify three kinds of space by function. Excluding storage areas, there's *private space*, or areas needed for sleeping, dressing, lovemaking, bathing, and studying. There's *social space*, or areas for being with others, entertaining, relaxing, and recreating. And there's *transitional space*, or places, depending on the circumstances, where either private or social activities can occur.

To discuss interior zoning in relation to those areas, we must study traffic that enters and exits the house, traffic that moves within the house itself, plus room-to-room relationships.

TRAFFIC ENTERING AND EXITING THE HOUSE

Service Access

It might sound snobbish, but there should be a definite entrance to be used by servicemen, repairmen, and individuals delivering items they have to carry into the house. Such an entry should be wide enough, direct, and as short to service areas as possible. The kitchen, laundry, basement, and utility rooms should be the prime considerations here, since those areas are the places most frequented by servicemen and vendors.

This entrance should be a logical alternative to protect the living room from unwanted intrusions by casual visitors such as messengers, salespersons, or unexpected visitors for whom a proper reception has not been prepared, such as your clergyman or parents-in-law. Ideally, this access, or a sidewalk that leads to it, should be visible and obvious from the front of your house so people who have never been to your place can determine which entrance to use by themselves. Otherwise, a small tasteful sign can be strategically placed at a sidewalk that leads to a side or rear entrance.

The most important idea of a service access is to reduce cross traffic through the living areas of the house whenever possible. Why invite a meter reader or other service provider to pass through your dining room while en route to the basement? It's wise to eliminate as much of this type of cross traffic as you can.

Guest Access

This entrance is traditionally for friends and guests of the family. It is the main front door, the entrance that usually faces the front street. It should be easily accessible from the driveway and the front street, and from all rooms inside the house so occupants are able to quickly answer the door when someone arrives.

This entrance should provide guests exterior shelter from the elements while they're waiting at the door, and should have a place to remove coats, a closet to hang them up in, and an area in which visitors can adjust to the surroundings (entrance hall, foyer, vestibule, gallery).

It should provide efficient access to those parts of the house guests are most likely to frequent. This includes the living room, dining room, recreation or party room, an office, a patio, the bathrooms—each family's pattern of living will determine the needs for guest accessibility. In addition, this access should give a pleasant impression to visitors, as well as a sampling of the quality and character of the house.

Day-to-Day Indoor/Outdoor Movement

Children need a good access to repeatedly go in and out while playing. Because very young children need almost constant supervision, a back door to their play yard may be a necessity. Excessive running through the house can be minimized further by locating toilet facilities near the door most often used by children.

Guests invited for outdoor activities usually enter the house by the front door then proceed to the location of the activity. This path should be fairly direct and avoid, if possible, passing through a room.

Because the outdoor living areas are likely to be the setting for picnics, barbecues, and similar events, the exits should be located near the kitchen. Here again, the availability of bathroom facilities for adult outdoor activities (in addition to the convenience for children) comes into play.

Removal of waste materials should involve a minimum of travel through the inside of the house. Containers for staging garbage and trash are usually located near the service areas, screened from public view.

If you have a basement planned, consider an outside door for the convenience of children who are playing downstairs. This lets them run straight outside without tracking through the rest of the house. And it's a great energy and time-saver if your laundry equipment is situated in the basement, where you can quickly walk outdoors to hang up wet clothes in nice weather. Also, when you're working outside in the yard, you can enter the basement, change clothes, and get cleaned up. It's nice to be able to bring large items in through the basement door instead of carrying them through the house and down the basement stairs. This means a lot when transporting clothes washers and dryers, freezers, pool tables, and other large objects. A direct basement access will also be a time-saver when you store outdoor equipment such as screens, storm windows, garden tools, and lawn mowers in the cellar.

In addition to the main front entrance, a separate side or rear access usually serves as the family entrance for grocery shopping, for children going to and coming from school, for family members taking out the laundry from a first-floor utility area, plus other informal activities.

General Guidelines for Entries

For safety's sake, install a peephole or window in your front and rear doors so you can see who is ringing or knocking.

Again, it's not a good idea to have a front door that opens directly into the living room. A main entrance center hall or foyer should both shield you and your visitors from an inrush of wind, snow, or rain, and keep your living room privacy intact. Although the main entrance should lead to the living room area, it shouldn't encourage people to pass through the living room on their way to the rest of the house. If so, it causes interruptions, wear and tear on the carpet, and other inconveniences. A good floor plan will provide access to all main living areas through hallways or foyers rather than directing traffic from one main room to another. This also means that you should provide the ability, even in open-style plans, for direct access to the kitchen and bedrooms without intruding on living room activities. Thus children can come and go without interrupting a conversation you are having with guests in the living room.

The access from the front door to the kitchen should be easy and direct, as this path is frequently used. There should be a convenient sheltered entrance to the kitchen from the garage, carport, or driveway, so groceries can be brought into the house and put away without a lot of effort and fuss.

You'll want good guest circulation with the ability to move the guests from the front door to the coat closet, bathroom, and living room. A clothes closet is essential near the front and side/rear entrance, not only for guests but for family members as well.

The remaining components of traffic planning and zoning in a house deal with internal movement and room-to-room relationships.

INTERNAL MOVEMENT

Here are five points to consider when developing your floor plan:

1. The living, sleeping, and work areas should be separate from one another. Yet they should be positioned properly in relation to each other and to additional factors such as orientation to the street, the sun, and even to scenic views. It's important to weigh your feelings toward "bedrooms" versus "work and play noise," or "entertaining guests" versus "bothering sleeping children." In other words, how much of a buffer zone between the bedrooms and the rest of the house do you think you'll need?

A two-story house contains natural zoning, with the kitchen and living rooms on the first floor—a full story below the bedrooms. In a single-story house the living and sleeping areas should generally be located at opposite ends of the house, neatly connected by the kitchen and utility room.

2. Try to separate quiet rooms from noisy ones by distance. Keep bedrooms as far away as possible from the living, food preparation, and utility areas. Isolate study rooms from play areas, hobby rooms, party rooms, and workshops. Adequate sound-absorbing features become particularly important in moderate-size houses with open kitchens, combined living and dining room areas, and all-purpose family rooms, and also in children's play areas and adult workshops.

3. In the interest of silence, though, don't get carried away. Make sure no key area is completely isolated (laundry rooms and bathrooms especially), and also see that there's a safe place for children to play while you're entertaining in the living room.

4. In houses where stairs are necessary, the head of the stairs should be centrally located. This not only minimizes the need for halls, it also frees exterior walls for windows and adds natural lighting and inexpensive ventilation. In two-story houses the stairway to the basement is usually positioned beneath the stairs to the second floor. The problem with this setup is one of arranging your plan so the head of the basement stairs is located near the service or rear/side door so items can come and go from the basement in an efficient manner.

5. For ease of internal movement, many people favor an open plan. Open planning attempts to achieve a feeling of spaciousness; the interior of a house is made to appear larger than it really is through the elimination of solid walls between activity centers and by substituting partial walls, screens, or open room dividers.

A small dining room will appear larger if no solid wall stands between it and the living room. The uninterrupted expanse of ceiling visually increases the appearance of the dining room, and it has the same effect in the living room. The two rooms "borrow" space from each other.

Similarly, a kitchen will appear larger if it opens to a family room or dining space. This can be accomplished by using a breakfast bar to separate the two spaces. The open feeling is not lost even if you opt for a cabinet over the bar. Space between the bar and cabinet, and the cabinet and the ceiling, as well as the absence of a door between the two areas will be sufficient to retain the openness.

Of course, there are disadvantages to the open plan: a lack of privacy, conflicting activities can be distracting, and incorrectly grouped furniture might "float" without unifying walls.

ROOM-TO-ROOM RELATIONSHIPS

Although you might have already read about some of these points in the first two chapters, many are so important that they bear repeating. A main consideration to keep in mind is that your traffic patterns should not take people through the middle of several rooms (or even one room) while en route to another.

The Kitchen

This is considered to be the most important room of a house. Certainly it's the heart of a house, a place used by the entire family for a variety of activities. It's most often placed adjacent to both dining and living rooms and close to a patio or deck where a barbecue can be located. If you have a first-floor family room, this too should be within easy reach of the kitchen, so that the dishes used for snacking are not far from the sink.

The kitchen should be centrally located to have "control" over the entire house. Here are other considerations:

- It should be easily accessible to the front door so guests can be received, and to the family entrance at the rear or side so a car can be unloaded and deliveries accepted.

- From the kitchen you should be able to keep an eye on children playing either inside or out.

- The basement stairs should be close by, especially if you have any food storage down there, or if your laundry is in the cellar.

- Having a bathroom within a few steps of the kitchen saves a lot of time.

- Consider that an open area from the kitchen to the dining or family rooms allows for free conversation and visiting while you're cleaning up or preparing something to eat. An island or peninsula, while still "open," can help separate the kitchen from a family room to keep curious hands away from hot pots, pans, and other kitchen hazards.

- Think twice about a kitchen that steps down into a family room. It may be harmless to household members who are used to this arrangement, but it could result in children and guests unfamiliar with such a step taking spills through the years ahead.

- Ideally a kitchen has no more than two doors, one to the dining area or front of the house, and one to the service/family entrance or garage. Within the house there should be alternate ways to reach those areas without going through the kitchen. If there are three or more doors in the kitchen they should be located in one passageway that doesn't break up the kitchen work traffic.

- After the kitchen's location is decided upon, appliances should be arranged so that distances between the central cooking area (range), the preparation and cleaning area (the sink), and the food storage area (the refrigerator and pantry) are no more than 7 feet each (Fig. 3.1).

- If possible, the kitchen should have at least one, and preferably two, outside walls in which to place windows. An open kitchen room arrangement and windows facing the backyard enable parents to keep an eye on their children during meal preparation and cleanup. Window screens will enable grease fumes and cooking odors to be removed. Windows also serve as pleasant distractions for the busy cook by providing scenic and interesting views when available.

A kitchen work triangle.

- Although the kitchen should have a convenient central location, watch out for any traffic patterns that route individuals from the living room to the bedrooms by passing directly through the kitchen or dining areas.

The Laundry Area

This feature is usually placed in one of four areas within the house:

1. In or next to the kitchen. This allows much of the required housework to be done in the same general vicinity, without wasted motions.

2. In the basement. But this forces you to constantly go up and down stairs when doing the wash, and if you don't have a direct outdoors access from the basement, it makes hanging up clothes in the yard cumbersome.

3. Near the bedrooms. This makes it handy for changing out of your soiled clothes and putting away clean garments.

4. In warmer climates where basements aren't included with many houses, a popular place to put the laundry is in a mud room attached to part of the garage or in a breezeway.

No matter where the laundry room is, you'll need easy access to the outdoors, you'll need space for a clothes washer and dryer, soaps and cleansers, and you'll need enough room nearby to set up an ironing board.

The Utility Area

This is where the furnace, air-conditioning unit, water heater, and possibly a humidifier are set up. From the standpoints of maintenance, efficiency of operation, and cost of installation, this area should be somewhat centrally located in a basement, but not out in the middle of the cellar floor. It should be close to a wall to avoid breaking up a large portion of otherwise usable space. Although the furnace, water heater, and related appliances are typically located in the basement, when no basement is included they're placed in a mud room, garage, or integrated into their own area right inside the house.

Again, in the basement, the furnace, water heater, heating and air-conditioning ducts, humidifier, main electrical box, central vacuum unit, plumbing pipes, water filters/conditioners, main water supply isolation valve, water fixture isolation valves, sump pump, burglar alarm panels, staircases, clothes washer and dryer and laundry sink/tub, freezer, storage shelves, and related appliances should be positioned out of the way, or at least where you want them—in case you decide to finish off part of the space later. Yet the equipment needing preventive maintenance and eventual repairs should be laid out in a manner to allow easy access. At least one window should be large enough for an emergency exit—if no outside basement doors are planned.

Bathroom Facilities

Here are some considerations:

- Avoid having bathrooms visible from other rooms, especially from the living room or head of the stairs.
- Be certain that guests can easily get to a bathroom without being under direct observation from the living room.
- Position at least one bathroom near the bedrooms.
- A bathroom should be simple to get to from the rear or side entrance for children playing or adults entertaining outdoors.

Bedrooms

Bedrooms should be placed together in one part of the house, protected from outside noises as much as possible and also convenient to bathrooms. This makes parental supervision easier and simplifies the problem of maintaining a quiet sleeping area.

- Don't situate bedrooms one after another in a series requiring passage through each other.
- When dressing, people should be able to move between the bedrooms and the main bathroom without being seen from the living areas.
- There should be a buffer zone between the living and sleeping areas so parents can entertain while children sleep. The placement of bathrooms, hallways, closets, bookshelves, utility rooms, fireplaces, or other interior masonry walls can serve as sound barriers between the various quiet rooms and the noise-producing ones. Avoid "closet" walls that have only a thin plywood or fiberboard backing as the barrier between two rooms.

The Dining Area

The dining area should be adjacent to the food preparation space. For quick meals many people use a bar that is part of the kitchen work counter. Others rely on a table in the kitchen, or position a table in the family room or breakfast room. Still others choose to have a separate formal dining room next to the kitchen.

The Living Room

The living room should be near the main front entrance. It's used for such activities as reading, visiting, and entertaining guests. If your house won't have a separate family room, you can use the living room for watching television and listening to music. In any case, this room should be at a dead-end location to discourage unnecessary traffic from interrupting conversations and other activities.

Storage Areas

As mentioned earlier, storage is a vital consideration when planning your home. Keep in mind the following points:

- There should be ample storage in all rooms of a house.

- Each bedroom should have its own closet(s).

- It is convenient to have storage space in bathrooms either under the sink or in a separate closet.

- The hallway leading to the bedrooms should have a linen closet for clean sheets, pillowcases, blankets, and other bedding and bathroom linens.

- Plan closets near all of the entrance doors: front door, side door, and rear door. These closets are needed to keep guest and family member coats, hats, boots, umbrellas, and similar personal clothing and care items.

- If there's no formal laundry area, consider a laundry closet near the kitchen or bedrooms.

- In the kitchen, a pantry closet for storing canned foods and appliances is a true plus.

- A broom closet in the kitchen is needed to store dust mops, brooms, sweepers, ironing boards, and other unwieldy items.

GENERAL GUIDELINES

Make sure the size and arrangement of your rooms allows for flexibility of living arrangements. Check that your house plan has enough windows to provide plenty of natural lighting and cross ventilation, yet that the windows will not severely limit the wall space for your furniture and decorations.

✔✔✔✔✔ **COMMON MISTAKES CHECKLIST**

Before you go to the next chapter, on size planning and future expansion, here's a checklist of things people often overlook or fall for:

___ No separate entranceway or foyer to receive visitors.

___ No window or peephole in the front and rear doors, so the occupants can't see who's knocking or ringing the doorbell.

___ No roof overhang or similar protection over the front door.

___ An isolated carport or garage with no sheltered direct access from the car to the house.

___ No direct access route from the driveway, carport, or garage to the kitchen.

___ No direct route from the back- or side yard to a bathroom so children can come in and out with a minimum of bother.

___ Are gas, electric, and water meters planned for the inside of the house? In the garage or basement? If so, move them outside to eliminate the need for meter readers to clomp through the house every other month.

___ A fishbowl picture window in the front of the house exposes you to every passerby.

___ Accident-inviting basement doors that open inward toward the cellar steps.

___ Walls so cut up by windows and doors that furniture placement is extremely limited. Plan ahead to accommodate your furnishings. Is there sufficient wall space? Develop a sense of scale and dimensions as you evaluate room sizes and window and door locations. The height of the window sills are important factors. Desks, bureaus, chests, dressers, and buffets all require wall space. If the window sills are

✔✔✔✔✔ COMMON MISTAKES CHECKLIST *(CONTINUED)*

high enough, some of the furniture can be placed beneath windows. Many major furniture pieces are between 30 and 32 inches high.

___ Windows in children's rooms that are too low for safety, too high to see out from, and too small or difficult to escape from in case of a fire.

___ A hard-to-open double-hung window over the kitchen sink is a big pain in the neck. An easy-to-crank casement window is best here, and a sliding window second best.

___ A window over the bathtub causes problems. It can result in cold drafts as well as rotted window sills from condensation.

___ Bathrooms located directly in the line of sight from living areas, or directly in view from the top of the stairs so everyone knows when others are using the bathrooms, makes for embarrassing situations.

___ Having only one bathroom is especially tough in two-story houses and split-levels.

___ No light switches at every room entrance/exit.

___ No lights or electrical outlets on a porch, patio, or terrace.

___ No lighting outside to illuminate the approach to the front entrance.

___ Noisy light switches that go off and on like pistol shots. Silent switches cost only a little more.

___ Child-trap closets that can't be opened from the inside.

___ Small closets that are hardly large enough for half your wardrobe. Also watch out for narrow lost doors that keep much of the closet out of easy reach unless you happen to use a fishing rod. Be careful of basketball-player shelves too high for a person of normal height, and clothes poles fastened so low that dresses and trousers can't hang without hitting the floor.

___ Avoid a situation where there is no room for expansion. Sometimes, due to how the dwelling is placed on the lot, or because of building or zoning restrictions or construction methods, a house simply cannot be expanded.

___ Watch out for rooms that are too small to be practical. There's competition among builders and developers to get the largest number of

✔✔✔✔ COMMON MISTAKES CHECKLIST *(CONTINUED)*

rooms in a given square footage, at the lowest price. A dining room is too small if you cannot walk around the table and chairs.

__ A floor plan that provides poor circulation in and out of the house and from one room to another.

__ No interior zoning: the living, working, and sleeping areas are all jumbled together, each infringing on another's integrity.

__ No consideration to the number of floor levels—one, one and one-half, two, or multilevels—that offer the most advantages and greatest living conveniences to *your* family.

__ A house interior that's dark and drab from a lack of ample window and glass placements. Strategic windows and glass sliding doors can go a long way to make your house bright, cheerful, and attractive. But don't overdo them; hang on to your privacy as well.

__ A kitchen that's situated at one end of the house, not centrally located.

__ A poorly designed kitchen. An inefficient work triangle, skimpy counter space and storage, no place to eat in comfort, and a lack of outdoor access. If any room of the house deserves the most attention to detail, it's the kitchen.

__ Inadequate storage space throughout the house might not become apparent for a few years, but when it does, that lack of space will be most frustrating. Make sure the closets are large enough for storing household items, linen, and laundry, as well as for personal possessions—seasonal and routine items.

▶▶▶▶▶ POINTS TO PONDER

1. The living, sleeping, and work areas should be as separate from each other as possible. Quiet rooms can be separated from noisy ones by distance. For example, in a single-story home, the living and sleeping areas should generally be located at opposite ends of the dwelling, neatly connected by a kitchen and utility room.

2. "Open" planning encourages easy movement from one area to another and gives a feeling of spaciousness.
3. Adequate sound-absorbing features in ceilings, floors, and walls become particularly important in moderate-size houses with open kitchens, combined living and dining rooms, and all-purpose family rooms.
4. There should be enough windows in your floor plan to allow for plenty of natural lighting and cross ventilation, yet not too much glass to severely limit furniture and decorative item placements.
5. Bathrooms should be positioned so their entrance doors are as private as possible.
6. There should be a direct route from the back- or side yard to a bathroom so children and adults can come in with a minimum of bother.
7. The kitchen should be centrally located whenever possible—not at one end of the house.
8. There should be a direct access from the driveway, carport, or garage to the kitchen.
9. An outside entrance/exit from the basement can be a great labor- and time-saving feature.
10. In houses where stairs are necessary, the head of the stairs should be as centrally located as possible, to reduce the need for hallways and to free exterior walls for windows for natural lighting and efficient ventilation.

Size Planning

Before you begin drawing your final plans and prints, within the best of your abilities try to determine how large your house should be and whether you can realistically afford it just yet. If your dream house is financially out of reach, face the facts. You'll have to decide exactly what's necessary and what can be scaled down, completely eliminated, or added on at a later date. If you elect future expansion as the best option, then plan for that expansion long before your new house is begun.

To start you out on the right track, this chapter covers two important subjects:

1. How to arrive at the correct size house to suit your present and future needs.

2. How to prepare your house for future expansion.

DECIDING ON THE SIZE OF YOUR HOUSE

The size of a house is generally expressed, as mentioned earlier, in total square footage of finished floor area. This is the key figure used today for determining building value.

Often a higher-priced house offers more square footage for the money, or more value in space per dollar than that offered by an inexpensive dwelling. Thus cheaper houses are frequently more costly per square foot. Of course, it also depends on special items and options built into each home but, all things equal, smaller houses tend to be more expensive per square foot of living space.

That holds true because smaller houses incur overhead costs comparable to those of larger houses, and in smaller dwellings those same overhead costs must be spread out over a lesser amount of square footage. In a sense, it's like buying groceries in bulk. The smaller packages usually cost more per ounce or per pound than their larger-size counterparts. On the other hand, smaller homes generally use less energy to heat and cool, plus there are fewer square feet to maintain and keep clean.

To get a handle on how the costs in a typical house and lot are broken out, those expenses can be separated into three relatively equal categories (Fig. 4.1): one-third of the costs result from the land and improvements to that land. Improvements can include a water well, septic system, utility connections, landscaping, a driveway and sidewalk, and even road construction if needed. Another one-third of the costs go to the house structure from foundation to roof, including the house shell and entire framework. The remaining one-third of the costs come from the vital organs of the house, which include the plumbing, heating, and electrical systems, and also the kitchen and bathrooms.

If you study that division of costs, it becomes evident that when the first and last categories remain fairly constant in price, you can considerably add to the size of the house by increasing the dimensions of the basic structure at a substantially reduced cost per square foot of living space.

Here are some pointers to weigh when size planning:

1. When considering the overall size of your house, the number of bedrooms can be used as an acceptable guide. At least three bedrooms are recommended even if you have no children or are planning no children in the future. A

FIGURE 4.1

A breakdown of house/lot costs.

two-bedroom house is for the most part more difficult to sell because fewer people are looking for them. Anyway, you can always turn a spare bedroom into a study, sewing room, or game area.

2. To economize on materials and labor, view the space inside your house in terms of actual requirements. Determine what each individual room will be used for, and then decide on its size and shape. You might realize that certain rooms such as walk-in closets are a waste for you.

3. When designing and planning rooms, consider your present dwelling. Are the rooms there too small? Or too large? Think about rooms in other houses you've been in. Focus on ones that are close to what you want. If you can, measure the ideal rooms to leave no doubt in your mind. And don't leave out the work area in the kitchen that will have to accommodate appliances, cabinets, and closet space.

4. The housing requirements of a typical family change about every five years, as time marches on. You might want to keep that in mind while laying out the size and shape of your new house. How do you fit into the following typical household scenario?

   - Using a young couple just starting out together as the initial family unit, all their living requirements could be contained in a small dwelling, from a one-bedroom kitchenette/bath apartment to a two-bedroom house.
   - Between 5 to 10 years, with the addition of one or two children, the needs go up to at least two and possibly three bedrooms, larger living spaces, and more storage.
   - Between 10 to 15 years, the typical family, if three children are present by then, needs more sleeping space, a second bath, and more living and storage area.
   - From 15 to 25 years, this 10-year span while the children are maturing is likely to be stable unless the wage-earner's business requires a change of locale or an upgrading of living standards.
   - At 25 through 40 years, during each 5-year period it's likely that one child will fly the nest—for marriage or at least for college or career.
   - Over 40 years, the family is once again down to two people, and large amounts of space can become a hindrance rather than a help.

Planning for Future Expansion

For any of a variety of reasons you might not be able or be willing to start out with the size house you'd like to eventually have. If you want to avoid jumping from house to house every few years as your housing needs increase, consider the following:

1. Initially plan a house that can be easily expanded at a later date.

2. Review the house design you want in relation to the ease or complexity of making additions. Allow space and structure adaptability to add a garage, foyer, family room, bedrooms, second bath, or whatever it may be that you didn't initially build into your house.

3. When more space is required of a single-story ranch or two-story house, the construction of an addition to the rear or side of the house may be the best (but not the cheapest) answer. In both types of houses, it's a good idea to begin with dwellings that are able to accept additions without having their overall architectural character ruined by those additions. Consider how roof slopes, window types, exterior finishes, dormers, and similar features will be affected by the modifications you're planning. Also pay close attention to property line construction setbacks, so they won't rule out your ability to expand in other ways at some future date.

4. If your expansion plans call for knocking out a wall or walls later to enlarge part of your house, plan for that *before* the house is completed. Leave plumbing out of the walls that will be removed. Support the above ceiling or floor independently of the affected walls. Build the framework for the new entrance right into the wall so all you need to do is knock out the rest of the wall when the time is right. Electricity is not a problem; light switches and outlets are easily moved.

5. When working with large unfinished places that will eventually be rendered into living areas, place doors and windows in such a way that easy-to-install partitions can be erected to turn big, open spaces into several individual rooms, as desired.

6. Although it might not be the way for you, there's no doubt that building up or down is cheaper than building out.

When Expanding Upwards

If you start out with a Cape Cod, a two-story, or even a ranch house having unfinished upper levels or attics, there are a number of technical points to be addressed when planning the initial structure.

To permit maximum expansion without resorting to exterior modifications, the roof slope must be steep enough (or a gently sloped roof raised up enough) to provide adequate head room for new living areas. For example, on a house having a width of 24 feet or more, make sure your roof slope—if the roof is not stepped up or raised up substantially—has a minimum of 9 inches of height for every 12 inches of travel or run toward the peak. Also make certain the floor joists of the unfinished floor or attic are large enough to carry typical floor loads (Fig. 4.2).

Whatever your plan, you'll have to comply with local building codes that usually require one-half of a room's ceiling area to have a minimum floor-to-ceiling height of 7½ feet. Thus, if your attic space has windows at the gable ends, sufficient head room, and properly

FIGURE 4.2

A cutaway of an attic expansion.

sized floor joists, the construction of one or more rooms is a relatively simple and inexpensive project, with no need for exterior remodeling. Extensions of existing heat, air-conditioning, and return air ducts that had already been installed to and capped off at the area to be finished and activation of the already rough plumbing and wiring should result in a satisfactory expansion of your existing house at a nominal cost.

To attain increased floor area and more wall space for windows, dormers are recommended. Two types of dormers may be used: the shed dormer, and the window or gable or "eye" dormer (Fig. 4.3).

The shed dormer is the most practical because it adds a great deal of floor and wall space and is relatively simple to construct. However, because it's not as pleasant to look at as the window dormer, it's generally built at the rear of the house. A window or "eye" dormer offers less space, but it's still a major improvement over nothing. The illumination, ventilation, and increased floor space it brings can transfer an otherwise little-used space into a cozy bedroom or study. This addition of dormers can often be accomplished without removing the existing structure's entire roof.

FIGURE 4.3

Shed and gable or eye dormers.

When Expanding Downwards

If you start out with a house having a basement, and you plan on eventually using that basement for additional living space, then keep the following points in mind:

1. Make sure you have enough clear area to allow for basement expansion. You wouldn't want your water heater, furnace, stairs, and other items to be laid out so they break up the entire cellar.

2. Use larger-than-normal basement windows for extra light and ventilation, and consider an outside access so you don't have to walk through the main part of the house every time you want to go in or out of the cellar.

3. If you plan to add a bathroom to your basement in the future, be sure to locate the sewer drain pipes below the cellar floor. If the sewer pipes enter the basement midway up the wall, you're in for extra expense and inconvenience when you have to add a pump system to push the refuse upwards.

In conclusion, you'll find that interior expansion is always more economical than exterior expansion. But exterior expansion provides extra space without sacrificing attic storage or basement areas.

No matter which direction you plan to expand in—whether it be up, down, or out—make sure your furnace/air-conditioning units will have the capacity to handle the extra load.

All in all, a small increase of effort in the initial planning, plus a little additional cost, can make enormous differences in the ease and expense of expansion at a later date.

▶▶▶▶▶ POINTS TO PONDER

1. As a rule, because smaller houses incur overhead costs comparable to those of larger dwellings, a larger home built on the same lot with the same quality of construction would likely cost less per square foot of living space than would that of the smaller house.

2. When considering the size of your house, the number of bedrooms can be used as a general guideline. At least three bed-

rooms are recommended even if you have no children or are planning no children in the future, because—unless you're in an area heavily populated by retirees—two-bedroom homes are more difficult to sell because fewer people are looking for them.

3. Consider your present residence. Are the rooms there too small? Or too large? Measure ideal rooms to leave no doubt in your mind as to how large they are.

4. The housing requirements of a typical family change about every five years, as time marches on. Consider your family's maturation and living needs as you lay out the size and shape of your new home.

5. If you're unable or unwilling to start out with the size home you'd eventually like to have, consider initially planning and building a house that can be easily expanded later.

6. If expansion plans call for knocking out walls later to enlarge part of the house, plan for that *before* the home is completed. Leave plumbing out of the walls that will be removed. Support the above ceiling or floor independently of the affected walls. Build the framework for the new entrance right into the wall so all you need to do is knock out the rest of the wall when the time is right.

7. When working with large unfinished spaces that will eventually be rendered into living areas, place doors and windows in such a way that easy-to-install partitions can be erected to turn those big, open spaces into several individual rooms, as desired.

8. Dormers are excellent ways to attain increased floor area and more wall space for windows.

9. When expanding upward with a Cape Cod, a two-story, or even a ranch house having unfinished upper levels or attics, the roof slope must be steep enough—or a gently sloped roof raised up enough—to provide adequate head room for new living areas. And make sure the floor joists of the unfinished floor or attic are large enough to carry typical floor loads.

10. When expanding downward into a basement, make sure that the basement is high enough (9 feet is not too high), that the heating/cooling equipment and stairs are laid out so they won't break up the entire cellar, that larger-than-normal basement windows are used for extra light and ventilation, that an outside access is considered, and that there's a logical place to install a bathroom.

Prints and Drawings

Now that the first four chapters have touched upon most of the major options involved when a house is planned, such as dwelling styles, types, floor plans, individual rooms, and sundry accessories, you can see how inefficient it is to just go to a builder and describe what you want in vague generalities.

WHY YOU SHOULD CREATE THE PLANS

To walk into a skilled contractor's office and hint merely at what you think you need, and then let the builder charge ahead and build it using his or her own discretion, is in a sense like going into a clothing store and—without even browsing through the racks—telling a salesperson who knows neither your size nor your taste in clothes to please select an entire suit of clothes, right down to the shoes, that you'll be sure to like. The salesperson would be astonished. No one ever leaves that many decisions up to a total stranger, however knowledgeable about clothes the salesperson might be. Naturally, the salesperson would start asking questions, inquiring what *type* of clothes? Sports, leisure, business, or social? What *size* slacks do you take? Made of which materials, in what colors? For winter or fair-weather use? And what price range are you looking in?

To take the analogy a step further, what about the purchase of an automobile? A new car is a major expenditure to most of us. You decide what style, type, and size vehicle is best suited to your needs, desires, and pocketbook. Few people will stroll into a dealer's showroom and request a "four-door sedan," and fewer yet will ask a salesperson to simply suggest something out of the blue. Try it sometime and see what happens. It's human nature for a salesperson to try to convince you to purchase whatever is being pushed at the time by the dealer. And salespeople are good at that. That's why they're in sales.

Builders are a different breed. Builders are accustomed to dealing with people who walk in cold, having only a foggy idea of what they want. By far, most builders will play fair with their customers, will try to help a potential homeowner arrive at a suitable house design. Some, however, especially during times when plenty of work is available, become irritated by customers who come expecting counseling services to help plan an entire dwelling from scratch. These builders will invariably suggest a stock plan—a house they're thoroughly familiar with, perhaps one they've built within the past few months.

Other builders, when faced with an undecided client, will ask dozens of questions such as "How large do you want the bedrooms?" and "What size garage?" Then they try to piece together an appropriate plan from your answers.

Somewhere along the line each builder is going to have to know how much material to order. How else can he bid the job? To know that, he's going to need a set of plans, a set of blueprints and drawings to use as a guide. And just as a cook needs to follow recipes in the kitchen, so does a builder need prints and drawings to follow in the field.

If you're still not convinced that you should participate fully in the creation of the prints and drawings by making many of the optional construction decisions yourself, then consider that the builder wants you to be pleased with the finished product, but rarely does that concern go too far past the technical level. Do you really think it will register on a contractor if you say "Gee, you should have made the family room 2 feet longer so we could fit our overstuffed sofa in front of the fireplace"? What else can he say but "I'm sorry. It was on the plans you approved." To mention that the basement has heaved up and it's full of water—now *that* will register. Builders can handle complaints centering on the actual construction—the carrying out of the original agreed upon plans. But if you chastise a contractor after he erects the house that the garage should have been located on the other side of the dwelling to act as a shield against prevailing winter winds—your efforts will likely fall on deaf ears.

FINAL SET OF PLANS

No matter where you get them, your final set of prints and drawings should in some way address the following:

Floor Plans

One blueprint for each floor. These are working drawings showing overall dimensions, room and hallway sizes, location and sizes of doors and windows, location of interior partitions and wall thicknesses, location of electrical switches, plugs, and appliances, plumbing fixtures, water supply, drains, and other information needed to complete the house (Fig. 5.1).

Lot Plan

The lot plan shows the original contour of the land, the proposed finished contours, original trees and the ones which will be left standing, the location of a water well and septic tank if applicable, the driveway, electrical service, and the placement or orientation of the house on the building site (Fig. 5.2).

Foundation Plan

The foundation plan shows the height of the sill (where the house frame rests on the foundation or top of the basement) above grade, the chimney location, the extent of excavation and grading required, plus the location of water and sewer hookups and easements (Fig. 5.3).

Elevation Drawing

The elevation drawing depicts the lines of the house from its four or more sides. You might need a front, rear, and two side views, depending on the complexity of the house. It will show where windows and doors go, and their respective sizes. Exterior material types can also be indicated here (Fig. 5.4).

FIGURE 5.1

A floor plan.

FIGURE 5.2

A lot plan.

FIGURE 5.3

A foundation plan.

BOARD AND BATTEN

FRONT ELEVATION ¼"= 1'0"

12" X 12" FLUE

12 / 8

BEVEL SIDING

CEILING HT.' 8'0"

BRICK

SIDE ELEVATION ½"= 1'0"

FIGURE 5.4

Front and side elevations.

SEE WINDOW DETAILS
C.6

CLOCK

DOOR TO GARAGE

FIRE RAT.

POS. ELEC. OUTLET

REF.
TFF-12 D

4¼ X 4¼ TILE

RANGE
LOC.
BY OWNER

D.W. BY
OWNER

DK. OAK CABINETS   W/ SEMI GLOSS
POLYURETHANE FINISH

12"   2'4"   5'6"   36"   4'-6"

6"   36"   18"   36"

FIGURE 5.5

An interior sketch.

Interior Sketch

If the interior has any unusual or distinctive features, you might want artist's renditions to help you visualize what the interior will look like. An example would be an elaborate bathroom or special kitchen cabinet setups (Fig. 5.5).

Perspective Sketch

The sketch shows what the completed house will look like from the outside, including landscaping if desired.

Finally, you should request at least four and possibly five complete sets of plans—one for the builder, one for the lending institution, one for the local building department, one for yourself, and, just in case, an extra set for your records.

PREPARING YOUR PLANS

There are a number of ways you can complete the plans you'll need before going to contractors and soliciting bids.

1. Have an architect do them for you, with your help.

2. Purchase a set of stock plans through a mail-order company.

3. Prepare them yourself with help from books, magazines, and friends.

4. Use packaged planning kits.

5. Employ a personal computer and special home designing software.

Architects

The truly great houses in the world have practically all been designed by architects. Indeed, architects are wonderful at custom engineering houses that require complex construction techniques or unique materials. If you've got a building site in the middle of a swamp, or on a ledge of solid rock, an architect will be able to figure out how to build on it. And due to the nature of their business, they stay abreast of the latest energy-saving techniques and other technical innovations. Whether an architect is right for you depends on the complexity of your design and building site, and your bank account. Like any professionals, architects are well compensated for their efforts.

Stock Plans

If you'd prefer not to draw your own initial plans, and hiring an architect is out of the question, consider stock prints and drawings that have already been prepared by professionals and are available through mail-order companies. Even if you can't find exactly what you want, plans can always be modified to some extent by your builder/architect. Remember that care must be taken, because major changes can cause structural problems—especially when altering a foundation to match a lot or when changing load-bearing walls.

One advantage to using stock plans is simple economy. They're inexpensive themselves, and their dimensioning of rooms and spaces for suitable structural members are made with a minimum amount of waste by using standard lumber. This is because stock plans are prepared by experienced home design experts who have accumulated a broad range of planning ideas over a considerable length of time. Some are licensed practicing architects.

Do-It-Yourself

To help you commit your ideas to paper, there's a wonderful invention available at nominal cost: graph paper. Graph paper is an ideal medium for expressing room sizes and relationships of a floor plan. A good scale to work with is ¼-inch equals 1 linear foot. You'll also need a roll-up steel or plastic tape measure at least 25 feet long, plus some home design books and magazines that will give you average dimensions and proportions of various features in houses such as hallway widths, door heights, and wall thicknesses. Many of these dimensions can be found within this book.

Once you finish your plans the best way you know how, the builder can use his knowledge of construction materials to point out where adding a few feet here, or taking away a few inches there, can result in substantial savings. If plywood sheets come in 4- by 8-foot sheets (and they do), it would be silly to spec out a room that would require coverage by ten sheets of 4½- by 8-foot sheets. That would result in sizeable waste.

Builder/architects can take your estimates and customize them—still keeping your plan's original integrity—to dimensions that lend themselves to standard building material sizes in order to reduce waste and give you more for your money. Builder/architects have a realistic feel for how to stretch materials to the maximum. They'll be able to take your rough drawings and show you where you can pick up efficiencies, and where you could use substantially less materials—perhaps by merely altering a particular dimension in some minor way.

Packaged Planning Kits

If you'd like to explore a simpler method of creating your own house plans, packaged planning kits are available from a variety of companies and publishers. They consist of scaled grid sheets or boards and appropriately sized furniture; construction parts such as windows, doors, and walls; and even landscaping trees and shrubs. They're simple to use, and they can help plan how much furniture your house will need and where it should go.

The kits come with instructions and most are designed with a ¼-inch scale. They can help you reduce the cost of professional drawings; the designer can do the drawings a lot faster if he or she just copies from your layout.

Most kits are manufactured in two-dimensional style, but some offer three-dimensional planning—a great help if you have a difficult time conceptualizing and visualizing whether a room design you are planning would fit the space allotted. The 3-D kits tend to be twice the scale of the others to give you a better grasp of the cardboard, plastic, or foam furniture replicas. These life-like objects include plumbing fixtures, televisions, stereos, sofas, toilets, even pianos. Some kits use decals, and plastic or cardboard printed in 3-D style. Other kits supply foam furniture that you can paint or even upholster to try out color schemes.

Computer-Assisted Plans

For the ultimate in home design at your fingertips, turn to the personal computer. Architects have been using CAD (computer-assisted design) graphics and engineering packages for years, but now that the personal computer has become so affordable and easy to use, it's certainly an interesting option.

Software is available to help you draw your own designs on a monitor or computer screen. And computer screens are great to work with because they're so easy to change, with no harm done if you make a mistake. With some programs you can look at the drawings in 3-D; you can rotate them right on the screen to see all angles of a room or entire floor plan. You can save the drawings on disks and print them out on a printer whenever you need a copy.

The details on these programs are incredible—down to the patterns on wallpaper. You can ask for overhead and side views, and you can even fast-forward a newly planted landscaping scheme to see how it will look years in the future, when fully grown.

These accurate designs can help reduce the effort and cost of having professionals complete your set of plans.

BEFORE APPROACHING THE BUILDER

It's important that your plans are as detailed as possible before you meet with contractors; otherwise, you'll be at a disadvantage in regard to the bids. In order to protect themselves against work that is not clearly spelled out, they might pad their bids. At the same time, some could attempt to make you do without items you are taking for granted, which are not initially specified.

▶▶▶▶▶ POINTS TO PONDER

1. Unless you have absolutely no opinion on what you're going to be living in, at the very least, provide some active input into the planning of your new home.
2. An ideal set of home plans includes floor plans, a lot plan, a foundation plan, an elevation drawing, an interior sketch, and a perspective or outside sketch, with landscaping if desired.
3. There are different ways to complete new house plans. You could use an architect; purchase a set of stock plans through a mail order company; prepare them yourself with help from books, magazines, the Internet, and friends; use packaged planning kits; or employ a personal computer with home-designing software.
4. Architects are great but expensive.
5. Stock plans are good—and they can be modified to some extent by your builder/architect. They're usually quite economical because they're prepared by experienced home design experts who have accumulated a broad range of planning ideas over a considerable length of time.
6. Do-it-yourself plans are entirely possible. Don't be afraid to try. A good builder can take your drawings and have a complete set of technically correct plans made, adding efficiencies when drawing from his knowledge of available construction material dimensions.
7. Two-dimensional and 3-D packaged planning kits are available for a simple way of creating house plans. They can help you reduce the cost of professional drawings because the designer can do the drawing a lot faster if he or she just copies from your layout.

8. If you're computer literate, some excellent software programs are available to walk you through numerous home design scenarios and can print out a variety of overhead, side, and even landscaped views.

9. It's important that your plans are as detailed as possible before meeting with the contractors. Do your homework in advance. Make all of the decisions you can beforehand.

10. Remain open, however, to good suggestions offered by builders. Don't be reluctant to modify your plans in reaction to new information that would better suit your purpose.

How to Build It

If you never even lift a hammer throughout the entire construction process, it still pays to know how a house can and should be put together. How else could you make educated decisions concerning the building specifications that are so crucial to a dwelling's quality of construction and overall durability, safety, and comfort? Often the difference between mediocre and excellent construction involves a ridiculously small materials cost. Knowing construction methods and materials will also assist in your dealings with whichever contractor you choose.

While it's not necessary to be able to recite good specifications from memory, it's important that you have a sense of how the contractor should go about fulfilling his obligations. Chapters 6 through 27 cover what should happen from foundation to rooftop and point out essential decisions that need to be made and should be made with your input.

Footers and Foundations

No house will be solid enough to reach its full life expectancy unless it's carefully constructed on adequate footers and foundations.

FOOTERS

A *footer*, as the name implies, is that lowest part of a house upon which the rest of the dwelling is placed. And like anyone's foot, if it's not firmly planted on the ground, proper posture or position of the rest of the body (or in this case, the house) becomes difficult if not impossible to maintain. A house footer serves to firmly situate the building onto and into the ground. And because it plays such a basic and critical role, it's important to make sure that the footer is done correctly. Footers are largely inaccessible once covered and landscaped over, and if ineptly constructed, major problems will result in huge expenses and inconveniences to homeowners.

Few people realize exactly what a house sits on, and how the house is joined to the earth. There are right and wrong ways to construct a footer; the main idea is to evenly spread or distribute the weight of the house over a large enough area of soil so that settling or moving will never occur. The chief enemies are gravity and time. Downward pressure that's not evenly supported from below will ultimately result in cracked floors, foundations, and telltale symptoms such as doors that will not close, cracks in plaster, and worst of all, an obvious tilting of the house.

Construction Guidelines

Consider the following when planning your footer:

1. It must be built on virgin soil if conventional building practices are to be followed. Sure, some houses are constructed on swampland—but they require extra engineering, expense, and effort. The standard-type house should rest upon solid ground. This means shy away from a building lot that has been filled in and graded to bring its surface up to a respectable level.

   Consider arranging for a soil test hole to be dug where the basement will be. It will identify soil types and may detect the presence of water or boulders below grade. Digging the test hole will also help get more accurate prices on excavation, foundation, and drainage work, plus it will prevent major surprises and possible delays.

2. If you realize the land consists of recently filled loose soil, and you still desire to build on it, several options exist. You can have the soil compacted through mechanical means. Contractors can use a heavy-duty tamper that hammers the soil down, plus huge rollers that pass back and forth over the surface, compacting as it moves. Together these machines press the soil until the proper "load level" or ability to support weight is reached that's similar to that of virgin earth (undisturbed ground).

   If the depth of uncompacted soil is too great to be efficiently compacted, and a deep cellar might lend itself to the house's structure, you could excavate and remove the disturbed ground until you hit virgin soil, then build from there.

   A last and most radical alternative could apply if virgin ground is entirely too far below grade to fix by either compacting or excavating. Here the solution is to architecturally design a one-of-a-kind footer of the floating nature to adequately support the house you plan. In most cases, though, the expense is too great to bother with. It is better to find a more suitable site.

   Either of the first two options will also cost more than an ideal lot, but they're necessary if you are to prevent the house from shifting and being subject to the difficult-to-correct ailments described earlier. Unless concrete is poured onto undisturbed or properly compacted soil, its weight, when coupled with that of the foundation and the rest of the house, will slowly press down the loose soil below. This will result in cracks, heaving, and tilting which naturally will disturb the framework of the rest of the house. Suddenly the windows won't go up as easily, the doors will no longer fit their frames, plaster walls will crack—all indicating that stressful pressures are at work that will probably brand the house as shoddily constructed.

3. The frost line must be taken into account. The earth is an insulator, and in northern sections some of the top ground freezes and offers protection to the unfrozen soil below. The frost line is an imaginary undulating plane located at some depth below the surface, or the average depth of ground that can be expected to freeze during winter, year after year. In the northern parts of the United States for instance, it ranges from about 2 to 5 feet below typical ground level. If a footer is not placed below that frost line, the alternate expansion and contraction of the earth above the frost line might cause the footer to move—to heave upward or list downward, causing cracks to occur in rigid concrete footers and foundations, with their accompanying ill effects. In general, national building codes recommend that footers should be located at least 12 inches below the frost line (Fig. 6.1).

4. The type and condition of the soil must also be taken into consideration. For example, it's an unwise practice to build on organic type soils such as peat: they haven't the proper loadbearing strength to support the weight of a house. Groundwater content likewise influences the ability of the soil to support weight and greatly affects the

FIGURE 6.1

A footer and foundation below the frost line.

installation of proper drainage to prevent water from seeping into lower levels. Be careful not to build over a spot where a large tree root system still exists: the roots will slowly disintegrate, leaving voids that will undermine the footer and lower-level floor. Major tree roots should be removed and the holes left by them filled in and compacted.

5. Naturally, the contour of the building site and the distribution of the house's weight can have a major effect on the footer's construction demands. A two-story dwelling with one floor directly above another, even if it weighs the same as a multilevel that's spaced out over more area of ground, will distribute its weight in a different manner—thus the need for a different footer than that of the multilevel's. In many cases, footers must be custom designed for lots having substantial slopes. "Steps" are commonly included to compensate for grade differences (Fig. 6.2). When preparing for a block foundation, as a general rule, the depth of

FIGURE 6.2

A step footer.

POST FOOTING

CHIMNEY FOOTING

PILASTER FOOTING

WALL FOOTING

FIGURE 6.3

A straight footer, wall, post, pilaster, and chimney footers.

each step should be in a multiple of 8 inches, which happens to be the height of the standard concrete building block. That helps build uniformity into the foundation so you won't end up having to add a half-course of block somewhere along the top of the foundation, with the accompanying waste and bother.

6. When a full basement is specified for a house, there should be an excavation of proper width, length, and depth to accommodate the foundation walls, piers and support columns, pilasters, entryways, fireplaces, chimney stack, basement floors, garages, patios and porches, and an adequate drainage systems (Fig. 6.3).

7. Pour separate footers wherever steel-support columns will be located (concrete columns that support the house's main steel beam or beams). This helps relieve downward pressure and will help prevent the basement floor from cracking. A footer for a pier, post, or column should be square and should have a pin or fasteners to securely anchor the post bottom. Check local building codes.

FIGURE 6.4

A footer with gravel and rebar.

8. A bed of gravel must be laid under and around the planned footer and foundation wall, no matter which type of footer is used (Fig. 6.4).

9. Footers for single-story and one and one-half-story houses should be at least 8 inches thick and 16 inches wide; for a two-story dwelling, 12 inches thick and 24 inches wide. Larger footers are needed for homes constructed on unstable earth or on filled land. In general, a rule of thumb is that footers be at least as deep as the foundation wall is thick, and twice as wide (Fig. 6.5). With concrete slab construction, contractors often simply increase the thickness of the slab under the load-bearing walls instead of pouring separate footers. The width of footer and foundation walls should be increased when brick or stone veneer is used on the exterior of the house. A single-story-home footer may go from 8 by 16 to 12 by 24 inches with foundation walls 12 inches thick. The contractor's engineer and local building code should determine the proper footer size and foundation wall thicknesses. In all cases the footer must meet the local building code minimum specifications. When the footer excavation takes place, make sure it's not dug too deep. You don't want the excavators to backfill fresh soil before the footer and basement floor are poured. It's critical to pour both onto virgin soil.

FIGURE 6.5

Footer design.

10. As mentioned before, if the earth on a potential building site is unstable, you would do best to avoid such a lot in favor of another with virgin soil. If you decide to build on a filled lot anyway, have a structural engineer design the

footer. He or she may have to go extra lengths to compensate for soil weaknesses.

11. The concrete used in footers should have a strength of at least 4,000 or more pounds per square inch. The footer strength must also meet local building code requirements.

12. Reinforce a footer for extra strength. This applies to all footers, including those for fireplaces and support columns or piers. In normal situations, embed at least three steel reinforcement rebars lengthwise throughout the footer (Fig. 6.6). Typically, steel rebar should be at least ⅝-inch thick and elevated from the ground during and after the concrete pouring through the use of "foundation chairs" concreted right in, about every 6 feet. Thicker steel rebar may be required depending on the application, and on local building codes. The bars are usually situated so they will be covered by a minimum of 3 inches of concrete at all points. Overlaps should occur wherever the bars meet, and those overlaps should be wired together. The use of 20-foot or longer rebar rods will minimize the

REBAR

FOUNDATION CHAIR

FIGURE 6.6

Footer reinforcement—rebar on chairs.

number of overlaps necessary. The overlaps should occur in straight runs, never at corners, and parallel runs of rebar should have staggered overlaps so two or three overlaps will not occur at the same point in a run. The rods should be bent and continued in single pieces around corners. The local building code may specify rod and overlap dimensions. Vertical support rods for the foundation walls should also be placed in the footer before the footer is poured, so those rods are securely anchored.

13. If you're going to have solid poured concrete foundation walls, consider placing a 2-inch keyway in the footer. Once the footer is poured and setting up, a 2-inch keyway can be formed into its top to allow the solid poured concrete wall to have a solid water resistant connection with the footer.

14. Allow concrete used for footers two days to set to gain most of its strength before anything is done on top of it. Make sure footers are level, with no visible cracks.

15. Depending on the type of foundation your house requires, there are a number of items that might have to be prepared for while the footer is being installed. These include drains and sewers, plus water, gas, electric, and phone lines. If the necessary holes or trenches are dug for these items while the backhoe/shovel is present for excavating the footer and basement, they can be completed at less cost. The backhoe/shovel won't have to come back a second time, nor will the contractor need costly labor to dig them by hand.

16. Special attention to the sewer or septic lines prior to pouring the footer will prevent basic sewage problems. If your house will be connected to a street sewer, this connection should be made at the excavation/footer/foundation stages of construction. The sewer usually runs under a wall footer and basement floor to the main stack location. If a septic system will be used, the same sanitary sewer pipe installation must be made from the septic tank location to the stack. In any case, you don't want to end up with your house sewer discharge line below the line it needs to be hooked up to.

17. Last, make sure the contractor grades and stones the driveway while the footer is going in—before the construction of the foundation and rest of the house begins. An early graded and stoned drive where the finished driveway will go is convenient for receiving material deliveries and for simply getting onto and off the site in bad weather. It will also encourage the heavy cement trucks needed for the footer, foundation, and basement floor to pack down the gravel and earth driveway long before the finished driveway will be poured or asphalted. All of the heavy equipment and delivery traffic will result in a stronger driveway base.

FOUNDATIONS

To put it in simple terms, the foundation of a house is what sets directly above the concrete footer and below the wood-frame living levels. Another way of describing most foundations is to call them basement walls. In houses without basements, a slab foundation also incorporates the dwelling's footer in one continuous piece of concrete.

The foundation must be strong enough, whatever its construction, to support the house sills (heavy horizontal timbers or planks attached to the upper part of the foundation to serve as a starting point for the house walls) and other related members of the house structure, as required.

From a structural standpoint, the foundation performs several key functions:

- It supports the weight of the house and any other vertical loads, such as snow.

- It stabilizes the house against horizontal forces such as wind.

- It acts as a retaining wall against the earth fill around the house.

- In some cases, a basement might be needed to act as a barrier to moisture or heat loss.

No matter which foundation type you must have, or elect to have, some general points apply. All foundations, whether slab type, crawl spaces, basements, or any others, should extend above the final grade enough so that wood members of the house are some distance above the soil. That distance might be regulated by local building codes. However, keep in mind as the specs of your foundation are laid out that if local building codes are being used as a guide, they'll help, but they could still fall short of what many people would consider optimum construction. Local specs lay down minimum rules for safety and health, but that's about all. In other words, you might want to go a few steps beyond what they recommend. In this case, it's better to position the top of your foundation slightly higher, away from the ground level, for added protection against moisture and insects.

When excavating is necessary—and that's likely for any of the foundation types you will consider—have the valuable topsoil scraped off and saved. It should be pushed into a pile and kept out of the way until the house is completed and the landscaping is roughly finished, so you can spread the topsoil around to provide a fertile base in which to plant grass seed or to lay sod. Don't let the topsoil become "lost" amidst the rest of the soil that's excavated and used to fill in around the foundation.

Slab Foundations

The slab foundation, as mentioned earlier, generally involves a combination of footer and foundation into a single slab of concrete (Fig. 6.7). They're popular wherever basements are impractical or impossible to have, in certain parts of the Southwest and South for instance, or in areas with high groundwater levels.

The "floating" slab is unique in that the finished concrete floor, foundation walls, and footers are reinforced together with steel mesh and metal rods and poured as one integral mass over a bed of gravel (Fig. 6.8). The entire slab thus floats on top of the ground while functioning as the floor of the house. However, the depth of the concrete should not be equal throughout its overall area: the slab must be thicker beneath support walls if the footer is considered part of the slab.

In cases where the terrain is not relatively flat, a footer must be poured separately from the slab and terraced or stepped down. Then a

SLAB ON GRADE

FIGURE 6.7

Slab foundations.

SILL

ANCHOR BOLT

SLAB

8" MINIMUM

WIRE MESH

VAPOR BARRIER

FILL

GRAVEL LAYER·6 IN.

GRADE

REINFORCING RODS

FIGURE 6.8

A floating slab foundation.

foundation, usually of concrete block, is constructed to a certain level height so a concrete slab floor can be poured. A slab foundation can be very trouble free and economical when built in adherence to the following construction points:

1. First, the site must be properly graded and compacted, and the footing trenches dug.

2. If the slab will be placed directly on soil, make sure the area is free of biodegradable tree roots and debris.

3. Granular fill makes a better base than soil. Bank or river gravel, crushed stone, or slag can all be used, in sizes from ⅜- to 1-inch thick. A 6- to 12-inch-thick granular bed of fill will suffice.

4. At this stage all of the following underground utilities should be installed: plumbing, drains, sewers, heating service lines and ducts, radiant pipes, electrical work, and any other public or private utilities. Steel sleeves with foam insulation inside should be placed over all water and sewer pipes where those pipes protrude

from a concrete slab, allowing the pipes to "give" if a slight adjustment is needed when the connection is made. Remember that if your house will have a slab foundation, you're going to end up with one continuous slab of concrete. If anything is done wrong and not corrected after the concrete is poured and before it dries, just think of the trouble and expense you'd have to go through to simply get at the problem, let alone to fix it. Take precautions to see that the utilities are all accounted for and installed in a safe and correct fashion.

When run beneath a concrete floor, water lines should be laid in trenches deep enough to prevent freezing (below the frost line).

Pressure-check the plumbing for leaks before the concrete is poured. The water should be turned on with all faucets and shutoffs closed to make sure there are no leaking seams, cracks, or holes through which concrete could seep, to solidify and plug water or drainage lines.

Make sure copper pipe is wrapped in a rubber or plastic tape wherever it will come in contact with concrete. An undesirable chemical reaction occurs when bare copper meets concrete. It's another simple precaution that can save a lot of time, expense, and inconvenience at some later date.

5. The subgrade for the slab should be dressed up or smoothed out in preparation for the concrete pour. Whether the subgrade is gravel or slag, it must be thoroughly compacted. It should end up higher than the surrounding grade so water will drain away from the house and so the top of the slab is comfortably higher than ground level.

6. At this stage, a vapor barrier is placed over the sub-base to stop the movement of liquid water and water vapor into the slab. Among materials used as successful vapor barriers are heavy-duty sheets of roofing material, polyethylene plastic, and construction paper. They act as both an insulation and moisture control, holding dampness in the ground rather than permitting it to penetrate cracks that could form in the slab foundation.

7. The slab should now be reinforced with steel rods. Although the steel reinforcement will not assure the prevention of cracks, it might reduce the magnitude of cracks that would otherwise occur. For best results, the steel is placed horizontally through the mid-

dle of the slab and held in position until the concrete dries. A common practice of placing the reinforcement rods on the sub-base, then pulling it up to the center of the slab with a rake or hook should not be permitted. It's virtually impossible to accurately control the location of the rods or wire fabric with this method. Instead, steel bridging or "chairs" can be anchored into the sub-base. The chairs will stick up to about the midpoint of the slab and will correctly hold the reinforcement when the concrete is poured. Naturally, the chairs will be concreted right into the slab, along with the reinforcing steel.

8. In addition to steel rods, welded wire fabric or mesh is required for slab foundations. Again, this material makes the concrete less likely to break loose from itself. Wire joints should be overlapped and wired together according to your building code, unless the entire job can be done with a single piece.

9. In an application where a foundation is required to hold up a concrete slab (with the interior filled with bank gravel to support the slab) then the top block—if it's a concrete block foundation—or the top ledge—if it's a poured foundation—should be a header or shoe block form in which a portion of the block/concrete has been cut/left out to provide a base for the concrete slab to be fastened to or supported on (Fig. 6.9). Vertical reinforcement rods should also come up from the foundation walls and be bent into the slab. This will help hold the walls to the floor slab. More about this type of construction can be found in the crawl space/basement section of this chapter.

10. Before the concrete is poured, a means by which the house sill—the wooden horizontal planks that support the main upper structure of the house—can be secured to the foundation must be arranged. Anchor bolts can be positioned about every 3 feet around the perimeter of the slab so they'll be embedded into the slab when the slab dries and cures. Check the local building code for the proper size and spacing of anchors.

11. When the slab is framed and ready to be poured, it should hold the top of the floor about 8 inches above the ground, and the surrounding grade should be sloped away from the foundation to keep water running away from the house. If an elevated floor slab is used, it should be a minimum of 4 inches thick at any part.

FIGURE 6.9

A foundation that supports a concrete slab.

12. If a smooth finish is desired, specify that the concrete should be troweled by hand or by power-driven machines. A textured finish can be obtained by dragging a broom across the surface before the concrete is fully set.

Advantages

1. They're very economical to build, especially when compared to crawl space or full basement foundations. Most slab foundations take much less labor and time to construct.

2. They're worm- and rot-proof.

3. They can't catch fire.

4. They're basically wearproof and are certainly more secure than any other kind except solid rock.

5. They can store heat from the earth and are naturals for use in a passive solar heating system.

6. They require little insulation from the elements.

7. As foundations, slabs are outstanding because they simultaneously act as one gigantic footer. Consequently, they impose the lowest soil loading per square foot of all foundations.

8. They experience less problems from ground moisture . . . there's no leaky basement from a slab.

9. The slab is more adaptable to filled or unstable soils where conventional foundations would settle unevenly and crack.

10. The slab-on-grade foundation eliminates the need to frame a floor on the first level.

11. They are not affected by underneath drafts.

12. Vinyl flooring and wall-to-wall carpeting can be installed directly onto the top surface of a slab.

Disadvantages

1. If a problem occurs with a utility that's concreted into or positioned beneath a slab, it's extremely expensive and troublesome to access the malfunction, to make repairs, and to restore the foundation to the way it was.

2. Slab foundations can be efficiently used only on relatively flat lots. They require substantial site-work when employed on uneven ground, whereas a crawl space or basement foundation readily adapts to hilly terrain.

3. Floors constructed over a crawl space or basement foundation are easier on the feet and legs.

4. Plastic and other moisture barriers must be punctured for pipes and electrical wires to pass through, thus allowing some underground dampness to rest against the bottom of the slab.

5. Because the slab is mostly below ground, no ventilation reaches its lower surfaces. The slab tends to adjust to room temperature very slowly and instead follows fluctuations in ground temperatures whenever they occur.

Concrete and Block Wall Foundations

Many houses built today sit on foundation walls that form either a crawl space under the house, a partial basement, or a full basement. These types of foundations are more common in northern locations where deep frost lines are encountered, but are also found, conditions permitting, in the South. They're constructed of either solid poured concrete or concrete blocks, and if either has the edge over the other, it's concrete blocks. Both foundations will not only support a dwelling, they'll also protect it from water, frost, and insects while providing (when desired) a basement to be used for storage or expanded living space.

If proper foundation construction is not followed, the result will be a below-standard foundation and possibly a house that tilts, floors that sag, walls that crack and leak, doors that won't fit their jambs, and windows that won't open or close—all of the same defects that can also be attributed to a poorly executed footer.

Although crawl spaces are frequently left with soil or gravel floors, both the solid concrete and the block wall foundation floors should be poured with concrete to provide cleanliness, to prevent moisture and insect encroachment, and to supply a useful floor for storage or additional living areas.

The National Building Code requires a foundation to start at least 1 foot below the frost line. Local building codes can tell you how deep the frost line is in your area. Should bedrock (solid rock) be encountered before the prescribed depth is reached, digging can stop because bedrock will not move no matter what happens or how cold it gets. Even if you build where there's never freezing temperatures, still see that the foundation is situated at least 1 foot below grade (ground level) to assure a firm and level base for the framing structure.

Crawl Space Foundations

These foundations are cheaper to construct than basements, and acceptable when the storage, utility, and living spaces otherwise found in basements are neither needed nor desired (Fig. 6.10).

Advantages

1. A crawl space foundation is cheaper to construct than a partial or full basement.

FIGURE 6.10

Crawl space foundations.

2. Because a crawl space is relatively low to the ground, there's not much risk of cracked walls.

3. The crawl space foundation takes considerably less time to build, thus speeding up the overall construction time of the house.

4. A crawl space provides ventilation below the first floor, separating the living areas from contact with the ground and letting the floor follow suit to the temperatures maintained by the living spaces (unlike a slab, which is more affected by ground temperatures).

Disadvantages

1. A crawl space foundation is practically useless for storage or living space (for humans).

2. A crawl space can't accommodate large or tall appliances such as water heaters or furnaces.

3. Crawl spaces will attract a variety of small furry creatures (notably rabbits, squirrels, chipmunks, skunks, possums, and mice).

4. Water or sewer lines that run through crawl spaces must be insulated extra well to prevent pipes from freezing.

Partial and Full Basement Foundations

There's a convincing argument that since the house will be placed over a footer anyway, you might as well put the potential space below the regular living level to good use, too (Fig. 6.11).

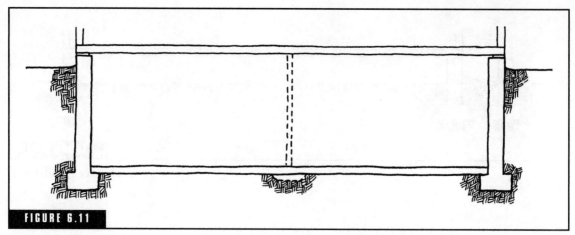

FIGURE 6.11

A basement foundation.

Advantages

1. The functional living areas of the house can always be expanded into a basement's lower level. A recreation room can be installed there at a minimal cost.

2. The partial or full basement can easily accommodate a water heater, furnace, and other major appliances such as freezers, washing machines, and clothes dryers.

3. A basement can include a separate entranceway into the house on the lowest level.

4. These foundations provide considerable storage and workbench areas.

5. Like the crawl space, a basement also insulates the main living areas from the ground.

Disadvantages

1. Basement foundations are more expensive to construct.

2. Because of their height, the walls of a basement foundation are more likely to crack and develop problems.

3. A basement foundation can at times be virtually out of the question in areas where the water table is high.

4. Basement foundations take a relatively long time to construct and string out the entire housebuilding process.

FOUNDATION CONSTRUCTION

Once you decide on the type of foundation that you think best fits your requirements or is intrinsically suited to the house you are planning, you then must decide how that foundation should be constructed. Three options are concrete block, poured concrete, and precast concrete walls. All can be used to provide crawl space foundations (usually built up from a footer having walls 18 to 24 inches above ground level), or basement foundations that are typically 7 feet high on the inside.

Concrete Block Construction

You probably already know what concrete blocks are. They're rather rough-feeling, heavy, gray, and have several rectangular holes running through their insides, vertically (Fig. 6.12). When installed, they're laid one course or row on top of another, staggered so their vertical joints don't coincide with each other. The staggering of joints makes for a stronger interlocking bond. At the same time, the center rectangular holes are large enough to overlap so the courses can be tied together with reinforcement rods that are inserted vertically and then filled with wet concrete.

On a foundation, the concrete blocks begin at the footer and are laid to form the desired height of the house foundation or

FIGURE 6.12

Concrete blocks.

basement. On houses using brick exterior finishes, the brick may also start with the footer and follow the house blocks right up. This will help support the brick veneer and strengthen the entire foundation. An alternative for brick exteriors is to go with a wider foundation block that provides a ledge at the outer top of the foundation walls on which the brick can be conveniently laid or begun from.

Advantages

1. Concrete block walls permit a stop-and-go schedule during construction.

2. Concrete block walls are easier to repair than poured concrete walls.

3. Concrete block construction is often preferred by builders costing out the foundation job because block construction eliminates the need for concrete forms.

4. Concrete block walls absorb sound better than solid poured walls.

Disadvantages

1. Concrete block walls are strong, but not as strong nor as impenetrable as solid poured concrete walls.

2. A concrete block wall is more likely to develop small cracks that can allow air infiltration, moisture, and even insects inside the foundation.

Solid Poured Concrete Construction

Solid poured concrete foundations, even though not as common as block foundations, are desirable in a number of situations.

Advantages

1. They have a slight advantage in strength and load-carrying capacity over block wall construction.

2. They offer the best protection against air infiltration, moisture, and insects. They're also less likely to result in wet basements. This can be a major advantage where rainy weather is common.

3. They can often be cast integrally with the footer, at a substantial time and cost savings.

Disadvantages

1. They can be more expensive than block construction.

2. It's somewhat difficult to be sure that you'll get as good a mix of cement as specified. There's an element of risk involved. It means, again, dealing only with reputable contractors for the concrete. Established builders will do so, but vanishing or marginal builders might not. A defective mix might not be detected until the house is up and the contractors are long gone. By then it will be a nightmare to correct major flaws or problems.

Precast Concrete Construction

Precast concrete stud wall construction provides an interesting alternative to concrete-block masonry construction. Precast walls are strong and capable of being efficiently installed as both foundation walls and walls above grade.

Precast wall panels are built with steel-reinforced concrete studs (typically about 7½ by 2 inches), 1-inch rigid insulation board, rebar reinforced top and bottom bond (footer) beams, along with a concrete facing about 2 inches thick. The bond beams and concrete facing are cast in one continuous pour. Studs are connected by encapsulating vertical rebars plus galvanized hooks and pins that protrude from the top, bottom, and back of each stud. The galvanized pins protruding from the studs secure an approximately 2-inch-thick face pour. Pressure-treated furring strips are preattached to the inner face of each stud. This construction provides a base for the homeowner to finish the basement without having to add any additional studding. Holes are cast into each stud to accommodate wiring and small-diameter plumbing (Fig. 6.13).

Precast Construction Points

- Custom-made panels are made to support door and window openings.

- All precast panels, and each individual concrete stud, should include vertical rebar reinforcement. This gives considerable tensile strength to the entire structure.

- The rebar-reinforced top bond beam typically has a perforation about every 24 inches to enable the secure bolting of a sill plate

SUBFLOOR

INSULATION

REBAR

SILL PLATE BOLT HOLES

HOLE FOR WIRING

CONCRETE FACE

INSULATION BOARD

CONCRETE STUD

REBAR

2 × JOIST

EXTRUDED STYRENE INSULATION

FIGURE 6.13

Precast wall panel.

to the top of the wall. The beam also provides strength and helps to equally distribute the weight of the home.

■ Insulation built into the wall supplies an insulating value of about R-5. The wall's cavity, about 7½ inches deep, permits a thick blanket of insulation to be applied. Combined with the 1-

inch thick polystyrene panels between the concrete studs and the concrete skin, those components can yield an effective cumulative rating approaching R-24.

Advantages

1. The panels come with ready-to-finish interior walls. A treated wood nailer is factory installed to the inside of the reinforced concrete studs, ready for the application of a vapor barrier and wallboard.

2. The panels resist moisture, mold, and mildew well.

3. The insulation panels also provide a thermal break and vapor barrier.

4. Precast panels can be installed in almost any weather. There's no danger of the concrete freezing before it cures or curing too quickly from excessive heat.

5. These panels save time when being finished in a basement, because there's no need for additional framing to support the insulation batts, vapor barrier, and drywall which can be attached directly to the furring strips with no loss of space.

Foundation Construction Points

Here's a collection of various construction specs and procedures used in proper concrete block, poured concrete, and some precast concrete foundations:

1. The minimum thickness for any home in the most ideal situations requiring minimum loadings is 8 inches. However, 10 inches is preferable and safer. The minimum thickness should be increased to 10 inches if the walls will be subjected to any lateral pressures such as large snowdrifts, if the walls are more than 7 feet below grade, if the walls are longer than 20 feet, or if the house is going to carry a heavier than normal load. This can be the case if you elect a two-story home or if you plan on having considerably heavy furniture and items such as a grand piano, pool table, waterbeds, or exercise equipment. For extra-deep basements, use 12-inch concrete block. As the block size increases, so should the footer.

2. Before the foundation floor is concreted, all necessary plumbing and sewer pipes should be installed. Make sure all pipe cleanouts are present in the foundation walls and floor. Once the rough (underground) plumbing is situated in the foundation, the plumbing inspector may wish to check that the drainage system, when full of water, will hold up without leaking; check for proper pipe slope or fall; check the cleanouts; inspect the piping for proper sizing.

3. Once the foundation walls are up, the floor of the crawl space, basement, or garage should be filled with 6 to 12 inches of ¾-inch stone, with 3- to 4-inch drainpipes running through the stone. The stone (or gravel) should be compacted as it's put down. Over the drainpipe and stone, a plastic vapor barrier should be placed to seal out dampness. This is especially important if the foundation is a crawl space. A concrete floor at least 4 inches thick will hold the water and dampness down into the ground, and the drainpipe will direct the water to a sump hole. Should the sump hole ever fill up, a sump pump can be installed to pump out the water and pipe it away from the house.

4. If concrete block is used, the first layer of blocks against the footer should be special drain blocks with grooved or weep holes along their bottoms. This will prevent a buildup of water pressure against the walls. Instead the water will flow into the 6-inch gravel bed beneath the concrete floor. The drainpipe running through the gravel will convey the water to the sump hole.

5. Along the outside of the foundation, 4-inch rigid plastic pipe having openings or perforations along the top should be placed end-to-end on a gravel base along the footer, pitched toward the spot where the water will be piped away from the house. This pipe should be lower than the basement floor and not simply resting on the footer. With this setup, water flowing against the wall of a home has a place to go. These drainage pipes need to be continuously sloped toward the discharge end; otherwise, sediment might build up at a low point and completely block the line. If the soil is full of clay or silt, consider installing a soil-filtering fabric to protect the stone and the drain piping from becoming plugged with sediment washed down from the backfill. The water table should

be maintained no higher than the elevation of the pipe under the entire basement or crawl space so water pressure is held at a minimum. This perimeter drainage pipe system should be covered with approximately 12 inches of ¾-inch stone.

6. On some lots there is no place to discharge the house drain pipe from the foundation to daylight. In this situation, footer drains can be run inside to the basement sump hole.

7. A sump pump should be installed in the foundation floor when necessary (Fig. 6.14). Some foundations, either crawl space or basement types, might never need one, while others may have to employ one year-round. Many building codes have been making it mandatory to include a sump hole so a pump can be added later, if needed. For the most part, sump pumps are set up so that if water backs up to a certain level and threatens to flood the cellar, the pump will automatically kick in and pump out the water into an outside drainage line that will carry it away from the house. The sump hole itself should be 24 inches in diameter or 20 inches square and should extend at least 30 inches below the bottom of the basement or crawl space floor. The sump hole should be covered to prevent people and pets from stepping into it and moisture from escaping it into the basement.

8. One aspect of the foundation that deserves special attention is waterproofing. Damages due to water and moisture are among the most serious causes of home deterioration. They cause wood rot, unsightly paint peeling, mildew, rusted appliances, and other maladies. They can even affect the health of the occupants. To prevent damp and wet basements, good waterproofing techniques, proper drainage, vapor barriers, correctly graded lots, appropriate landscaping and positioning of shrubs and trees, generous roof overhangs, and plenty of gutters and downspouts are necessary.

9. If you're going to have a basement, have the septic disposal system line or the sewer line located below the basement floor if possible. Otherwise, wastewater and solids generated in the basement have to be pumped up to the level of the main lines for disposal. If the disposal lines cannot be lowered, the simplest solution is often to completely avoid any sanitary drains in the basement (that means no toilets, wash basins, showers, or laundry equipment). Then the

FIGURE 6.14

A foundation interior with sump pump and drainage.

house sewer or septic lines can be suspended beneath the first-floor joists and run through openings cut in the foundation walls. The same thing can be done with a crawl space foundation if necessary, as long as precautions are taken to prevent the lines from freezing.

FOUNDATION REINFORCEMENT

Reinforcement of a foundation's floor and walls is a critical part of the housebuilding process that can be easily slighted by marginal builders. Most home buyers don't realize what's involved and depend solely on the recommendations of contractors who can, at times, underemphasize the specs that are needed for a sturdy foundation.

WATERPROOFING

Wet and damp basements can be more than just uncomfortable. Unchecked moisture allows mold and fungi to flourish, which can cause allergic reactions in people and pets and can result in peeling paint; rotting wood; and warped drywall or other wall, floor, and ceiling components.

With either a basement or slab foundation, in addition to applying a ½ inch of parging masonry (or cement) on the outside surface of basement walls, followed by two coats of a bituminous tar sealant, make sure good drainage is achieved around the entire dwelling. Grading or sloping the soil away from the home's perimeter is essential to effectively controlling roof and outside wall water runoff. As a rule of thumb, the soil should slope downward at least 6 vertical inches in the first 10 horizontal feet of travel from the foundation wall or outer vertical surface of the slab.

Some of the best drainage systems direct water that comes near the foundation down toward the level of the home's footing, where clay, concrete, or plastic drainage tiles or pipes collect and convey the water away from the dwelling, or collect and discharge the water through a sump pump. For drainage lines to work efficiently, they must be securely installed in beds of porous material—usually washed gravel. To achieve good drainage at window wells, the washed gravel should continue from the bottom of the wells to the foundation drainage tile. The window well should be wider than the window and frame and deep enough for at least two inches of washed gravel to be placed at the bottom of the well—while staying below the lower portion of the window's frame. It's important to prevent any chance of water getting up to any part of the window's frame.

To address the "open" nature of window wells, galvanized steel window wells are available to hold back the earth, and sturdy grating should be fitted at the well's top to prevent someone from stepping into the well. Plastic covers can also be placed over the top of window wells to keep out rain and snow.

Downspouts that carry rainwater away from roof gutters should be connected to a mostly horizontal (slightly sloped) length of pipe that carries the water several feet away from the foundation. If a sidewalk is in the way, drain tile can be used to run the water beneath the walk to open ground or a catch basin, depending on the landscaping serviced. If a downspout empties into a catch basin, then into a drain pipe, the catch basin should be positioned far enough away from the foundation so runoff during a heavy rain will not overshoot it and yet close enough to catch the slower flow during a light rain. The water can also be conveyed to a bubbler or "dry well" where the water is allowed to simply drain off or dissipate into the surrounding ground. Bubblers or dry wells should never be located within the drip line of large trees—where the soil could become saturated for long periods of time and could allow the tree to fall over (roots and all) in high winds.

On flat or level building sites where there's no room for or possibility of establishing surface drainage slopes, a "trunk and arm" drainage system can help handle water runoff (Fig. 6.15). Such a drainage system consists of a perforated drain tile (usually 6-inch diameter), which acts as the trunk and runs parallel to the home's foundation, and solid drain tiles (usually 4-inch diameter), which act as the arms, attached to the trunk with T connectors. The arm tiles run perpendicular to the trunk, spaced about 10 feet apart from each other and slope underground to dry wells filled with washed gravel, where the surface runoff water can collect and slowly dissipate into the surrounding earth.

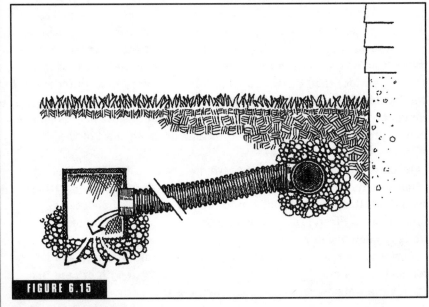

FIGURE 6.15

Trunk and arm drainage system.

This cost-cutting philosophy can lead to big problems later, at the homeowner's expense.

Here are some guidelines for the reinforcement of foundation floors and walls:

FIGURE 6.16

Foundation block pilaster.

1. A concrete floor should be strengthened with reinforcement rebar. The rebar should be elevated to the middle of the floor's thickness on steel bridges or chairs set so they're positioned evenly across the floor before the concrete is poured with ends overlapped. If welded wire fabric is used along with the rebar, its joints should overlap. Material overlap should meet local building code.

2. If a foundation has long walls or walls subjected to above-average stresses, they can be strengthened with pilasters (Fig. 6.16). A pilaster is a vertical block or concrete column poured or constructed adjacent to or adjoining a foundation wall, located at about the middle of the wall's length. More pilasters are often needed along unusually long walls. By having thicker walls at selected points, this extra support lessens the overall stress on the walls and helps prevent cracking. Steel rebar at least ⅝-inch thick, with four rebars to a set should be installed in and extend the full height of the concrete-filled pilaster voids.

3. Another modern and commonly used method of reinforcing the walls of a foundation is to place long pieces of ⅝-inch-thick rebar the length of the wall, in sets of four, through the rectangular openings of every other concrete block, vertically, and then to fill in those reinforced holes or "cores" solidly with concrete (Fig. 6.17). The same rebar can also be embedded in the footing pour as a tie from wall to base, especially when high walls must withstand considerable pressures from slopes, water, or backfilling. All house foundations should have either the pilasters or the reinforcement rebar for vertical support. For a stronger foundation wall, use both pilasters and vertical reinforcement rebar throughout the walls.

FIGURE 6.17

Vertical concrete block wall reinforcement.

4. For horizontal support, reinforcement wire should be placed in the mortar bed joint of every other course of blocks (Fig. 6.18).

5. Block walls that are quickly erected and backfilled require bracing within the crawl space or basement for temporary support until the concrete and mortar dries, to make sure the structure is tightly knit before stresses are applied. Leave temporary wood supports up in the basement as long as possible, especially during and after backfilling takes place.

6. Load-bearing foundation walls should not be joined or tied together with a masonry bond unless the walls join at a corner. Instead, steel tie bars vertically spaced not further than 4 feet apart (check local building code) will form a strong bond (Fig. 6.19). If the walls are concrete block, strips of lath

FIGURE 6.18

Horizontal concrete block wall reinforcement.

FIGURE 6.19

A steel tie bar.

or steel mesh can be laid across the common joints in alternate layers or courses (Fig. 6.20). If a nonbearing wall will be constructed at a later date, ties should be incorporated into the first wall, to be left half-exposed so they'll be available when needed for the second adjoining wall.

FIGURE 6.20

Steel mesh reinforcement.

Masonry Joints

If using brick or block for foundation walls, you have an option to select any of the following mortar joint types that would best go with your style of construction: flush, struck, V, concave, raked, beaded, extruded, and weathered (Fig. 6.21). The V and concave versions are the most popular since they look neat and do not form a miniledge that could accumulate water. Beneath the grade, or the ground level, where appearance does not count, the joints are typically left flush.

Concrete Forms

If you're using poured concrete walls, make sure you realize that the quality of the concrete forms directly affects the finished appearance of the walls. Concrete forms must be tight, smooth, defect-free, properly aligned, and well-braced to resist lateral pressures created by the poured concrete.

FOUNDATION FLOOR SUB-BASES AND FLOORS

The floor sub-base should consist of a compacted layer of ¾-inch stone 4 inches thick. Plastic sheathing that comes in 4- or 6-mil thicknesses or other suitable vapor barrier materials are placed over the subbase to form an effective insulating moisture barrier before the floor concrete is poured.

The concrete floor should be a minimum of 4 inches thick, with welded wire mesh and rebar running through it for strength, and the concrete should be sloped to the floor drains. If you desire a smooth finish on a basement floor, it will be necessary to specify that you want the concrete steel-troweled. Should you desire a textured finish, it can be obtained by having brooms dragged across the surface before the concrete is set.

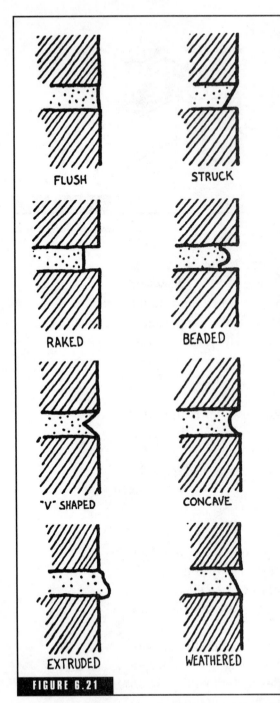

FIGURE 6.21

Types of mortar joints.

FOUNDATION WALL TOPS

On top of all foundation walls anchor bolts (Figs. 6.22 and 6.23) should be installed or partially embedded at approximately 3-foot intervals (check local building code), with protruding bolt lengths long enough to securely fasten the sill plates (wooden planks that join the upper framing structure to the foundation).

Have foundation walls constructed of concrete block capped with a course of solid masonry blocks that will act as an insect barrier and help distribute the weight of the house's upper structure. When solid blocks are not used, the cores or rectangular holes in the top course can be solidly filled with mortar or concrete. To do this, a strip of thin metal lath must be placed in the mortar joint under the top course. The strip, which is just wide enough to cover the block cavities, forms a base for the concrete that fills the top course cavities.

WALL COVERINGS AND INSULATION FOR THE FOUNDATION

Exterior

The foundation will be less susceptible to frost damage, moisture transfer, leaking, and insects if the walls are insulated on the outside (Fig. 6.24). Concrete block walls should be pargeted (plastered) with a ½-inch of cement mortar.

The half inch of mortar can be applied in two coats for superior holding power. Apply ¼-inch thick layer of portland cement to a moistened masonry wall. The

2" X 10" SILL

STANDARD ANCHOR BOLT

CONCRETE SLAB

FIGURE 6.22

Anchor bolt in a poured concrete wall.

first coating should be put on roughly and allowed to dry for 24 hours. When ready for the second coating, the first should be moistened, then the second ¼-inch coating can be smoothed over the first and kept moist for about 48 hours while it hardens.

For any foundation wall, request two coats of tar or bituminous waterproofing material to be troweled on. Troweled tar is the best, but brushed on or sprayed on waterproofing is better than nothing. If local weather conditions are severe, protection can be further improved with a layer of sheet polyethylene or asphalt-impregnated membrane. Make sure there are no sharp surfaces that could tear or damage the membrane when the membrane is applied. Remove any large rocks or roots from the backfill so the poly membrane won't be damaged during backfilling.

Internal insulation inside the blocks can be accomplished by installing rigid foam insulation inserts that are friction fit into conventional block holes before the block is laid to increase R-values. Block

FIGURE 6.23

Anchor bolt cemented into top course of a concrete block wall.

holes that will be concrete filled are skipped. This type of insulation is out of view and protected from the elements. (See Fig. 6.25.)

Exterior insulation can be installed using extruded polystyrene rigid foam that's 1½ or 2 inches thick tongue and groove for a good seal. It will provide good thermal protection and moisture resistance above and below grade. The joints should be taped with product from the manufacturer. The manufacturer will supply installation instructions.

Above-grade foundation wall exteriors can also be protected with stucco or treated plywood.

Interior

To reduce heat loss, to prevent moisture and water leakage, and to further prevent the possibility of insect penetration, foundation interior walls can be insulated and covered.

A thick waterproofing white paint that's brushed onto the interior surface will reduce moisture penetration and discourage insects from

Exterior of a foundation wall, cutaway.

Concrete block insulation inserts.

infiltrating interior walls (Fig. 6.26). Foundation wall interiors can be insulated by first putting up furring strips and then applying blanket insulation in the usual way (Fig. 6.27).

FLOOR SUPPORT BEAMS OR GIRDERS

To support the house, one or more girders (load-bearing beams that help support the first-floor joists) as determined by the contractor's structural engineer should be installed. Steel I beams make the most reliable girders, but wood girders constructed of planks joined together by bolts or nails are also used (Fig. 6.28). Steel I beams are rather consistent in quality. The wood girders will vary in quality because they're dependent on the quality of their individual component planks. Girders either rest in pockets formed in the tops of the foun-

Interior of a foundation wall, cutaway.

INSULATION

MASONRY WALL

FURRING STRIPS

POLYETHYLENE VAPOR BARRIER

FIGURE 6.27

Foundation wall furring strips and insulation.

dation walls or on top of corresponding masonry pilasters. In any event, the steel girder tops are generally made flush with the top of the wooden sill with wood planking that's laid along the top of the entire steel beam (Fig. 6.29).

FOUNDATION VENTILATION

Ventilation in foundation walls can be accomplished either with windows or with vents. Basement windows are discussed in the chapter on windows. If vents are decided upon, have them installed near or at the top course of concrete blocks, or as high as possible in the foundation walls at the rate of one every 50 linear feet, each being about the size of a concrete block: 8 by 16 inches (Fig. 6.30). They should be the type that can be closed during cold weather. At least one vent should be positioned at each corner of the house, with cross ventilation arranged for a minimum of two opposite sides. If the house is located in an area experiencing high humidity during much of the year, increase the number of vents to one for every 15 linear feet.

On a crawl space foundation, in addition to vents, there should be at least one access door of not less than 32 by 36 inches installed. If it's a large crawl space of 2,000 square feet or more, or an unusual shape, more than one access door should be included. Confirm this with local building codes.

BACKFILLING

Once the foundation work has been completed and before backfilling occurs, you should make a formal inspection. Backfilling is simply the pushing back of excavated soil around the house to fill in the construction ditches. Backfilling should only occur after the first floor is framed and the walls are framed up so the added weight of the structure will stiffen the walls and make them less likely to bulge from the pressure of the backfilled soil.

ANCHOR

BLOCK WALL

SILL PLATE

BUILT UP GIRDER

FIGURE 6.28

Wood girder.

ANCHOR

BLOCK WALL

SILL PLATE

PLATE

I-BEAM

PILASTER

FIGURE 6.29

A steel I-beam girder.

SUBFLOOR

FLOOR JOISTS

FOUNDATION VENTILATOR

WIRE MESH BELOW TOP COURSE

SLOPED SILL

FIGURE 6.30

Foundation wall vents.

To avoid subjecting a "green" foundation that isn't fully cured to pressures that could damage it, plank or timber bracing should be installed inside the crawl space or basement, supporting the walls at about 12-foot intervals. The house's central longitudinal support beam or girder, plus the first-floor joists and floor decking should also be erected to help strengthen the foundation walls before backfilling takes place.

As a general rule, backfill height from footer to grade should not exceed about 7 feet.

The waterproofing must be protected during the backfilling, since rocks and other hard materials in the backfill could scratch and penetrate the waterproofing and allow moisture seepage. If the soil that will be pushed back contains large rocks, the contractor should apply 4 by 8-foot or 4 by 10-foot sheets of impregnated sheathing or equal material for protection. The final grade must slope away from the foundation.

◀F☺CUS

STORM SHELTERS

Sometimes referred to as tornado shelters, these units are typically set within the ground and temporarily protect household members who may seek shelter during major storms. A good time to have one installed, of course, is when the home's foundation is being constructed and the backhoe or other piece of heavy equipment is already there anyway to excavate.

The most popular types of storm shelters are manufactured out of fiberglass—a forgiving material that withstands considerable movement and settling of earth, resists corrosion, mold, and mildew, and is very durable (Fig. 6.31). Units are available that seat up to 10 adults. These shelters are often anchored at the bottom of excavations, in poured concrete foundations that hold the units below ground level. To provide enough air for the inhabitants to breathe, storm shelters need multiple ducts and vents that rise far enough above the ground to prevent surface water and runoff from entering. The vent openings should also be covered with insect screens.

Outside doors should be low profile to permit simple landscaping and to avoid tornado or hurricane winds from affecting the unit.

Some of the more important features found in storm shelters include the following:

- Prewiring for a television and phone. This would allow shelter users to stay in contact with what's in the news or what's going on outside, and to phone for help in case problems occur.
- A safe or storage box to hold valuables.
- Skid-resistant steps with handrails.
- A lifting jack inside the unit, in case the doors become blocked by a downed tree branch, for instance.
- A carpeted floor.

Other alternatives for tornado- or hurricane-resistant home protection include "in-residence shelters," which employ more conventional construction methods to encase an interior room of a house with concrete or steel and to then bolt the reinforced room to the foundation. Such rooms can have practical uses as well—as closets, storage areas, or even photographic darkrooms.

FIGURE 6.31

A storm shelter.

SAFETY NOTE

With any storm shelter, make sure that a number of relatives, friends, or neighbors know of its existence and get them to agree to come looking for you following a major storm if you don't check with them immediately afterward.

ROOT CELLARS

A root cellar may sound a bit old fashioned, but for households fond of gardening, farming, and cooking, a root cellar can be an interesting and useful addition. Root cellars are still standard fare in Europe and many other parts of the world—small- to medium-sized rooms or portions of cellars carved out of or built into the earth. Their name has evolved from two of their characteristics: root cellars have been used for centuries to store root vegetables such as potatoes, carrots, parsnips, turnips, and onions (as well as canned and pickled foods) that keep longer in dark, cool places; and second, because roots of trees and live plants had often grown directly into the root cellar over the years.

The perfect time to build a root cellar is when the excavation and foundation are under way. Because a root cellar needs to be shaded from sunlight, the basement provides the best location, where it will help resist temperature swings and has a natural ability to keep stored items cool. One way is to take a corner of the basement—a northern corner, if possible—with the greatest exposure to cold outer walls (concrete or concrete block) and frame in a rectangular room (large enough to suit your needs) with insulated studded walls. Another way—if the home will have a concrete porch or patio that rests on top of a full foundation wall—is to simply build the root cellar within that part of the foundation wall. It's typically a large enough area and will need only one insulated wall and door to enclose.

A third option is a root cellar that has three sides carved out of the soil, again, so only one insulated wall and door separates the space from the rest of the basement. Any enclosing wall (or walls) should use 2 by 6 inch studs with fiberglass or rigid foam insulation. The ceiling needs to be insulated as well. Protect both sides of insulation from moisture in the air with polyethylene air-vapor barriers. The ceiling needs the same barriers running up and around each joist, above the insulation, and below the insulation, too. A finish layer of drywall can be placed over the insulation and air-vapor barriers to protect against punctures. For access, an insulated steel door will do a good job here with a tight seal around its edges and extra rigid foam insulation bolted to the inside of the door with large flat washers. Because the door needn't be fancy, contractors often suggest making it out of 2 by 2s,

2 by 4s, and plywood. Wood doors, however, will likely warp over the long haul, and lose their temperature-tight seal.

A root cellar must also be ventilated. A small louvered metal vent the size of a concrete block works well. The louvers can be adjusted or closed as needed throughout the year.

Last, make sure the contractor builds and installs whatever shelving you need to maximize storage space (Fig. 6.32).

FIGURE 6.32

Root cellar shelving.

POLE AND PIER FOUNDATIONS

A less frequently used foundation is the pole and pier arrangement (Fig. 6.33). It's a good setup for small homes built in steep terrain, or for vacation homes and cottages. Poles or piers are firmly implanted into solid ground so they're stationary (frequently cemented right into the ground) and then the frame of the house is constructed on top of them. For this type of foundation, concrete tubes (concrete-filled cardboard cylinders) and telephone poles are very popular.

Advantages

1. It lends itself to steep terrain where there is considerable variation in the height of the piers and where a regular masonry foundation is impractical.

2. Grading isn't required. There's a minimum of site preparation involved.

3. It's an inexpensive foundation and easy to build.

4. There's plenty of natural ventilation between the ground and the living levels.

FIGURE 6.33

A post and pier foundation.

Disadvantages

1. With the underside floor surface fully exposed to the elements, in cold climates the floor must be exceptionally well insulated.

2. It allows wind and small creatures to get beneath the building.

3. It is practically useless for any kind of storage or future expansion.

MISCELLANEOUS ITEMS

1. In locations with large populations of termites or carpenter ants, consult a qualified pest-control company to provide appropriate treatment. The company should provide a guarantee on their work that covers repairs if insects re-infest the treated areas.

2. Specify if you want windows in your foundation: their size and make, how many, and their location if in a full or partial basement.

3. Specify if you want a rear or side outdoor entrance to the basement. Use concrete or steel lintels for door openings. Precast lintels are

simple to install because they're made to match the height and width of concrete blocks. They should be long enough to overlap (per building code) on the bearing block. Another method involves forming and pouring a lintel on the site, using wood forms and reinforcement rods.

The outside stairwells should begin at a point lower than the basement floor, to prevent water from entering the house. A 6-inch sill protecting the basement door is standard. Or, a built-up curb could be constructed as a partial remedy. A decision should also be made if you want the stairwell opening covered by steel doors.

4. Don't let the contractors confuse the topsoil that was pushed to the side when the construction first began with the soil that was excavated for the foundation. The topsoil should only be used for finished site grading, not as backfill around the foundation.

Trees you want saved should be marked with bright ribbons or spray paint so the contractors won't damage or knock them down. The agreement should specify that all scrap tree stumps and brush must be pulled out and hauled away. If you get your builder to agree up front, hardwood trees that need to be removed could be cut up and piled for firewood.

5. It's not a common request, but poured concrete walls and floors can be colored by the addition (when wet concrete is being mixed) of mineral pigments sold by ready-mix concrete and block producers, lumberyards, and building material dealers. Reds, greens, yellows, browns, grays, and other colors are available.

6. If you're going to have a full basement, and you plan to eventually put in a recreation room, try to locate it as closely as possible to the basement stairs. Opt for larger windows than normal so the room will have adequate light and ventilation during the day. Check building code requirements related to any partitions you plan to install around the furnace and water heater; you might have to meet clearance and surfacing requirements.

Avoid placing partitions, present or future, too close to plumbing-heating-electrical elements such as sump pumps, water meters, shut-off valves, and waste cleanouts. Give them an extra inch or two clearance to permit quick access in case of trouble.

When possible, plan a workshop area close to an outside access and also near an unexcavated sheltered area where a crawl space can be used for lumber and storage of other long materials.

The typical cellar wall should be 11 courses high (or 88 inches). But if any rooms on the floor above it will be sunken, consider an extra course (12 courses total) in case you someday decide to finish off the basement. If you go the extra block, you'll still be able to have a normal ceiling height when finished.

All basements should have at least one water drain in the floor, and those cellars larger than 900 square feet should have two drains. The floor should taper toward the drains, and the drains should transport water to the house's sump hole or exit drain.

The local building code and the contractor's engineer should specify properly sized steel beams, girders, and vertical columns.

▷▷▷▷▷▷ POINTS TO PONDER

1. The main goal of a footer is to evenly spread or distribute the weight of a house over a large enough area of soil so that settling or moving of the dwelling never occurs.

2. If the building site you select consists of recently filled loose soil, the loose soil must be either excavated out, compacted through mechanical means, or built upon by custom engineering and construction of a footer for the exact home you are building.

3. The frost line must always be taken into account when constructing footers and foundations. If a footer is not placed below the frost line, the alternate expansion and contraction of the earth above the frost line might cause the footer to move—to heave upward or list downward—causing cracks in rigid concrete footers and foundations, with their accompanying ill effects.

4. The type and condition of the soil must be taken into account; check it by having a soil test hole dug. Organic types of soils (such as peat) groundwater content, and large tree root systems can all interfere with traditional concrete footers and foundations.

5. Paying special attention to the sewer or septic lines prior to pouring a footer will help prevent basic sewage and drainage problems.

6. Concrete foundations should extend above the final grade enough so that wood members of the house are some distance above the soil, for protection against moisture and insects.

7. Concrete block or panel or poured concrete foundation walls enclosing a basement should be a minimum of 7 feet high, from the basement floor, and consider up to 9 feet if you know you'll be finishing off parts of the basement later.

8. Achieving efficient outside drainage around a home's foundation is absolutely critical to prevent basements from developing moisture and leaks. So are good waterproofing techniques, vapor barriers, correctly graded lots, appropriate landscaping and positioning of shrubs and trees, generous roof overhangs, and plenty of gutters and downspouts.

9. Don't allow the contractors to confuse the topsoil that was pushed to the side when the excavation first began with the soil that was excavated for the foundation. The topsoil should only be used for finished site grading, not as backfill around the foundation.

10. Consider the addition of a root cellar and/or storm shelter to be excavated at the same time your home's footer and foundation are being installed.

Floor Framing

The wood frame of a house has been compared to the skeleton in a human body, in that it forms the shape and size and provides the strength to a dwelling. Even with a brick house (in today's modern construction this usually means brick veneer), the framing actually supports the brick, not the reverse as many people think. It's critical that the framing be erected correctly; it's not an area in which to compromise to reduce costs. Any errors discovered after the framing is complete are likely to be expensive to correct.

As a rule, the sills, girders, floor joists, and subflooring are the first members of the wood-framed structure placed on the foundation walls. These are followed by the outside wall studding and corner posts.

LUMBER

All the lumber used should be air- or kiln-dried and of No. 2 grade or better. Regular lumber while seasoning after it's nailed in place, can shrink away from the shank of a nail, reducing friction between the nail and the surrounding wood and causing *nail popping*, the protrusion of heads of nails from lumber they had previously been nailed flat against.

Besides an increase in strength and nail-holding power, air- or kiln-dried lumber holds screws and glue better, and results in superior adherence of paints and preservatives. It's also a better thermal insulator than regular lumber, and is less likely to be attacked by fungi or insects. Only pressure-treated lumber should be used for framing members that are exposed to moisture.

Here are some guidelines:

- .25 CCA (pounds salt solution per cubic foot) for above-grade applications, such as decks and railings.

- .40 CCA for lumber that comes in contact with the ground, such as columns supporting decks.

- .60 CCA for lumber located below grade, such as in an all-wood foundation.

SILL PLATES

The sill or sill plate is the timber (usually made of 2 by 10-foot wood planks) that's secured to the top of the foundation walls to form a link between the foundation and the home's upper structure.

Some sill plates are laid in a bed of wet mortar. Most, however, are installed in the following manner: anchor bolts are partially embedded in the concrete foundation wall tops, then a resilient, waterproof layer of sealer (similar to felt or Styrofoam) is pushed over the protruding bolts down onto the top surface of the foundation walls. The sill plate, having holes drilled in it to correspond with each anchor bolt, is then placed over the bolts onto the fiberglass layer, pressing the fiberglass flat against the top of the foundation walls. The sill plate is secured along the foundation top with sturdy lock washers and nuts tightened onto each anchor bolt (Fig. 7.1).

SUPPORT BEAMS OR GIRDERS, AND POSTS

As mentioned in chapter 6, floor joists that traverse long spans between foundation walls must be supported by longitudinal beams or girders. These structural members can be steel I beams (the best alternative) or wood planks nailed or bolted together, as determined by the contractor's engineer. The ends of these longitudinal beams or girders rest either on pockets (rebar/poured concrete reinforced) in the foundation walls, or on concrete block or poured pilasters. The girders should bear or rest on each foundation wall. The top surface of a longitudinal beam or girder must be made level with the top surface of the foundation wall via a wood plank secured on top.

Vertical posts of steel support the beams or girders through the interior of the span (Fig. 7.2). To prevent sinking, the vertical posts should be located over piers (concrete-filled holes about 18 inches across and 8 inches deep) set in a gravel floor or beneath a concrete floor so the weight the posts support will be distributed over a broad area.

FLOOR JOISTS

Floor joists are horizontal structural planks placed on edge against a house's sill plate in an orderly fashion to distribute the weight of the wood framing to girders and sills and to provide a base for floor decking. Joist ends rest both on the sill plates and on interior longitudinal girders of steel or wood (Fig. 7.3). The joists should be of sufficient strength, stiffness, and number to support the floor loads over the area spanned, with no perceivable deflection or "give" that could result in cracked plaster or pulled-apart drywall seams.

In good construction, joists are placed either 12 or 16 inches on center, and are made of planks 2 by 10 inches or 2 by 12 inches. Planks running around outside wall perimeters that floor joists are fastened to are called *headers* (Fig. 7.4).

FIGURE 7.1

Securing and sealing the sill plate.

FIGURE 7.2

A vertical support post.

FIGURE 7.3

Floor joists support.

Double-thickness floor joists—two planks fastened together—should be used in certain situations, for example, wherever the first- or second-floor walls run parallel to the floor joists. This will also occur at openings around a stairway (Fig. 7.5), near a fireplace chimney, or at any major change in joist direction such as where partitions are built to provide clearance for hot air ducts and returns, under cast-iron bathtubs, or to provide additional support where joists cross a girder (Fig. 7.6).

When choosing the floor joist material, ask your builder about engineered wood I-beam floor joists. Engineered wood I beams are made with a top and bottom lumber flange (typically 2 by 3 inches or 2 by 4 inches) with a grooved center to accommodate a center web (typically plywood) (Fig. 7.7). Special hangers with blocking are needed to secure these beams.

Engineered wood I-beam floor joists offer many advantages:

- Good strength.

- Excellent clear span on large rooms. Span longer distances than regular wood.

- Always standard and consistent in dimension.

- Laminated construction eliminates crowning, warping, twisting, and bowing.

- Won't shrink or crack.

- Floor sheathing lays flatter initially and remains that way since these beams don't shrink. Helps prevent squeaky floors.

- Wide flanges allow the plywood to be screwed straight down (not

Header-joists construction view.

Framing a stairway opening.

FIGURE 7.6

Double thicknesses of floor joists.

FIGURE 7.7

Engineered wood I beam for floor framing.

angled as when trying to hit half a 2-by lumber) while staying back from the edges.

- There is more bearing surface for glue and support.
- Typically lighter than dimensional lumber.
- Can come with predrilled knockouts for wire and plumbing.

HEADERS

Again, a floor-framing header is a wood plank that the floor joists are nailed perpendicular against on two opposite sides of the house, and parallel against on the other sides. It's erected vertically on its long edge, resting on the sill plate along the exterior of the foundation walls. Many contractors also use the term "rim joists" when referring to the floor header joists.

FLOOR DECKING

A number of structural materials, mostly wood or composition wood products, are used to cover floor joists and to construct the first-floor platform on which all subsequent house framing rests. These are mainly walls that are bearing units for the upper floors and the roof structure, and walls that form interior partitions. The most popular materials are plywood, hardwood boards, and particleboard. Thicknesses of the floor should range from 1⅛-inch and thicker. Remember to consider what you're going to have as furnishings. For example, if a room is expected to include a complete set of Olympic weights, with a variety of exercise benches and machines, it will likely require a thicker floor.

Plywood is one of the strongest and most convenient floor materials available. It not only makes an effective floor, but also serves as a strong structural tie between the floor joists and wood beams or girders.

Hardwood boards are available in many sizes and thicknesses. They are often used as floor coverings, and alone over the joists as the main floor structure as well.

Particleboard is popular because of its low cost and lack of sheet curvature (it's stiff and straight). When used with an underlayer of plywood, what results is a thick, sturdy floor. If you use a two-layer floor with particleboard as your second layer, do not leave this material exposed to the weather. It will absorb moisture and swell up.

An excellent all-around floor construction consists first of ⅝-inch thick (or thicker) plywood sheets glued and screwed to the floor joists.

The glue helps eliminate squeaks and nail popping and increases the stiffness of the plywood-to-beam bond from 10 to 90 percent. In fact, the adhesion of mastic-type glue is so strong that plywood and joists tend to behave like integral T-beam units. Screwing the flooring to the joists is superior to nailing. Screws have proven the most efficient; they'll help prevent springiness, uplift, horizontal shifting, warpage, and nail-head popping. When used along with glue, they'll provide a trouble-free floor.

The plywood and other sheet materials should always be attached so that the joints don't line up in a regular fashion (Fig. 7.8). On the

UNDERLAYMENT JOINTS OFFSET WITH RESPECT TO SUBFLOOR

LEAVE 1/16" SPACING BETWEEN EDGE AND END JOINTS

UNDERLAYMENT

SUBFLOOR

STAGGER END JOINTS (OPTIONAL)

FIGURE 7.8

Joints should be irregular.

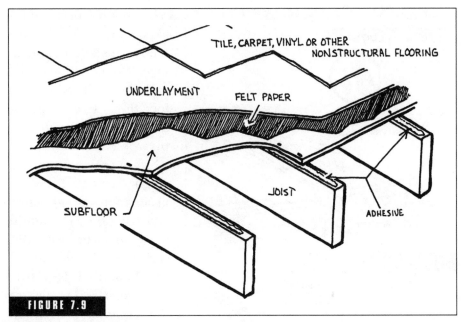

FIGURE 7.9

Covering the floor joists.

first layer of flooring, it's best to arrange the plywood sheets so their lengths run at right angles to the joists for maximum strength. Once the 4 by 8-foot sheets of plywood are laid down, they should be covered with 15-pound asphalt-saturated felt paper. Then a second structural layer of particleboard (⅝-inch) sheets can be fastened to the plywood— again staggered so none of the seams coincide (Fig. 7.9). If additional strength is desired, the second layer can also be plywood sheets (⅝-inch). In either case, the result will be a sturdy, quiet floor.

When you select plywood, make sure that the contractor uses a good CDX grade, one that contains exterior glue lines on both sides. This grade of plywood, made with an exterior-type glue that is waterproof, will stand up to prolonged exposure to the elements during construction. The bottom plywood layer is first screwed down with an automatic screw gun, it should then be screwed along the vital joints— where one piece of plywood faces another—to prevent squeaking. Gaps of ¹⁄₁₆-inch or more, depending on the humidity levels in your area, should be left between the sheet edges and end joints in all plywood layers. Plywood expands when it absorbs moisture and will buckle if it doesn't have enough room. Higher humidity areas may

FIGURE 7.10

Plywood tongue-and-groove sheets.

FIGURE 7.11

Cross bridging of floor joists.

require more of a gap for expansion. Even correctly installed single-layer floors will squeak and give if the sheets are too thin. Use 1⅛-inch-thick tongue-and-groove plywood

if you're going with a single layer. Plywood used for single-layer construction should have an approved APA stamp on it, or be of equal quality (Fig. 7.10).

Formerly known as the *American Plywood Association*—the "APA" now refers to *The Engineered Wood Association*'s trademark. That association's member mills produce about 75 percent of structural wood panel products made in North America.

In any event, plywood subflooring should always end directly over a joist. The subflooring stabilizes the joists and keeps them from twisting or buckling.

CAULKING

Make sure that parallel beads of caulk are run between the bottom of the floor decking and the sole plate as well as between the top of the floor decking and the outside wall framing. This will reduce the loss of heat due to air infiltration.

BRIDGING AND BLOCKING

To stabilize the floor joists, bridging or blocking must be used. They help keep the joists properly aligned so the floor decking has a continuously level base to rest upon (Figs. 7.11, 7.12, and 7.13).

FIGURE 7.12

Metal bridging of floor joists.

Bridging consists of pieces of wood (or sometimes metal), usually 1 by 3 inches, nailed crossways between the top and bottom of adjacent joists at about the center of each joist span. There should be no more than 8 feet between individual rows of bridging, and nailing is easier if the bridging is slightly staggered along individual rows (Fig. 7.14).

Blocking refers to 2 by 10-inch or 2 by 12-inch wood blocks fit and nailed firmly between joists at the center of each joist span. Again, there should be no more than 8 feet between individual rows of blocks.

Blocking not only holds the joists parallel and plumb, but will also act as a firestop that will retard the horizontal spread of flames. In homes where bridging is used to support the floor joists, a row of blocking can also be installed for fire protection.

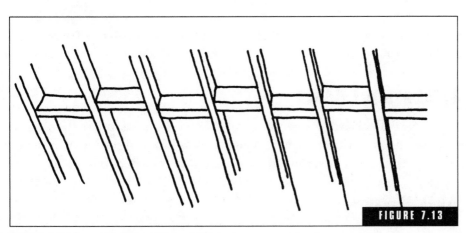

FIGURE 7.13

Solid bridging or blocking of floor joists.

SOLID BRIDGING

SUBFLOOR

DOUBLE JOISTS
UNDER PARTITION

CROSS BRIDGING

FIGURE 7.14

Staggered bridging.

Solid bridging should be used under load-bearing partitions for support (Fig. 7.14).

STONE AND TILE FLOORS

If your plans call for stone or tile floors in areas other than bathrooms, allow additional space where needed for the setting of stone or tile in a thin bed of cement by dropping the floor decking.

FLOOR EXTENSIONS

Give careful consideration to house designs that call for floor extensions that protrude outside the basic perimeter of the walls. They might be needed for such features as porches, second-story overhangs or decks, or bay windows. A sizeable protrusion could require supports outside of the foundation wall or even an actual adjustment to the foundation.

TERMITE CONTROL

Termites frequently enter a housing structure near the first-floor level. It's best to consult a qualified pest-control company to make sure the necessary treatment is provided. The best companies give a lifetime guarantee on their work that will cover repairs if insect damages eventually result. Construction design precautions include, on a hollow-block foundation, filling the top courses of block with concrete, and installing a metal termite shield along the foundation wall. Such a shield must be made of noncorroding metal and must be installed so no gaps exist along seams or where the shield is attached. This continuous strip of thin metal, attached between the foundation and sill plate, should extend at least 2 inches out and 2 inches down from the foundation wall, bent downward at a 45-degree angle.

FLOOR INSULATION

The usual procedure for installing an effective vapor barrier is to place 15-pound building paper between the first and second layers of floor decking (if there are two layers), or else between the only layer of structural floor decking and the floor covering (Fig. 7.15). In addition, if required by your climate and house type, blanket or batt insulation can be installed between the floor joists beneath the floor decking. An integral vapor barrier should also be situated against the underside of the floor decking. This will prevent the movement of moisture from the living area into the insulation.

Insulation from noise can be an important feature in a home. An example of a soundproof type of floor, starting at the top, consists of a layer of carpet, the carpet pad, a ⅝-inch plywood top floor deck, a layer of 15-pound felt paper, a ⅝-inch plywood bottom floor deck, 8-inch-thick fiberglass batt insulation with a vapor barrier at the top against the warm side of the structure, and finally, a layer of ½-inch fire-resistant gympsum board nailed to special resilient channels attached to the joists.

FIGURE 7.15

Floor insulation cutaway.

 POINTS TO PONDER

1. Lumber should be air- or kiln-dried No. 2 grade or better. It's already seasoned, it won't shrink as much as regular lumber will, it holds screws and glue better, provides increased thermal insulating values, holds paint and preservatives better, and is less likely to be attacked by fungi and insects.

2. Only pressure-treated or exterior grade lumber should be used for framing members that will be exposed to moisture.

3. Sill plates must be fastened to the foundation in a positive way, typically with anchor bolts that are partially embedded in the concrete foundation wall tops.

4. To prevent air, moisture, or insect intrusion through gaps or cracks which could otherwise exist between the foundation top and sill plate bottom, a resilient, waterproof layer of sealer (sometimes of or similar to felt or fiberglass or Styrofoam) is pushed over the protruding anchor bolts so that it is sandwiched and tightly squeezed between the foundation and sill plate.

5. In good construction, floor joists are placed either 12 or 16 inches on center and are made of planks a minimum of 2 by 10 inches or 2 by 12 inches.

6. Double-thickness floor joists—two planks fastened together—should be used where extra strength is needed: wherever the first- or second-floor walls run parallel to the floor joists, for instance, or at openings around a stairway, near a fireplace chimney, under cast-iron bathtubs, or at any major change in joist direction.

7. To stabilize floor joists, bridging or blocking must be used to help keep the joists properly aligned so the floor decking has a continuously level base to rest upon.

8. Give careful consideration to house designs that call for floor extensions that protrude outside the basic perimeter of the walls. They might be needed for porches, second-story over-hangs, decks, or bay windows. A sizeable protrusion could require supports outside of the foundation wall or even an actual adjustment to the foundation.

9. If you live in termite country, consult a professional exterminator and arrange whatever precautionary work that's needed. Construction precautions may include filling in the top two courses of foundation blocks with concrete and installing a noncorrosive metal termite shield that extends at least 2 inches out and 2 inches down at a 45-degree angle from the foundation wall.

10. Insulation from noise can be an important feature in a home, especially in single-story dwellings with basement recreation rooms.

Wall Framing

The wall frame is the next logical part of the house to erect after the first-floor decking is attached to the foundation. Wall framing performs three basic tasks. First, it supports the home's upper floors, ceilings, and roof. Second, it acts as a base on which outside and inside coverings can be fastened. Third, it provides space for and conceals essential wiring, pipes, heating ducts, and insulation. In its most general sense, wall framing also includes room partitions that are constructed within the outer perimeter of a dwelling.

TYPES OF WALL FRAMING

There are four types of wall framing worth noting: platform, balloon, post and beam, and pole.

Platform Framing

In platform framing, each floor is built separately, one on top of the other, with the first floor providing a work platform for the second level, and so on (Fig. 8.1).

Balloon Framing

In balloon framing, the studs or vertical members of the exterior walls are continuous from the sill plate of the first floor to the top plate

DOUBLE TOP PLATE

2ND FLOOR JOIST

SUBFLOOR

HEADER

DOUBLE PLATE

STUD

SOLE PLATE

SOLE PLATE

HEADER

SILL

SUBFLOOR

1X6 LET-IN DIAGONAL BRACE

FIGURE 8.1

Platform framing.

FIGURE 8.2

Balloon framing.

FIGURE 8.3

Post and beam framing.

of the second floor. These long studs are more expensive than the studs used to frame single-floor levels, and the labor to erect the longer studs, due to scaffolding required, is higher (Fig. 8.2).

Post and Beam Framing

Post and beam wall framing uses long, thick structural members—often rough-hewn posts and beams. There are fewer framing pieces required, and those pieces must span lengthy open spaces. Wooden planks are used for the floors and roof. In fact, they supply the sole support over long spans in both, being nailed at their ends to wood beams. Consequently, post and beam framing doesn't employ joists for the floors or ceiling. This type of framing is very popular where exposed beams and beamed wide-open ceilings fit the particular style or decor of a home (Fig. 8.3).

Pole Framing

In certain situations this uncommon type of framing has an advantage over studded wall framing in that long wooden poles, if properly pres-

PURLIN

OUTSIDE POLE

FLOOR JOIST

BLOCKING

LEDGER

FIGURE 8.4

Pole framing.

sure treated, can be embedded deep into the ground to provide a total bracing effect for the walls against the force of strong winds (Fig. 8.4).

STUDDED WALLS

By far, studded walls support most of the floors, ceilings, and roofs of modern dwellings. This conventional wall framing consists of a combination of header, studding, and top plate, which should be doubled (Fig. 8.5).

Exterior Studded Walls

The header for the exterior walls runs on and along the top outer edge of the sill plate and against the perimeter of the first floor joists and decking. It should possess greater width than individual wall studs—usually 2- by 10-inches. Specify the quality of all framing lumber to be KD No. 2 BTR SPF or better grade and a species appropriate for the span, spacing, and load.

Many contractors will suggest the use of 2- by 4-inch studs in the wall framing. Don't be swayed by a builder who advocates such construction. By going with 2- by 6-inch studded walls, you'll end up with stronger walls that will accommodate thicker blankets of insulation—that will, in turn, yield greater energy efficiency for a proportionally small increase in construction costs.

Have the wall studs spaced 16 inches on center to provide a sturdy base for exterior and interior wall coverings to be attached to. Use a double-width top plate of 2 by 6-inch lumber to hold the top of the walls together.

Interior Studded Walls, or Partitions

Conventional interior wall framing consists, as does the exterior wall, of a combination of sole plate, studding, and top plate

FIGURE 8.5

A studded wall frame, with double top plate.

(often doubled) to receive the weight of the ceiling joists. The sole plate generally runs across the floor decking, parallel or perpendicular to the floor joists, depending on the direction of the partition. The ceiling joists are typically positioned directly over the supporting studs applicable.

The partition tops should also be capped with two pieces of 2-inch thick boards, which are lapped or tied into exterior walls wherever they intersect.

If your house is a one and one-half-story or two-story design, it will require the installation of one or more load-bearing partitions before the structural framing work is completed. Later, interior partitioning consists of fitting the other various room and intersecting partitions to load-bearing partitions and exterior walls.

In a conventionally framed two-story home, the load-bearing first-floor partition should be placed directly over the main longitudinal support beam or girder that rests on the foundation walls. Load-bearing partitions on a second floor should likewise be positioned over corresponding members on the first floor, so weight will bear down upon the main girder(s) beneath the first floor.

Remember, due to their size and shape, combination bathtub/shower units must be installed during the wall partition and framing activity (Fig. 8.6). Select the models and colors well in advance so they can be ordered and received in time for the plumbers to erect them when the framing crew is ready.

Corners

The corners of wall frames need extra support because they must provide stability to both intersecting walls. They involve the assembly of "posts" with insulation, and corner bracing for strength, also with insulation (Fig. 8.7).

Posts

The posts are block assemblies of 2- by 6-inch planks with blocking used at cor-

FIGURE 8.6

A bathroom tub/shower unit and framing.

FIGURE 8.7

Exterior corner post construction.

ners of wall frames and where interior partitions abut an outer perimeter wall. They should be constructed to provide a good nailing surface for exterior and interior wall coverings, and because they're hollow, they must be filled with fiberglass or other insulation so that heat is not wasted through the thermal break they'd otherwise create (Fig. 8.8). The insides of posts must be insulated as they're being put together. It can't be done later, when the posts are covered over.

Corner Bracing

If plywood at least ½-inch thick is used as the outer sheathing on the wall frame corners, depending on where you live (i.e., a location where strong winds and storms are common), other bracing may not be necessary (Fig. 8.9). But if the outer sheathing is a material that's not very strong, such as particle board, additional bracing will be needed. An effective corner brace to specify is the diagonal support that's "let into" or inset into the outer corner studs (Fig. 8.10). This type of brac-

FIGURE 8.8

Post construction.

ing is achieved with either 1- by 4-inch or 1- by 6-inch boards that fit snugly in notches cut at appropriate angles at the proper height of each wall stud crossed. The inset boards on both sides of a corner rise to meet each other in the shape of a triangle (Figs. 8.11 and 8.12).

OPENINGS IN WALL FRAMING

Remember that it's the outer walls of a home that protect the occupants from winds and inclement weather, noise, and unsightly views.

FIGURE 8.9

Plywood corner bracing.

FIGURE 8.10

Diagonal corner bracing.

Openings should be strategically placed as well as being soundly framed. Here are some pointers to consider when planning the openings in your wall frames:

1. It's important to know far in advance of the wall framing, the size, type, and brand of each window and door you want so the rough opening dimensions can be secured from the manufacturers and passed along to the carpenters who will be erecting the wall framing.

2. In good construction, board cuts and joints should be accurate and tight at the junction of the roof rafters and the ridge board, at the headers of windows and doors, and at all intersections. Cuts and joints that result in large, obvious gaps create weaknesses in the framing that you should not accept.

3. Wherever an interior door or window will be hung, there must be double

FIGURE 8.11

Corner bracing.

DOUBLE PLATE

STUD·CONTINUOUS
BOTH FLOORS

JOIST

FIRE STOP

BLOCKING

1 X 4 RIBBON
(LET · IN)

CORNER POST
3 STUDS

1 X 6 LET-IN
DIAGONAL BRACE

1ST FLOOR JOIST

SILL

FIGURE 8.12

Corner bracing.

studding around the opening to make up for the support studs that would otherwise go in place of the door or window opening. Double studding also presents a needed place to nail door and window trim. A double horizontal lintel or header is used to support short studs that reinforce the top plate of the wall above the opening (Figs. 8.13 and 8.14). The planks for the headers should be 2 by 10s.

4. If any of your exterior walls will have brick veneer coverings, you'll need steel lintels to support the brick veneer over the tops of window and door openings (Fig. 8.15).

5. If you desire, blocking can be installed to the right and left of each window between the studs to provide a solid backing to which curtain rods can be mounted. Anywhere you plan to hang heavy or often-used objects such as large pictures, trophies, or hanging bookcases, arrange for blocking between the studs to take the weight. Keep this in mind in the bathroom, for fastening towel racks, soap dishes, and toothbrush holders to the wall.

6. If your bathrooms call for any flush-mounted medicine cabinets in which

FIGURE 8.13

Door-opening reinforcement with double header.

FIGURE 8.14

Door and window reinforcement.

FIGURE 8.15

Masonry steel lintel reinforcement over window.

FIGURE 8.16

Plywood sheating construction.

the storage portion of the cabinet is recessed into a wall, additional framing must be installed to accept them. Select the cabinets well in advance so you'll have the correct dimensions of the rough openings to give to the framing crew.

7. Make sure the framing crew remembers to install nailers to which drywall or plaster lathing can be attached, especially in odd corners and spaces where regular framing isn't used.

VENTILATION

Plan the openings—especially window openings—for cross ventilation as far as possible. Good airflow occurs when the air inlets and outlets are approximately the same size. A better airflow results from a larger outlet than inlet.

SHEATHING

One of the last operations of the wall framing is the installation of the exterior sheathing that's attached to the wall studs. Six materials are typically used, mostly in 4- by 8-foot sheets: CDX plywood, particleboard, fiberboard insulating sheathing, exterior gypsum board (if you plan to stucco), rigid foam insulating sheathing, and Styrofoam insulating sheathing (Figs. 8.16, 8.17, and 8.18).

Exterior sheathing performs three functions:

1. It braces the structure. Plywood is the strongest, most rigid of the six, followed by particleboard. If plywood is used, at least on the corners, it may eliminate the need for diagonal bracing. Diagonal boards with plywood corners will provide superior structural bracing.

For best results the sheathings should be applied vertically in 4- by 8-foot or longer sheets with edge and center nailing.

2. It provides insulation. If insulation, not strength, is the main concern, rigid foam and Styrofoam board are the winners here. They can be purchased with tongue-and-groove edges to provide a tight fit to reduce air infiltration.

3. Sheathing provides a weathertight base for the exterior siding. Plywood and particleboard sheathings are a strong base for exterior siding. Make sure the sheathing you choose will provide the needed base for the exterior siding you have selected. Be aware that there are two types of plywood: exterior and interior. Definitely, only exterior-grade plywood should be used for the outside of a house. Exterior CDX plywood is made with high-quality veneers and is bonded with water-proof glue. It offers the best durability and its glue won't weaken with age or with long exposure to foul weather.

Last, with rigid foam or Styrofoam sheathing, review with the manufacturer and your contractor where an additional vapor barrier may be needed. Besides a vapor barrier applied to the inside of wall studs to prevent movement of moisture

FIGURE 8.17

Particleboard.

FIGURE 8.18

Styrofoam or fiberboard.

from living areas into insulation, a vapor barrier may also be needed on the outside of wall studs. If where you live rigid foam or Styrofoam traps any moisture inside an exterior wall, it will condense as it reaches its dewpoint and create water. The water will soak the insulation and rot the sill plates over time.

NAILS

As minor as they might seem, nails are what hold much of a house together. Only galvanized nails should be used on exposed materials, both inside and out. Unless the house is roofed over immediately, a sudden downpour could cause regular steel nails to rust and streak the surfaces in just one night.

If your walls will have studs with 24-inch o.c. (on center) placements instead of 16-inch o.c. as recommended, nailers will have to be installed so drywall or plaster lathing can be securely attached. Nailers are small 2- by 4-inch or 2- by 6-inch blocks attached perpendicular to the studs, in between pairs of studs. The nailers will also give extra support and stiffness to the walls and will act as a fireblock to discourage flames from spreading throughout a wall.

It's a good idea to specify that exterior wall sheathing be applied by hand nailing only. Some of the more fragile sheathings such as polyurethane board can be easily torn and damaged by power nailing equipment.

For optimum efficiency, nails should be spaced 6 inches on center (o.c.).

ENERGY

Energy is of great interest no matter which part of a house is being discussed. But here, with the exterior walls, insulation takes on a special importance. Naturally, you want to reduce the consumption of energy for heating and cooling and to increase the level of comfort in the home by muffling the effects of the elements. That's another reason why openings should be carefully planned to prevent unwanted heat loss or heat gain and to allow for natural ventilation and heat gain when desired.

The major obstacles to well-insulated, sealed walls are doors, windows, and electrical outlets. Again, eliminating as many potential problems as possible in the design stages is the first and most logical step. Place wall switches and outlets on interior walls when possible, and use as few windows, glass sliders, and doors as practical. Have reasons for everything that goes into the exterior walls. When you can, incorporate features that must be inset into a wall, within interior walls, where the interruption of insulation is not a factor.

Because wall insulation is so important, the use of 2- by 6-inch studs is stressed over and over. Old-fashioned 2 by 4 studs were fine in their day, when energy was inexpensive, but only 3½ inches of fiberglass batt or blanket insulation will fit into such walls. With 2 by 6 studs, 5½ inches of the same kind of insulation can be laid (Fig. 8.19). That makes a big difference in energy use.

SOUND INSULATION

There are two ways to arrange effective sound insulation for interior walls. The first employs staggered 2- by 4-inch studs erected on a 2- by 6-inch plate. The studs should be positioned 16 inches o.c. Because the studs are staggered, this technique eliminates the touching of drywall or plaster on both sides of the wall by any single stud, thus reducing the wall sound transmission capabilities. The air voids between the studs are "woven" with 3½-inch fiberglass blanket or batt insulation, which will further deaden noise transmission.

In the second procedure, interior walls are constructed with 2- by 6-inch studs and 5½-inch or 6-inch batt or blanket insulation. The additional wall thickness makes up for sound transmission deficiencies.

FOIL BACKED INSULATION STAPLED FLUSH WITH STUDS

STUD

SOLE PLATE

UNBACKED INSULATION

STUD

FINISH WALL

POLYETHYLENE FILM STAPLED TO STUDS

FIGURE 8.19

Wall insulation views.

VAPOR BARRIERS

In addition to being insulated, living areas should also be sealed with a moisture-proof layer or vapor barrier that's applied to the inside of the wall studs to prevent the movement of moisture from the living areas into the insulation. Insulation will lose some of its thermal qualities if it becomes damp or wet, and if the moisture within the living spaces is retained within the house, the occupants will still feel comfortable with less heat, due to the inside humidity. Consult local building codes for guidance on specific vapor barrier requirements. Depending on your climate, whether it's hot, humid, or dry, vapor barrier needs vary.

There are several methods for applying a vapor barrier to exterior walls: install insulating batts or blankets faced with vapor barrier backings such as treated Kraft paper or aluminum foil. The vapor barrier should always be placed closest to the living area that's heated. If unfaced batts or blankets are used, a vapor barrier or polyethylene film not less than 3 mils thick (or an equivalent) should be applied.

If you elect loose blown insulation, establish a vapor barrier by stapling or nailing polyethylene sheet material to the interior of the wall studs. You can also install aluminum foil–backed drywall before the insulation is blown between the studding.

BEFORE THE WALLS ARE CLOSED

Before the walls are closed up, the following items should be completed, if applicable:

- Sink drains
- Vents
- Water supply for sinks
- Cold water for toilets
- Water for showers and tubs
- Hot water for a dishwasher
- Hot and cold water for a clothes washer
- Gas lines

- Appliance vents
- Built-in vacuum system
- Electric wires and doorbell
- Intercom system
- Internet connections
- Phone lines
- Alarm systems
- Heating and cooling ducts
- Wall insulation
- Plumbing installed

≣INSPECTION

WALL FRAMING

After the wall framing is complete, check the following:

- Vertical walls are plumb.
- Opposite walls of rooms are parallel.
- Horizontal members (joists, headers, and subfloors) are level.
- Exterior sheathing is not damaged or punctured.

>>>>>> **POINTS TO PONDER**

1. Again, if you're using wood, use only air- or kiln-dried No. 2 grade or better framing lumber. You don't need the warping and shrinking that could result from unseasoned lumber.
2. Don't be swayed by a builder who suggests the use of 2- by 4-inch wood studs in the wall framing to save a few dollars. By using 2- by 6-inch studded walls, you'll end up with stronger walls that will accommodate thicker blankets of insulation.
3. Conventional wood studding should be spaced 16 inches on center to provide a sturdy base to which exterior and interior wall coverings may be attached.
4. Use double-width or double-thick top plates of 2- by 6-inch lumber to hold the top of the walls together.
5. In a conventionally framed two-story home, load-bearing first-floor partition(s) should be placed directly over the main longitudinal support beam(s) or girder(s) that rest on the foundation.
6. Remember, due to their size and shape, combination bathtub/shower units must be installed during the wall partition and framing activity or you won't be able to simply carry them into place later—they're too big.
7. Corners of wall frames need extra support because they must provide stability to both intersecting walls.

8. In addition to being insulated, living areas should also be sealed with a moisture-proof layer or vapor barrier that's applied to the inside of the wall studs to prevent the movement of moisture from the living areas into the insulation.

9. Sound insulation is important for establishing privacy between bedrooms, bathrooms, and other living areas.

10. While wall framing is still exposed or open, make sure as much of the plumbing, electric, communications, doorbells, security alarm systems, certain types of insulation, central vacuum systems, heating and air-conditioning components, plus various vents, drains, built-ins, window and door openings, and other applicable items are completed.

Roof Framing

There's no getting out from under it: the roof of a house is often all there is between you and the sky. And as such, the roof will protect you from such inconveniences as snow, sleet, hail, rain, sunrays, wind, dust and dirt, acid rain, insects and animals, moonlight, and noise. It will, when constructed and insulated properly, keep cool air in the house during summer, and warm air outside. Then conversely, during winter, the roof keeps cold air at bay and warm air inside.

The typical roof also serves, however infrequently, as a platform for contractors to walk on when they're performing maintenance and repairs—to renew the flashing on a chimney, for instance, or to dislodge a stubborn bird nest from a false flue.

A roof must be securely fastened to the rest of the house, not merely "tacked onto" the upper level. It has to be able to resist updrafts of wind that would otherwise yank a roof right off.

The roof and ceiling frame of a home's upper level needs to be sturdy enough to support whatever covering or options are planned, including heavy tiles or slates, solar panels, and skylights. At the same time, however, it should be noted that any irregularities or impediments to simple rooflines provide opportunities for water or moisture to seep through the roofing. This includes chimneys, vents, roof lights, and anywhere the roof has a valley or dormer where one roofline intersects another.

Other practical considerations to be made with the roof frame are the size and shape of the area between the upper level's ceiling and the rooftop, commonly known as the attic space. In certain types of houses, this space can be constructed in a variety of ways. It tends to follow patterns dictated by the shape of the rest of the house, tempered by basic aesthetics. Although it should be in correct proportion to the surrounding architectural components, certain decisions must be made regarding roof pitch, materials, and construction techniques.

The roof overhang—the part of the roof that protrudes beyond the exterior walls—protects the exterior sheathing or siding, windows, and doors from the elements, especially rain and sun. A wide overhang will block the sun on summer days when the sun rises high overhead, then will let the sun rays enter during winter, when the sun travels a much lower route in the sky.

ROOF STYLES

Six styles of roofs account for the lion's share of roofs, old and new: gable, gambrel, hip, mansard, flat, and single-pitch or shed. The first three are the most widely used (Fig. 9.1).

Keep in mind that the following styles are not restrictive of each other. A single dwelling can and will often have a combination of several roof styles.

The Gable Roof

The *gable roof* is the single most popular roof style built today. It consists of two usually equal-sloped roof planes that meet at a topmost ridge. In fact, it's the ridgeline running the entire length of the house, or at least on the parts of the house having that style of roof, that most characterizes the gable style. The gable also means the upper triangular area formed on each end of such a roof. Gable or shed dormers are frequently added to plain gable roofs to break monotonous lines or for the practical purpose of providing natural light, air, and additional space to make an attic area more useful.

The Gambrel Roof

In general, the *gambrel roof* is a gable roof having two separate roof slopes on each side of the topmost ridge, the flatter or least-sloped of

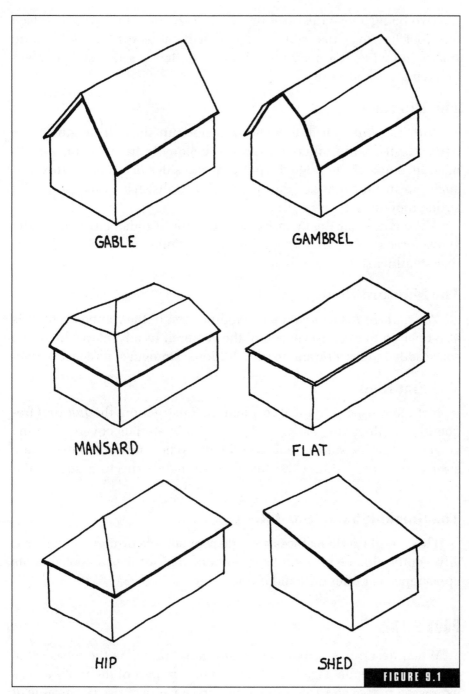

GABLE

GAMBREL

MANSARD

FLAT

HIP

SHED

FIGURE 9.1

Roof styles.

the two being above the level of any dormer windows. An advantage this roof has over the gable roof is that it increases the usable attic space, and when dormer windows are installed, it's almost equivalent to having a second story.

The Hip Roof

With the *hip roof*, the ridge does not run the full length of the house. Instead, hip rafters extend up diagonally from each corner to meet the ends of the ridge. Essentially, the sides or slopes of this roof angle up in four planes from the outside walls. It's an exceptionally strong roof design.

Although by far the majority of houses built today have one of the above three roof styles, there are an equal number of lesser-used styles that should also be mentioned.

The Mansard Roof

The *mansard* is a variation or modification of the gambrel roof. It is also referred to as a hip version of the gambrel. Its advantages lie in the space added to the attic and in the additional strength of its construction.

The Flat Roof

Not often used in typical residential construction, the *flat roof* frequently employs the use of rubber roofing materials covered by fine gravel. Naturally, such a roof would have to be constructed extremely strong for any building located in a climate expecting substantial snowfalls.

The Single-Pitch or Shed Roof

This simple style features a single roof surface or plane that's usually gently sloped in a single direction. It's not a bad roof, but its appearance is rather dull and uninspiring.

ROOF PITCH

When describing a roof's configuration, "pitch" is the measure of its steepness or the degree of slope the roof or part of the roof has. It's expressed in two corresponding numbers: a value of rise per a value of run (Fig. 9.2). "Rise" means just what it says—a vertical distance.

"Run" addresses the horizontal travel it takes to reach a given rise. A 4–12 pitch means there are 4 units or measures of rise for each 12 units or measures of run (Fig. 9.3). It can as easily be expressed with inches or feet. Whatever measures are used, the ratio remains constant. Generally, when it comes to roof pitch, builders tend to do their thinking in inches. A very low-pitched roof will have a substantially smaller rise than run: 1–12 or 2–12, for example. Medium-sloped roofs range up to about 6–12—about the steepest slope that a novice can comfortably walk around on. A roof having a 45-degree angle is considered steep, having a pitch of 12–12.

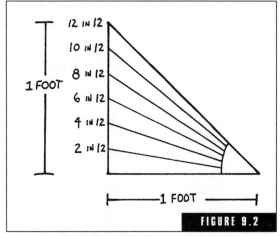

Determining roof pitch or slope.

The pitch of a house roof is influenced by a variety of factors, including expected snowfall, the heaviness or lightness of construction materials, how much storage or living space you want beneath the roof, how much insulation is planned, and of course, how the house should look so it's architecturally balanced. Different climate conditions and different house types will call for different roof pitches. Here are the main characteristics of a low-pitched roof:

1. It will shed water well in warm climates, and will, if built soundly, retain snow for added insulation in colder climates.

2. The area directly under roof will consistently be a wider, more open space, providing extra room with pleasantly sloped ceilings.

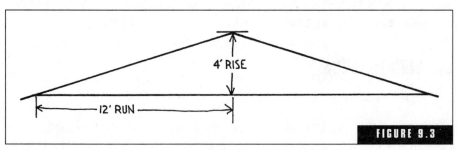

A pitch of 4–12.

3. The low pitch will make both interior and exterior maintenance safer and less expensive.

4. Since its initial construction requires less material due to its minimal surface area, it's also less costly to build than a steeply pitched roof.

To balance out our roof picture, here are some characteristics of a steeply pitched roof, from 6–12 to 12–12 and above:

1. A steeply pitched roof sheds just about everything in a hurry. Rain races off its surface, and snow is less likely to accumulate there. A steeply pitched roof rarely leaks. It doesn't give the moisture a chance to penetrate.

2. Although certain individuals can benefit by lofty storage spaces provided within a steeply pitched roof, care must be taken to avoid ending up with inaccessible, unpleasant attic rooms. Let no one sway you into believing that every inch of an attic constructed beneath steeply sloped roof planes can be gainfully employed.

3. A steep pitch makes maintenance and repairs tasks for professionals, especially when the exterior must be accessed. That means inconvenience and high expenses for both.

4. Since more surface area is involved, a steeply pitched roof requires more materials at an initially larger cost outlay.

5. Steeply pitched roofs are good for placing solar collectors on in cold and warm climate locations.

Keep in mind that the pitch of your roof might limit or even dictate what roofing materials you can use. Wood and asphalt shingles, wood shakes, and tile or slate can require a pitch of 4–12 or steeper. Roofs sloped less than 4–12 are uncommon, and might need to be covered with an industrial-type flat roof of rubber or tar and fine gravel.

BUILDING METHODS

There are two common methods of constructing roofs:

- The *stick-built system* uses individually erected rafters, ridge boards, ceiling joists, and collar beams assembled on the job.

■ The *prefabricated truss system* is a newer method in which trusses are made to your roof's specifications by a fabricating company that specializes in this work.

Stick-Built Roofs

Figure 9.4 shows an example of a stick-built roof.

CEILING JOISTS

When all exterior and interior walls are framed, plumbed, and nailed, and after the top plate has been fastened in place, the ceiling joists go up to tie the walls together and to form a structural base for the erection of the roof. In most cases, these joists must span the width of the house, one overlapping with another, supported by a load-bearing collar beam toward the center of the house. The size of lumber to

FIGURE 9.4

A stick-built roof.

use for joists is determined by the distance to span, the type of wood used, and the load that will have to be supported above. The dimensions of the lumber used for ceiling joists should be specified in the plans. Do not settle for anything less than 2- by 6-inch planks.

In a two-story home, the ceiling joists at the second level become floor joists for the attic, and it's reasonable to assure they must be as sturdy as those used below and constructed in a similar fashion.

The spacing of the ceiling joists may vary, but, as with studs, 16 inches o.c. is considered standard good construction. The doubled top plate of the wall frame supplies sufficient strength. It makes sense to locate joists over the wall stud positions (Figs. 9.5 and 9.6). Install wood blocking between ceiling joists where bracing is needed for ceiling lights and fans.

Ceiling joists serve several purposes: they resist the outward thrust imposed upon the walls by the roof rafters, they provide nailing surfaces for the ceiling and the upstairs or attic flooring, they support any weight placed on the upper floor. Because of their place in the framing scheme, joists must be securely nailed to the top plate of every wall that their ends rest on and to every load-bearing partition wall that they cross or join on.

Note that ceiling joists are not used with houses having truss framing. The bottoms of the trusses, normally constructed of 2 by 4s or 2 by 6s, become the ceiling joists.

RAFTERS

Rafters are wood planks or boards that span the distances from the top of the exterior walls to the roof ridgeline or peak to form the skeletal structure that the roof deck is fastened to. The size of the rafters

FIGURE 9.5

A stick-built roof construction view.

RAFTER

JOIST

NAIL JOIST
AND RAFTER TOGETHER

NAIL JOIST TO PLATE

TOP PLATE

FIGURE 9.6

Positioning the ceiling joists and rafters.

varies with the distance they must span and the steepness or pitch of
the roof. It's often computed by referring to tables that show the load-
bearing capacities and deflection qualities of various woods and
boards. When sizing your rafters, many variables go into selecting the
proper dimensions, such as length of span, spacing of structural members, wood species, lumber grade, plus expected wind forces and
snowfall. Depending on the conditions, your rafters may need to be 2
by 8, 2 by 10, or even larger.

When selecting roof rafter joists ask your builder about using engineered wood I-beam roof rafter joists.

Engineered wood I beams are made with a top and bottom lumber
flange with a grooved center to accommodate a center web (typically
plywood) (Fig. 9.7). Special hangers with blocking are needed to
secure these beams.

Engineered wood I-beam roof rafter joists offer many advantages:

■ Good strength.

■ Excellent clear span on large rooms. Span longer distances than
regular wood.

FIGURE 9.7

Engineered wood I-beam roof rafter joists.

- Always standard and consistent in dimension.

- Laminated construction eliminates crowning, warping, twisting, and bowing.

- Won't shrink or crack.

- Roof sheathing lays flatter initially and remains that way since these beams don't shrink.

- Wide flanges allow the plywood to be screwed straight down (not angled as when trying to hit half a 2 by lumber) while staying back from the edges.

- There is more bearing surface for glue and support.

- Typically lighter than dimensional lumber.

The rafters should be spaced in the same manner as ceiling joists are erected, then each rafter can be tied or nailed to a companion joist as well as to the plate.

Advantages

1. Dormer expansions are relatively simple to make with rafter framing. If you think you might want to expand into an attic, it's a must to use rafters instead of prefabricated trusses. And if expansion is likely, then increase the size of your floor joists.

2. The rafter or stick design is also the better choice when adding dormers because it's much easier to tailor the roof to accept the dormer framing.

3. Rafter-built roofs allow you to have cathedral ceilings.

Disadvantages

1. The main disadvantage of rafter roof framing is that load-bearing interior walls must be relied upon for support.

Truss-Built Roofs

Roof trusses, unlike ceiling joists used with rafters, span the entire width of a structure (Fig. 9.8). They are triangular with wood interior

Truss-built construction.

bridging (W-shaped) for strength. Mathematically, the principle that gives what appear to be flimsy components the strength to span such long distances is the inherent rigidity of the triangle. Trusses simply rest upon and are fastened to opposite exterior walls. The individual truss units should be spaced 16 inches o.c. to avoid the risk of a sagging roof deck.

If you are using a truss-built roof, consider the following three points:

- While some contractors use 2 by 4 trusses, a 2 by 6 truss provides a stronger design. A major disadvantage of 2 by 4 trusses is truss uplift. When the top chords of a 2 by 4 truss are heated in the summer, they expand slightly causing the bottom chord to bow up in the middle. The interior ceiling drywall or plasterboard is attached to these chords and is pulled upward separating corners and cracking the joints. If 2 by 4 trusses are being used, consider requesting 2 by 6 bottom chords to help resist bowing.

- Trusses limit attic space as a result of the cross member supports. To alleviate the space loss, ask your contractor if "W" trusses will support the roof load. "W" trusses have the inner cross member angled to provide more attic space.

- Make sure wood blocking is installed between trusses where bracing is needed for ceiling lights and fans.

Advantages

1. Ceiling joists aren't needed in the attic.

2. Trusses are built using smaller dimensional lumber than is used by the stick-built rafter system.

3. Despite the small lumber, the truss design still provides adequate strength to a roof.

4. Savings in framing costs can usually be realized due to the reduction of materials and labor involved with truss installation.

5. The greatest advantage of a trussed roof is that it eliminates the need for load-bearing interior walls. Trusses are engineered to span entire distances between opposite exterior walls without relying on intermediate support. Thus, complete design freedom in the planning of interior space is possible.

Disadvantages

1. The diagonal members used to reinforce the truss design greatly restrict the amount of usable attic space. To many homebuilders it comes down to the question of free use of living areas versus the importance of storage space.

THE ROOF DECK

The roof deck is what gets fastened to the exterior of the rafters and what the finished roofing shingles, shakes, tiles, or other materials are fastened to (Fig. 9.9). It consists of a structural sheathing and a moisture-resistant underlayment.

Roof Sheathings

Most roof sheathing is done with plywood sheets in thicknesses suitable to properly strengthen the rafters and to correctly prepare for whatever roof covering will be used. Here are some construction points to remember about plywood sheathing:

1. The type of plywood to specify is CDX. This comes with a clear (C) or smooth side to be seen, and a rough side (D) to be hidden. The X means it's all held together with exterior-type glue.

2. The plywood thickness for roof sheathings should be at least ⅝ inch, and preferably ¾ inch. Review your local building requirements. The added thickness of ¾ inch gives superior resistance to high winds and affords better penetration for shingle nails. Plywood roof sheathing should be on 16-inch on center roof framing,

FELT
OVERLAP

PANEL CLIP
IF REQUIRED

ROOFING FELT

PANEL SHEATHING
INSTALL WITH LONG DIMENSION
ACROSS SUPPORTS, STAGGER THE VERTICAL JOINTS

FIGURE 9.9

A cutaway of the roof deck.

with metal "H" clips fastened between the edges of the plywood sheets to reduce the potential of the sheathing to sag and to give extra support between the framing rafters or trusses.

3. For the greatest overall strength, the 4- by 8-foot or larger sheets of plywood should be laid crossways to the rafters or trusses—similar to their use over floor joists—to tie the greatest number of framing members together as possible with a single sheet.

4. The joints should also be staggered by at least one rafter or truss so that there is no continuous joint line from a cornice to the roof ridge board. No adjoining panels should abut over the same rafter or truss.

Roof Underlayments

The second step toward completing a roof is to place a layer of underlayment or saturated roofing felt paper on top of the plywood sheathing. The roofing felt should be a 15-pound or 30-pound material, which means that the weight of the amount of felt paper that would cover 100 square feet in a single ply is 15 or 30 pounds, respectively. The shingle manufacturer may specify which felt to use so the warranty remains in place.

Roofing paper should be applied with 6-inch end overlaps and head overlaps along the edges of 3 inches. Many felt papers have white stripes on them for indicating the correct overlaps, and such stripes can also be helpful guides for coursing the shingles.

There are three basic reasons that felt paper is placed over the sheathing before the final roof topping material is laid:

- It provides additional weather protection for the roof.

- It's a resilient padding between the shingles and the wood sheathing.

- It keeps the sheathing dry until the final roofing material can be applied.

It's a good idea that the roofers try to paper a roof on a mild-weather day. If the temperatures are too cold, the paper becomes brittle and tears easily. If the weather is too hot the paper becomes soft, and likewise tears easily. Of course, building paper must be applied perfectly flat to avoid bulges on the finished roof. Although numerous roofing underlayments are available, many contractors have been using ice and water guard underlayments, especially where water and ice plays a role, such as along valleys, drip edges, dormers, chimneys, and other roof parts.

VENTILATION

When closing a car door from the inside, have you ever experienced pressure on your ears because the car is practically airtight, and there's barely any means for the air to escape? Or how about storing fresh mushrooms in an airtight plastic bag? Any cook knows that to do so invites spoilage: if air cannot freely circulate around the mushrooms to remove "expired" moisture, then that moisture will quickly condense onto the mushrooms and will cause them to deteriorate, even if they're kept cold.

The same principle holds true with houses, especially when it comes to roofs. A house/roof combination that's too "airtight" is unhealthy. Moisture that's given off from a variety of our appliances and fixtures such as toilets, showers, clothes washers and dryers, dishwashers, cooking surfaces, and even from our own breathing—not to mention periods of high-humidity weather—becomes an agent that will, if not removed, rot wood, wreak havoc with insulation, and even go right through to the underlayment of a roof and affect asphalt or wood shingle roofing materials themselves—all from within. Materials stored in moist environments will also tend to be ruined by mildew over the long haul.

Thus, an airtight, self-contained roof/house combination is not only undesirable, but is downright dangerous to have. Many old houses were constructed without vents. Instead, the owners relied upon large double-hung windows and screens positioned at the gable ends, opening them for a cross breeze. That worked fine until the windows rotted or "froze" shut and couldn't be opened or were closed during rainstorms and times of high humidity. That's why you'll find so many old houses with rotting wood roofs and musty-smelling attics that are extremely hot in the summer and freezing in the winter.

Hot air accumulates in the attic as heated air rises from the home's living areas, while sunrays superheat the roof. Trapped hot air in an unventilated or improperly ventilated attic will defeat the best efforts of air conditioning, insulation, and even shade trees to help keep a home cooler during summer. On the other hand, effective attic ventilation reduces heat buildup, helps keep the living quarters comfortable, cuts cooling costs, extends shingle life by keeping the roof cooler during hot weather, helps reduce moisture buildup that encourages mildew growth and rot on the roof's framing members and sheathing, and also minimizes the buildup of ice dams on the roof and gutters during winter.

Nowadays, all good builders realize that attic or roof vents are necessities, and the builders supply one or a combination of several vent types to let the house breathe and rid itself of unwanted moisture. Consider, too, that roof ventilation also allows heat that rises to the upper reaches of the roof interior to escape, and does the same for dangerous gases or fumes that could collect there in the event of an accident or emergency.

How much ventilation is needed? Your builder should have a good feel for that. It can be affected by the direction of prevailing winds, the amounts of shelter from the sun, or even from the positions of neighboring buildings or parts of the house itself. Some rooflines can channel wind toward a certain part of the roof, while others might hinder particular airflows from having desired effects. Roof ventilation is especially important to houses exposed to continuous sunshine and equipped with air-conditioning.

Proper ventilation helps remove warm, moist air from the attic, making your home more comfortable and helping to reduce cooling costs in the summer and prevent ice dams in winter. An effective year-round ventilation system provides continuous airflow through the attic, with air entering via soffit vents and exiting at ridge, gable, turbine, or roof vents as well as roof fans.

The following are five popular types of vents that can be used on new houses (Fig. 9.10) along with window and roof fans.

Ridge Vents

Because the ridge line is the highest part of a roof, it offers an efficient location for a ventilator. A ridge vent typically consists of a long channel or "crack" covered by an upside-down gutterlike vent running along the roof ridge that permits air to escape from the house and prevents rain from entering.

A ridge vent will vent your entire peak, working with the wind to siphon moist, hot air out of the attic spaces and protecting your roof and keeping your house more comfortable.

Ridge vents should be durable and weather-resistant. They typically come in metal or plastic. When choosing yours, make sure it offers the following qualities:

- Rain- and snowproof, prevents both from entering
- Rated to withstand high winds (in excess of 100 mph) and blizzard conditions
- Bug- and insectproof
- Resists denting and cracking
- Warp-proof

FIGURE 9.10

Types of roof ventilators.

- Unibody construction, rugged and durable, with no pieces to come loose

- Crushproof design

- Rustproof

- Design that allows for expansion and contraction during temperature extremes

- Allows shingles to be attached on its top so it blends in with the roof

A gable vent.

Gable Vents

Gable vents are the most widely used roofing vents (Fig. 9.11). These are the triangular slatted arrangements you'll notice on practically every house that has gable ends. Frequently made of galvanized metal, gable vents do a good job of getting rid of heat because they are located close to the roof ridge. Depending on the location of the house, a cross breeze will sometimes result.

Roof Turbines

A roof turbine vent.

Turbine vents help get rid of heat and moisture. Roof turbines and fans are galvanized or aluminum vent units fastened to a side of a roof, on one of the slopes, positioned to act like a wind-powered turbine or fan when the wind blows, and like a free vent when the air is still (Fig. 9.12). The turbine vent utilizes a series of specially shaped vanes to catch the wind and provide the rotary motion to pull hot and humid air from the attic. They can be electrically powered to assist in removing hot air during summer, to augment an air-conditioning system so that it doesn't become overloaded. Look for a turbine vent with sturdy rust-free construction (typically aluminum) that has permanently lubricated upper and lower bearings, rated to operate from as little as a breeze of 1-mile-per-hour through regular winds, and be able to withstand the strongest winds expected in your location.

FIGURE 9.13

A soffit ventilator.

Roof Vent

Roof vents are galvanized or aluminum vents that fasten to the side of a roof, on one of the slopes, that allow the attic air to vent out. The quantity used will depend on the size of your roof.

Soffit Vents

Soffit ventilators are similar to gable vents, except they're positioned at the eave or soffit areas of the roof (Fig. 9.13). Install a continuous pattern of soffit ventilation under the eaves to allow fresh, cooler air to enter the attic. Fresh air flows in through the soffit openings into the attic and then stale air is expelled through the gable vents, roof vents, ridge vents, turbines, or fans.

Make sure your contractor does not block the soffit vent spaces between rafters just above the exterior walls, where baffles should be installed to allow air to move past the insulation. Without ventilation baffles, effective airflow up and out the ridge vents may be hindered.

And finally, because air will be drawn into the soffit vents, the vents should include a fine screen mesh to prevent insects from entering. Of course, soffit vents should be made of nonrusting materials, such as aluminum or plastic.

Window Fans

When any or all of the preceding vents do not provide enough air circulation, an attic window fan might be necessary to draw out hot air and rid the attic of unwanted moisture. If you plan to install an attic

FIGURE 9.14

A roof fan.

ventilation window fan, make sure the builder includes large enough gable or other vents to permit the passage of enough air so the fan can operate efficiently.

Roof Fans

Roof fans, also referred to as attic fans, have traditionally been electric ventilators that mount on a side of the roof and can quickly exhaust heat and humidity from the attic (Fig. 9.14). The fan motor is typically activated and shut down by a built-in thermostat that monitors the attic temperature. When the air rises above a set temperature, the fan comes on; when it falls below that temperature, the fan shuts down. A manual shutdown switch is normally placed in the hallway to allow turning the fan off. These units continue to be very popular in homes. They lower the attic temperature, save on air-conditioning, and make a home more comfortable.

Due to the situation—a roof fan is most needed when the sun is shining during times of hot weather, it's an ideal candidate for solar power. An energy-efficient solar fan provides an excellent way to vent an attic or garage by using the sun's rays to exhaust heated air (Fig. 9.15). Their energy source is free and plentiful, with no electrical wiring or complicated controls to attach.

These relatively inexpensive fans operate fastest during the hottest parts of the day, then at lower speeds during early morning or late afternoon when inside air is cooler and needs less circulation. Since sunshine access by the roof-mounted solar fan is so important, the units work best when facing south or southwest.

Consider these points when shopping for solar fans:

FIGURE 9.15

A solar roof fan.

■ Solar fans should be able to be set to come on at one temperature, and turn itself off at another, lower temperature.

■ The fan design should accomplish positive venting by creating negative air pressure that will draw heated air, including moisture, out from beneath the roof.

■ A baffle system should enable heated air to exhaust but keep rain and snow from entering.

■ The unit should provide ventilation even later in the day or night if temperatures within the space remain elevated. This can be accomplished with a rechargeable backup battery charged by excess energy generated during the day by the solar cell. When fully charged, the battery should have the capability to operate the vent for nearly three days' worth of dark or cloudy weather conditions.

■ A heavy-gauge screen should be attached around the top edge of the inside housing to keep out insects, birds, and other critters.

Chimney Vents

Although they have little to do with attic airflows, chimney vents also pass through the attic and roof, or are positioned directly adjacent to them. Especially if it's a manufactured metal chimney that has a built-in air space, it should be located at least 2 inches away from any nearby wood frame. The top of a chimney should clear the roof ridge by 3 feet.

INSULATION

Insulation of the attic and roof is a task that must not be taken lightly. In cold-climate locations, the heat generated by a furnace or fireplace rises, and it's the attic insulation that prevents it from escaping. In warm climates, heat from the sun beaming down on the roof tends to make the rooms that are directly beneath the attic too warm. Again, it's the attic and roof insulation that will prevent heat from passing through the attic floor into the living areas.

Attic and roof insulation is covered in Chapter 20.

▶▶▶▶▶▶ **POINTS TO PONDER**

1. The roof overhang—the part of the roof that protrudes beyond the exterior walls—protects the exterior sheathing or siding,

windows, and doors from the elements, especially rain and sun.

2. A wide roof overhang will block the sun on summer days when the sun rises high overhead, then will let the sun rays enter during winter, when the sun travels a much lower route in the sky. This means a wide overhang is usually preferred over a narrow one.

3. Simpler roofs, with fewer angles, valleys, and intersections, are typically less-expensive roofs, due to simplicity of installation.

4. Stick-built roofing systems use individually erected rafters, ridge boards, ceiling joists, and collar beams assembled piecemeal on the job site.

5. Stick-built roofs allow for simpler dormer expansions and cathedral ceilings.

6. Prefabricated truss systems employ trusses made to your specification by a fabricating company that specializes in this work. They're simpler to erect on site than stick-built systems.

7. Include a complete ventilation system with soffit vents that allow outside air to enter and higher-level vents (ridge, gable, turbine, roof) or fans to provide air an exit.

8. If an attic is desired, trusses will not work as well as stick-built roofs because the truss components take up most of the otherwise usable attic space.

9. An airtight, self-contained roof/house combination is not only undesirable, but is dangerous to have. Attic and roof vents are absolute necessities.

10. Remember that the steeper the roof pitch, the more dangerous it is to be accessed for maintenance and repairs.

Roof Exterior Finishing

The exterior roof covering is an important milestone in the house construction process because it brings the job's progress to the point of being closed in against the weather, or in the terminology of many builders: under roof.

The reasons for reaching this stage as quickly as possible are to protect the already completed construction from extensive damage due to rain, snow, and exposure, and to provide cover and enclosure so that further construction can proceed despite inclement weather.

ROOFING MATERIAL SELECTION

Good reasons exist as to why you should explore the various types of roofing materials available for your house. Indeed, your selection may be influenced by the following:

1. *The desire for fire protection.* At one time, the combustibility of a house's roofing material substantially influenced the fire insurance rate charged. Certainly, if you're miles away from the nearest hydrant, you might want to think twice about wood shakes or shingles.

2. *The effect that weather elements have in the area you live in.* Certain roofing materials hold up better in certain climates than others will.

3. *The life expectancy of the roofing.* The price of the labor needed to replace a roof is high. Therefore, it's important to pick out a roofing material that will last. Don't make the mistake of selecting a material that will need replacing in less than 10 years. A quality product should last for 20 to 30 years of normal use.

4. *The type of house and how the house is positioned on the lot.* If large expanses of sloping roof will be visible from the ground, try to choose a material that will contribute to the overall attractiveness of the home. Too often an owner will select expensive siding materials only to downgrade the building's appearance with a cheap roof. Instead, give careful attention to your roof; use materials that add color, patterns, or textures as desired.

TYPES OF ROOFING

There are basically six types of roofing that cover about 95 percent of the residential roofs: asphalt shingles, fiberglass shingles, wood shingles and shakes, slate shingles, tile shingles, and metal shingles.

Asphalt Shingles

By far, asphalt shingles (Figs. 10.1 and 10.2) are the most common roofing material in both warm and cold climates. Sometimes they're also referred to as *composition shingles.*

These durable shingles, depending on their weight, have a life expectancy of 15 to 30 years. They're made of a heavy paper known as felt, which is coated with hot liquid asphalt then covered with fine rock granules.

Asphalt shingles are manufactured in many different colors by many different companies. These shingles vary in weight from about 165 pounds per roofing square (a roofing square equals 100 square feet of roof area) to about 340 pounds per square. The heavier shingles are more expensive and have greater textures and longer life. They also take more time and effort to put up, and most roofers will charge a higher rate for applying them.

FIGURE 10.1

An asphalt three-tab shingle.

FIGURE 10.2

Asphalt shingle installation.

There are many different kinds of asphalt shingles. The minimum grades weigh about 165 to 235 pounds per square, the medium grades run about 235 to 250 pounds per square, and the top grades weigh above 250 pounds per roofing unit. If a medium- or heavy weight shingle is selected, the house framing will have to be strengthened enough to support the additional weight. The heavier the shingle, the longer the life expectancy. A 300-pound or heavier asphalt shingle should last between 20 to 30 years. Besides being more durable, premium shingles are offered in better colors, colors that do not fade as quickly as the less-expensive models do. The 250- to 340-pound shingles are also less susceptible to wind damage than the lighter shingles because of their heavier, stiffer construction. But even if you live in a severe windstorm or hurricane area and decide to use the heavier asphalt shingles, they should have self-sealing tabs so curling doesn't result.

Winds can play havoc with asphalt and other shingles. To prevent such damage from occurring, choose only shingles with self-sealing tabs, plus opt for the interlocking types having tabs and slots used to hook each shingle together with the adjacent ones. Consider that light shingles have a tendency to get blown around in heavy wind.

Last, although asphalt shingles are the most popular selection for roofing materials on new construction, they should be used warily on roofs having pitches of less than 3–12. With very low slopes, water seepage can occur under the shingles, especially during times of high winds.

Fiberglass Shingles

These shingles are similar in appearance to the asphalt variety, but are more resistant to fire. Ask your insurance agent about the possibility of reduced premiums for your homeowner's policy if you elect to go with fiberglass shingles. As with the asphalt type, the heavier fiberglass shingles are the more durable. Stick with self-sealing or interlocking shingles for protection against wind and curling. Along with the asphalt shingles, fiberglass ones should not be used with a pitch of less than 3–12 unless a properly installed underlayment is laid first.

Fiberglass is a popular choice due to its favorable combination of appearance, price, and durability.

Wood Shakes and Shingles

Wood shakes and shingles are available in several species of wood, with red and white cedars the most popular, followed by cypress and redwood (Fig. 10.3). The term "shingle" means that the wood has been sawn, whereas "shake" indicates that the wood has been split. The shake is usually thicker and has a more rustic appearance.

Supply and labor costs to install wood shakes or shingles can be four to five times that of installing standard asphalt or fiberglass shingles. Homeowners, though, consider wood shakes and shingles a step up in quality and beauty.

SHINGLE
(SAWN)

SHAKE
(HANDSPLIT)

FIGURE 10.3

A wood shake and shingle.

"Hand-split" wood shakes and wood shingles have been popular for quite a while in the western United States, but did not reach the Midwest and East in appreciable numbers until the late 1960s. Their increasing popularity is attributed to their textures, deep shadow tones, longevity, weather resistance, and compatibility with Colonial, Modern, and Contemporary house styles.

The main drawback to wood shakes and shingles is their flammable nature.

Slate Shingles

Slate is one of the finest roofing materials available, and one of the most expensive (Fig. 10.4). Certainly it's one of the most durable shingles you can cover a roof with. But it also can weigh over 3,000 pounds per square (compared with 165 to 350 pounds for asphalt and fiberglass, and 200 to 450 pounds for wood), so a slate roof frame must be designed strong enough to support such an ambitious load.

Roofs made of slate shingles can add considerably to the value of a house. Pieces of slate are available in smooth commercial grades or rough quarry runs, in different colors and variegated shades depending on where they come from. They make a beautiful roof and, if cut from a good mineral bed, will last 100 years and more.

It's unfortunate that slate has been given a bad name from older homes where tree-damaged roofs or roofs undermined by rotting wood supports caused by a lack of proper ventilation result in loose and

PREDRILLED NAIL HOLES

FIGURE 10.4

Slate shingles.

FIGURE 10.5

Tile shingles (clay or cement).

FIGURE 10.6

Metal shingles.

fallen slate roofing. People have heard horror stories about the high costs of repairing old slate roofs and have unjustly grown overly wary of the slate shingles.

Tile Shingles

Clay or cement tile shingles are especially popular in the sunbelt areas (Fig. 10.5). They come in all kinds of decorator shapes and colors and textures. They're simple to install but physically taxing because of their incredible weight—from 800 to 2,600 pounds per square. As with slate shingles, a tile roof needs to be well braced to support its own weight. The tiles are apt to be expensive, especially in areas where they aren't frequently used (outside of warm-climate locations), but they are durable and have a long life expectancy.

They should be used sparingly for flat-sloped roofs, and should generally be applied where the pitch is steep enough for water to run down quickly to avoid water backup and leaking roofs.

Metal Shingles

Metal roofs, especially ones made of high-quality copper, terne (tin/lead alloy), or aluminum are very durable (Fig. 10.6). At the same time, they're relatively expensive and can be noisy to the point of aggravation in a rainstorm.

Aluminum shingles are lightweight when compared with other roofing materials (about 40 to 60 pounds per square) and come in many modern colors, shades, and styles, mostly in a shake-type texture. They'll last a long time if fastened securely with aluminum nails.

ROOFING COLOR

If your roof is a complex one, with many dormers, valleys, and varying planes, medium to dark roofing shingles will tend to pull it all together in a nice way.

Check other houses that are already completed in the area or on the street you're planning to build. If several or many of them are using similar colors, it might be wise for you to select something different so your home doesn't "blend in" with the rest of them, to break the monotony.

Be aware that a light-colored roof reflects heat and is more desirable in areas where air-conditioning is the greatest energy user. Whites and light grays are the most effective shades and when it comes to keeping roofing and attics cool under strong sun rays. Other colors and darker shades convert more of the sun's rays to heat.

In humid locations and places where tree leaves and debris tends to fall on roofs, algae and mildew growth may be a problem. This can be seen as dark areas or streaks on light-colored roofs. If your site has these conditions, select algae-resistant shingles. They have a slight amount of copper in the surface granules. Copper ions retard the growth of algae.

If you live in a warm climate and still decide to select a dark-colored roof, make sure you have sufficient ventilation, insulation, and air cooling to negate the additional warmth absorbed by the shingles.

VENTILATION AND SOFFITS

The roof and attic should be assured of adequate ventilation to allow for the escape of heat and humidity (Figs. 10.7 and 10.8). All ventilation units installed on the roof or in gable ends should be designed to shed rain and snow and not permit any moisture penetration. In addition, the free opening vent areas must be screened to protect against entry by insects, bats, rodents, squirrels, and similar invaders Soffits, the flat painted surfaces under a roof or overhang, should be constructed of prepainted or vinyl-coated sheets that are maintenance free (Fig. 10.9).

They're available with either a smooth unbroken surface, but also with perforated or slotted surfaces that will encourage ventilation of the attic or roof space. You need a steady pattern of perforated soffits

FIGURE 10.7

Gable ventilation.

FIGURE 10.8

Soffit and gable ventilation action.

FIGURE 10.9

Soffit under an overhang.

to ensure effective air flows for circulation. Eave soffit vents work by allowing circulation of air through an attic to prevent moisture condensation and its consequential damage to roof structure and insulation. When installing the soffit vents, insulation must not plug the spaces between the rafters just above exterior walls. To prevent this from happening, consider the installation of baffles that will allow air to move past the insulation. Also remember that venting the eaves alone is insufficient. Because warm air circulates upward, roof or gable vents mentioned earlier should be used in addition. There must also be enough free opening areas near the top of the attic to match the collective opening space of the eave soffits.

Because ventilation is so important, a ventilation system may include soffit vents with a combination of roof ridge vents, louver vents, metal dome vents, gable vents, and turbine vents, any combination of which will:

- Allow outside air to flow naturally upward and out of the attic.
- Promote a cooler, drier attic.
- Prevent moisture from becoming trapped within insulation, structural wood, shingles, and roof deck.
- Help prevent rotting, mildew, drywall damage, peeling paint, and warped siding.
- Provide year-round performance for consistent ventilation, lowering the overall energy consumption.

FLASHING

Protecting framing and insulation from rain, snowmelt and moisture is critical. All can cause great amounts of damage and inconvenience. At the very least, uninvited moisture in its many forms can reduce the insulating value (reducing energy efficiency) and damage your ceilings and walls.

Flashing is sheet metal or other material used to prevent the leakage or driving in of rainwater and general moisture infiltration at joints near openings or where different materials or planes meet, such as around chimneys, vents, roof valleys, and stacks (Figs. 10.10, 10.11, 10.12, and 10.13). If a material projects horizontally from the surface of the house, as at window and door trims, or at the insulation around a foundation, flashing is required. It's also needed wherever roofs and walls join, as with a split-level house or a two-story having an attached garage (Fig. 10.14). Flashing is important at the juncture of a dormer's siding with a main roof, to prevent water from leaking through (Fig. 10.15).

Aluminum is the most common flashing material. It's produced in long rolls in several widths and is inexpensive, lightweight, and resistant to corrosion except in industrial areas and near the seacoasts. It has one drawback—a shiny appearance that must be painted. And aluminum does not paint well.

Galvanized steel and terne are also employed as flashing; but they must also be painted. Stainless steel, zinc alloy, and even lead have all been used in similar fashion.

An excellent, though expensive, choice for flashing is copper. It seems to last forever and requires almost no maintenance. One advantage it has is that its corners can be soldered for a watertight connection.

Asphalt roofing material is sometimes used for valley flashing on roofs, and plumbing stacks are frequently flashed with special neo-

FIGURE 10.10

Exterior flashings.

FIGURE 10.11

Flashing around a chimney.

FIGURE 10.12

Flashing around a vent pipe.

FIGURE 10.13

Valley flashing.

FLASHING AT ROOF AND WALL INTERSECTION

SIDING

FIGURE 10.14

Flashings at roof and wall intersections.

FLASHING

FIGURE 10.15

Flashing around a dormer.

prene plastic collars. Vinyl materials in various colors are also on the market. Vinyl is an excellent choice and costs substantially less than copper.

Chimney Flashing

Because the chimney's exterior can be a frequent source of unwanted water intrusion, a few words on its flashing will perhaps save considerable trouble in the future. For sure, water seepage around the chimney can enter the attic or spaces beneath the roof and ruin the insulation there, do damage to the roof sheathing and framing, and eventually ruin the ceiling below. When there is such a leak, the problem is usually with the chimney flashing. The sheet-metal flashing around the chimney is supposed to keep the intersection between the chimney and roof watertight.

An effective way to seal a chimney is with two flashing layers: flashing and counter-flashing. The first layer is called step flashing, where sections of L-shaped sheet metal are "woven" into the surrounding shingle courses and lapped snug up against the chimney sides.

This flashing is installed in a stair-step fashion starting at the bottom or lower side of the chimney, working toward the upper part, fastened to the roof only, not to the chimney. Next, a small lip of the counter-flashing metal is embedded in the chimney mortar joints, and folded down to cover the tops of the step flashing. Then when the roof moves with winds or from shrinkage, the two pieces of metal flashing move or slide against each other to prevent bending or damage while maintaining protection from water. The corners of this arrangement are especially vulnerable, and an effective installation will leave only a small spot that must be sealed with high-quality caulk.

A special situation occurs when a chimney is positioned at or near the bottom of a roof slope. In such a case, a "cricket" or "saddle" should be installed at the intersection of the chimney's high side and the roof to divert and prevent water from rushing down the roof into or against the up-roof part of the chimney (Fig. 10.16).

FIGURE 10.16

A chimney cricket or saddle.

A cricket also prevents leaves, twigs, and other debris, snow, and ice from collecting behind the chimney—which can cause rain or snow melt to back up beneath the shingles and leak through the roof. If the cricket is large and exposed to view, it should be framed, sheathed, and finished with the same shingles and flashing used on the rest of the roof. Smaller crickets unexposed to view, can be covered with metal, but must still be flashed at all joints with the roof and chimney.

INSTALLATION

No matter how good a roof's materials are, the roof won't be able to do what it's supposed to do if the installation is shoddy. Here are some things to watch out for:

- The ice and water guard or similar underlayment, which is needed to protect your roof deck from ice damming and wind-blown rain, should be flexible, self-adhesive, and waterproof.

- A 3-inch galvanized metal drip edge eave should be installed nailed at least 10 inches on center. Roofing ice and water guard or a similar underlayment should go beneath this drip edge.

- All roofing felt should have at least a 6-inch vertical overlap.

- Ice and water guard, a water-resistant underlayment (Fig. 10.2), provides superior roof deck protection and helps prevent damage caused by freeze/thaw cycles, pooled water, wind-driven rains, and normal water flow that occurs around roof valleys, vents, skylights, and chimneys. It should also be installed under shingled roofing eaves to protect against water backup from ice dams and hard rains.

- When anchoring the underlayment and topping materials, power staple guns are the most economical way to go, *but* they don't do as sturdy a job as nails do. If your roofing is self-sealing asphalt shingles (shingles with glue underneath each tab that will stick to the shingle below it when baked in the sun), consider that it takes at least one and preferably two hot summers for them to "melt" together to form a strong bond. Up until that time, staples will not provide the holding power of wide-headed nails. High winds are more likely to blow stapled shingles from a roof.

■ Roofing nails must meet the shingle manufacturer's specifications to protect the shingle warranty requirements. At the very least, roofing nails will have very sharp points, flat head diameters, and length long enough for full penetration of the roof sheathing.

■ All roofing nails should be nailed flush with shingles.

■ When wood shakes and shingles are applied, the manufacturer's installation instructions must be followed exactly, especially regarding spacing and fastening.

■ Because of the high asphalt content in asphalt and fiberglass shingles, it is recommended that temperatures be over 50° Fahrenheit when installed, as they are susceptible to cracking in cold weather.

■ Make sure masonry and metal chimneys, skylights, and other obstructions are in place before the roofing begins. Otherwise, the roofers will have to make an extra trip to complete the remaining shingles and flashing, at extra expense.

■ All materials should conform to or exceed requirements of the local building code.

WATER DRAINAGE

Gutters and downspouts work together to collect runoff water from the roof and divert it away from the house so foundation seepage can be prevented (Figs. 10.17, 10.18, and 10.19). They can divert water away from foundations, plantings, decorative details, basements, siding, sidewalks, driveways, and roof edges, while increasing the width of roof overhangs and helping to prevent snow and ice slides during winter. They're vital necessities in most cases, but can be troublesome to maintain—tree leaves, seeds, and twigs tend to collect in them and clog the downspouts, squirrels and chipmunks use them as freeways and store winter food in them, plus they can be damaged by ice that collects and hangs from their not-too-strong edges. Here are some important points to consider when planning gutters and downspouts:

FIGURE 10.17

A roof drainage system.

1. The least-expensive gutters to buy are galvanized steel models, but they have to be painted before they can be secured to the fascia or rafter ends of a roof.

2. Another inexpensive option is to use unpainted aluminum. It's durable enough unless exposed to salt air near seacoasts or air laden with chemical contaminants. Even when no pollutants are present, however, this gutter should be painted for the sake of appearance.

RECTANGULAR   BEVELED

STYLE 'K'   SEMICIRCULAR OR HALF-ROUND

FIGURE 10.18

Metal gutter shapes.

3. Your other choices of gutter materials are much better: aluminum with factory baked-on enamel, and aluminum covered with a thin layer of vinyl. Vinyl gutters (solid vinyl) are also available. All three are in the long run durable, economical, and require little maintenance. Vinyl tends to be brittle in very cold weather, but it never requires refinishing because the color

is integral to its form. Copper gutters are also available at substantially higher prices than the others.

4. Metals used in gutters and downspouts vary in thicknesses; 26-gauge galvanized steel is quite strong and common, but 24-gauge is stronger.

5. Cleaning gutters and preventing downspouts from getting clogged can be easily done if you specify removable caps or screens. Then you can just pop off the caps or screens when necessary and flush the small accumulation of silt from the gutters with a garden hose.

6. Gutters should be mounted on the fascia boards (especially when the fascia is not made of or coated with vinyl) so the gutter backs are offset slightly, with an airspace between the fascia so the fascia surface will not deteriorate from lack of ventilation.

7. Large houses with great expanses of roof require that both the gutters and the downspouts have sufficient capacity to handle expected volumes of rainwater. While 5-inch gutters are common, 6-inch gutters may be required to handle roofs having very long spans.

8. A roof plane will collect water during any rainfall, especially if there is wind. The higher the roof ridge, the more true roof area there is and the faster water will race into the gutters. If you plan a steep roof, try to be generous with gutter sizes regardless of the roof area size.

9. Gutter troughs are to be sloped toward downspouts approximately 1 inch for every 12 lineal feet.

10. Your downspouts may be rectangular or round, and plain or corrugated (Fig. 10.20). In cold-climate locations when there is a

FIGURE 10.19

A gutter and downspout arrangement.

CORRUGATED ROUND

PLAIN ROUND

PLAIN RECTANGULAR

CORRUGATED RECTANGULAR

FIGURE 10.20

Standard downspout shapes.

possibility of standing water freezing in the downspouts, the corrugated type is preferable because it can expand without damage.

11. Downspouts are to be fastened to the wall every 5 to 6 vertical feet.

11. The water discharge can flow from the downspouts into drainpipes that run to storm sewers or to a natural runoff area, perhaps to the street or a storage cistern or rain barrel—as long as it meets building code requirements and does not run into the foundation or form a swamp on adjacent ground.

COLUMNS

Depending on the construction of your house, unsupported roof overhangs can protrude from the house a considerable distance. But beyond a certain point they must be supported around the outer edges by columns (Fig. 10.21).

Although wood columns, except in very small sizes, are hollow, they still have the strength to bear a substantial load. Trouble is, they're so intricately made that they cost a fortune.

Factory-painted aluminum columns are the answer. They cost considerably less, are maintenance-free, and because they're hollow—made only of thin metal—they can be installed around a weight-bearing wood or steel post.

▷▷▷▷▷ **POINTS TO PONDER**

1. When shopping for roofing, pay particular attention to fire resistance, the severity of weather the roof will face, the roofing's life expectancy, and the roof's appearance.

2. It takes about the same time, effort, and cost to put on a low-quality, marginal roof as it does one of the highest quality.

STEEL SUPPORT POST

ALUMINUM COLUMN →

FIGURE 10.21

A column.

3. Roofing material should not be skimped on. The roofing market is competitive; and you'll usually get what you pay for. It's worth doing comprehensive reviews and inspections of a wide variety of materials and models.

4. Selecting premium roofing materials is almost always a wise decision. They not only last longer and provide better protection against the elements, they'll also make the home look considerably more handsome.

FINAL INSPECTION

- Shingle pattern and color should be even and uniform from close up and far away.
- Shingles should fit tight around all stack vents and skylights. Areas should be well sealed with an asphalt roofing compound.
- Shingles should lie flat with tabs sealed/glued down.
- Shingles should extend over the edge of the roofing deck by at least 3 inches.
- Shingles should match or exceed the required fire rating stated by local building codes.
- Vents and roof flashing should be painted the proper color with exterior rustproof paint.
- Check vents to make sure they are not blocked with insulation or other obstructions.
- Make sure adjustable attic and other vents and louvers work correctly.
- Downspouts should be secure so that a strong wind will not affect them.

5. If your roof is a complex one, with many dormers, valleys, and various planes, medium or dark roofing shingles will tend to pull the roof together in an attractive way.

6. Be aware that light-colored roofs reflect heat and are more desirable in areas where air-conditioning is the greatest energy user.

7. In colder climates, the reverse is true. Black absorbs heat from the sun, so a darker color is clearly the more practical choice.

8. The roof and attic must be assured of adequate ventilation to enable heat and moisture to escape.

9. Flashing is an important component of roofs. It belongs where different construction materials or planes meet, such as around chimneys, vents, roof valleys, and stacks, and when materials project horizontally almost anywhere from the surface of the house. Simply put, it prevents water, air, dust, and other materials from entering cracks and gaps in the roof and in the rest of the home's outer shell.

10. Be generous with large, quality gutters and downspouts that are appropriately selected to complement the appearance of both roof and outer shell.

Exterior Wall Finishing

The exterior wall covering is the single most dominant feature of a home's outer appearance; its color and texture are the first things noticed by anyone approaching the house. Good design calls for simple lines, common sense in the selection of materials, harmonious textures and colors, plus good proportions and scale. A hash of materials such as a bit of stone here, some brick over there, with shingles and clapboards and stucco all mixed above, will give the impression that the house is desperately trying to trick observers into liking *some* detail, and more often than not will ruin a dwelling's appearance.

Beyond its cosmetic nature, the exterior wall covering also acts as the final protective layer between a home's occupants and the great outdoors. More specifically, it is this outer "sandwich" layer that, along with its interior counterpart, envelops whatever insulation is chosen to help protect family members from temperature extremes, and minimizes the need to import or purchase additional energy required for comfort. Attached to the frame or masonry walls can be wood siding in various forms, brick, stone, stucco, aluminum and vinyl sidings, shingles of metal, asphalt, or plastic, and many other lesser-used siding materials.

MATERIAL REQUIREMENTS

When selecting the material for your home's siding, consider how the following characteristics stack up against those materials in the running.

- Cost of materials
- Cost of installation labor, ease of handling by size, weight, and shape
- Resistance to natural weathering, chemical attack, and atmospheric pollution
- Resistance to scratching and impact
- Appearance of color and texture
- Dimensional changes resulting from temperature and moisture
- Resistance to moisture penetration
- Combustibility
- Sound insulation and absorption
- Strength under conditions of compression, bending, shear, and tension to carry applied loads and resist the pressure of wind
- Adaptability to future expansions and other modifications
- Susceptibility to insect damage

ALUMINUM AND VINYL SIDINGS

Aluminum and vinyl sidings are available in many different colors and shades, textures, and forms for both horizontal and vertical installation. When used alone or in combination with each other to cover exterior wood surfaces, they'll practically eliminate the need for future wood refinishing and painting chores. These sidings can also help provide additional thermal and sound insulation when installed over polystyrene or similar backer boards.

Indeed, recent manufacturing innovations enable many sidings to have wood-grain finishes or textures that look, and often feel, just like painted wood, smooth "clear" cedar, cedar shakes, weathered cedar, teak, or fir, roughsawn barnboard, and other varieties. All feature

TRIPLE 3" CLAPBOARD

DOUBLE 4" CLAPBOARD

DOUBLE 5" CLAPBOARD

DOUBLE 4½" SHIPLAP

FIGURE 11.1

Horizontal siding types with wood grain.

sturdy locking mechanisms so that individual panels will resist wind and weather.

For example, horizontal siding panels generally interlock where they overlap, as do the panels of double 4-inch clapboard, double 5-inch, and triple 3-inch, plus double 4½-inch wood-grain shiplap (Fig. 11.1).

Aluminum Siding

Aluminum siding is a low-maintenance exterior wall covering that won't rust in the ordinary sense. Its baked-on finish lasts for 20 to 40 years, depending on the grade purchased. Aluminum siding won't rot, split, warp, or crack. It's manufactured in a wide variety of colors and shades from light pastel tints to whites to deep rich tones, and comes in numerous textures and finishes—some resembling wood siding. The difference in price and insulating qualities is small, but if you're

"Double-four" aluminum siding.

planning top-notch construction that calls for aluminum siding, opt for the thicker gauge because it's stiffer and holds up better to abuse. The width of the horizontal type of aluminum siding is a single panel of 8 inches, or "double-four" panels that are essentially single panels, each having a horizontal crease across the middle so it resembles two 4-inch-wide lengths of clapboard (Fig. 11.2). There are also clapboard-like panels with 5-inch exposures, 9-inch exposures, and two beveled edges to give the appearance of two strips of beveledge siding.

For vertical applications, aluminum siding is available in many of the same colors and finishes as the horizontal panels, so the two materials can be mixed and matched on the same dwelling. The vertical siding comes in 10-, 12-, and 16-inch-wide board and batten strips, plus in V-groove and other styles.

There are several drawbacks to aluminum siding you should know about. First, unless reinforced by being installed directly over a stiff polystyrene or Styrofoam backer board material, aluminum siding will dent when soundly struck by a baseball, rock, or other hard object flung by a neighbor's 10-year-old son. Second, the surface color can be scratched off, exposing the silvery bare aluminum beneath. Third, bare aluminum exposed to industrial pollutants and seacoast environments can gradually react to the airborne chemicals in a negative way. And fourth, aluminum siding can be expensive. That's because the cost of aluminum siding is naturally tied almost directly to the cost of aluminum, which can fluctuate considerably due to the overall supply and demand. Conditions involving wars, tariffs, or the industrialization of China and other nations can all have dramatic effects on the price of aluminum.

Vinyl Siding

Vinyl siding is another popular low-maintenance wall covering that's manufactured essentially in the same forms as aluminum siding. As with aluminum siding, vinyl can be backed with a polystyrene or other board reinforcement both to give the siding a strong base and an

STUDS

HOUSE WRAP

EXTERIOR SHEATHING

ALUMINUM SIDING BACKED WITH POLYSTYRENE INSULATION

FIGURE 11.3

Aluminum siding installed with backer board.

insulating R-value (especially when also backed with several layers of house wrap). A major advantage to vinyl siding is that the color is molded throughout the entire thickness of the material, so a scratch will do little damage (Fig. 11.3).

Neither will vinyl siding dent; it's resilient nature allows it to spring back into shape after all but the most violent blows. Look for a vinyl siding that's a double thick .088-inch rolled-over nail hem design that increases wind resistance and stiffens the panel. Such a design may withstand wind load pressures up to 180 miles per hour when installed with nails and up to 235 miles per hour with staples.

This siding panel should feature a true .044-inch thickness for outstanding strength and durability. Most modern vinyl sidings have one-

FIGURE 11.4

Caulking around a window.

step panel locking systems for secure installation and perfect horizontal or vertical alignment. Too, the color goes clear through the vinyl, so scratches won't show, and a special sunshield technology is often used to protect the surface from harmful sun ultraviolet rays.

Drawbacks to vinyl are that it's inclined to buckle or ripple if not installed exactly correct, and it's not as readily adaptable as aluminum is to cover unusual or unique exposed wood trim.

No matter which type of aluminum or vinyl siding is selected, make sure the contractor correctly applies caulking around the doors, windows, and corners—wherever the siding forms a seam across its grain or meets with different building materials (Fig. 11.4). The contractor should also use aluminum nails for fastening the siding materials to exterior walls. Aluminum nails won't rust and form unsightly streaks.

MASONRY EXTERIOR WALL COVERINGS

Masonry exterior walls of brick and stone have always held a certain attraction for individuals who prefer the beauty, feel, and apparent strength of brick and stone construction. Masonry also enjoys an intangible prestige value that houses sheathed with wood, aluminum, or vinyl sidings seem to lack.

It's true that brick and stone sidings are more expensive than most other exterior wall coverings, mainly due to installation costs. To use brick or stone, a contractor must either move exterior walls inward 5 or more inches to allow space for the full masonry veneer so the specified outer wall dimensions can be retained or can keep the load-bearing foundation walls and exterior walls true to their specified dimensions by installing the brick veneer against the outside of these walls (Fig. 11.5). To permit the latter method, a separate outer foundation must be constructed to support the brick or stone walls (Fig. 11.6). In either case, there must also be a space between the masonry and interior wall surfaces, and this space should contain proper insulation and a vapor barrier (Fig. 11.7).

The first choice (of moving the walls inward to accommodate the thickness of bricks or stones) should require no change in the home's roof structure, particularly to the overhang and exterior trim. The second choice (of building out) might, however, require alterations in these areas to accommodate the wider dimensions of the outer limits to the exterior walls.

Advantages

1. Brick and stone make beautiful, unique exterior wall coverings.

2. They hold onto their looks indefinitely, with little maintenance.

3. Brick and stone houses have historically held their value well and have enjoyed good resale demand.

4. They're durable and have a reputation of permanence.

5. Because of their strength, they don't "sway" as much in the wind as wood-sided homes and will not develop as many interior plaster or drywall cracks and imperfections as in less-rigid non-masonry dwellings.

6. Their resistance to fire is excellent.

7. They help reduce exterior noise.

Masonry/brick construction.

Masonry/brick construction on supporting footer.

FIGURE 11.7

A space between the brick veneer and frame wall.

Disadvantages

1. They add considerable extra expense to the purchase price of a house.

2. It's difficult and expensive to make modifications to the exterior walls or additions to a structure. Removal of part of an old wall is expensive, and matching up the brick for the new walls can be difficult.

3. Brick and stone have low insulating values. Despite popular belief, even the thickest masonry offers exceptionally poor insulation properties, which is why masonry houses seem particularly cold and are hard to heat. Consequently, the proper amount of exterior wall insulation must be insisted upon regardless of the type of brick or stone used.

Brick

Brick makes a very attractive exterior, with numerous colors and textures available. All of one color can be used, or a mottled effect can be had by using many different shades or colors in the same surface. The best way to arrive at what you'd like is to take a drive through neighborhoods that have plenty of brick homes. A few color snapshots of what most appeals to you can be handed to your contractor, who will be able to tell you where those bricks can be purchased or ordered.

It should be noted that most bricks are manufactured with holes in their centers. When mortar is applied to the bricks, some of it fills those holes and provides additional bonding strength when dried. If the top of any bricks need be exposed, enough solid bricks without holes should be ordered along with the others. The same principle applies to textured bricks where

FIGURE 11.8

A textured brick.

typically only one side—the exposed side—is textured (Fig. 11.8). When bricks are needed to have a textured surface exposed on two or three or four surfaces, special bricks that are textured all around will have to be ordered. Remember that a brick wall will cover a structure, but won't support it. The stud wall provides the support. Instead, metal anchors tie the brick wall to the frame wall.

Make sure the contract specifies that the masons must finish the job by cleaning the brick with the brick manufacturer's cleaning solvent. Muriatic acid can stain brick.

Stone

Stone also makes an attractive exterior that's durable and practically maintenance-free. It has most of the advantages and disadvantages of brick.

Stonework is usually more costly than brick. In general, stones cut with rectangular corners are more commonly used for covering exterior walls. Rubble or fieldstones having irregular shapes and no corners can be employed in a feature wall for dramatic effect to create a rustic appearance.

Openings in Masonry Exterior Wall Coverings

Due to the weight of brick and stone, door and window openings require special supports to hold the brick or stone securely in place

STUD WALL

STEEL LINTEL

BRICK VENEER

FIGURE 11.9

A steel lintel.

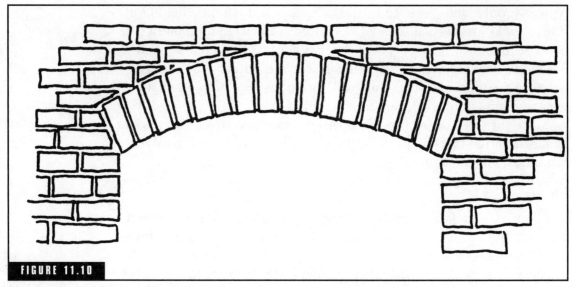

FIGURE 11.10

A curved brick arch.

FIGURE 11.11

A flat brick arch.

above those openings. There are three common ways to provide such support: with steel lintels, curved brick arches, and flat brick arches.

The steel lintel is the simplest to install (Fig. 11.9). It consists of "angle iron" of appropriate length that overlaps the top of the door or window opening on either side, so the weight of the brick or stone above the opening can be transferred to and distributed throughout the adjacent masonry structure. The curved brick arch is constructed of standard size and shape bricks or stones to span the opening (Fig. 11.10), and the flat brick arch is formed with specially cut bricks (Fig. 11.11).

WOOD SHINGLES AND SHAKES

Wood shingles and shakes are usually made of cedar, but can be made of redwood or cypress (Figs. 11.12 and 11.13). Cedar shingles or shakes are used as siding when a homebuyer wants an eyecatching rustic appeal to the home and a

Wood shingle construction.

"warm" siding that's naturally resistant to decay and is an excellent insulation. Cedar has a golden brown color when new, that gradually darkens with age, and finally weathers into an attractive silver-gray, depending on the climate (the amount of sunlight and humidity) it's located in.

The difference between shingles and shakes is that both sides of shingles are sawn smooth, while shakes have at least one rough-textured side created by splitting it from the mother log. These are the same shingles and shakes that are also used for roofing.

While cedar, redwood, and cypress shingles and shakes can be installed in some climates without being coated with preservatives, weathering everywhere is best controlled by applying recommended weatherproofings every five or six years. Pressure-treated Southern yellow pine is also an acceptable substitute, when available.

The best wood shingles and shakes are free from knots and pockets of pitch. You

Wood shake construction.

can tell the difference between the best and lower grades by the wood grain—it should be regular and clear with few or no defects.

Drawbacks to wood shingles and shakes include their cost: they're expensive and time-consuming to apply. Unless you opt for shingles and shakes prefabricated into 8-foot panels, each shingle or shake must be hand nailed into place, one at a time. They're also susceptible to fire.

Only nonrusting nails that provide sturdy holding power should be used to fasten wood shingles and shakes to the walls. Common nails won't hold well enough and will rust and streak the siding.

Molded "Cedar" Shingles

Molded shingles that look like wood are available in vinyl, polypropylene, and other plastic materials. Models include both half-

FULL PERFECTION SINGLE PANEL

FULL HALF ROUND SHINGLE PANEL

FIGURE 11.14

Molded "cedar" shingles.

round shingle panels and "full perfection" shingle panels. While offering the look of real wood, these panels are practically free from splitting, warping, cupping, twisting, fading, or streaking. They also need no painting or repetitive surface protection. The panels are typically about 0.100-inch thick with ribbed backer components that add structural stability. These molded shingles hold up well in rainy, windy, and coastal climate locations, especially when backed with reflective building foil (Fig. 11-14).

SOLID WOOD SIDING

Almost any type of wood can be used for solid plank siding, including such species as cedar, redwood, fir, cypress, pine, spruce, and hemlock. Redwood siding in particular is very durable. It resists deterioration from the weather and from insects. Unpainted redwood surfaces will darken season by season to a deep grayish brown.

Solid wood siding comes in many styles for horizontal and vertical applications, including beveled, dropped, and beaded planks for horizontal sidings, and V-groove, tongue-and-groove, board-and-batten, and channel vertical sidings (Figs. 11.15, 11.16, and 11.17).

Beveled horizontal wood siding is probably the most popular of all solid wood exterior wall coverings because it so nicely complements most styles of architecture. It consists of long boards, available in varying thicknesses and widths having beveled edges and tapered to exag-

FIGURE 11.15

Solid wood siding.

FIGURE 11.16

Board-and-batten wood siding.

FIGURE 11.17

Vertical application of wood paneling.

FIGURE 11.18

Siding corner construction.

gerate the deep, long horizontal shadow lines at the lower edges of the planks that help provide character to a dwelling's appearance. The individual boards are usually installed over a sheathing and building paper, nailed through them to the exterior wall studs. Corners are covered with either metal corner pieces or wood corner boards (Figs. 11.18 and 11.19). The thickness of the corner boards should be at least 1 inch to provide a substantial caulking base.

The old-fashioned clapboard siding that once covered (and still covers) many a home consists of wood planks of uniform thicknesses.

All solid wood sidings should be weatherproofed with water-repellent treatments, oils, varnishes, preservatives, or exterior paints and other coatings that will have to be periodically renewed as needed. A vapor barrier beneath the wood siding is also required to prevent condensation from within the home from causing paint to peel and wood to rot.

FIGURE 11.19

Siding interior corner construction.

PLYWOOD SIDING

Plywood siding can be supplied in many varieties of wood and patterns at varying costs (Fig. 11.20). Check with your local suppliers to see samples. Only exterior types of plywood should be considered— those having their layers of veneer bonded together with a tough waterproof glue.

Plywood panels are manufactured in 4-foot widths and 8- to 12-foot lengths that, due to their size and ease of installation, help hold down labor costs. If you plan to use plywood siding, match the correct length panels to the requirements of your home to have as few horizontal joints as possible, because they'll detract from the overall appearance and can be a source of water and moisture leaks if not correctly installed.

FIGURE 11.20

Plywood panel vertical application.

Because of its strength, plywood siding is sometimes applied directly to the wall studs, without the use of an underlayment sheathing.

HARDBOARD SIDING

Hardboard sidings are manufactured panels consisting mostly of wood products. They come in more finishes and textures than plywoods, but are not as strong.

On the positive side, factory-made hardboard sidings are free from natural defects. Their panels are stiffer and less likely to warp or bend. Both the texture and depth of wood are presented in authentic-looking wood grains and grooves. The better hardboard or wood fiber sidings are over 50 percent denser than real wood planking and won't crack, split, check, or delaminate. They can also be purchased primed—ready for custom finishing in multiple lap sheets that are easy to install without having to nail narrow individual boards.

Remember that even factory-finished hardboard sidings will probably have to be refinished eventually.

STUCCO

Stucco is that plasterlike material so popular with English Tudor construction. It's an excellent exterior finish, having a long life span and needing very little maintenance. It's really a version of Portland cement that's troweled on like plaster to either masonry or frame walls, with no seams or joints. It's usually made in white, but can be colored with any paint manufactured for application over masonry. There's also a wide selection of pigments available that can be added to the stucco mix. If deeper hues are desired, the stucco can be painted in the same fashion as concrete block.

Stucco can be applied as a finish coat to both existing houses and new construction. It can be finished to give a number of interesting textures to conform with traditional or modern architectural styling.

Three coats with a total thickness of about ¾ inch are generally recommended. When stucco is applied over the sheathing of a wood-framed house, a layer of stucco wrap can be placed over the sheathing. Stucco wrap is a type of engineered construction fabric or membrane (also see house wrap, in the section on Vapor Barriers). Stucco wrap creates a drainage path for water and moisture to escape. It will take water and moisture that may enter the walls from the interior spaces and around windows, doors and other joints, and channel it outside. It thus helps prevent water and moisture from harming the sheathing, framing and insulation—which can cause expansion and contraction, leading to stucco fractures and cracking.

Stucco wrap is also good at managing the hydration process of the stucco material during the curing. The scratch coat will not absorb water from the other stucco coats because, again, the stucco wrap channels the water and moisture toward the outside. Because the scratch coat will not absorb extra water, it won't expand and contract much during curing. The result is a dramatic reduction of cracking in the scratch coat. This helps create a strong, stable stucco, with each layer drying at a similar rate, front to back. A white stucco wrap is often preferred because it won't absorb much heat from the sun, and the cooler surface further extends the stucco drying time, so cracking is even less likely. Less stucco cracks makes a more solid energy efficient exterior wall.

Next comes the application of metal lathing nailed to the exterior wall. The lathing should be self-furring or should be applied with self-furring nails. The most important point in the application of the stucco is that the scratch or first coat of material must be pushed through the metal lathing and behind it to form a solid layer between the lathing and studs or sheathing.

Where stucco is applied over large uninterrupted areas, control joints should be installed to permit expansion and contraction of the stucco material. Without these control joints the stucco will crack. As a general guide, control joints are planned for at least every 3 feet of travel.

The second coat is applied over the scratch coat (the first coat) after allowing sufficient time for the first coat to dry. And finally, after the second coat has dried, the third and finishing layer is applied with whatever pattern you have selected—smooth, stippled, swirled, or other (Fig. 11.21).

When applying stucco over masonry, the finish coat can be troweled directly to the block or concrete. Make sure exterior outlets and fixtures aren't accidentally covered, and ask about the stucco warranty. Strong stucco will better withstand building movement, wind pressure, and other stresses.

FIGURE 11.21

Stucco application.

VAPOR AND AIR-INFILTRATION BARRIERS

It was apparent decades ago, since the 1950s, that builders needed to protect their houses from the harmful effects of unwanted air drafts and moisture. Back then, they used tar-impregnated paper and similar building papers and sealing materials.

The living areas between the exterior walls should be sealed with appropriate material applied to the inside of the walls to prevent the movement of unwanted air and moisture from the outside in, and also from the inside living areas into the exterior wall insulation and outer wall coverings (Fig. 11.22).

To reinforce why vapor and air-infiltration barriers are needed, it's been estimated that the typical home can have close to a half mile of undesirable cracks and crevices in its outer shell that can let out warm air during winter, and cooled air during summer.

In addition, unwanted moisture that enters walls can lead to mold, mildew, and rot. Wall moisture originating from within a building can sometimes be more damaging than outside moisture penetration.

Daily activities within a household such as showering, cooking, washing clothes and dishes, and even breathing—produce moisture vapor that needs to escape. Again, without proper vapor barriers, as the temperature increases within a home, inside water vapor is transmitted

FIGURE 11.22

A vapor barrier view.

into walls, where it condenses. This condensation results in a wetting of structural materials and in a loss of the insulating qualities of exterior walls. It also gives rise to such serious problems as chemical, physical, or biological deterioration of the wall materials, and promotes corrosion of metal, spalling of brick, and rotting of timbers.

House wrap—an engineered construction fabric or membrane—can be used on the outside of a wall, against some wall sheathings, to protect the sheathing from water and moisture. If properly installed, exterior house wrap placed over certain exterior sheathings can improve comfort, energy efficiency, and will protect against moisture and water damage.

Installed over wood or certain insulation sheathings, and under siding or other exterior coverings, house wrap provides a protective barrier which helps seal against leaks and drafts (air infiltration).

On the other hand, as some manufacturers of rigid sheathing panels point out, if their panels are properly installed, there should be no air leaks through cracks or seams (or very minimal air leaks). If that's true, they say, then additional installation of house wrap over those panels may actually create harmful conditions by trapping eventual residues of wood starches from siding materials and from cleaning detergents that may become trapped within the house wrap fabric (thus plugging the fabric meshing so it can no longer breathe).

In many other situations, though, house wrap works hand-in-hand with insulation. Using a clothing analogy, the home's insulation traps air in tiny pockets (like a thick cable-knit wool sweater does) to slow the transfer of heat, while house wrap functions like a Goretex windbreaker does, when layered over the wool sweater. Where properly used, house wrap should thus cover or seal:

- Gaps between sheathing pieces or panels
- Joints between the sole plate and sub floor along exterior walls
- Gaps in drywall or plaster board and top and bottom wall plates
- Where framing members meet in an outside intersection and form a crack
- Around window and door frames
- Electrical and plumbing penetrations through top and bottom wall plates.

An effective house wrap design resists tears in all directions, stands up to windy conditions, with good tensile strength. Also, it should only enable condensation to evaporate or drain away from the house sheathing. Around windows and doors, house wrap can be used in the sill rough openings before a window or door is installed. A straight flash wrap is available for straight heads and jambs of windows and doors to effectively seal gaps. House wrap tape is manufactured for taping house wrap seams, tears, and openings such as holes and open spaces around electrical boxes, venting ducts, and similar construction components and materials. Before deciding on a vapor/air infiltration system for your home, at least be aware of the various strategies, and discuss them with your builder.

Make sure the particular house wrap or rigid panels are compatible with the planned siding. For example, certain cedar and other wood siding may need special add-ons to enable the siding to breathe from both sides. Consider that many new products are in the process of coming to market, so carefully research their pros and cons, then consider your house style and the weather conditions in your locale. It's far less expensive, and a much simpler process, to design the barrier system for installation during construction—than to try to upgrade or change systems at a later date.

Insulating batts in the exterior walls should have a vapor barrier backing such as treated Kraft paper with the vapor barrier on or toward the living-area side. If blown insulation or unfaced insulation is chosen, aluminum foil–backed drywall can be used, or friction fit or other types of insulation can be applied after polyethylene sheet material is stapled or nailed to the interior of the wall studs and ceiling joists. The polyethylene film should not be less than 3 mils thick.

INSULATION

Underneath the sheathing and exterior wall covering, between the studs, one of the following types of insulation will generally be used:

- Batts or blankets—these are prepared thicknesses of expanded glass fiber, mineral fiber, or organic fiber that are placed in the walls between the studs. They should be faced (having a vapor barrier on one side) in order to hold their form well.

- Blown or poured—this is composed of loose expanded mineral or organic fibers that are placed or blown into frame spaces. They're more useful for insulating existing buildings when it would be impractical to completely remove the inner or outer wall sheathings. On the down side, blown or poured insulation may eventually settle and lose some of its insulating value.

If you choose to use vinyl or aluminum siding, remember that polystyrene and similar backer boards can be used behind the siding panels to provide extra insulation as well as added strength.

Or, this leads us to another recent product development that's become especially pertinent in this time of rising fuel costs, that of *exterior rigid foam insulation*. Exterior rigid foam insulation is made of extruded polystyrene or similar material that has an R-value of about R-5 per inch of product thickness. It contains literally hundreds of millions of densely packed air cells. Since air is one of nature's most effective insulators, the sheer volume of this compressed trapped air gives this insulation exceptional thermal performance. It also prevents air infiltration and resists moisture penetration.

In some cases, these panels can be installed over exterior sheathing (as long as the total vapor/air-infiltration barrier system isn't over engineered to prevent at least some healthy "breathing"). For example, a cost-effective way to achieve a R-19 wall system is to install 1-inch extruded polystyrene foam insulation to the exterior sheathing of a 2" by 4" wall cavity filled with R-13 fiberglass insulation. Exterior sheathing, siding, and interior drywall typically provide an R-value of R-1. A 2" by 6" wall cavity filled with fiberglass insulation will give an even greater R-value. The exterior layer of foam insulation will also help reduce road noise, will help prevent air infiltration, and will increase comfort through less radiant heat loss because the entire mass of the wall structure is covered.

Again, when dealing with barrier products, it's important to have a strategy that manufacturers and builders will somewhat agree upon, so the combination of several different products will work in your favor—and will not inadvertently cause moisture or air circulation/breathing problems.

ENERGY-SAVING OUTDOOR PAINT

Many of these paints use microscopic insulating ceramic spheres in their composition to help create a sturdy reflective, radiant barrier to ward off the sun's heat, especially in white and lighter shades of color. They also protect against moisture, and provide an excellent choice when sealing joints and narrow cracks and spaces around vents, trim, and fastening devices.

Paints with insulating ceramics resist stains, corrosion, mold and mildew, and can be scrubbed clean, help deaden sound, and are effective in hot and cold climates. They can be applied with brush or roller, and are simple to use for touch-up tasks.

Table 11.1 lists insulation values of sidings.

INTAKE/EXHAUST HOODS

Request that the siding contractor provide waterproof maintenance-free hoods in colors that match your siding for dryer and other intake/exhausts (Figs. 11.23 and 11.24).

TABLE 11.1. Insulation for Resistance Values of Siding Material

Material	Thicknesses in Inches	Resistance Rating
Airspace	¾ or wider	.91
Aluminum foil (sheet type with ¾-inch airspace)		2.44
Blanket insulation	3	11.10
Common brick	4	.80
Cinder block	8	1.73
Concrete	10	1.00
Concrete block	8	1.00
Gypsum board	½	.35
Insulation board	1	3.03
Plywood	⅜	.47
Roofing roll vapor barrier	⅛ to ¼	.15
Sheathing and flooring	¾	.92
Shingles		.17
Stone	16	1.28
Wood siding	¾	.94
Window glass (single)		.10
Window glass (double)		1.44

MOUNTING PLATES

Color-matching mounting plates for mailboxes, hose reels, electrical outlets, coach lamps, and other lights and fixtures are usually available in vinyl and plastic. While these may sound like "small" details, they can all contribute to a handsome exterior—without ungainly distractions caused by mismatching hardware (Fig. 11.25).

FIGURE 11.23

Dryer vent.

ILLUMINATED HOUSE NUMBERS

Many police, paramedic, or fire department personnel will tell you about the amount of time lost nights trying to locate a house for an emergency call when the home's address numbers are not readily identifiable. Consider asking the contractor to quote on a decorative low-voltage address number fixture.

They're inexpensive to operate and easy to read, day or night. They're made from maintenance-free vinyl or plastic products that also come in colors to match the siding (Fig. 11.26).

AWNINGS

There's something old-fashioned about a good set of fabric awnings. Maybe it's the additional level of privacy they provide when installed over windows, doors, decks or patios. Or maybe it's the additional color they add, or their ability to be adjustable. They also protect—to a certain extent—against rain, wind, and sunlight. In fact, canvas and other fabric awnings block out or absorb up to 99 percent of the sun's harmful ultraviolet rays, and can reduce the amount of sunlight and

FIGURE 11.24

Intake/exhaust vent.

glare passing through windows by as much as 94 percent. Awnings can thus reduce heat gain through windows—up to 77 percent on eastern and western windows.

They'll also protect indoor furnishings such as carpeting, curtains, and furniture from sunlight fading, while keeping the inside environment cooler, with lower air-conditioning costs. On the down side, awnings eventually wear out. They'll need maintenance and eventual replacement as well as routinely being put up and taken down, depending on seasonal weather patterns; this could raise safety issues, especially with second-story installations. One possible answer to durability concerns is that of rigid awnings, awnings constructed of aluminum, plastic, or composite materials.

FIGURE 11.25

Hose faucet mounting plate.

Especially where snow and ice are not issues, rigid awnings can provide many of the advantages of their fabric cousins and can be left in place year-round.

There are many types and styles of awnings. Consider these features if you decide to investigate their use on your home:

- Do the units require minimal maintenance?

- Are they self-storing?

- Is the awning material resistant to ultraviolet light, mildew, and water?

- Is the awning operated with a manual crank, or is motorized?

- Is it an under-the-eave mount, or flat-wall mounted?

- Does it have stainless steel or other hardware that will not rust or deteriorate?

FIGURE 11.26

Illuminated house number.

■ Are there oil-impregnated bearings, so there's no need for lubrication?

■ Do the units have strong, lightweight, rustproof frames with a baked enamel finish?

VENTILATION GABLES

Ventilation gables can be critical to planning for sufficient air movement into an attic or other "open" spaces beneath upper reaches of the roof. Air movement will help remove dampness and hot air, thus helping the insulation and lumber there. Some manufacturers offer co-polymer construction gable vents with ultraviolet-stabilized colors molded throughout, and fully screened for insect, bat, and bird protection. These units can be installed on all types of exteriors, including wood, vinyl, aluminum, stucco, hardboard, stone, and brick.

SIDING GENERAL CONSIDERATIONS

■ It's a good idea to view the work of masons the builder is planning to use on your siding. Ask to see recent completed projects whether they're in brick, stone, or stucco.

■ Decide if you want a matching stoner brick mailbox or light posts on either side of the driveway or walk before masonry siding is applied.

■ It should be stated in the contract that the builder should see that only OSHA-compliant scaffolding is used for all elevated work.

■ The exterior siding contractor should also quote on any wrought iron railings needed.

■ The exterior siding contractor should figure in trim around the doors, windows, and at the corners of the home. Flashing must be installed at the head and sill of all door and window openings. Trim should be securely fastened and well caulked wherever needed. Request tinted caulk that matches the siding color.

■ House wrap fastened over plywood will help keep out wind and water. Flashing at the base of the wrap will help carry off water from the wall, and weep holes between bricks, stones, or in the vinyl or aluminum siding will allow water to escape.

- Wood siding should clear the ground surface for less chance of wood-boring insect damage and decay from moisture.

- The agreement should specify if any brick, stone, shingle, or shake siding must be treated with water repellant after the siding has had sufficient time to "dry out." For example, the contractor should not paint right after installation of wood, but should wait until the wood has a chance to dry. If it shrinks after being coated, that will leave unpainted strips of wood where the pieces overlap.

- No matter which siding you plan, ask the contractor to hand-pick the best material for the front and back of the home, where appearance is most important.

- See that only exterior, nonrusting fasteners are used in all siding applications.

- Nails must be driven flush or countersunk.

- All laps of siding must be parallel, and all joints should be staggered between courses.

▶▶▶▶▶▶ POINTS TO PONDER

1. The exterior wall covering is the single most dominant feature of a home's outer appearance; its color and texture are the first things noticed by anyone approaching the house.
2. Good design calls for simple lines, common sense in the selection of materials, harmonious textures and colors, plus good proportions and scale.
3. A hash of contrasting materials, such as a bit of stone here, some brick over there, with shingles and clapboards and stucco all mixed together can lend an unattractive garish look to the dwelling—even though individually those sidings are quite attractive.
4. Brick and stone are more expensive than most other wall coverings, mainly due to installation costs. But they do make beautiful, unique exteriors, hold their looks indefinitely, need little

maintenance, and have reputations for durability and for helping home resale values.

5. Although cedar, redwood, cypress, and pressure-treated Southern yellow pine shingles and shakes are sometimes installed in hot, dry climates without being coated with preservatives, weathering everywhere is best controlled by applying recommended weatherproofing every few years per the manufacturer's recommendation.

6. Only nonrusting fasteners should be used to attach exterior wall siding, to prevent unsightly rust leaching and staining.

7. Stucco is a plaster-like material so popular with English Tudor construction. It provides an excellent exterior finish, having a long life span and needing very little maintenance. It's really a version of portland cement that's troweled on like plaster to either masonry or frame walls, with no seams or joints.

8. The vinyl, aluminum, and related siding industry is constantly engineering improved materials. Do a thorough review of these sidings before making a final decision. Consider the material's appearance, plus its ability to resist dents and scratches, to hold its color and resist fading, and to provide insulation value. Again, it costs about the same to install an inferior material, as it does to put up quality siding.

9. After you decide on what kind or kinds of siding you want, select only high-quality siding(s) and sealing caulks.

10. If your home is being constructed near others, consider how the appearances of those neighboring dwellings may affect or limit your own siding (and roof) selections. In other words, it's prudent to consider the appearance of your home within its setting.

Stairs

Who can forget the dramatic confrontations in *Gone with the Wind* between Rhett Butler and Scarlet O'Hara on a huge, spectacular staircase?—the dominating structural feature of the deep-South estate of Tara. And what about the shrieking panic of Martin Balsam in Alfred Hitchcock's *Psycho*, as he tumbles backwards away from the murderer—down a stark wooden flight of stairs.

No doubt, staircases are custom-made for grand entrances and exits. At the same time, stairways can be convenient and dangerous, healthy and harmful, attractive and ugly, space-saving and space-stealing. They're less expensive and much more practical than elevators or escalators, and they enable us to make better use of small building sites by permitting several living levels to be positioned one atop another. Staircases can be made of wood, metal, stone, concrete, or any combination of construction materials having the strength to do the job.

A *stairwell* is the term for a shaft or opening through one or more floors of a house in which a staircase is constructed or placed. A completed stairway consists of the following (Figs. 12.1 and 12.2):

■ Stringers—diagonal or circular supports for the steps.

■ Treads—the horizontal upper surfaces of individual steps, the part your foot steps on.

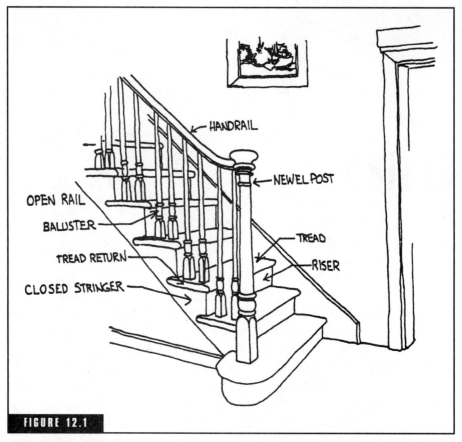

HANDRAIL

NEWEL POST

OPEN RAIL

BALUSTER

TREAD

TREAD RETURN

RISER

CLOSED STRINGER

FIGURE 12.1

An open main stairway.

- Risers—the vertical pieces between the treads. Some basement stairways don't have risers, but are wide open between the wooden treads (Fig. 12.3).

- Handrails.

- Newel posts—the posts at the top or bottom of a flight of stairs that support a handrail, or the central upright pillar around which the steps of a winding staircase turn.

- Balusters—any of the small posts that support the handrail of a railing. In olden times, these were frequently elaborate woodwork. Latter-day balusters, railings, and posts are more likely to be black wrought-iron or simple wooden handrails attached to the sides of the stairwell walls.

FIGURE 12.2

Staircase parts.

GENERAL STANDARDS

1. *Stairway angles.* In staircase design and construction you'll find a rise and run similar to that of a roof's slope. The angle of a stairway is determined by the arrangement of the tread depths and riser heights.

2. *Stairway treads and risers.* For safety's sake, all treads should be equal and all risers should be equal in any one flight.

3. *Stairway widths.* Main stairways should be at least 3 feet wide, clear of the handrail(s) (Fig. 12.4). A basement stairway can be slightly narrower, with a minimum clearance of 2 feet 10 inches.

FIGURE 12.3

A basement stairway with open risers.

FIGURE 12.4

Stairway dimensions.

4. *Stairway landings.* The minimum dimensions for a regular stairway landing is 3 feet square. For safety, landings must be level and free from intermediate steps between a main up flight and a main down flight.

5. *Stairway framing support.* This is the required vertical structural framing built to support all stairways from underneath.

Table 12.1 provides a checklist for interior stairways.

TABLE 12.1. Checklist for Interior Stairways

	Minimum	Best Quality
Vertical rise	7½"	6½"
Horizontal run	10"	12" to 14"
Tread width	3'	4'
Railing	Firm	Solid
Baluster spacing	10"	6"
Number of landings	0	2
Natural lighting	Fair	Excellent
Artificial lighting	Fair	Excellent
First-floor foyer	Skimpy	Generous
Second-floor stair hall	Skimpy	Generous
Two-story-high walls	2	0

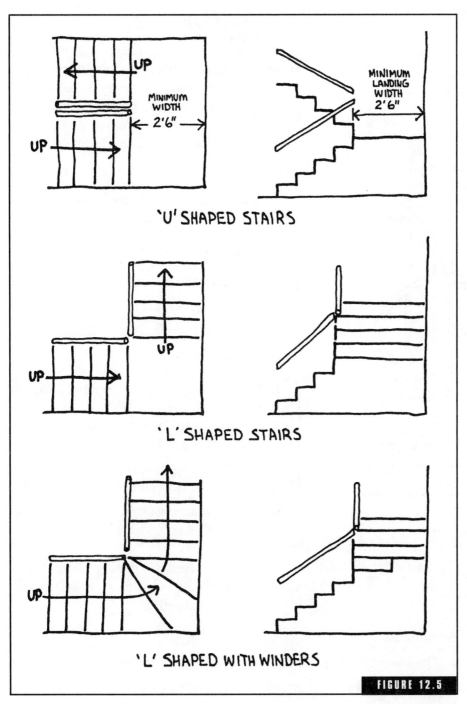

'U' SHAPED STAIRS

'L' SHAPED STAIRS

'L' SHAPED WITH WINDERS

FIGURE 12.5

Stairway types.

FIGURE 12.6

A spiral staircase.

STAIRWAY TYPES

There are four basic types of staircases used in modern houses: straight stairways, L-shaped stairways having a landing or winders at the turn, U-shaped stairways having a landing or winders at the turn, and spiral staircases (Figs. 12.5 and 12.6).

Straight

Straight stairways are by far the stairways used in most house construction today.

Advantages

1. They cost the least to build.
2. They're the easiest to carry bulky items and materials on.

Disadvantages

1. They're dangerous. If someone happens to trip at the top, a fall all the way to the bottom could result. Small children especially must be protected from them.
2. They're tiring to climb because there's no space to stop and catch your breath.
3. They're not very attractive.

L-shaped and U-shaped

Both of these stairway types were used frequently during past decades when individual carpentry efforts were more predominant than today's prebuilt and space-saving methods.

Advantages

1. They have landings to rest on to catch your breath.
2. The landings provide good spaces to hang decorations or art.
3. They can be so attractive as to add character to a house.

Disadvantages

1. They're more difficult to work into a house's floor plan.

2. They're more expensive to build.

3. They make it harder to carry large items such as bedroom furniture up and down. This is especially true of narrow U-shaped stairways.

Spiral and Circular

Only people thoroughly familiar with spiral staircases should plan them into their houses.

Advantages

1. They save space. Spiral stairways can be installed where you cannot possibly fit conventional stairs.

2. Because they're rarely enclosed, they serve as attractive decorative units that generally become focal points of the rooms they're in.

3. They're good for outdoor use to provide access to second-story balconies, decks, and regular rooms.

Disadvantages

1. The treads are not full depth at both sides. If you fall from the top you can tumble a long way. Most people aren't used to them. Spiral stairways require a different gait to ascend than to descend; visitors unaccustomed to them might find this a nuisance.

2. They're almost impossible to use for moving large items such as bedroom furniture between floors.

STAIRWAY STYLES

Regardless of their shape, stairways can be open on both sides, open on one side, or closed in by walls on both sides. The most attractive seem to have one open-type support or stringer. That way at least one wall provides a surface to hang artwork or plants, and the stairway still looks and feels spacious—even if it isn't.

As an added note, if you're planning to use stairwell walls as a gallery, arrange for blocking in between the studs while the wall is being erected. Then heavy items can be fastened to the blocking if need be, and not just into the weaker plaster or drywall.

WIDTHS AND HEADROOM

A staircase should be wide enough so two people can pass each other on the steps and furniture can be transported up and down with a minimum of trouble. Consider 36 inches as a minimum width to be safe; 42 inches, if space permits, is ideal. Extra inches are especially handy if a staircase is closed or makes a turn and involves winders as in L-shaped and U-shaped types. If wider, they're a lot easier to maneuver large pieces of furniture on.

The stairs should also be plenty deep for a good step. Twelve to 14 inches deep for individual treads is both the maximum and ideal range. The headroom between any part of the tread on any individual step and the nearest vertical obstruction should not be less than 7 feet, preferably 7 feet, 6 inches (Fig. 12.7).

7'0" MIN. HEADROOM

FIGURE 12.7

A stairway's minimum headroom.

RAILINGS

Stairway railings can be fun to think about. Should you have a flashy brass rail? Or maybe an intricately carved wooden one? Then again, maybe it would be better to put up a half wall and top it off with a nice modern slab of sanded-smooth oak with a great, round finial (ornamental post top) at the bottom to keep youngsters from using the rail as a slide. Above all, a railing must be sturdy. Although local building codes must be followed or exceeded, they often define "sturdy" as being able to support a weight or push of 200 pounds at any point of the rail.

Stairway railings can add a lot to the safety and decor of your home, so keep the following in mind:

- Stairways should be equipped on each side with permanent and substantial handrails 36 inches in height from the center of each tread. Narrow stairs can get along with one rail, but wide stairways should have two.

- The railings should be continuous from floor to floor, even when there are landings.

- All handrails should have rounded corners and a surface smooth and free of splinters.

- Since you're going to need *some* kind of railing(s) anyway, you might as well use railing that adds to the attractiveness of your home.

FOLDING AND EXTENSION STAIRWAYS

Folding or extension stairways are widely used for necessary and convenient access to attics, finished living quarters, or out-of-the-way closet storage spaces (Fig. 12.8). Some models, especially the wider ones, have handrails on both sides. These are preferable.

Many of the narrower models, with only a single handrail, are best installed to drop down along an adjacent wall, if possible. The use of these stairways also saves the floor space of the room or area below the device, which allows for freer planning. Most folding or sliding extension stairways come completely assembled for installation in a prepared opening and are attached to a ceiling door so you just have to reach up and pull them down. The two most popular types are rigid extension units that slide up and down parallel with their pull-down door, and three-section units held together with hinges. When not in use, the hinged sections fold up into a compact bundle that's stored on top of the closed door.

FIGURE 12.8

A pull-down extension staircase.

Although these setups provide somewhat less sturdy means of access than access gained by permanently fixed stairs, the folding and extension models are not used as frequently and are the better choice for top-level spaces.

The folding units fit into homes with floor-to-ceiling heights of 7 feet 6 inches to 8 feet 9 inches. Rigid extension stairways are available in many more sizes ranging from 7 feet 6 inches to over 16 feet.

All folding and extension staircases that fold or slide up into unheated areas such as attics must not be overlooked when it comes to insulation and air infiltration. The door of a pull-down stairway should be hinged on one side of the frame and equipped with latches so that when closed, the door can be snugly pulled against a rubber seal to prevent drafts.

Insulation to match the other parts of the attic floor should then be placed on top of the door and around the sides of the frame. Caulking compound can be applied around the seam at the juncture of the door frame and subfloor.

SAFETY POINTERS

BASEMENT STAIRS

Due to the "hard" nature of typical basement staircases, coupled with the fact that they usually lead to a plain concrete floor, take extra precautions to safeguard them from babies, toddlers, and other young children. Consider the use of a closure on the basement door, one that slowly shuts the door after someone goes through, similar to the setup on a storm door. To remain effective, the unit should also have a cylinder that can hold the door open if something needs to be transported up or down the stairs. Another feature to arrange for is plush-type, padded carpeting at the bottom of the basement stairs, securely fastened to the floor or placed with nonslip backing, so that it won't pose a tripping hazard. If someone accidentally slips down the stairs, the plush padded carpeting at the stairs' bottom will help soften the impact.

FIGURE 12.9

Outdoor basement stairs.

EXTERIOR STAIRWELLS

Exterior stairwells that lead from basements and lower living levels directly to the outdoors face special problems that are solved by construction specifications different from those used for inside stairways (Fig. 12.9).

1. Exterior stairwell sidewalls are normally formed with poured concrete or concrete blocks.

2. The steps are practically always made of poured concrete.

3. The entrance doors, single or double, can be wood, but should preferably be steel with a wood center or core. These composition steel/wood doors hold up very well against moisture in all climates.

4. The bottom of an outside stairwell should be lower than the basement to prevent a direct flow of water into the house. A 6-inch sill is standard, with a stairwell drain installed to convey excess water into an appropriate drainage area.

▶▶▶▶▶ POINTS TO PONDER

1. Although stairway appearances are important, they're not as important as stairway safety. Safety considerations should come first with stairways.
2. Main stairways should be at least 3 feet wide.
3. Stairs should be plenty deep for a good step. Twelve to 14 inches deep for individual treads is an ideal range.
4. The headroom between any part of the tread on any individual step and the nearest vertical obstruction should be between 7 and 7½ feet.
5. There should be at least one sturdy handrail on each stairway.
6. Stairways must be well lit, with lighting controls at the top and bottom of each stairway.
7. Folding or sliding stairways, such as pull-down units to attics, must be frequently inspected for loose fasteners caused by opening and closing actions, vibrations, and even alternating hot/cold temperature changes.
8. Consider putting up a barrier in the attic around a pull-down stairway so that no one accidentally steps, kneels, or leans against the folded stairway from above (which could cause the stairway and the person to tumble to the lower floor).
9. Be aware that hardwood stairs can be beautiful, but they can also be quite slippery, especially when wet or when people walk on them in stocking feet.
10. If you're planning to use stairway walls as a gallery, arrange for blocking in between the studs while the wall is being erected. Then heavy items can be fastened to the blocking if need be, and not just into the weaker plaster or drywall.

Windows

Imagine a house without windows and you're likely to conjure up some prison-like dwelling or subterranean earthen home constructed into the side of a hill. Windows, large and small, perform many important functions in the typical home. First of all, they provide natural lighting. Second, they admit fresh air for ventilation and allow oxygen-depleted used air to be expelled. They also provide access for passive solar-heating sunrays, and openings in the house's outer shell for air-conditioning units. From within the house, they enable the occupants to attain a visual continuity with the outdoors and provide exits to those same outdoors in case of emergencies.

GENERAL CONSIDERATIONS

When planning for and selecting windows for your house, keep the following points in mind for each potential window candidate:

■ Insulating and anti-air infiltration properties.

■ Ease of operation.

■ Necessary maintenance.

■ Ease or difficulty to clean.

■ Its style and how it will fit in with your overall exterior scheme.

- Price—a cheap window could cause a loss of any initial savings through consequential increases in heating, cooling, and maintenance costs.

DRAWBACKS

Like any other feature in a house, windows can also have their drawbacks:

1. Large expanses of glass increase heat loss during periods of cold temperatures and become a source of unwanted, and at times uncontrollable, solar heat gain during warmer months.

2. In the summer, windows not only let the hot sun in to make the inside of a house uncomfortably warm, but they also permit sunlight to fade the color from carpeting, paneling, furniture upholstery, and practically anything else.

3. In addition to providing views that might not always be pretty, windows can turn a house into a goldfish bowl by enabling outsiders and strangers to see into the interior living areas.

4. Windows require a fair amount of washing—a chore no one enjoys. Every now and then a child's softball smashes through one, or a limb from a nearby tree gets blown too close, and they must be replaced.

5. Windows are the first surfaces in a house to fog up when the interior humidity rises. They can stream with condensation, which might ruin the finish on the sills.

6. Windows can admit annoying neighborhood noises.

7. When not secured properly, windows provide encouragement to burglars and intruders.

8. Windows become ugly black mirrors from inside when you turn on the lights at night.

9. Windows require expensive curtains, draperies, and blinds that also need periodic cleaning.

10. If not carefully and tastefully selected and located, instead of improving the appearance of a house, they can actually detract from it.

WINDOW TYPES

When selecting from the 11 basic window types used on today's modern houses, there's no reason why you can't employ two or three types of them as long as they look nice together. At the same time, there's no reason why you can't combine one type of movable window with a fixed window, or even with another type of movable window in the same opening. The tightest-sealing and most energy-efficient window types, including casement, hopper, tilt-turn, and awning use long-lasting compression-type weather strip seals.

Casement Windows

A casement window is a miniature version of a hinged door, except it's opened and closed with a crank or lever mounted on the inside of the window sill (Fig. 13.1). Thus, you don't have to disturb a screen or additional storm sashes, which might be mounted on the inside—although add-on storm windows and screens can also be installed on the outside of casement windows. A latch locks each sash tightly.

Advantages

1. Because of their method of operation, casement windows are ideal for installations behind counters and hard-to-reach or difficult-to-

FIGURE 13.1

Casement windows.

move furniture. Wherever you can't stand right next to the window for leverage, or can't reach the entire window due to its high placement, you won't be able to comfortably position a double-hung window and should opt for the casement.

2. They offer excellent sealing against air infiltration when they latch against compression weather stripping.

3. Depending on the particular design, interior and exterior surfaces can be cleaned from inside the house.

4. Since the entire sash opens, a casement window admits 100 percent of an available breeze.

5. Casement windows can be outfitted with automatic openers.

Disadvantages

1. You have to carefully consider where you locate casement windows in relation to outdoor activities. They shouldn't open out onto terraces, porches, decks, or sidewalks where people can bump into them.

2. Because the screens or storm windows are fastened to the inside, they hinder fast exits through the window openings if needed during a fire or other emergency.

Double-Hung Windows

These are the most common windows found in construction today. The double-hung window has two sashes or panes that slide up and down in channels or tracks called stiles. As a rule, the sashes are the same size; but in some cases, the bottom sash is taller than the top sash. The two sections are held in place by either springs or friction. If by friction, it's a sign of a good, tight fit (Fig. 13.2). Look for models with ventilation limit latches that enable the windows to vent in a partly open position, for recessed tilt latches that allow easy window cleaning access, and for a sloped sill for rainwater runoff.

Advantages

1. Because they're held firmly in place, double-hung windows rarely warp or sag.

2. Unless they're painted shut, double-hung windows are simple to open and close as long as you can stand directly adjacent to them for good leverage.

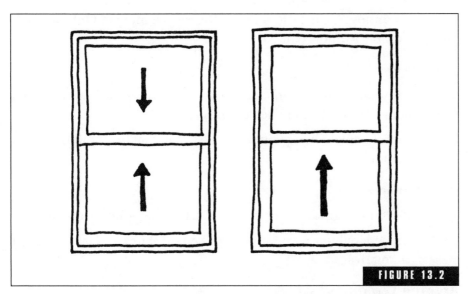

FIGURE 13.2

Double- and single-hung window operation.

3. Relatively little air leakage occurs around the edges.

4. They can be cleaned from the inside if the sash is removable. The older models had pulleys and weights suspended within the walls to help the windows open and close—they had to be cleaned from the outside. Some modern double-hung window sashes can be popped out of their stiles, to the inside, for convenient cleaning and replacement.

Disadvantages

1. If you will have to reach over a counter or piece of furniture to open and close them, double-hung windows will be difficult to operate and shouldn't be used.

2. These windows can never open to more than half of their total area.

3. Even when they're open only an inch or two, double-hung windows are likely to admit hard-driven rain.

4. If the sashes aren't removable, the only way to clean them is from the outside—with a ladder when they're located on second-story levels.

Single-Hung Windows

Not as popular as their double-hung cousins, the single-hung window looks exactly like the double-hung unit but differs in that the single-hung window's top sash is fixed. It can't be moved. Only the bottom half of the window can be screened.

Advantages

1. Because half of this window is sealed shut, there's somewhat less maintenance and less chance of air leakage.

2. The cost of a single-hung window is less than that of a similar double-hung model.

Disadvantages

1. Ventilation is limited to the bottom part of the window opening.

2. Washing a single-hung window can be a problem unless the lower sash is removable.

Awning Windows

Awning windows are hinged similarly to casement windows, but along their top edge so they swing out and up when you turn a crank or lever or simply give them a push (Fig. 13.3). Some units are made with special hardware that provides pivot action—the top of the sash moves down as you push the bottom outward. The screens and storm windows are installed from the inside.

Advantages

1. They can be opened wide enough so you can get almost 100 percent of possible ventilation—even during a rainstorm—without letting in water.

2. They can be used as clerestory windows, placed high in walls to provide natural light and ventilation while assuring privacy and leaving a maximum amount of wall space for furniture placement.

3. They offer an excellent seal against air infiltration when they latch closed against compression weather stripping.

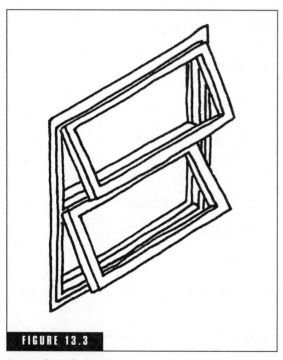

FIGURE 13.3

An awning window.

Disadvantages

1. Awning windows shouldn't be installed overlooking porches, decks, terraces, or sidewalks because someone might run into their open projecting sashes.

2. Because they slant, open sashes are so exposed that they become dirty in short order and require more frequent washing than any other type of window.

3. As with casement windows, having storm windows and screens mounted on the inside can hinder a quick escape.

Hopper Windows and Tilt-Turn Windows

A hopper window.

Hopper windows are the reverse models of awning windows. Hinged or pivoted at their bottom, they open inward and downward from their top so that the entering air flows upward (Fig. 13.4). Operated by a lock handle at the top of the sash, they're most commonly used in basements and clerestories. Screens and storm windows are installed on the outside.

A tilt-turn window is a variation of a hopper window in which, by turning one handle on a tilt-turn window 90 degrees, the window switches from a hopper design (tilts in at the top just a little) to a swing-in casement window (Fig. 13.5). In the hopper position, the window can be left open in a rainstorm without water leakage. In the casement position, they are easy to clean from indoors. Tilt-turn windows are also very airtight and efficient because the weather stripping seal gets compressed when the window is closed.

Advantages

1. Hopper windows provide almost 100 percent of possible ventilation.

2. Both their inner and outer surfaces can be easily washed from the inside.

FIGURE 13.5

Tilt-turn window opening positions.

3. They offer an excellent seal against air infiltration when they latch closed against compression weather stripping.

Disadvantages

1. Hopper windows interfere with draperies and curtains and are impossible to darken with shades when opened.

2. Because they stick out inside a room or hallway they can cause traffic problems in living areas of a home.

3. Because of their unusual open position they can be difficult to exit from in case of an emergency.

Horizontal Sliding Windows

In effect, a horizontal sliding window is a double-hung or single-hung window laid on its side (Fig. 13.6). With some units, both sashes slide from side to side in a channel; in others, only one sash (usually the right sash) slides. In still others made with three panels of glass, the two outer sashes slide to the center over a fixed sash that is twice

FIGURE 13.6

Horizontal sliding windows.

the width of each sliding sash. Look for ventilation limit latches that enable the windows to vent in a partly open position, for recessed tilt latches that allow easy window cleaning access, and for a sloped sill for rainwater runoff.

Advantages

1. As with double-hung windows, because they're held firmly in place they won't warp or sag.

2. They're easy to open and close as long as you're standing next to them.

3. Relatively little air leakage occurs around the edges.

4. Washing is usually easy because many sashes can be removed from the inside of the house.

5. Horizontal sliding windows are a good choice in locations where you want an operating sash with a large expanse of glass and a minimum number of framing members to obstruct the view. No other operating unit fills this requirement as well.

Disadvantages

1. Horizontal sliding windows cannot be opened to access more than 50 percent of their possible ventilation space.

2. They will admit driving rain into the house.

3. If you must reach over a counter or piece of furniture to open and close them, horizontal sliders are difficult to operate and should not be used.

Fixed Windows

Fixed windows are panes of glass mounted in frames that are installed directly into a wall (Fig. 13.7). They can't be opened and closed, and can be ordered in a variety of sizes, shapes, and glass types.

Advantages

1. They're the most weather-tight windows available.

2. Because they can't be opened, they don't require screens or hardware.

3. They're less expensive than other windows.

FIGURE 13.7

Fixed windows.

Disadvantages

1. They can provide no ventilation.

2. They're impossible to exit from in case of an emergency.

3. They must be cleaned from the outside.

Glass Block Windows

Glass block windows are installed like concrete blocks, course by course. Glass blocks allow light to enter a room and, at the same time, provide privacy. Standard (plain) as well as fancy "designer" glass blocks are available. These blocks are not solid glass. Instead, each unit consists of two hollow ¼- to ¾-inch-thick glass half-blocks fused together under high temperatures. As the air inside the fused block cools, an insulating partial vacuum is formed within the block (Fig. 13.7).

Advantages

1. When set in mortar, glass blocks are airtight, reducing the likelihood of drafts, dirt, allergy-causing particles, noise, and even burglar entry. They're efficient year-round and minimize interior glare and the fading of carpet, furniture, and furnishings.

2. Some "designer" glass blocks have patterns etched in their glass such as wavy finishes, raised diamonds, stippled textures, or fluted surfaces. Any of those can add character to a room.

3. Glass blocks can be purchased with color tints to blend or contrast with interior designs.

Disadvantages

1. They can't be opened or seen through.

2. They can't be escaped through.

Bay Windows

A bay window consists of three adjacent windows or sections of windows in a series. Two side sections are angled back from each side of a straight center window or section of windows (Fig. 13.8). An entire bay window unit can be made from combinations of windows such as casement or double-hung windows on the sides and a fixed center section.

FIGURE 13.8

A bay window.

Bay windows are ideal when you want to increase both the real and apparent size of a room. They'll also add a graceful note to an otherwise rather severe facade.

Advantages

1. They open up a 180-degree view and add space to a room.

2. They not only increase ventilation but also enable you to scoop in breezes traveling parallel to the house walls.

3. They form a delightful niche for sitting or dining near. They're often featured in designer rooms and houses and they provide considerably more light than conventional window arrangements do.

4. They provide an excellent place for growing houseplants.

5. Bay window roofs may be shingled to match the house roof, or they can be roofed with copper for a distinctive, traditional look.

Disadvantages

1. At least the center part of a bay window must be cleaned from the outside.

2. Because this arrangement protrudes out from a wall, it's not as energy efficient as other window installations.

Bow Windows

The bow window is a close relative of the bay window, and they're often confused with each other (Fig. 13.9). The bow window is gently curved rather than angled and is considered a more graceful feature when used in a house's living area. The bow window receives its name from the arrangement of a series of windows that arc out from the house's exterior walls.

Because of their curved shape, bow windows are necessarily made up of relatively narrow sashes or of many small fixed panes. When

FIGURE 13.9

A bow window.

sashes are used, they're generally the casement and occasionally the double-hung type. With casement windows, either all of the sashes can open, or only the two end panels, or only the end panels and every other intermediate panel. When double-hung windows make up a bow, only the end panels open. Bow windows are also available in models in which none of the sashes open, with fixed large- or small-pane styles.

Advantages

1. They open up a 180-degree view.

2. Not only do bow windows increase ventilation, they enable you to scoop in breezes that run parallel to the house walls.

3. They form the same kind of delightful niche found with bay windows, for dining near, growing plants in, and sitting in.

Disadvantages

1. Because they protrude, they are not as energy efficient as windows closer to the walls.

2. These windows are usually narrow or small, so there's little opportunity to escape through them in case of an emergency.

3. Some of their sections are normally fixed, and cleaning will have to be done from the outside.

FIGURE 13.10

A garden window.

Garden Windows

Garden windows, also referred to as greenhouse windows, project from a home's exterior by about 12 inches and have glass roofs as well as vertical glass panes (Fig. 13.10). Inside glass shelves or expanded metal shelving across a garden window allows the placement of plants and admits sunlights from top to bottom. The insulated glass and tight seals minimize winter heat loss. Some models have insulated curved center window sections that eliminate the need for center frames.

Others use side-opening casement windows that hinge on the side near the house. Many come with double lock latches on each side for security and an airtight seal when closed and latched.

Numerous units employ vinyl frames (some foam-filled for extra insulation value) that come in white, tan, and brown. For severe cold climate locations, certain models afford extra protection for the plants during winter, with rigid foam insulation sandwiched between the seat and sides.

Advantages

1. They offer practically the same excellent spaciousness and ventilating possibilities as those available with bay windows.

2. They are great for growing cooking herbs in or near the kitchen.

Disadvantages

1. They cannot be easily escaped through.

2. They may be difficult to clean.

Jalousie Windows

A jalousie window is made up of a series of narrow horizontal panes or glass slats that open outward with a crank. (Fig. 13.11)

Advantages

1. They can be opened far enough to gain virtually 100 percent of available ventilation.

2. They can be opened during rainy weather without admitting water into the room.

3. The airflow from jalousie windows can be adjusted in any amount or vertical direction.

4. They're easy to open over a counter or furniture.

FIGURE 13.11

A jalousie window.

Disadvantages

1. They possess many small glass sections that need to be cleaned.

2. They're difficult to wash from the inside.

3. They're very poor for preventing air infiltration.

4. Jalousie windows are impossible to exit from in case of an emergency.

Skylight Windows

Skylight windows do two things better than other windows can: they admit more natural light and distribute the light more evenly.

They also make rooms look larger and can help equalize the light in a room that might have windows on only one side. Frequently, the skylight chosen is a fixed window unable to be opened. Fixed skylights come in many shapes—dome, smooth, low-profile curb, pyramid, and ridge (Fig. 13.12). The same windows also are available in models that can be opened and closed.

Another kind of roof skylight window is a single sash that pivots at the sides about a third of the way down from the top. When opened, the bottom swings out and the top swings in. It can be held open at any angle—even completely reversed for easy washing from the inside.

In a third type of roof window, the sash is hinged at the top and raises like an awning window to give an unobstructed view while keeping out rain. The outside of the more progressive models is washed with a special tool provided by the manufacturer.

Skylights and roof windows should generally be installed on the south side of homes located in cold-climate areas, or on the north side of dwellings located in warm-climate places. In colder areas, consider a clear skylight or roof window combined with an insulating shade or storm window. In warmer areas, use frosted or tinted skylights that open to vent excess heat and have shades for blocking out the sun when needed. The tinted glass will help reduce illumination while cutting down on glare and heat gain.

Sun-screening capabilities with skylight or roof windows include Venetian blinds, pleated shades, and roller shades. Venetian blinds come in thermal units operated manually or electrically. Pleated shades offer lighting gradations from soft filtered light to darkness.

DOME

LOW PROFILE CURB

SMOOTH

PYRAMID

RIDGE LIGHT

FIGURE 13.12

Skylight windows.

Various colors and shades are available, with different insulation values. Roller shades are often a choice of homeowners looking to work within a limited budget.

Roof windows can be installed in convenient-reach locations such as attics and "extra" or "nook" rooms. Some of these windows open to a full 45-degree angle to satisfy egress requirements for emergency escape.

Ventilating skylights are available in low-e insulated glass, with optional insect screens. Units positioned out of a person's normal reach can be operated with a number of control systems (with manual or motorized control rods), including the following:

- Electric programmable units with timers that can be set to open or close the windows automatically at desired times

- Electric control systems with switch keypads

- Units with infrared remote controls similar to a hand-held television remote control, for convenient operating of vent skylights and sunscreening accessories

Advantages

1. Skylight windows permit installation of smaller and fewer windows and simplify interior decoration and furniture placement by allowing more uninterrupted wall space in a room.

2. They can be used to illuminate rooms and areas that share no outside walls for regular windows, such as inside bathrooms and halls.

3. They supply privacy without sacrificing any natural lighting. Also, some models open for fresh air.

4. Skylight windows can provide more flexibility in the planning of a house because you needn't have to include sidewall windows in every room and because they can effectively add useful space (such as in attics) to spaces otherwise dark and dreary.

5. During winter, the pros and cons of a high-quality skylight are about a wash, as the skylight loses more heat than does an insulated attic floor or ceiling, but *does* reduce the need for electric lighting during the day and provides some passive solar heat gain during sunny weather. However, during summer, a vent skylight is an energy saver since the hottest indoor air rises to the ceiling where the skylight vent exhausts it. This creates a natural air flow, drawing fresh cooler outside air indoors.

Disadvantages

1. Because heat rises, skylight windows tend to be less efficient than a plain windowless roof or ceiling in cold weather, especially during times when the sun is not shining. Because of this, consider only skylights that have a minimum of double-glazed glass (not all of them do).

2. They can be difficult to clean. The fixed types must be cleaned from above. Leaves, dust, and even ice buildup during winter can pose real problems.

3. Provisions need to be made for draining off water—either condensated moisture or water that collects from rain and melting snow.

TYPES OF GLASS

There are three types of glass panels typically used to construct modern windows: plate glass, tempered glass, and insulating glass panes.

Plate Glass

This is the standard glass normally used in house windows. It can be plain or tinted to reduce glare and can be doubled up to sandwich in a thin airspace for insulating qualities. When struck or put under stress, it shatters into pieces that are usually very sharp. It's an excellent material for windows, though, because it can be manufactured free of flaws and distortions.

Tempered Glass

Tempered glass panes are three to five times stronger than those made of ordinary plate glass. Tempered glass should be used in doors and in glass panels adjacent to doors and other areas where it is likely that people, especially children, might run into or fall against them. In fact, many building codes require the use of tempered glass in wall areas that are within 4 feet of any door. When struck or put under stress, tempered glass develops hairline cracks or breaks into many small, rounded pieces instead of into the sharp, ragged pieces that come from standard plate glass. Auto windshields are a common example of tempered glass.

Insulating Glass

This glass exists in two forms. One is a special double or triple sheet of glass (double or triple pane/double or triple glazed) separated by an airspace(s) with the glass edges welded or formed together to make airtight center spaces much like the liner for a thermos bottle. The other consists of two or three sheets of glass held in the frame with an insulating airspace in between. Double-pane insulating glass used in most stock windows is made of two panes of sheet glass having a ⅜ to ½ inch of airspace between them. Triple-pane glass windows consist of three panes of glass with approximately ⅜ inch of airspaces between each pair of panes (Fig. 13.13).

DOUBLE PANE

TRIPLE PANE

FIGURE 13.13

Insulating glass double- and triple-pane windows.

In this day and age, it no longer makes sense to install windows having only a single thickness of glass. Instead, all exterior windows located in living areas or heated areas of a house should be double- or triple-paned. The additional expense is well worth it; you should save enough in fuel and energy costs to more than make up for the initial investment within a few years and have a more comfortable home in the meantime.

More advantages to using double- or triple-pane windows as opposed to a combination of single-pane sashes and storm windows are that the multipanel windows offer a better appearance; are easier to clean; and provide increased soundproofing, a permanent installation, and even a better overall price. In all multipane windows, specify that the thickness of the sash is at least 1⅜ inches.

Self-Cleaning Glass

Several manufacturers produce windows made of glass that's designed to self-clean. Due to chemical compounds embedded within the surface of the molten glass during manufacturing, when the window is exposed to sunlight a chemical reaction helps disintegrate many foreign materials that collect on the glass, such as tree sap, pollen, or dead insects. Also, water doesn't bead up on self-cleaning glass; instead it spreads out in sheets that wash away loose debris like a squeegee.

While windows with self-cleaning glass cost more, they enable more of the sun's rays to enter through the cleaner glass—warming interior spaces during winter and helping to reduce energy costs.

Additional Glass Options Include:

- *Low-e glazings* are special coatings that reduce heat transfer through windows. The coatings are thin, almost invisible metal oxide or semiconductor films placed directly on one or more surfaces of glass or on plastic films between two or more panes. The coatings prevent heat loss during winter and slow heat from entering the house in the summer.

- *Spectrally selective coatings* are considered to be the next generation of low-e technologies. These coatings filter out from 40 to 70 percent of the heat normally transmitted through clear glass, while allowing the full amount of light transmission.

- *Insulated glass* contains at least double panes surrounding a sealed air space, offering an insulated layer between you and the elements, plus warm-edge spacers that minimize heat and cold conductivity between outdoors and indoors. Filling the gap between the panes with a low conductivity harmless inert gas adds about another R-1 of insulation value to the window, and also helps block out noise.

- *Heat-absorbing glazings* are glass that has tinted coatings to absorb some solar heat (but they can't absorb it all). Some heat continues to pass through the glass by conduction and re-radiation.

- *Warm-edge technology* uses low-conductance spacers to reduce heat transfer near the edges of insulated glazing. The edge spacers are what hold the panes of glass apart and provides an airtight seal in an insulated glass window. The better models carry a long warranty against spacer and seal failure. New glazing technologies with warm edges and insulated frames not only reduce energy costs, but make homes more comfortable as well, even helping to reduce incidents of frost and condensation.

- *Reflective coatings* greatly reduce the transmission of daylight through clear glass. Although they typically block more light than heat, reflective coatings, when applied to tinted or clear glass, also slow some heat transmission. These coatings are commonly applied in hot-climate locations, where protection from the glaring sun is critical to comfort. Care must be taken, though, since the reduced cooling energy that results may be somewhat offset by a resulting need for additional artificial lighting.

- *Visual transmittance (VT)* identifies the see-through quality of the glass. Windows with high visible transmittance are easy to see through and admit plenty of natural daylight. The VT in residential windows ranges from a shady 15 percent for some tinted glass, up to 90 percent for clear glass (the higher the number, the clearer the glass). To most people, glass with VT values of 60 percent or more looks clear. Any value below 50 percent begins to appears dark and/or reflective. Besides giving you a nice view, high-VT windows can save energy in certain conditions because you'll need less artificial illumination. But can you have your high-tech insulated glass and see through it too? Not all of the time. Some tints and coatings that block heat also reduce visual transmission, so make sure you actually *see* and *look through* any special glass you may be considering, before specifying it for your home.

CONTROLLING HEAT

Windows, for all their wonderful qualities, can also be considered as thermal holes or passageways. An average home may lose up to 30 percent of its heat or air conditioning energy through low-quality windows. Energy-efficient windows save money every month. Their higher initial cost can be offset in many ways. One way is that a smaller, less expensive heating and cooling system would be acceptable. Energy efficient, durable windows will certainly cost less in the long haul because of less energy used, lower maintenance costs, and avoidance of replacement expenses that will otherwise inevitably come into play if inferior windows are selected.

All of this, plus the occupants will be a lot more comfortable in a dwelling that's built with good windows—due to the ways the windows help control heat. In short, when sunlight strikes a window, visible light, ultraviolet rays, and heat are either reflected, absorbed, or transmitted into the building.

During winter, a window with a lower glass temperature feels colder partly because more heat is radiated from a person's body toward the window, than from the window to the person. Cold glass can also create uncomfortable drafts as air next to the window is cooled and travels downward to the floor. This sets up an air movement pattern that feels drafty and promotes heat loss. High-performance windows installed with efficient weather stripping result in higher interior temperatures in winter, and thus greater comfort. During summer, windows with low solar heat coefficients reduce the solar radiation coming through the glass, with its overly warm discomfort.

Windows lose and gain heat by conduction, convection, radiation, and air leakage (Fig. 13.14).

■ *Conduction* is the movement of heat through a solid material. With less conductive material, head flow is impeded. To control conduction, look for multiple-glazed windows with an approved low-conductance, inert approved harmless gas trapped between panes of glass. Thermally resistant edge spacers and window frames will further reduce conduction.

■ *Convection* is another way heat moves through windows. In cold weather, heated indoor air presses against the interior surface of window glass. The air cools off, becomes dense and sinks toward the floor. As this cooled air drops, warm air rushes in to take its place along the surface of the glass. The cycle then repeats itself over and over, or at least until the glass becomes too warm to continue to cool the indoor air. What actually happens is the occupants feel too cold for comfort

FIGURE 13.14

Windows lose and gain heat.

and turn up their thermostat control. Unfortunately, this is where excessive energy costs come into play. Each 1 percent increase in thermostat setting requires an increased home energy usage of about 2 percent. This heat loss or transfer is expressed with U-values, or U-factors. U-values are the mathematical inverse of the R-values commonly used to measure the effectiveness of thermal insulation. That means the lower the U-value, the higher its insulating value. Your window U-value should be below 0.35 to be efficient.

■ *Radiation* is a third way heat can enter or leave a dwelling. You can help control this process to your advantage with low-e glass coatings, transparent metal oxides that reflect up to 90 percent of long-wave heat energy, while passing shorter waves of visible light. The shorter wavelength visible light is absorbed by the floors, walls and furniture. It re-radiates indoors from those surfaces, all while the long-wave heat energy is reflected back outdoors. In cold climates, the low-e glass reflects the internally produced *radiant* heat waves back into the house, again while admitting visible light. The shorter wavelength visible light is absorbed by floors, walls and furniture, and re-radiates from those surfaces at the same time the long-wave heat energy is reflected back inside. For heating, low-e coatings thus work best when applied to the internal or inter-pane surface of the interior window pane. Conversely, for cooling, low-e coatings work best applied to the inter-pane surface of the window's exterior pane.

■ *Air leakage* is a fourth way that heat is lost (or gained) from a home. In short, air leakage siphons a large percentage of an average home's heating and cooling energy to the outdoors. Some of this is unavoidable, of course. When someone enters or exits a dwelling, there's bound to be some exchange of indoor and outdoor air. It's the avoidable air escape and exchange that windows (and doors) must address. To control air infiltration, quality windows need durable weather stripping and secure closing devices. Hinged windows such as casement and awning types tend to clamp more tightly against weather stripping than do double-hung windows. But the difference can be slight; well-made double-hung windows are certainly acceptable.

How well the individual components of the window are joined can also affect air leakage. Glass-to-frame, frame-to-frame, and sash-to-frame connections must be well-fit and tight. The technical measurement specification for window air leakage is measured in cubic feet of air per minute per square of window. Look for windows with certified air-leakage rates of 0.01 to 0.06 cfm/ft or less. Lowest values are best.

TYPES OF WINDOW FRAMES

There are three primary types of materials used in window frame construction: wood, metal, and plastic.

Wood Frames

Wood frames are the most handsome window frames available and are often preferred for this reason alone. They can be purchased with their exterior and side surfaces (the parts that abut the tracks or stiles and face the outdoors) covered with a layer of tough vinyl or a layer of aluminum with a coat of factory-applied, baked-on paint. The only part of such a window frame that retains its wood surface is the interior section—what you can see that faces the inside of a room. That inside surface is the most important part of a window frame from an appearance point of view. It can be stained, varnished, or painted to match or complement the rest of a room's decor. The choice of colors for either the vinyl- or aluminum-clad surfaces are usually limited to white, brown, or bronze.

Because no staining, varnishing, or refinishing is ever required to the non-wood surfaces, maintenance there is extremely infrequent. And the wood part of the frame, the part you can see from inside the room, will rarely need attention either, because it isn't exposed to the elements. Vinyl-clad or aluminum-clad factory-finished wood frames are excellent choices (Fig. 13.15).

EXTERIOR RIGID VINYL COVERING

FIGURE 13.15

Vinyl-covered window construction cutaway.

Advantages

1. A primary advantage of wood-framed windows is their appearance. They look less clinical than aluminum or steel sashes. As such, wood is favored in many residential applications because of its appearance and traditional place in house design.

2. Condensation is not much of a problem with wood frames as, it is with steel and aluminum ones.

3. Wood frames can be successfully used with all architectural styles.

4. Wood frames are poor heat conductors, so they provide effective insulating qualities.

5. Provided you select the wood frames having vinyl- or aluminum-clad exteriors, the outer and inner track surfaces will be practically maintenance-free.

6. The interior surfaces of wood sashes can be painted to match any color scheme or can be stained and finished in natural tones to match inside wood baseboard and other trim. Exterior surfaces of wood sashes can also be painted to easily change color schemes if desired.

Disadvantages

1. If the exterior surfaces are not vinyl- or aluminum-clad, they'll need refinishing, especially if no awnings or substantial overhangs are in place to shield the windows from rain, sun, and snow. If uncovered wood frames are not treated to resist decay and moisture absorption, they'll rot in short order.

Metal Frames

Metal window frames are available in aluminum and steel models, in natural finishes or various selections of anodized coloring. Aluminum windows became popular because people thought aluminum models suffered from none of the problems associated with wood—that they wouldn't rot, swell, contract, warp, or need refinishing. This, however, proved not altogether true. Near seacoasts and corrosive industrial locales, aluminum frames can corrode so badly that they need to be painted for protection. For these reasons, it's advisable to purchase aluminum or steel windows that are protected by factory-applied finishes.

A traditional heat conduction problem for aluminum frames can be addressed during their manufacture by including a thermal break, splitting the frame components into interior and exterior pieces by using a less-conductive material to join them.

Advantages

1. They cost less than wood frames.

2. They lend themselves nicely to places that receive rugged use, such as basement windows and garage windows.

3. They're easy to operate.

4. They won't warp.

5. Aluminum window frames are light, strong, and easily extruded into the complex shapes required for window parts.

6. Aluminum frames are available in anodized and factory-baked enamel finishes that are extremely durable and low-maintenance.

Disadvantages

1. Because aluminum and steel are excellent conductors, they permit high heat loss from within a house through the window frames.

2. Also due to their conductivity, they cause excessive moisture condensation on the interior portion of the frames when significant temperature differences exist between the inside and outside of the windows. If you insist on aluminum- or steel-framed windows, make sure you select a brand that has a thermal break—where an insulating material separates the interior and exterior sections of the frame. The most efficient and practical insulating materials include plastic, urethane, epoxy, and vinyl.

3. Aluminum and steel frames often provide a looser fit than that of wood frames, allowing for more air infiltration.

Vinyl Frames

Vinyl is an option for your consideration. Vinyl allows very little heat and cold transference and is practically maintenance-free. Vinyl-clad wood makes for top-quality frames that combines wood's extra insulating properties with vinyl's easy care. Most vinyl-framed windows use multichambered hollow extruded frame and sash sections. These chambers create multiple "dead" airspaces that provide insulation U-value and strength. Several manufacturers offer foam insulation inside the frame chambers. The major difference between insulated vinyl and standard vinyl frames is improved thermal insulating capabilities.

Advantages

1. They are energy efficient and help reduce noise transmission.

2. They have good air and weather seals for reducing dust and pollens.

3. Vinyl comes in wood grain finishes, and one model actually has a real wood composite on the side that faces the inside of the home.

4. Vinyl window frames do not require painting. Because the color goes all the way through, there is no finish coat that can be damaged or will deteriorate; therefore the surface is maintenance free.

Plastic Frames

An available option on some window types is plastic frames. Plastic frames are lightweight and corrosion-free.

Advantages

1. Painting is never needed unless you decide to change their color.

2. They're easy to operate.

3. They're not as expensive as wood frames.

4. Plastic is not a good conductor; it doesn't have the condensation or heat transfer problems of aluminum or steel.

Disadvantages

1. The main drawback is their lack of strength. Wood, aluminum, and steel frames are much stronger. Plastic frames are more likely to break, especially during cold weather, when plastic turns brittle.

Fiberglass Frames

Fiberglass-framed windows can cost a bit more, but they may be worth it to you. They seldom need to be caulked or painted and possess high insulation values. Some fiberglass windows are available with real wood interior sides. The strong fiberglass exterior sides provide the stability and can resist gale winds and driving rains while the wood interior sides give the home a warm, comfortable look and feel.

Advantages

1. They remain airtight because fiberglass frame material expands with temperature changes at almost the identical rate as window glass, so the fit stays true during temperature swings.

2. The fiberglass exterior provides excellent strength and rigidity, which makes these windows favorable choices in rough-weather locations subject to gale-force winds and driving rain. Models are available in many colors, and since fiberglass resists high temperatures, the paint can be baked on. These frames can also be hand painted with good success, should you decide to change the décor of a single room or of the entire house.

3. Many fiberglass-framed windows offer optional foam insulation filling for additional energy efficiency.

4. Because fiberglass is stronger than most vinyl/plastic, it can have smaller cross-sectional pieces and thus provide a proportionally larger clear window area, allowing more free passive solar heating during winter.

WINDOW SIZE AND ALIGNMENT

Make certain that the size of some windows, particularly in bedrooms, is large enough to escape from in case of a fire. As mentioned previously, all sleeping areas should have at least one easy-to-open window having an opening of not less than 7 square feet. Check local building code requirements for window opening width and height, as well as the sill height above the floor.

Also be aware that the size and placement of windows will limit where you can comfortably arrange furniture. Major items such as desks, sofas, bureaus, dressers, china cabinets, and buffets all normally require wall space. However, if window sills are high enough, some furniture can be placed beneath them. Many pieces of furniture are only 30 to 32 inches high.

Windows should be aligned in a pleasant manner, especially when viewed from the outside. That typically means that windows across each living level conform to one long horizontal line. Small windows should line up with the top or bottom halves of large windows. Then for maximum effect, have the tops of exterior doors line up with the

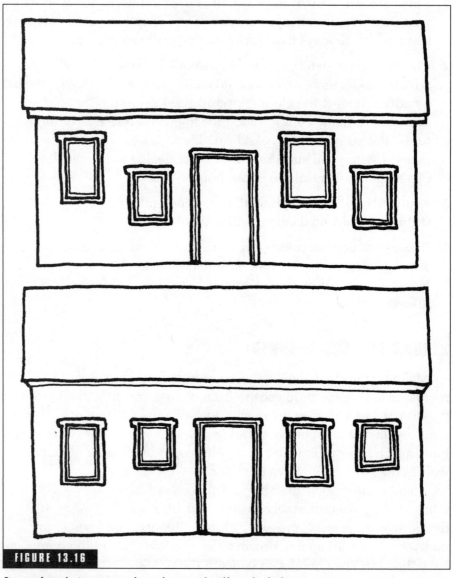

FIGURE 13.16

Comparison between poorly and correctly aligned windows.

window tops on the first level (Fig. 13.16). When possible, arrange vertical window placements directly above one another.

WINDOW LOCATION

No matter where you locate your windows, all exposures will be able to provide a sufficient amount of natural light (Fig. 13.17). Southern exposures, with their high sun angle, offer the most light and the best opportunity to control and use sunshine to good advantage. East and west exposures are the most difficult to control, having low-angled rays, with the west being particularly troublesome. Northern exposures, lacking direct sunlight, are the easiest of the four to control. For the typical home, windows on the north side of the house are discouraged. However, when windows are required due to an unavoidable or advantageous orientation or positioning of the dwelling—such as a master bedroom overlooking a scenic view—a northern exposure can be well suited to the dwelling.

Other points to remember:

■ Horizontal window openings are especially useful for controlling light from southern exposures.

FIGURE 13.17

Good window location.

- Vertical window openings are most useful for controlling light from eastern and western exposures.

- Windows located high in a room offer the most illumination and the deepest penetration by natural light.

- Clerestories and skylights offer good possibilities for lighting interior spaces in a home.

- Windows can be located to illuminate parts of a house or room where specific tasks will be undertaken. Of course, artificial lighting should also be arranged for times of insufficient daylight or during evenings.

WINDOW VENTILATION

In addition to providing natural light, the second major function of windows is to provide ventilation to get rid of stale air in the home (Fig. 13.18).

Large openings allow for the best natural ventilation when arranged to encourage a crosscurrent of air. Openings should be oriented to pick up prevailing summer breezes.

Good airflow occurs when the inlets and outlets are approximately the same size. Better airflow can be attained by having a larger ratio of outlet-to-inlet area. A combination of openings can direct airflow as desired; openings placed lower in the wall surfaces result in better cooling than those placed higher in a room.

Exterior features such as overhangs, porches, fences, garages, shrubs, and trees can be used to block or encourage airflow.

If you plan to install central air-conditioning in the house, you won't need side windows for cross ventilation. By not putting them in, you'll save their installation costs, plus money on energy costs.

STORM WINDOWS

Storm windows cut down on conductive heat losses and gains, depending on the season, by impeding air infiltration and by providing an airspace between inner and outer panes of glass (Fig. 13.19).

On most types of windows (double-hung, single-hung, awning, sliding, and jalousie) conventional storm windows are put up in the

FIGURE 13.18

Window ventilation.

CHANNEL FOR EACH OPERATING PANEL

SCREEN

STORM PANELS

WEEPS

FIGURE 13.19

A triple-track storm window arrangement.

fall and taken down in the spring. But they can also be used to keep cool, conditioned air in a home during summers in warm-climate locations. On casement windows, storm windows are frequently fastened to the outside of the sash.

Combination aluminum-framed storm windows and screens are used on double-hung, single-hung, and sliding windows. In cold-climate areas, they have generally replaced conventional storm windows because combination storm window/ screens can be left in place year-round. In winter, they keep out the cold, and during summer, the insects.

Two kinds of combination storm windows are available: double-track and triple-track. Both include an upper panel of glass, a lower panel of glass, and a single panel of screen. In the double-track arrangement, both glass panels are fitted into separate channels or tracks so they can move up and down independently of one another. In summer, when ventilation is required, the lower panel of glass slides to the top of its track and the screen panel is inserted into the lower half of the track. During winter the screen is removed entirely and stored.

The triple-track storm window arrangement eliminates the necessity for putting in and taking out the screen because each of its two glass panels and the screen all fit into their own tracks. You can convert from a storm window to a screen by simply sliding the lower glass panel up and pushing its replacement screen down. In winter, the screen can conveniently be stored in the top part of the frame, within its own track. Although definitely more expensive, this setup is highly desirable if it fits into your budget. You gain the flexibility to have screens at a moment's notice, or storm windows, and it sure beats having to lug and store screens someplace where they could get damaged during the off-season.

When planning for storm windows, consider that caulking is needed around permanently installed units, at the outer edges of their frames. Two weep holes must be kept open at the bottom edges of each storm window to provide drainage and some ventilation, or wooden sills might rot. To prevent corrosion and maintain a good appearance, select only storm windows that have frames finished in baked enamel or that are coated with a layer of maintenance-free vinyl or similar material.

Key points to look for in a storm window are:

- Installation with quality stainless steel screws.

- Low air infiltration rating.

- No-gap weather stripping. The entire perimeter of the closed sash should be sealed.

- Baked enamel finish on the frames.

- Tie-bar horizontal stiffeners result in a more rigid assembly.

- Double-strength glass.

- Thick-gauge aluminum.

- Low-e coating

- Adjustable sill extender permits a tight fit, even to uneven sills.

- Energy Star labels present.

SCREENS

Most screens installed in today's homes are made of aluminum mesh (Figs. 13.20 and 13.21). Screens are wonderful conveniences. They let air in (or out) and keep out insects and vermin. One recent innovation is a window with built-in screens that pull down and roll up out of sight within the window frame.

FIGURE 13.20

A screen in place.

FIGURE 13.21

Screens.

Aluminum Screening

Aluminum screening is rustproof and resilient. It comes in bright or natural (silvery) finish, charcoal, and black. Charcoal and black tend to be the most popular because they provide excellent outward visibility. Black aluminum is a top-of-the-line screening product. It actually seems to disappear into the background while you look through it to the outdoors.

Fiberglass Screening

Fiberglass screening is typically vinyl-coated for strength and durability. It's especially well suited for coastal areas. It will not corrode, rust, or dent and is very easy to handle.

Solar Screening

Solar screening products are made of vinyl-coated fiberglass, heavy-duty vinyl-coated polyester, and louvered aluminum. They provide protection against insects while blocking out two-thirds of the sun's heat and glare—and still allow good outward visibility. Less heat and less glare means less summer energy consumption.

Pet Screening

Pet screens are heavy-duty, pet-resistant screens made from strong materials such as vinyl-coated polyester. This screening fabric resists tears, punctures, and other damages caused by pets, toddlers, or heavy wear in high-traffic areas. They're available in black and gray and are ideal for windows, doors, and porches likely to take abuse.

SHUTTERS

The main purpose of outside shutters is to beautify the exterior of a house, to harmoniously balance out the appearance of the windows. Maybe years ago they would prevent an Indian's arrow or a marauder's bullet or grizzly bear's paw from entering a window, but they don't anymore. In fact, most of them no longer even close.

You can save money by using ornamental shutters made of vinyl, plastic, or aluminum. Vinyl and plastic shutters are typically available in maintenance-free colors and shades that will match or contrast with whatever siding you choose. Their rigid one-piece construction comes with the color molded throughout, and no paint to chip or flake like the finishes of traditional painted shutters can. Deep wood grain textured models are also on the market, in both open louvered or raised panel designs. They're less expensive than wood and don't require costly operating hardware. Vinyl, plastic, and aluminum shutters are made in louvered and raised-panel designs—usually in black, brown, green, or white (Fig. 13.22). Aluminum units are the stronger of the three, but because the finish is only baked

LOUVERED   RAISED PANEL

FIGURE 13.22

Shutters.

on, and they're exposed to the rain, sun, and snow throughout the year, they'll eventually need repainting. Vinyl-covered shutters, on the other hand, are integrally colored so they don't have to be touched up even if damaged.

Shutters are typically installed by fastening them to window casings or adjacent wall surfaces with screws. But that also means there's no easy way to clean out wasps' nests, bats, or debris that can accumulate behind the shutters.

Wood shutters present an additional problem: if they're not adequately treated with wood preservative, they'll rot. They require frequent stripping, sanding, and painting or staining, which can be quite a time-consuming process, especially if the shutters are louvered. Like the other site-painted items, painted wood shutters won't clean as easily as those having factory finishes. On the positive side, wood shutters can be custom-finished and refinished to match any decorating scheme.

FIGURE 13.23

Snap-in muntins.

DIAMOND AND RECTANGULAR PANES

If you'd like to have windows with either small diamond—or rectangular-shaped panes, you could invest a small fortune into obtaining them. Alternatively, you could buy single-pane windows and turn them into multipane ones with devices called snap-in muntins. The muntins are made of plastic or wood, painted or coated to match the window frames. They snap onto the back of the window, on the inside, depending on the style of window. You can remove them quickly when you wash the windows, then snap them back into the sash when the glass is clean (Fig. 13.23).

Seen from the inside of a house, muntin inserts are difficult to distinguish from permanent muntins. From the outside, although you might be able to tell that they don't project through the glass, the insets impart an appearance and effect of the real thing at a much lower cost.

EXTERIOR CONTROL OF SUNLIGHT

Regular double- or triple-pane windows, even though they're great for controlling the loss or gain of heat through conductivity, cannot prevent sunrays from entering and heating a room. This is good in winter and bad during summer. There are tinted window coatings that act like tinted glass when applied (as in a car windshield) or, to a certain extent, like sunglasses.

Wide roof overhangs, like wide-brimmed hats, will effectively shade windows facing south. The same overhangs will also admit winter sun that strikes at a much lower angle. Overhangs, though, are not very effective at shielding east and west windows, because the morning and afternoon sun rises and sets at low angles all year round.

Canvas, plastic, or aluminum awnings can successfully provide the overhang needed to shade most windows during warm weather (Fig. 12.24).

Also consider motorized awnings, which can enhance the appearance and comfort of an existing porch, deck, or patio while stopping direct sunlight from hitting windows and raising the house temperature. In addition, they protect carpeting and furniture from sunlight fading and stop the associated degrading effects that gradually weaken the fibers of indoor furnishings. Beyond installing canvas, plastic, or aluminum awnings, deciduous trees can be the answer (Fig. 13.24). Deciduous

FIGURE 13.24

An aluminum awning.

shade trees planted on the south, west, and east sides of a home will provide much appreciated shade during summer, and because they lose their leaves toward the end of each autumn, sunshine will be let through when you need it the most—during winter.

Sun Control Window Film

Window film is a relatively inexpensive feature to consider from day one with your windows. It should be installed and approved by the window manufacturer to protect the window warranty. It's a clear high-tech protective layer that's applied over window glass to increase the window's visual clarity, shatter resistance, and ultraviolet (UV) and other light-blocking ability. The film is treated with a variety of thin metal coatings which result in a wide range of colors or shades, appearances, and performance. Quality sun-control window film has the following features:

- Can block up to 99 percent of the sun's harmful ultraviolet rays. Ultraviolet light causes most of the deterioration and discoloration in furnishings.

- The film also helps block out intense visible light that contributes to fading of more sensitive colors and materials such as natural dyes and fibers or works of art on paper.

- Window film can reduce the amount of solar heat that passes into the home. Solar heat levels build up on and damage furniture and fabrics, which get almost hot to the touch. It causes temperature changes that lead to dryness, warping, and general deterioration—particularly with wood, paper, and natural fabrics.

- Can provide a clear, practically colorless appearance that's critical for a good view—while reducing glare and eye discomfort (similar to what a good pair of sunglasses does for the eyes).

- Is wipable and scratch-resistant.

- Helps holds the glass together if struck, for additional security against violent weather, intruders, and accidental breakage and personal injury.

- Saves energy by reducing cooling needs during summer, and by reflecting heat back inside the home during winter. It effectively increases the insulation value of windows.

INTERNAL CONTROL OF SUNLIGHT

Be aware that curtains and drapes can be purchased with linings that provide considerable insulating values. Look at the options before making a choice. In addition to conventional curtains and draperies, you can also help control energy loss with roll-up shades, honeycomb shades, cellular shades, Venetian blinds, and vertical blinds. Roll-up shades come in many colors, patterns, and textures. The least-expensive ones are made of a thin layer of vinyl. Vinyl-coated cotton shades are better. Fiberglass laminated to vinyl results in the most durable and nicest-looking shades available. While most of these materials are translucent or semitranslucent, some are designed to give complete darkness. Also on the market are shades that are coated on the back to prevent and reflect the incoming sunrays. The alternatives to fabric shades are those constructed of slender strips of wood, metal, or semirigid vinyl.

When choosing blinds, honeycomb shades made of spun polyester are extremely flexible, making them good choices to fit windows with unusual shapes. The combs give this product a distinct look. They do a fine job trapping air for good sound and thermal insulating qualities. Some manufacturers claim R-values as high as 4.8. Cellular shades are also good sound and thermal insulating, while the use of Venetian blinds is another common way of regulating available sunlight (Fig. 13.25). Venetian blinds of horizontal wood, metal, or plastic strips or louvers are made in two basic styles. The standard blind features 2-inch-wide slats held in place by wide cloth tapes. The miniblind has 1-inch-wide slats held by slender cords. Simply because it's made of heavier material, the standard blind is more rugged, flaps less in a breeze, and can be used to darken rooms more effectively. But the miniblind is more attractive in every way, and when it's opened wide, the slats are almost invisible. These and other size units come in a great range of colors and dimensions up to a maximum of about 100 square feet.

Vertical blinds are, in effect, venetian blinds turned on their side (Fig. 13.26). They take the place of draperies and conventional blinds or shades on windows of above-average size and are particularly suited to unusually tall or wide windows. They're ideal for glass sliding doors because they can be set to shut out glare without barring the view, and won't catch in the doors like draperies will.

When choosing blinds, consider the single-cord control, which eliminates the looped cord design. Better yet, some advanced models operate on a remote control system. No cords, no wiring, just batteries. A few even feature a memory stop system to adjust the shades in the same desired position each time.

FIGURE 13.25

A venetian blind.

HEAT LOSS THROUGH WINDOWS

The loss of heat through window openings can be reduced by the following:

- Adding additional layers of glass (storm sashes or panels).

FIGURE 13.26

Vertical blinds.

- Sealing cracks around glass, sashes, and window frames to prevent air infiltration.

- Making sure that weather stripping and thresholds seal the door edges tightly.

- Installing heavy drapes on the inside to trap an additional layer of air next to the glass.

- Providing shelters for window openings in the form of overhangs, baffles, recesses, or plantings.

WINDOW INSTALLATION

- Proper installation will protect the indoors from wind and moisture, and will help lengthen a window's useful lifespan.

- The rough opening for the window should be wrapped with house wrap or prepared using an equally efficient insulation material.

- As the frame is set into the opening, it should be adjusted to be perfectly square, plumb, and level. The distance between the frame sides should be measured precisely to make sure there is no bowing that would result in overly tight or loose sashes.

- After the frame is fastened in place, the top must be flashed with a copper or aluminum cap. To be effective, the cap must extend up under the siding.

- The gap between the window frame and wall frame should be filled with a nonexpanding approved insulation.

WINDOW ENERGY-SAVING CONSIDERATIONS

- Grilles mounted between double-glaze windows eliminate the task of removing and replacing standard grilles whenever the windows need cleaning. With the use of interior grilles, all you do is wipe the glass clean.

- The same goes for blinds that are enclosed between glass layers—their individual slats won't need meticulous cleaning over the years, and they're protected from being accidentally caught and damaged by children, cats, or clumsy bystanders. Cordless models are available in which a sliding handle can raise, lower, and tilt the slats. Some are adjustable by remote control.

- Keeping the glass clean will help take advantage of solar heat in the cold months and will admit higher illumination levels all year around, reducing the need for indoor artificial lighting.

- Double weather-stripped window sashes and compression seals all the way around save energy.

- In warm climates, look for windows with double glazing and spectrally selective coatings that reduce heat gain.

- In climates with both heating and cooling seasons, select windows with both low U-values and low solar heat gain co-efficiencies.

- Another quality to look for in windows is an air-leakage rating of 0.01 to 0.06 cubic feet of air per minute, or less.

- Quality-built windows help your house stay cleaner due to less air infiltration. Humidity is easier to control, and less electricity will be used running vacuums for cleaning.

- Awning windows can stay open through more types of weather without needing to close.

- Windows should be located for cross-ventilation to help reduce cooling system use. Also, try to locate them away from high-noise areas so you will be able to leave them open more often, for longer durations. In general, try to avoid placing windows on the west side in hot-climate locations, and on the north side in cold-climate locales.

- General window features to look for include tilt-in sashes for easy cleaning, removable screens, double- or single-hung or sliding windows with interlocks at the panel's meeting rails to seal out air and water, tempered or "safety" glass for shatter resistance, and fusion-welded frames for superior strength and weather resistance.

- Energy Star labels on the windows mean energy savings at home.

- Multi-pane windows having ⅜- to ½-inch spaces between panes that are filled with low-conductivity inert gas.

- Windows have traditionally been a weak link in a home's exterior when it comes to insulation capabilities. Insist on windows with high R-values (or low U-values). That means storm window arrangements and at least double-pane (and sometimes triplepane) windows made of glazed low-e glass. The *e* stands for *emissivity*, a measure of the ability of glass to reflect or block out long-wave radiant energy or heat and ultraviolet rays. The lower the emissivity, the better the insulating qualities of the glass. Low-e glazing and coatings reduce the fading of furniture, curtains, carpeting, artwork and paints.

- What's next? Researchers have discovered that thin transparent films made from metallic compounds such as nickel hydroxide and titanium dioxide, when sandwiched around window glass, can yield effects similar to those available from "reactive" sunglasses that automatically darken as light levels increase. Simply, these "smart" windows can remain transparent or clear when the sun is low in the sky (or not out at all) and will slowly darken as the sun rises and shines more forcefully later in the day. By blocking out midday heat from the sun, these photochromatic windows will reduce the amount of energy needed to run air-conditioning and cooling units. As the sun sets and outdoor light levels decrease, these windows gradually turn clear again.

▷▷▷▷▷▷ POINTS TO PONDER

1. Windows provide natural lighting, ventilation, passive solar heat, openings for air-conditioning units and fans, visual contact with the outside, and exits during emergencies.
2. Consider the following characteristics when selecting windows: insulating properties, ease of operation, necessary maintenance, simplicity or difficulty to clean, and how the style fits in with the overall exterior schme, and price.
3. Avoid making decisions on window selections mainly on price. Inexpensive windows could really cost literally thousands of dollars worth of unnecessary heat loss over the years.
4. When choosing windows, ask yourself where and how the windows will be used, then match your needs with the most logical window types that will satisfy them.
5. When comparing windows, carefully review their insulating values.
6. All sleeping areas should have at least one easy-to-open window having an opening of not less than 6 to 7 square feet. Check local building codes for the opening height, width, and sill height from the floor.
7. Be aware that the size and placement of windows will limit where you can comfortably arrange furniture.
8. Horizontal window openings are great for controlling light from southern exposures; vertical window openings work well with light from eastern and western exposures.

9. Windows located high in a room offer the most illumination and the deepest penetration by natural light.
10. Clerestories and skylights offer good possibilities for lighting interior spaces in a home.

Doors

There's absolutely no doubt about it. You can't have a house without doors. Even primitive people had them—hides draped from poles or vines. The Egyptians used woven reed mats that rolled up and down, and early Britons employed huge stones that pivoted in a circular fashion. Doors as we know them came into vogue during the Middle Ages—sturdy wooden models held together by strips of wrought iron or tightly fitted dowels.

A door provides a lot more than a simple entrance or exitway in a house. A door is a moving part. It lets in air and seals out weather, dirt, and noise. It takes up space, gets in the way, batters walls and furniture, and gets battered in turn.

Doors protect our privacy and belongings. They keep out the heat and cold and allow ventilation of a closed-in space, even when shut. They provide an access for natural light and bring the outdoors inside. They'll hold warmth-giving heat indoors during winter and cool air in the summer. They'll even pull teeth in a pinch.

When considering the entrances/exits that your house will have, here are some questions to ask yourself about each door:

- Will it operate easily and reliably?

- Will it close securely?

- Will it permit easy passage of people and objects?

- Will it interfere with the use of space on either side of the door?

- Will it effectively close off whatever is supposed to be closed off?

- Will it retard the spread of fire?

- Will it minimize the transmission of sound?

- Will it permit you to see through to the other side?

- Can you hang things on its back side?

- Can it cause injury if someone walks into it?

DOOR TYPES

There are five main types of doors that a house can contain: exterior, interior, storm, patio/garden, and basement.

Exterior Doors

In addition to providing privacy and security, exterior doors can serve as effective weather barriers and sound reducers (Fig. 14.1).

They're about 1¾ inch thick, 3 feet or more wide, and at least 6 feet 8 inches high. There should always be a secure layer of weather stripping around an exterior door's edges to ensure a tight weather seal.

A house's front door deserves extra attention because it's the part of a home visitors see first. The main entrance can make an impression that adds considerably to a dwelling's appearance, and even to the home's value and saleability. Because of the special importance of front doors, they're constructed differently in some respects from just "plain" exterior doors. Details such as door caps, exterior moldings and panels, windows or lights in or to the side of the door, and reeded or fluted pilaster trim at the jambs all help make the front door something to be approached by its own sidewalk, lit up from the outside at night, flanked by landscaped shrubbery beds, and protected by a roof overhang.

Home security should not be forgotten in connection with any exterior doors. Security means a combination of the proper door locks and

Exterior doors.

hardware plus the ability to see who is calling before the door is opened. One way that front entrance visibility can be accomplished is by the installation of sidelights. Sidelights are narrow glass panes or panels that run the height of an entrance door, placed either at one or both sides of the door for added beauty and natural light. Two draw-backs are their relatively poor insulation value and their susceptibility to intruders who, if the sidelights are not positioned correctly in rela-tion to the door's locks, can break the glass then reach inside to unlock the door. Sidelights vary in size, but are normally less than 1 foot wide. They're available in many finishes and textures, some with low-e insu-lated glass for increased energy efficiency.

If there are no see-through sidelights, opt for a peephole to see who's outside before opening the door. Electronic touch pad and remote-type entrance locks are available that eliminate fumbling for keys at night.

FIGURE 14.2

A louvered door.

For a side door or rear door having large clear energy-efficient glass panes, consider a unit with built-in blinds. Because the blinds are sealed between tempered safety glass, there's no dusting or cleaning of the individual slats; they should operate for years with practically no maintenance involved. Such inside-the-door or -window blinds will tilt a full 180 degrees, which allows you to control sunlight levels and privacy with fingertip adjustment. Some units even come with an option that enables raising or lowering the slats just like that of a traditional blind.

Interior Doors

Interior doors exist mainly for privacy and noise reduction. To be effective for each, they must be well fitted. However, if the house heating system depends on a free flow of air from room to room, interior doors should be undercut at least ½ inch above the finished floors to permit air passage. Although this doesn't apply to areas having their own air supply and return outlets, remember that door fit is still important. You don't want doors to work too tightly, especially over carpeting, because large amounts of friction will be created when the doors are opened and closed.

Interior doors are available, in addition to flush and paneled models, in full louvered, top and bottom louvered, or partially louvered with either a top or bottom of paneling (Fig. 14.2). Louvered doors, while more expensive than flush or paneled doors, are particularly useful in locations requiring a free flow of air—namely closets or rooms containing mechanical equipment that must "breathe" to operate safely and efficiently, such as water heaters and certain heating units and furnaces.

Storm Doors

If you elect to include an enclosed patio that leads to your back or side door, it will provide an efficient air lock when you enter the house from there during cold weather. Otherwise, storm doors provide protection from harsh weather and direct sunlight for your primary doors.

They supply additional security, offer natural ventilation in the summer, and help control heat loss and drafts during winter and cool air loss during summer (Fig. 14.3), when, in both seasons, the storm door creates an insulating dead air space around the main door it protects. Most storm doors are designed for easy changeovers from screens in summer, with fiberglass or other screening that will not rust or corrode, to energy-efficient glass inserts during winter. A storm door is nothing to skimp on: good styling on the front entrance storm door can add a lot to the appearance of a house, and can also cover up a nondescript front door.

When selecting your storm doors look for the following:

FIGURE 14.3

A storm door.

- The main frames and frames for the glass and screen inserts should be strong. If you can easily bend or flex the frames, they're too weak to make an adequate door.

- A wrought-iron door with deadbolts and heavy hinges makes a secure and decorative storm door. But well-constructed storm doors are available in many materials as well, including wood, aluminum, steel, and fiberglass.

- Doors having a foam insulation core between their outer panels or skins are very efficient. This sandwich-style construction forms a rigid door with airtight seals, some with refrigerator-type magnetic closure strips.

- A functional design will typically enable you to remove the glass and screen inserts from the inside of the house, in a simple manner. Separate screen doors with particleboard or wood cores beneath their outer skins are rigid and durable.

- A front storm door with a lot of screen/glass having attractive bevels, or stained glass provides efficient ventilation and an attractive entrance.

Home's Appearance

The most decorative glass panes are beveled, etched, frosted, colored, or accented with brass and other accompaniments. Smaller windows, such as ornate ovals, are energy efficient. Low-emissivity glass with insulating inert argon gas in the gap is one of the most energy-efficient panes available.

- For the front storm door, select glass that helps enhance the apearance. In some models, the decorative glass panes are further sandwiched between two outer panes, creating additional insulating air gaps.

- For a functional rear screen door, consider a unit having less glass and an extra-strong frame. In hot climates, tinted glass panes will help your air conditioner.

- Look for weather tightness to prevent the entrance of water, cold air, dust, and insects. A triple-track system is one of the best designs, especially for the back storm door. If you lower the top glass and raise the bottom glass panels a little, it creates a natural air current ventilation path. With such a system, you never need to remove the screen or glass panels.

- For ease of maintenance, a storm door with a self-storing glass or screen has less glass area, so that the glass or screen panel can be slipped down and hidden inside the door.

- Make sure storm doors have easy-to-work locking mechanisms. Some of the most secure units feature decorative wrought-iron or aluminum channels, reinforced latches, anti-theft stops, deadbolt pins resembling the pins from bank vaults, and non-removable pin hinges. In addition, there is an increasing demand for storm doors having keyed deadbolts that you can lock from the outside for additional security.

Screening

Retractable Screen Systems

In our ever-present quest to save energy whenever possible, consider that improving natural ventilation instead of using air conditioning can help lower utility bills and improve indoor air quality. Enter retractable screen systems.

Retractable screen systems feature a narrow tubular housing mounted vertically on a door frame (Figure 14.4). One small aluminum track is attached to the floor, and another to the top of the door opening. A magnetic latch is fixed on the other side of the door opening, as seen in the illustration. When you open the door to go in or out, or just for ventilation, you pull the handle on the screen that's coiled up within the cassette housing. The screen unrolls from the cassette housing and adheres to the magnetic latch; there is a slight spring tension on the screening to keep it taut and attractive. Premium screening kits use ball bearings in the cassette for smoother operation. Nylon or other reinforcement strips along the upper and lower edges of the screen increase the unit's durability.

SUN AND PET CONTROL SCREENING

This screen material can be used to block intense summer sunlight when a window is open and also when the same window is closed, since the screening is located on the outside of the window. A durable woven vinyl-coated fiberglass product, its ribbed weave is designed to block up to 70 percent of the sunlight's heat and glare. In addition to reducing the amount of solar heat gain (and keeping insects out) during summer, it can also reduce heat loss during winter. Another handy option for pet lovers is special dog- and cat-resistant screening made of special vinyl coated polyester. It's about seven times more tear-resistant than ordinary screening.

Awnings

An alternative to a storm door is a retractable awning, installed above its companion exterior door. Many retractable awning models open or close in just a few

FIGURE 14.4

A retractable screen.

seconds. An awning can protect the door from rain and sun. It can keep the outer surface of the exterior door from not getting wet— which also prevents water from dripping off the door onto the interior floor each time the door is opened when wet. An awning will give you the chance to open an umbrella as you first go outdoors, and an opportunity to be out of the rain as you unlock the door to go inside.

Patio/Garden Doors

Sliding glass doors and French doors will bring the outdoors inside and will provide convenient access to a patio, deck, or garden. They'll make whatever room they're part of appear larger than it really is, and they'll supply a flood of natural air and light when their screens are in play. Practically any house built today will use one of these doors somewhere within its walls (Fig. 14.5).

FIGURE 14.5

A glass sliding patio door.

Factors to consider when selecting patio/garden doors are thermal insulation quality, weather tightness, a secure locking system, and a nice appearance.

Sliding glass doors are generally the bypass type. All units include at least one fixed and one sliding panel. Some three-panel models are available having a center panel that slides open in one direction. For larger wall spans, four-panel models can be installed having two center panels opening in opposite directions to make a convenient access to large decks or patios. Sliding glass doors cover a large span, so the strength of the frame is critical. Typical frame material options include fiberglass, vinyl, wood, vinyl- or aluminum-clad wood or aluminum. Wood frames allow for a great range of styles and contours; they should come treated with a water-repellant coating.

Fiberglass frames are very energy efficient, easy to maintain, durable, and can be easily painted. Fiberglass expands and contracts with temperature changes at a similar rate as the glass panes. This reduces stress within the door and results in a long-term airtight seal that helps prevent fogging. Fiberglass or vinyl frames should contain foam or similar insulation inside the cavities for improved comfort and lower utility bills. For a wood door appearance, select a model having real oak or other veneer fastened to the fiberglass. A patio door has a large amount of glass area compared to the frame area, so the type of glass you select has a greater impact on energy efficiency than does the frame material. For hot climate locations, consider doors with tinted glass. For cold climate locations, opt for triple pane systems with low-e glass.

French doors generally have a single panel that swings while the other panel remains stationary (Fig. 14.6). Their wide frames are attractive, strong, and can be energy efficient because there is less glass area to lose or gain heat through. Grids inside the panels have thick rails, stiles and transoms, with stained, beveled or etched thermal glass. For exterior wood French doors, look for units that have a waterproof material inserted in the bottom of each door stile to prevent moisture damage. The block is covered by veneer so you can't see it, and the bottom rail and stile secured with glue and dowel pins. The bottom rail needs to be sealed with waterproof material.

FIGURE 14.6

French doors.

Basement Doors

Outside basement doors allow you to transport such items as screens, storm windows, and garden tools inside and out without lugging them through the living areas. As mentioned earlier, basement doors are ideal for lower-level laundry rooms and will provide children with a means of getting to the back and side yards without having to pass through the rest of the house. A basement door should be at least 36 inches wide to accommodate large appliances.

Although basement doors should be able to effectively withstand the weather and provide security against theft by themselves, attractive basement stairwell covers can be purchased in ready-to-install packages for use in all types of houses. They're typically steel double door covers that enclose and protect the outer stairwells leading to basement doors.

DOOR STYLES

There are six basic styles of doors used throughout today's modern house: hinged, bifold, sliding, pocket, folding, and cafe.

Hinged Doors

A hinged door is essentially a simple rigid panel that swings open and closed on hinges. It's the most common type of door. Hinged doors come in several architectural styles: flush, contemporary, Colonial (six-panel), and glass (Fig. 14.7).

SOLID FULL LENGTH - 3 HINGES

FLUSH   CONTEMPORARY   COLONIAL WITH GLASS

FIGURE 14.7

Hinged doors.

Advantages

1. When closed, hinged doors seal very well, curbing energy loss and limiting the amount of sound transmission.

2. They're initially one of the least costly type of doors to purchase and hang.

3. They require a minimum amount of maintenance and cleaning.

4. They're great for providing (on their back sides) space for door-hung shoe racks, necktie racks, belt racks, and for fastening all-purpose hooks to.

Disadvantages

1. They take up precious room to swing in. Consequently, they can't be used where there's an obstacle in the way of their swing.

Bifold Doors

Bifold doors are similar to those used in telephone booths, except house bifolds open outward (Fig. 14.8). They're used indoors only, because there is no way to seal the cracks around their edges. The most

FIGURE 14.8

Folding doors.

common bifold door consists of two fairly narrow vertical panels that are hinged together. One panel pivots next to the door jamb; the other glides in an overhead track. To open a bifold door, you either shove the track-mounted panel toward the opposite door jamb or pull the knobs fastened to the panels near the hinged edges. Both methods of opening force the panels to fold together back-to-back at right angles to the doorway opening.

For small openings, a single bifold door with two narrow panels is adequate. For larger openings, the door is made with wider panels or a double bifold door is employed having four panels hinged together. These doors are designed to be operated from one side only and are best suited for closets. They're useful in providing wide door opening coverage to shallow closets, making the most of the available square footage.

Advantages

1. When both sections of a bifold door are completely opened, you have an almost clear view through the doorway. Or, you can have access to one-half of the same closet without disturbing the door covering the other half.

2. Bifold doors are ideal in cases where there is little room to swing a regular door outward.

3. They allow the maximum opening to a closet with the minimum extension into the room. Extending the height of the doors a full 8 feet to the ceiling eliminates headers and permits full-width shelves and access to the upper area which would otherwise be lost.

4. In walk-in closets, space used for the "walking in" cannot be used for storage. In shallow closets with bifold doors, however, the users do not enter the closets—so almost all of the space within is available for storage.

5. Bifold doors come in styles that include solid or louvered panels. The louvered doors have a beautiful appearance that alone makes them popular with many homeowners.

Disdvantages

1. Bifold doors can come untracked or malfunction easier than simple hinged-hung doors can. They won't take the abuse that other types of doors can take.

2. Bifold doors are somewhat more expensive than their counterparts.

3. Bifold doors cannot be used where a tight weather seal is required, nor where the door must be operated from two sides.

4. Bifold louvered doors are time-consuming to clean and difficult to repaint or resurface because of the many individual slats.

Sliding Doors

Sliding doors consist of usually two and sometimes three door panels that slide by each other (Fig. 14.9). These units hang from and

FIGURE 14.9

Sliding doors.

move along double or triple tracks installed against the underside of conventional head jambs. To prevent operating problems, sliding doors made of glass should be of top-quality construction with sturdy tracks, double or insulated shatterproof glass, and mohair or other stripping laid along the door's tubing edges for maximum insulation.

Advantages

1. Sliding doors can be used wherever doors are needed, but door swing space or projections are not permitted.

2. Sliding doors are easily maintained and cleaned.

3. Glass sliding doors are wonderful for expanding a view and for making rooms seem a lot larger than they really are.

Disdvantages

1. Sliding doors give access to only half (or when three doors are involved, to one-third) of an opening at once.

2. These doors are sensitive to any settling that might occur in a house. The sliding doors can stick against the bottom floor guide, which causes the doors to ride up and either jump or damage the hanging tracks and trolleys.

3. Sometimes the screen inserts to glass sliding doors can be a nuisance if they're not fitted exactly because they tend to pop out of their tracks.

4. A cheaply made closet sliding door, when handled gently, will do the job, but a cheaply made glass slider that isn't weather tight and fitted correctly will let in a lot of cold or hot air and can be difficult to operate.

Pocket Doors

A pocket door slides in and out of a pocket built into the wall framing of partition walls. Their use with load-bearing walls is usually

TOP VIEW

FIGURE 14.10

A pocket door.

impractical. One excellent use is with a small bathroom or mudroom, to prevent the room's occupant from having to squeeze around the door. (Fig. 14.10).

These space-savers can have silent-action rollers and rubber stopping bumpers inside the pockets so the doors will work without clatter. A pocket door recedes or slides in and out of a pocket built into the wall framing, instead of swinging out in an arc like a hinged door does. Standard hinged doors waste a lot of space; they take away from possible furniture placements, picture hanging, shelving installations, and the like.

A well-placed pocket door will save roughly 8 to 10 square feet of floor space. Also, while pocket doors themselves may not directly lower your utility costs, they will allow you to build a smaller square footage house that provides the same usable amount of floor space. A smaller house has less wall and roof footage, thus less area to heat and cool.

Another energy benefit of pocket doors is that they allow heating and cooling systems to operate more efficiently because when you open a pocket door there is no restriction to air movement, allowing better circulation. Standard hinged doors can hinder air movement and cause (however slightly) heating and cooling systems to work harder. Manufacturers offer beautiful wood pocket doors made from oak, cherry, walnut, and others, supported by sturdy steel-reinforced split studs.

Advantages

1. Pocket doors are useful in locations where there is little room to swing a standard hinged door out of the way due to interference with traffic or the operation of other doors.

2. When open, pocket doors are completely out of the way (disappeared into a wall). They take up no floor or wall space and they don't obstruct the door opening even a fraction of an inch.

Disdvantages

1. Pocket doors should be installed only in partition walls, not walls that are load bearing.

2. A wall that has a door pocket built into it should not contain electric wiring in that section of wall. You'll have to place electrical outlets and the light switch on the other side of the doorway.

3. Avoid locating a pocket door in a wall that will be tiled. Vibrations from frequent opening and closing of the door could eventually crack the grout and loosen the tiles.

Folding Doors

Folding doors are made of many thin, narrow vertical strips or creases that fold back-to-back into a compact bundle when the doors are pushed open (Fig. 14.11). The simplest folding models have very small strips that are tied together with cords. Most, however, have wooden or metal slats about 4 inches wide that are hinged together with vinyl fabric. In all cases, these doors hang from and run in a track. They open and close between the door opening's side jambs.

The main applications for folding doors are in closets, laundry niches, and some storage pantry-like areas in the garage, basement, or hallways. They can also be used to divide large open spaces into two smaller rooms.

Advantages

1. They don't swing out or protrude from doorway openings. Their accordion sections fold up into a small bundle when opened.

Disdvantages

1. Folding doors give scant protection against fire and noise.

2. They don't operate very smoothly. They're not made as sturdily as other doors and cannot stand heavy use well.

3. A main objection of homeowners is that folding doors *don't* look like doors. Rather, they resemble stiff draperies. Folding doors are generally neither strong nor secure and they have a tendency to wave in a strong draft.

Cafe Doors

These are the doors you've probably seen a thousand gunslingers walk through, into television and theater saloons. They're the double swinging doors on the

OPEN

CLOSED

FIGURE 14.11

Folding doors.

FIGURE 14.12

Cafe doors.

short side—about 30 to 60 inches long—installed on opposite sides of an opening roughly midway between the top and bottom of a passageway (Fig. 14.12). They're attached to the opening's walls or jambs with gravity pivot hinges that enable the doors to be pushed open in either direction, only to be closed automatically once a person passes through them. Cafe doors are available in both louvered and paneled designs.

Because you can push your way through them without using your hands, these doors come in handy in places where you're likely to have your hands full, such as between a kitchen and dining room, where the cook is likely to shoulder his or her way from the kitchen carrying a holiday turkey. Cafe doors don't provide much privacy from noise or odors (then again, who wants to hide the delicious smells that waft from a kitchen stove?), but they will block the sight of stacks of dirty dishes in the kitchen sink from guests in the dining room.

Advantages

1. They're inexpensive and easy to install.

2. They're simple to use.

3. They add a unique and attractive character to the interior of a home.

Disdvantages

1. They provide little protection from fire and noise.

2. Because people are constantly pushing against them, they're difficult to keep clean. If louvered, they're time-consuming to wash or resurface.

3. Children can be injured running in and out of them.

DOOR OPENINGS

Door openings are permanent features of a house that should be well thought out in advance. Here are some pointers to consider:

1. Door opening heights should be a minimum of 6 feet 8 inches or 7 feet. For greater flexibility, though, consider a front door opening that's 8 feet tall and 42 inches wide, for moving large pieces of furniture through. An alternative is to select a door having a decorative side light panel that opens. The extra 14 inches or so will greatly save time that would otherwise be spent by movers who must carefully lift and manipulate large furniture pieces sideways, backwards, or upside down.

2. A front door should be a minimum of 36 inches wide—which is still a tight fit for numerous oversize pieces of furniture available on the market today. If the front door width is any less, then the house should have another outside door at least 36 inches wide so you'll have the ability to move large items in and out. The recommended thickness of a 36-inch+ exterior door is at least 1¾ inches.

3. Secondary outside door openings to a basement, kitchen, laundry, or garage can be 32 inches wide, with thicknesses of 1⅜ inches.

4. If you happen to position a bedroom door at a right angle to the end of a hallway, make sure the hallway is extra wide, and the door opening is 36 inches, or you'll never be able to maneuver large pieces of furniture such as dressers and headboards into the room.

5. Consider each individual passageway if you want interior doors to open inward or outward, as safety and convenience dictate. Basement stairway doors should always open away from the stairs.

6. When planning patio/garden openings, figure that they consist of sliding and stationary glass panels with widths of at least 36 inches per panel.

HINGED DOORS

Because hinged doors are used in every house in some fashion, exterior or interior, they deserve additional comment:

1. They are easier to open and close than all other doors except swinging cafe doors.

2. They permit you to use their backsides for storage space, a major advantage in closets.

3. Their operation is noiseless except when slammed.

4. When properly hung, exterior models close tightly and stop drafts, dirt, and insects from penetrating around the edges.

5. Exterior and interior doors should be hung with three hinges. Ball-bearing hinges typically provide the smoothest operation. The middle hinge helps support the door while maintaining correct alignment. At the same time, on hollow doors there is typically a horizontal reinforcement board placed through the door center to provide a sturdy base or support for the doorknob hardware. If you plan to install a doorstop with a hollow door, position the stop where that center reinforcement board runs. If the doorstop is placed elsewhere, it may punch a hole in the unsupported facing.

6. Interior doors should swing into the rooms they close off from hallways. Otherwise they interfere with hallway traffic.

7. Doors on hall closets must obviously swing into the hall, however, and it's often advisable to swing a kitchen door into a hall so it doesn't create traffic problems within the kitchen work areas.

8. Whenever possible, bathroom doors should swing in; but if the bathroom is too cramped, the door can be hung to swing outward.

9. Doors between adjoining rooms other than bathrooms can be swung whichever way will cause the least inconvenience.

10. Doors at the head of stairways must swing away from the stairs.

11. Whether a door should be hinged on the right or left depends on which position will interfere less with furniture placements and passage through the doorway.

12. Ideally, storm doors should be placed so that they can swing back into a corner out of the way.

13. Every exterior hinged door (and other types for that matter)— front, back, or side—should have a step down to the outside, a sill

forming the bottom part of the frame and entrance. This 8-inch step down is to prevent water from entering the house during heavy rains or snows.

PET DOORS

In warm-climate regions if you own a dog or cat, you might consider installing a pet door next to one of your side or rear entrances (Fig. 14.13). Several companies manufacture ready-to-install units that are two-way, self-closing, silent, chewproof, energy efficient (fitted with a weather seal), and lockable.

The main reason that pet doors are energy efficient is because a pet exiting and entering through a small pet door prevents the full-size exterior door from opening for those same tasks. A full-size exterior door opening allows a substantial amount of heated or cooled air to escape outdoors. Then whatever conditioned air is lost must be replaced, thus increasing energy usage and cost. Units are also available with foam insulation inside the metal rise and the height adjustment components for further energy savings and noise reduction.

Consider that pet doors are available for practically any situation, even panels constructed to fit in a glass or screen door track, as are units available having ½-inch dual pane insulated glass with foam weather stripping on both edges. Some models have a locking steel close-off cover that keeps animals in or out. A pin lock is available for security.

FIGURE 14.13

Pet door.

Advantages

1. You needn't be present to let your pet in and out during the day or night.

2. You needn't worry about heating or cooling the great outdoors by leaving a front or rear door propped open while you peer into the darkness and whistle for your pet to come home.

Disadvantage

1. What might happen if your neighbors install the same types of door for their pets?

PET DOOR CONSIDERATIONS

■ Units can be purchased that mount between 2 by 4 or 2 by 6 framing studs. Other designs include units that are complete panels which mount in a sliding glass patio door track with a pet door built in at the bottom. Units are also on the market to custom-frame in an irregularly sized door.

■ The pet door or panel should have a fully weather stripped, soft, two-way flexible flap, with magnetic closures to keep the flap secure, or an electromagnetic release equipped with two collar keys that have a beeper to indicate when a unit's battery is running low. A collar key is a tiny device that attaches to the pet's collar—typically operates on two AA batteries. Without a signal from the key, the pet door will not open. This system effectively keeps out neighbor's pets, plus squirrels, rodents, and other wild animals.

■ Some models have settings such as "In Only," "Out Only," "Locked," or "Full Open," in case special circumstances arise, such as your cousin visiting with his or her pet that also needs to go in and out throughout the day.

■ Several units come with an "in/out" indicator that lets you know which way the pet went last: in or out.

■ A "break-in" alarm is available on some models, which goes off or "chirps" if the pet door is forced open or smashed in.

■ Some manufacturers claim their doors will help wipe off mosquitoes and other bugs as the pets come and go.

DOOR CONSTRUCTION

The construction of interior and exterior doors is substantially different from one another (Fig. 14.14).

Interior Doors

Interior doors can be built out of wood, plastic, metal, or any combination thereof. A solid wood door is the best and most expensive interior door available. Solid wood doors do a good job controlling sound between rooms. They are made by sandwiching a wooden core between two sheets of high-quality hardwood veneer such as birch, oak, mahogany, or pine. Lighter-duty hollow-core doors can have the same expensive veneer faces, but sheets of sturdy wood-grain plastic also make a practical, easy-to-clean surface. The lowest-priced hollow-core models are frequently covered with less durable wood composition board.

When selecting door veneers, keep in mind that birch and oak doors hold up better than mahogany or pine. Oak and birch are harder woods that can resist greater impacts.

FIGURE 14.14

Door construction.

Exterior Doors

Exterior doors can be categorized as wood, steel, and composition patio doors.

THRESHOLDS AND SILLS

No matter what kind of door it is, a sturdy threshold is needed. Door models having an adjustable threshold are excellent choices. An adjustable threshold can be easily adjusted up or down with a screw driver—which can help make and keep the door airtight, quiet and energy efficient while sealing out dust, dirt, moisture, and drafts (Fig. 14.15). At the same time, located on the bottom of exterior doors, a multi-fin threshold seal provides further defense against air penetration (Fig. 14.16). For ultimate protection in high exposure severe weather areas, look for a composite substrate bumper swing-out sill.

FIGURE 14.15

An adjustable threshold.

FIGURE 14.16

A multi-fin threshold.

The accompanying seal increases with pressure against the door to keep out air and water. When an exterior door is installed, it's critical that a generous amount of caulk be applied beneath the door's threshold, with a few beads run on top of the sill plate, and that insulation is carefully placed around the rest of the door frame to keep out drafts.

EXTERIOR WOOD DOORS

There are two basic styles of exterior wood doors: flush and paneled. Flush doors are simple flat-surfaced doors that can be constructed with particleboard cores between two outer surfaces of a durable wood such as a high-grade fir, or a solid lumber core between the two outer faces. The latter are much stronger—a better choice, and the most expensive. Paneled doors have decorative designs cut into them. Both flush and paneled models can be made with various amounts and shapes of glass inserts. If you desire the highest insulating efficiency along with the beauty of real wood, several manufacturers produce real wood exterior doors having insulated cores, and, for a weather-tight fit, triple weather strip seals. There are even models featuring engineered wood for additional strength.

Advantages

1. They're beautiful, particularly when stained to show off their grain.

2. They lend themselves to an infinite variety of designs and can even be customized by a manufacturer to your specifications.

3. They can be sawed and planed to fit existing door openings or new openings that are not carefully made, or openings that later warp because of settling.

4. Solid-core and insulation-core wooden doors have good insulating qualities and are relatively soundproof.

Disdvantages

1. If not taken care of, they may expand, warp, crack, shrink, and cause sealing problems.

2. They must be periodically refinished.

3. Wood doors are combustible.

EXTERIOR STEEL DOORS

Most steel doors are really part steel and part wood: steel sheets fabricated around a wooden frame in which urethane foam or another insulation material is sandwiched to provide outstanding protection against cold and heat.

Steel doors are more practical than doors made of wood. They're designed to prevent the principal cause of wood door failures—warpage that results in improper closure and air infiltration. They also resist cracking, splitting, splintering, shrinking, and bowing. Newer door frames provide a thermal break between interior parts and exterior surfaces, eliminating winter condensation inside.

Other features that apply to many steel door models are adjustable thermal-break thresholds, magnetic weather stripping for uniform sealing, and fire-resistant qualities that result in excellent safety ratings. The steel-skin design makes these doors efficient and maintenance free, with the thickness of the steel skin and door width being fairly good indicators of overall door quality. Thicker steel provides better stability and dent resistance and offers considerable protection against intruders.

Remember, when comparing steel doors, a lower gauge number represents a thicker steel skin. Partly for security and partly to maintain a tight fit, units are available with a multipoint deadbolt lock—the deadbolt engages the door's frame in three locations from top to bottom, operated by a sturdy rack and pinion system hidden inside the door. Another safety feature of quality steel doors is a rugged heavy wood lock block. The insulated foam placed in the hollow can provide insulating values of R-14 and greater.

Exterior steel doors come in many styles and finishes and are commonly fitted with glass inserts and peepholes for viewing. They're also available with real natural oak and other veneers permanently bonded to the steel skin all sandwiched around a core of insulation. The steel doors with magnetic gaskets along their edges grip like seals on a refrigerator door give the tightest seal against the weather. For ease of installation, they're available with integrated framing systems that coordinate framing components, sills, door bottoms, corner pads, and weather stripping as a single packaged unit, completely pre-hung with hinges. The cost of steel doors is quite competitive with those made of wood.

Make sure that any steel door you buy is predrilled by the supplier to accept the door hardware (handles, knobs, and locks) you desire. If you don't, it could cost you extra to have it done at the job site because some carpenters don't have the right tools to drill this type of door.

Advantages

1. They provide an excellent seal against air infiltration; some have magnetic seals.

2. They're well insulated.

3. They're difficult to force open, cut open, or break through.

4. They're not affected by moisture and won't crack, rot, or warp.

5. They're fire resistant.

6. Plastic decorator panels are available for some steel door models to provide elaborate and varied finishes.

7. They come in 20-gauge, dent-resistant wood-grain finishes that are stainable to achieve the warm look of wood.

8. Steel doors can be purchased with stained wood, steel, or vinyl-coated aluminum.

9. Steel doors are available with fully adjustable oak or vinyl caps to provide energy-efficient fits.

10. Multiple-blade sweeps (on door bottoms) eliminate drafts.

Disdvantages

1. They come in standard sizes and are not easily adjusted to slightly uneven openings or odd-sized openings.

EXTERIOR FIBERGLASS AND CARBON DOORS

Factory-finished or stainable fiberglass and carbon doors have sturdy construction and a foam core that gives them high insulating values. These doors will hardly shrink or expand with changing seasons, maintaining a tight air and moisture seal that is often further ensured by the use of magnetic weather stripping with brass-plated steel trim strips inlaid in the door's edge. Of the two, carbon expands or contracts less with temperature changes, making a tighter seal.

Carbon door skins also require less forming pressure during the manufacturing process, so the surface remains more porous and able to take stain very well. Triple-locking mechanisms with heavy-duty blocks such as those found on better wood and steel doors are also available on fiberglass and carbon door models.

COMPOSITE PATIO DOORS

Patio doors are typically sliding glass doors framed with steel, aluminum, or wood, or French doors that provide access to a patio, porch, deck, or garden. The wood frames are frequently clad in vinyl to eliminate the need to repaint or refinish the wood.

Double- or triple-pane glass that has a good insulating value should be used in these doors, and weather stripping must be included along the door edges. Design improvements have separated the inner and outer faces so that the frames will not easily transmit heat or cold.

Advantages

1. Glass allows a view of the outside surroundings.

2. They require very little maintenance.

3. They're great if lots of light and sunshine are desired.

Disdvantages

1. They're easy to force open if proper precautions are not taken.

2. Poorly constructed ones will sweat.

3. When constructed without thermal-type double or better glass, they have poor insulating value.

4. Even with the better patio doors, the wear and tear caused by the regular door movement across the sealing material is prone to leaks in the sealing that will allow air and moisture infiltration.

GENERAL DOOR CONSIDERATIONS

Make sure you check the operation of each door after the doors are installed. Because doors are used so often, minor imperfections or operating deficiencies can become very annoying.

See that:

- All knobs, locks, and deadbolts work properly, without sticking, and that doorknobs and latches line up with latch inserts. You shouldn't have to yank a door closed to latch it, or push downward or upward on the handle to engage the latch. This is especially important for a basement door. If it won't close securely, a small child could open it and fall down the stairway.

- Doors hang level, with hinges that don't squeak or bind. All doors should swing freely, without noise or obvious friction. The door installation must be square, with an even gap between the door frame from top to bottom.

- Opened doors should hold their position and not swing closed or farther open by themselves.

- Door frame and casing nails should be set below the wood surface and puttied.

■ There should be no leaks around the weatherstripping or thresholds.

■ When choosing interior doors, you can increase the appearance of interior lighting while making the room look larger by selecting mirrored doors. Interior doors are available having a mirror built into one side. Mirrors reflect lighting, so the lighting travels around the room farther, illuminating things on its way. At least one manufacturer offers mirrored doors with framed and frameless mirrors on doors that swing, slide, and bi-fold open and closed.

■ At times, we all receive unwanted visitors at our front door. During summer or winter, heated or cooled air is lost when the front door is opened so that unrequested solicitors can be spoken with or asked to leave. For safety's sake, and to limit the need for opening the door unnecessarily, consider the installation of a wide-angle peephole. Models are available that offer excellent views of the outside. One unit even projects the view onto a screen that's several inches wide.

■ To protect a door's integrity, install a door stopper that will protect both the door and its adjacent wall. Look for a model that does not put pressure on the door itself.

■ For exterior doors, consider a built-in battery-operated burglar alarm that, when the door is locked, any shaking of the door sets off an audible alarm for a short time. The alarm sensitivity level can be adjusted.

▶▶▶▶▶ POINTS TO PONDER

1. When selecting a door, ask yourself if it will operate easily and reliably, close securely, interfere with the use of space on either side of itself, retard the spread of fire, deaden sound, and allow you to see to the other side.

2. A home's front door is often the first thing a visitor (or potential buyer) sees. It helps form an impression of the rest of the home, for good or for worse. In short, the main entrance can make an impression that adds considerably to a dwelling's appearance and even to the home's value and saleability.

3. A little extra invested for a unique entrance door that's more attractive than those typically found with comparable homes will be worth it in the short and long run.

4. Storm doors for all outside entrances/exits are a must in cold climate locations, and also desirable in warmer locations because they can help conserve cool air, screen out insects, and provide ventilation.

5. If you've ever seen or had a child accidentally run through the regular glass panel of a storm door, you know why only safety glass should be used with storm doors.

6. Pocket doors, once popular years ago, are useful in locations where there is little room to swing a standard hinged door out of the way due to interference with traffic or the operation of other doors.

7. For security's sake, exterior hinged doors must have standard hinges positioned on the interior side of the door so that the pins can't be removed by a potential intruder to gain access.

8. Make sure that all latch mechanisms line up correctly with their matching plates, so the doors can be positively closed and won't accidentally swing open in response to window or fan drafts or pets or toddlers pushing on them. This is especially important with bathroom and basement doors.

9. For ease of operation, European-type latch handles provide greater leverage and a more comfortable grip than do round doorknobs.

10. Bifold doors are ideal for closets. They allow a maximum opening with minimum extension into the room. Extending the height of the doors a full 8 feet to the ceiling eliminates the need for headers and permits full-width shelves and access to the upper area that would otherwise be lost.

Garages

The garage is not often given the attention it deserves by the typical homeowner. A brief analysis of the situation reveals no sound reason to skimp when it comes to this important part of a house. To be sure, many owners don't realize that a garage costs considerably less per square foot than the rest of the house: it doesn't have as much electrical, plumbing, lighting, or floor or interior wall finishing costs. Consequently, instead of being stingy with your garage money, you're better off building one a little larger than you initially want. It won't cost much more (Fig. 15.1).

When you do plan your garage, here are some ideas to keep in mind:

1. Few garages built today are constructed apart from the house. The conveniences of initial construction, maintenance, and home-owner traffic patterns of an attached garage far outweigh the disadvantages.

2. However, an attached garage requires safety features not necessary in detached models. In some locations, the ceiling and wall connecting the garage and house must be plaster, masonry, or some other fire-retardant material, and the door from the garage to house must be solid wood or covered with sheet metal.

FIGURE 15.1

A view of a garage interior.

3. One disadvantage with attached garages is that carbon monoxide fumes can gather within them and seep into the house's living quarters. Carbon monoxide fumes are heavier than air and can travel into a basement or lower living level if the garage is on that same level or higher. To prevent this from happening, your building code will state the required stepdown measurement from the house to the garage. A curb can also be a partial remedy. In any case, if you plan a house with an attached garage, realize that there will always be a potential danger with exhaust fumes if a car is allowed to idle in the garage with the garage door closed.

4. Request a minimum of two electrical wall outlets in the garage, as well as an outlet or outlets centered above the overhead garage door(s) so you can put up automatic door openers at a later date if desired.

5. Besides having at least two overhead lights installed in the main level of the garage, if there's a garage attic in your plan, specify a light fixture there also.

6. Provide adequate ventilation in any garage attic.

7. If you want to heat the garage, have the outer walls as well as those of adjoining living spaces insulated.

8. Proper flashing should be installed between the garage roof and the wall of the house, or vice versa, to prevent water seepage there.

9. If the back of a fireplace chimney will protrude into the garage, make sure you take this into consideration when planning the garage's length.

10. To keep out the elements, soil, and energy-wasting summer and winter temperatures, make certain that the garage car doors will seal tightly against the floor and sides of their tracks when closed.

11. For appearance's sake, specify if you desire the trim around the car doors to have "cut corners" at the top. This can add an interesting flair to a garage for a minimum cost.

12. If you're having a two-car garage, decide if you'd prefer two separate car doors or a single larger model. Two doors might look more attractive, but they require two separate door openers and need a support post in the center, which reduces the opening clearance that might be wanted for maneuvering a boat trailer in. Such a center post between two doors can also become an expensive obstacle for inexperienced drivers to crunch into.

13. A single-car garage should be no smaller than 12 feet by 14 feet to provide enough space for an automobile plus general equipment such as lawn mowers, snowblowers, ladders, garbage cans, bicycles, and other sports items. A two-car garage should be at least 24 feet by 24 feet to comfortably handle two autos and equipment storage. The ceiling height in either case should be at least 12 feet, with plenty of room to install an electric garage door opener.

14. Have a water faucet installed somewhere inside the garage. The best place is usually on a common wall with the living quarters of the home, to avoid winter pipeline freeze. An ideal arrangement is a utility sink center. A utility sink center will allow you to complete cleanup chores before going into the living areas of the house. This includes messy tasks such as bathing a pet and washing off fruit, tools, greasy hands, or clothes. A variety of units are available. An inexpensive one that does a good job is a plastic sink 24 inches wide, 24 inches long, and 12 inches deep.

15. A telephone in the garage offers numerous conveniences. When you're working in the garage or yard it will save you from tracking through the house in dirty clothes, and you can at times grab a call you'd probably otherwise miss.

16. Having a window or windows (other than in the garage door) helps increase illumination and air circulation. From a safety standpoint, that means you can see more of what you're doing, and you can get rid of fumes from a car's exhaust. An awning window is a good choice because it can be cracked open for ventilation even in times of inclement weather.

17. Depending on your garage's design, you may want to consider one or more skylights for additional natural light and ventilation. Skylights can also help dissipate heat during summer, when having a cool garage will help prevent the rest of the house from becoming uncomfortable or needing air conditioning. Electric venting skylights are available to be operated from either a remote control or a convenient fixed location near the entrance door to the garage from the house. Some models even feature rain sensors that automatically cause the window to close at the first sign of rain or other moisture. A model that fits perfectly between the trusses or other roof supports should be selected.

In some climates, not enough heat from the home radiates into the garage, especially during winter. A heat vent or wall heater installed in the garage is frequently the answer. Either one offers the following benefits:

- Snow and ice will melt/dry off cars and the garage floor.
- Fluids and foods stored in the garage will not freeze.

- Working on a car, snowblower, and any other project can be done in relative comfort.

- You won't have to scrape ice and frost off your car windows in the morning.

GARAGE DOORS

Since a home's garage car door often makes up a major part of the dwelling's structure and curb appeal, it's important to select a door that will contribute as much beauty, security, and insulation as possible. That means avoiding marginal-quality units that eventually may shake, rattle, warp, stick, and deteriorate, and selecting only quality garage door and opener systems.

Modern car doors on garages either swing or roll up out of the way. Old-fashioned sliding bypass types and hinged garage doors are much less practical. The typical single garage car door is 7 feet high and 9 feet wide, while a double garage car door is the same height and at least twice as wide (Fig. 15.2). Some doors have reinforced, high-impact nylon rollers with solid steel shafts. These rollers enable the door to glide easily, smoothly, and quietly.

Insulation values can range from about R-6 to R-7. Windows in the door will typically lower the overall insulating value. Naturally, favor doors with higher R-values. Also, review the various decorative window design options available with doors you are considering. There are frosted and beveled panes and assorted decorative glass inserts. All, however, should be the shatter-resistant type.

In general, the better units feature strong warranties on the doors and their openers.

Garage doors are constructed in a variety of materials. Below are the pros and cons of each type of construction.

WOOD DOOR CONSTRUCTION

Advantages

1. The wood can be painted or stained to a desired color or finish.

2. Intricately carved or rough sawn panels are available to suit a home's exterior decor.

FIGURE 15.2

Garage doors.

3. Wood doors can be precision-cut from solid ¾-inch redwood or hemlock, offering a beautiful natural finish when stained and covered with a clear-coat protectant.

Disadvantages

1. Will periodically need to be repainted or refinished.

2. It doesn't clean well.

3. It's capable of warping and rotting.

FIBERGLASS DOOR CONSTRUCTION
Advantages

1. It's lightweight.

2. Doesn't need to be painted or stained.

3. Can be easily cleaned.

4. Resistant to salt, air corrosion, and to rusting and warping from exposure to moisture.

5. Lightweight and easy to lift without an automatic opener.

6. Is relatively inexpensive and requires little maintenance.

Disadvantages

1. Low strength.

2. Some fiberglass doors come with minimal insulation.

3. Not as strong or secure as steel doors.

STEEL DOOR CONSTRUCTION

Steel-door "sandwich" construction is by far the most popular with builders and homeowners. It consists of two outer steel "skins" sandwiched or pressure bonded around a rigid polyurethane foam, polystyrene core, or similar panelized material. Panelized insulation materials offer added strength plus predictable heat and consistent noise insulation qualities, while injected foam insulation may decompose and develop cavities. In short, this method of construction results in high-strength, dent-resistant, well-insulated, attractive doors. Additional desirable steel door features include the following:

- Heavy gauge high-tensile steel skins (26- or 24-gauge) with deep embossing to help resist denting.

- The steel skin "layering" can include zinc/steel plating, hot-dipped galvanizing, primer coatings, and exterior/interior finish coatings to resist rust formation. Paint colors are often white, tan, brown, almond, or others. Some doors feature wood-grain outside finishes and textured inside coatings that simply wipe clean, like those of a kitchen range or refrigerator.

- Durable heavy-duty hinges that are galvanized and coated.

- Heavy-duty steel backup plates laminated under the inside steel skin to support each hinge.

- Painted galvanized steel end stiles to give hinges and rollers extra support and a clean interior appearance.

- Heavy-duty steel step-plates, inside and out, which help make the door easy and safe to close without the automatic opener.

- Steel door panels that are mechanically interlocked along their entire length for additional strength.

- Steel door panel joints should have seals to prevent wind, rain, and snow from entering between sections. There are two popular types of panel seals—compression and tongue and groove (Fig. 15.3). The compression type has an excellent seal, but tends to wear over time. The tongue-and-groove panel seal is effective and almost maintenance-free.

Advantages

1. With exterior skins of at least 26-gauge steel, they have good strength and durability.

2. The insulation value, given a thickness of 2 inches of material, is about four times that offered by a conventional wood door.

FIGURE 15.3

Steel door panel joint seals.

3. Painting maintenance will be minimal as long as the exterior and interior door skins are precoated with an epoxy primer plus a top-coat of polyester white, brown, or other color of baked enamel.

Disadvantages

1. They're heavy.

2. If scratched, touch-ups are difficult to complete.

3. Cleaning is often difficult.

Aluminum Door Construction

Advantages

1. Light in weight.

2. Painting and maintenance needs are minimal, given primer and enamel precoatings similar to those available on steel doors.

Disadvantages

1. Some models are lacking in strength.

2. Scratch touch-ups are difficult to make.

3. Cleaning can be difficult.

Swing-Up Doors

These are less expensive than roll-up doors. They can be made on the building site from the same materials used for the house's siding. Often, though, swing-up doors consist of thin sheets of exterior plywood that are easy to work with and light enough for the owners to open with little bother. The drawbacks to this type of door are that it's so lightly constructed it often has problems operating on its tracks, it can warp easily, it's not very energy efficient, and it's not as attractive as roll-up doors (Fig. 15.4).

FIGURE 15.4

Swing-type garage door.

Roll-Up Doors

Roll-up doors are the most popular and practical garage car doors available. They come in wood, steel, aluminum, fiberglass, plastic, masonite, and composite models. Insulated garage doors made of plastic, aluminum, or steel having fiberglass insulation inside are terrific for saving energy. The plastic doors are also maintenance-free, with the door's color an integral part of its makeup so it never needs resurfacing. Any roll-up door should be trimmed on the bottom with an astragal (rubber) strip to ensure a tight seal with the floor.

Specify the type of roll-up door propelled by torsion springs for operating safety and ease. All roll-up doors can be efficiently connected to automatic door openers.

Garage Door Features

Perimeter weather sealing with jamb and header seals along the exterior sides and top of the door is critical. To prevent air infiltration the door should be equipped with the following factory-installed seals (Fig. 15.5):

- Between each section joint
- Self-adjusting jamb seals on the end stiles
- Top section header seal
- Adjustable U-shaped bottom rubber or astragal seal with the ability to conform with irregular floors to effectively seal out the elements

The bottom weather seal retainer should be made of aluminum or other rustproof sturdy design; its thickness will likely affect the door's durability. At least 2 inches of insulation, pressure bonded between the sheets of steel or other material, reduces energy loss and improves noise reduction.

Tongue and groove section joints provide excellent weather sealing. Look for a door model with a pinch-resistant joint design that helps prevent fingers from getting caught in the door panel joints. A full plastic thermal break will reduce metal-to-metal contact between the interior and exterior of the door's surface while adding to insulating efficiency. Garage door windows should be watertight and at least double-glazed.

FIGURE 15.5

Garage door seals.

Torsion springs should be computer-calibrated to match your door load. The springs should be made from oil-tempered wire and must be mounted on a continuous cross-header tube or shaft that's appropriate to the door's torque load. Torsion springs mounted without a tube or shaft are dangerous because if they snap unexpectedly they'll whip through the air with a powerful force.

Automatic Door Openers

It's nice to come home late at night in a thundering rainstorm or blizzard and push a tiny button from within the car so that your garage door raises open for you, like magic. For the sake of convenience and safety, automatic garage door openers are relatively inexpensive and reliable contraptions.

```
SAFETY»NOTE
```

GARAGE CAR DOORS

Some garage car doors feature "safe" hinges designed to reduce the chances of fingers getting pinched between sections of a closing door. Finger shields "hide" and restrict access to section joints on the door's outer side. Other brands offer pinch-resistant designs where the closing sections actually push fingers away from the section panel joints as the door closes. The parts of some of these pinch-preventers are made from the same prepainted steel as the door panels themselves so they blend in with the rest of the door face.

Advantages

1. Convenience. You never have to get in/out of your car to open/close the garage door, especially in bad weather. An inside wall button lets you open and close the door while standing at the garage man door from the house.

2. Safety. A built-in lamp brightens the way as you head into the garage, or out of it.

3. Security. The opener itself acts as a garage lock, making it difficult for anyone to jimmy open the garage door. Plus, the door is automatically locked when closed.

4. Weather protection. The opener's shock absorbing spring(s) allow the door to close tightly against the floor, assuring a good weather seal.

Check for the following features:

1. There should be an easy disconnect pull cord for manual operation in case of a power failure or other emergency. It should automatically reconnect when the radio control or wall push button is pressed after the power is restored.

2. A ⅓-horsepower motor will handle a single-car door, but a ½-horsepower unit is recommended for double doors.

3. There should be separate up and down door travel limit nuts that are easy to adjust for fine tuning of the desired open and closed positions.

4. A heavy-gauge metal cover should protect the inner workings. It should have a maintenance-free decorative surface.

5. There should be safety switches that are obstruction sensitive. They'll make the door automatically reverse itself if it contacts any object.

6. An electric eye. Even if you aren't planning to have children or pets, include an electric eye to supplement the obstruction switches. It will stop a descending door and send it back up when a child or animal passes through the beam.

7. A keyless entry mounted to the garage overhead door jamb that allows access from the outside via a private (and changeable) security keypad code, thus eliminating the need to leave the garage door open for long periods just because someone will be arriving later and needs access (such as children or other relatives). This also comes in handy when there aren't enough door remote units to cover all of the family vehicles.

8. Plastic strap track drives, belt drives, and worm screw drives are quieter than chain drive openers.

9. Remote-control coding. So the code can be changed by flipping small switches in the remote to any up/down configuration you desire.

10. A high-impact plastic light cover for the lamp that turns on automatically for five minutes when the door is either being opened or closed.

11. Consider an opener with two-socket lighting. This allows for two light bulbs to do the illumination. When one bulb burns out, the other will continue to provide some light, providing time for the bad bulb to be changed. This is particularly important for someone with limited mobility who needs help changing out an overhead bulb.

12. A vacation switch. The switch renders the opener deaf to all radio signals, including those from its own remote, while you're gone.

13. Some units come with a lighted keyless four-code entry pad that installs unobtrusively on the outer door frame. It has its own flip-up weather protection cover and allows the homeowner to press in the correct code from the outside to open the door.

12. Fixed door opener codes can lead to thieves stealing or cracking the code with sophisticated code-cracking devices; then, while you are away, the thieves may open the garage door to survey what they could take. Even if nothing appeals to them, they may leave the door up during the middle of winter as they disappear, allowing cold air in and leaving your garage open for further vandalism. To defeat these thieves, some keyless entry pad systems feature anti-burglary coding mechanisms that automatically change the access code to one of billions of new codes selected each time the remote control unit is activated.

15. Consider a unit with a soft start/stop that prevents jerking when starting or stopping. Again, make sure that the opener you select will reverse itself automatically if it encounters any obstacles (such as a small child) while closing toward the garage floor. Also arrange for the control buttons to be positioned high enough so children can't reach them. This is especially important for the buttons near the inside garage man door to the house. Children will sometimes push a control button to close the door then attempt to dash through the opening before the door is fully lowered.

16. Units are available that operate off a direct current (DC) motor instead of with a standard alternating current (AC) motor. The DC motor can operate on less energy, will provide a soft start and stop feature for smooth operation, less noise, reduced door wear, and greater reliability.

17. A polymer-lined rail reduces metal-to-metal contact between movable parts for less resistance and noise during operation.

18. Units are available with a light control having an energy-saver shutoff. There's also a motion-detecting control panel that will turn the garage door opener lights on when someone enters a dark garage from inside the home. A timer should automatically shut off the same lights after a few minutes. Another option is a multi-function remote control that will turn on the opener's lights independently of the garage door operation, and even activate or deactivate house lights. This is helpful when a person must enter through the small door and wants the lights on in advance.

19. Consider the feature of having a red light inside the kitchen or other room that goes on whenever the garage car door is in a raised position. That may save the door from being accidentally left open all night.

Garage Door Screens

If included, this handy feature offers the pleasure of using your garage during warm-weather days and evenings for sitting, socializing and partying without being annoyed by insects or dampened by rain.

Man Doors

A man door entrance to the garage should be included to permit access into the garage from outdoors without having to raise the garage overhead door. The best man doors are steel-covered. They're strong, burglar-resistant, and fare well against the weather. As with all other outer man doors, garage entrances should be insulated with weather stripping. Depending on your lot, if the back of the garage faces the backyard you might consider having a second man door installed there.

SAFETY》**NOTE**

GARAGE DOOR OPENERS

Remember, a photo-eye positioned near the floor across the garage door's plane of travel must not be the automatic door opener's only or main method of preventing injury. Although the photo-eye beam mechanism—when working correctly—will prevent someone from being struck and will reverse the door's travel, it does not react upon the door's edge striking something on its way down. Indeed, sunlight, rain, or snow can make the photo eye malfunction, as can collections of dirt or other debris on the lens, and even a simple bump of the eye by a child's foot or basketball can disable the beam from proper operation. Instead, the unit's main safeguard must be a sensor in the opener's drive mechanism, set so the door will automatically and immediately stop and reverse its travel upon encountering a change in pressure or resistance (such as the presence of a child's head or arm) when the bottom edge of the door strikes the same on its way down.

SAFETY》**NOTE**

GARAGE DOOR OPENERS

Some manufacturers offer a wall control inside the garage with an illuminated open/close button in case the door must be opened in the dark.

GARAGE FLOORS

The following points should be considered to ensure a trouble-free garage floor:

1. It should have a 4-inch gravel base covered by a sheet of polyethylene or similar moisture barrier. Drainpipes should be laid under the gravel, and the gravel should be tamped before the concrete floor is poured.

PM POINTERS

GARAGE DOOR OPENERS

Monthly

- Examine cables for fraying. Carefully run a rag along the cables. If the rag catches or tears, have the cables inspected by a professional.
- Inspect the garage door springs, rollers, pulleys, and other hardware for signs of wear. Make sure nuts and bolts are tight. If any component is broken, contact a professional for repairs and avoid using the door until they're completed.
- Per the manufacturer's instructions, periodically lubricate the door rollers, bearings, hinges, and drive mechanism.
- Test the emergency release used for power outages, then test the balance of the door to see if the springs are properly adjusted. Follow the manufacturer's guidelines, or close the door and disconnect the automatic operator. You should then be able to lift the door waist high with relative ease. The door should stay open in that position by itself. If it doesn't, the door spring tension should be adjusted by the door company repair person until it does.
- Test the reversing features on the opener monthly by seeing if the photo-eye works and by placing a 2- by 4-inch block of wood on the floor to obstruct the door to see if it will reverse direction, as it should. If either of these safety features fails, disconnect the door opener until it's repaired.

2. If no garage floor drains will be installed, the garage floor should be poured so it begins about ½ inch above the driveway's surface then slopes up to about 2 inches toward the back of the garage.

3. If possible, include floor drains, one for each car space. Naturally the floor should be sloped toward the drains to prevent any standing water.

4. To support the edges of the garage floor where the fill around the footer might settle, specify 6- by 6-inch reinforcement wire to be used throughout the entire floor.

5. The concrete should be poured at least 4 inches thick.

6. The garage (and basement) floor should be steel-troweled to achieve a smooth finish. This is a time-consuming task that requires going over the surface with a trowel many times during an 8-hour period or until the surface hardens.

7. The part of the garage floor that sticks out past the garage door—normally about 6 inches—should taper away from the door down toward the driveway, ending ½ to 1 inch higher than the driveway surface. By tapering it down toward the driveway, rainwater and melting snow will not drain into the garage. Keeping the floor slightly elevated prevents water from backing up into the garage from the driveway.

8. Before parking cars on a new garage floor, the floor should be cleaned with a solution of muriatic acid, then coated with two or three applications of a clear sealer. The sealer improves the floor's appearance by preventing oils, grease, and dirt from staining the concrete and by making the floor a lot easier to clean. It will also prevent cement/concrete dust from rising and will help water flow more quickly toward the drains.

GARAGE ATTIC STORAGE

The garage attic, even when trusses are running through it, can be used to store off-season equipment of all types, including holiday decorations, lawn furniture, spare tires, kids' swimming pools, bicycles, and gardening supplies. To make this space accessible, cover or "finish" the attic floor and specify a set of pulldown steps. Folding or roll-down type stairways (Fig. 15.6) are in most cases the best option. At the same time, with attic space in the garage quite high off the garage concrete floor, these types of stairways are far safer than using conventional stepladders.

Make sure whichever model you choose has handrail(s). Also, when closed, the unit should latch securely against a rubber seal to prevent drafts and insects from entering the attic.

There should be adequate lighting installed in the garage attic so you can see and move freely about in a safe manner. The switch for the light should ideally be located on a wall in the garage so you can turn it on before climbing the stairs. A less-desirable alternative is a pull string you can grab as you reach the top of the attic stairs.

If it applies to your location, avoid the use of fluorescent bulbs, which take too long to activate in cold temperatures. Also make sure

FIGURE 15.6

Folding pulldown stairway.

exposed bulbs are not situated where they'll be easily bumped into and broken.

An important consideration for a garage attic is ventilation. A thermostatically controlled ventilation fan is an excellent choice to help remove excess summer heat and car exhaust fumes. Such a system will also prevent dampness and mold problems. Ridge, roof, gable, and soffitt ventilation can also be employed with satisfactory results.

Electrical outlets should be installed throughout the attic so that you can plug in tools or a vacuum cleaner.

GARAGE STORAGE

In years past, there was a time when garages fit the automobiles for which they were built like a glove. Now garages are erected not only to hold cars, but to shelter a wide variety of other work, maintenance, and leisure-time items.

Consider the following ideas when planning your garage storage space:

1. Provide enough space to store lawn mowers, snow blowers, bicycles, and other bulky objects along a side wall, and a place to keep even larger items such as garden tractors or small boats along the back wall.

2. No matter what size garage you plan, many cubic feet of relatively inactive storage space can be salvaged by building one or more shelves 24 to 30 inches deep around the two sides and the back of the garage about 6 feet above the floor, attached by brackets fixed to the walls. This will accommodate the storage of spray cans, garden tools, box of rags, auto parts and supplies, and so on.

3. A huge rack for storing screens, oars, water skis, and other long articles can be hung from the ceiling over each car bay. If built over a "walking area" at the sides or in front of where a car is stored, the rack should clear the floor by at least 7 feet, but where it hangs over the car it can be dropped to within 6 feet of the floor because it isn't over a highly traveled pedestrian zone.

4. The more you can keep items elevated off the floor, the easier and faster you'll be able to clean out the garage.

5. You'll find it handy to leave one wall with the framing studs and planks exposed—not covered with plaster or drywall board. This permits you to attach large sheets of Peg-Board directly to the studs and will provide an airspace to arrange hanging pegs into the Peg-Board itself. Peg-Board is ideal for hanging all sorts of hand tools, garden tools, hoses, and many other items. If Peg-Board will be secured to finished walls, you must leave an airspace behind it using 2- by 2-inch studs to establish a gap.

6. Heavy garden tools and items such as hand mowers, empty lawn rollers, and long wooden extension ladders can be hung from 4-

FIGURE 15.7

Garage storage.

inch boards nailed across open studs when steel brackets are fastened to the top edges of the 4-inch boards.

7. A lockable tool/equipment cabinet keeps small items and tools organized and extra secure.

8. On the bottom of the exposed stud walls, and below areas having Peg-Board, you can build 12-inch shelf inserts between the studs on top of the block, at an elevation approximately 12 inches above the floor (Fig. 15.7). It will work well for storing wash pails, step stools, jack stands, bags of seed, fertilizer, and so on.

GARAGE POSITIONING

This subject is covered in the chapter on house orientation and positioning, but in a nutshell: the garage must fit on the lot without encroaching on an adjacent site. It should also conform to the slope of your lot. For instance, when a garage is located on a downward side sloping lot, instead of completely lowering the garage to meet the natural lot line or placing load after load of fill dirt to raise the lot level, it's best to reach a compromise between the two solutions.

Position a garage to reduce energy loads. In cold-climate areas garages should be located on a northern part of the house, if possible. In hot-climate areas, a garage is best suited on the east or west side of the home to help reduce heat gain.

$\blacktriangleright\blacktriangleright\blacktriangleright\blacktriangleright\blacktriangleright\blacktriangleright$ **POINTS TO PONDER**

1. A garage costs considerably less per square foot than the rest of the house costs. Instead of planning a garage that's just large enough for your needs, go a few steps further. It won't cost much more.

2. A garage can be positioned as a buffer between cold prevailing winds and home living spaces, or on the east or west side of the dwelling to help shade interior living areas, depending on your location and climate.

3. If you plan to heat the garage, have the outer walls, as well as those of adjoining living spaces, insulated. If you insulate, consider that when a warmed car is pulled into the garage after a drive, heat radiating from the parked vehicle will be retained longer within the garage, and will even help insulate the adjoining part of the house.

4. Have a water faucet or utility sink center installed somewhere on a common wall with the living quarters of the home.

5. Install a garage floor drain, or better yet, a strip drain (a rectangular lengthwise concrete drain covered with pieces of removable grating for cleaning mud or debris) so the floor can be hosed down when needed throughout the winter.

6. A telephone located in the garage provides numerous conveniences. Otherwise, the opening and closing of the house door will waste energy as the home's heated or cooled air is lost. Also consider installing a cable television outlet there, for watching favorite programs while waxing a car or pursuing various hobbies and housework activities.

7. Automatic garage door openers must have automatic reverse safety features and should also have an electric-eye beam which stops a door's downward travel when someone or something crosses the floor in the door's path.

8. It usually makes sense to have a garage attic that can be accessed by a set of pull-down stairs.

9. Garage attics should have lighting, a sturdy floor, and adequate ventilation.

10. Plan garage shelves, Peg-Boards, racks, and hangers with the goal of keeping items in the garage stored off the floor, so the floor remains uncluttered and easy to be kept clean.

11. Fluorescent lighting will allow you to spend long periods of time performing various activities in the garage without receiving a high electricity bill.

12. Sunlight Tubes installed in the garage can help provide an inexpensive source of natural illumination.

13. To maximize lighting efficiency, have the walls painted white or another bright, light color or shade.

Fireplaces

The first fireplaces were logical extensions of an open campfire—
functional features that were designed to provide heat,
illumination, and a way to cook foods in early dwellings. They were
originally a necessity in all but the warmest climates and supplied
homeowners with basic needs for centuries.

Then, rather quickly, other mechanisms were invented that more
efficiently heated our houses, illuminated our rooms, and cooked our
foods. Consequently, fireplaces lost some of their functional value and
became more decorative options than necessities. They still, however,
remained a part of our houses for the atmosphere they created and the
warmth that homeowners appreciated on cold winter evenings. But
once the energy crunch hit, fireplaces were accused of being the
energy-wasters they really were, and fell further out of favor.

Not to be upstaged, hundreds of large and small companies set out
to modify the standard fireplace into units which, through various
add-on tubes, gadgets, and heat exchangers, would burn fuel much
more efficiently.

So today's fireplaces can be divided into two main types: those
used primarily to heat a room, area, or entire house; and those used
primarily as decoration or novelty. Even with continuing concerns for
energy usage, the latter models—the fireplaces installed for decoration
and atmosphere—are still the most popular. They're included in mod-

ern homes because of what they add to a room, in ways that excite our senses of sight, sound, and smell. They're a bit of the past to which we still cling.

Any fireplace should at least do five things:

- Permit combustion of fuel.
- Exhaust the by-products of combustion from the house.
- Deliver as much heat as possible into the house.
- Function safely.
- Be located so people sitting in all areas of a room can enjoy it. In a long, narrow room, for example, it's better to plan a fireplace on one of the long side walls than on a short end wall. Because people tend to cluster around a fireplace, if it's located at one of the short walls in an end of a long room, the opposite end of the room (without a fireplace) would likely go completely unused.

Advantages

1. They can provide additional heat.
2. They can provide *all* the necessary heat in mild-climate locations.
3. They enhance the appearance and comfort of any room in any house in any climate.
4. They provide a traditionally romantic and reassuring atmosphere.
5. They can burn as fuel certain combustible materials that would otherwise be wasted, such as coke, briquettes, and scrap lumber.

Disadvantages

1. A major concern with a typical fireplace is that it uses substantially more air than needed for combustion. The room air used for fireplace combustion has already been heated by the primary heating system, and much of it is ultimately lost up the chimney. Rather than assisting the primary system in its heating function, the fireplace can interfere with its operation and usually increases the workload of the primary system. As much as 80 percent of the heat produced by a wood fireplace can dissipate up and out of the

chimney. To address this concept further, you can review the Fireplace Energy Efficiency Points toward the end of this chapter.

2. A fireplace heats by radiation only. Much of the air that comes into contact with the hottest surface of the fireplace ends up outdoors.

3. Some warm air from the house will go up the chimney even when a fire is not lit and the damper is closed.

4. Because brick and stone are poor insulators, a fireplace and chimney can create a thermal opening in the wall of a dwelling if located somewhere in the building's outer shell.

5. A fireplace adds to the cost of a new house.

6. When positioned within a building, a fireplace occupies valuable floor and wall space.

7. When positioned in an exterior wall, a fireplace can occupy scarce land.

8. A fireplace requires periodic maintenance and occasionally the services of professional chimney cleaners.

9. Fireplaces can be messy. Storage space for wood and other fuel is needed, and so are places to keep dirty fireplace tools such as pokers, tongs, and shovels.

10. Fireplaces can be dangerous when incorrectly built, installed, or used. They can be hazardous when small children have free rein throughout the house.

TYPES OF FIREPLACES

With the development of modern manufacturing processes, materials other than traditional stone and brick have been made available for fireplace construction. Today there are numerous fireplace designs that come ready-made or can be custom-built to suit any application.

Masonry Fireplaces

These are the original models that are still popular today. They consist of a stone or brick exterior having a lining of firebrick—a brick that can stand high temperatures encountered when wood or other fuels are burned. Of course, built into the masonry are various operating accessories such as grates to hold the wood while it's being burned and dampers to regulate the amount of airflow through the chimney passages (Fig. 16.1).

There are several basic masonry fireplace designs, including fireplaces with a single opening constructed against a single wall (the most popular); fireplaces constructed into a wall that divides two rooms so the fireplace has two openings, one per each of the back-to-back rooms; fireplaces built into an outside corner, open to two sides; and even circular fireplaces of brick and stone having sheet metal chimneys suspended from the ceiling that flare out over the round firebox like an inverted funnel.

Because these masonry units must be built from scratch on the building site, the labor construction costs of masonry fireplaces are high. Once a masonry fireplace is up, however, its maintenance expenses and efforts are minimal. The beauty, durability, and reputation of its brick or stonework can enhance the overall appearance of a house's interior and exterior and will increase the home's saleability and value.

An all-masonry fireplace.

Stone generally costs more than brick and requires a higher degree of skill on the mason's part. If you opt for an all masonry fireplace, make sure that whoever will be putting it up has had experience completing others as well. There are many tricky steps to masonry fireplace construction, and unless they're all done exactly right, they can cause serious structural and safety defects that might appear years later. All-masonry fireplaces, because of their weight, require at least an 8-inch-thick concrete footer for adequate support.

Masonry and Steel Box Fireplaces

This type is similar to the all-masonry fireplace except that the firebox, or where the fuel is burned, is prefabricated of steel instead of being constructed from firebrick. The rest of the fireplace is all masonry. Masonry and steel box fireplaces are less costly than all masonry units, and they still retain a handsome appearance and low-maintenance characteristics (Fig. 16.2).

Circulating Fireplaces

A typical circulating fireplace consists of a specially designed prefabricated steel shell with firebox and damper. It greatly simplifies construction because all a mason has to do is build the foundation and hearth, set the prefabricated fireplace shell on the hearth, and lay finishing bricks or stones up around the shell. The shape and approximate exterior dimensions of the fireplace are already determined.

The prefabricated shell more than makes up for its restricted authenticity with increased efficiency. The real advantage of a circu-

FLUE

SMOKE CHAMBER

WARM AIR OUT

STEEL LINTEL

STEEL FIREBOX

COOL AIR IN

FIGURE 16.2

A masonry and steel box fireplace with circulator vents.

lating fireplace is that it heats not only by radiation (as a conventional fireplace does) but also by circulating heated air directly into a room or adjacent area. As a result, it provides almost twice the heat output of a conventional fireplace.

The walls of most prefabricated circulating fireplaces consist of two layers of steel separated by an airspace. Cool air enters the airspace through grilles installed at the floorline next to the fireplace. As air passes through the bottom grilles and moves between the hot layers of steel it gets heated and then expelled through other grilles installed near the top of the firebox or high in the wall. To encourage constant air movement and an even amount of heat, manufacturers offer air inlets containing electric fans. Fans can also be used with the warm-air outlets placed in adjacent rooms. The chimney may be of conventional masonry construction or made of prefabricated steel.

Prefabricated Built-In Fireplaces

This type of fireplace not only reduces construction costs but makes it possible to install a traditional design almost anywhere in an existing house. The prefab built-in fireplace consists of a steel firebox complete with hearth, damper, and a prefabricated chimney as well. Prefabricated built-in fireplaces are made with either one opening in the front, or with one front and one side opening. Most are constructed with close clearances. The manufacturer should detail the necessary clearances and proper floor construction required. Choose a unit that bears the UL label, and check what clearances your building code specifies (Fig. 16.3).

Another advantage to the prefabs is that they don't weigh much, so there's no need to place them on an elaborate and expen-

FIGURE 16.3

A prefabricated fireplace.

sive masonry foundation. Instead, they can be set directly on a non-combustible floor, and a fire-resistant forehearth can be integrated into the finished flooring directly in front of the fireplace's main opening.

Freestanding Fireplaces

Freestanding fireplaces are the least-expensive fireplaces and the easiest to install. All it takes to erect one is to set it in position and run a flue through the roof or the nearest exterior wall. Freestanding units are usually made of steel or cast iron and come in a variety of designs and shapes—round, square, hexagonal, egg, even triangular. They're typically finished in bright porcelains or enamels of red, green, yellow, black, white, and other tones. They're modern-looking but give off plenty of old-fashioned heat because the sheet metal chimney, in addition to the firebox, also gives off radiant heat directly into the room (Fig. 16.4).

These fireplaces can be placed right against unpainted masonry walls, but if a wall is constructed or surfaced with combustible materials, a clearance of several inches is needed behind them and even a greater safety margin is required on the sides.

Woodburning Stove Fireplaces

To someone looking for more heat than glamour, a wood- or coal-burning stove is a good choice. Made of either steel or cast iron, freestanding stoves can provide over 90 percent of the available heat from wood or coal combustion. And because they're not constructed at the building site, they'll definitely keep installation costs low. Another plus is that many models have doors that can be swung open so all the pleasures of an open fire can be enjoyed (Figs. 16.5 and 16.6).

When strapped for funds, a home buyer can elect to install a freestanding wood-burning stove after the house is constructed, without much trouble.

NONCOMBUSTIBLE MATERIAL

FIGURE 16.4

A freestanding fireplace.

FIGURE 16.5

A Franklin wood stove.

FIGURE 16.6

A wood stove.

Like freestanding fireplaces, stoves must be set out from combustible walls, and although most of them stand on legs, they should be centered on a noncombustible pad of some kind.

FIREPLACE DESIGN

Fireplace efficiency depends largely on proper design (Fig. 16.7). Here are some important considerations to review if you're thinking about including one or more fireplaces in your house:

1. A common but inefficient way to include a fireplace in a home is to have it built so it employs a chimney at a side or end of a house where three sides (the back and two sides) of the chimney are exposed to the weather (Fig. 16.8). As mentioned in the chapter on insulation, brick and stone are of limited insulating value. They'll lose much more heat to the outdoors than they'll save for the indoors.

2. Don't settle for a fireplace with a large throat and a flue without an adjustable damper. An adjustable damper will limit the amount of warm air lost up the chimney to only that necessary to remove the smoke.

3. The best place for a fireplace to be located is away from outside walls, so most of the heat stored in its brick, stone, or metal parts is eventually delivered into the house.

4. A low chimney is a dangerous design feature.

5. The most efficient fireplaces follow established guidelines, mathematical relationships between the firebox, opening, throat diameter, and flue diameter dimensions. If the front opening is proportionally too large, the draft will be poor. A cheap way to decrease the acceptable size of the opening would be to raise the hearth, but because a fireplace requires a size-able draft, savings on energy expenses in this manner would be insignificant—and very often negative. You don't have to actually *know* what all the technical points are before you plan a fireplace, but you should be able to throw out a few ideas so your builder thinks that he's dealing with someone who understands and will accept only letter-perfect work.

Even though fireplace dimensions vary tremendously, as a general rule, the height of the opening should be about three-quarter of the width, and the depth of the firebox should be two-third to three-quarter of the opening height. For openings up to 6 feet wide, the height should usually not exceed 3½ feet; 4 feet is a good maximum for fireplaces over 6 feet wide. The average fireplace has an opening 30 to 40 inches wide and 30 inches high. The depth is between 18 and 24 inches. A typical fireplace facing will be 6 feet wide all the way from floor to ceiling.

FIGURE 16.7

Cross section of conventional fireplace design.

6. A fireplace should be more or less in scale with the room it will be located in. As a rule of thumb, there should be 5 square inches of fireplace opening for every square foot of floor area.

7. Each fireplace should have its own flue, and it's not a sound idea to vent any other heating unit, such as a furnace, into a fireplace flue.

FIGURE 16.8

A three-sided fireplace chimney exposure.

8. Glass doors will eliminate lazy drafts and reduce smoking, plus they're good safety features to have.

9. If natural gas is available in your area, it's smart to include a gas starter in a fireplace, for convenience. Make sure an isolation valve is included on the gas line to the starter in case eventual repairs or maintenance tasks are needed.

10. To operate safely and efficiently, a fireplace should be positioned level to the floor.

WHERE TO LOCATE THE FIREPLACE

Keep in mind that once you decide where a typical fireplace will be positioned, and once it's installed, you won't want to move it to somewhere else in the house.

Whenever possible, outside wall locations should be avoided. Why heat the outdoors? The heat loss from a placement along an outside wall is nearly 25 percent. A chimney that's exposed to the weather along its entire length on one or more sides is bound to cool off quickly when the fire is low. Then, when the fire is rekindled, the products of combustion must try to force their way out of a chimney filled with dense, cooled gases. In contrast, heat that escapes through the chimney walls from an inside wall fireplace will help warm the house or at the very least the garage (Fig. 16.9).

By locating a fireplace on any inside wall, especially the wall separating the garage from the living areas, the part of the fireplace and chimney facing the garage does not need a facing of finished brick or stone. Thus, by locating a fireplace in the way most favorable for energy savings, material and installation costs can also be lowered.

There should be ample room around a fireplace for furniture. But the furniture placement shouldn't interfere with traffic in and through the room, and it shouldn't be situated closer than 6 feet away from the fireplace front opening. Chairs and sofas positioned closer than 6 feet

FIGURE 16.9

A fireplace chimney through a garage.

will likely make occupants uncomfortably warm no matter what the outdoors temperatures are.

FIREPLACE SUPPORT

A masonry chimney is usually the heaviest part of a house. It must rest on a solid foundation to prevent settlement. Concrete footers are recommended. They must be designed to distribute the load over an area wide enough to avoid exceeding the safe load-bearing capacity of the soil. They should extend at least 12 inches beyond the chimney on all sides, and be at least 8 inches thick for single-story houses and 12 inches thick for two-story houses with basements. If there is no basement, the footers for an exterior wall chimney should be poured on solid ground below the frostline.

CHIMNEYS

Stone and brick fireplace chimneys can be dominating features no matter whether they're located at the exterior of a home, or the interior.

Chimney Walls

Walls of chimneys with lined flues, not more than 30 feet high, should be at least 8 inches thick if made with brick or reinforced concrete, and at least 12 inches thick if made of stone. A flue lining is recommended.

Chimneys can contain more than one flue. Building codes generally require a separate flue for each fireplace, furnace, or boiler. If a chimney contains three or more lined flues, each group of two flues must be separated from the other flue or groups of two flues by buck divisions or *wythes* at least 3¾ inches thick.

Neither the chimney nor the fireplace should touch any wood or flammable materials in the house structure. Check the local building code for the proper clearance the chimney must have from any combustibles as it passes through floors, walls, or roofs.

Chimney Height

Proper chimney height on any house depends on the shape of the house's roof as well as the positions and sizes of surrounding trees, buildings, and even hills. The chimney should extend or rise at least 3 feet above flat roofs and at least 2 feet above a roof ridge or raised part of a roof within 10 feet of the chimney. A chimney hood should be provided if a chimney cannot be built high enough above a ridge to prevent trouble from wind eddies caused by breezes being deflected from the roof or nearby trees. The open ends of a chimney hood should be parallel to the ridge (Fig. 16.10).

Chimney Lining

Although a chimney can be lined with brick, there's less chance of soot accumulating inside the flue if a clay tile lining at least ⅝-inch thick is used instead. The joints between such tiles must be completely filled with mortar and finished smooth on the inside. The lining is surrounded with a brick, stone, or concrete block wall at least 8 to 12 inches thick. The inside of the fireplace will be finished with firebrick sides and back.

Chimney Mortar

Brickwork around chimney flues and fireplaces should be laid with cement mortar. It's more resistant to the action of heat and flue gases

Chimney heights.

than is lime mortar. Firebrick should be laid with fire clay. Mortar will not stand up to intense heat as well as fire clay will.

This is an example of why it pays to have only experienced masons work on fireplaces. It's a shame, but they're a disappearing breed, the fireplace specialists—going the same way as plasterers and stone masons. Even some of the masons who claim to know what they're doing, do not. They leave behind a trail of fireplaces that smoke, draw poorly, and have flues that are constantly accumulating thick deposits of creosote. That's why, when putting up a masonry fireplace, it's best to select someone (or make sure the contractor chooses someone) who is a proven professional.

Chimney Damper

The fireplace and chimney are large heat gobblers, particularly when they're not in use. Because of this, a fireplace chimney should be equipped with a metal damper that can be closed when the fireplace is not in service, to prevent a continual draft. The damper should be the kind that opens and closes by increments, so airflow can be regulated when the fireplace is needed. A fireplace damper is typically about 36 inches wide.

Chimney Cap

The chimney cap, by definition, is placed at the very top of the chimney (Fig. 16.11). The top surface of the chimney cap should be given a slight downward slope for water to run off. This watertight cap prevents moisture from entering the brick, stone, and flue lining. Typically, the cap is made of concrete.

Spark Arrestors

Each year many fires are caused by sparks or flying embers escaping from chimneys. Those same sparks and embers can also damage roofs. A chimney spark arrestor is a metal device with metal caging on the sides and a solid metal top. It is fastened over the chimney top opening to not only stop sparks, embers and pieces of burning material from getting out of the chimney, but also to prevent rain, leaves and animals from entering. Spark arrestors can also reduce "down drafting," which is smoke that either starts to travel up the chimney but then backs down the chimney, or smoke that has escaped from the top of the chimney that "pushes back" into the chimney due to wind or air-movement patterns created by nearby structures or trees. Select only spark arrestors that are UL labeled.

FIGURE 16.11

Chimney cap.

Chimney Flashing

The intersection of the chimney and roof should be flashed with metal shingles which extend at least 4 inches under the roof shingles and 4 inches up the outer face of the chimney. They should also overlap each other by 3 inches to provide a watertight seal along the chimney. Counterflashing should be installed over the top of the metal shingles, again overlapping by at least 3 inches. Counterflashing should be embedded at least 1 inch into the masonry (accomplished, of course, as the chimney is being constructed, so the 1-inch counterflashing lip can be mortared in between a course of bricks or stone) to prevent water from running behind the flashing and into the house. The flashing seams where it meets the shingles should be caulked and then coated with a rustproof paint (Fig. 16.12).

Chimney Sealing

Once the chimney is complete and cured, the contractor should seal the outside masonry with a transparent penetrating water-repellant sealer developed for stone, brick, concrete, and general masonry. It should be a sealer that's specifically made for the application—that establishes a moisture barrier yet allows the surface to breathe.

FLASHING INSERTED INTO BRICK JOINT

COUNTER FLASHING

BASE FLASHING

FIGURE 16.12

Chimney flashing.

The exterior walls and cap will naturally encounter rain, snow, ice, wind, and other conditions as time goes on. Those exterior chimney components, if not treated, may eventually absorb water. If water gets into the chimney wall, it could cause cracks and chipping, especially in cold climates, with their alternating freeze/thaw cycles. Eventually the moisture could work its way into the house and cause damage to your insulation and ceiling. The masonry sealer will help keep your chimney in good condition from the very start, and it will also help prevent spalling and efflorescence. It should be reapplied as recommended by the manufacturer, as a planned preventive maintenance measure.

Chimney Cleaning

All wood fires produce some creosote, and flues should be inspected periodically to check the amount of creosote present inside them. Creosote can build to thick deposits that become extremely flammable and can result in dangerous house fires.

When the flue's insides are coated with uneven surfaces of black gummy-looking material and you can't discern the tile and mortar joints, it's time for a cleaning. The term "chimney sweep" isn't really accurate. Creosote is so hard and gummy that it can't be swept loose. Rather, it has to be chipped away from the masonry with a blade. In the meantime, care must be taken not to knock out mortar joints or damage the flue lining. Because it's such an infrequent and important task, and specialized tools are needed, it's best to hand the job over to a commercial chimney sweep or cleaning outfit.

HEARTHS

The fireplace hearth is really an extension of the fireplace floor that protects the surrounding room floor area from catching fire. Typically, it's the brick, stone, or concrete pad beneath and in front of the firebox. Practically any noncombustible material can be used, including brick, concrete, adobe, terrazzo, quarry tile, marble, mosaic tile, slate, fieldstone, and even bronze or copper if laid over a noncombustible base.

Because the hearth cannot safely rest on the floor or wood framing, it should either be cantilevered out from the foundation or the foundation should be extended under it. It must be supported from the ground up, beginning with a concrete pad 12 inches thick or more typically part of the entire fireplace footer, and then brought up to the sub-floor level with concrete block.

A hearth should extend at least 20 to 24 inches into the room and at least 6 to 8 inches on both sides of the fireplace opening. It can be flush with the floor so that sweepings can be brushed into the fireplace, or it can be raised. Raising the hearth to various heights and extending its length is a common practice, especially in contemporary designs. This can create a natural seat for people to rest on and warm up for brief periods after a cold winter evening of skiing or tobogganing. When done on a smaller scale, though, raised hearths can also present a hazard for tripping over.

COVERS AND SCREENS

Suitable screens should be placed in front of all fireplace openings to minimize the dangers from sparks and exploding embers, and to keep young children from playing with and in the flames. Some wire mesh screens tend to be messy looking, especially when they're not permanently attached to the sides of the fireplace opening. It's better to go with ones that are suspended across the opening and can be removed when the fire needs tending. Glass screens or doors are even better because they're ideal for safety, are attractive, and they can be closed at night to reduce heat loss that would otherwise go up the chimney during cold weather. They can also be used to prevent any smoke from being blown back down the chimney into a room by a strong fluke downdraft.

MANTELS

There's no strict rule dictating that every built-in fireplace must have a mantel. Many do not; quite a few contemporary designs carry the wallcovering material—usually brick or stone—right up to the edges of the fireplace opening. Most traditional fireplaces, however, still have mantels. Mantels can be made of practically any sturdy material, from a slab of rough-hewn oak, to granite, marble, slate, and even concrete. Some consist of elaborately carved wood.

All wood mantels must be set back from the fireplace opening edges to keep the wood from catching fire. The minimum clearance from the front of a fireplace is at least 14 inches away from the opening.

ASH PITS

A fireplace ash pit or soot pocket is formed in the hollow space within the foundation walls and is connected with the fireplace by a small metal door called an ash dump. Some fireplaces have them and others don't; it depends on the fireplace design and how often the owners will be burning wood. With an ash pit, to get rid of ashes and soot you simply open the ash dump door and scrape or shovel the ashes into the pit. Then they're removed through a tight-fitting metal cleanout door (about 10 by 12 inches) located in the foundation wall of the basement. In houses without basements, the pit takes the form of a metal bucket that is lifted out through the hearth when full.

In recent years, the ash pit is often placed on the outside of the chimney. This arrangement is workable in houses with or without basements, providing access to the ash pit from the outside, where the ashes are ultimately disposed of anyway.

DIRECT-VENT GAS FIREPLACES

Are you reluctant to fuss with all of the activities associated with wood-burning fireplaces, such as the procurement, cutting, storage and handling of firewood, disposing of ashes, as well as performing chimney and flue cleaning and maintenance? Then consider direct-vent gas fireplaces.

They come in a variety of attractive designs. Contemporary models include corner, three-sided peninsulas, see-through, arched, bay-front and other styles. The burning process is totally sealed from indoor air. Combustion air is drawn from outdoors and the flue gases go back outside through one special dual-channel pipe. No air is lost during the process, and there are no drafts or dust involved. They burn clean, efficient gas and need only an access through an outside wall right behind or above the fireplace for the exhaust hardware (Fig. 16.13). No expensive chimney is required.

Direct-vent gas fireplaces are efficient, too, up to 80 percent. Using one of these units can cut utility bills because it allows the home ther-

A direct-vent fireplace.

FIGURE 16.13

mostat to be set lower. For convenience, you can select a model with a hand-held remote control, which allows you to simply push a button to start a fire in the hearth. Other remote buttons control flame size, heat output, room temperature, and optional blower speeds.

Many of the better models have optional battery-powered ignition systems, or generate their own electricity from a pilot light. They will operate during an electrical power outage even when your furnace won't.

FIREPLACE ENERGY EFFICIENCY

The two major keys toward maximizing the energy efficiency of a fireplace are by reducing the amount of already heated up room air that escapes up a chimney, and, by directing or sending more heat from the fire out into living spaces. Then, by running a furnace blower or other blower on continuous air circulation, the heated air in the fireplace room can be distributed throughout the home. There are numerous steps you can take to accomplish the above, including:

1. The fireplace can be completed with tight-fitting glass fireplace doors with adjustable air openings. These glass doors not only block large amounts of indoors heated air from being drawn up the chimney while the fire is burning, but also when there is no fire. Some doors use magnets to keep the doors closed; others use cam mechanisms. High-temperature silicon gaskets provide excellent seals. These doors are available in attractive finishes such as polished nickel, copper, and pewter.

2. A heat-circulating grate and blower installed in the fireplace will greatly assist heat distribution. The quiet built-in blower draws cool room air into the grate so that air can be heated as it circulates through grate tubes before being blown back out into the room. The grate is typically constructed of steel pipes, that, again, enable cooled air to enter and heated air to be blown out. Since the grate base is only a few inches high, it fits under the glass doors (Fig. 16.14). The heat output can be as high as 40,000 Btu per hour.

3. Models with a built-in thermostat and a variable-speed blower provide the most control over heat output and noise levels. The thermostat turns the blower on automatically when it senses about 110 degrees Fahrenheit, and off again at about 90 degrees Fahrenheit.

FIGURE 16.14

A heat-circulating fireplace grate.

4. Consider the installation of a fireback, made of heavy cast-iron plate. Such a fireback positioned at the back of the fireplace will get very hot. It helps absorb—and then radiate—additional fireplace heat into the room, heat that's otherwise lost up the chimney. Many commercial firebacks have decorative patterns cast into their face (Fig. 16.15).

▶▶▶▶▶ POINTS TO PONDER

FIGURE 16.15

A cast-iron fireback.

1. Before you rule out a fireplace, check with local real estate brokers. Buyers in your area, when looking at homes similar in type and size to the one you're building, may expect at least one fireplace to be included. If you don't put one in your home, it may eventually hinder the resale value or your ability to sell.

2. Many people install fireplaces but are reluctant to use them because they have installed a light-color plush carpeting in the room, or they have no place to stack the wood, or they simply don't want the ashes and debris from burning and handling wood in the house. If you definitely plan to use your fireplace(s), plan the room's furnishings and wood supply storage accordingly, so a bit of ash or dirt here and there won't create a federal case.

3. Why not select fireplaces that deliver as much heat as possible into the house? Even though they may be more expensive up front, they'll have a continuing positive effect on energy consumption during cool to cold weather conditions.

4. For hundreds of years, Europeans, Russians, and numerous other groups have been using modular masonry fireplace units in which hot fires are stoked with wood or coal, and the surrounding firebrick and attractive glazed tile absorb the heat, store it, then gently release/radiate it throughout the day or evening, warming the unit's surroundings. Similar units are presently available through a number of manufacturers and distributors.

5. Prefabricated built-in fireplaces not only reduce construction costs, but make it possible to install a traditional design almost anywhere in an existing house.

6. Freestanding fireplaces are the least-expensive fireplaces and the easiest to install. They're typically made of steel or cast

iron, but are also available in soapstone—a handsome, durable fireplace and stove material.

7. If natural gas is available in your area, it's a good idea to include a gas starter in a fireplace.

8. By locating a fireplace on any inside wall, especially the wall separating the garage from the living areas, the part of the fireplace and chimney facing the garage does not need a facing of finished brick or stone, plus absorbed heat can radiate into the garage instead of being lost directly outdoors. This will save energy and material and installation costs.

9. Don't operate an open fireplace without the minimum protection afforded by spark screens. Glass screens and doors, however, are much safer.

10. For safety's sake (and to ensure operating efficiencies), fireplaces, flues, and chimneys need to be put on a routine cleaning, inspection, and maintenance schedule.

Plumbing

The plumbing and electrical systems in any dwelling can be considered the actual lifelines of the house. Without them practically all modern conveniences would be impossible. Due to their importance, both systems are strictly regulated by local and national codes, and both are included in ambitious inspection programs required to ensure the occupant's safety. This chapter focuses on plumbing.

The entire plumbing system of a house can be broken into five basic categories: water supply, pipe types, fixtures, water heaters, and drainage.

WATER SUPPLY

Your water source can be either public, private, or a combination of both. Public water systems are the most worry-free, from a homeowner's point of view. Large water pipes called *mains* deliver the water directly to your house in practically all urban locations, ensuring adequate water pressure and supply. Large private water systems often do the same thing for subdivisions beyond the reaches of public water mains. These latter full-blown water systems, both public and private, have strict rules and codes to follow that guarantee proper hookups to residential and other dwellings (Fig. 17.1).

FIGURE 17.1

Water supply system.

■ Homes with basements should have as much plumbing as possible run parallel along the floor joists then up through the floor. Try to minimize the number of holes drilled so piping can run perpendicular through the joists. Similarly, don't allow notching to the bottoms of the joists to make room for piping. In both cases, the holes and notches reduce the carrying strength of the joists. If piping absolutely must go through joists, the holes should be cleanly drilled

Joint center.

through the center of a joist, just large enough for the pipe (or wire) with some clearance to prevent a hot pipe from contacting a wood joist (Fig. 17.2). Check local building codes; they will provide guidelines. All told, it's best to discourage hole drilling.

Water Filters

If you plan to filter your water, you might as well have a filter unit installed on the main water supply pipe as soon as it enters the house (Fig. 17.3).

■ A filter can remove sediment, lead, rust, sand, silt, sulphur, dirt, excess chlorine, and many other undesirable elements—depending on what's in your water supply.

■ By removing impurities, a filter can reduce odors and improve the water's taste.

■ Installing filters from the start protects pipelines and water equipment, (water heaters, cooling

Water filter.

equipment, washers, dishwashers, and ice makers) from any harmful scale elements.

■ Installing filters can possibly protect household members from potentially harmful elements.

Water Wells

Beyond the big water supply systems, things get personal. Since the first settling of America, private wells or springs have provided rural farms and homesteads with their water. Wells are not as regulated as large water systems, and if you need one it's best to consult local professionals familiar with the conditions and special situations that exist in your area. There are certain constants, however, you should be aware of when putting in a well as your main source of water supply:

1. Locate the well as close to the house as possible, yet as far away from any septic disposal system as practical—preferably uphill from it. You certainly don't want to contaminate your water with sewage leachate. Also consider the possibility of sewage systems that future neighbors might install to the sides or back of your property, and keep in mind that presently uncontaminated rivers, streams, lakes, ponds, and swamps might not always remain so. Try to position the well at least 50 feet away from any of them.

2. When the well is completed, have it tested for water flow, purity, taste, and even color. If any irritating characteristics persist, such as "hard" water (having higher than usual concentrations of dissolved solids), a metallic taste, or a cloudy or off-color appearance, determine if those qualities can be effectively handled with a water softener/treatment unit that attaches to the well.

3. Protect the pipe that transports water from the well to the house from freezing temperatures. This can be achieved by burying the pipe below the frost line, lagging or wrapping it with insulation, or attaching electrically heated wire to the pipe (heat tape). It won't matter how good the rest of your plumbing is if the supply line freezes in midwinter. Frozen pipes are expensive to thaw and can cause a lot of damage if they burst.

PIPE TYPES

Cast-Iron Pipe

Cast-iron pipe might be heavy and awkward to handle, but it's so strong and durable it's been in general use for drain, sewer, and vent lines for years. Compared with plastic pipe, cast iron has two major advantages. First, it delivers its contents with much less noise. If you can't avoid running a waste pipe through a wall adjacent to a living or dining room, cast-iron pipe will prevent many uncomfortable moments you would otherwise be spending listening to water and waste gurgle through the line. Second, cast-iron pipe is more durable, and able to withstand the rigors of the "Roto-Rooter" and other mechanical and chemical pipe-cleaning equipment.

Galvanized Steel Pipe

Galvanized steel pipe is what was most commonly used for transporting water before copper lines gained widespread acceptance. It's available in various lengths and diameters, and has a rust-resistant coating on its inside and outer surfaces. Connections are usually made by cutting threads into the pipe, and because this is done after the protective coating is applied, any exposed threads will rust.

Because of its strength and wall thickness, steel pipe has a long life expectancy even when buried and is frequently used to supply natural gas as well as water. It's still a popular choice whenever a "rough" plumbing line is called for. The principal drawback is the pipe's roughness, which contributes to water-flow friction and the collection of mineral deposits and sediments that over the years tend to reduce the inside diameter of the pipe in the same way that cholesterol can accumulate and restrict a person's arteries.

Copper Pipe

Copper makes an excellent pipe. It comes in soft, flexible, and hard varieties, has a very long life, and—if not spliced into galvanized steel pipe—is generally not affected by corrosion. It's the number one choice to supply hot and cold water throughout today's modern houses. Copper lines are somewhat more expensive when compared with other piping, and so is the labor needed to install them. Individual pieces are connected by soldering them to copper unions, Ts, elbows, and other fittings. A major advantage of copper pipe is that it can be bent or curved rather easily, a characteristic not available with cast iron, galvanized steel, or most plastics. However, due to their nature, copper pipes require special pressure chambers to prevent "water hammer"—a shuddering, rapping noise created by a sudden turning off (or on) of the water. Like most other pipes, copper can be ruptured by water freezing inside.

Plastic Pipe

Plastic pipe is substantially less expensive than copper, galvanized steel, or cast iron. Plastic pipe is also simple to install and keeps labor costs low. There's no need to solder with torches, and no measuring and threading the ends of galvanized steel stock. There's only convenient plastic fittings, easy-to-cut plastic pipe, a can of plastic cement, and a brush. Almost anyone can do it.

There are other advantages to plastic pipe. It's extremely lightweight and easy to support. Plastic is chemically inert and unaffected by corrosive materials. The smooth inside surface of plastic pipe aids the movement of materials through the lines.

A few major disadvantages, though, eliminate the use of plastic lines from several parts of a house. It's not as strong as cast iron, galvanized steel, or even copper, plus it doesn't have the bending capability of copper. Because of its tendency to crack under heavy loads or stress, it shouldn't be used beneath or within a concrete slab where long, strong lengths of pipe having no splices are needed. As mentioned before, to the unwary, the noise that water makes when running through plastic lines can be a serious source of irritation if used above or near first-floor living areas, especially in multilevel houses. Plastic pipe will also burst when water freezes inside it.

A good-natured battle wages between the proponents of cast iron, galvanized steel, copper, and plastic for dominance over the entire house plumbing material question. The most sensible approach, and one favored by many residential plumbing experts, is to employ each kind of material where its strong characteristics can be used to best advantage. This means cast iron and steel for drainage pipes and for piping that's embedded in ground or concrete, copper for water supply, and plastic for venting.

PIPE INSULATION

While traditional construction methods prescribe that pipes—especially water pipes—exposed to cold temperatures should be insulated to conserve warmth or prevent freezing, we take pipe insulation recommendations to another level. Indeed, consider having *every* pipe—"hot" or "cold"—insulated with heavy-duty fiberglass or polyethylene foam tubes, their seams sealed with insulated tape. This should be done in the home's initial construction stages. Early on, it's simple and inexpensive to do. Later, once walls, ceilings, and floors are enclosed or covered, simple access will be lost.

A couple of points to consider regarding insulating pipes follow:

■ Piping in attics, garages, crawlspaces, and outside walls is especially vulnerable to freezing if nearby cracks and other openings let in cold air. If any areas of piping will be exposed to extremely cold temperatures, consider using a combination of insulation sleeves or tubes with electrical heat tape or a thermostatically controlled heat cable. Insist that the contractor use only products approved by an independent testing laboratory such as Underwriters Laboratories Inc., and make sure products intended for outdoors use are labeled that way. Manufacturer instructions must be precisely followed.

■ Insulated pipes, hot or cold, will maintain more consistent water temperatures. They will prevent hot water from losing heat and cooling off within the line, and, conversely, will prevent cold water from absorbing heat and warming up while it sits in the line. With insulated piping, water won't have to "run" as long to reach the desired hot or cold temperatures at the faucet. In other words, more hot water will stay hot longer within an insulated line, so it comes out of the faucet at the desired temperature sooner than would hot water standing in an uninsulated line that loses its heat in a cool basement and has to run out (being wasted) at the faucet until hot water fresh from the water heater can be drawn into its place. Thus, insulated pipes deliver water at desired temperatures with less waiting, less wasting of water, and less energy needed for heating. That's a savings of water, time, and money.

PLUMBING FIXTURES

Plumbing fixtures include the water heater, sinks, tubs, showers, toilets, and even outside faucets. The time and effort you spend planning their locations will be the most important part of their installation.

A major consideration is where to position the water heater, and how to keep as much of the plumbing as possible concentrated in one area of the house. Hot water will cool off if it must stand in sizeable lengths of pipe or travel long distances between supply and outlets.

For ease of installation and savings on materials, bathroom fixtures should line up along one wall, and, depending on the floor plan, the other side of such a "wet wall" full of plumbing could perhaps accommodate the plumbing support systems of a kitchen, a laundry, or another bathroom. Compact fixture placement will keep the plumbing clean and simple.

Another benefit of compact plumbing is that certain fixtures can share vents. Whenever possible, locate the toilet between the tub and sink, so the vent from the toilet can perform extra duty. Rookie bathroom planners sometimes ask builders to put the toilet on one wall, and the bathtub on the opposite wall. That causes unnecessary piping to be installed at an extra cost.

To save yourself from headaches later on, make certain every fixture can be turned off, preferably via a local or easy-to-get-at water shutoff valve, in case it's necessary to isolate the fixture so it can be serviced or repaired.

Don't ignore the economy that can be realized through careful planning of the house's entire plumbing system.

◀️ᖴOCUS

SHUTOFF VALVES

A shutoff, or "isolation" valve, stops water or other liquids or gases at some point within a pipeline or tank system, typically so maintenance, repair, or installation work can be performed downstream from the valve. Localized shutoff valves should be installed for all individual fixtures, such as faucets, bathtubs and showers, hot water heaters, boilers, dishwashers, and others. Don't allow the plumbing and fixtures to be installed without these shutoffs, or future maintenance will be difficult to accomplish without shutting off and draining main portions of the home's plumbing. Shutoff valves should include the following:

- Valves should be located beneath each faucet in the house.
- Shutoff valves should be present at the washing machine, dishwasher, and refrigerator ice maker.
- Toilets will have one cold-water valve usually installed under the water tank.
- Hot-water heating systems have a cold-water shutoff valve near their boilers.
- Bathtub and shower valves should be located behind the faucet controls.
- In addition to providing shutoff valves the contractor should cut an "access door" or a simple rectangular hole in the back of the plumbing wall that can be kept covered with a thin, discrete removable cover—they're often located out of sight within an abutting hallway or bedroom clothes closet. The door will allow access for any needed maintenance once the plumbing is isolated.
- The plumbing system should have an indoor shutoff valve to each sill cock (outdoor) faucet, which enables those faucets to be shut off and drained from the pipe to the faucet—reducing the risk of water freezing in the outside part of the faucet and piping during winter (Fig. 17.11).
- Each plumbing system must also have a main shutoff valve, typically located where the waterline enters the house and just before the water meter, on municipal water systems (Fig. 17.1). The idea is to be able to quickly shut off the entire water supply in response to serious leaks or emergencies. Again, if the water must be shut off at the main valve, remember to follow the boiler or water-heating tank instructions for proper shutdowns. Remember that any fire protection sprinkler systems will lose their water pressure as well.
- Test all shutoff valves, from the main valve to the individual fixture shutoffs, with the entire plumbing system activated, to see if they individually work or hold.
- Insist that the contractor tag basement shutoff valves with labels that tell what each valve shuts off, to prevent errors from being made if you ever have to activate them during an emergency.

DRAINAGE

Sufficient capacity and pitch, tight sealing, proper venting, and provisions for cleanouts are all important to a good, effective drainage system. Used water and the waste it carries must be disposed of, both for convenience and for the sake of your health. Waste creates unpleasant and potentially harmful gases that must be expelled. A drainage system therefore has two functions: to transport water and solid wastes to a sanitary sewer or septic tank, and to dispel noxious gases into air you won't be breathing.

If everything has been well planned, the waste water and materials will flow by gravity alone. Consequently, all drainage parts must be pitched or sloped downhill. These parts must be connected with special fittings and be large enough in diameter and smooth enough inside to prevent accumulation of solids at any point. This also means the fewer drainage parts, the better. It might not sound very exciting, but it's true: the entire plumbing installation is generally planned around the drainage system—to drain as many fixtures as possible with the same main pipe, and, the fewer main pipes, the better. This setup makes venting easier, too.

There are four topics important enough to discuss by themselves when it comes to drainage: the plumbing lines that drain the house's internal plumbing fixtures, the private, individual sewage system or septic tank, cleanout plugs, and venting.

The Fixture Drainage Lines

All drainage lines must be pitched toward the sewer pipe. Tests have proven that a ¼-inch pitch per foot of run will allow practically all waste to move freely, even though it doesn't seem like much of a slope. At the other extreme, a pitch of 45 degrees or more (1 foot of pitch per foot of run) provides a much stronger flow. If a straight run can't be accomplished with a sizeable pitch of ½ inch per foot maximum, the largest part of the run should be made using the latter pitch and the remainder sloped at 45 degrees.

Drainage line piping should use 45-degree elbows to minimize flow resistance, instead of 90-degree elbows. Using 90-degree elbows will slow down the drainage flow and increase the chance of a drainage plug up.

The slope and size of the trenches required to be excavated for the disposal lines are also important, and depend on the type of soil and the contour of the land. Ideally, excavators will dig all the drainage trenches at the same time they are completing the foundation preparations.

Septic Systems

Because drainage systems that malfunction can affect the health of the entire community, there are usually stringent regulations governing private or individual sewage systems.

The best all-around individual sewage system is the septic tank (Fig. 17.4). The septic tank system consists of a house drain, a septic tank, an outlet sewer, a distribution box, and a disposal or leachate field.

The location of a septic tank and leachate field on a building site will be partly determined by the lay of the land, since the drainage must be downhill and away from the water supply. Also remember that you need access to the tank when it must be serviced or repaired.

FIGURE 17.4

A septic tank system.

TANK INLET

TANK OUTLET

TO DISPOSAL FIELD

FROM HOUSE SEWER

TANK PIT

GRAVEL

FIGURE 17.5

A septic tank cutaway.

The soil pipe is the main drain from the house to the septic tank. It's usually made from a sturdy 5-inch cast-iron pipe that's pitched at an ideal slope.

The septic tank will most frequently be tar-coated steel or concrete (Fig. 17.5). Concrete costs more but lasts longer. When raw sewage enters the septic tank, bacterial action breaks down the solids into liquids and gases that drain off through an outlet sewer into a box that distributes them into the disposal field. This field is an area beneath the surface of the ground that "absorbs" and "cleans" the waste through natural processes of decay. The size of a septic tank is important because a tank that's too small will accumulate sludge that can back up into the house.

If you will need a septic system, be careful when you select your building site. Building sites seem to be getting smaller all the time. Once wide-open land is being built up. The space required for safe waste disposal is dwindling, and in some close-quartered neighborhoods, nonexistent.

FOCUS

SEPTIC SYSTEMS

A septic system is one of those hidden support systems that nobody thinks about until something goes wrong with it. To city dwellers who are used to the effortless convenience of sanitary sewers, septic systems are mysterious subterranean pipes and tanks that surely must take care of themselves.

Well, nothing could be further from the truth. Ask anyone who was raised on a farm. A septic tank system biologically breaks down household sanitary wastes. Bacteria within the system helps decompose the solid wastes. As these tiny microorganisms grow, feed, and breed in the septic tank and lines, most of the wastes are rendered into liquids that are trickled or leached into the ground through a "leaching field" of perforated pipe laid in underground beds of gravel. Some of the waste-laden sewage water that leaches through the disposal lines is additionally decomposed or purified by natural bacteria found in the ground from 2 to 6 feet deep. Other wastes, however, remain inside the septic tank in the form of a sludge that gradually accumulates. A wide variety of factors can influence a septic system's operation.

The contractor who installs your septic tank should supply you with information so you can inspect and arrange for maintenance services on the entire system. The following points are likely to be similar to the advice you should get.

SEPTIC SYSTEM INSPECTIONS: WHAT TO LOOK FOR

- Septic tanks that are filling with sludge.
- Remove the access cover or cap and measure the depth of sludge by inserting a long stick into the tank. When the total depth of solids exceeds one-third of the tank's capacity (certainly no more than one-half), it's time to have the tank pumped out and the solids removed. On many septic systems, if the sludge is allowed to accumulate it will eventually fill the tank so there is no room for waste to enter from the house. If this happens, the tank may overflow and saturate the surrounding grounds with horrible-smelling raw sewage.
- Sluggish or plugged waste in sewer lines.
- When septic tanks are not functioning properly, a side effect is that lines running from the home's toilets are slow to convey wastes from the toilets to the septic tank. Solids and waste paper begin to settle and accumulate in the lines. Eventually, the whole system could back up.
- Unusual foliage displays above leaching fields.
- Look at the grounds above and adjacent to the leaching field. Abnormal or luxuriant lawn conditions are an indication that the soil is being overloaded with waste-laden nutrients. Wet, soggy soil is another characteristic of failing absorption fields or clogged septic tanks. A good time to inspect leaching fields is during very wet weather. The size and composition of the leaching field should be sufficient to absorb household wastes and rainwater at the same time. If a heavy rain overloads the system, and turns the leaching field into a swampy mess, improvements should be considered—perhaps adding more lengths of drainage pipe. Most problems are caused by the quality of soil around the

leaching field. If there's a lot of clay present in the soil, good drainage will be almost impossible to achieve.

- Trees and large shrubs growing on leaching fields.
- Roots can reach into the absorption beds and clog perforated piping. Make sure trees and large shrubs are not encroaching over or immediately adjacent to septic system leaching fields.

SEPTIC SYSTEM REPAIRS AND MAINTENANCE

As far as repairs go, few individuals look forward to working on septic systems. Special tools and equipment such as heavy-duty pumps and vacuum units are often required.

1. Septic tanks should be cleaned periodically, or when they need it. Most should be checked twice, or at least once a year to see that they're in working order. Typical septic tanks need cleaning about every two or three years. Ideally, the cleaning can be done in the spring. Because the waste material can give off obnoxious odors and may contain disease bacteria, and warm weather accelerates bacteria action, it's best to pump and get rid of the waste before hot weather sets in. Cleaning a septic tank is not recommended as a do-it-yourself project. There are qualified companies that specialize in working on septic, well, and similar plumbing systems. They'll have the knowledge and equipment, and they'll also know where to get rid of the waste. It can't and shouldn't just be dumped anywhere.

2. Leaching fields should be kept free of trees and shrubs.

3. Avoid connecting nonessential home wastewater streams to a septic system. Runoff from gutters should be channeled elsewhere, as should discharge water from swimming pools and sump pumps.

4. Review with other family members what household wastes should not be put into septic systems.
   - If you have a kitchen garbage disposal, try not to grind and dispose of large amounts of vegetable and fruit matter. It's much better to dispose of them in an above-ground composting bin or pen, along with grass clippings, leaves, and similar vegetable and plant matter. Kitchen sink waste that's introduced to a septic system takes more time to be broken down by bacteria than do human wastes. If kitchen sink wastes are sent to the septic system, it will probably mean more frequent septic tank pumping and cleaning.

- Avoid using drain cleaners and high-foaming detergents if the plumbing they go into is connected to the septic lines. Those substances will kill bacteria that's needed by the septic system to break down regular wastes. Low- and nonfoaming detergents are okay to wash with. So are nonphosphate and biodegradable laundry soaps.
- Never let petroleum products, paint thinners, solvents, cleaning fluids, dyes, cigarettes, plastics, or similar materials enter a septic system. Most are harmful (or neutral) to the bacteria that grows, feeds, and breeds in the septic tank.
- Grease from cooking juices and related activities should be reduced as much as possible. Grease, animal fats, and related food particles tend to float and accumulate in the top layer of lighter-than-water scum and slime that's present in all septic tanks. It's usually pumped out during regular maintenance of the tank. Naturally, never pour grease down a kitchen sink. Instruct family members to scrape and wipe as much grease as possible from cooking pans before immersing the pans in soapy water.
- Also avoid placing modern "flushable" sanitary napkins into a septic system. Naturally, that goes double for regular types of sanitary napkins as well.

NEW SEPTIC INSTALLATIONS

When planning a new septic system, the most critical factor is the type of soil the ground is made of. Soil having good drainage will make things easier. As a general rule, a three-bedroom house should have, at minimum, a 900-gallon septic tank. A four-bedroom dwelling should have a tank with at least 1150-gallon capacity. Since the septic tank and system is so critical to the daily operation of a household, leave nothing to chance. Get some professional help. Check with companies that have installed systems near your location. They'll know what to look for and what to look out for as well. Also consider the following options, all designed to take the pressure off of the septic system:

- In many areas, building codes insist that all toilets must be connected to a sanitary sewer or septic tank. These codes have not caught up with all of the advances made by toilet manufacturers. There are toilets available that perform their own decomposing operations, channeling the waste (along with a very small amount of water) to relatively small tanks that are usually installed in a basement. These tanks need to be emptied as few times as once per year. And by then the waste has been broken down into a practically odorless material. Composting toilets thus greatly reduce the amounts of solid wastes going to a septic tank, and the overall amount of water used in a bathroom.

- A less-radical option is one of a number of new toilets designed to use less water per flush. Since even now, at this very moment, new designs are on the drawing board, check with local plumbing supply houses for news on the most water-efficient models.

- Another workable idea is to use two separate septic tanks: one for solid waste and the other for what's known as gray water. Gray water is wastewater that's not heavily laden with solids. It includes rinse and other water from clothes washing machines, dishwashers, showers, bathtubs, and even sump pumps. The gray water can be routed through its own tank to the leaching field, so it won't overload the main septic tank.

NOTE

- Large vehicles should not be allowed to drive over septic tanks or leaching fields. Be especially wary of large, heavy rigs such as concrete trucks, front-end loaders, bulldozers, drilling outfits, and the like.

SEPTIC TANK QUICK CHECKLIST

1. Septic tanks should be cleaned out when the total depth of solids within it exceeds between one-third and one-half of the tank's capacity.
2. Have septic tanks inspected at least once a year, typically during spring.
3. Keep trees and large shrubs from growing over the system's leaching field.
4. Avoid routing gray or nonsanitary wastewater to the septic system.
5. Keep kitchen wastes out of the septic tank. Same with petroleum products, paints, solvents, and similar materials.
6. Don't use drain cleaners or high-foaming detergents if the plumbing they drain into is connected to a septic tank.

Cleanout Plugs

The importance of cleanouts in a plumbing system becomes apparent as soon as there's a blockage somewhere. Plumbing stoppages occur due to a number of reasons, including the following:

- Foreign objects lodged in a drainage line

- An accumulation of hair or other matter

- Deposits of grease, fat, or other congealed substances

These materials can completely block the discharge through drainage lines, or at least greatly reduce effective flows. Complete blockages cause considerable damage to the lower floors when wastewater backs up. Even partial stoppages can create conditions in drainage lines that interfere with proper venting. In turn, poor venting results in the escape of foul gases and odors into the living areas of the home.

Pipe drainage cleanouts should be accessible for servicing. The contractor should provide an out-of-sight access door for any that are located within a wall.

Venting

A *plumbing* or *building trap* is a device installed in plumbing that prevents the intake of sewer gas into the interior piping system. A cleanout at the trap offers access to the house's sewer line between the dwelling and the outside street sewer facilities. Other gases and odors in a home's plumbing are kept in check and vented from the house through piping that runs up through the roof. At the same time, this prevents gurgling or sucking sounds after a fixture is drained and protects trap seals from siphonage and back pressure.

It's best to specify that the vent pipe or pipes be installed near the rear of the house so that they're not readily visible from the street (Figs. 17.6 and 17.7).

WATER HEATERS

Until fairly recently, most homeowners had only one basic water-heater type available for their home hot-water use: a tank water heater. Today, tank water heaters still make the majority of water heaters sold and installed for home use. But another type of system is likely to con-

FIGURE 17.6

A drain/waste/vent plumbing system.

FIGURE 17.7

Toilet venting.

tinue to gain wider acceptance in the near future: that of the tankless water heater. Most water heaters are fired by either natural gas, propane, oil, or electricity.

Tank Water Heaters

The capacity of a tank water heater is an important consideration. The water heater should provide enough hot water at the busiest time of the day or night. The ability of a water heater to meet peak demands for hot water is indicated by its "first hour rating," which accounts for the effects of tank size and the speed by which cold water is heated. A standard tank of 40 or 50 gallons is usually sufficient for a family of four living in a house having two and one-half bathrooms, but larger tanks are available for high-volume water users.

A number of points regarding water tanks should be kept in mind:

1. Look for a unit that has a self-cleaning system that creates a turbulent swirling action as water enters the tank, thus fighting sediment build-up, improving operating efficiency and lengthening tank life.

2. Some tank heaters are available with set-back adjustable thermostats. Units with multiple temperature settings are convenient

SAFETY NOTE

HOT-WATER-HEATING SYSTEM SHUTOFFS

When shutting the water off to the boiler or other parts of a hot-water-heating system or to a hot water heater (tank), carefully follow the manufacturer's instructions. If a boiler or hot water heater runs out of or low on water, serious damages (including explosion and fire) and injuries can result.

FOCUS

WATER SOFTENERS

Also referred to as water conditioners, when the quality of available water is less than ideal, the installation of water softeners or conditioners can provide a number of major benefits, including the following:

- Filtering potentially harmful contaminants out of the water
- Removing miscellaneous unpleasant tastes and odors from the household's drinking water
- Softening hard water reduces build-up of hard-water soap curd, which can gum up the insides of appliances. Less soap-curd deposits can mean dishwashers, clothes washers, and water heaters will operate more efficiently, for a longer lifetime.

Hard water typically contains unusually high amounts of minerals and metals, including iron, calcium, and magnesium. This water can wreak havoc within a home, causing soap scum and lime deposits to form on numerous appliances, fixtures, and plumbing components. Hard water will leave streaking windows, bathtub and toilet rings, tainted appliances, plugged showerheads, restricted flows in pipes, and other nagging problems. Water softening is by far the most common treatment required to hard water supplied by wells and some private or municipal water authorities. Advantages of softening hard water are many. They include the following:

- Hard water causes lime scale buildup. Lime scale coats moving parts in appliances, causing them to operate less efficiently. Lime scale collects within water heaters, reducing heat exchange efficiencies and increasing the cost of heating water. Lime scale clogs pipes and fixture internals and slows the delivery of water throughout the home.

- Hard water will discolor bathroom and kitchen fixtures.
- Soft water works far more efficiently with soaps and detergent cleaners. For clothes, shorter wash cycles and cooler water will suffice when soft water is employed. In some cases, for the same results, twice as much cleanser is needed when used with hard water. Hard water can also reduce the life span of clothes when lime "curd" deposits cause difficult-to-remove yellowish or gray stains. For people and pets, bar soap and shampoo usage will be reduced with soft water. Hard water can dry skin and hair because the minerals within the water combine with the soap to form a sticky residue that's hard to rinse away.

People who use hard water tend to use more skin-softening lotions and hair conditioners.

SELECTING WATER SOFTENERS/CONDITIONERS

Consider the following points when reviewing your water softener or conditioner needs:

- First, test your water so that you know exactly what problems, if any, you need to solve. A local water treatment company expert can perform a preliminary analysis, usually at no charge.
- Conventional softening equipment works via an ion exchange. The softening tank is full of tiny porous plastic spheres that attract hard calcium and magnesium ions. When the spheres are full of these hard ions, a regeneration cycle starts to clean off the spheres so that they can be used again to soften more water. For maximum savings, look for a sphere-cleaning system that uses a salt solution and water. Further, a demand-initiated regeneration system actually meters water usage and only regenerates on demand—unlike units that use timers to regenerate at preset intervals, which can require twice as much salt and water. Give serious consideration to a twintank system that allows switching from one softening tank to the other as they exhaust their softening capability, to provide an uninterrupted flow of soft water 24 hours per day.
- Lean toward reliable systems not subject to electric timer malfunctions or power outages. Cost should not be the main issue when it comes to water softening and conditioning. You'll want equipment that operates without interruption, is easy to care for, and produces consistent desired results.

and can save energy costs when water can be kept cooler during certain times. Some models are manufactured with a timer and integral thermostat that automatically raises or lowers the water temperature in the tank up to four times per day, to conserve energy. If need be, each day can be programmed differently. This control system enables the unit to reduce the temperature temporarily when hot water is not in demand, such as when you're asleep or at work. A manual override can be accessed when a pre-set schedule must be changed.

3. Install them near the highest hot-water demand areas in order to reduce wasted energy from running the water long distances. If your house will have two equal demand areas, try to center the water heater between them. If your furnace and hot water tank vent through the chimney, they will logically need to be near each other. However, many of the high-efficiency furnaces and hot water tanks have their own direct vent system, allowing them to be vented straight to the outdoors. Because a hot water heater or tank will wear out in time, you should be able to easily access it for removal, and the inspection panels and drain valve must also be simple to get at for maintenance and repairs.

4. Check to see if adding insulation to your water heater will affect the warranty. If additional insulation is desired, follow the instructions from the water-heater manufacturer.

5. A water heater tank must have a drain near the bottom so you can easily drain the tank when needed, and can periodically flush out sediments that collect at the tank's bottom. Unless you have soft water, it's important to drain water from the bottom of a water-heater tank periodically to help remove hard-water deposits that may accumulate on the tank's bottom. These deposits effectively act like insulation. They eventually surround the heating element and force it to work harder and harder at heating the tank's water. Removing these sediments by periodic draining of small amounts of water from the tank's bottom will help keep the system healthier and less expensive to operate.

6. When locating a gas water heater in a garage, keep it raised off the floor so when the pilot ignites the gas burners it doesn't cause any floor-hugging gasoline fumes from a lawnmower or auto to explode.

Tankless Water Heaters

Also called "demand" water heaters, these tankless units provide alternatives to the standard hot water tank. Why consider tankless units? There's less risk of a water rupture—with all of the water damage such an unexpected event can cause. Also, tankless water-heating equipment will likely last longer than components of a tank heating system. Tankless components are less subject to corrosion. The highest quality models use stainless steel, copper, and brass for parts that contact water. If a component malfunctions, it can be repaired. There's no tank to rust out, so the entire unit never has to be replaced.

Too, tankless systems provide hot water where and when you need it, without relying on a preheated inventory of heated water. Considerable energy is lost from heated water that simply stands in the tank all day and all night. Tankless units also virtually eliminate standby water heat losses—energy wasted when hot water cools down in long pipes or while sitting in a storage tank. By providing heated water immediately where it's used, tankless water heaters waste less water. People don't need to let water run as they wait for warm or hot water to reach a remote faucet. A tankless water heater, correctly sized, provides almost unlimited instant heated water as long as the system is used within its capabilities.

For example, when someone opens a hot-water faucet within a home's plumbing system, the tankless water heater "senses" this—starting the gas burner or the electric elements that heats the water as it flows toward the faucet. By using standard fuels such as electricity, gas, or propane as a heat source in this remarkably efficient system, tankless water heaters can reduce a household's water-heating bill by 10 to 20 percent, or more. The top models have modulating gas-valve or electric-heat output, and solid-state controls maintain a steady hot-water temperature. These designs ensure a constant water temperature from a faucet's trickle to a shower's full-force spray.

As a rule, tankless water heaters are a lot smaller than water-heater tanks; some are only 36 inches high and hang on a wall (Fig. 17.8), others are about the size of a bread box. When compared with bulky water tanks, those units use far less of valuable square footage living space. Direct-vent models are available, as are units with electronic ignition to save energy otherwise consumed by a continuously burning pilot light.

FIGURE 17.8

A tankless water heater.

Are there any downsides to installing tankless water heaters? One could be that in the event of an electrical failure, a tank full of already heated water is *not* available, on standby, as would be with a hot-water tank system. Another could be dependent on the affected electrical power utility—tankless electric units draw more instantaneous power than tank water heaters because water must be heated quickly to the desired temperature. If electric rates include a demand charge, operation could be relatively expensive.

PLUMBING INSPECTION

It's likely that the plumbing in a new house will be put together satisfactorily from a technical viewpoint because local codes usually specify that licensed plumbers must perform the work, and all of that work must then be inspected and certified. But no matter what the situation is with your house, it's still up to you to determine if the plumbing is installed in a fashion that you feel is adequate. Here are some guidelines to help you evaluate your plumbing system:

PLUMBING CHECKLIST

Few things in a house can be as irritating, as destructive, and as expensive to repair as plumbing. When it's working, it's taken for granted. When it's not, look out. Keep yours out of trouble by identifying and following the applicable items in this checklist. And also be aware of the choices you can make in the selection of various fixtures.

1. Plumbing Item Specs

___ Sewer pipe from street to house: preferably cast iron or steel.

___ Sewer pipe under the house: preferably cast iron.

___ Exposed sewer and vent pipes: plastic, cast iron, or copper.

___ Cleanouts in enough locations.

___ Sewer pipe from street to house: preferably cast iron or steel.

___ Sewer pipe from street to house: preferably cast iron or steel.

___ Cold and hot water supply pipes: preferably copper.

___ Sewer pipe from street to house: preferably cast iron or steel.

___ Sewer pipe from street to house: preferably cast iron or steel.

___ Natural gas piping: preferably "black" steel pipe.

___ Toilet: specify type, manufacturer, model, and color.

___ Bathtub: specify fiberglass, steel, or cast iron, manufacturer, model, and color.

___ Molded shower/tub unit: specify type, manufacturer, model, and color.

___ Bathroom vanity top/sink: specify porcelain or cultured marble or other, type, manufacturer, model, and color.

___ Kitchen sink: specify stainless steel or enamel; type, single-, double-, or triple-basin; manufacturer, model, and color.

___ Faucets: specify single- or double-handle type; chrome, brass, or other; manufacturer, model, and color.

___ Refrigerator: include a water connection for an ice maker.

___ Shower heads: specify type, manufacturer, and model.

___ Garbage disposal: specify manufacturer and model.

___ Dishwasher: specify manufacturer, model, and color.

___ Clothes washer and dryer: specify type, manufacturer, model, and color.

✔✔✔✔✔ PLUMBING CHECKLIST (*Continued*)

___ Laundry tub: specify manufacturer, model, and color.

___ Water heater: specify electric, natural gas, or oil heat source; gallon capacity; and manufacturer.

___ Water softener: specify manufacturer and gallon capacity.

___ Water wells and pumps: specify size and type.

___ Septic tank: specify size and type.

2. Plumbing Minimum Drain Specs

___ Toilet: 3 inches

___ Shower stall: 2 inches

___ Clothes washer: 2 inches

___ Laundry tray: 1½ inches

___ Tub and shower: 1½ inches

___ Bathroom sink: 1½ inches

___ Kitchen sink: 1½ inches

___ Dishwasher: 1½ inches

3. Pipe Insulation

___ Bare pipes do not conserve energy, so they should be insulated. Insulating cold-water pipes prevents cooling the warm air around them during winter, which can cause a heating system to run harder than necessary.

___ Insulating hot-water pipes is useful year round. During late spring, summer and early fall, pipe insulation will prevent the heat from the hot water inside the pipes from radiating and warming the surrounding air, which forces the air-conditioning system to run more often. Insulating hot-water pipes also helps prevent hot water in the lines from cooling off before it reaches its destination faucet or appliance.

___ For pipe insulation, consider ¾-inch-thick-wall preformed pipe insulation tubes, some constructed of flexible rubber or polyethylene foam. These tubes can be purchased in bulk, or by the piece, often 3- or 6-feet long, pre-slit and self-sealing.

___ Make sure that whatever type you choose is rated to safely handle the highest temperature your system can produce. If the insulation

PLUMBING CHECKLIST *(Continued)*

is not suited for the application, the insulation could deteriorate or even catch fire. Insulate bare steel-jacketed burst-proof hoses with flexible pipe-wrap insulation with ¾-inch-thick walls.

4. Miscellaneous Plumbing Points

___ You should be able to conveniently turn off the water or gas supply pipes to each plumbing fixture in the house with shutoff valves (Fig. 17.9).

___ A neat way to arrange the plumbing needed by the clothes washing machine and laundry tub is to have the plumber install an in-the-wall-plumbing box (Fig. 17.10). This box will dress up the installation and provide protection to any plaster or drywall that might be placed behind your laundry area. It's a good method to achieve the plumbing compactness mentioned earlier. All of the faucet, supply, and drain piping is conveniently tied together. A laundry room clothes washing machine will be safer and more energy efficient if insulated steel-jacketed burst-proof water supply hoses are used.

SHUT-OFF VALVE

FIGURE 17.9

Sink shutoff valves.

✔✔✔✔✔ **PLUMBING CHECKLIST** (*Continued*)

FIGURE 17.10

An in-the-wall plumbing box.

___ Make sure that piping run through the basement does not "break up" otherwise usable living space.

___ Include enough sill cocks. A sill cock is nothing but an outside cold water tap for lawn watering, car washing, and other outdoors use (Fig. 17.11). A typical dwelling should have at least two of them,

A sill cock.

PLUMBING CHECKLIST *(Continued)*

and very large houses as many as four—so you needn't rely on excessively long and unwieldy garden hoses. Have the sill cocks staggered around the house with one near the driveway. In cold-weather locations where freezing occurs, sill cocks should be of the freeze-proof variety to protect your exterior faucets from freezing and rupturing. A freeze-proof outside faucet having a long stem shuts water off a foot or two back within the house, where things stay warm and above freezing.

___ Locate a sill cock or water faucet in the garage, preferably on an inside wall bordering the heated part of the house.

___ Insist that single-unit bathtubs or shower stalls be installed while the house is being framed for a more custom built-in look.

___ Even if you're not including a basement bathroom with the initial construction, it's a good idea to include a "service stub" or connection arrangement for one sink, one toilet, and one tub/shower unit, so they can be easily installed later.

___ Vinyl, ceramic tile, and wood flooring should be installed in rooms that will receive plumbing fixtures. You'll have a much neater looking floor if these materials are laid down first. If carpet is the selected floor covering, the carpeting underlayment should be installed before the plumbing comes through, then the carpet itself can be laid after the fixtures have been set.

___ To prevent cluttering up the appearance of the front of the house, have waste vents exit through the roof at the rear of the house.

___ All roof stacks should be made of galvanized or other nonrusting metal or material.

___ A floor pan should be installed under a clothes washer if the washer is located upstairs.

PLUMBING

1. Bathtub/shower hot and cold faucets operate correctly, with no dripping when shut off. The drains work quickly.
2. All sink faucets and drains work as they're supposed to.
3. Toilets flush properly, fill to correct lines, with no seepage or running sounds.
4. Turn on all sink faucets and flush all toilets at the same time to see if they'll all work without a major reduction in water flow.
5. Allow faucets, tubs, and drains on upper floors to run for a while. See if any stains form on downstairs ceilings beneath those fixtures. Best to catch problems early, before the home is painted or wall-papered.
6. Garbage disposal operates smoothly.
7. Dishwasher operates evenly, with no leaks. Run through an entire cycle.
8. Run the clothes washing machine; make sure the drain discharge doesn't leak.
9. No scratches, dents, or chipped surfaces on appliances.
10. Test the water heater drain valve. See if it opens easily and seals shut when closed.
11. Operate the sump pump, the humidifier, the baseboard heat, and all other plumbing components that may apply. Check for leaks.
12. Try all outdoor spigots. Make sure they close easily and completely.
13. Check that isolation valves are tagged as to what they shut off. Test the isolation valves, with the system activated, to see that they hold. Make sure with hot water heaters and boilers that the manufacturers' instructions are followed.
14. If the home has natural gas, ask the utility company to test or "sniff" the gas lines, gas appliances, and areas in which those components are present for leaks, loose fittings, and other problems. Many utility companies will do such a check as a complimentary safety service.

1. All piping must be well supported. Nothing should just hang there, wobbly or vibrating when liquids and waste materials pass through.

2. Pipes should run parallel to inside wall studs. If any pipe runs parallel to an exterior wall stud, make sure insulation is arranged between the pipe and both the interior as well as exterior part of the wall.

3. Check to see if the plumber installs the correct number of shutoff valves and cleanouts as called for in the prints.

4. Before the walls and floors are closed up by the contractor, the rough plumbing must be inspected by the municipal inspector. You should also make a mental note (or drawing) of what's getting covered up. Check that all water piping has been insulated.

5. The regular plumbing lines should be water-tested and inspected for leaks, and if there's a gas line, it must be subjected to pressure leak tests as provided by the building code.

6. One of the most obvious ways to conserve resources and energy is to prevent leaks. A faucet that leaks hot water wastes both. That's why you should select only faucets that come with a strong warranty. The extent of coverage specified is a good indication of the manufacturer's quality standards. For a top-notch faucet, look for an all-inclusive warranty, one that applies to all of the parts as well as to the outside finish. Consider washerless, drip-free faucets as desirable alternatives to old-fashioned units with washers and seals—the main reasons for troublesome leaks.

7. Request outside faucets: one in the garage (on a warm wall), one at the home's front, and two at the back to allow simultaneous lawn sprinkling, car washing, or garden watering.

▶▶▶▶▶▶ POINTS TO PONDER

1. The time and effort you spend planning the location of plumbing fixtures is the most important part of their installation.
2. A major consideration is where to position the water heater, and how to keep as much of the plumbing as possible concen-

trated in one three-dimensional area (from basement or lowest level to top level) of the home.

3. The plumbing should be planned, if possible, so waste water and materials flow by gravity alone.

4. Drain a few gallons of water from the water heater tank at least once a month. At the same time, check the tank's pressure valve.

5. Know where plumbing shutoff valves are. The contractor should label each valve as to what it shuts off. Operate each valve several times a year to keep them in working order.

6. All piping must be well supported to prevent wobbly or "hammering" lines.

7. For maximum energy savings, insulate water heater tanks (following the manufacturers' instructions) and water lines. Install water heaters near the highest hot-water demand areas to reduce wasted energy from running the heated water long distances.

8. When planning your landscaping, keep large trees and large shrubs from being planted over septic tank leaching fields, and also avoid, if possible, connecting nonessential home wastewater streams to a septic system. Runoff from gutters should be channeled elsewhere, as should discharge water from swimming pools and sump pumps.

9. If a gas water heater is located in a garage, make sure it's raised off the floor so when the pilot ignites the gas burners it doesn't cause any floor-hugging gasoline fumes from a lawnmower or auto to explode.

10. Whenever you have the option, elect water-saving appliances such as low-demand toilets, smaller bathtubs, and low-flow faucets and showerheads.

Electric

If there is one system in a house that shouldn't be skimped on, it's the electrical. Like the plumbing in a house, the electrical system is taken for granted until something goes wrong with it or there's not enough to go around. To properly understand your prints and drawings, familiarize yourself with the symbols in Table 18.1.

TABLE 18.1 Basic Electrical Symbols

1.	⊖=	Is a duplex wall outlet. This supplies your power to lamps, vacuum cleaners, and other household devices and appliances.
2.	S	Means a single-pole switch. This provides on and off control to outlets from one position
3.	S_2	Signifies a double-pole switch. This provides on and off control from two locations. For example, it lets you turn off lights from either of two entrances to a room.
4.	S_3	Is a three-way switch.
5.	S_4	Is a four-way switch.
6.	Ⓢ	Is a pull-switch in the ceiling.
7.	S_{CB}	Is a circuit breaker.
8.	=⊖wp	Means a weatherproof outlet.
9.	⊙̣	Denotes a ceiling light fixture.
10.	TV	Is a television antenna outlet.

THE POWER SUPPLY

The minimum power supply recommended for most houses today is a three-wire 240-volt, 200-ampere service, especially if the house is larger than 3,000 square feet, if heavy-draw electric appliances such as electric cooking ranges or clothes dryers are planned, or if such features as central air-conditioning and swimming pool pumps will be installed.

A good indication of the power supply available at any site is whether two or three main wires enter the weatherhead fitting on the roof or side of the house. If only two wires are present, the dwelling has 110–120 volt power throughout. If three, then 220–240 is available at the meter.

The circuit box is where the main electrical service is split into separate circuits. There should be at least 12 to 15 circuits to handle the electrical needs for most homes. The cover on the panel should be able to be tightly closed, and the main wires entering the box should be neatly and securely affixed to the wall. Home wiring must be grounded properly. Proper grounding provides a path for electricity to safely travel from a defective appliance, tool, outlet, fixture, or other

✔✔✔✔✔ APPLIANCE WIRING CHECKLIST

When you think of it, there aren't many modern home conveniences that would work without electricity. Here's a checklist you can use to help plan your electrical service. Consider electrical service for the following:

___ **Telephones** (kitchen, living areas, bedrooms, basement, garage)

___ **Doorbells** (front and side or back doors with different tones) with illuminated buttons

___ **Refrigerators** (kitchen plus spare for basement, garage, or wet bar)

___ **Freezers** (kitchen plus spare for basement or garage)

___ **Furnace blowers**

___ **Thermostat controls**

___ **Cooking ranges/stoves**

___ **Microwave ovens**

___ **Water heaters**

___ **Televisions** (electrical, cable, antenna service)

___ **Smoke alarms**

APPLIANCE WIRING CHECKLIST (*Continued*)

___ Carbon monoxide alarms

___ Cable television hookup

___ Video players and games

___ Personal computers-Internet access

___ Attic fans

___ Bathroom fans

___ Garage door openers

___ Dishwashers

___ Clothes washers

___ Clothes dryers

___ Hi-fi speaker systems

___ Intercoms/cassette or stereo systems built into walls

___ FM antenna hookups

___ Burglar alarms

___ Garbage disposals or compactors

___ Electric grills

___ Sun lamps in bathrooms

___ Water pumps

___ Sump pumps

___ Vent hoods for cooking ranges

___ Central air-conditioning

___ Dehumidifier

___ Humidifier

___ Jacuzzi motor with timer switch

___ Overhead circulating fans and whole-house attic fan with timer switch

___ Electric heat-circulating fan built into a fireplace

___ Bathroom heater, vent fan, lights

___ Attic power ventilator

___ Electric baseboard heaters, if main or supplementary heat source

___ Central vacuum system

component, to the earth or ground. Your local building code will state what is required for proper grounding in your area.

Electric clothes dryers and cooking ranges require special 240-volt receptacles. These receptacles differ slightly but significantly, so make sure the dryer and range receptacles will fit your appliances. Electric water heaters are wired directly to the house's electric cable. Electric ranges can also be wired directly.

Because most major appliances run on electricity, you'll want to

- Make sure the brand is reputable
- Consider if the features of each appliance will do what you need them to do
- Evaluate the warranties on each one
- Check for energy efficiency
- Know if service contracts are available

ELECTRICAL OUTLETS AND SWITCHES

The rule for electrical outlets is one duplex outlet for every 12 linear feet of wall, because lamps and household appliances usually have 6-foot-long cords. When a doorway comes between, the outlets around it should be located closer than 12 feet apart or you might have to use extension cords in that part of the room. Kitchen outlets are best located above the countertop to handle appliances safely. A duplex wall outlet for every 4 linear feet of kitchen counter space will do nicely.

Here are some other guidelines:

1. There should be light switches at every entrance to every room, and, for safety's sake, at the top and bottom of stairs and at garage and basement doors. These switches should be about 3 feet away from the steps so that the user will not trip on or down the steps while trying to access the light.

2. Insist on "intermediate-" or "specification-" grade outlets and wiring. There are also "competitive" grades of cheaper quality for only a minor difference in cost. Specification grade, the best of all, is usually recommended for heavy-duty commercial installments,

but is worth the extra cost if you want top quality, particularly in the kitchen and in all switches.

3. Wall switches should control overhead lighting. If a room has more than one entrance, install double- or triple-pole switches so these lights can be turned off and on from each doorway.

4. If a room has no overhead lighting, such as a living room or family room, wire at least one duplex outlet to a wall switch so a lamp that's plugged into the outlet can be turned on and off at the switch on a wall near the room's entrance.

5. Include at least three outside electrical outlets (two in front, one in back), and for a large, sprawling ranch home, four. They should be equipped with ground fault circuit interrupters for protection from the electrical hazards posed by wet lawns and driveways, as well as a weatherproof cap that covers each receptacle.

6. Install ceiling outlets in the garage for automatic garage door openers even if you're not planning to use openers at first. If you decide to add such a convenience later, you can do it without having to spend a hefty price for a service call.

7. Be certain to plan several receptacles in the garage for power tools, an extra freezer, a vacuum cleaner, and other items.

8. All ceiling fixtures such as lights and fans must be securely fastened to the house framing structure and not dependent on the outlet for anchoring.

9. There should be at least one ground-fault circuit interrupter (GFCI) duplex safety outlet above each bathroom vanity top for hair dryers, electric shavers, and other personal care appliances. Such outlets will help prevent shock.

10. All receptacles should be the three-hole grounded type. These are much safer than the old two-hole ones. If an appliance becomes faulty, the current will pass through the third wire (the ground wire) in the receptacle rather than through you.

11. Make sure you allow for a sufficient number of outlets throughout the home, especially for plugging in and unplugging electronic equipment. Many of today's home electronic items use electricity even when turned off—they go into "stand-by" mode so that they'll

instantly ready when needed. This stand-by energy loss is sometimes referred to as "leaking electricity." Consider that to save this type of energy from enlarging energy bills, try to remember to unplug home electronics and appliances when they're not in use.

12. It's easy to overlook the basement when planning for outlets. Consider that refrigerators, freezers, hand tools, vacuums, dehumidifiers, sump pumps, and extension cords all require electricity.

13. Locations of certain light switches and outlets you want in special places can be marked in advance with chalk.

LIGHTS AND LAMP WIRING

1. Wire for overhead lights in the dining area, kitchen, kitchen sink and counter, laundry room, bedrooms, bathrooms, hallways, garage, and basement.

2. Avoid putting recessed lights in ceilings with unheated space above. They can't be properly insulated and will leak air badly. Recessed lights should be the Insulated Ceiling (IC) type. Confirm from the manufacturer that the units will not become hot enough to be fire hazards.

3. Include recessed lights in all closets, with wall switches mounted outside the closet near the closet door (Fig. 18.1). Even shallow closets having bi-fold doors will need lighting on occasions.

4. Consider some outside spot or floodlights to provide illumination for general use of the yard and for security reasons. Ideally, some yard lighting should be controlled from the master bedroom as an additional security measure.

FIGURE 18.1

Closet recessed lighting.

5. Make sure there's wiring for lighting at the front and back doors and wherever someone can enter the house, with convenient switching at those locations. Lighting should be wired near the main electric service panel so you can see the circuit breakers and their labels without using a flashlight.

SURGE PROTECTORS

A power surge may not sound dangerous, but if it strikes your PC, TV, or other piece of electronic equipment, it can cause expensive problems. The average home gets almost a dozen surges from lightning every year—power surges that can damage electronic microchips. And lightning is not the only source of high-voltage surges. Local businesses and utility companies with electrical equipment going off and on can also help create potentially damaging power surges.

These surges may not damage an electronic device right away, but the cumulative effects can definitely ruin equipment over time. Each surge results in an electrical "hammering" that wears and tears at the weakest parts of the electronics, eventually causing failure. Power surges come from both outside and inside a home, for numerous reasons, and can even travel through phone and cable television lines.

The remedy? In addition to individual outlet plug-in surge protectors, whole-house voltage surge protectors are available for installation with a home's main electrical system. Such a combined two-stage method protects electronic equipment from almost anything short of a direct lightning strike.

Whole house surge protectors help protect every television, phone, computer, modem, microwave oven, programmable thermostat, stereo, fax machine, security system...the list goes on and on. Some whole-house surge protectors are installed at the circuit breaker box, while others are engaged at the electric meter—generally installed by the supplying utility company. These surge protectors use very little energy and can literally save hundreds of dollars in appliance repair and replacement costs because modern appliances are often operated through delicate electronic controls that can be instantly damaged by high-voltage surges.

With less power spikes and surges traveling through the home, appliance energy-efficiency capabilities and life expectancies are increased; even simple light bulbs will last longer and burn brighter. The surge protectors should have monitor lights that indicate if the units are working. Before specifying whole-house surge protection, discuss the options with your builder or electrical contractor.

ELECTRICAL INSPECTION

Here are some wiring features to watch for as the house nears the plaster/drywall stage, and how the electrical inspection proceeds:

1. See that in exterior walls, cables installed horizontally run along the top of the bottom plate. This provides the least interference with wall insulation. Most electric cable is sufficiently flexible to comply.

2. Be careful how electric wiring is installed in bathrooms. It should not be run through the area around the bathtub. Wiring should also stay clear of places where long screws may be used to fasten shelving, soap dishes, or towel racks to the wall.

HOME CONTROL SYSTEMS

Individuals with busy schedules can employ relatively sophisticated home control centers by simply touching bedside controls or clicking the mouse of a personal computer. These units can operate various home equipment functions even from remote locations through code numbers sent via Touch-Tone phone lines. Homeowners can better manage their heating, cooling, and ventilation systems to save money and increase comfort. These electronic units can control functions such as the following:

- Setting/checking security systems before leaving the home or retiring at night
- Setting lawn sprinklers for the next morning or evening
- Automatically turning off/on house or Christmas lights
- Setting what time a VCR/television should wake you up or record a program
- Automatically starting kitchen or other appliances

3. Wires should not be placed too close to any plumbing to avoid damage from the plumber's propane torch.

4. After all the rough wiring is completed—known as the "roughing out"—and checked over, the electrician will contact both the Underwriters Laboratory inspector and the local building code inspector who will inspect everything and, if satisfied, will issue a certificate and notify the utility company. The utility company will then send a representative to connect power to the house.

5. The electrician can now wire all the outlet box receptacles as soon as the walls are insulated and covered. To finish this work, the electrician must know how you plan to complete the walls so that the boxes can be set to project the right amount through the finished walls.

SPECIAL ELECTRICAL FEATURES

Remember to give some consideration to the following features:

1. Noiseless, no-click light switches. There are also silent touch-button switches that require only slight finger pressure. There are flat-plate models that are set flush against the wall. Slight pressure on the top turns a light on, and pressure on the bottom turns it off.

2. Ivory, colored, metallic, and other decorator switchplates are available instead of the standard plastic brown, off-white, or tan models that might clash with your decor. Electrical and lighting suppliers carry them in a wide variety of models and materials. These unique switchplates can give your house an interesting finishing touch overlooked in most dwellings today.

3. Dimmer controls enable you to adjust lighting intensity up or down according to your needs. Illumination in a room can be dimmed to a candlelight glow for a dinner party, kept subdued for television watching, or turned up brightly for reading. Dimmers are used chiefly for living and dining rooms, but can also be used in a bathroom night-light arrangement.

4. You can have built-in automatic switches that turn on the closet lights when the doors are opened, and then turn them off again when the doors are closed, similar to the refrigerator interior lighting setup.

5. Remote-control lighting is surprisingly simple to install. It can permit you to turn indoor and outdoor lights on or off from a central location such as the kitchen or master bedroom. A remote kitchen switch can control front door or garage lights, for example A control panel next to your bed can eliminate that final tour of your house and grounds every night to turn out all lights.

6. Electrical snow-melting panels are available for sidewalks and driveways, and electrical snow-melting wire strung along your roof gutters will prevent the accumulation of dangerous snowdrifts and icicles on the roof slopes and gutters (Fig. 18.2).

7. No-shock outlets can be installed to prevent children (who frequently insist on jabbing hairpins or anything metallic into receptacles) from receiving shocks.

8. As already mentioned, safety-type grounded outlets can be added protection against shocks and help prevent the possibility of electrocution in a bathroom. A ground fault is a partial short circuit in an electrical device. A person can be the electrical ground (electricity will travel from an outside source through the person and into the ground) when using an appliance or tool in a damp or wet area such as a bathroom, laundry room, basement, garage, or backyard. The partial short circuit allows a small amount of electrical current to flow through the individual's body—a condition that could be harmful or even fatal. Regular household appliances work by drawing power from one side of a wall receptacle through one prong on the plug, and returning it through the other prong to the other side of the receptacle. If the GFCI (ground-fault circuit interrupter) detects extra current within the circuit, it will trip a little breaker within itself and interrupt the current. GFCIs belong wherever household members are likely to

FIGURE 18.2

Snow-melting wire.

encounter wet or moist conditions (Fig. 18.3). These outlets are safeguarded by a groundfault circuit interrupter (GFCI), a safety device that acts as a second fuse and kicks out the socket's power in the event of a malfunctioning hair dryer, electric shaver, or other appliance. The socket can simply be reset with the push of a button. As with any bathroom receptacles, these outlets should not be within reach of a bathtub or shower.

CHILD-SAFE ELECTRICAL OUTLETS

SAFETY POINTERS

For electrical protection of children, consider installing outlets with a nightlight on the top outlet and with the bottom outlet blocked with a cover that flips down when electrical access is needed.

FINAL INSPECTION

ELECTRICAL

1. Furnace/heating unit starts and stops okay.
2. Cooling system runs.
3. Washer, dryer, sump pump outlets operational.
4. Central vacuum system works.
5. Bathroom vents and heaters work.
6. Jacuzzi pump motor operational. Timer switch is not reachable from the tub.
7. Electric range/stove operates properly. Electric pilot light on gas range is connected and working correctly. Range hood, down-draft, and light work.
8. Garbage disposal, dishwasher, trash compactor all work. Refrigerator outlet is functional.
9. All lights work.
10. Door chimes work.
11. Garage openers work.
12. Thermostat/power ventilators on roof are connected and working.
13. Electronic security system operational; each individual sensor tested.
14. No scratches, dents, or other damages to electrical appliances.

FIGURE 18.3

Ground-fault circuit interrupter.

9. Even if you don't initially plan to have a security alarm system, the wiring for one can be easily installed within the walls at the time of construction. The system can then be inexpensively completed at a later date, if desired.

▶▶▶▶▶▶ **POINTS TO PONDER**

1. Insist that no "competitive" or cheaper grades of electrical wiring and related components are used.
2. Make sure that the main electrical supply wire is properly grounded and sturdily attached to the house, and free from encroaching tree limbs or other wires and cables.
3. Remember to specify electrical outlets in the basement, garage, and attic, plus near outdoor front and rear entrances, and patio and deck areas.
4. All circuit breakers in the home's main circuit box must be clearly marked by the electrical contractor, so electricity can be turned off to certain parts of the home if necessary, and so areas where electrical overloads occur can be identified.
5. Major appliances that are heavy users of electricity should have individual circuits to themselves.
6. For a modern look and ease of operation, consider using large push-on, push-off light switches instead of standard wall switch controls.
7. Any electrical outlets positioned in areas where water is expected to be present, such as outdoors, in kitchens, bathrooms, laundry rooms, garages, or near swimming pools need to be ground-fault circuit interrupters (GFCIs).
8. To protect against appliance- and computer-damaging power surges, have a whole-house voltage surge protector installed with the main electrical system.

9. Research available electronic home communications and control systems for possible installation and use in your new home.

10. Consider wiring the home for motion detector lighting, outdoors and indoors. Motion-sensing wall switches exist that activate when a person enters a room or area.

Lighting

Along, long time ago, before humans discovered how to use fire, when it got dark, it got dark. There were no switches to flip on, and no battery-powered flashlights to illuminate pathways. Once we mastered fire, we not only increased our comfort, safety, and gastronomical enjoyment, but the light we gained supplied us with more time to constructively work with.

The first lamp could easily have been a lit pool of fat drippings that shimmered in a shallow depression near the glowing embers of a cave campfire.

Then clay and stone lamps came onto the scene—little more than saucer or cup-shaped receptacles for oil, grease, or tallow. They were either open or covered, with a carrying handle on one side and on the other a small trough or gutter in which a wick rested. This simple lamp persisted for about 10,000 years, resisting change even into the eighteenth and nineteenth centuries, when people were still using dangerous iron lamps that burned disagreeable-smelling whale oil.

Throughout the ages, light has always been something sacred to humans. It has been a symbol of religion, of ideas, of knowledge and understanding. It has enabled us to take advantage of our most important sense: sight.

Lighting in these days, however, often takes a back seat. People will frequently buy lights because they fancy the fixtures, not the effects those features will provide. When you think of it, that's kind of silly. It's like buying food for only its looks, or for how it might conveniently fit into a refrigerator or freezer, with no regard to taste or nutritional value.

There's often little advance planning for lighting. While homeowners pride themselves in knowing the last little detail about stereo systems, kitchen ranges, or video players, the lights that illuminate their private worlds are completely taken for granted. That's too bad, because precise lighting can create a variety of moods within a room and can help exaggerate strong points while downplaying shortcomings. Lighting can increase efficiency in work areas. Consider how important lighting is to theater and dance. What show, what film, what live performance have you ever seen that didn't include strategic lighting as a major part of its overall effect? Consider museums and art galleries, and how they can make their showcase works stand out by merely lighting them properly.

The same principles hold true for lighting in home use, in the average household. Unfortunately, most people are afraid to make advance plans they feel might be too radical and difficult to change. Nothing radical is needed, however, to lend a home a pleasant lighting scheme. It doesn't take many built-in lights to add a distinctive touch.

TYPES OF LIGHT SOURCES

Sunlight

Sunlight, or "natural" daylight, as it's sometimes called, is plentiful—at least during the day—and free. Natural light can lift a person's spirits, can help display colors more accurately, and provides excellent illumination for reading or for doing intricate tasks.

People and plants function better in a natural light-filled environment. Of course, sunlight intensity can be somewhat reduced by clouds, weather, foliage, plus the seasonal position and tilt of the Earth's axis. Days get longer and shorter and longer again, and some sunlight is considerably stronger in certain locations and places. Unfiltered sunlight, or rays strengthened and concentrated by certain types of glass and windows, can send ultraviolet and other light waves into the home to discolor and fade furnishings and to dry out and burn skin on people, pets, and plants.

Naturally, the chief source of natural light is glass in windows, sky-lights and doors. In earlier editions of this book, discussions about skylights were presented only in the chapter about windows, where they were mentioned regarding their roles providing ventilation and natural light. Numerous advances in skylight technology, however, made it far more logical to include some information in this, the lighting chapter, as well.

Electric Lighting

There are only two major kinds of electric lamps or "bulbs" as most people call them: incandescent-filament lights and fluorescent lights.

INCANDESCENT-FILAMENT LIGHTING

The first practical incandescent-filament lamp was perfected by Thomas Edison in the late 1800s. An incandescent lamp produces light when its filament (usually made of tungsten) is heated by an electric current to a regulated temperature, at which point it glows and emits the amount of light it's engineered for (Fig. 19.1). The quality of light from incandescent-filament bulbs is warm in color and gives a friendly, homelike feeling to interiors. Beneath incandescent lights, colors such as oranges, reds, and browns are enhanced, while the cool colors such as blues and greens are subdued.

These bulbs provide a source of light that can be focused or directed over a restricted area if desired, and because most incandescent household bulbs have the same size base, the lighting from fixtures or lamps can be increased or decreased within limits by changing to bulbs of different wattages. Most types of incandescent lights are less expensive than fluorescent types. And the incandescent lighting fixtures themselves are generally less expensive to purchase because they require no ballast or starter—a part of a light bulb that provides a high voltage for starting the bulb and a low voltage for running it.

FIGURE 19.1

Incandescent-filament light.

FLUORESCENT LIGHTING

Fluorescent bulbs operate by an entirely different principle. They've typically been long and tubular in design, either straight, circular, or angular in the case of neon signs used for advertisements. They're coated on the inside of the glass with phosphors, substances that give off light when subjected to ultraviolet radiation generated by a low-pressure electric charge. The low-pressure electric charge is regulated by the starter or ballast that forces the charge through a mercury vapor inside the bulb (Fig. 19.2).

Fluorescent bulbs offer greater lighting efficiencies, up to three or four times as much light per watt of electricity as incandescent bulbs have. They'll also last from seven to ten times longer, largely due to their cooler operating temperature range. Hot-burning incandescent lights, by their very nature, burn themselves out more quickly.

Fluorescent bulbs provide lines of light and are excellent choices in work areas where light coming from several angles is needed to effectively eliminate bothersome shadows. These lines of light are also frequently used over mirrors, kitchen work surfaces, in window valences, corners and covers, and other architectural features. Due to their long life spans, fluorescent bulbs are favorites in places that can't be conveniently reached for bulb changing. Circular fluorescent tubes have traditionally been used in high kitchen ceilings, for example.

When considering their use, remember that some fluorescent bulbs aren't as quiet as incandescent lights. Most fluorescent models produce faint humming sounds, which admittedly are noticeable only if a room is library quiet or if you're listening for the noise. A newer wrinkle to the lighting scene has been the emergence of smaller, more compact fluorescent bulbs or lamps.

Compact Fluorescent Lights

As a general guideline, although they can cost many, many times what a comparable incandescent bulb costs, compact fluorescent light bulbs are about four times more energy efficient, provide equivalent illumination for considerably less wattage,

FIGURE 19.2

Fluorescent light.

produce less heat, and last up to 6 to 10 times longer. Many take the form of coil-type spiral bulbs that will fit in traditional incandescent fixtures (Fig. 19.3). Others are manufactured in straight, longer styles that may not fit traditional fixture shades or globes designed for incandescent bulbs.

For sure, compact fluorescents are great for hard-to-reach places where changing bulbs may be both an inconvenience and a safety issue. When planning your lighting, remember that not all compact fluorescents are equal. Some are constructed with electronic/iron ballast in each bulb; cheaper models with this kind of accompanying ballast tend to flicker at startup,

FIGURE 19.3

A compact fluorescent spiral bulb.

and may buzz. When planning for compact fluorescent fixtures, consider fixtures with built-in ballasts that take pin-based replacement bulbs (Fig.19.4), which will save money because you won't have to replace the ballast within the bulbs every time you change a bulb.

FIGURE 19.4

Compact fluorescent pin-type bulbs.

Just be sure you know how much the replacement bulbs will cost, where to buy them, and that pin-type fixtures will not accommodate standard screw-threaded incandescent bulbs. Also be aware that many compact bulbs cannot be dimmed with dimmer switches. If you want to dim one, you'll need to purchase a bulb designed for dimming. If applicable and desired, make sure the same bulb can be used with photo sensors, electronic timers, or motion detectors. Fluorescent bulbs come in numerous makes, models, and sizes, including three-way and floodlight styles.

Some, however, have certain restrictions on what they should be used for, such as: only indoor use, outdoor use, low-temperature use, cannot be installed within a glass globe, or cannot be installed in an inverted position. Compact fluorescent lights are components that are constantly being improved, and you can expect numerous advancements in the near future.

Skylighting

Again, you'll find a separate discussion of skylights in the window chapter. Although it's hard to review the same subject here without some overlap, there are several important points worth re-reviewing:

A skylight is basically a casement window mounted in a ceiling or section of roof framing to provide natural daylight, and sometimes ventilation, so the need for additional active daytime electric light, and possibly powered ventilation, is reduced. Since hot air naturally rises, opening a vented skylight will exhaust such heated air and create a comfortable breeze inside the dwelling without relying on air conditioning. Some models are fixed in place, and do not open or vent at all.

On skylights that do open or vent, control options range from a manual crank, to an electric motor operated by sophisticated electronic and/or hand remotes.

Many skylights come with laminated or tempered glass having low-e and tinted coatings that effectively control heat transmission and ultra violet radiation. Compare U-value, heat transmission, and light transmission rates of all skylights you may consider for your home.

Sunlight Tubes or Tunnels

Sunlight tubes or tunnels are, essentially, highly reflective cylindrical skylights that run from the roof down into an interior room or space (Fig. 19.5). These natural sunlight skylights are complete roof-to-ceiling systems for efficiently bringing natural sunlight into the home.

In frequently used rooms requiring ongoing lighting, a sunlight tube or tunnel offers natural lighting that saves turning on electric lights every time you enter, say, a bathroom, kitchen, or other room where such a natural lighting system is installed. There are lots of makes and models available, but they all operate under the same principle. Sunlight enters through a clear acrylic plastic or similarly made dome on the roof.

Acrylic does not yellow from sun exposure, and it naturally filters out some of the damaging ultraviolet rays from the sun. In its domed shape, it is very resistant to breakage, even from hail. Rain will usually be enough to keep it clean. Some domes incorporate a prismatic lens, like a "fly eye," that helps bend and collect low-

FIGURE 19.5

A sunlight tube.

angle or early morning light and late afternoon light down into the tube or tunnel. Some units provide interior seals and a double-insulated diffuser lens component that creates insulating dead-air pockets similar to those of a thermal pane window.

The insulation rating on some models is as high as R-22. Collected sunlight travels from the roof dome through a rigid or flexible tube or tunnel. The rigid tube or tunnel is lined with one of several types of silvery, highly reflective linings of aluminum or equally good quality. A rigid tube is fine for passing through an open attic; the fewer bends (elbow joints), the better, because even though the tube is highly reflective, some light intensity is lost each time the light bounces back and forth inside the tube. Flexible tubes or tunnels employ sturdy construction that can be easily bent around obstacles such as chimneys, furnace ducting, beams, and other construction components, without using elbow joints. The captured sunlight, after being transported down the tube or tunnel, is then diffused into a room or space through another prismatic diffuser lens.

On sunny days, this natural skylight can easily provide the equivalence of between 600 to 700 watts of incandescent light. Even on cloudy days there is still enough natural light to approach the illumination level of a 100- or 150-watt bulb, and what's more, on nights with a clear sky and full moon, an out-of-this-world moon glow within the room is not out of the question.

HOME LIGHTING USES

Few homes will rely on one or the other type of bulb exclusively. Most dwellings employ a combination of incandescent and fluorescent fixtures. What follow are three different ways in which both types of lights can be used in modern dwellings.

General or Background Lighting

General or background lighting is a low level of illumination required for general living activities. It's the level of lighting provided by ceiling fixtures such as overhead lights in a bedroom, or from lighted valances (shields affixed to the wall that direct light from a source behind them upward, downward, or both ways), coves, cornices (shields affixed to the ceiling that direct light from a source behind them downward), and wall lighting, or portable lights in groups of three or more that cast relatively low but adequate levels of light throughout a room.

Local or Task Lighting

Local or task lighting is the light you want focused on relatively small areas or limited areas used for specific activities such as reading, playing cards, typing at a computer keyboard, playing billiards, sewing, painting, shaving, cooking, and eating. These are the lamps and fixtures people are most familiar with, including floor, desk, and table lamps, and other lighting arrangements such as recessed ceiling downlights in a bathroom to illuminate a bathtub or hand basin.

Accent or Decorative Lighting

Accent or decorative lighting comes from fixtures planned to create certain moods and atmospheres, plus fixtures designed and positioned to emphasize artwork, plants, and any other items important to a person's lifestyle or interior decor. Many different kinds of fixtures and bulbs can be used in creative ways here, limited only by the owner's imagination. Spotlights, floodlights, all sorts of decorative lights, and even candles, will create a host of effects.

While planning your home you have to decide how much of each of the lighting types you need. Then look through designer books, magazines, and lighting sales literature for ideas, and, if possible, visit actual houses that pay attention to lighting schemes. It doesn't take many well-placed lighting built-ins for a house to be considered unique, and such a home will gain a special quality not found in the vast majority of dwellings that treat lighting merely as a necessary afterthought, not a part of the house to be carefully planned for maximum effect.

With general lighting, the light rays are usually diffused over a wide span. This diffusion is best accomplished by translucent glass or plastic. In a room in which the light is completely diffused, it will be coming from all sides, either directly or indirectly (bouncing off other surfaces) including the floor and ceiling, so no shadows are cast.

Dimmers can be useful to increase control over a variety of lights by taking charge of the voltage or current applied to the bulb or tube, thus giving a full range of light intensities.

FIGURE 19.6

A light switch with a dimmer slide control.

Dimmer Lights

Dimmer light switches that come with intensity slide on and off controls (Fig. 19.6) allow you to simply turn a light on or off without setting or resetting the dimmer intensity level each time. By operating lights at less than their maximum output, energy savings can be realized. Dimming can also add an interesting mood to a room while quietly extending the life of affected light bulbs. Light bulbs dimmed just 10 percent on a regular basis are estimated to last about twice as long as a bulb burned at full brightness. For flexibility, dimmer switches are available that allow dimming the same light fixture from multiple locations.

Under-Cabinet Lights

The kitchen is one room to consider for the installation of low voltage under-cabinet lighting that will make counters brighter and safer at a savings compared to operating overhead fixtures that illuminate the entire room. Because basic kitchen lighting can place the fixture at the center of the ceiling, cooks working at counters frequently find themselves working behind their own shadows. This will make food preparation difficult and sometimes even dangerous. Under-cabinet lighting gives an effective lighting output that can be focused directly on tasks at hand. Fixtures are available with swiveling heads that allow home cooks to pinpoint illumination exactly where it's desired.

Automatic Light Switches

Also called motion-activated light switches, these "automatic" controls (see Focus on Motion Detector Lighting) are typically activated by a sensor that detects a moving object that emits heat, such as a person or animal. When the activating creature leaves the room, the light will automatically turn itself off, preventing lights from being left on unintentionally. These switches should also have electric eyes so that the lights do not come on if there is already enough daylight present. Units having adjustable daylight sensors for this purpose will allow the level of darkness to be preset for when motion will begin to turn the lights on. For rooms where you spend a lot of time in the evening, watching television or reading, you can install a light control that gradually brightens the lights as night falls. It senses the current conditions and maintains a preset desired brightness level within the room. Automatic light switches can be great indoors for bedrooms, kitchens, stairwells, closets, garages, attics, and laundry and utility rooms. It's nice not having to reach for a light switch if your hands are full of groceries

MOTION DETECTOR LIGHTING

Motion detector lighting can provide both convenience and cost-efficiency. No more fumbling for light switches when entering a closet, garage, basement, attic, or laundry room—especially when your arms are full of groceries, tools, or laundry. Feel more secure when you come home to an illuminated entryway, deck, or patio (Fig. 19.7). Some units

FIGURE 19.7

Motion detector lighting.

can be adjusted to sense motion up to 50 feet away and within a 120-degree radius. It's also convenient for visitors to park their vehicles outside in a well-lit driveway, and to approach the home's entrances on illuminated walkways. Motion-detecting units can come with solar-powered security lights. The solar panels are normally tethered with long cords so the panels can be located in a remote place. Solar units are also available with amorphous collectors that make use of energy present in low-light levels during morning, dusk, and even overcast and rainy days. Heavy-duty batteries allow units to work in below-freezing temperatures.

Indoors, why allow lights to be on for long periods of time, especially if you have children who are constantly forgetting to turn them off?

Motion-sensing wall switches exist that activate when a person enters a room or area. Lights can easily be "tuned" to stay on for 1 to 10 minutes after no motion is detected. Sometimes a wide field of view for a sensor works best for a particular situation, and other times a narrow field is desired. Motion-detecting units are available for both. Installation of these convenient components can be specified along with the main electrical system.

or laundry. The electricity savings from not leaving the lights on by accident will quickly pay back the cost of the switch, and when children are involved, the savings can be even greater.

LIGHTING TERMS

Lighting terms are constantly being tossed about by various experts and publications. Here are a few that you should be familiar with:

- Semi-direct—light is directed 60 to 85 percent downward.

- Semi-indirect—light is directed 60 to 85 percent upward.

- Recessed—lighting fixtures affixed flush to a ceiling, wall, or other surface (Fig. 19.8).

FIGURE 19.8

Recessed lighting.

- Valance—light sources shielded by a panel attached parallel to a wall, usually employed across the top of a window. Valance lighting provides illumination both downward and upward, unless the valance possesses a top (Fig. 19.9).

- Indirect—a system in which over 85 percent of all the light is cast upward toward the ceiling.

- Direct—over 85 percent of all the light is cast downward toward the floor.

- Accent—directional lighting to emphasize a particular area or object (Figs. 19.10 and 19.11).

- Cornice—light sources shielded from direct view by a panel of wood, metal, plaster, or diffusing plastic or glass parallel to the wall and attached to the ceiling, and casting light over the wall through direct or downward lighting (Fig. 19.12).

FIGURE 19.9

Valance lighting.

FIGURE 19.10

Accent light.

FIGURE 19.11

Accent light.

FIGURE 19.12

Cornice lighting.

FIGURE 19.13

Cove lighting.

FIGURE 19.14

General diffuse lighting.

- Cove—light sources shielded by a ledge and casting light over the ceiling and upper wall, usually through indirect or upward lighting (Fig. 19.13).

- General diffuse—almost an equal amount of light produced in all directions, such as the light emitted from a suspended globe (Fig. 19.14).

- Luminous—a lighting system consisting of a false ceiling of diffusing material with light sources mounted above it (Fig. 19.15).

- Track—one electrical outlet supplying a number of separate fittings that can be positioned anywhere along a length of electrified track. It's very versatile for ceilings or walls, with vertical or horizontal tracks (Fig. 19.16).

- Wallwashers—when installed about 3 feet away from a wall, wallwashers will light up the wall evenly from top to bottom or bottom to top, without spilling or wasting light away from the wall into the room. Angled closer to a wall of paintings or art groupings, wallwashers will splash light onto varying surfaces, leaving interesting shadows contrasted in between.

- Downlights—round or square metal canisters that can be recessed into a ceiling, semi-recessed, or ceiling mounted to cast pools of light on the floor or on any surface below them. They can be a spotlight, a floodlight, or an ordinary bulb. A spotlight will throw a concentrated circle of light. A floodlight will cast a wider, cone-shaped light. An ordinary bulb will provide soft, diffuse, all-over lighting.

- Uplights—fixtures put on the floor, behind sofas, plants, or other appointments, under glass shelves, and in corners where they will lend a beautiful dramatic accent, bouncing reflected light off ceilings and into the room, creating moods that could hardly be imagined possible by day.

Exterior Lighting Considerations

- Consider solar powered security lights (Fig. 19.17), where solar panels collect free natural light during the day and store it as energy in rechargeable batteries. No exterior supply wiring is needed. For motion-sensing models, at night, a halogen bulb

FIGURE 19.15

Luminous lighting.

FIGURE 19.16

Track lighting.

turns on automatically when any motion is detected and remains on a certain length of time—30 seconds or so—after the motion stops. Other models are triggered by timers or automatic photocell electric eyes set to specific darkness levels (that turn on automatically at night, and off in the morning).

There are units available that work by solar panels so the light itself can be located in a shady area if need be. Some can function in temperatures reaching 40 degrees Fahrenheit below zero. You can aim, test and adjust the solar lights via test switches, and weatherproof housings

FIGURE 19.17

A solar-powered security light.

seal for protection against the elements. Some units will operate for nights without an intermediate charge. Different styles of solar-powered lights can solve a variety of specific lighting challenges. Wall-mounts, hanging units, column-mounted coach lights similar to a lamp post, pagodas, and tier lights that are wall-mounted or ground-supported cover most situations.

For entryways, decorative lantern units are common choices. Many have adjustable motion sensitivity and manual override so you can activate the light from a standard wall switch. Motion-sensing flood lights directed at rear and side entranceways or walkways are recommended by many security experts. Even on cloudy days, built-in batteries will keep them working. At dusk, an electric eye automatically switches on an accent amber LED. When motion is detected within about 20 feet of the light, a bright halogen bulb comes on for about 3 minutes to scare away unwanted visitors. Remember that the key factors to consider when selecting a motion-sensing light are the sensitivity range and field of view. Those two factors determine the area of security coverage for an individual light fixture.

■ To assist evening delivery persons, visitors, emergency service providers, and others, solar-powered house number lights are available. Numbers 4 inches high illuminate at night and can be clearly seen from the street. They need only a couple hours of sun during the day and are completely weatherproof. Mailboxes with solar-powered lights also use rechargeable batteries that can be activated at night by a remote control feature that allows you to turn on the lights from inside your home.

- Hanging garden lights are another outdoors option. They come with an adjustable height hanging hook. They're ideal for illuminating steps, walkways, entryways, porches, decks and patios.

General Lighting Considerations

- Use lower-watt bulbs for nonworking spaces.

- Choose light fixtures that are easy to access and clean. Remember that dirt absorbs light.

- To get the most from your lamps, walls and ceilings painted white will maximize the amount of reflection into the room.

- Lighter color and shades of furnishings such as carpeting, draperies, and upholstery will minimize the amount of artificial light required by a room.

- Mirrors spread light within a room. By strategically placing mirrors where they will not be blocked by furniture, illumination can be spread and extended to where needed.

- Selecting fluorescent-bulb fixtures over incandescent-bulb fixtures results both in energy savings and longer individual bulb life. This becomes especially important with fixtures that illuminate from hard-to-reach areas inside garages, stairwells, foyers, attics, or anywhere you need a ladder to change the bulbs. Standard 4-foot-long bulb fluorescent fixtures with reflective backing and electronic ballasts are great for workroom, garage, and laundry areas.

- Bulbs having the Energy Star label, though they typically cost more to buy, run with less pollution, less energy, and will last longer.

- Use lamps and other fixtures having three-way controls (for bulbs having three separate wattage levels, such as a bulb for a table lamp set up as a reading light, with the brightest intensity setting to read by). Three-way bulbs enable you to use the lower settings when the brightest is not necessary.

- When choosing night lights, consider 4-watt mini fluorescent or electro luminescent models. Some use as little as a few cents per year to operate. Some have auto-off features that will turn the light off after 10 to 30 minutes; after 9 or 29 minutes the bulb will blink twice—signaling that it is only 1 minute away from turning itself off.

- Have you ever been frustrated by children who leave closet lights on forever? Then consider door frame buttons that turn on the light as the door opens—similar to that of a refrigerator. As the door is closed, it pushes the button in and the light turns off. Of course, you've got to train those same children to keep the closet doors closed, or install an automatic door closure.

- To provide cost-effective security lighting while you're gone, consider electronic timer/light switches. The best ones enable you to set different light schedules (six on/off times) for each day of the week. Some even have random lighting schedules. Even for just an evening out, it's an effective strategy to have indoor lights go on at dusk, or at other times while no one is home.

- Remote control entry door locking and lighting controls allow you to illuminate and unlock an entry door from as far as 30 feet away, providing both security and convenience. This helps save energy by eliminating the need to leave your outdoor lights on all evening until you return, and allows you to use both hands to carry items to the door, instead of using one hand for keys. With the remote, you may need one less trip back to the car, as well as one less opening and closing of the entry door. Each time the door is opened, heated or cooled air can escape.

▶▶▶▶▶▶ POINTS TO PONDER

1. Built-in lighting—opposed to lighting fixtures simply added on after the rooms are planned—will add a distinctive touch to any home.

2. Fluorescent lamps offer greater lighting efficiencies than do incandescent-filament lamps. Initially, setting up for fluorescent lighting is more expensive, but those expenses will eventually be recaptured with lower energy costs.

3. Fluorescent lamps—due to their cooler operating temperature range—will typically last up to ten times as long as many incandescent bulbs. That's why fluorescent lamps should be considered in places that can't be conveniently reached for bulb changing.

4. If absolute quiet is a major factor, such as in a small office or library, remember that fluorescent bulbs aren't as quiet as incandescent light. Most fluorescent models produce faint humming sounds. On the other hand, so do personal computers—and few individuals notice or complain about computer background noise.

5. Most homes are constructed with plenty of general or background lighting such as overhead lights in bedrooms. Identify places where local or task lighting will be needed and try to plan recessed or track lighting units to focus on those areas.

6. Dimmer switches make sense wherever accent or decorative lighting is installed. Dimmers increase control over lamps by taking charge of the voltage or current applied to the bulb or tube, thus allowing a full range of light intensities.

7. Make sure fixtures are rated for the bulb wattages you plan to use in them. For example, avoid burning 100-watt bulbs in fixtures rated for only 60 watts.

8. If your children are notorious for leaving certain lights on all the time, such as bright lights over a makeup table, consider putting the lights on a 15-minute (or so) timer switch that will automatically turn off the lights unless the timer is manually reset.

9. Make sure all stairways have adequate lighting that's controlled by switches at both ends of the stairway.

10. Consider twice before installing fixtures in places that are extremely difficult to access, such as in vaulted ceilings and two-story-high entrance foyers. At the very least, plan how the bulbs will be replaced without the use of extra-long ladders. Also, avoid putting recessed lights in ceilings with unheated space above. They can't be properly insulated and will leak air badly.

Heating and Cooling

Y ou could plan the most attractive and utilitarian home design imaginable, locate it on a site with a breathtaking view, and furnish it with the finest appointments, yet unless the temperature and humidity within such a dwelling are maintained properly, the house would be unpleasant to live in. Heating and cooling systems are probably the hardest working components of any home, especially in homes located in climates having temperature extremes.

For discussion purposes, heating systems can be broken down into two topics: types of fuel, and types of heat production and delivery systems.

TYPES OF FUEL FOR HEATING

There are six primary types of fuel available for home heating use: electricity, fuel oil, gas, coal, wood, and solar.

Electricity

Electricity is readily available almost anywhere.

Advantages

1. It's a clean fuel that leaves no residue to contaminate the house or the atmosphere.

2. It requires no chimney to vent exhaust fumes and smoke.

3. It's a fuel that can be depended on in the future because it can be produced from almost any other type of fuel—gas, oil, coal, nuclear, solar, wind, and hydro or water power.

Disadvantages

1. Its fuel rate charge depends on the local utility company.

2. Breaks in the main supply line could leave you and your neighbors temporarily without supply.

Fuel Oil

Like electricity, fuel oil enjoys a comprehensive, efficient distribution that makes it readily available practically everywhere.

Advantages

1. If the oil fuel burner is routinely serviced and adjusted for maximum efficiency, fuel oil is a relatively clean source of combustion.

2. The supply is stored on the property. Once it's in place there's no worry about it being cut off.

Disadvantages

1. It must be stored in a tank that's usually located underground. The tank requires certain safety and fireproofing precautions, all of which combine to make the initial setup cost fairly high.

2. Money is tied up in the inventory stored.

3. The use of fuel oil may require a chimney.

4. If burned in an out-of-tuned unit, fuel oil will give off dirty emissions that will soil the interior of a home.

5. Fuel oil is not a renewable resource.

Gas

Gas comes in two forms: natural and liquid. Natural gas is not available in certain areas. Liquid or bottled gas can be purchased almost anywhere.

Advantages

1. Gas is a clean fuel.

2. Natural gas requires no on-site storage.

3. The liquid type can be maintained on the property.

Disadvantages

1. The natural gas supply and rate depend on the local utility company.

2. A liquid gas supply requires a storage tank.

3. Liquid gas ties up money in inventory.

4. The use of gas may require a chimney.

5. Gas is not a renewable resource.

Coal

Coal is an old-fashioned fuel that, while remaining a popular fuel supply for the generation of electricity, is rarely used any more to heat individual homes. It's not readily available in all areas.

Advantages

1. Its supply can be maintained on the property.

Disadvantages

1. If you've ever read Victor Hugo's *Germinal*, then you know what a dirty, filthy substance coal is—even *before* it's burned.

2. It's dirty when burned, too.

3. Coal leaves large amounts of ashes after combustion occurs.

4. Naturally, the use of coal requires a chimney.

5. It's a hot-burning fuel that possesses above-average risk of starting house fires.

6. Its supply requires substantial storage capacity, as well as money tied up in inventory.

7. It's not a renewable resource.

Wood

The availability of wood depends on the local supply of hardwoods such as oak, ash, maple, cherry, and elm.

Advantages

1. The supply can be maintained and even grown on the property.
2. If you have the equipment and time you can procure the supply yourself.
3. It's a renewable resource.

Disadvantages

1. Substantial labor is required to place or have the hardwood put in storage, to move it to a stove or fireplace, and to remove the ashes after combustion.
2. If handling and preparing the wood yourself, there's danger involved with using chainsaws, hand axes and mauls, and power splitters.
3. The inventory takes up a lot of room and ties up money.
4. The use of wood requires a chimney.
5. There's some risk of house fires.
6. Wood can bring dirt, insects, and fungi into the house.
7. The combustion of unseasoned wood can cause smoke to taint interior furnishings.

Solar

Solar energy depends on the amount of sunshine available.

Advantages

1. It's clean.
2. There's no charge for sunshine.
3. It should be readily available for the next few billion years.
4. It lessens the reliance on endangered and imported fuels.

Disadvantages

1. Unless substantial expense is incurred, not much long-range solar energy can be stored up. Even at best, it's minimal when compared with the storage capacity of other fuels.

2. How often have you known your local weather forecaster to be 100 percent accurate? There's an inability to predict with assurance the amount of sunlight that will occur during any one season.

3. Backup systems are needed.

4. It's relatively expensive to plan and install a solar system.

TYPES OF HEAT PRODUCTION AND DELIVERY SYSTEMS

When it comes to selecting a heating system, there are four major types to consider: forced-air, hot-water, heat pumps, and electrical. Beyond those are lesser-used solar and wind-powered units.

Forced-Air Heating Units

These systems burn fuel to create a supply of warm air that's blown (or forced) by a fan through a duct system to various parts of the house. During its operation, this type of furnace heats air that's drawn from the rooms and then sends it back through ducts and registers out again into the rooms (Figs. 20.1 and 20.2). The enclosures that route the air back to the furnace are known as the return ducts, and those supplying the air are supply ducts. Before the air comes back into the furnace from the return ducts, it goes through an air filter where most of the fugitive airborne dirt and dust is filtered out to protect the furnace from fouling its working parts.

Advantages

1. Forced-air systems are very versatile. Air can be heated, cooled, humidified, dehumidified, filtered, and circulated, all through the same distribution system.

2. A forced-air system is quick to respond manually or automatically via the thermostat to temperature changes.

3. There's no freezing of pipes to worry about.

Forced warm air heating system.

4. Forced-air units can operate with a pilotless ignition that uses an electrical spark generated only at the moment the fuel flow begins.

5. A forced-air unit requires simple, low-frequency maintenance. The filters need occasional cleaning or changing, and the electric motors and a few moving parts may need a few drops of oil periodically. Only once a year will a typical furnace *need* tuning up by a professional. In units that are heavily run, though, such tune-ups will usually save more in energy than they cost to have done.

FIGURE 20.2

Wall register with damper.

6. The installation price of forced-air heat is fairly low.

7. The distribution system requires less floor or wall space when compared with radiators for water or steam heat or electric baseboard heat.

8. The forced-air system is adaptable to all six main types of fuel supplies.

9. Forced-air systems can be designed with more than one blower or with special devices so the heated air can be directed to particular locations, with each having its own thermostat. The ducts can also have fins inside them, or movable baffles that can be used to regulate the airflow to various rooms.

Disadvantages

1. Some of the by-products of combustion—the unburned gas, oil, soot, or other contaminants—can come out through the registers. A poorly maintained, dirty forced-air furnace, for instance, will inevitably transport small amounts of airborne soot through the supply ducts and onto walls, floors, and furnishings. This process is likely to be so gradual and insidious that the graying of white walls, for instance, might only be revealed by washing a small area near one of the registers or by removing an old picture from a wall.

2. Another disadvantage of forced-air heating is heat cycling. Because the blower operates on an off-and-on basis, the room temperature varies near the thermostat setting from an over-warm to under-warm condition and then back again. There's a constant over-compensating going on.

3. If a blower motor is too large, or a duct system has not been properly designed, the movement of air in a room can be uncomfortable.

4. The sounds of the blower unit can be conveyed all over the house through the ductwork.

Forced-Air Heating Considerations

1. Consider opting for a forced-air furnace with a high-efficiency (over 90-percent efficiency) condensing unit that exhausts directly outdoors via a pipe. Condensing furnaces can use true sealed combustion air drawn through a small pipe, minimizing the chances of backdrafting, carbon monoxide poisoning, and chilly indoor drafts. A lower-cost alternative is an energy-efficient (over 80 percent efficiency) conventional forced-air furnace that exhausts through a chimney flue.

2. The furnace's casing and blower compartment should be insulated.

3. The furnace operation should be quiet, with a direct-drive blower.

4. Look for an easy-to-change filter arrangement. Some units have filter doors/covers that attach magnetically, enabling the cover to be pulled off and put back on without the use of tools. If it's difficult to access the filter, you'll be less likely to change the filter as often as should be. The filter should be replaced or cleaned regularly to remove accumulations of dust and other particles.

5. See that there's a drain installed for condensation discharge.

6. The air-intake pipes and furnace exhaust port should be located above the snow line in cold-climate locations. In all areas, they must be kept unobstructed and clean.

7. Some forced-air furnaces are two-stage models with low and high heat output levels. They use two-stage burners, operating in low-output mode during moderately cold weather, and high-output mode during cold temperatures. The furnace adjusts its own mode of operation to best suit the circumstances. Since the furnace runs longer in a low-heat stage (than it would in a high-output stage), there is more continuous air circulation for household comfort and more effective air cleaning.

   Two-stage heating models offer the following advantages:

   - Increased heating comfort
   - Quieter operation

- High heating capacity to ensure comfort on coldest days
- Longer and fewer heating cycles which provides
- Increased air circulation
- More consistent house temperatures
- Improved indoor air quality
- Reduced drafts
- Less wear and tear on the furnace

8. Variable-speed blowers that automatically adjust to heating needs are superior to single-speed blowers and are able to deliver better air quality and comfort. That's because different airflow capacities are needed for different heat output levels. Once a furnace starts its cycle, the blower motor on a variable-speed unit operates slowly, then softly ramps up to full speed—preventing chilly drafts while conserving electricity. When shutting down, the variable-speed unit ramps down into slow speed and brings itself to a stop.

   Variable speed motors offer the following advantages:

- Quieter heating and cooling operation
- Improved electrical efficiency all year long
- Increased comfort in both heating and cooling
- Economical use of continuous fan
- Increased cooling efficiency
- Better humidity control in cooling

   Important features can be had with variable-speed blowers:

- Furnaces with soft start and soft stop are considerably quieter and use less energy than units without those features. They maintain a more constant temperature, without the push and pull of cold then warm, then cold, then warm corrections that commonly occur with single-speed blowers.
- They also achieve better humidity control while cooling the household air because they run longer in the low speed.
- They reduce furnace-caused "drafts" and minimize the shock of blowers that abruptly come on at full speed and abruptly stop.

9. Forced-air "zoning" features a system that operates via individual area thermostats and motorized duct dampers. They allow a home to be segmented into zones that are individually controlled with their

own thermostats. The units typically come with a clean air filter reminder and indoor relative humidity display, with fully modulating dampers and adjustable temperature set points. Energy is saved by cutting back heat to zones where and when it's not needed.

Hot-Water Heating Units

With this type of system, water is heated in a boiler by a gas, oil, or other burner and then pumped throughout the house via a piping network equipped with radiators that ultimately distribute heat into the rooms (Fig. 20.3). Two basic types of radiators are used. One is the familiar under-the-window style modernized with an attractive grilled cover (Fig. 20.4), and the other is the low-profile baseboard radiator (Fig. 20.5). The disadvantages of the former are that they jut into a room and interfere with furniture placements and drapes. The baseboard system gives more outside wall coverage and efficiency. For these reasons it's generally the favored of the two. The best baseboard models are the long, low kind about 6 to 10 inches high and up to 10 feet long, and longer. They're often made with copper or aluminum heating fins. The most elite, quiet, and expensive baseboard units are the cast-iron makes.

Advantages

1. Hot-water heat is a clean, effective, and fairly quiet way to heat a home.

2. Hot-water heating systems are adaptable to many of the more popular solar heating arrangements.

COPPER TUBING WITH FINS

FIGURE 20.3

Hot water radiator.

3. Hot-water heating can be zoned to allow you to maintain different temperatures throughout the various parts of a house.

4. Hot-water heat is a more even heat than the heat supplied by forced-air systems.

5. Hot-water gives a moist, warm heat that won't dry people or furnishings out.

6. Hot-water does not create or stir up dust, relieving allergies and easing home cleaning requirements.

FIGURE 20.4

Radiator.

Disadvantages

1. Humidifiers, dehumidifiers, air cleaners, and air conditioners must be added as separate systems, thus incurring extra expense. There's also no ductwork already in place to provide for the movement of air needed by such add-ons.

2. Hot-water units can be difficult to keep clean. The insides of the pipes can develop mineral deposits that reduce heating efficiencies.

3. Some hot-water systems tend to rattle and clink when the heat goes on and off.

4. If a pipe breaks, a whole floor could get soaked.

FIGURE 20.5

Cast-iron baseboard heating unit.

5. The actual production of heat is not spontaneous; it takes time for the process to start up and become operational. The complete cycling of the water takes time initially when compared with the immediacy of forced-air heat.

6. This type of heating system is generally more expensive than forced-air units to purchase and have installed.

7. Having to keep furniture away from the radiators can be annoying.

8. If a home with hot-water heat will be idle during periods of freezing temperatures, there's the possibility of frozen and broken pipes, or else the entire system might have to be winterized.

Hot-Water Heating Considerations

1. Look for a gas or oil "high-tech" hot-water boiler heating unit with direct venting for greatest efficiency.

2. If your home is in an area with frequent temperature swings, a two-stage low/high heat output noncondensing gas boiler will allow for increased efficiency. When temperatures are extremely cold, the burner operates in the high-output mode. The rest of the time the boiler will run in low-output modes. This translates to less energy use and increased comfort.

3. A water heater coil can be added to hot-water home heating systems to increase water-heating efficiencies.

4. Dust on radiators or baseboard units acts as insulation, and wastes heat. These components must be accessible to be kept clean in order to operate efficiently.

Electrical Heating Units

Another popular but less used heating system than forced-air and hot-water is electrical. Straight electrical heating systems use electricity directly as a heat source. In essence, electricity is converted to heat when it moves through conductors that resist the flow of current. The conductors or heating elements become hot and give off heat. The heat is then typically distributed via baseboard heaters that come in a wide range of sizes (Fig. 20.6), with different output ratings so they can be used for general heating or for supplementary purposes.

Advantages

1. An electric heating system is one of the simplest and least-expensive heating systems to install. There's no ductwork, plumbing, or expensive furnace or boiler needed.

2. It's an unobtrusive and practically silent heat.

3. Depending on the circumstances— where and how it's used—electric heat can be very cost-efficient. Each room can have its own control, permitting variations in the amount of heat provided. If these controls are judiciously used, the cost of operation can be quite low.

Electric baseboard heating unit.

4. Maintenance is practically nonexistent. There's no furnace or boiler to service, repair, or replace.

5. Electric heating units offer the cleanest heat available.

6. Because there's no fuel burned, there's no need for a chimney.

7. Electric heat is adaptable to wind and other locally powered electrical sources.

Disadvantages

1. Electric heat is a very dry heat. Humidification is usually necessary during times of low humidity.

2. Sometimes electrical heating element surfaces get hot enough to pose a danger to young children.

3. The practical justification for electric heat can depend heavily on what the local electric rates are in the area: how they compare with other fuels economically.

Heat Pump Units

Earlier editions of this book contained brief discussions about heat pumps, because years ago, the verdict on them was still out. Now, the verdict is in, and heat pumps are certainly heating and cooling systems to be seriously considered. Just ask your local electric company.

Essentially, there are two basic types of heat pumps: air-to-air (or air source), and geothermal. They collect heat from the air, ground, or water outside the home and concentrate it for use inside. They both also function as central air conditioners, cooling by collecting heat inside the house and then effectively pumping it outdoors.

AIR-SOURCE HEAT PUMPS

These units (Figs. 20.7 and 20.8) employ air to store and deliver both heat and coolness, depending on which is needed at the time. The most common is the split-system heat pump. The main compressor, fan, and heat exchanger coil are located outdoors in a unit that looks like a central air-conditioning compressor. Another fan and heat exchanger coil is located inside the house within a unit that resembles a furnace.

FIGURE 20.7

Air-source heat pump system.

Air-source heat pump system.

In simple terms, an air-source heat pump heats the home during times of cool or cold outdoor temperatures by pumping refrigerant through a tubing or piping system that absorbs heat from the outside air (believe it or not, there is heat available to be drawn from cold air), carries the heat into a coil within the indoor unit, where a blower forces the heated air through ducts to various rooms. When outdoor temperatures are very cold, a backup electric strip-heating system kicks in to help deliver heat throughout the home. During times of warm or hot outdoor temperatures, the heat pump refrigerant absorbs heat from the air inside the house, then pumps it through the outside tubing or piping where the heat is released outside of the home.

Advantages

1. One unit can provide year-round comfort.

2. Units are fairly quiet.

3. No fuel delivery problems.

4. The units operate cleanly—no ashes, smoke, or soot is created. The walls, furniture, and draperies stay clean longer.

5. Units are safe—no flames, no combustible gases, no storage of flammable fuels, no flue.

6. No worry about the future availability of heating fuels.

Disadvantages

1. Supplemental heating may be needed in areas with extreme cold temperatures.

Air-Source Heat Pump Considerations

1. Look for two-level output capability: either two separate compressors (a large and small one) or a single two-speed compressor, both with variable-speed blowers. With two-level output, each setting can be tuned to run at the most efficient speed. The low-output level will be run most of the time and will switch to the higher level during very cold or hot weather.

2. External fittings installed in a totally sealed manner to prevent system leaks.

3. To reduce compressor operating sounds, a well-insulated compressor compartment.

4. Air filters located within the return air duct or at the indoor section of the system.

GEOTHERMAL HEAT PUMPS

Geothermal units take advantage of the Earth's relatively constant ground temperature to provide very efficient heating and cooling in any season. These are also referred to as ground-source or water-source pumps. After all, the earth is like a huge solar sponge, soaking up energy from the sun and holding it about 6 feet below the surface, where the soil's temperature is between 50 and 55 degrees Fahrenheit. Geothermal heat pumps, via heat transfer solutions traveling through piping buried 6 to 8 feet underground, use the natural thermal mass of the Earth to withdraw heat during cold weather and to transfer heat into during hot weather.

Geothermal heat pumps are made from two main components:

1. An indoor unit, with a compressor to circulate refrigerant, an evaporator coil to provide heat exchange between the heat transfer solution and refrigerant, a reversing valve to "switch gears" from heating to cooling or cooling to heating, and a blower fan to send warm or cool air through the household.

2. The underground heat-exchanger piping that's run underground, which allows heat transfer solution to collect heat from the ground during winter and disburse home-captured heat to the ground during summer.

HEAT PUMP BACKUP HEAT

A geothermal heat pump does not create heat; rather, it just moves heat from inside out, or outside in. In moderate climates, a backup electric resistance heating system or a warm-air furnace may not be needed. However, in extreme climates, such a backup system should be in place.

- With auxiliary electric resistance heat, consider getting a "smart" controller that monitors the home's temperature level and brings up just enough resistance heat, in small stages, to raise the outlet air temperature as needed.

- When a warm-air furnace is the backup, electronic controls choose between the operation of the heat pump or the furnace, depending on the weather. As the outside temperature drops, the heat pump becomes less efficient (it's harder to draw heat out of colder air). When the outside temperature drops to the point where it's no longer economical to run the heat pump, the controls automatically switch the heat pump off and turn the furnace on. That way, the heat pump and furnace operate at maximum efficiency. The installation of this system costs more than typical heating systems, but it's very efficient and results in very low energy usage.

There are two basic types of piping delivery/collection systems: closed end and open end.

A closed-end system uses a solution of water/antifreeze that circulates (is pumped) through a closed ground loop of pressurized piping that's connected to the indoor heat pump. The Earth has the ability to store heat energy. To use that stored energy, heat is extracted from the earth through the liquid antifreeze solution and is pumped to the heat pump or heat exchanger. There, the heat is used to heat the home. In the summer, the process is reversed. Indoor heat is extracted from within the home, then transferred back to the soil, where it dissipates. The ground pipes are typically buried in narrow trenches 6 to 8 feet deep. In a small yard, the pipes can be placed in vertical holes drilled deep into the ground. To save the possibility of expensive repairs later on, make sure the installing contractor pressure tests the piping loop before covering up the trenches (Fig. 20.9).

The other option exists for homeowners with access to a pond or well—an open-end system for drawing water from a well, lake, or

FIGURE 20.9

Closed-end geothermal heat pump system.

pond and using it as a heat-transferring solution. Since ground water is at a relatively constant temperature year-round, it provides a good heat source. First, however, because of strict water usage regulations, check the local and state laws, ordinances, codes, covenants, or licensing requirements to see if it's even an option. Also understand the quality of the water that will be used. It should be tested for hardness, acidity, and iron content before the heat pump is installed. Unacceptable water quality can cause mineral deposits to build up inside the piping and related components, which could clog the system and make it inoperable within a relatively short time (Fig. 20.10).

The installation of geothermal units should be completed only by experienced contractors who know how local building codes apply, who know exactly what to do, and who supply the homeowners with accurate, detailed records of the heat exchanger piping arrangement

FIGURE 20.10

Open-end geothermal heat pump system.

and location. Such information will be necessary for any future construction or maintenance required by the system.

Advantages

1. These units are very energy efficient. Ground- and water-source heat pumps require less supplemental energy to operate than air-source pumps need because the ground and water provide more consistent temperatures year-round. It's much easier during the winter to pump heat from 55-degree soil, than it is from frigid outdoor air. In the summer, the situation is reversed, when it's simpler to draw heat from inside the house and transport it to the 55-degree, cooler ground than to, for instance, a 92-degree, moist, midafternoon atmosphere.

2. The closed "earth loop" piping system is inherently quieter than noisy outdoor condenser fan units with other types of systems.

3. Added safety with geothermal units—there are no fuel tanks, no flame, no fumes, no emissions, and no need for flues. They eliminate dangerous by-products of combustion, such as carbon monoxide. This also results in improved household air quality.

4. A clean energy source—no ashes, soot, or fumes. Walls, furniture, and draperies stay cleaner longer.

5. No fuel delivery problems.

6. The geothermal unit within the home is sheltered from rain, snow, hail, and extreme temperatures and from pests such as squirrels, rodents, and birds.

7. Additional energy savings can be realized by diverting indoor heat to the home's water heater for practically free hot water all summer and for adding supplementary heat during winter, for reduced-cost hot water then.

8. Although initial installation costs of a ground- or water-source heat pump system is higher than that of many other systems, when comparing all fuel types, these heat pumps are among the most economical heating and cooling alternatives available today. Such a system, with its low energy consumption, will be an attractive feature for buyers if the home is ever put on the market.

9. Geothermal systems are reliable and have low maintenance and a long life span.

10. One unit can provide year-round comfort.

11. Some electric companies have offered financial assistance or rebates to encourage the installation of heat-pump systems.

12. Some states and provinces have tax credits for installing geothermal systems.

Disadvantages

1. Supplemental heating may be required in areas of extreme cold temperatures.

2. Initial installation costs will probably be higher than other heating/cooling systems.

Geothermal Heat Pump Considerations

1. Cabinet and compressor compartments should be insulated for noise control.

2. Look for two-level heat pump output capability and a variable-speed blower.

3. Consider purchasing an optional water heater that can be used for heating the house water with the heat pump. Some manufacturers offer a hot-water de-superheater that produces hot water for household use whenever the unit runs in the cooling mode.

4. Another option is the "space-heating-priority water-heating system." If both the house and water heating tank need heat, the heat pump first kicks in to take care of the home heating system, and then to take care of the water heater.

5. Check out the warranty on the system's underground piping. Naturally, the longer the warranty, the better. Fifty years is not unheard of.

Solar Units

A typical solar heating system that uses the sun for an energy source includes four major components:

- Collectors to harvest sunlight and convert radiant energy to thermal energy
- A storage medium that can hold enough heat to last through a night or through periods of cloudy weather
- A distribution system to convey the heat to points of use
- A backup system that will take over when stored solar heat is exhausted because the sun has not been cooperating

The collector is often a heat-absorbing metal plate with an array of tubing that can be an integral part of the plate or merely bonded to it. Usually this assembly is in a black frame with a layer of insulation at the back and a glass or plastic-covered airspace on the surface that should face the sun.

The heat transfer can be made through liquid or air that passes through the collector, picks up heat, transports it to storage, and later distributes it through the house.

Electric Thermal Storage Units

An electric thermal heating system can be an excellent solution for new homes, can meet the requirements of hard-to-heat rooms, and can easily be added at a later date for additions to home living spaces or basements. These units employ electricity to create heat and store it in ceramic bricks, crushed rock, or water for later use (Fig. 20.11). If the homeowner's electric utility company offers lower rates for consuming electricity during off-peak hours, this type of heating system can have considerable cost advantages.

Electric thermal heating systems come in central heating systems and individual room systems.

Electric thermal heating units create enough heat to warm the home immediately at night and heat their storage mediums (ceramic bricks, crushed rock, or water) during off-peak hours when electrical demand is least (and less costly), typically late at night. Then during peak electrical usage times, typically during the day and early evening, the heating elements are automatically turned off or down while the stored heat is released to warm the household. It's a great way to use electricity late at night when it's less expensive, convert the energy into heat, and store the heat for later use.

THERMAL INSULATION

HEAT STORAGE CORE

WARM AIR OUT

FAN CONTROL

FIGURE 20.11

Electric thermal heating system.

Various types of electric thermal storage heat delivery systems are available:

- Forced-air systems
- Radiant baseboard hot water
- Radiant/convection room heaters

Advantages

1. Units operate fairly quiet.

2. Units are dependable, the heating elements have no moving parts, which means long life.

3. Units are located indoors out of the weather.

3. No fuel delivery problems.

4. The units operate cleanly; no ashes, smoke, or soot is created. The walls, furniture, and draperies stay clean longer.

5. If the electric utility offers low off-peak hour rates, they can make efficient use of electricity.

6. Units are safe—no flames, no combustible gases, no storage of flammable fuels, no flue.

7. No worry about the future availability of heating fuels.

Disadvantages

1. If individual room units are used, their placement in rooms will take up wall space.

2. These units are designed for heating only, cooling would involve separate equipment.

Electric Thermal Storage Units Considerations

- An option that exists in some units, when stored radiant heat isn't enough to keep the room temperature at the desired thermostat setting, a quiet fan will circulate air through the core of heated bricks or stone and warm the spaces by convection.

Radiant Floor Heating Systems

Radiant floor heating can provide a cost-effective, quiet, gentle heat, with delivery by warm-water piping or electric wiring floor panels or mats. If you're serious about investigating radiant floor heating possibilities, consider meeting with contractors experienced in their installation. There are numerous flooring situations for which this type of heating will work, but the components must be customized and installed to suit the type of floor planned. For instance, hydronic (liquid) hot-water piping systems use small-diameter piping laid within the floor in "wet" installations where the tubing is embedded in a concrete foundation slab, or over a previously poured slab, or even within a relatively thin thickness of concrete that's been poured over the top of a subfloor. Ceramic tile has typically been the floor of choice for radiant heating, but that has been changing lately, as radiant floor heating options expand. "Dry" installations still involve tubing, but the tubing is either suspended beneath the subfloor or is laid between two subfloor layers, or is actually built into a sandwich-style subfloor.

This form of home heating has recently seen considerable innovation, so do a last-minute check on what's available before making a decision. In any case, the piping or tubing holds hot or warm water heated by a gas, oil, or similarly-fired boiler and/or a circulation pump (or geothermal heat pump) that circulates the water to heat the flooring. A manifold of valves controls the water distribution, and a thermostat controls the temperature—some control the temperature of water in a boiler, while others may control the room temperature. Another alternative for smaller homes or homes in locales with low heating demands, is simply using a standard water heater/tank to supply the radiant floor heating. Water piping systems may cost a bit more to install, but they're very efficient.

Carpet, tile, vinyl, engineered wood flooring types can all be positioned over the hot-water piping that's typically installed in a masonry floor by a plumber or HVAC contractor. Electric panel elements provide another option for radiant floor heating. They're relatively inexpensive to install, but may cost more to operate, especially if reduced off-peak energy rates are not available from the local electric utility company.

Advantages

1. It's quiet, even, comfortable heat.

2. It's clean, there's no dust generation.

3. Radiant heat does not dry out the air, there are no drafts, and less outside-air infiltration.

4. It's invisible, blending nicely into the home's structure, with no bulky ductwork or registers.

5. It's a safe heat, with no or very few moving parts.

6. It's energy efficient.

7. It warms from the floor up, and feels great on the feet.

Disadvantages

1. Maintenance on the piping or electrical panels could be costly.

2. A separate system is usually needed for cooled-air delivery.

3. It's not as responsive as other forms of heat; it takes a long time for a floor to heat up.

4. Electric heating can be relatively costly unless the electric company offers off-peak rates when radiant floors can be heated up or "recharged" at night.

Radiant Floor Heating Considerations

■ Recent innovations in concrete and other masonry flooring make suitable matches with radiant floor heating. Consider that contractors specializing in custom-concrete counter tops, table tops, and other furniture and furnishing innovations are rapidly becoming more available to general contractor, architects, and the housing industry in general.

■ Laminated wood flooring is often preferred over solid wood, which reduces the possibility of wood shrinking and cracking.

■ Early versions of radiant floor heating systems often failed due to leaky tubes caused by corrosion from chemical reactions that took place between the metal piping and concrete. Now plastic, ceramic-coated, rubber, copper, and other noncorrosive tubing is in use by most manufacturers.

COOLING SYSTEMS

Because all of the same ductwork will be shared, most forced-air heating units are readily adaptable at a modest surcharge to include mechanical air-conditioning. The heat pump automatically includes it because the same equipment is used for both heating and cooling operations. If your primary heating system is not one requiring ducts, and you still want central air-conditioning, it will have to be a separate system.

For the highest comfort, a multilevel cooling output model is best. It matches the cooling output to changing cooling requirements of the home. A two-speed unit is like having two systems in one: a low-speed system for mild days and a high-speed system for hot and humid days. Such a dual system usually operates about 80 percent of the time in low speed. Longer low-speed cycles mean better dehumidification, air cleaning, and air circulation, for increased household comfort. Some available cooling systems have two separate, different size compressors in the outdoor unit. When the outside air temperature is below about 85 to 88 degrees, the small compressor runs the system. When the outside air temperature reaches the high eighties and beyond, the system switches to the larger compressor. On very hot days, when neither compressor alone can handle the desired cooling requirements, both compressors kick in at once, for maximum effort. A second style of multilevel output unit employs two-speed compressors. These multilevel output units are most effective when they use variable-speed indoor blowers that automatically adjust to match the cooling output required. The blower motors should have a quiet soft-start feature so they'll slowly ramp up to full speed, then slowly ramp down when proper cooling levels are reached.

There are a number of important points that shouldn't be overlooked when you're considering the installation of air-conditioning:

1. When comparing bids from air-conditioning contractors, look at the seasonal energy efficiency ratings (SEERs). That's how the various units are compared. Seventeen or 18 are excellent. Fifteen or 16 are good, and thirteen or 14, acceptable.

2. Don't oversize a system in hopes of getting quick cooling. If oversizing is much greater than 15 percent, a fast cool-down of the air will occur, but without efficient moisture removal. The result will be cold, clammy, very uncomfortable air.

3. If possible, locate outdoor compressors away from decks, patios, bedroom windows, and dryer vents. Also avoid interior corners that tend to accentuate the compressor noise. Try instead for a shaded area out of the limelight. That way the noise won't bother anyone and no direct sunlight will unnecessarily increase the compressor coil's workload.

4. A well-designed unit's top will keep dirt, leaves, and debris from clogging the insides, so hot air can be discharged upward away from adjacent plants, patio, or grounds.

5. If you're not starting out with air-conditioning and you plan to add it later, arrange for a large enough heating equipment room so the

air-conditioning coil, air cleaner, and humidifier can be comfortably installed.

6. Provide a means of draining condensation water from the coil to a nearby fixture.

7. If you plan on expanding your home at a later date, make certain the size of your air-conditioner will accommodate it.

8. If you're not going to have a forced-air system with ductwork, consider having the proper ductwork for air-conditioning installed when the house is being constructed even if you're going to wait to have the air-conditioning put in.

9. Make sure that refrigerant used by any proposed cooling system will be readily available in the future and is not being phased out to comply with existing or expected environmental regulations. The refrigerant must be both ozone- and environmentally safe.

DUCTS

Ducts can be considered the main delivery vehicles for heated and cooled air within a home having heating and cooling systems serviced by some type of air-moving blower unit. Two kinds of material are used in combination to manufacture ductwork for forced-air heating and independent air-conditioning or cooling systems: galvanized sheet metal and fiberglass.

Galvanized sheet metal ducts are manufactured in a shop and brought to the job site for installation. These ducts offer good support and are put together using strong fasteners, including rivets. By themselves, however, sheet metal ducts can be annoyingly noisy. Insulating the outside of the duct with 2-inch thick fire-resistant fiberglass duct wrap insulation with a vapor-retarding face or liner will cut down on noise vibration, will help control moisture condensation, and will give thermal support by preserving the heated or cooled air temperature as the air travels to its destination. When the sheet metal ducts are manufactured or installed, the seams, joints, and corners should be of a good design and craftsmanship, tightly fitted to form a good seal. Sheet metal construction offers numerous advantages: it's durable, its smooth surfaces offer little resistance to air flow, it can be custom-fitted to odd shapes and sizes, it isolates the outer insulation jacket from the air stream—preventing penetration of the insulation by dirt and dust—and cleaning can be easily accomplished on the smooth surfaces with yearly dust vacuuming or in response to special situations such as smoke or ash contamination from a fire.

Duct System Considerations

1. Insulate the outside of sheet metal ducts using 2-inch thick fire-resistant fiberglass insulation with a vapor barrier.

2. To make cleaning easier, access port doors or covers can be installed. Although few builders or home buyers think of this, duct access ports provide the means for vacuuming collected dust from ductwork once a year. It will keep the system, the air it supplies, and the entire household cleaner and healthier.

3. With forced-air units total duct travel distances, as well as the number of bends and turns in the ductwork, should be minimized. The more 90-degree bends or Ts used, the shorter the allowable or functional run can be, due to increased resistance to the airflow experienced by air swirling and losing momentum in curves and bends. Wherever possible, 45-degree bends should be used instead of 90-degree components to improve airflow efficiency. Ducts with curved sides move air more efficiently than ducts with sharp corners.

4. In cold climates, have ducts run within heated areas of the house. This will help maximize the amount of heat retained within the ducts and will place more heat where it's wanted, at a lower cost.

5. If there's a basement, make sure a few heat outlets are placed there to help supply warmth when needed and to cut down on dampness. They can simply be adjustable louvers installed in one of the main heat supply ducts.

6. Warmed or cooled air that's blown down a main or "trunk" duct line will bounce off an end cap and disperse down the various branch lines. If there's a duct opening or open line at the end of the trunk, much of the conditioned air will take the path of least resistance and continue down that path—starving the rest of the ducts.

7. There should be dampers on each branch where the branch comes off the main trunk, so that the amount of air entering any particular duct branch can be somewhat controlled. An unused bedroom may

thus be "sealed off" during winter and left unheated if desired. To set dampers once the system is running, use a thermometer to check individual room temperatures, then adjust the airflow dampers as needed.

8. Ducts with humidifier connections will need a nearby water source and drain.

9. Finally, do not locate air return ducts in bathrooms or kitchens; they will pull undesired humidity back into the system from showers, baths, and cooking.

In short, carefully plan the location of furnace ducts and their outlets. Once your house is finished and occupied, you must keep furniture, rugs, and other obstructions away from the return registers, heating and cooling vents, and related components.

REGISTERS

The purpose of heating and cooling outlets or registers is to supply the heat or cooled air where it's most needed, usually near the exterior walls and windows (Fig. 20.12).

Two or more are often needed in large rooms or along extended walls beneath long picture windows. What's needed is a "curtain" of warm air or cold air thrown up (or down) from the registers around the perimeter of the house, between the occupants and the outside temperatures. The heat sources work best when they're located along the bottom of a wall beneath the windows. This position counteracts the most likely places where cold might seep into the room. In warm-climate areas the registers can instead be located in the ceiling, directly over windows on exterior walls, because cool air falls.

Here are some other considerations:

1. Make sure that no registers contribute to unwanted noise transmission between rooms. Two-sided or double-opening registers that serve two rooms at once are fine in certain instances, but be on guard against any doubling up that violates someone's privacy. These double registers can be a big source of interroom noise transmission.

2. Floor-mounted supply registers are more efficient than the baseboard type. It remains a good practice, however, to use the base-

board registers in rooms such as kitchens, bathrooms, and laundries to prevent water, wax, or other materials from entering the duct system.

3. Return registers are best mounted on the walls in the interior of a home. They should be positioned near the floor in cold-climate areas and along the ceiling in warm-climate locations.

4. After the completion of the heating/cooling rough-in, the heating contractor should install temporary covers over all outlets and registers, both supply and return, to prevent debris, dust, and other materials from getting into the ductwork during the remaining construction. If temporary covers are not installed, fine dust particles will enter the duct work and eventually coat every room in the house when the blower turns on. Even so, it's a good idea to request that air ducts be cleaned at the end of construction, because even

FLOOR

CEILING

OUTLETS

WALL

FLOOR

CEILING

WALL

INLETS

FIGURE 20.12

Registers.

with attempts to temporarily cover the registers, some dust, dirt and debris may still inadvertently enter the ducts. On a related note, make sure the heating/cooling system is disconnected and cannot operate when the registers are covered, because restricted air flow can damage the entire system.

5. The more areas that can be tapped for return air, the faster and more efficient the system will be. The best systems include many more than the minimum number of inches required for return air.

6. Registers should be scratch-resistant rustproof, with easy to operate and set dampers.

THERMOSTATS

Thermostats shouldn't be placed where they'll be affected by drafts, or in the hottest or coldest parts of a home, or in places where they'll interfere with furnishings and decor. Place thermostats on inside, not outside walls.

Thermostats should be located away from heat sources such as fireplaces and registers, and from cold sources such as doors and windows, for dependable readings.

Programmable Thermostats

Programmable thermostats are electronic conveniences that can save lots of energy. They'll allow a heating or cooling system to be turned down or back automatically at preset times, so heating or cooling units won't be running full blast while occupants are sleeping or away. Although these controls aren't recommended with heat pumps or radiant flooring heating systems—units meant to be run under steady operation or systems that are difficult to shut on and off—they'll work wonders with many other systems.

Programmable Thermostat Considerations

1. Look for a programmable control that can store and repeat multiple daily settings, for wake-up, daytime, evening, and sleep times. Some "smart" units will even learn how long it takes to heat or cool the house, so that it "knows" when to start heating or cooling in the future. Many of those same units are also able to remind the occupants when to clean or replace the system's air filter.

2. Thermostats for heating and air conditioning should be positioned on an inside wall where they will not be subject to draft, or heat from televisions, lamps, and other appliances.

3. Units exist which retain programmed settings during a power outage. Better units need no batteries and operate off memory chips.

4. Some models offer a temporary program override feature for away-from-home vacations or holidays. You can override the program and set the temperature down for the time you will be out of town.

5. If you go with zoned hot-water heat or have adjustable fans on your forced-air system (dual-control fans), consider having more than one thermostat strategically located in the house.

6. One of the newest designs is a thermidistat. It controls the furnace, air conditioner, blower, and humidifier independently, for total comfort.

NOISE

A noisy heating or cooling system can be annoying. There's no justification for such noise, except that it costs the manufacturer a trifle less and saves the builder a trifle more.

Ask to be taken to a home that already employs the heating/cooling system that you're considering. Listen to it start, operate, and stop. Be sure you do all three because sometimes a burner fires with a bang, or pops when the flame goes out. Sometimes the motor that runs a circulating pump or blower is noisy. Fan noises can be transmitted through the ductwork (like through an old-fashioned speaking tube), and quite often the noises created in boilers are carried throughout the house in the metal piping.

How much attention you pay to these noises depends on your sensitivity to disturbing sounds.

SIZE AND LOCATION

You shouldn't go with an oversized furnace or air-conditioner unless it's in anticipation of a room or space you plan on adding at a later date. An oversized unit will run inefficiently in a smaller space than it was engineered for.

Try to locate the furnace/air conditioner in as central a location as possible to get an even distribution of heat and coolness. The air conditioner's outside compressor, as mentioned earlier, should be installed in an out-of-the-way place in the shade where it won't annoy anyone.

AIR CLEANERS

Forced-air heating and air-conditioning systems are ideal for the application of electrostatic air cleaners. They not only clean the air, but tend to make it smell fresher too, which is a feature that's becoming more important with today's comprehensive sealing of houses. The accompanying reduction of air infiltration has actually reduced the amount of fresh air that used to move into homes through various uninsulated surfaces and cracks in the outer shell.

Air cleaners remove up to 95 percent of airborne dust, bacteria, and even viruses. Air cleaners have many benefits:

- They can filter out unseen microscopic particles that float in the air, including dust, pollen, mold, plant spores, bacteria, viruses, dust mites, pet hair, dander, cooking smoke, and other miscellaneous particles—making the air cleaner and more comfortable for everyone, pets included.

- Air cleaners also keep heating and cooling equipment coils cleaner, protecting operating efficiencies and lowering costs.

- Cleaner air minimizes time required for cleaning dust and soil throughout the home.

The other types of heating systems aren't so accommodating to the air cleaners, and separate units must be installed in individual rooms.

HUMIDIFIERS

Heat tends to dry out the air inside a house and make it uncomfortable. This is particularly true of forced-air systems. If mechanical means for supplying moisture are not available, the humidity inside the home can drop to the level of dryness found in a desert. This condition causes shrinking of wood and other materials, which might open gaps in the house structure and shell and permit air infiltration.

Low humidity causes a variety of problems:

- Dry, itchy skin, dry-throat coughs, and cracked nasal membranes on people and pets
- Sharp static electrical shocks
- Ceiling and wall cracks that may allow hot or cold air to enter hurting energy efficiency
- Dehydration of some house plants
- Excessive wear of fabrics, carpets, and other furnishings. Wood shrinks; floors creak, banisters wobble, drawers loosen, gaps appear in moldings
- Household members often feel colder in homes having dry air

As with air cleaners, humidifiers can be installed directly onto a duct system (Fig. 20.13). They can be hooked up to a constant water supply so they'll continually and automatically put needed moisture into the air. For houses heated with systems other than forced-air, humidifiers must be placed in appropriate areas throughout the home to accomplish the same thing.

Dehumidifiers can also be needed in certain locations and times of the year, usually in basements during hot and wet weather conditions. Individual units run by electricity will usually do the job.

CEILING FANS

Running a ceiling fan allows you to raise an area's air conditioner thermostat by as much as five degrees for the same results. In winter, reversing the fan's rotation direction will send warm air near the ceiling to gently flow outward and down along the walls. Some ceiling fans also function as air cleaners, with air filters hidden inside each blade. As the fan circulates room air, the air constantly passes through and is cleaned by the blade filters.

General Heating and Cooling Equipment Considerations

1. No matter what type of heating unit is selected, the indoor mechanical equipment location must not break up the interior floor plan. If the main unit is placed in the basement, consider how it will impact

FIGURE 20.13

Humidifier.

the living spaces there, but remember that it will need plenty of air circulation and must be easily accessible for maintenance and repairs.

2. For the sake of noise reduction, the main unit should be placed away from quiet living spaces such as bedrooms, family rooms, and offices or libraries.

3. A whole-house humidifier adds needed moisture to the air in a home during seasonal dry spells and other times of low humidity. Properly humidified air feels warmer than drier air of the same temperature, so you can effectively lower your indoor settings and still enjoy comfortable conditions.

4. Wherever it's placed, the mechanical equipment needs to be accessible for maintenance. Filters should especially be easy to get at, with an overhead light nearby.

5. For any heating unit that's exhausted through a chimney, make sure the chimney has the proper liner to safely handle the exhausting. Water vapor is a by-product of fuel combustion and can condense on inside masonry chimney surfaces, especially those on exterior walls. Resulting water can then be absorbed by the chimney and transferred through walls. This can result in damp patches on interior and exterior walls, blistering paint, peeling wallpaper, stains on the ceiling around the chimney, and white stains on the outside surfaces of the chimney itself. During winter, chimneys may be subject to numerous freezes where the condensation freezes and expands. This "works" on mortared joints, bricks, or blocks, and could cause cracks and crumbling masonry which could, in turn, lead to openings in the flue and possible incursions of dangerous carbon monoxide into the home.

6. Rubber isolator (vibration) pads placed beneath the corners of a forced-air furnace or heat pump blower unit will help absorb vibration and lessen operating sound levels.

7. If you choose hot-water baseboard heat but also want separate forced-air central air-conditioning, the air-conditioning sheet metal ductwork with outside insulation should be installed overhead with outlets in the ceiling. The most efficient air-conditioning is where outlets are overhead (cool air falls). The most efficient heating runs along the floor (heat rises).

8. If you're putting in hot-water baseboard heat, and know that you'll want central air-conditioning at a later time, prepare for that eventuality by having the sheet metal ductwork with outside insulation installed overhead, complete with ceiling outlets.

1. Forced-air heating and cooling systems are very versatile. Air can be heated, cooled, humidified, dehumidified, filtered, and circulated, all through the same distribution system.

2. A hot-water system is a clean, effective, and fairly quiet way to heat a home. It can supply heat to specific areas or zones in a house, and withhold heat from seasonally unused parts of that same house. It also can be adapted to some household water heaters and some solar heating arrangements.

3. An electric heating system is one of the simplest and least-expensive heating systems to install. There's no ductwork, plumbing, or expensive furnace or boiler needed.

4. Although initial installation costs of a ground- or water-source heat pump system are higher than that of many other systems, when comparing all fuel types, these heat pumps are among the most economical heating and cooling alternatives today—when their low energy consumptions are considered.

5. Don't oversize an air-conditioning system in hopes of getting improved performance or quicker cooling. If oversizing is much greater than 15 percent, a fast cool-down of the air will occur, but without efficient moisture removal.

6. If possible, locate outdoor air-conditioning compressors away from decks, patios, bedroom windows, and dryer vents.

7. In warm climates, it's better to place heating and cooling registers in ceilings. In cold-climate locations, they should be positioned at floor levels. If you have separate heating and air-conditioning systems (i.e., hot-water baseboard heat and forced central air), the heating should be at floor level with the air-conditioning in the ceiling.

8. If you're not going to have a forced-air heating system with ductwork, consider having the proper ductwork for air-conditioning installed when the house is being constructed, even if you're going to wait to have the air-conditioning put in.

9. Heating and air-conditioning ducts should be insulated on their outside, not inside.

10. To prevent "false" readings, thermostats should be located away from heat sources such as fireplaces and registers, and from cold sources such as doors and windows.

Insulation

There aren't many people who live in a climate where they don't have to worry about protecting themselves from temperatures that are periodically too hot or too cold. Since the oil embargoes and the realization that many of the energy sources on which we depend are not unlimited, insulation in houses has taken a position of high priority no matter what the location.

In its most universal application, insulation belongs inside or against any barrier located between a heated space and an unheated space, or between a cooled space and an uncooled space. Applied to the structure of a house, this means that insulation should be within all exterior walls, in attics or under roofs, beneath floors exposed to the outside as well as floors covering unheated crawl spaces or slabs, and in extremely cold locations, on walls in a heated basement.

In short, insulation should envelop all living areas of your home, leaving no openings except doors, windows, and necessary vents. As discussed in the heating and plumbing chapters, the heating or cooling ducts and hot water heater and pipes must be insulated to provide energy efficiencies, especially when such ducts and pipes pass through unheated or uncooled spaces.

Fortunately, sealing a home against heat conduction and air infiltration is a relatively simple process if done during construction of the house, and it's fairly inexpensive, considering the energy saved in the long run. If insulation is not properly planned and must be added at a later date after the house has been completed—now that can run into big problems and big expenses.

Most insulation is installed after the framing is complete and the electrical, plumbing, and heating systems have been roughed in and inspected.

R-VALUES

Insulation quality is often expressed in "R-values." An R-value is merely a quantitative expression of the ability of any material to resist the passage of heat. For example, a fiberglass batt 6 inches thick has an R-value of approximately 19. The same material in batts 12 inches thick will possess an R-value of about 38. The greater R-value, the greater the material's resistance to the passage of heat (or coolness), and the better its insulation value.

Table 21.1 gives an insulation materials comparison. Table 21.2 lists some of the same kinds of insulations, and shows what their most common thicknesses equal in insulating values.

Because heat rises, the potential heat loss in a house is greatest through the roof, and least through the floors. Therefore, different recommendations exist for insulating those areas as well as the walls—each with a different, appropriate R-factor.

Here are some conservative recommended R-values for your house: walls—R-20; floors—R-27 (above grade), which includes overhangs, cantilevers, and below projecting windows; and ceilings—R-40.

Table 21.1 Comparison of Insulation Materials

Form	Type	Approximate R-Value Per Inch of Thickness	Relative Cost 1 = least, 5 = most
Blankets	Fiberglass	3.1	1
and Batts	Rock Wool	3.7	1
Boards	Fiberglass	4.5	5
	Polystyrene	3.5 to 5.4	5
Loose Fill	Rock Wool (blown)	2.9	1
	Fiberglass (blown)	2.2	1

Table 21.2 Thicknesses of Various Insulations and Insulating Values

R-Values:	R-11	R-19	R-22	R-30	R-38
Fiberglass blankets/batts	3½"–4"	6"–6½"	7"–7½"	9½"–10"	12"–13"
Rock wool blankets/batts	3"–3½"	5"–6"	6"–7"	8"–9½"	10½"–12"
Fiberglass loose/blown	5"	8½"	10"	13½"	17"
Rock wool loose/blown	4"	6½"	7½"	10"	13"

U-VALUES

On occasion you might find the thermal qualities of an insulation material expressed in terms of "U." The U-value is the reciprocal of the R-value and can be determined by dividing the R-value into the numeral value. For example, a fiberglass batt having an R-value of 19 has a U-value of ⅟₁₉, or .053. Basically, the lower the U-value, the greater the thermal resistance of the material, and the better its insulation quality.

TYPES OF INSULATION

While it's true that each material used to make up your house possesses some insulating value, the effectiveness of individual types of materials varies greatly. For example, a 1-inch-thick blanket of fiberglass insulation has the same insulation value as approximately a 3½-inch thick layer of pine wood planking, a 22-inch-thick wall of common brick, a 40-inch-thick layer of solid concrete, or a 54-inch-thick (4½ feet!) layer of stone.

The most popular types of insulation used in modern homes are blankets and batts of fiberglass and rock wool, rigid boards of polystyrene, fiberglass board, rigid foam boards, and various loose forms of fiberglass and rock wool.

Fiberglass and Rock Wool Blankets and Batts

These two products make up about 90 percent of all homeowner insulation (Figs. 21.1 and 21.2). They're made of compressed fibers that come

FIGURE 21.1

Blanket insulation.

FIGURE 21.2

Batt insulation.

in a continuous roll form (blanket) or in rolls having perforations along every few feet or yards so you can pull off regular rectangular pieces (batts). Both blankets and batts are available in various thicknesses and widths, and with or without facing material or vapor barrier material on one side.

Fiberglass and rock wool also come in shredded forms for hand-pouring or machine-blowing applications. Be aware that both of these materials can be irritating if they come into direct contact with your skin. Rock wool is the less bothersome of the two. Although loose insulation is more economical to purchase and install, it will eventually settle and lose some of its insulating value, and it's difficult to move out of the way, if need be.

Fiberglass and rock wool insulation can be used throughout the entire house, for ceilings, walls, floors, basements, around windows and doors, or anywhere else energy might otherwise be lost to conductivity and air infiltration. They both have good insulation values and are among the most economical types to purchase.

Rock wool insulation batts are available in semirigid models with unique flexible edges designed to compress as the batt is placed into walls, attics, ceiling, and floor frames. The flexible edge springs back, expanding against whatever it is filling, to give a tight fit.

Rigid Boards

Rigid foam and Styrofoam insulation "boards" are used for basement walls, concrete slabs, cathedral ceilings, and exterior walls before finishing (Fig. 21.3). Rigid boards are manufactured in a variety of materials:

POLYSTYRENE RIGID BOARDS

Polystyrene is a plastic that, in rigid board form, dents easily and is highly combustible, but is also very weather- and moisture-resistant.

It's excellent for below-grade or exterior wall applications. Used indoors, it's a fire hazard unless covered by ⅝-inch-thick sheets of fire-resistant gypsum board.

FIBERGLASS BOARD

Fiberglass board is made of compressed fiberglass wool sandwiched between tough facing materials that together form a semirigid board. Its insulation value is average among the rest of the rigid board insulation family. It's often covered by ⅝-inch-thick fire-resistant gypsum board on interior walls and ceilings.

FIGURE 21.3

Rigid board insulation.

RIGID FOAM BOARDS

These boards have the highest insulating qualities of all rigid board materials. They form their own vapor barriers, too. Foam board dents easily and must be handled gently. Like many other rigid board insulations, because of its flammability, it should be covered by ⅝-inch thick fire-resistant gypsum board on interior walls and ceilings.

Loose Insulation

Loose insulation can be hand-poured or blown into walls and other voids (Fig. 21.4).

FIBERGLASS AND ROCK WOOLS

By far the most popular loose insulation. It's efficient and inexpensive.

PLACES TO INSULATE

Even if you live in an area having a mild climate, your home will be more comfortable if it's well insulated. It's not possible to have too much insulation in the walls and top floor ceiling, or in floors over carports, garages, porches, and other areas exposed to the weather, provided the insulation is installed correctly.

FIGURE 21.4

Loose fill insulation.

To prevent fire hazards, always keep insulation away from chimneys, exhaust flues, attic ventilators, and, in general, all other heat-generating components and fixtures. Local building codes and product manufacturers provide clearance guidelines and requirements.

There are six primary areas that should not be overlooked: basements, floors, walls, attics, ducts and plumbing, plus cracks and joints that require caulking.

Basements

Insulation should not be installed against a wet or damp wall. Before insulation can be applied, a dry wall in necessary; after, basement or masonry interior walls may be insulated by several methods:

- First, by putting up furring strips followed by applying insulating blankets or batts in the usual way, with a vapor barrier facing the living area of the basement.

- Another method is to attach rigid board insulation to wood nailing strips which are bolted to the walls. Sheets of extruded polystyrene foam are very efficient per unit of thickness. The foil-faced vapor barrier should be placed toward the living spaces.

For either insulating method, consider using a separate vapor barrier on the back side of the insulation to prevent moisture from wall dampness from entering or collecting against the insulation.

After basement insulation is put up, it should be covered with an approved fire safety-rated finishing material such as ⅝-inch-thick fire-resistant gypsum board. Find minimum guidelines for this in your local building code.

1. In general, rigid sheets of extruded polystyrene foam are the most efficient per unit of thickness. They're good to add to any masonry or concrete surface.

2. The exterior of basement foundation walls may be insulated with extruded polystyrene rigid foam insulation. Rigid foam insulation, with its tongue and groove design, also makes an excellent barrier against moisture and air infiltration. It can be used below grade because of its exceptional moisture resistance, for applications such as concrete and masonry walls.

3. When foam panel board installation is complete, all joints should be sealed with construction insulation tape.

Floors

Prudent insulation of floors can save 5 to 15 percent of your heating costs. It's easy to insulate under floors during construction, and not very expensive. Here's what to consider:

1. Insulate between the top of the foundation wall and the sill plate under the first-floor decking. This will stop air infiltration more than it "insulates," which is important when it comes to overall energy efficiency and savings. Resilient polyethylene foam insulation strips are used to make an airtight seal between the masonry foundation and the sill plate (Fig. 21.5).

FIGURE 21.5

Insulating under sill and sole plates.

Insulation cutaway.

2. The subfloor junction with the sole plate should be sealed. The framing crew can place a double bead of caulk on the subfloor before the sole plate is put in place (Fig. 21.5).

3. Underfloor insulation is important unless the first floor sits over a heated basement. On a house with a basement, typically the furnace is located in the basement with ducts (if a forced-air system) running to the upper floors. Some heat will be released from the furnace and ducts in the basement, heat that rises and helps warm the floor above. If your house is instead built over a crawl space, consider that a floor over an unheated crawl space can be insulated by laying blanket insulation with a vapor barrier that faces up (Fig. 21.6). The insulation bottom must be covered with approved material per your local building code so it's not exposed. To insulate over a concrete slab, lay a hard, rigid board such as plywood, over the top of the slab.

4. Seal where pipes, electric wires, or telephone and television cables penetrate the sole and top plates.

5. Seal around plumbing drains, and beneath bathtubs by blocking large openings with pieces of construction sheathing and sealing the remaining cracks with expanding foam.

6. For soundproofing, insulate the floors between a first and second story. You can use blanket or batt fiberglass or rock wool insulation.

7. Fiberglass batts are excellent for insulating along or between the perimeter joists. There should be a vapor barrier that faces the living side, and the insulation should be covered with a fire safety-rated material that's specified or approved by your local building code. One example may be ⅝-inch fire-resistant gypsum board.

8. All floors above cold spaces, such as vented crawl spaces, must be insulated, and so must floors in a room that is cantilevered beyond exterior walls below.

9. Floors of slabs built directly on the ground need insulation.

10. With crawl spaces, the insulation should be positioned with the vapor retarder toward the warm side of the structure (in cold-weather climates). The insulation can be supported with nylon banding or metal insulation supports. The bottom of the insulation should be protected or covered by a material specified or approved by your local building code.

Walls

Sides, tops, and bottoms of windows and doors should be insulated, with all cracks around window and door sashes and frames filled with insulation loosely pressed into place, then sealed with strips of vapor barrier tape, which serves as a vapor barrier. Tape should be stapled into wood so it holds firmly.

Conduit, electrical outlets (notorious energy wasters), switch boxes, and other fixtures and built-ins should be insulated. Fiberglass can fill larger holes and gaps around the conduit, electrical outlets, and switch boxes. Heat-generating electrical items must have a clearance from insulation. Reference your local building code and the fixture manufacturer's recommendations.

1. The openings formed near corner studs, cavities, and T-junctions created during the framing construction should all be filled with

insulation before the entire framing is completed. Otherwise it will be very difficult, if not impossible, to get insulation into some of those places.

2. The spaces between wall studs should be lined or filled with blankets or batts during framing. The insulation should be placed in the stud cavities with a vapor barrier facing the living area of the house.

3. For additional R-value, use insulated sheathing or apply rigid board insulation to the outside of regular sheathing that might have a low insulation value.

4. Interior walls should be insulated if you want soundproofing. Fiberglass works well for sound control.

5. If the exterior walls of a house are covered with house wrap prior to the application of the siding, air infiltration will be greatly reduced.

6. Drafts can be prevented around electric light switches and wall outlets with inexpensive fire-retardant plastic foam gaskets that fit behind the cover plates. The contractor should use only UL approved products.

7. Insulation should be placed behind plumbing access panels and warm-air registers.

8. Insulating the garage walls and enclosing them with drywall or plasterboard will help retain the heat from your vehicles during winter.

9. Knee walls are partial walls that extend from the floor to the rafters, commonly found in one and one-half story homes and most frequently used for bedrooms or bonus spaces. They should be insulated.

10. Stipulate in the contract that the contractor is responsible for the initial cleaning, both interior and exterior, of windows. Dirty glass can block as much as 40 percent of available solar energy coming through during the day, which could contribute to as much as 3 or 4 percent of your heating bill.

11. If your walls have metal frames, consider having continuous insulation sheathing placed over the outside of the wall framing, between the metal framing pieces and your exterior siding.

12. Consider having window coverings quoted as part of the house contract. Window insulation is available in a variety of shutters, shades, draperies, and panels. Most curtains, blinds, shades, and drapes provide some insulating value when closed over a window. During sunny winter days, windows receiving direct sunlight should be uncovered, since they will let in more heat than they'll lose.

    Qualities to look for in window coverings include the following:

    - Flame-retardant materials that won't produce dangerous fumes if ignited

    - Moisture resistance

    - Durability

    - Quality of opening/closing mechanisms

    - Ease of operation

13. Unless exterior doors come with bottom seals, request door sweeps be installed and positioned so the door bottom seals when closed.

14. Openings that have been made in walls for plumbing or heating components should be plugged to keep air and sound from traveling through. Larger openings and gaps where the walls and floors were drilled for pipes and wiring can be packed with unfaced fiberglass insulation. Smaller cracks and openings can be sealed with silicone caulking.

15. Foam panels installed over the outside of exterior wall sheathing can increase insulating values. Some tear-resistant foam panels unfold over sheathing to form a nearly airtight seal all around the house. This rigid foam panel board siding is made of "fan-folded" panels that minimize the number of seams and greatly reduce the potential for air infiltration. Once the few existing joints are covered with construction insulation tape, an efficient seal is complete.

16. Exterior walls can receive added protection from the application of house wrap after taping the joints or sheathing and caulking/that helps block the chill from wind, rain, and snow.

Ceiling insulation.

Cathedral ceiling insulation.

Attics

Particularly in a single-story house, most heat loss occurs through the attic. By installing sufficient attic insulation you can cut up to 30 percent of your fuel bill.

1. The most common method of insulating an attic is to staple blanket insulation between the ceiling joists with the vapor barrier on the side closest to the home's living areas (Fig. 21.7). Attic insulation should be at least 15-½ to 18 inches of standard fiberglass batts. In cold-climate areas consider insulation with even greater R-values.

2. If you have cathedral ceilings, the proper way to insulate is to install batt material between the roof rafters against the underside of the roof sheathing or deck before the installation of dry wall or plasterboard (Figs. 21.8 and 21.9). There should be an airspace of at least 3 inches between the top of the insulation and the underside of the roof sheathing or deck. This space is needed to ensure proper ventilation and to provide enough space for attic rafter and other vents to function properly.

3. Any attic overhead pulldown doors should be hinged on one side of the door frame and equipped with springs so that when closed, the door can be snugly secured. The insulation that fits over the attic side of such a door should be able to be pulled over the opening before the door is closed, unless it's permanently attached to the top of the attic door itself. There should also be a rubber seal around the door frame to stop any possible air infiltration.

4. Soffit vents must not be blocked by insulation. In the attic ceiling, baffles can be placed where the attic ceiling insulation approaches

ATTIC RAFTER VENTS

AIR AIR

ROOF SURFACE

RAFTER

CEILING SURFACE

BATT INSULATION

FIGURE 21.9

Cathedral ceiling insulation with attic rafter vents.

soffit vents to help maintain airspace required between insulation and roof sheathing. The baffles help prevent insulation from blocking soffet vent air flow into the attic, and help prevent insulation from blowing into unwanted areas. (Fig. 21.10).

Attic baffles are typically extruded polystyrene, used to help maintain constant airflow from soffit vents through the attic to the ridge vent, preventing heat buildup. They increase attic cross ventilation; reduce cooling energy loss; minimize moisture buildup, heat gain, and roof ice dams; and help extend the useful life of the roof. They also keep insulation out of unwanted areas, prevent insulation from blocking airflow from soffit vents into the attic, and keep loose fill insulation away from recessed light fixtures or other heat-producing devices and from spilling over attic hatch door openings.

5. Attic accesses should be insulated—the back of the hatch or door with a piece of fiberglass blanket or rigid board. The bottom of the hatch or door should be weather-stripped to prevent heat from transferring into the attic from below.

6. Connections between the heated space and the attic, such as plumbing and vent stack openings, must also be sealed.

Attic rafter vent baffles.

One access cover design available is molded from lightweight polystyrene plastic to form a hollow shell. The shell is then filled with fiberglass insulation. The insulated cover is large enough to cover attic stairs. Double foam weather stripping seals are attached to the bottom edge, providing an airtight seal around the opening. It's hinged on its side to attic joists for easy opening.

7. Recessed lighting fixtures can be a major source of heat loss, but you need to be careful how close insulation is placed next to a heat-producing fixture unless the fixture is marked "I.C."—which means "Insulated Ceiling," which further means "designed for insulation contact." For all recessed lighting fixtures, verify local building codes and light fixture manufacturers recommendations for proper insulation clearances.

DUCT

VAPOR BARRIER

DUCT TAPE

FIGURE 21.11

Duct insulation.

Ducts and Plumbing

By insulating heating and cooling ducts, pipes, and water heaters, you can reduce your annual heating costs by as much as 10 percent.

1. Wherever heating ducts run through unheated parts of a house, such as through attics, basements, or garages, they can waste as much heat or more than they deliver. That means the occupants pay for a lot more heat than they receive. Two-inch-thick blanket insulation is manufactured in sizes designed for wrapping around ductwork and pipes (Fig. 21.11).

2. Well-sealed vapor barriers should exist on the outside of the insulation on cooling ducts to prevent moisture buildup.

3. Water pipes need insulation, too, especially cold-water pipes exposed to freezing temperatures in winter and hot-water pipes installed between a water heater and fixtures. The pipe insulation will also muffle gurgling noises and will prevent the irritating problem of condensation during warm temperatures when cold-water pipes tend to "sweat" and drip condensate onto basement floors, carpeting, and furnishings (Fig. 21.12).

4. For hot-water tanks, carefully read the manufacturer's instructions to see if additional blanket insulation is allowed. Some companies may void the warranty if insulation is applied over the tank. If addi-

TAPE

CYLINDRICAL PIPE INSULATION

FIGURE 21.12

Pipe insulation.

tional insulation is permitted, instructions must be followed to the letter, because many critical parts cannot be covered safely or effectively. The top or bottom of the tank, the thermostat control, pilot access, drain valves, pressure-relief valves, power supply wiring, air vents, hood drafts and other components could become hazards if covered with additional insulation. In all cases, make sure the tank air vents and hood draft are clear at all times for safe ventilation to the outdoors. If a tankless water heater is selected, follow the manufacturer's instructions as to where pipe insulation can be installed.

5. Outside faucets should be able to accept a pre-made foam faucet insulation cover for the winter, as a temporary weatherization to prevent freezing winds from entering the house. The cover should fit flush and securely against the exterior wall.

6. Wherever ducts penetrate a wall, ceiling, or attic floor, there must be effective fits and tight seals. On hot water heaters, air vents or hood draft openings must not be blocked with insulation—which could prevent toxic fumes from being properly vented outdoors. Likewise, neither should the top or bottom of the tank, the thermostat control, pilot light access, drain valves, pressure relief valve, power wiring, or any other critical parts be blocked. Follow the instructions from the water heater manufacturer for installing insulation.

Caulking

A house is made of many different materials. With age, temperature changes, vibration, and general wear, cracks will develop where the different construction materials meet. Even when doors and windows are weather-stripped, air can infiltrate through these other cracks and joints in the floors, walls, and roof. Individually, these small cracks might seem insignificant, but together they can cause chilly drafts and raise heating or cooling costs.

They also invite insects, leaks, and rot-causing moisture. Although you can't expect to seal up your house completely, by caulking it thoroughly you can curb most of the drafts and heat loss. It's a simple and inexpensive process, yet it can cut up to 10 percent off your heating bills.

The caulking itself is an ideal solution for sealing narrow gaps and cracks. It's a soft, rubber-like material that will conform to any opening, will stay supple, and won't crack or deteriorate for at least several years, or—depending on the type of caulk used and the application—for many years.

The following checklist presents key areas that should be caulked in the typical house:

CAULKING CHECKLIST

___ Around window and door frames

___ Anyplace a crack occurs between brick or pieces of siding

___ Between the foundation and the house framing walls

___ Around the outside of an air-conditioning unit that protrudes from a window

___ Where the wood sill meets the foundation

___ Where exhaust hoods and fan covers pass through a wall

___ Where plumbing pipes enter the house (severe cold wind chill at a tiny opening can cause a pipe to freeze)

___ Where telephone, cable, and electric wires enter the house

___ Where trim meets wood siding, brick, mortar, and other materials

___ Where door or window frames meet walls

___ Under window sills

___ Where floors meet walls

___ At corners formed by siding

___ Between porches and the main body of the house

___ Where chimney or masonry meets siding (chimney caulking is needed here)

___ Around fireplace glass door jambs (special heat-resistant caulk needed here)

(Continued)

✔✔✔✔✔ CAULKING CHECKLIST *(Continued)*

___ Around heating and cooling ducts and pipes running from a separate outside central air-conditioning unit

___ Around pipes going to sinks and behind toilets

___ Around roof flashing vents, and pipes

___ In gutter and downspout joints

___ Around vents and fans

___ At mortar joints

___ Where two building/siding materials meet (i.e., brick meets stucco or wood)

___ Around exterior basement doors

___ At window stops

___ Make sure weep holes at the bottom of storm windows are not caulked or otherwise plugged. They allow moisture from condensation to drain out or evaporate.

___ At seams between door jambs and door stops

___ Underneath metal or wooden door thresholds

___ Between window and door drip caps and siding

___ On split or broken siding

___ Where framing meets flooring

___ On gaps in the attic around pipe penetrations under the insulation, and anywhere else cracks or gaps exist between the living area and attic.

Note: Silicone caulk stays flexible and is ideal for gaps where movement or seasonal expansion/contraction occurs. However, most makes of silicone caulk cannot be painted. They need to be purchased in appropriate colors. When caulking, for gaps of ⅜-inch or more, the crack should be packed with foam backer rod before the caulk is applied, so the seam won't crack later.

VAPOR BARRIERS

In addition to insulation, a home's living areas should also be sealed with appropriate material (called a vapor barrier) applied along the inside of the studs, the ceiling joists, and the floor joists—mainly to prevent the movement of moisture from the living areas into the insulation. Insulation loses some of its efficiency when it becomes damp or wet, and if moisture is not retained inside the living spaces of a home, the occupants won't be as comfortable and will need more heat to achieve a satisfying inside temperature. In humid locations, however, where air-conditioning is often running to remove moisture from the inside air, the vapor barrier will prevent outside moisture from entering the living areas.

Vapor Barriers for Walls and Ceilings

There are three methods for applying a vapor barrier to exterior walls or ceilings:

1. Install insulating blankets or batts having faces of vapor barrier backing such as treated kraft paper or aluminum foil placed on the living area side of the wall or ceiling.

2. When unfaced blanket or batt insulation is used, a separate vapor barrier must be provided. Aluminum-backed plaster and drywall are not effective choices because their seams don't overlap.

3. Staple or nail polyethylene sheet material to the interior of the studs and ceiling joists. This is probably the most effective vapor barrier.

Vapor Barriers for Floors

If blanket or batt insulation is applied between the floor joists, a vapor barrier (per local building code specifications) should be installed against the subfloor. The covering of the insulation on the bottom should likewise be per code specifications.

A Safety Note

Peel back insulation and flammable vapor barriers away from the heat-producing components or features in a house. Chimneys, flues, stoves, electric fans, and heating sources can all be potential fire starters. The heat-producing equipment manufacturer and your local building code should provide guidelines for proper clearance.

SUMMER AND WINTER PROTECTION

Where possible, provide shade for sunny east, south, and west walls and windows. Use roof overhangs, shade trees, sun screens, shades, or interior draperies. Try to be flexible; shade makes for easier cooling in summer, yet sunshine streaming in through a window in winter can be a welcome sight.

Consider placing evergreen trees on the north side of the house to help block the cold northern winter winds.

✔✔✔✔✔ SOUND CONTROL INSULATION CHECKLIST

__ Consider using fiberglass insulation in walls, ceilings, and floors to control sound.

__ Install thick padding and carpeting to reduce impact sound. Heavily padded carpets absorb sound far better than bare or tiled floors will.

__ Choose solid wood (not hollow core) interior doors with threshold and jamb seals, where privacy is desired.

__ Have all windows, wiring, and piping holes caulked.

__ Use at least double-pane storm windows to help reduce sound transmission.

__ Telephone hookups, doorbells, intercoms, or audio built-ins should be installed on interior walls only, never on common walls or corridor walls.

__ Wiring, where it penetrates connecting structures, should be insulated with nonhardening caulk or dry packing.

__ Ceiling fixture openings need to be sealed, using before-mentioned precautions around heat-producing components.

__ Electrical outlet holes should be neatly cut out to reduce sound leaks.

__ Fire-retardant plastic foam gaskets may be included behind all electrical outlets and switch covers on both sides of common walls they're placed in, blocking a direct route between rooms for airborne noise.

__ A well-planned layout will minimize flowing water noise.

__ Plumbing fixtures and wall plates need caulking.

__ A nonhardening silicone or butyl-based caulk is also need for the perimeter of drywall panels. Caulking around the floor, corner, and ceiling of drywall or plasterboard must be done before the panels go up against the wood studding. This makes sure acoustical gaps from

SOUND CONTROL INSULATION (*Continued*)

warped or uneven studs are filled. The flexible caulk will help reduce vibration.

__ Window treatments can help minimize sound transmission from the outside. Heavy draperies and quilted or pleated shades will help absorb noise better than thin metal or vinyl blinds or curtains will.

FIGURE 21.13

Resilient channels.

__ An additional sound control relies on resilient channels, U-shaped metal strips, applied to wall studs and ceiling joists with a ½-inch by 3-inch gypsum nailing strip at the bottom. The channels help break up sound waves and isolate noise. Fiberglass or mineral wool batts should be stapled in the stud spaces. Since the channels are resilient, they deaden sound transmission (Fig. 21.13).

(Continued)

SOUND CONTROL INSULATION (*Continued*)

___ Another sound-controlling wall features studs that are staggered within the wall so no individual stud actually touches both inner surfaces of the wall. Insulation is snaked through the studs along the entire length, leaving no gaps for sound to get through.

INSULATION

■ All insulation is tightly installed, with no air gaps.

■ Vapor barriers face the interior of the home sides that are heated.

■ No punctures have been made in vapor barriers. Any rips or tears have been repaired.

■ Ductwork is insulated.

■ Plumbing is insulated throughout the house.

■ All openings to the outside for plumbing, wiring, and gas lines are sealed.

▶▶▶▶▶▶ POINTS TO PONDER

1. Insulation should envelop all living areas of your home, leaving no openings except doors, windows, and necessary vents (which may, in turn, be individually insulated, too).

2. Heating and cooling ducts, and water piping should be insulated to provide energy efficiencies.

3. Much of the insulation should be installed after the framing is complete and the electrical, plumbing, and heating systems have been roughed in and inspected.

4. Because heat rises, the potential heat loss in a house is greatest through the roof.

5. Although interior walls and floors are not exposed to outside temperatures, they should also be insulated to provide sound barriers between rooms.

6. Insulation belongs between the top of the foundation wall and the sill plate under the first-floor decking. Insulation should also

be stuffed into the cracks and small spaces between rough framing and the jambs, heads, and sills of windows and doors, and used to fill spaces behind conduit, electrical outlets, switch boxes, and other built-ins. Enough air space should be included between insulation and any devices that produce heat or get hot.

7. Seal where pipes, electric wires, or telephone and television cables penetrate the sole and top plates. Insulating foam is a viable alternative to caulk when large gaps must be sealed because foam fills cracks, holes, and other voids, assuming the shape of the cavities. It does not shrink and sticks to most surfaces, including wood, metal, masonry, glass and most plastics.

8. Make sure that contractors don't skimp on the quality of caulking they use. There isn't much additional cost that separates medium-quality caulking from top-quality caulking. If special color caulking is used (as with stucco), see that you receive a few tubes for future touch-ups and so you can purchase more of the same caulk later.

9. Insulation loses effectiveness when damp or wet. Vapor barriers must be applied between the living areas and insulation to prevent movement of moisture from the living areas into the insulation.

10. Where possible, provide shade for walls and windows with roof overhangs, trees, blinds, shades, or interior draperies, and plant evergreen trees and shrubs for wind blocks.

Wall Covering and Trim

The materials you select to cover your inside walls, plus the trim that's installed along corners and joints, are features that should weigh heavily in your decorating scheme. They're part of a home's inside cosmetics—what you and your visitors will see—and part of the home's structure.

WALL COVERINGS

There are a number of possibilities to select from when it comes to covering or finishing off the inside walls. The most popular materials are drywall, plaster, and paneling. If drywall or plaster is selected, then specify if you want the finished surfaces painted or wallpapered.

Drywall Installation

Drywall consists of large (usually 4- by 8-foot) panels of prefabricated gypsum plaster sheathed on both sides with paper (Fig. 22.1).

- Panels are measured to fit, cut to fit, and screwed (or screwed and glued for extra strength) to the rough walls.

- The screws must be slightly countersunk or driven so that the heads pass slightly through the surface of the drywall.

PERFORATED TAPE AT INSIDE CORNER

SCREWS HIDDEN WITH JOINT COMPOUND

SCREWS 6"-8" O.C.

BEVELED EDGE

EXTERIOR SHEATHING

INSULATION

STUD

OUT SIDE CORNER METAL CORNER BEAD

OPENING FOR ELECTRICAL OUTLET

FIGURE 22.1

Drywall—vertical application.

- A smooth continuous surface is achieved between adjacent panels through filling in and troweling over the joints, cracks, and spaces with a plasterlike "joint" compound after a thin water-saturated paper tape has been applied to each crack or space.

- Screw depressions from the countersunk screws are filled in with the same joint compound, then troweled smooth.

- Lightweight but sturdy metal angles are installed wherever two pieces of drywall form right angles, to strengthen the corners. Edges are then troweled smooth with a thin layer of joint compound.

- Once the joint compound dries, it's smoothed out with fine-grit sandpaper. A second coat of joint compound should then be applied and also sanded smooth when dry. The second coat should then be followed by a third and final coat.

Final finishing is accomplished with more sanding and by last-minute "point-up" work—taking care of any minor irregularities and making edges sharper. When everything is dry and sanded smooth, the entire surface is painted, usually white. Once painted, there should be no evidence of panel joints or nail indentations.

At an additional cost, special finishes may be applied to drywall (and ceilings) in "skim" coatings of topping compounds similar to plaster. A skim coat can be left smooth, swished, dappled, ridged, or otherwise be finished to obtain a variety of unique textures (Fig. 22.2). Some contractors will apply a coating of material, and while it's still wet, take a large sponge and press it against the surface, drawing out the plasterlike material in many tiny points that look like miniature stalactites. It's a way to have your own walls and ceilings finished in a manner that you'll find nowhere else.

Drywall Considerations

- Drywall should not be applied in extreme heat or cold, to avoid the possibility of warping or shrinkage.
- Drywall should be carefully fit to minimize the number and sizes of gaps.
- Specify that contractors must use approved scaffolding for reaching ceilings and high walls. Some contractors actually use stilts to reach indoor heights—a dangerous practice.
- When specifying drywall, look for ⅝-inch thick fire-resistant gypsum board. Check to make sure it meets your local builing code.
- When extra strength is desired, wall adhesive can be applied to all studs before installing drywall.

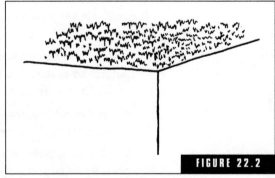

FIGURE 22.2

A textured ceiling—dappled finish.

- Screws provide better holding power than nails will, with less chance of "pop outs," where fastener heads loosen and work their way back through the surface of the drywall.

- Request that all joints be taped, with three separate coats of joint compound, each sanded smooth. Each successive coat should leave a wider swatch or track and a smooth finish.

- Special moisture-resistant gypsum drywall must be used along all wall areas around shower stalls and bathtubs—and wherever else there's the likelihood of water or moisture present.

Advantages of Drywall

1. Drywall is relatively inexpensive to purchase and install.

2. It's less inclined to crack than plaster.

3. It's easier to repair than plaster.

4. Drywall can be installed quickly and doesn't take as long to set up as plaster does. The rest of the finishing work can proceed without much delay.

Disadvantages

1. Drywall must be painted because its finished appearance is not uniform. All joints, screw indentations, and repairs are whiter—due to the joint compound—than the rest of the drywall surfacing, which

 DRYWALL INSPECTION CHECKLIST

The following is a checklist of items that shouldn't be overlooked with drywall:

__ Cuts should be clean around register openings, wall switches, and outlets so that covers and fixtures do not allow gaps or exposed spaces in the drywall.

__ When viewed lengthwise, there should be no warped or bumpy surfaces. Nor should there be uneven surfaces to the touch.

__ Inquire as to how long the contractor will guarantee the drywall against defects.

is a gray or buff color (whatever the shade of the drywall's outer paper layer).

2. The modular construction and the taping of drywall sections can sometimes be discerned, especially if it's a less-than-perfect installation. This can be worse than an occasional crack in a plaster wall.

PLASTER

Before drywall was invented, plaster was the number one way to finish off a home's interior walls.

Plaster Installation

Plaster is a mudlike building material that's applied over plasterboard lathing which supplies a secure base for the plaster to adhere. The lathing is a wallboard that usually has a gypsum core sandwiched between layers of paper and a cardboard or foil backing that serves as a vapor barrier. The outer layers of paper absorb water quickly so that plaster sticks to the lath before it begins to slide. The inner layers are treated to resist moisture.

- Specify ⅝-inch-thick fire-resistant gypsum board, if it meets your local code.
- The lath may be solid or perforated. Perforated material improves bonding capabilities between the plaster.
- Gypsum lath should be applied to the studs with screws. If extra strength is desired, it can also be glued to the studs.
- Gaps between applied sheets should be minimized.
- Plaster is typically applied in either a single ½-inch-thick layer or two ⅜-inch-thick coats, one on top of the other.

Plaster Considerations

- Plastering should not be done in extreme heat or cold.
- Contractors should use approved scaffolding to reach high areas (not stilts).
- Screws, not nails, should be used to fasten lath to studs; for extra strength, also apply glue to the studs.

■ Plaster can be finished in smooth or textured surfaces to complement any decor. Ask the plaster contractor to show you samples of the various options. If possible, view homes featuring different plaster options to compare looks.

■ Specify how you want the plaster finished in each room. In bathrooms and kitchens consider smooth surfaces for easier cleaning.

Advantages

1. Together with its lathing, a plaster wall is thicker and provides better insulation values than drywall.

2. A plaster wall is more fire-resistant than a surface finished with drywall.

3. Plaster, with its lathing screwed to the studs, is more rigid than drywall, and less likely to bend or buckle.

4. It provides better soundproofing than drywall.

5. With plaster, a wider variety of creative artistic effects are possible. The topping layers on drywall cannot create such startling designs and surface modifications.

Disadvantages

1. Plaster costs more to install.

2. Plaster cracks easier than drywall does and is more difficult to repair.

✔✔✔✔✔ PLASTER INSPECTION CHECKLIST

The following is a checklist of items that shouldn't be overlooked with plaster:

___ Cuts should be clean around register openings, switches, outlets, and fixtures, so no voids in the plaster show.

___ When viewed lengthwise, there should be no undulations or bumps in the plaster's surface. Nor should there be any uneven surfaces to the touch.

___ Inspect closely for cracks.

___ Ask how long the contractor will guarantee the plaster work against cracks and other defects.

3. Plaster takes longer to install. It takes time for it to dry or set up that could otherwise be used for completing more of the wall finishing work.

PANELING

Prefabricated panels of wood and other materials are used to cover walls because of the panels' beauty, variety, low-maintenance qualities, and simple installation methods (Fig. 22.3). In fact, the finishing job on drywall or plaster walls that will be covered by paneling can be less than perfect, thus saving time.

You can find panels constructed to look and feel like a wide selection of building materials, including marble, stone, brick, and stucco. There are even panels that simulate a wallpapered surface. These handy prefabricated sheets are becoming increasingly popular in kitchens, bathrooms, foyers, and even in main living areas planned

FIGURE 22.3

Paneling.

in today's modern dwellings. They are still not, however, as widely accepted as wood and wood-simulated paneling designs.

Plywood makes very good paneling for walls. It's durable and will add a rich look to a family room, recreation room, study, den, or dining area. Wood species such as elm, pecan, birch, and certain kinds of walnut lend themselves nicely to use on the plywood veneers.

Paneling should be installed against walls that have already been roughly finished in drywall or plaster, so the paneling will have sufficient backing to prevent waviness or buckling. Care must be taken to ensure that all sections of paneling are plumb and fitted tightly together, with adequate nailing along their edges.

Advantages

1. Paneling will not show cracks in the walls.

2. It is easy to install.

3. It adds to the insulation and sound proof values of the walls.

4. It can create many different moods for a room or area.

Disadvantages

1. Making repairs to damaged paneling can be very difficult.

2. Paneling adds to the overall expenses of wall finishing beyond the costs of drywall or plaster.

3. It's another step in the construction of a house that takes additional time.

TRIM

Look in any home and you'll see wood or other trim installed wherever different construction finishing materials intersect: along joints for instance, and corners, door frames, windows, and other built-in house features. Trim makes an otherwise unattractive meeting place of two planes or surfaces (such as plastered walls and wood flooring, drywall and carpeting, wood paneling and vinyl flooring) into an attractive border accent.

Trim can also have functional applications: it can tightly hold down edges of paneling, carpeting, and linoleum, and when placed in dining areas at chair-back height from the floor, it will prevent the chairs from scratching the walls.

The cost of a house's interior trimwork will vary, depending on what you specify. Here are some general points to consider before planning the trim for your house:

1. Even though hardwood trim is more expensive, it's the best and most common choice because it's more durable than softwood trim.

2. Decide whether you want the trim to be stained, sealed, varnished, or painted. Some contractors will charge extra, depending on how the trim will be finished.

3. Specify where you want trim to be used. Some places in a house are not necessarily trimmed unless you make specific arrangements for them, such as around open doorways or around closet exteriors.

4. Be careful not to mix or have too many different molding shapes. Match up the kind of trim material you select with the basic style of your home.

Trim Considerations

- If you plan to have bookshelves, get quotes along with the trim.

- Trim needs to be protected before installation. It should be kept out of main traffic areas to avoid dents, scratches, and waste.

- Whenever possible, all of the trim should be purchased from the same supplier, so pieces match. Otherwise, different shades, grades, finishes, and dimensions may not match well together. Top grade no. 1 trim material is well worth the relatively minor extra cost.

- Specify in which finish you want the trim stained.

TYPES OF TRIM AND MOLDINGS

The following types of trim are a good representation of what's available on the market and what each is most commonly used for (Figs. 22.4 through 22.11):

FIGURE 22.4

Trim/molding.

FIGURE 22.5

Trim/molding.

CROWN · AND · BED TRIM

FIGURE 22.6

Trim/molding.

FIGURE 22.7

Trim/molding.

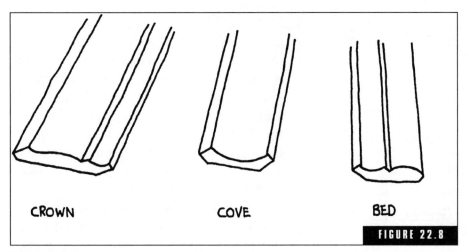

CROWN   COVE   BED

FIGURE 22.8

Trim/molding.

CORNER
GUARD
TRIM

FIGURE 22.9

Trim/molding.

SIDING

FLASHED METAL DRIP

DRIP CAP

WINDOW CASING

SASH

FIGURE 22.10

Trim/molding.

CHAIR RAIL

APPROX 32"

FIGURE 22.11

Trim/molding.

CASING TRIM

Casing trim is the molding applied around doors and windows to cover the junctions of the door or window frames and finished wall. It's available in several styles and sizes. Doorway casing runs all the way to the floor, past and adjacent to baseboard trim that stops snugly against it.

BASE OR BASEBOARD TRIM

Base trim or molding covers the gaps between the floor and the finished walls. Its style is usually the same as the door and window casing, but larger in size. Plasterers and drywall finishers will assume that the baseboard is at least 2½ inches high and will leave unfinished that part of the wall that is less than that distance from the floor. If you select base that's less than 2½ inches, check with your contractor to ensure that the drywall or plaster walls will be finished near enough to the floor so no unfinished wall will show above the baseboard.

BASE SHOE TRIM

Base shoe trim is molding applied between the finished floor and the baseboard. It's very flexible and can fit tightly along both the floor and baseboard trim, despite any irregularities of the structure that can be present even in the best of wood construction.

BASE CAP TRIM

These narrow sections of trim may be used to handsomely "cap" the tops of plain flat baseboard moldings. If you choose to use them, they'll also close any gaps that might exist between the wall and the baseboard.

CROWN-AND-BED TRIM

Crown-and-bed trim is a decorative molding used to soften sharp lines where two planes meet. Usual applications are at corners where walls and ceilings intersect. Such moldings are ideal for decorative trimwork, around a fireplace mantel for instance, or to make picture frames. The backs on most crown trim sections are hollow.

STOP TRIM

Stop trim is molding nailed to a door jamb to stop a closing door. It's also used on windows with sliding sashes.

STOOL TRIM

Stool trim is molding used at the bottom of windows to provide a snug joint with the lowered sash.

PICTURE TRIM

Picture trim molding was so named because it was originally designed as a perimeter trim from which pictures could be hung. It can still be used that way, but a more modern application is to use it as a substitute for crown trim.

SHELF EDGE OR SCREEN TRIM

This molding is designed to cover the raw edges of screening on doors or windows, to decorate the edges of wood members such as shelves, or to conceal exposed plywood edges.

CORNER GUARD TRIM

Corner guard trim is used to protect and finish outside corners.

DRIP CAP TRIM

Drip cap trim can be installed for use at top edges on the exterior side of doors and windows to prevent moisture from getting inside the walls.

CHAIR RAIL TRIM

Chair rail trim is a decorative and functional molding installed about 32 inches above the finished floor or at whatever height is best for a particular application that would protect the walls in a room from dining room chair or other furniture damage.

WAINSCOTING

Wainscoting can be wood planks with tongue-and-groove arrangements, paneling, or other similar materials installed on the lower portions of interior walls, often between the baseboard and a chair rail. The wainscoting is applied first, then the chair and baseboard trims are fastened over the wainscoting's bottom and top edges.

PLY CAPS

Ply caps are moldings used at the top of wainscoting to provide a smooth finish. They're also effective for edging plywood and for framing any panel, especially if the panel will be used as a slab for, say, a table top.

ROUNDS

Rounds can be purchased as quarter-rounds, half-rounds, and full rounds (Fig. 22.12). Typical applications for full rounds are as closet poles, curtain rods, and banisters; for half-rounds, as decorative surface trim or seam covers; for quarter-rounds, as decorative trim for inside corners and as shelf cleats.

HANDRAILS

Handrails are installed along one or both sides of a staircase (Fig. 22.13).

▶▶▶▶▶ POINTS TO PONDER

1. When planning major-installation wall coverings such as wood paneling, stone, and tile, give them plenty of thought because they're expensive and difficult to replace.

2. Even heavy-duty paneling should be installed against walls that have already been finished in drywall or plaster, so the paneling will have sufficient backing to prevent waviness or buckling.

3. Consider that paint and wallpaper are the simplest wall surfaces with which to make subtle and dramatic decorating changes.

4. Between drywall and plaster, remember that drywall is less expensive, easier to

FULL ROUND   HALF ROUND   QUARTER ROUND

FIGURE 22.12

Rounds.

A stairway with a handrail.

FIGURE 22.13

repair and work with, and is less inclined to crack than plaster. Plaster, however, lends itself to a wide variety of finished textures when professionally applied. A plaster wall is also more rigid, more soundproof, and more fire-resistant than drywall.

5. Whenever you have a choice, go with stain-resistant, washable wall surfaces. Avoid the use of flat paints for kitchens, bathrooms, and children's rooms. Instead, opt for semigloss or gloss coatings.

6. Even though hardwood trim is more expensive, it's a good choice because it's more durable than softwood trim. If the trim will be painted, though, softwood can be an acceptable choice (dents and scratches can be filled with wood filler and coated with touch-up paint).

7. Any home can benefit from the use of unique molding. Moldings can provide architectural details—at relatively small costs—that can make the interior decor of a home far more attractive than it would otherwise be.

8. Be careful not to mix or have too many different molding shapes. Match up the kind of trim material you select with the basic style of your home.

9. Consider asking the contractor for extra pieces of trim and molding, finished exactly like those used throughout your home, in case you eventually need to replace or add pieces for repair/addition/maintenance reasons. Naturally, make this request before the main trim is installed, and realize that you may have to pay a minimal charge for the extra pieces.

10. Inexpensive vinyl trim is often an acceptable material for use in utility rooms, sunrooms, and basement bathrooms. Extensions of a room's carpeting can also be used as wall trim if it suits the decorating plan.

Burglar-Proofing Your Home

It's true that crimes of violence, though on the rise, occur much less frequently than crimes against property. But it's also true that crimes against property, such as burglary, can easily turn into crimes of violence if an intruder is discovered and confronted.

Most thieves, burglars, and housebreakers are amateurs. Sure, on television shows they sand their fingertips, pick combination locks, scale buildings with grappling hooks, dress in color-coded outfits, and perform near-perfect crimes; but in real life they're not that classy. Instead, most are opportunists searching for unlocked doors, open windows, and unattended pocketbooks.

According to law enforcement experts, these amateur burglars and housebreakers worry about three things:

- Delay in getting into your home.
- Being forced to work where they can be observed.
- Having to make noise in the process.

In other words, they don't want to cause a commotion. They don't want to get caught. That's why they'll pass by a house that has good door and window locks and other characteristics that will delay or announce their entry.

DOOR LOCKS

Older homes and apartments were usually built solid, with doors of thick oak—heavy, sturdy, impossible to kick in. Unfortunately their locks were often flimsy by comparison.

Many were mortised locks that were recessed into a hole or slot cut from the door's outer edge near the knob. Sometimes their locking bolt fit securely into its door frame receptacle, other times not. If the door was "hung loose" or wobbly, often only ⅛ inch of bolt kept the door locked.

Most of the remaining old-fashioned locks had keyholes, the kind you can look through. They could be operated with skeleton keys, the same keys that sell for under a dollar per set in any hardware store. Not too safe.

Because skeleton locks are so easy to defeat (to open through picking or simply using other skeleton keys), many residents installed chain units to supplement their protection. A chain lock is merely a short chain permanently fastened to the door or door frame that, when attached to its receiving fixture, prevents the door from being opened more than a few inches. Again, not safe. The chains afford little safety from a determined intruder. All the intruder has to do is kick or smash the door with enough force to rip loose the screws holding the chain's receptacle to the door or frame.

Since the days of keyhole locks, safer locks have been designed and put into use . . . some of the time. Other, unsafe locks have also come onto the market and are being frequently used in new construction because they're inexpensive to produce and easy to install.

These relatively new locks are called key-in-knob locks. To open the door from the outside you insert a key directly into a hole in the knob, and turn. To lock it when leaving, you simply push a button on the inside knob, or push the inside knob and turn, then slam the door shut. The locking bolt is spring-operated.

A key-in-knob lock is the easiest modern lock to thwart. Unless antidefeating features are built into the lock, it can be broken into in several ways:

1. By force. Most of these locks are constructed of flimsy materials. By placing a piece of widemouth pipe over the outside door handle, the knob can be snapped off. And because its locking bolt is always short and beveled, a crowbar or similar tool can often pry the door open from its frame.

2. By guile. The simplest way to defeat a key-in-knob lock is to loid it. To loid it? Yes, *loiding* is a new word, invented in honor of the key-in-knob lock. You probably won't find it in your dictionary, but it comes from the word "celluloid." It means to open a lock by inserting a thin plastic strip (like a credit card) between the bolt and jamb so the plastic strip releases a spring-operated catch.

If you are not yet convinced that key-in-knob locks, by themselves, are unsafe, inquire at your local police department.

From the worst, let's jump to the best: a single cylinder deadbolt, operated by a key from outside and a thumb-latch inside. It throws a 1-inch rectangular (not beveled) bolt into its receptacle, and if installed properly, cannot be pried or loided.

There is a hitch, however: if any glass is situated in or near the door someone could break it, reach in, and turn the thumb latch from inside. In this case, two options are available:

1. Replace the glass.

2. Replace the single cylinder lock with a double-cylinder model—a lock operated by key from inside and out.

The first option is the safest. That's what most locksmiths and law enforcement agencies recommend. A lock that requires a key on the inside could be hazardous in case of a fire or other emergency. Avoid using double-cylinder locks.

Doors already equipped with a key-in-knob lock can be made safer by having good single-cylinder deadbolts installed above the key-in-knob lock.

In most cases, strike plates (what the door bolt or latch locks into) should be fastened into the door frame or jamb with long screws, preferably 3-inch (Fig. 23.1).

WALL STUD
DOOR JAMB
DOOR STOP
STRIKE PLATE
THREE INCH SCREWS

FIGURE 23.1

Securing a strikeplate.

This setup will resist heavy blows or force that might otherwise defeat the lock by ripping the strike plate right out of the door frame.

A lock cylinder having six pins instead of the typical five makes it substantially harder to "pick" open. Also, unusual key designs such as dimpled faces are harder to duplicate by illegal means.

One newly marketed door lock can be operated with either a key or by turning the knob after a 3- or 4-digit access code is entered. This means you could never accidentally lock yourself out, ever again. Temporary access codes can also be set up so guests, servicepersons, or relatives could let themselves in for some specific purpose without knowing your master code. Various alarm settings are available to scare off intruders who might try to turn the knob while attempting to guess the code.

Remember, your door will be a lot more secure if it's soundly constructed and well-fitted to a sturdy frame. Doors having solid wood construction at least 1¾ inches thick and metal doors will both do the job.

DOOR HINGES

Door hinge pins should be located on the *inside* of all doors that lead outside your home; otherwise an intruder could gain entrance by prying up the pins with a screwdriver.

DOOR PEEPHOLES

As mentioned in the chapter on doors, peepholes should be installed in doors to the outside that afford no other view of callers. Plastic lenses will fog, scratch, and deteriorate in a short while. Quality glass peepholes, with a viewing field of 180 degrees, will last a lifetime.

SLIDING DOORS

Sliding glass doors are usually situated in a family room or kitchen dining area, facing the rear of the property. That's great for housebreakers. Remember, they like to work in dark places where no one can watch them.

Although most sliding doors consist of two glass panels, usually only one of them is permanently fastened. To safeproof sliders you must—if the window/door manufacturer has not—prevent intruders from sliding the movable door open by force, and prevent them from prying the movable door up and out of its track.

Probably the most common way to prevent someone from opening the movable panel by force is to place a long wooden dowel or piece of broom stick in the bottom track. This is not foolproof, however, because it won't prevent someone from simply prying the door away from and out of its track. A special steel or wood bar that locks into the sliding track (frequently called a "Charley Bar") will prevent house-breakers from prying the panels off their tracks and may be purchased commercially.

In addition, a simple cylinder lock will pin a bolt through both doors where the doors overlap. The pin must be able to be released quickly by anyone indoors in case of an emergency. Make sure to use a single-cylinder lock that does *not* require a key to open from inside.

WINDOW LOCKS

If determined housebreakers can't negotiate your exterior doors, chances are they'll turn their attention to your windows.

The windows most vulnerable in an average house are the basement windows. They should be capable of latching and locking securely closed from the inside.

Other windows should be locked or fastened in fixed positions, either closed all the way or opened a few inches for air in warm weather.

Double-Hung Windows

These windows are probably the most commonly used today. They operate upward and downward, and lock with a simple metal latch. Approach a locked double-hung window from the outside. Try sticking a knife blade up the crack and see if you can jiggle the latch with it. An experienced housebreaker can open all but the most tightly fitting windows in this fashion. Older windows often suffer from dry rot around their latches, and the screws that fasten the latch to the wood can easily be pulled out.

Make certain your double-hung windows all have effective locking mechanisms.

Casement Windows

These windows operate by means of a crank near their bottom. A latch locks the window to a center post. Don't include any casement windows without effective locking latches.

Sliding Windows

These windows can be secured the same way as sliding glass doors.

Skylights

Skylights should be locked with latches when not in use. The openings can be protected with metal grilles latched close.

MAKING YOUR HOME SAFER

Here is a list of things you can do to help prevent burglars and other intruders from selecting your home as a target.

1. When leaving home for several days or more, stop mail, milk, and newspaper deliveries. Arrange for other services, when needed, to continue as usual, such as lawn mowing and snow removal. Consider keeping a spare car or one of your neighbor's cars parked conspicuously in the driveway.

2. Also, when gone, use automatic timers to turn on one or two lights at night to fool a burglar into thinking that someone's home. A good choice is a bathroom light (a bathroom with an outside window). That's a room that could be in use at any hour of the night.

3. While on vacation, have a relative or friend visit your home to alter the positions of drapes and blinds and change the settings on timers that activate lights, radio, and television so regular patterns are not obvious.

4. Consider hiring or arranging for a house sitter during extended absences.

5. Give your neighbors phone numbers to call in case they observe any unusual activities that need to be reported or investigated. Offer your assistance to them in return.

6. Never leave a key hidden outside. Instead, trust a nearby friend or relative with one in case the police are summoned while you're absent. Don't mark the key or your key ring with your name or address. If you're nervous about losing your keys, keep one or two extra sets, one at home, the other with a relative or trusted neighbor.

7. Register any alarm system and advise local authorities who to contact if your alarm goes off while you're away.

8. Even if you don't have burglar alarms, alarm system decals placed on doors and windows will make burglars think twice before taking on your home. It could steer them in another direction to a different residence.

9. Ideally, maintain lighting at all points where an intruder could gain entry.

10. Photosensitive outside flood- and door lights that automatically turn on and off at dusk and daylight do a good job of illuminating the grounds.

11. If your neighborhood is dimly lit or completely dark, ask local authorities to replace existing bulbs with others of higher wattage, or to add new posts and lamps.

12. Keep landscaping shrubs and trees a reasonable distance from entrances and windows, or at the very least trimmed low and tightly cropped against the house. If too large and close they could give burglars cover to work from.

13. Strong door locks, particularly deadbolts as mentioned earlier, encourage burglars to move on because "forced entry" time with less-sturdy locks is much shorter.

14. Consider installing storm windows and doors with locks.

15. Garage overhead doors that can be opened from inside an automobile by a radio remote-control unit eliminate the need for you to get out of the car until you're safely within the garage. They also act as a locking device when the door is in the closed position.

16. During the day and early evening you can leave a child's toy, a scooter or wagon, outside, up against the house, to make it appear that someone's home.

17. It's best not to display your sex and marital status on your door or mailbox.

18. Telephone answering machines are good if programmed with a message saying you are unable to come to the phone now, but you'll call back soon. Never leave a message that you're on vacation and will be gone until a certain date.

19. A barking dog of any size will usually scare off all but the boldest of burglars.

20. Don't let strangers look into your home through your windows. Venetian and other blinds, shutters, and window treatments prevent burglars from casing the inside of your house.

21. Peepholes on exterior doors having no windows are a must.

22. Door speakers or intercoms will allow you to speak with whoever's at the door before opening it.

23. Request that your water, gas, and electric companies call in advance, if possible, and arrange your appointments so you know they're coming ahead of time.

24. The police in your area will probably perform a free security inspection if you schedule it with plenty of advance notice. It's one of the best ways to learn if you're leaving yourself open for trouble.

Further Safeguard Your Valuables

Record the descriptions and serial numbers of valuable items and engrave the ones without them. Polaroids or other photos can be used for insurance records. Include articles such as bicycles, guns, cameras, stereos, televisions, binoculars, sewing machines, and power tools on your protected list. Keep the records in a safe place, but not inside your home.

Use a safe deposit box for valuables that needn't be kept in the house.

MONITORING SYSTEMS

Also known as burglar alarms, monitoring systems have come a long, long way since "turn-the-Doberman-pinscher-loose-in-the-locked-house days":

- In-House Monitoring Box System. Located at an out-of-the-way location in the house. When activated by an intruder's entry, it will set off a loud horn, siren, or bell. This usually works fine as long as neighbors are close enough to hear and respond to the alarm if you're away.

- Central Monitoring System. Monitored by a central base outside of the home, for a monthly fee. It directly and swiftly summons police, fire, or medical emergency assistance. It dispatches personnel to respond to, inspect, and reset the alarm. It will notify any other designated party as directed by the homeowner and will also trigger an outside alarm.

Central monitoring systems can be linked from the home to the central base in a variety of ways.

1. *Directly Connected.* By special telephone lines leased specifically for that purpose, which can also be tied into police and fire departments. In addition to alarm signals, these lines will indicate line faults or cuts to the receiving base.

2. *Digital Dialers.* These, too, send alarm signals over telephone lines to a central monitoring office or to the police department. The difference is that they send the signals over regular phone lines. Regular lines won't indicate faulty or cut wires. To remedy this situation a local sounding device should be installed to go off if the telephone line is disturbed or cut.

3. *Automatic Dialers.* These dialers deliver a prerecorded message or a coded signal to the alarm company office, to an answering service, to the police station, even to a neighbor, over regular phone lines. This type of alarm should also be equipped with a local sounding device to indicate if telephone line problems or tampering occurs.

4. *Long-Range Radio Signals.* These alarm signals are sent to a central base station direct, by radio transmitter. They avoid the telephone

line problems and tampering, but require test signals to be transmitted occasionally to verify if the system is functioning.

Sensory Devices

These sensors are the eyes, ears, and other intruder-sensitive senses of the monitoring systems.

EXTERIOR MONITORING SENSORS

- Electric eyes/motion detectors will alert you of someone's approach. Can also be triggered by animals and can lead to frequent false alarms.

- Magnets for gates on fenced-in yards can alert you when the gates are opened. Easily defeated, however, if an intruder climbs over the fence.

PERIMETER SENSORS

- Magnetic switches are attached to doors and windows and adjacent frames. They're wired to signal a control unit when a magnet moves away from its switch.

- Plunger contacts are concealed, recessed into doors or windows. They operate the same way as a hidden light switch on automobile and refrigerator doors.

- Current-conducting foil consists of thin ribbons attached to windows, door panels, and walls to monitor any breaking of the surface. Unless trickily camouflaged by modernistic decor, the foil is very noticeable.

- Vibration or shock detectors monitor someone or something shaking or breaking through walls, doors, or windows.

- Special screens are available to cover windows and other openings. They contain inconspicuous alarm wires to protect against forced entry through the screen material. They're installed so an alarm will also sound if the entire screen is removed from the opening while the system is on.

INTERIOR SENSORS

- Photoelectric beam eyes are simple and effective. They cast an invisible infrared light beam across hallways, rooms, stairs, and other locations. When a beam is interrupted or "broken," an alarm sounds.

■ Heat detectors, although installation is simple (just plug into a wall outlet), these units are very sensitive and can result in false alarms more often than other types of monitor sensors, especially if pets are kept in the house. Anything that generates body heat passing near the device is detected by the sensor.

■ Pressure mats are flat switches placed beneath mats, which, when pressed by footsteps, alert the monitoring/alarm system.

■ Motion detectors fill the area with microwaves that are monitored in a specific preset pattern. By entering the area, a person changes the pattern and triggers an alarm. Air-conditioning and heat vents, loose-fitting windows, phones, or anything else that might interrupt the microwave pattern could result in faulty alarm soundings.

■ Closed-circuit television uses a hidden camera to show outside the door or other exterior views around the house. This setup is of little use to a homeowner when he or she is asleep or away from home.

Alarm System Features

1. Automatic Shutoff. Make sure the unit will automatically turn itself off after five minutes or so. A burglar isn't going to stick around to wait for it to stop and if you're not home you don't want the alarm to sound indefinitely. This feature is particularly beneficial if you're not at home and the alarm is triggered accidentally (a false alarm).

2. Area Zones. Consider a monitor box that has various area zones to allow identification of the problem area.

3. Battery Backup. If the alarm system is not battery-powered, be certain it at least has battery backup. Battery-operated systems should have a way of automatically reporting impending battery failure. A service/maintenance contract that includes automatic battery replacement when needed is a nice safeguard.

4. Wired/Wireless. The wired systems involve hiding the wiring installation to protect the system from being disabled and defeated.

Wireless systems are more costly and involve conspicuous sensors, but are easily installed by anyone. It's a good idea to inspect places where each type has already been installed.

5. Disarming Codes. A system that permits you to readily alter the entry disarming codes for added security.

6. Changeable Delay. Each system will give you time to enter/exit before the alarm is set to operate. Check that the system you choose allows for the delay time to be changed according to your needs.

7. Instant Arming. See if the system can be set for instant arming to protect you the very moment you enter the house.

8. Panic Button. A button or device that lets you manually sound the alarm if you know or suspect something is happening. Some systems offer portable wireless emergency buttons that resemble garage door openers.

9. Smoke Detector Connection. The monitor has a place for a smoke detector to be added on line.

10. Range. Wireless systems must be powerful enough to cover the whole area of your house.

11. Warranty. Investigate the length and coverage. Some are good for two years, parts and labor.

12. Insurance Discount. Check if the system you're considering will enable you to get a discount on your homeowner's policy.

13. Access Panel. Installed at the door or other strategic location to allow you to arm and disarm the system. Push-button pads are replacing lock-and-key arrangements because the push buttons are easier to reset.

14. Malfunction Signal. Some visual or audible signal should be provided to alert you to a problem within the system.

15. Tamper Resistance. Any components that can turn the system on and off or render it otherwise inoperable or ineffective should be tamper-resistant.

16. Instructions. They should be detailed and legible, so you'll understand the system's operations very thoroughly. Be aware of what the system will and will not do.

17. All components should meet requirements of the Underwriter's Laboratories and other standards such as Factory Mutual, as well as all applicable local standards, regulations, and codes.

ALARM INSTALLATION COMPANIES

When evaluating a burglar alarm company, consider the following points:

1. When responding to television, radio, newspaper, or phone book ads, don't give out your name, address, or phone number right away. First request and check references. Favor a well-established company having a record of successful operations.

2. When checking company references, find out what bonding organization covers them and for how long. Ask which manufacturer they buy from and find out if it's reputable. Personally call on people who have bought the installations of whichever company you are asking about. Check with the local Better Business Bureau, Consumer Protection Agency, Chamber of Commerce, and the police to see if many complaints have been filed against the company in question. Find out how long the company has been in business.

3. Review the various alarm features so you know what you want and need. Investigate their approximate cost so you will be talking from a position of strength when the contractor enters the picture, and so the installer cannot sell you devices you don't require.

4. Once the installer arrives, he or she will carefully inspect all doors and windows, furnishings, and valuables in order to recommend what equipment you should have installed for optimum protection. Remember, though, the more elaborate the system, the more profit the installer makes. If the contractor realizes you know little about alarms and what they cost, understands your financial worth and living habits, and perceives that you are fearful of intruders, he or she may target you for as expensive a package as possible.

5. Evaluate the service policy. What's warranteed and how long does the coverage last? A quality system should cover parts and labor from both the manufacturer and the contractor for two years from the date of installation.

6. All components and installation methods must meet the requirements of all applicable local standards, regulations, and codes.

7. Since any system of this type will require service from time to time, you must be sure that the company you deal with can supply prompt service. Ask what a service call will cost and get the answer in writing.

8. Insist on receiving verbal as well as written instructions covering all the important details of the system's operation.

9. When considering overall costs, remember to think about the distance to the alarm company if you're using them as a central monitoring station, the amount of wiring required in and to your home, and the cost of local line rates.

10. An intruder should not be able to easily disarm the system. The parts and wiring should be concealed as much as possible.

▶▶▶▶▶ POINTS TO PONDER

1. Remember, there's nothing a burglar likes more than privacy. Make a point to "case" your new home by walking the building site before and as the dwelling is being erected. What would a potential intruder see from the front street, from the sides, and from the backyard? Use that information to help make your new residence less "burglar friendly."

2. Use lighting (especially motion-detecting and other intruder-resistant) fixtures to your advantage.

3. The same goes with landscaping components. Consider that some "small" shrubs and trees stay relatively small throughout their lives, while others will grow to be huge unless regularly pruned back. Don't let your landscaping overpower the place. Keep door and windows tastefully free from heavy foliage.

4. Insist on quality, sturdy locks for all exterior doors and windows.

5. View the home's exterior shell as an envelope that attempts to seal the inside living areas against opportunistic intruders from the great outdoors. What are the weakest points? Find them in advance, and make sure they're reinforced by your burglar-proofing plan.

6. Remember that even though "secondary" interior doors—such as doors leading from the kitchen to a garage, breezeway, or sunroom—may have sturdy deadbolt/locking mechanisms, the outer doors of garages, breezeways, and sunrooms also need to be outfitted with similar strong locks to prevent burglars from gaining entrance to areas where they can work sight unseen.

7. Watch out for simple installation mistakes such as hinges/bolts positioned outside instead of inside, or open access wiring to exterior security lighting or alarms.

8. Make sure pet doors are not large enough for a slender person to slip through. Burglars have indeed sent children into homes in such a fashion, to pop open locked doors from within.

9. Before building, enlist someone from your police department's crime prevention unit, or from your insurance company's loss prevention department to give recommendations on how to build security into your plan.

10. Occasionally test the effectiveness of your security. Ask a trusted friend, relative, or neighbor to determine how he or she would try and gain entrance (without using heroic means).

Bathrooms

Bathrooms rank right up there next to kitchens when it comes to the most important rooms in a home. As such, the quality and number of bathrooms in a house can greatly affect the dwelling's resale value. Bathroom components will also contribute considerably to the amount of energy the family uses. Unless those components are chosen with water and energy conservation in mind, too many energy dollars will be going down the drain. Naturally, your family's needs will also help determine how many bathrooms you'll want, and how they'll be appointed.

In a nutshell, bathrooms usually consist of a hand sink or lavatory, a toilet, and a tub/shower unit (Fig. 24.1). Bathroom lavatories or sinks are available in numerous types, styles, sizes, and colors.

TYPES OF BATHROOM SINKS

The main types of bathroom sinks or lavs include vitreous china, porcelain/enamel over cast iron or steel, marbleized bowls or counter units, solid composites, and concrete.

Vitreous China Sinks

These sinks are inherently acid resistant, and although they can be stained by rust, copper corrosion, and certain other persistent staining

FIGURE 24.1

A full bath.

FIGURE 24.2

A vitreous china sink.

substances, vitreous china is considered an excellent material, with good resistance to chipping (Fig. 24.2). Vitreous china can also be formed into very fancy bowls and even into original works of art that are substantially more expensive than most other bathroom sink units.

Porcelain/Enamel over Cast Iron or Steel

These are practically the least-expensive sinks you can purchase. They're less durable and more susceptible to chipping and normal wear than the others mentioned here.

Marbleized Bowl/Counter Units

There are two kinds of marbleized bowl and counter units: acrylic plastic and cast methacrylate, both of which can contain veining that simulates, in a highly polished surface, that of marble (Fig. 24.3). They're even referred to as synthetic marble. Both come in various colors and finishes, including high-gloss "onyx" models.

FIGURE 24.3

A marbleized sinktop.

These sinks are frequently integrated into a vanity countertop, with one-piece construction. They have a popular appearance, are easy to clean, and can be molded into beautiful patterned bowls (in the form of a seashell, for example).

The main drawback to marbleized surfaces is that the finished layers are very thin. A heavy scratch can penetrate the coating and expose the white material underneath, which is difficult to cover up or repair.

Solid Composites

Sinks and counters made of solid composite materials are made with the color, often a bone white, all the way through the material. If scratched there's no color change and the mark can be easily removed with steel wool or fine sandpaper. Solid composites can also be sawn, drilled, and filed with standard carpentry tools for custom applications. It's one of the better materials for bathroom (and kitchen) counters and sinks, but it's also one of the most expensive.

Concrete

Sinks and countertops made of concrete that's custom-formed, stained and sealed can be created right on site by individuals who specialize in finished concrete work. (See the section on kitchen countertops.) It's an option that you may want to consider if you like components that are artistically stylish and one-of-a-kind.

STYLES OF BATHROOM SINKS

More and more people are turning to designer and continental-style lavs and lav sets. The following styles of sinks can be purchased in a wide range of materials and prices in round, oval, or sculptured bowls.

- Wall-hung lavs requiring no floor supports or pedestal—for more openness and ease of cleaning.
- Lavs supported by cabinets or pedestals.
- Lavs supported by metal legs.
- Lavs built into ceramic-tile surfaced counters.
- Lavs recessed into countertops of plastic laminate. China sinks are popular with plastic laminate countertops.
- Single-piece sink and counter units, either molded or sculptured.

BATHROOM SINK INSTALLATION

A bathroom sink should be large enough for comfortable use, especially if it must suffice to wash your hair or bathe an infant. Try not to select anything smaller than 20 by 24 inches. In master bedrooms, consider a double-bowl arrangement.

Every sink should have at least a narrow backsplash along the back of the wall it's mounted against, to protect the wall from spilled or splashing water. A drip edge should be included at the front and side ends of the countertop or around the tops of basin lavatories to prevent water from overrunning the top surfaces onto the floor. Sinks should also have an overflow prevention catch hole that drains water after it reaches a certain upper level in the bowl.

TOILETS

Toilets or "water closets" are made in various grades, from low-cost models to luxurious units with gold-leaf seats. The best buys are usually in the middle of any manufacturer's range. Toilets also come in water-saving designs that operate with less water than standard models—an especially helpful feature if you're in an area having metered water, if you draw water from a well, or if you experience periodic water shortages.

Most toilets are made of vitreous china, although some manufacturers carry injection-molded ABS plastic tanks as well. The important features to look for in a water closet are:

■ Sanitary self-cleaning action

■ Size of the free-flow water passage

■ Quietness of the flushing action

FIGURE 24.4

A siphon-jet toilet.

Types of Water Closets

There are only three basic types of toilets that you should be aware of: siphon-jet, reverse-trap, and washdown. The first two are the only ones you should consider for inclusion in your home.

SIPHON-JET BOWLS

The free water surface in a siphon-jet toilet bowl covers practically the entire visible bowl area (Fig. 24.4). Water and wastes exit the siphon-jet from the rear of the bowl.

1. A siphon-jet bowl is usually manufactured in an elongated oval form that's attractive and comfortable.

2. It's the most sanitary of the three types mentioned.

3. The free-flow water passage is the largest of the three, with less chance of becoming obstructed.

4. It's the quietest type of the three.

5. It's available in a one-piece wall-mounted unit that makes cleaning the bowl itself and the bathroom surfaces around it simple.

6. When made in a single piece, however, the cost is quite high because any chip or flaw destroys the entire unit at the factory and in your home. When the bowl and tank are separate units the cost for the combination drops.

FIGURE 24.5

A reverse-trap toilet.

REVERSE-TRAP BOWLS

A reverse-trap bowl is a shorter type of toilet than the siphon-jet (Fig. 24.5). Like the siphon-jet, water and wastes exit the reverse-trap from the rear of the bowl. The reverse-trap toilet has a free water surface covering roughly two-thirds of the bowl area and has a smaller water outflow passage.

1. It's a little less sanitary than the siphon-jet.

2. It's moderately quiet in flushing action, and the most popular type with builders of middle-priced houses because it costs quite a bit less than siphon-jet models in similar combinations of tank and bowls.

WASHDOWN BOWLS

Washdown bowls are old-fashioned type toilets that can be distinguished by their vertical front profiles. They have very small free water areas, half that of the siphon-jet and the smallest of the three types mentioned. Water and wastes exit the washdown models from the front of their bowls.

1. It has a noisy flushing action.

2. It's not effective in self-cleaning.

3. It's the least sanitary of the three types mentioned.

BATHTUB AND SHOWER UNITS

A typical home features one bathroom having a combination bathtub and shower, and another bathroom with only a shower (Fig. 24.6).

Bathtub and Shower Sizes

Choose bathtub and shower units you'll feel comfortable in, and plan them in advance so the bathroom framing can be erected to size.

FIGURE 24.6

A bathtub/shower unit.

Many sizes of bathtubs are available. The usual widths are 2½ to 4 feet, and lengths, 4 to 6 feet. Typical tub depth is 12 to 15 inches above its floor surface. Numerous special models such as sunken units and old-fashioned tubs with legs are on the market. Remember that the deeper bathtubs will result in less water splashing.

A small shower stall is only about 30 inches square. It's preferable to go with one that's between 36 and 48 inches in both width and depth.

FIGURE 24.7

A fiberglass tub and shower.

Types of Bathtubs and Showers

FIBERGLASS TUBS AND SHOWERS

Fiberglass tubs and showers are extremely popular units that come either as a single molded piece complete with walls, or with separate walls that are assembled around the tub (Fig. 24.7). Most new construction uses the single unit tubs/showers having molded walls.

Advantages

1. They're easier to clean than other types.
2. They tend to resist mildew better than ceramic tile surfaces.
3. They solve the age-old problem of getting a watertight joint between the tub's edges and the adjoining wall surfaces.
4. These units can be purchased with their own ceilings attached.
5. Fiberglass units are warmer to the touch than the harder models, especially during cold weather.
6. They don't soil as quickly as conventional porcelain.
7. They can be purchased with molded-in soap holders and seats.
8. They're very attractive and come in numerous colors.
9. They're soft and forgiving.

Disadvantages

1. They flex under the weight of even a medium body. Sufficient support must be placed beneath the units during installation to prevent the fiberglass floor from "giving."
2. When the shower water strikes the bottom of a fiberglass unit, it tends to be somewhat noisy unless insulation is installed between the bottom of the shower and the top of the floor, to absorb sound.

ENAMELED CAST-IRON OR STEEL BATHTUBS

Cast-iron or steel tubs finished in regular enamel rarely come in any other color than white. The same tubs finished with acid-resisting enamel, however, come in white and colors. Because you can't tell by observation which grade of enamel is used on white tubs, the manufacturer's warranty must be requested. Elect the models with acid resistant enamel if a cast-iron or steel bathtub best suits your decor.

The walls above a cast-iron or steel bathtub can be finished with a number of coverings including ceramic tile and glazelike hardboards. Tiles come in a huge variety of colors, sizes, and patterns. The glazed hardboards work well when installed with adhesive over a suitable backing material such as gypsum board. Their joints, corners, and edges are trimmed in color-matching metal moldings in various shapes to fit the junctures. A few manufacturer's lines of glazed hardboards have unusual patterns and themes such as of ferns, lace, multiple lines, metallics, antiqued and textured woodgrains, and other modern surface representations.

Advantages

1. They're exceptionally sturdy.
2. They're a lot quieter than fiberglass.
3. The adjoining walls can be finished off in practically any way that would best suit your decor.

Disadvantages

1. The enameled or porcelain surfaces chip very easily.
2. These tubs tend to show water stains after a period.

CERAMIC TILE BATHTUBS AND SHOWERS

Ceramic tile bathtubs and showers are just that—tubs and showers built in place with walls and floors of ceramic tile. Often people going with this type of bathing facilities elect to have the tub sunken beneath the floor level. Ceramic tile applied with cement is the most permanent installation. Tile applied with mastic glues is second best because its performance is highly dependent on well-maintained caulking. If water works its way through the joints, the mastic base could deteriorate.

Advantages

1. They're unique and colorful.
2. They offer unlimited patterns, designs, sizes, and shapes. They can provide the ultimate customizing possibilities.

Disadvantages

1. They're expensive.
2. The tile installation must be of superior workmanship or the tiles will eventually loosen and the tub will leak.
3. Tiles are more difficult to clean than the other types of tub and shower surfaces (especially the small mosaic tiles).

WHIRLPOOLS

Whirlpool bathtubs—once found only in expensive, exclusive homes—are now available for most budgets and have become standard

FIGURE 24.8

Whirlpool.

fare with many contractors. Whirlpools, in addition to lending beauty to a bathroom, are also functional. Available in a huge variety of attractive materials and colors, with many equipment options, whirlpools provide relaxing comfort for their owners and will often improve a home's market value and sales potential (Fig. 24.8).

Present-day whirlpools are more energy efficient than ever—some models giving up as little as 1 degree in temperature every 15 minutes, with electricity to run the whirlpool circulation pump costing only a few cents per use. During winter, the warmth that's slowly "lost" from the hot water can help heat the surrounding room space. The main cost of operation is heating the water that's used from the hot water tank.

Some important features to select from are the tub material (cushioned models are available); the number, power, and control of water jets; plus the shape and size (gallon capacity) of the tub. Massage jets in the whirlpools inject an adjustable mixture of water and air to control the jet force. The size or horsepower of the pump and number of speeds are often good indicators of the relaxing and massaging capabilities of the unit.

WHIRLPOOL OPTION CONSIDERATION CHECKLIST

___ Digital water temperature and timing controls

___ Waterfalls are available on certain models

___ Rotating deep massage jets

___ Review the number, power, and control of water jets

___ Multispeed pumps

___ Check the pump size and number of speeds

___ Colored mood lighting

___ Check the energy efficiency

___ Sample the tub material for comfort

___ Consider the shape and size of the tub

___ Whirlpool motor accessibility for future maintenance

FIGURE 24.9

Wall framing around tub/shower unit.

Bathtub and Shower General Considerations

A number of points should be considered while you plan your home's bathing facilities.

1. The plumbers should set any tub or shower unit in place before the framing is completed (Fig. 24.9). Some of the larger molded fiberglass units won't fit into the house once the framing work is finished.

2. If a tub/shower unit comes from the manufacturer covered with protective plastic or paper, fine. The covers will protect the unit's finish while construction work goes on around it. If not, it's advisable to tape plastic around the inside of the tub, with some thick paper on the bottom for padding, so somebody can step inside and work around the tub without damaging the finish.

3. A tub/shower unit should be securely fastened to the walls. This is especially important with tubs that use ceramic tile for wall protection. Any movement later on will cause the tub to crack away from the tile.

4. The floor of the tub/shower should have a nonslip surface.

5. The tub/shower unit should have handles that you can live with.

6. Remember not to place the bathtub beneath a window. This design fault will mean providing some form of shower curtain to cover the window, especially if the tub is equipped with a showerhead. In cold weather, a window over the tub can create unpleasant drafts, and whenever the window must be opened, you'll either have to reach across the tub or step into the tub to get enough opening leverage.

7. Specify tub/shower color.

8. Insulation should be placed in the shower walls, as well as under the tub and in the cavities surrounding it. The insulation will help retain the heat in the shower stall or tub. Consequently, the tub will require less hot water to stay warm.

9. All plumbing holes or penetrations through walls and floors should be sealed with urethane foam or a similar insulation. Remember the hole in the sub floor around the tub drain; it can be a major source of heat loss.

10. One additional possibility, when planning tub and shower enclosures, is the use of custom-formed concrete that's stained and sealed. It can be of the same type, style and finish as concrete that's used for the room's sink and sink countertop.

FAUCETS

The selection of faucets is a matter of personal taste. Many, many styles are available, from high-tech to old-fashioned, constructed with many different materials. One thing for sure, the quality faucets will last longer and retain their appearance over the long haul.

They will also likely come with aerators. An aerator is another device that can help save energy within your water supply. Shower and faucet aerators are typically located in place of the standard faucet or shower head screen. They add air to the spray to lower the flow.

High-efficiency aerators can reduce water flow from between 2 to 4 gallons per minute to less that 1 gallon per minute, which is sufficient for most bathroom sink activities. The aerator simply reduces the amount of water in the flow, which saves the energy that otherwise would have been needed to heat the amount of water saved. There is a slight reduction in flow pressure, but it will barely be noticeable There are three basic grades of faucets: good, marginal, and cheap.

Good faucets are constructed with solid brass innards having tough coatings of chrome, nickel, brushed or polished brass, or other durable materials. Marginal faucets are usually made of lightweight zinc or aluminum castings that will tarnish quickly, drip, and look dreadful within a short time. Cheap faucets can be identified by their crosslike handles, with four horizontal spokes coming out from their center.

Faucets really get a good workout from the average family. Cheap faucets just won't do the trick. One drippy faucet may waste as much as 50 gallons of hot water per day! Literally, money down the drain. That's a powerful reason for selecting a quality-made reputable brand.

In general, faucets having luxury features cost more than the straight models. Push-pull or dual-control handles, or single-lever-control faucets are certainly convenient, though, and are made in models of high quality.

You might realize a better price if you select all your plumbing fixtures, sink, tub, and shower, from the line of a single manufacturer.

Once the faucets are installed, check to see if the cold water is on the right-hand side of each fixture. Believe it or not, people have been scalded while discovering that their faucet handles had been reversed by mistake.

✔✔✔✔✔ SHOWER/BATHTUB SAFETY VALVE CHECKLIST

___ Select a unit that will maintain constant water temperature.

___ Look for a model where you can set the sensitivity comfort zone range between two temperatures so it's simple to fine-tune water temperatures.

___ Some units feature a preset temperature memory, which lets you set the water temperature where you like it and the faucet "remembers" to return to that temperature the next time it's turned on. Certain units allow as many as three preset bathwater temperatures to be programmed—to accommodate different people's preferences.

___ The fixtures should restrict water flow entirely until the set temperature is reached to prevent hot or cold water shocking.

___ Some units have safeguard rotation-limiting mechanisms or stops that prevents a control handle from accidentally being bumped into a fully "hot" position.

___ Last-temperature memory is a feature that many homeowners find convenient.

___ Temperature limit stops allow you to limit how far the hot water can be turned on. This is a feature that's important when children or elderly users are involved.

___ The best units are corrosion-, clogging-, scalding-, and erosion-resistant.

___ Volume controls allow the water delivery rate to be adjusted as desired.

___ Some are self-cleaning.

SHOWER NOZZLES

It usually takes substantially more water for a bath than for a shower, as long as a person spends a reasonable amount of time in the shower, and doesn't overdo it. Even so, an efficient shower head is a component that can help save energy and water costs. Regulating the water going through the shower head to match the needs of the task can greatly reduce waste and save on heated water usage. Flow restrictors with a shut-off valve and temperature controls will help with the shower head's efficiency.

■ *Flow Restrictors:* A shower-head flow restrictor can effectively reduce the water flow from around seven gallons per minute in the heaviest volume showers, to as little as a gallon and a half per minute, without cutting back on pressure and without appreciably decreasing the quality and effectiveness of the shower spray. On average, they'll cut a family's total energy expenditure for hot water by over 40 percent. A shower head control should allow the spray to be shut off altogether while a person lathers up, shampoos, or shaves, and then to turn it on again at the same temperature and pressure when needed to rinse.

■ *Temperature Control:* This is a shower handle control with scald guard protection that maintains the temperature even if there's a change in water pressure. It prevents wasting water while you try to get the desired temperature setting back.

The shower nozzle you choose should have a flexible ball joint for directional control, plus a control to adjust the spray. Self-cleaning showerheads make the most sense to buy. Consider a unit that's hand-held, with a pullout hose and adjustable spray and pulsating massage sprays. Cheap nozzles offer little or no control of spray direction or quality.

An automatic diverter control should come with a combination tub/shower. It automatically diverts the water back to the tub faucets after someone has taken a shower. Such a setup prevents the next person who might want to take a bath from being pelted with hot or cold water. Omission of the diverter, an inexpensive item, can also cause accidental scalding of children.

Shower Shock and Bathtub Shock Safety Valves

Shower and bathtub "shock" occurs when water pressure fluctuates because of changing water supply demands. For example, turn on one faucet, and the water flow may be very strong. Turn on a second faucet at the same time, and the pressure of the first may drop somewhat. If, while someone showers, a toilet is flushed, or a dishwasher or clothes washer turns on, the person showering may be jolted by a "shocking" change in water temperature (as, for instance, less cold water makes it to the shower, and the shower water comes out hot). With traditional faucets, a sudden change in water temperature is what we notice most. The actual thermal shock event is a change in water pressure. In the case of traditional bathroom faucets, if there is a demand for cold water elsewhere in the house, the cold water pressure at the faucet is reduced, leaving mostly hot water in the mix. An additional demand for hot water causes pressure on the hot side of the faucet to lessen, leaving mostly cold water in the mix. Flow further weakens with each new water outlet put into operation, causing rapid temperature swings which could either scald or chill.

Water "shock" can be prevented by specifying bathroom plumbing equipped with either pressure-balance or thermostatic valves. Such valves provide a measure of safety by eliminating surges of hot or cold water from the shower.

Pressure-balancing valves detect changes in pressure and instantly adjust water flow to keep temperatures constant. Pressure balance valves are designed to keep hot and cold water pressure equal at all times. Valves use diaphragms or pistons to accomplish these feats by adjusting the inlet ports of the faucet's control valves.

Thermostatic valves cost more but allow you to dial in a desired temperature, which will be maintained even as water pressure varies.

Thousands of people are injured every year from thermal shock. The most severe scalds are caused by high-temperature water flowing into a tub or shower. Young children and the elderly are particularly at risk.

A second common scald injury is when someone slips in the shower or tub and bumps the valve handle or grabs it as he or she falls, and it gets fully turned to hot. If a person who so falls does not move immediately, serious burns can result. The elderly often have reduced temperature sensitivity and can unknowingly scald themselves. Thermal shock can also cause broken bones and other impact injuries that occur as victims try to escape burning or freezing water.

Shower and tub thermal shock can be avoided through the installation of pressure-balancing or thermostatic bathtub or shower fixtures. These fixtures will hold the bath or shower water temperature steady to within a few degrees even though toilets are flushed or dishwashers are started elsewhere along the home's plumbing lines. The installation of these valves can also save on heating costs and water bills. With fluctuating shower temperatures, time and water can be wasted just trying to arrive at an optimum shower water temperature. Some build-

FIGURE 24.10

A medicine cabinet with diffusion lighting fixtures above.

FIGURE 24.11

A medicine cabinet with sliding door.

ing codes in areas of the country now require water shock safety control valves for new construction.

BATHROOM CABINETS

There are two types of cabinets that you should consider for installation in your bathrooms: medicine cabinets and lavatory cabinets.

Medicine Cabinets

Medicine cabinets are used for storing medicines, razors, toothpaste, and other items of personal hygiene. These cabinets come in a variety of styles. Four of the most popular are as follows:

- A rectangular door and mirror with diffusion lighting fixtures above the mirror (Fig. 24.10).

- A sliding door operation, again with a light fixture positioned above the mirrored doors (Fig. 24.11).

- Hinged mirror door cabinets with lighting fixtures positioned on both sides (Fig. 24.12).

- And more economical cabinets consisting of single mirror doors on recessed cabinets without lights (Fig. 24.13).

Lavatory Cabinets

Lavatory cabinets, also referred to as vanity bases, frequently support the sink and sink counter in addition to providing storage space below (Fig. 24.14).

Lav cabinets, when compared to the smaller medicine cabinets, offer consider-

FIGURE 24.12

A medicine cabinet with lighting fixtures at sides.

FIGURE 24.13

A medicine cabinet with no lights—the most economical.

ably more storage space. They also eliminate unsightly plumbing connections below the sink, help develop the bathroom decor, and can even be used to accommodate a built-in clothes hamper.

TOWEL WARMERS

Towel warmers (Fig. 24.15) are clever devices that come in a number of different types and models. All of them supply the luxury of warm towels after a shower, bath, or morning face wash. Some units use electric low-wattage heating elements. Many towel warmer bars or "tubes" are oil-filled and permanently sealed to provide safe, even heating. Some towel warmers are simply extension units of hot-water radiator/registers, and heat the towels

FIGURE 24.14

A lavatory cabinet.

✔✔✔✔✔ TOWEL WARMER CHECKLIST

___ Choose only models with UL approval.

___ Look for models with on/off timers that can be set in advance. Programmable timers can be set to come on 15 to 30 minutes before the warm towels will be needed. These timers should automatically turn themselves off in case you forget to.

___ Built-in thermostats are also nice features that will tell how warm the towels get during the heating process.

___ The units should be able to be installed out of young children's' reach.

FIGURE 24.15

Towel warmer.

while heating the room. Warm towels can also save energy by reducing the need to crank up the heat in the morning for a shower.

SPACE HEAT

Raising the heat throughout the house in order to warm the bathroom is a common practice, but it isn't very energy efficient. When you want a warmer bathroom, it's far more effective to simply raise the temperature there instead. The three most common ways to do that are:

1. Electric radiant heating panels installed on walls, ceilings or floors provide heat on demand. For walls or ceilings, even a small panel can supply the warmth needed. Because of their radiant nature, these panels heat people and objects with a gentle warmth without overheating and drying out the room's air. Radiant units are ideal for just one room. In a bathroom, people can stay warm while in the tub or drying off even though the temperature of the air in the bathroom is the same as the air in the rest of the house.

2. In addition to the electric radiant panels, radiant floor water heating systems are particularly popular with people who have allergies. That's because radiant systems cause very little air

movement, compared with that of more traditional ducted forced-air heating systems. There are less fugitive particles in the air, such as airborne dust, mold spores, and animal dander.

3. A third common method of direct bathroom heating is the ceiling forced-air fan heater. Some models also provide a built-in ventilation fan and light.

VENTILATING FANS

Energy Star-rated ventilating (or exhaust) fans, vented to the outdoors, should be installed in bathrooms to control moisture levels. The shorter and straighter the ductwork is from the fan to the outside, the more efficient the fan will be. If the duct must pass through an attic or other unheated space, all ventilation ductwork should be insulated.

Excessive moisture can quickly deteriorate building materials and furnishings, will promote the growth of mold, and can cause allergy problems with many individuals.

Operating a vent fan is typically more efficient than simply opening a window. The fan should be designed to quietly run for the proper amount of time to remove moisture and odors. If it runs too long, it draws excessive heated or cooled air from the house. If it runs too little, then mold, fungus, and wall material damage could occur. One of the best and most energy efficient features to have is a quiet automatic timer switch. (Fig. 24.16). The fan goes on when you start the timer, then shuts off when the desired time period ends.

Depending on how much moisture and humidity is present, and what the bathroom temperature is, you simply touch the 5-, 10-, 15-, or 30-minute key to set the timer, or bypass the pre-set keys if a different time is needed. Another reason that having a timer is convenient is that it gives you the ability to remove humidity

FIGURE 24.16

A ventilation fan timer switch.

FIGURE 24.17

Automatic ventilation fan and light.

VENTILATION FAN CONSIDERATION CHECKLIST

___ Is the unit UL approved?

___ Is the unit grounded with a ground-fault circuit interrupter (GFCI)?

___ Does the unit have a built-in damper that eliminates metallic clatter while preventing backdrafts?

___ Is there a balanced high-efficiency blower?

___ And a permanently lubricated motor?

___ Resilient motor mounts for isolating vibration?

___ Quiet performance? Listen to a demo unit before agreeing to a particular model.

___ Is there a built-in nightlight control switch?

___ Size the vent fan properly for quiet operation. Don't buy more fan than you need. No matter how well the unit is designed, all other things equal, the larger the airflow capacity, the louder the fan noise.

for up to 30 minutes after you leave the room without the worry of forgetting to turn the fan off later. For maximum efficiency, match the bathroom ventilation or exhaust fan to the size of the room based on cubic feet the fan moves per minute. That's typically how the fans are rated.

If your calculation falls between two sizes, look at the different brands and models to find the best match. If there's not a model with a perfect fit, go up to the next higher fan based on cubic feet per minute. The best exhaust fans will combine a heater, fan, room light, and nightlight into a single unit. More advanced units also have heaters that circulate warm air while removing moist air at the same time.

Automatic Ventilation Fans

Automatic ventilation fans, mounted in bathroom ceilings, will automatically activate lamps and ventilation fans (Fig. 24.17) based on need, to help prevent cosmetic and structural problems that can be caused by excessive moisture buildup. Most automatic fans are operated either by:

1. Motion sensing, where sensors automatically turn on the fan, light, or both when a person enters the room. If the user forgets to activate or deactivate the light or fan as he or she enters or leaves the room, the unit will do it anyway. There's typically an adjustable automatic shutoff time, from about 5 minutes to 60 minutes after motion stops. There should also be an adjustable sensor where the sensing field can be modified to match specific conditions.

BATHROOM CHECKLIST

The following is a checklist of items that shouldn't be overlooked when you're planning bathrooms:

___ A waterproof shower light.

___ A low-permeability vapor barrier on the inside surface of the bathroom framing to help prevent moisture from condensing in the wall cavities.

___ Electrical outlets well out of reach of the shower, tub, and lavatory water.

(Continued)

BATHROOM CHECKLIST (*Continued*)

___ Soap holders at the lavatory, tub, and shower.

___ Toothbrush holders.

___ Shutoff valves at each fixture so water can be turned off for repairs without turning off the main water supply to the house.

___ Consider having a built-in linen closet.

___ Consider that the plumbing plan include the installation of a PVC pan underneath the shower as a protection against leaks.

___ A toilet paper holder located so it's not subject to splashing water from sinks, tubs, or showers, or to dripping from washcloths hanging on a towel bar above.

___ A grab-bar or safety bar should be installed to serve two purposes: to help a person using the tub to get up easily, and to help the bather step out of the tub safely.

___ One 36-inch towel bar (the longest standard bar available) for each person using the bathroom. This gives ample space for a folded bath towel, hand towel, and washcloth. Use towel rings only for supplemental towel or washcloth storage, or for drying off wet towels.

___ Install the shower soap dish as far from the shower head and as high up on the back wall as practical. Centering the dish between the ends of the tub or shower stall results in the rapid melting of the bar soap under prolonged exposure to the water spray.

___ A combination ceiling unit that includes an exhaust fan, an electric fan-forced heater, and a light. A good ventilation fan or exhaust fan is important for removing odors and excess humidity in the air. Such humidity can be harmful to the walls, paint, paper, and insulation.

___ Consider installing several tasteful garment hooks.

___ Specify whether you want glass sliding doors or a shower curtain for your shower. Doors cost considerably more, but to some people, doors are marks of luxury. To others they represent more surfaces to clean.

___ The best way to select fixtures is to compare brands and see what line of fixtures most appeals to you. Stick to one brand for each line of fixtures. In selecting colored fixtures such as nonwhite tubs and toilets, remember that there is a good color match between fixtures of the same brand, but noticeable variations in the same color when fixtures of different manufacturers are compared.

BATHROOM CHECKLIST (*Continued*)

___ Anywhere sinks meet walls, or where tub or showers meet flooring, needs to be caulked.

___ Moisture-resistant insulation should be installed along tub/shower bottoms and sides to help maintain constant water temperatures.

___ When selecting faucets, make sure they're compatible with the models of lavatories you're planning.

___ Have ground-fault circuit interrupters (GFCIs) specified on all receptacles.

___ Allow no electrical switches within 60 inches of any water, if possible.

___ Have a clear walkway space of at least 21 inches in front of the lavatory and toilet.

___ Have the toilet paper holder installed within easy reach from the toilet.

___ Install one or more grab-bars for safe bathtub or shower entry/exit.

___ Be sure all shower and bathtub faucets are protected by pressure balance temperature regulators or temperature-limiting devices.

___ Be sure bathroom, bathtub, and shower flooring are slip-resistant.

___ Install a removable handheld showerhead for flexibility when showering.

___ Be sure there is generous storage space, including
 – Counter/shelf space around lavatory
 – Grooming equipment storage
 – Shampoo/soap storage in shower/tub area
 – Hanging space for linens
 – Towel storage/towel warmers

___ Be sure bathtub faucets are accessible from outside the tub.

___ Make child toilet seats available. They have smaller openings and wider seat areas to make small children feel secure. They can include molded hand grips on the sides for children to hold onto.

___ Install a toilet tank bowl with an insulated liner to help provide quieter operation and prevent tank sweating that could eventually damage the floor.

___ Be sure bathroom fasteners are rustproof. Even toilet seat and toilet lid fasteners will eventually rust.

___ Specify the desired colors of bathroom items (tubs, showers, sinks, toilets, and so on) so that it's figured in the quote.

2. Humidity sensing, where monitors detect rapid increases in humidity brought about by the bath or shower, and the fan turns on automatically.

Inline Ventilation Fans

A remote inline vent fan is a quiet and effective bathroom exhaust option. Sometimes called "tube" fans, these units are mounted in attics, attached with a flexible dryer duct to a grille in the bathroom ceiling. Since the fan motor is located away from the bathroom, the operation is practically without sound (but will not have other built-in options such as lights or heaters). Also, the units must be turned on and off as needed with wall switches. By using a T duct fitting, one inline fan can vent two or more areas simultaneously (such as two separate bathrooms).

ELECTRIC MIRRORS

This interesting product is often overlooked as a possibility, but it's a great bathroom feature. If you dislike waiting for a fogged-up bathroom mirror to clear after a hot shower or bath with the ventilation fan working overtime, an electric mirror could solve the problem. An electric mirror gently warms enough to prevent condensation, thus allowing you to finish in the bathroom more quickly and to waste less energy there.

LIGHTING FOR THE BATHROOM

All bathroom lighting, especially lighting in bathrooms without windows, has to be well thought out. You need general plus very good task lighting for shaving and applying makeup. And don't forget lighting to read by in the bathtub.

Some of the most successful lighting for bathrooms is created by indirect rather than direct light sources. Light can be bounced off a white ceiling, concealed behind battens, and doubled off mirrors. Where ceilings are low, choose flush recessed fittings so that you won't hit them while toweling off.

Lighting can also create interesting focal points that are particularly important for internal bathrooms without windows. In fact, lighting can even be employed to create a fake window effect.

> > > > > > **POINTS TO PONDER**

1. The quality and quantity of bathrooms in a house may greatly affect the home's resale value.

2. Elect water-saving fixtures whenever possible. Toilets, faucets, showerheads, and even bathtubs all can be purchased in models that take less water per use than standard units do.

3. Remember that many one-piece bathtub/shower units may not be able to be used in bathroom additions or expansions because they're too large to fit through typical stairways. They need to be installed along with the original home wall framing.

4. Make sure bathtub and shower units have nonslip surfaces.

5. Tub and shower glass doors should be made of safety glass, and so should all mirrors used adjacent to the tub or shower.

6. Bathroom electrical outlets should all be GFCI (ground-fault circuit interrupter) types.

7. Consider installing safety railings or support handles near tubs, showers, and toilets.

8. Whirlpool off and on switches should be located far enough away from the tub that no one in the tub can turn on the unit.

9. Don't skimp on the bathroom ventilation fans; a quality fan system is required to address moisture control and healthy air movement.

10. You should be able to unlock a bathroom from the outside in case a child or other person locks himself or herself in.

Kitchens

If there's one overall most important room in a typical house, it's the kitchen. Just look through the shelves of any library, bookstore, or magazine rack. Dozens and dozens of books have been written entirely about kitchens, and countless magazines devote their pages to the same subject. Kitchens have spawned enormous manufacturing invention, variety, and capacity with seemingly limitless amounts of materials, appliances, and other items designed and marketed specifically for home kitchen use.

It used to be that the kitchen—with its fireplace in constant use—was the most regularly heated room of the house. It was the family gathering place, where household members cooked, ate, talked, studied, and played cards and other games. Today, even without a wood burning fireplace, the kitchen is still the most frequented room in the typical home.

Ask any real estate agent which room in a home will best up the dwelling's market value, and he or she will invariably answer "the kitchen." As discussed in chapter 1, a kitchen functions as the hub in any household. In kitchens, we prepare our meals, eat our meals, socialize, relax, and work.

One way to look at kitchens is to think of their four major components: dining facilities, countertops, appliances, and cabinets.

DINING FACILITIES

Even if you plan to have a formal dining room, you'll still find dining accommodations in the kitchen a convenient necessity. Consider one or both of the following two options:

1. A table placed in the kitchen, out of the traffic flow (Fig. 25.1). Such an arrangement, also referred to as a breakfast nook, can be openly situated between the kitchen and another room (a family room, for example). In some homes, the kitchen table is simply put in a corner out of the way. Wherever it's located, the kitchen table and chairs should always be as close as possible to food preparation and cleanup areas.

2. A snack bar or counter is frequently used instead of a table with chairs (Fig. 25.2). The counter itself can be employed to separate the kitchen from an adjacent family room or eating area, whether

FIGURE 25.1

A kitchen with dining space.

it be a nook or formal dining room. A counter is especially nice because it encourages excellent communications and socializing; it allows whoever is working in the kitchen to carry on conversations with family members or friends while those guests comfortably enjoy food and drink at the counter.

COUNTERTOPS

Of all parts in a kitchen, countertops get the most use. And they're not only used regularly, but are also subjected to the greatest abuse and the most frequent cleaning. To be truly serviceable, a countertop surface must be able to resist moisture, heat, color fading, sharp knives

FIGURE 25.2

A kitchen with a snack bar.

and blows, scratching, and staining from all sorts of nasty foods and substances such as grape juice, beets, and Easter-egg dyes.

Countertop materials include plastic laminates, wood, ceramic tile, solid composites, stainless steel, and concrete. And these are not your old-fashioned versions. A lot of innovative engineering and manufacturing has gone into modern countertops. As result, they've got great appearances and even greater durability. Most are simple to care for and will last practically a lifetime.

Plastic Laminates

Plastic laminate countertops are by far more popular—due to a combination of price, availability, and utility—than all the rest. They come in many different styles, designs, and colors. The best ones are factory-made in a single laminated piece consisting of a rigid base covered by a hard, heat-resistant plastic topping about 1/16 inch thick. This topping is formed or molded under heat and pressure with a rolled front edge and a vertical "backsplash" that abuts whatever wall the countertop is mounted against.

Plastic laminate countertops come in two types of construction: custom and postformed. The custom-made top has an advantage of greater flexibility in shape—it's made to fit. But it also has a joint between the top and backsplash section that is difficult to keep clean, plus a seam in front that's exposed to wear and, like all laminate seams, might come apart if the cement fails. A well-made top, though, even with seams, will last indefinitely with proper care.

The postformed top is molded under high pressure by machinery designed specifically for producing countertops. The result is a smooth countertop with a seamless rounded back joint that's easy to clean, and a seamless smooth lip or drip edge on the front that prevents spilled liquids from running off the countertop onto the floor.

Although it's not as nice a setup as factory-integrated laminated models, the same kind of hard, heat-resistant types of plastic can be adhered to flat plywood countertops, with square edges finished off in the same plastic through the use of narrow strips that are cemented onto the edge surfaces. The exposed edge corners are dark, showing the thickness of the plastic laminate itself. The edges can also be covered with stainless steel or aluminum trim. In the best countertop installations there are no joints in the worktop surface.

Less-expensive polyester and vinyl plastics can be used instead of the durable plastic previously mentioned. But both polyester and vinyl are more susceptible to heat damage from cigarettes, hot skillets, or other hazards.

Wood

Wood countertops are constructed of hardwood blocks or boards of maple, beech, birch, or oak glued together in a thickness of about 1⅛ inches or more. Wood makes an excellent, attractive surface for cutting on and for handling hot dishes, but requires more care in cleaning and maintenance. Plywood doesn't make an acceptable countertop by itself, but is commonly used as a base for other finishing materials. Wood in the form of compressed hardboards treated with a protective coating of tung or other oil is a low-cost alternative suitable for inexpensive kitchen designs.

Ceramic Tile

Ceramic tile makes a beautiful, easy-care countertop if well laid. It's colorful, distinctive, and heat- and fade-proof. It's also hard and noisy and can cause dish and glass breakage. Neither does it provide a good cutting surface (a wood or plastic chopping/cutting board can take care of that problem easy enough). Tiles can be large or small, glazed or unglazed with nonporous vitreous bodies, and laid plain or in patterns. Stone can also be used in place of ceramic tile.

Solid Composites

Solid composites are tough, nonporous materials. They're exceptionally durable and easy to work with. Because of their solid substance and homogeneous color, accidental burns or scratches can be rubbed out of the countertop with common household abrasive cleaners. These countertops also come with integrated sinks. This material is more expensive than laminated plastic, and the choice of colors is somewhat limited, but improving as new lines are being introduced.

Concrete

Since the last edition of this book, custom and production concrete countertops have made quite an entrance. It's not that they haven't been used before. They've been fairly common in many other parts of the world. It's just that these new and improved versions have recently been promoted by high-end users, architects, kitchen designers, writers, and builders. Now these countertops are finding their way into typical new construction, although they're still at upper price ranges because of the skilled labor needed to create them—not because of the cost of their raw materials (after all, like other concrete, countertop concrete is made simply of water, cement, sand, stone, and color pigments). When correctly mixed, formed, cured, and finished, concrete countertops can be artistic statements, their design limited by only the imagination.

They may include colorful tile and stone embedded in their surface, and can offer numerous colors and texture effects. Depending on the skill of the fabricator, features such as integral sinks, drain boards, and decorative splash plates and edges can all be included as part of the countertop, without seams or joints. The counters can be either pre-cast to fit a mold that's designed exactly to your specifications, or cast on site. At the same time, some owners opt for matching kitchen tables, decorative tiles, or other products that can be made with the same color and type of concrete. Some manufacturers offer ready-made finished concrete sections that can be arranged and installed as a countertop.

Concrete, though sturdy, does have its drawbacks. It must be carefully sealed in order to resist stains, and the seal needs to be protected with occasional waxings. Even then, the surface may need resealing within a year or so. Cutting on a concrete countertop will likely leave marks.

Stainless Steel

Stainless steel is another option. It's the first choice of commercial food service institutions such as restaurants and hotels. Stainless steel is hard, durable, sanitary, heatproof, attractive, and expensive. It's usually satin-finished to avoid any evidence of scratches, but constant cleaning will eventually polish the work area anyway. On the negative side, stainless steel is noisy and tough on dishes and glassware. And when dirty with gritty substances, it gives some cooks the shivers when they touch it.

Countertop Placement

Give careful thought to where you locate your counter space.

1. You'll want some near the entrance you use from the garage, to set groceries on.

2. Some should be placed adjacent to the refrigerator where you must put away groceries and take out food for meals.

3. If possible, try to arrange for continuous counter space from cooking range to sink to refrigerator. The refrigerator, however, should never be placed between the sink and the range because it would divide the counter and impede the kitchen work flow.

4. A countertop next to the range is convenient to temporarily put hot foods on before serving them.

5. There should be counter space on one side of the sink and dishwasher for rough cleaning and stacking of dishes and glassware and for placing food brought back from the dining area. Another clear countertop should be planned on the other side of the sink and dishwasher (usually to the left) for placing the washed and drying dishes and utensils.

APPLIANCES

The most basic kitchen planning concepts revolve around a very simple arrangement of three common-to-all-kitchen areas: the food preservation and storage area (refrigerator), the food preparation and cooking areas (range, oven, and microwave), and the food mixing and cleanup areas (sink, disposal, and dishwasher) (Fig. 25.3).

If you're going to have a well-planned, modern kitchen, it's wise to outfit it with top-rated appliances. Here are four considerations you can use to help select individual units:

1. Try to favor major appliances designed so their main components can be serviced and repaired from the front.

2. Self-diagnostic electronic controls make appliances more reliable and make it easier for service technicians or knowledgeable appliance owners to troubleshoot problems.

3. Always compare warranty coverages.

4. Investigate the availability, reputation, and rates of the local manufacturer's service dealer—if there is one.

Kitchen appliances.

APPLIANCE EVALUATION AND OPTIONAL SERVICE CONTRACTS

Product Evaluation

It's your first and strongest line of offense and defense against inferior appliances. Product evaluations are 95 percent of finding and purchasing the best values for your dollars. Many builders may be able to purchase whatever appliances you select. If you happen to pick out units that exceed the builder's allowance, you'll likely have to pay the difference, but you'll still be ahead because the builder's cost is typically at a hefty discount.

Here are some guidelines that have worked well for consumers:

1. Select appliances and other items with established brand names known for quality and dependability. Unfamiliar makes can be difficult and expensive to have repaired. Choose a model that best suits your requirements. It needn't be the least- or most-expensive model.

2. If possible, ask for a demonstration so you see the item in action and you can learn how to operate it.

3. Find out what the availability is of competent service technicians and spare parts. How quickly can a service call be arranged?

4. Read the warranty or guarantee made by the manufacturer. Resolve any questions before making your selection.

Service Contracts or Extended Warranties

It's becoming standard fare. Walk into any appliance store, electronics shop, automobile dealership, or real estate firm. Purchase what's offered, and some salesperson will invariably inquire if you also want to include, at extra cost, a service contract.

A service contract is really a form of insurance. Consider that no company in its right mind would offer an insurance policy—or a service contract—without fully understanding the possible outcomes based on known mathematical probabilities, and without making sure that those probable outcomes favor the company—not the consumer. For example, a two-year-long service contract on a new clothes dryer might cost $120. You can be sure that the manufacturer arrived at that price based on the knowledge that average repairs on the unit in question during the first two years of a typical owner's use will cost considerably less than $120. Well, if that's the case, then why would you ever consider or want a service contract?

There are reasons. Perhaps you're planning to use the appliance more frequently than the typical user does. What if you're the designated uniform washer for a grade school soccer team? You know that for the next few years—during your stint as uniform washer—you're really going to put 10 year's worth of usage into your new dryer. In that case, the service contract could likely come into play on your behalf.

Simply put, purchasing a service contract or extended warranty is a gamble. It's in your best interest to see that the odds are tipped at least as far as possible toward an outcome that will be favorable to you. If you simply feel more comfortable with and can afford service contracts and extended warranties whenever they're offered, so be it. You're well covered, and you'll be unlikely to experience any major repairs. But, unless you plan to use those items harder than most other individuals do, you'll probably be paying a premium for the coverage. For those purchases that will be used for routine service, that's why it's important to do your homework before you buy. Find out which makes and models have the least number of problems, are the least expensive to run and own, and are superior performers. If you buy the best-value items to begin with, and if no special or extenuating circumstances exist, you aren't likely to need a service contract. So, in a nutshell, before you go for any repair-type service contracts, you must have a clear understanding of what's being promised in all of the fine print, and you must do a thorough evaluation of your own needs and how you will be using the item in question.

Here are some additional considerations:

■ Is the contract already covered, in full or in part, by a manufacturer's warranty? This happens. A manufacturer will warrant its product and another company—a different company offering extended or other warranties—will accept payments for the same protection.

■ What does the contract include? Labor? Labor and parts? Must you pay for the repairperson's travel time? Some contracts cover only certain components, such as the motor in a washing machine, or the heating elements on an electric range, or the picture tube on a television.

■ What if the repair is needed at night or on a weekend? A hot water heater that fails on a freezing Friday night in February needs to be fixed before Monday morning. If the service contract doesn't specify seven-days-a-week repairs, a costly overtime charge could result.

■ Does the cost of the service contract rise as the item ages? It likely will. Naturally, expected repair costs are minimal during the early life of most appliances and major components. Ask about maintaining the contract in the third, fourth, fifth, or later years.

■ Never take a salesperson's word for what a contract covers. He or she may forget important details or may misunderstand the terms. Find out what a contract includes and excludes by reading it yourself. Pay attention to items such as the following: Where will the product be serviced? In your home? In a repair shop? In a manufacturer's service center? Is the contract transferable if you sell the item? How much time do you have to decide if you want the service contract?

■ Find out who is offering the service contract: the retailer or dealer you're buying the item from, the manufacturer, or an independent third party?

■ Find out who will be performing or who you can have do the repairs. Regarding appliances or individually manufactured units, will repairs be made by technicians trained to service your product?

■ To check on the reputation of a company offering service contracts, ask the Better Business Bureau or your local consumer protection office.

APPLIANCE CHECKLIST

1. Prepare before you buy. Compare and evaluate products and services.

2. If reasonable, favor established, reputable, local retailers.

3. Buy quality. Generally, select appliances and other items with established brand names.

4. Always ask for a demonstration.

5. Ask about parts and service availability.

6. Favor service contracts (or "repair insurance") if you plan to give unusually rough use to whatever you're buying.

7. When purchasing items for normal use, buy models offering superior performance and maintenance records, and you won't need a service contract.

Refrigerators

A refrigerator should be large enough to accommodate your expected family size and still be able to take care of all the entertaining you plan. Consider which modern options, if any, you'd like, such as automatic ice maker, fast freezer, or ice water spout. Make sure the model you want will fit into the spot allocated on the plans. And whenever possible, the refrigerator door should be reversible, so with a simple changeover it can open from the right or the left, in case you want to remodel some day or relocate.

Here are some available options for refrigerators:

- Adjustable rollers at the base so the unit can be moved without being lifted.

- Reversible doors.

- Recessed handles.

- A textured door that won't show dirt and smudges.

- A door heater to prevent excess condensation during hot, humid weather.

- Door lights that signal problem conditions such as power outages, an open door, warm inside temperatures, and dirty condenser coils.

- An automatic ice maker with dispensers for crushed or cubed ice and chilled water, conveniently illuminated by a nightlight.

- A front-door compartment that enables a built-in counter to drop out from the door to provide easy access to often-used items such as milk or juice.

- If lack of space is a problem, some units come only 24 inches deep.

- A self-defrosting freezer.

- Ice trays and buckets.

- Removable door dikes that allow you to completely remove the ice bucket.

- Removable covered storage containers/dishes that are designed for freezer, microwave, and dishwasher use.

- A vacation economy setting.

- Adjustable internal and door shelves.

- Humidity-controlled crispers.

- Extra cold meat compartments.

- Egg storage bins.

- Extra deep, movable door storage bins for gallon containers, 3-liter bottles, or six-packs.

- Movable retainers on door shelves to keep small, tall, or oddly shaped items in place.

- See-through compartments allowing viewing of food without opening them.

- Sealed snack pack compartment for keeping items such as cold cuts and cheeses fresh.

Ovens

The oven can be a part of the cooking range, situated under the burners, or it can be a separate unit built into the kitchen cabinets. Consider a double oven if you do a lot of baking or entertaining. Make sure the ovens aren't placed next to the refrigerator where cooking heat could affect the operation of the refrigerator.

Here are some available options for ovens:

- Self-cleaning.

- Electronic ignition. This takes the place of standard pilot lights in gas ovens, to save on fuel.

- Broiler pan/rack.

- A window plus a hand towel bar on the oven door.

- A clock with an automatic timer.

- A removable oven door.

- An electronic meat thermometer.

- An automatic rotisserie.

- Chrome finish for easy cleaning.

- A porcelain enamel-on-steel finish is also excellent.

Cooktops

The range or top burners can be a separate unit built into a countertop, with at least four individual burners. In some makes, the burner tops can be temporarily removed so other cooking devices such as grills and rotisseries can be substituted.

Popular new types of electric cooktops can be purchased with sealed elements that replace hard-to-clean drip bowls. Food spills end up on the cooktop around the heat element where cooler temperatures will not "bake" the spilled material onto the finish.

There are two kinds of new cooktops: inductive and glass ceramic. *Inductive cooktops* are made with electric coils located beneath a glass ceramic surface. Magnetic energy generated between the cooktop coils and the pots and pans placed on the cooktop surface creates heat that cooks the food. Because the glass ceramic cooktop surface is nonmagnetic, the current flows through it, reaches the metallic pots and pans, heats them but leaves the rest of the cooktop surface cool to the touch.

Cooking on induction stovetops has certain advantages:

- Cooking starts or stops immediately, with no preheating or cooldown time required. This means you can bring milk that is about to boil over back to the preboil temperature within a second of the heat being turned down.

- Cleanup is simple because spills don't bake on.

- Only the part of the cooktop that comes in contact with the pan heats, which helps to save energy.

- It's safer than heating with other types of cooktops.

- *Glass ceramic cooktops* use halogen lamps that provide instantaneous heat on demand. A resistance coil around the element's outer edge assures even heat distribution.

- Cleanup is easy because the surface of the cooktop around the elements remains cool.

- Heating is uniform across the element, and heat control is very precise. The reheating ability of the elements is extremely rapid.

- For safety, temperature limits are employed to prevent heat surges and to protect the elements from overheating.

Other considerations for cooktops include the following:

- Grime-resistant control knobs are the best. The most popular are plastic injection-molded knobs with markings that won't rub off and are flush with the knob so they don't collect grease, dirt, and grime.

- Removable cooktop sections that can be replaced with a grill, rotisserie, or griddle having easy-to-clean nonstick finishes.

- If the cooktop is mounted as part of a range, a cooking light should be furnished.

- "On" indicator lights will remind the cook when a cooktop surface unit is turned on.

- Some solid disc units contain temperature limits that will automatically reduce heat if a pot boils dry or if a unit is accidentally left on without a pot or pan on its surface.

Cooktop Ventilation

Whether gas or electric, most grill-cooktops have built-in ventilation systems. Their downdraft designs pull smoke, odors, moisture, and grease from the cooktop through a vent to the outside. This setup offers several advantages over ventilation that's positioned above a cooktop.

- A downdraft system uses a quieter and less-powerful fan than is required of an overhead ventilation hood.

- It provides design options for kitchens that can't accommodate updraft or overhead ventilation systems.

If your cooktop won't have a built-in downdraft ventilation system, the alternative is an overhead vent hood. Look for the following options:

- The fan should come with several speed settings.

- It should use removable grease filters.

- There should be a nightlight.

Microwave Ovens

Don't overlook the inclusion of a microwave oven. Inexpensive models are available for placing on a countertop or mounting in a wall cabinet or beneath a hanging cabinet. They're particularly useful in conjunction with freezers, because they eliminate the chore of defrosting food beforehand. Combination microwave/convection ovens are available that offer the best in both cooking methods.

Available features include the following:

- Countertop, built-in, or beneath-cabinet mounts
- A built-in clock/timer
- Window and interior light
- Multiple power levels
- Auto start
- Adjustable shelves
- Meat probes
- Humidity or weight sensors to calculate cooking time
- A defrost setting
- A ventilation system
- Combination cook: microwave and microbake
- Microwave/convection oven capable of cooking, roasting, broiling, baking, toasting, and warming
- A temperature cook/hold setting that allows food to be kept at a desired temperature for up to one hour or until the clear/off pad is touched
- Wood-grain cabinets

Dishwashers

Some people would never have a kitchen without a dishwasher. Others hardly ever use the one they have. It's up to your own personal preference. Here are some features to consider if you're planning to have a dishwasher in your kitchen:

- A warning alarm that signals a blocked drain.

- An energy-saving option that will shut off the heater in the drying cycle to save energy when dishes can air dry overnight or throughout the day.

- A soft-food disposal.

- A choice of wash cycles: normal, short, light, energy saver, china/crystal, rinse only.

- Changeable front panels that allow damaged panels to be easily replaced or existing panels to be replaced with different color panels to match changing decorating schemes.

Disposals

The disposal is another appliance that draws mixed reviews. Some people love disposals—the way they can just whirr through almost anything short of bones. Other people are afraid of them, of the noise and the blades—can they trust them with children?

If you plan to include one in your kitchen sink, look for the following:

- Stainless steel construction

- A model insulated for sound depression

- Continuous feed

- A noncorroding nylon hopper and polyester drain housing

- Child safety features

Food Processors

These appliances make it quicker and easier for both new and experienced cooks to tackle much of the work involved in food preparation. Small quantities of foods can be minced in seconds—onions, garlic, parsley, raw meat, cooked eggs, practically anything. Look for the following options:

- Continuous feed for processing large amounts

- An S-blade for chopping

- A reversible slicer/shredder disc

- Up-front controls for easy access

- On/off pulse action

- Bowl capacity of 4 dry cups and 2 liquid cups
- Cord storage
- A convenient opening for adding liquids while processing
- A lid to the processing bowl for food storage

Vacuum Meal Sealers

These neat devices seal food into plastic bags. Good points include the following:

- They expel the air from the package/food, locking in flavor and freshness.
- They extend storage life and reduce required cooking and heating times.
- They allow food to be boiled in the plastic bag or heated in a microwave.
- They come with instant on/off controls, a plastic bag cutter, and cord storage.

Automatic Coffee Makers

Consider the following features:

- A capacity for making 4 to 12 cups of coffee automatically
- A removable glass carafe server with cord-free convenience
- Stainless steel pump
- Automatic "keep warm" cycle
- Thermostatically controlled
- An automatic shutoff if left unattended for 2 hours
- A heat-resistant handle and base that stays cool to the touch
- An LED clock/timer
- A 24-hour automatic-perc time cycle on a digital clock auto timer with on/off/auto switch
- A flavor-neutral glass carafe
- Dishwasher-safe glass carafe server

- A removable water container that can be filled right at the sink

- A beverage indicator on an insulated carafe (coffee, decaf, tea, or other)

Cool-Touch Wide-Mouth Toasters

This type of toaster offers many features and advantages:

- Its "cool touch," sleek exterior remains comfortable to the touch, even when toasting.

- It is self-adjusting, capable of toasting thin to extra-thick bread, bagels, English muffins, croissants, and more.

- An extra-wide, long toasting rack accommodates French bread or oversize rolls.

- An electronic temperature control offers defrosting, warming, and various degrees of toasting.

- A convenient crumb tray makes cleanup a breeze.

Automatic Chrome Can Opener/Scissors Sharpener

This appliance should provide the following features and advantages:

- It will open cans, bags, jars, and bottles.

- It will automatically power-pierce lid, open can, then shut itself off. A magnetic finger securely holds lid.

- The sharpener hones household knives, shears, and other cutting instruments.

Cordless Wet and Dry Vac

This appliance is designed for wet, soggy, and dry cleanup tasks.

- It's great to have close by for spilled flour, beans, liquids, potting soil—almost anything.

- One option to look for is a motorized brush attachment that cleans carpets, upholstery, and bare floors.

- Other popular attachments include a crevice tool, a ceiling wand, a furniture brush, and a squeegee.

Sinks

Many of the best kitchen sinks are made of either stainless steel or enameled cast iron. Both are easy to keep clean and will retain their good looks over the years. There are also porcelain-on-steel sinks that look like cast iron but are hard to keep clean, chip easily, and lose their gloss quickly. The more expensive line of stainless steel sinks contain higher percentages of chrome alloys, which provide better appearances and a reduced tendency toward "water spotting."

The style of sink you choose should have at least two wash bays or bowls and a rinse spray gun.

A triple-bowl kitchen sink (Fig. 25.4) allows hand dish washing in one bowl, rinsing in a reduced-size center bowl, and placing items in a drying rack staged in the third bowl. This quick-wash and dry system enables dish washing to be completed while the washing water is still hot.

If desired, an optional garbage disposal makes cleaning dirty dishes and cookware faster and easier, but can be a headache if not properly used and maintained.

It's not absolutely necessary, but it sure is handy to include an automatic dishwasher. If you decide on one, place it next to the sink and be sure to allow at least 18 inches between any side wall or counter running at right angles to the machine's front. If you cram a dishwasher all the way into a corner, then two people won't be able to load or unload it at the same time.

FIGURE 25.4

A triple-bowl sink.

SINK/PULLOUT SPRAY FAUCETS

Consider purchasing a comfortable, palm-fitting pullout main kitchen sink faucet. It will allow easier washing and rinsing of larger items in the sink and the filling of containers that would otherwise be too large for a fixed sink faucet spout to handle. With fingertip control, this faucet's flow can change from an aerated stream for rinsing vegetables or cleaning around the sink, to a functional steady stream for basic sink use.

FAUCET FILTERS

When choosing a kitchen sink faucet, consider one with a functional "carbon block" filter. Unless you have included a main house water filter with your plumbing, take a look at faucets that come with replaceable filters right inside the faucet's neck, out of sight, and available in pullout models. These faucets and their filters accomplish the following:

- Reduce common impurities such as chlorine and lead.
- Should not remove beneficial fluoride.
- Improve water taste and reduce odor.
- Can typically be switched from filtered to unfiltered flow.
- Filter cartridge offers quick and easy replacement, right at the sink.
- Inconspicuous filters are positioned out of sight, inside the faucet.
- Units are stylish.
- Are available with built-in filter life indicators to provide visual and audible feedback signals for remaining filter life, for showing water is being filtered, and monitoring battery strength.

CABINETS

Kitchen cabinets have always been the focal point of any kitchen (Fig. 25.5). More than anything, they set the flavor of the room and make or break its appearance. It's no coincidence that they're usually

FIGURE 25.5

Kitchen cabinets.

the first to be changed when kitchens are remodeled, and countless home improvement contractors earn their living by replacing or giving facelifts to kitchen cabinets. Nowhere else in the typical house are so many different items kept. If it weren't for kitchen cabinets and drawers, chaos would prevent numerous cooks from staying organized and efficient in the kitchen.

Most kitchen and other cabinets (bathroom cabinets, for instance) are manufactured in one of three ways: custom-made, factory-made, and custom factory-made.

Custom-made cabinets are constructed in a local cabinet shop according to your exact plans. Such a method offers practically unlimited selection as to material, design, and finish, but it's also the most expensive. If your needs are unusual, though, custom-made cabinets could be your best option. Your builder should get bids from several cabinetmakers before you make a final decision.

Factory-made cabinets are built to the specifications of the different lines the factory carries. Your choices are thus limited in the selection of material, design, and finishes. These cabinets range in price from inexpensive to very expensive, depending on the individual manufacturers and lines.

Custom factory-made cabinets are assembled at a centralized plant in response to orders taken by local kitchen cabinet outlets. You can expect a much greater choice in material, design, and finish than with factory-made cabinets. Prices are usually less than those of custom-made cabinets and more than those of the medium and economy grades of factory-made models.

For your kitchen cabinets, give careful thought not only to cost, but to what cabinet style, type, sizes, quantities, and accessories will best suit your needs.

Cabinet Considerations

- Base cabinet depth should be around 24 inches.

- The floor-to-countertop height should be about 36 inches.

- Cabinets installed over countertops should be at least 12 inches deep and about 30 inches high.

- There should be about 18 inches of clearance between the countertop and the bottom of wall cabinets.

CABINET STORAGE CHECKLIST

Kitchen storage space is obviously most efficient when it's conveniently located. This is particularly true in the cooking area, where most kitchen work is done. It follows that, when planning a kitchen layout you must arrange for enough storage space of the right kinds to be made available near each of the major appliances for utensils, foods, seasonings, cleaning supplies, and other items that are used at the various work stations.

Here are some sample checklists of items you should plan storage space for near the kitchen cooking range, refrigerator, and sink.

(Continued)

✔✔✔✔✔ CABINET STORAGE CHECKLIST (*Continued*)

Near the range:

___ Seasonings, instant coffee, tea and cocoa, flour, cornstarch, cooking oils, and shortening

___ Saucepans, skillets, griddles, roasters, frying pans

___ Knives, large forks and spoons, ladles, tongs, shears, carving tools, measuring cups and spoons

___ Platters, serving dishes and trays

___ Hand mixers and blenders

___ Cooling racks

Near the refrigerator (this area usually serves as the food preparation area):

___ Baking sheets, pie and muffin pans, rolling pins, sifters

___ Casserole dishes, measuring cups and spoons, mixing bowls

___ Paper towels, sandwich bags, aluminum foil, waxed paper, plastic wrap

___ Seasonings

___ Bottle and can openers

___ Spatulas, ice cream scoops, refrigerator dishes

___ Ice bucket

___ Sandwich grill, waffle iron

___ Bowl covers

___ Bread and cake boxes, cookie jars

Near the sink (and dishwasher if you have one):

___ Soaps, cleansers, detergents

___ Paper and garbage bags

___ Paper towels and napkins

___ Scouring pads

___ Silver-polishing supplies

___ Window-cleaning supplies

___ Appliance waxes

___ Scrub brushes

CABINET STORAGE *(Continued)* ✔✔✔✔✔

___ **Coffee pots**

___ **Colanders and strainers**

___ **Cutting boards**

___ **Dishcloths, towels, mop**

___ **Everyday china and glassware**

___ **Draining rack**

___ **Double boiler**

___ **Juicers**

___ **Funnels**

___ **Saucepans**

___ **Tea kettle, pitchers**

___ **Garbage can and trash can**

Types of Cabinets

There are four basic types of cabinets you can select from: unfinished wood cabinets, stained wood cabinets, painted wood cabinets, and wood and plastic laminate cabinets.

UNFINISHED WOOD CABINETS

Like any unfinished product, unfinished wood cabinets can be purchased at a substantial savings if you decide to finish them yourself or have the house stainers do the job for you, before or after the cabinets are installed. If this method is selected, the cabinets can be finished off to exactly match other woodwork and trim throughout the house.

STAINED WOOD CABINETS

Stained wood cabinets are finished at the shop or factory in a carefully controlled environment that ensures an excellent application and curing of the many finishing coats that are available.

WOOD AND PLASTIC LAMINATE CABINETS

Wood and plastic laminate cabinets are finished either at the factory or at a local shop. They're constructed of wood or a wood product such as particleboard, and then covered with a plastic laminate. The plastic laminate offers a wide variety of bright and wood-grain colors and patterns, and is easy to clean.

Special Cabinets

Apart from the standard cabinets that are set squarely against a wall, other units are available to fill special storage space needs.

- Pull-out disposable and recyclable bins in the kitchen will permit easy handling of those materials without having to access the garage frequently.

- Two-way cabinets have doors on both their fronts and backs. When suspended from a soffit over a counter peninsula or island, they permit you to put dishes away from the sink side and to take the same dishes out from the dining-room side when setting the table. Matching two-way base cabinets can also be purchased.

- Quarter-round cabinets are used at open ends of cabinet rows to give a rounded-off look and to permit items to be stored on the front or side of the cabinet from several angles. Similar half-round cabinets and shelves can also be purchased when needed.

- Mixer cabinets are used for storing large electric mixers. A mixer cabinet is a base unit with a shelf that pulls out and up.

- A bottle cabinet is a base cabinet with pullout trays that are eggcrated to hold bottles.

- When wall and floor cabinets are located on both sides of an interior corner, a revolving round "lazy Susan" cabinet tray arrangement can make good use of otherwise hard-to-access space.

Cabinet Slide-Out Shelves

Consider having some of your lower shelves as pullout trays that will give greater visibility and ease for reaching their contents. Heavy pots and items can be brought into full view and easy reach by simply pulling a tray forward. Vertical drawers are particularly satisfactory below the sink, where often-used dishpans, strainers, and colanders are kept.

Special drawers are also available with dividers for canned goods if there is no pantry. Bread box and slide-out vegetable bins are good for storing onions and potatoes.

VENTILATION

A poorly ventilated kitchen will suffer from chronic condensation and the odors of your last meal. In addition to strategically placed windows and sliding doors with screens, an overhead lighted hood with a fan that's vented directly to the outdoors is one of the best overall solutions. But a fan built into a counter range top and vented to the outdoors is also very popular and effective. When considering hood exhaust equipment, look for:

- At least three fan speeds
- Multiple light settings
- Filter cleaning reminder
- Seamless construction in a metal hood; otherwise grease can collect under the edges where joints are welded.
- Hooded vents should be vented directly to the outdoors with straight, rigid, smooth, fire-proof metal sections to provide practically effortless airflow.
- The terminal (outdoor) vent should be kept as far as possible away from windows so exhausted air won't draft back into the house when the windows are open.

LIGHTING

The kitchen should have enough illumination, day or night, for cooking, work, or socializing. If possible, locate a window over the sink. Large windows and skylights are always helpful to the family chef.

A kitchen should have task lighting installed under wall cabinets, for the sink, range, and counters. The same goes for all other kitchen work areas and centers.

Consider fluorescent lights underneath cabinets that hang from a soffit over countertops to illuminate counter work surfaces. Plan recessed lights in plain soffits above work counters and ranges (if a light isn't already in a range hood).

There should be separate lighting over the main kitchen area. A light over a table with chairs or over an eating nook should be dimmer-controlled.

KITCHEN WALL FINISHES

The walls of a kitchen, especially the wall surfaces above the work counters, should be finished with an easy-to-clean material. Three popular, functional wall finishes are as follows:

- Fabric and vinyl wallpapers—these have excellent surface washability and durability characteristics. They come in a wide variety of colors and patterns.

- Predecorated wallboards—these colored and patterned vinyls come in factory-manufactured sheets that are easily cut to fit and applied to the walls.

- Ceramic tile—ceramic tile is durable and attractive, but it requires a little more maintenance and effort to keep clean.

MISCELLANEOUS

1. Make sure there are enough electrical outlets along the countertops.

2. Consider locating broom and pantry closets in or near the kitchen.

3. Specify on your prints the make, model, color, and style of the sink, refrigerator/freezer, dishwasher, range, oven(s), microwave, garbage disposal, and exhaust system.

4. Consider having a small desk in the kitchen where you can sit down to thumb through cookbooks, make out shopping lists, check bills, and make telephone calls. The desk should be large enough to accommodate a computer, too, for allowing Internet

access to cooking information and to enable family members to perform computer work between kitchen tasks.

5. A portable telephone in the kitchen is a must. If the phone rings while you're cooking supper, you can bring it over to the range top and keep stirring that sauce or stir frying those potatoes while talking.

6. Every surface in the kitchen should be easy to clean with a damp sponge: countertops, walls, floors, appliances, and cabinets.

7. There should be plenty of receptacles for portable appliances such as coffee makers, blenders, toaster ovens, radios, bread machines, and electric skillets.

8. Ground-fault electrical circuit interrupters (GFCIs) should be supplied in all kitchen and bathroom receptacles.

9. A fire extinguisher should be within an easy reaching distance to the cooktop, and smoke alarm protection should be included near the kitchen.

10. Allow enough space for at least two waste containers: garbage and trash.

▷▷▷▷▷ POINTS TO PONDER

1. When designing a kitchen, carefully consider its four major components: dining facilities, countertops, cabinets, and appliances.
2. Of all parts of a kitchen, countertops (or food preparation tops) are used the most. Plan generous amounts of them.
3. Make sure there are plenty of GFCI electrical outlets along the countertops.
4. Kitchen cabinets have always been the focal point of any kitchen. More than anything else, they set the flavor of the room and make or break its appearance. It's to your advantage to select quality-grade cabinets. They'll look better and wear longer.
5. Consider installing broom and pantry closets in the kitchen, if there's enough room. Cookbook shelves and a small computer

desk/work station have also become popular modern kitchen features.

6. If possible, a window should be located behind or to the side of the kitchen sink, to provide natural lighting during the day. Because food preparation tasks entail lots of fine handwork, plan enough task lights into the kitchen. Recessed or track lighting units make excellent choices.

7. Remember, when planning the location of appliances, that certain units, such as trash compactors, garbage disposals, blenders, food processors, and stove/cooktops with front-unit controls, should be off-limits to young children.

8. Good ventilation in a kitchen is a must. That can include window/screen units, sliding glass door/screen units, and rangetop fans.

9. The walls of a kitchen, especially the wall surfaces above the work counters, should be finished with durable, easy-to-clean materials.

10. Consider running two phone lines into the kitchen, in case the household cook plans on being on the Internet while preparing meals.

Floor Coverings

The selection of a particular floor covering depends on where it will be used, its appearance (available styles and colors), durability, ease of care and maintenance, price, and the buyer's personal taste. It's an excellent idea to visit a number of large home stores and specialized flooring stores to see available floor coverings, and get a feeling for what's new. There are certainly many floor coverings to consider when planning your home, including carpet, laminate, vinyl, linoleum, wood, cork, bamboo, tile, stone, brick and concrete.

CARPETING

An almost limitless array of carpeting is manufactured for home-owners to choose from. Practically any quality, basic material, texture, color, weave, or price range can be had for the asking. It's an all-around excellent floor covering that can literally be used anywhere in a home.

Certainly, carpeting is an interior decorator's dream because it can create as many moods as colors can influence. It can stretch small spaces into large, and shrink large spaces small. It can supply a rich, modern look to a room or create a statement of cool neutrality. It feels wonderful beneath bare feet and is equally enjoyed by small children who can tumble and fall on it without injuring themselves. It helps control sound from echoing through a home by absorbing noises and is relatively simple to replace when worn out.

On the other hand, it's tough to remove a cupful of spilled grape juice from a lily-white shag. Carpeting shows various stains and soils and can pose big cleaning problems if chewing gum, grease, ink, or various foods and drinks become embedded in its yarn tufts. Pet odors can also find refuge in carpeting, and during times of low humidity, static electricity can collect and shock people who touch metal lamps or even one another. Also, when carpeting is installed in high-traffic areas of a house, no matter what its quality, it will eventually show wear paths, can be marred by dropped cigarettes, and cannot be refinished in any way. When soiled, carpeting needs either time-consuming shampooing or must be professionally cleaned.

There are carpets custom-tailored to solve a wide variety of problem situations: fibers designed to control the static electricity that draws dust or gives shock on cold, dry days; carpets having soil resistance built right into the fibers themselves; industrial grade carpeting designed to take unbelievable punishment, indoors and out; textured carpets with a mixture of sheared yarns and loops engineered to camouflage stains and look good while doing so; and lustrous sheared velours and velvets that look so plush that people are afraid to step on them.

You can tell quality carpet by its material and nap or yarn density. Wool makes excellent carpet, but it's expensive. Nylon is the most popular, accounting for over 75 percent of all carpeting manufactured today. Acrylics, polyesters, rayon, and polypropylene or olefin are no longer as popular as they once were, but are all still used for specific applications, the latter, for instance, in kitchens and wherever indoor-outdoor carpeting is needed.

Carpets used to be woven, but are rarely woven anymore. Instead they're tufted—a process by which yarns are looped through a woven backing then locked into that backing with an adhesive and then another thin layer of backing. Then the yarn loops are cut or sheared to various lengths. The higher quality carpet contains a higher density of yarn, or more yarn per square inch. The higher the density of yarn, the greater the carpet wearability.

Because so many varieties of carpeting exist, here are some guidelines to help you plan the carpeting for your house:

1. The first decision to make is one of style. By area, do you want a plush, a shag, or some other style better suited for each application. After you narrow down the style, begin comparing fibers available in each of the style groups you've selected. A general rule is to seek deeper and denser piles (the configurations of the fibers) than you think you'll need. Remember that shag carpeting is intentionally manufactured with low-density yarn to achieve the "shag" look.

   Two of the most popular styles of surface texture for carpeting are the sculptured and the plush. The sculptured style is composed of designs created by alternate areas with and without heavy pile. The plush type has a constant pile thickness and is more likely to show footprint indentations.

   Another texture is the level loop pile, which wears well and hides footprints nicely.

   A fourth style is the frieze or twist type, which also thwarts footprints and hides dirt and dust fairly well. Like the level loop pile, the frieze or twist carpet stands up to rough use. And if it has a level surface, it's easy to keep clean. Frieze is ideal for installations where multiple small seams must be matched—for wrapping carpet around and between handrail supports on a stairway, for example.

2. When checking for carpet density, watch out for crimp. Crimp is exactly what it sounds like: mechanically induced zigs and zags in the individual carpet fibers that add bulk and fullness. A given amount of crimped fiber will fill more space than can otherwise be filled with the same quantity of regular, straight fibers. The actual crimping of the fibers is on such a tiny scale, it can't be seen at a casual glance. When crimped fiber is spun into yarn, air is captured between the zigzags; the yarn then looks straight and solid, but at the same time has a fuller, fluffier look than the noncrimped versions.

   This crimping technique is used to make "high bulk" yarns that are fluffed or tufted into some very stylish, elegant carpeting. It's one way to obtain a plusher-looking carpet without encountering a higher expense in the process. Crimped-fiber carpeting might look good at first. It might feel and even sound good, but all a consumer really gets is the same amount of fiber that's available in more "honest" versions with thinner piles—plus a lot of air.

3. When choosing carpet styles and types, consider the wear that they're likely to receive. You'll probably want the most beautiful carpet in your living room, but if the room will see heavy family traffic instead of being just a visitor's parlor, then you might be further ahead to avoid light-toned solid colors and favor an anti-soiling plush or textured carpet instead. In general, when it comes to the busier areas in a home—the living room, family room, halls, and stairways, for instance, you'll do better with carpeting that will stand up to the traffic it receives. Bedroom carpets receive relatively light duty and thus can be good places to either economize or go luxury.

4. Most carpeting should have a padding of some type laid beneath the entire surface covered. Padding helps lengthen a carpet's useful life by absorbing much of the footfall pressure that would otherwise grind the carpet backing against the hard and potentially raspy surface of the floor decking. It also makes a carpet seem plusher than the carpet really is by softening the impact of a person's footfalls so that walking on such a surface is more comfortable.

   Various paddings are available, manufactured from hair, felt, rubber-coated jute, cellular rubber, high-density sponge, latex foam rubber, and urethane foam. All are acceptable when purchased in ¼- to ½-inch-thick layers.

5. Carpeting should be installed on only smooth surfaces that are relatively uniform and ridgeless. Whenever a separate cushion or padding will be used, such undersupport should have all necessary seams covered with tape.

6. Carpeting should be planned so the least number of sections and seams will be needed. When possible, the seams should be positioned in low-traffic areas. Carpeting should always be laid in the same direction; that is, a butt end of a fresh roll shouldn't be seamed to a side of a previous roll.

Types of Carpeting

Here are brief introductions to the various types of carpeting materials available.

NYLON CARPETING

Nylon can go by various brand names such as Antron, Anso, Ultron, and Enkalure II. By any name, nylon is the most popular carpet available. It's especially good for entrance halls and stairways where traffic is heaviest. It can be purchased in many bright colors, has excellent resistance to abrasion and overall strength, and is relatively inexpensive.

Advantages

1. Fairly inexpensive to produce and purchase.
2. Available in a huge quantity of styles, textures, and colors.
3. Good to excellent texture retention.
4. Good wet cleanability.
5. Excellent durability.
6. Good to excellent appearance retention.
7. Easy to maintain.
8. Excellent resistance to abrasion.
9. Good to excellent resistance to alkalis and acids.
10. Excellent resistance to insects and mildew.
11. Good resistance to compression and crushing forces.
12. Good resistance to staining.
13. Long life expectancy.

Disadvantages

1. Nylon carpeting in particular needs a good backing material to attain dimensional stability.
2. Tends to pull and fuzz when abused.
3. Can retain oil and soil and "look dirty" easier than several other synthetic fibers can.
4. Some discoloration might result from prolonged exposure to sunlight.
5. Nylon has more sheen than wool and some of the other synthetics.

6. Can develop static buildup.

7. Offers little protection against cigarette burns.

ACRYLIC CARPETING

These synthetic fibers closely resemble wool in texture, appearance, and abrasion resistance. Some acrylic carpeting, though, is very flammable. Due to their resistance to staining and soiling, and their low-maintenance demands, acrylic carpeting works well in kitchens, bathrooms, basements, porches, patios, and poolside areas—wherever dampness could be a problem, or spills are likely to occur.

Advantages

1. Good colorfastness, with good resistance to sunlight.

2. Resembles wool in appearance and texture.

3. Resists aging well.

4. Good texture retention.

5. Good to excellent wet cleanability.

6. Good resistance to static buildup.

7. Good to excellent resistance to staining and soiling.

8. Excellent resistance to insects and mildew.

9. Good resistance to alkalis and acids.

10. Good resistance to abrasion.

11. Good resistance to compression and crushing forces.

Disadvantages

1. Offers little protection against cigarette burns. Some acrylics burn very easily.

2. Tends to pull and fuzz when abused.

3. Some loss in textile strength upon prolonged exposure to sun.

MODACRYLIC CARPETING

Modacrylic carpet fibers are acrylic fibers, chemically modified to reduce their flammability. They wear and look like acrylic carpeting.

POLYPROPYLENE OLEFIN CARPETING

Polypropylene olefin is synthetic material that has one of the lowest moisture absorption rates of all carpet fibers. It's easy to clean and very resistant to stains and soils. It can be used instead of acrylics in kitchens, bathrooms, basements, porches, patios, and poolside areas. Be aware, though, that it isn't as resistant to compression or crushing as the acrylics, and doesn't retain its texture as well.

Advantages

1. Good appearance retention.
2. Easy to maintain, with excellent wet cleanability.
3. Good durability and resistance to aging.
4. Excellent resistance to staining and soiling.
5. Excellent resistance to abrasion.
6. Good to excellent resistance to alkalis and acids.
7. Excellent resistance to insects and mildew.
8. Can be treated by the factory to give good resistance to direct sunlight.

Disadvantages

1. Does not afford much protection against cigarette and other burns.
2. Has only a fair resistance to compression and crushing forces.
3. Has only a fair retention of texture.

POLYESTER CARPETING

Polyester makes an attractive carpet with many fine features, but it's less favored than nylon, acrylics, and polypropylene because of its resiliency deficiencies.

Advantages

1. A soft luxurious appearance.
2. Good colorfastness.

3. Excellent resistance to insects and mildew.

4. Less static prone than wool.

Disadvantages

1. Resiliency of polyester is somewhat less than that of nylon and some other types so that dense, deeper pile construction is needed for the same performance.

2. Stains easily with oily materials.

3. Prolonged exposure to sunlight will result in some loss of strength.

RAYON CARPETING

Rayon is not generally recommended over any of the others. It soils easily and gives poor resistance to abrasive wear.

Advantages

1. Unaffected by most acids and solvents.

2. Can be an attractive flooring in areas of light usage.

Disadvantages

1. Poor resistance to abrasion.

2. Soils rapidly.

3. Fuzzy types are very flammable.

WOOL CARPETING

When it comes to beautiful, durable, top-of-the-line carpeting, there's no doubt that natural wool fiber leads the pack. Wool is a wonderfully durable fiber that has yet to be surpassed for its excellent appearance retention and resilience. Carpet wools are as varied as the different types of sheep across the globe, with fibers that range from fine and lustrous to coarse and springy.

Advantages

1. Excellent appearance and texture retention.

2. Excellent durability.

3. Good to excellent ease of maintenance.

4. Warm and comfortable to the touch.

5. Dyes well.

6. Good resistance to abrasion.

7. Good protection against cigarette and other burns.

8. Excellent resistance to compression and crushing forces.

9. Good resistance to staining and soiling.

Disadvantages

1. Expensive.

2. Offers only fair resistance to alkalis and acids.

3. Possesses only fair to good wet cleanability (but many other cleaning methods have been developed over the years).

Carpet Protection

Although frequent vacuuming prevents soil and miscellaneous bits of debris from becoming ground into carpeting, it also makes sense to start out with a quality grade of carpet that already has built-in protection engineered into its construction. When reviewing carpet specifications and manufacturers' claims, look for the following:

- Stain resistance. Spills should bead up on the carpet's surface, allowing easy blotting for quick removal.

- Soil resistance. Soil resistance helps repel dirt and prevents it from becoming embedded and damaging to the carpet's backing. It also helps prevent dust and tiny bits of debris from sticking to individual carpet fibers, making vacuum cleaning and other soil-removing methods far more efficient.

- Static resistance. Static electricity can build up to startling levels and may pose serious problems to youngsters, senior citizens, or anyone who happens to receive an unexpected sharp shock after touching a piece of metal such as a lamp base while going about routine activities at home.

- Wear resistance. This quality is typically reflected in the length and breadth of the carpet's warranty.

- Color/fading resistance. This feature is especially important in sunny climates and in contemporary homes using plenty of exterior glass.

Carpet Warranties

Any carpet you purchase should be covered by a warranty against manufacturing defects. The warranty comes directly from the manufacturer and is an assurance that the carpeting wasn't made in a slipshod manner (or if it *was*, by accident, the company will replace the damaged carpet or reimburse the owner). It's the consumer's protection against defects such as if the tufts pull out of the carpet, or if the face of the carpet comes apart from the backing, or if the dye bleaches out when shampooed.

Carpet warranties are very important, so important that you should never even consider buying a carpet that's not guaranteed against manufacturing defects. As important as such warranties are, though, remember that they don't guarantee performance over the long haul.

FOCUS

BUILT-IN CENTRAL VACUUM SYSTEMS

Central vacuum cleaning systems have come a long way since their introduction decades ago. They're now more powerful and more convenient. Main vacuum power units can be located in a well-vented utility room, basement, or garage—away from daily living activities providing quiet operation (Fig. 26.1). Tubing that runs beneath the floors or in the attic from one end of the house to the other connects hose inlets (Fig. 26.2) throughout the house. On many systems, when a portable hose attachment is inserted into an inlet, the vacuum starts automatically. The long hose attachment enables the vacuuming of stairs, walls, ceilings, and furnishings. The vacuum power plant is typically vented to the outdoors—but not onto or near a patio, deck, breezeway, window, or entrance.

Central vacuum systems are convenient for cleaning multistory homes where you'd otherwise have to lug a portable unit up and down; they're also good for keeping basements, garages, and automobiles vacuumed. Plus overall, the convenience and ease of using a central vacuum system helps encourage household members to clean more frequently than they otherwise might. Numerous cleaning attachments also make specific vacuuming tasks easy.

There's even vacuum dust pans, built into a cabinet toekick or baseboard, that accept dirt swept off vinyl, wood, concrete, and other hard floorings. Great for kitchens, baths, laundry rooms, mud rooms—with smooth flooring, they eliminate the need for dustpans or stooping. The vacuum system automatically activates with the flip of a toe switch (Fig. 26.3).

FIGURE 26.1

Central vacuum power unit.

FIGURE 26.2

Hose inlets.

FIGURE 26.3

Vacuum dust pan.

LAMINATES

Laminate floorings have recently found favor with builders, home buyers, and remodelers, and for good reason. Various patterns and styles can supply the look of wood, tile, and stone—without the accompanying care and maintenance hassles. Laminates are typically composed of four layers (if you count the printed photograph of the wood, stone or tile finish as a layer). The top layer, also called the wear layer, is usually made of an extremely durable material called aluminum oxide. The thickness of the aluminum oxide is often what sets the price and warranty length of the particular laminate in question. The thicker the layer of aluminum oxide, the more durable the product surface is. Beneath the clear surface layer is the decorative finish (the wood plank or stone or tile appearance) layer. Supporting the top layer is the middle or core layer which is often a sturdy fiberboard or particleboard. The bottom layer can be made of laminated products which sometimes include plastics and melamine. Together, the layers are fused by pressure and heat into a user-friendly flooring. The wear layer enables laminate flooring to withstand stains (even from notorious staining agents such as mustards, red wine, bleach, and some felt-tipped markers), impacts, and abuse that would damage most other types of floorings.

It's a good surface for high-traffic areas such as kitchens, recreation rooms, or exercise rooms. It's simple to care for and maintain, requiring little more than routine vacuuming and an occasional sponge mopping. It comes in a wide variety of styles, colors, and patterns that imitate wood (narrow or wide boards), tile, and stone. The better models even have realistic, textured grains or surfaces that match the wood, tile or stone appearances. Most laminates come in individual boards having tongue-and-groove edges. The boards are most often installed as a "floating floor" over a thin layer of foam, without nails, screws or glue. Although wet areas such as bathrooms and laundry rooms can potentially be a problem for laminates (water may leak through the tongue-and-groove seams), that problem is sometimes solved by using glue or sealants between each board. Check with your contractor if you plan a wet-location installation.

VINYL FLOORING

Vinyl is a synthetic material made of petroleum products. Vinyl flooring makes a fine floor covering for bathrooms, kitchens, recreation rooms, sunrooms, laundry rooms, or any other rooms for that matter. It offers wide selections of patterns, colors, and even textures, and is available at many quality levels and prices. Although it comes in tile and long strips, most vinyl flooring is manufactured in wide rolls so a room can be laid out with very few seams. Quality vinyl resists grease and other staining materials, and is overall, very durable. Lower-quality vinyl should be avoided. Some vinyl flooring never needs waxing, while other vinyls might need waxing from time to time.

Advantages of quality vinyl flooring

- Wear-resistant.
- Stain-resistant.
- Scuff-resistant.
- Tear-, gouge-, and rip-resistant.
- Should not discolor from mold, mildew, or alkalis.
- When installed properly, seams should not curl.

Vinyl floor considerations

- Seams should minimized and protected by seam coats.

- Vinyl flooring with greater percentages of vinyl makeup are tougher and more cushioned than models having less vinyl makeup.

- Thicker vinyl floorings are more comfortable and tend to be more tear- and puncture-resistant.

- Ask if the vinyl flooring you're considering comes in 12-foot widths, to minimize seams.

LINOLEUM

Before vinyl appeared decades ago, linoleum ruled the kichens, bathrooms, rec rooms, and laundry rooms throughout the country. The "lin" in linoleum refers to linseed oil, which is a product extracted from flax seed. For linoleum, the linseed oil is dried out and made into a cement powder that bonds ground wood, cork, resins, and other natural materials into an extremely durable material that's backed with a jute fiber or similar layer. Linoleum, in improved versions, is once again available. Don't avoid considering it because you think it's old fashioned. It's a natural, modern product that's entirely recyclable, a flooring that's recommended for individuals who suffer from allergies or asthma because it's hypoallergenic. Manufacturers also claim that linoleum does not emit gases, is a natural deterrent to bacteria, and resists the transfer of static electricity. Linoleum is used in many of the 12-inch square (and larger) commercial tiles you see in hospitals, stores, and other high-traffic businesses.

WOOD

Wood floor covering has been used for centuries. It comes in many types and styles and can be used in almost every part of a house.

Wood flooring is available in hardwood and softwood varieties. The hardwoods have excellent wearing qualities. The most popular species are white and red oaks. Standard hardwood flooring boards come in widths of 2¼ inches and random lengths. To achieve a more custom look, oak flooring can also be supplied in random widths with or without a distinct V-groove between the lengthwise side edges of each plank.

Softwood floors really mean pine wood planks. They come in standard and random widths and lengths. It's a lot less expensive than oak, but pine will show wear more quickly than oak. On the plus side, pine has a beautiful grain and takes staining very well.

Parquet flooring is another variety. It consists of small pieces of wood pressed and bonded together in a square tile. A parquet floor can be a thing of beauty, but it's more troublesome to take care of than plain plank flooring.

Wood flooring will not wear appreciably if its surface pores are filled in and the entire top is sanded, sealed, and periodically resealed with a protective finish of either layers of wax, varnish, shellac, lacquer, or hard polyurethane. If desired, wood stain can be applied before the polyurethane. Polyurethane is available in a matte (soft gloss) or a hard shiny finish. The choice is one of personal taste. In addition to giving wood flooring a pleasant appearance, polyurethane requires no waxing. Eventually, though, even polyurethane will have to be reapplied.

Wood floors have good grease and other stain resistance and are fairly simple to maintain.

While linoleum and carpeting must be torn out and replaced when worn, wood flooring can be resurfaced. It's the only floor that can actually improve with age and successive refinishings.

On the negative side, the periodic refinishings, with their laborious sanding, can be expensive and time-consuming. Hardwood floors can also be very noisy. You can soften up their effects by placing large area rugs in the living spaces and by hanging substantial draperies in the same room to absorb sound. And lastly, wood flooring not securely nailed will squeak when walked upon.

CORK

No, not the champagne bottle stopper, but rather, a surprisingly durable flooring or underlayment made of the replenishable bark of cork oak trees grown around the Mediterranean Sea, in North Africa, Spain and Portugal. Cork flooring has terrific sound absorption qualities, and makes for an extremely comfortable surface to walk on. When used as an underlayment beneath laminate, hardwood, and other floorings, it greatly reduces the sound transfer below and above the walking surface. Manufacturers stress that cork flooring, with appropriate finishes, is tough enough to install in living rooms, kitchens, family rooms, hallways, practically anywhere except places likely to get doused with water every so often, such as bathrooms and laundry rooms. Home hobby areas and hobby craft spaces are good candidates for cork, because users may spend a lot of time there on their feet, and can benefit from such a cushioned surface.

BAMBOO

Like cork, bamboo is a replenishable material that has recently been finding it way to flooring. Stronger than oak, bamboo is really a grass that takes only about five years to grow into canes large enough for flooring use. It sounds too good to be true, because when pressed and formed into boards, bamboo is beautiful, super-hard, durable, scratch- and gouge-resistant, and will not absorb as much moisture as hardwoods will. It's produced in a variety of horizontal- and vertical-grain models, colors, and board sizes. This flooring needs to be seen to be believed.

TILE

Tile flooring—individual square or other multisided tiles—come in a full range of colors, finishes, and sizes in two popular types: ceramic and quarry.

Ceramic tiles are generally glazed in bright, shiny colors and are used to create custom floor designs or mosaics that set or follow a room's decorating scheme. Many ceramic tiles are made in Italy and Portugal.

The term "quarry tile" is misleading. It isn't actually tile that comes from a quarry. Rather, it's made from a mixture of clay, shale, and grit that's baked at high temperatures. Quarry tiles feature muted, earthen tones that are not glazed or shiny. Their dull surfaces help create a natural look inside homes that are planned with unsurfaced or natural building materials and decor. The term "quarry" really hails from the old-fashioned word "quarrel," which means a four-sided stone.

Tile makes a floor covering that possesses a lot of character, and is often used in hard-service areas such as entrance foyers and patios, and is equally at home in bathrooms, kitchens, and sunrooms. Tile is ideal to use on floors that will be on the receiving end of passive solar heating designs. During the day the tiles will soak up heat that will, in turn, be gradually released during the evening.

Although tile is very durable and will withstand wear and tear well, it has many seams and joints that are susceptible to cracking and staining. These seams and joints should be periodically recoated with an impervious surface sealer. Aside from the grout or other joint cement, the tile itself requires little maintenance. For best results, with the exception of bathrooms, tile should be laid in cement mortar over a dropped or sunken subfloor.

Tile flooring has been around for many, many years, and lots of different types and grades of tile and substrates (material that tile is laid in or set on) exist. Some tile is selected for its resistance to water absorption. Others for slip resistance, stain resistance, or (for outdoors use) frost resistance. Final selections should be made only after consulting contractors and manufacturers with considerable tile expertise.

STONE

If you elect to specify a natural stone floor in a foyer or room, there's no doubt that such a floor will be one of a kind. There are dozens of colors and sizes of natural stones, from purple, red, and black slate, to multitoned granites, colorful quartzites, and the softer polished marbles.

Practically speaking, most stone used in today's homes is either slate or bluestone. Slate is a smooth gray, red, blue, or black sedimentary stone that splits easily and evenly into convenient slabs. Bluestone is a sandstone that can be gray, green, blue, or buff colored. Their most popular applications are foyers, hallways, kitchens, and sunrooms.

Although marble is the most luxurious stone that's widely available, it's a soft stone that tends (especially in the darker colors) to scratch easily and to absorb stains readily unless covered with a few coats of a good stone sealer. It's also slippery when wet.

What all well-cared-for stone offers is natural beauty and durability, plus ease of maintenance. The seams and joints, however, will need the same treatment as they receive with tile flooring—an impervious surface sealer.

Because natural stone is very heavy, depending on the thickness of stones selected, floor joists should be installed 12-inch on center for additional strength.

BRICK

If you're considering tile and stone, you might as well look at brick, too. It also comes in many colors, textures, and types. Brick is installed and cared for in a similar manner to tile and stone. All three can add a lot of character to select areas in your home.

CONCRETE

One more masonry flooring possibility is concrete. If you've never seen a stained and finished concrete floor, imagine that you're looking at a floor that resembles buckskin suede, or a soft blue aged Italian marble, or terra cotta in soft brown hues punctuated with bits of rust.

Circular saws can be used to cut the concrete surface to give to effect of tile or cut stone flooring. Stained concrete can be used indoors and outdoors. More and more independent contractors are learning how to stain, etch, and seal thin and thick concrete slabs, which results in competitive pricing. In addition, matching concrete furniture and countertops can be cast and finished—on site—to give a home a one-of-a-kind decorative look.

FLOORING INSTALLATION CARE

- The contractor should wait until the latter stages of construction before the home's flooring is installed—to prevent excessive wear and tear.

- No matter which floorings you select, make sure that when heavy appliances are delivered, the flooring is protected by a thin sheet of plywood or similar material.

- Remind the contractor that no smoking is allowed. Brand new floors can be badly marred by burn marks from dropped cigarettes or cigars.

- Make a point to look closely at the flooring before releasing the contractor's final payment.

POINTS TO PONDER

1. Don't skimp on the padding when it comes to carpet. A thick, resilient padding makes a carpet feel much plusher than it would with a marginal, thin pad. Even though you can't see it, padding contributes greatly to lengthening a carpet's useful life by absorbing much of the footfall pressure that would otherwise grind the carpet backing against the hard, raspy surface of the floor decking.

2. Through selective choice of colors and shades, carpeting can create desired "moods" or "feelings" in rooms. It can be used to liven up a simple floor plan, or tone down a starkly modern room or dwelling. It can make a room or area look smaller or larger. It can help separate one part of a room from another part.

3. Consider the type of use a carpet will receive before selecting carpeting type, style, and color. Review your needs with several trusted carpeting distributors for suggestions and information on the latest offerings.

4. Become acquainted with the benefits available from laminate flooring. If planning tile, stone, brick, or hardwood flooring, investigate those looks in laminates, then compare cost, care, and warranties.

5. Vinyl and linoleum floorings offer great appearance and wear, at relatively low cost. Some so closely resemble stone, brick, or wood that you can hardly tell the difference. Slip-resistant finishes are available for entrance foyers, kitchens, bathrooms, or wherever flooring is likely to get wet. The better grades of these floorings are virtually maintenance-free.

6. Major advancements have been made to all sorts of wood flooring products, coatings, and maintenance aids. Wood, when properly installed and cared for, has excellent wear qualities, but so do alternative flooring products such as cork and bamboo.

7. Selective use of tile flooring (sometimes with matching or contrasting wall tile) can add beautiful utilitarian, one-of-a-kind

floors to a home. The array of ceramic and quarry tile available is mind boggling. Tile is also very durable.

8. Proper installation of tile flooring is critical to the long-term life of the tile. Although the tile itself is rarely a problem, the grout or joint cement can crack or loosen. The stability of the base or underlayment the tiles rest on is also important. Make sure the installing contractors are experienced or specialize in laying tile.

9. Stone makes attractive, unique floors. Stones are also heavy and hard and need professional installation techniques in addition to extra sturdy floor framing to support the weight. Brick is installed and cared for in a manner similar to that of stone and tile. Keep an open mind when it comes to the unique, cost-effective looks of stained and sealed concrete.

10. Try to consider your entire flooring picture at the same time, instead of going from room to room. Too many different types, styles, and colors of flooring materials can result in a busy look that you may quickly tire of. Real estate brokers and flooring distributors can advise you on decorating traps to avoid.

Home Offices and Work Spaces

Anyone paying attention to today's demographics, social structures, and modern career paths will acknowledge that the days of family breadwinners starting out and finishing their careers with the same company have changed. As large corporations continue to redefine their own identities, and technological advances have powerful influences over manufacturing techniques and products, more people are finding themselves working out of their own homes or work locations.

Magazines for entrepreneurs are flourishing. The large "office" superstores are selling business supplies not just to small, medium, and large companies, but to millions of small business owners who are working a "regular" job during the day, then operating a janitorial service at night, or servicing furnaces on weekends, or buying and fixing up small income properties. Many individuals, realizing how tenuous their "regular" jobs are—and wishing to expand a part-time avocation into a full-time career, carve out some space for themselves in a loft above the garage, a corner of the basement, a spare bedroom, or a study—even a small desk in the kitchen.

In truth, a home office can be many things. It can occupy a corner of the dining room or be housed in the basement, a converted garage, a spare bedroom, even an attic. The nature of the business is what typically dictates how large or elaborate the office may be. Ask yourself questions. Will you be working alone, or will you eventually need employees? Do you need space for a showcase for your product or service? If customers or clients need to access the office, then it probably should be located and configured to give a favorable, professional appearance.

Do you have special tools or supplies that require considerable storage or must be kept away from curious children? What about the electrical requirements? Computers, faxes, copy machines, printers, and modems all need to be plugged in somewhere. Consider dedicated circuits and surge protectors for your office equipment—so other household appliances such as washing machines, refrigerators, coffee pots, and the like won't create internal power drains and surges that could affect electronic equipment or the information stored within. The surge protectors will also supply some margin of safety from power surges that come from outside the home, too. Storms or power blackouts can affect the way electricity is transmitted to your system. These changes or spikes in voltage can cause major damages.

Other considerations include lighting requirements—certainly, a productive office needs more light than that found in typical bedrooms or spare rooms. Ventilation, air-conditioning, and efficient heating are also critical to the comfort and well-being of office occupants. Sound insulation is necessary in households with active family members.

OFFICE SPACE PLANNING

1. List your office needs, such as equipment, supplies, and furniture. Will you need a mail room or setup? Video equipment? An exercise area or room for a hobby? What's important? It need not look like a traditional corporate office to be effective. If fact, it should be planned to enable you to carry out your activities in the easiest ways possible. How will you be spending your time there? Put some thought into this, so you can make those major activities your main planning focus. Will you be in front of a computer a good portion of the time? Do you need a lot of flat, clear space? Is there a ton of paperwork to keep track of? Do volumes and volumes of reference books need to be kept handy?

   A few pointers include the following:

- Consider setting up away from the busiest areas of the home. This means away from the kitchen, front door, family traffic.
- The office should be in a bright, well-ventilated area of the home. Although many offices are constructed in basements, that may not be your best option.
- Resist the urge to aim your desk and chair at the door or entrance of the room. Too many distractions.
- Remove nonessentials from the office. Put seldom-accessed items elsewhere.
- Keep essentials at or within reach of your desk. Especially small office supplies.
- Realize that a home office does not have to be a separate room. It can be part of a room, as long as there's permanent work space.

2. Sketch a plan, to scale. Putting your ideas to paper (or computer monitor) will help you visualize the setup. Don't fall into the trap of winging the purchase of desk and file cabinets and other storage components without knowing how everything will work together. People sometimes purchase items that are too large for their spaces, and the office room becomes too cramped for them to work comfortably.

3. Figure the amount of storage you'll need. There are two kinds of storage requirements—for items you'll need at hand, and materials that don't need to be close by. Try to arrange storage for "farther away" items somewhere else—out of your office, to reduce congestion. But usually, additional storage capacity will be greatly appreciated. Desk space can quickly be taken up with computers, keyboards, printers, faxes, and other bulky items. Make sure you have some space to spread out working papers, books, and magazines you might need at the time.

4. Lighting can make or break an office. Certainly, bad lighting will have an adverse effect on both a person's mood and behavior, while good, even lighting improves them plus productivity while contributing to a sense of well-being. Track lighting is an excellent choice. It can be installed on walls or ceiling, saving desk and table space for other uses. Dimmer switches are nice, too.

5. The decor of the room also helps create the right atmosphere for working. Even if you're the only one seeing it, it still matters. Certainly, if customers, clients, or visitors will be visiting your office, consider that you are trying to build a business, and you want to be taken seriously. The image you project through your office makes an important contribution to your efforts. Let your work environment show that you are serious and organized about the tasks at hand.

6. Noise control is important. Deaden the noise levels by installing the thickest, heaviest carpeting (with a thick pad) you can find. It doesn't have to be expensive—just substantial. You can also sound-insulate the walls, hang heavy drapes—cover those hard, echoing surfaces with sound-absorbing materials. Also, work spaces, when situated in the home, should have some sort of healthy take—allowing occasional mental and physical breaks.

We suggest you combine, whenever possible, your office space with a "health" space in which you locate the following:

Your business resources:

1. A personal computer with modem and Internet access.
2. A fax machine.
3. A printer.
4. A copy machine.
5. A double-line phone.
6. A file cabinet.
7. A reasonably nice desk, large enough to accommodate what you need, with at least two pullout leaves for writing on or temporarily keeping resource materials at hand. Because most desks become so cluttered with permanently positioned computer equipment and stacks of papers and files, there's little room for anything else.
8. A comfortable desk chair, and at least one other "side" or visitor chair.
9. Some 3-ringed binders.
10. A stapler.

11. A hole punch.
12. Some highlighting markers.
13. A pair of scissors.
14. A ruler.
15. Yellow lined 8½-by-11-inch pads.
16. A wall calendar.
17. A daily planner book.
18. Transparent tape.
19. Stationery and stamps.
20. Data required for the business/pursuits.
21. A telephone/answering machine.
22. Bookcases or shelves.
23. Wastebasket.

Your health resources:

1. An exercise pad.
2. One or several basic exercise machines, such as a step machine, stationary bicycle, treadmill, or combination home gym/exercise station.
3. A VCR/television.
4. A CD player/cassette player/radio/stereo AM-FM receiver.
5. A body weight scale.

Other design considerations

1. Situate office areas close to the kitchen or laundry so other work can be done between office tasks, and vice versa. If you have or are planning to have children—the ages of 13 and under—figure on locating the office away from the main kitchen/living spaces to avoid commotion.
2. Have a portable phone for greater mobility.
3. Have extra electrical outlets installed.
4. Prewire for coaxial and computer cable terminals, so you can enjoy the benefits of a small home network, and can perform the same computer work tasks from multiple locations.
5. Instead of built-ins, opt for furniture settings that can be simply relocated if your room needs a change—even temporarily.

SPECIAL PURPOSE ROOMS

The conventional office is not the only type of work-related space needed. Some individuals have hobbies they desire to turn into second incomes or eventually full-time careers. In those cases, special design components can be planned into a spare bedroom, a garage, a basement or attic.

For example, consider how a photography darkroom could be designed into any of those spaces. Or a sewing room, complete with natural and artificial lighting, plus space for cutting, fitting, pressing, and storing fabrics and completed items. As more of the baby boomers retire, they are looking for second or third careers involving activities such as painting, sculpture, and various crafts. For the artist it might mean a quiet, well-lit, ventilated attic loft.

Maybe it's a room used for appreciating music or films, or an indoors greenhouse. A cellar space for wine making, a second kitchen for recipe testing, canning, and cookbook writing, a room for showing collectibles, or even a padded room for coaching youngsters wrestling—are more examples of planning space for special activities. Consider that an extra bedroom may, with a little pre-planning, function as a special-purpose room for as many years as you wish—before being converted back into a bedroom when the house needs another conventional sleeping room, or must be sold. Other special purpose areas can likewise be deconstructed into plain attic, basement, or garage spaces if and when necessary.

▶▶▶▶▶ POINTS TO PONDER

1. It doesn't cost much extra to run plenty of communications lines and outlets to rooms you may eventually turn into offices, such as third or fourth bedrooms. It's a lot simpler to hide the wiring in the walls while the place is under construction, instead of drilling and fishing wires at a later date.
2. Although certain rooms can double as family rooms and offices simultaneously, consider that the IRS has strict rules for what an "office" is and may not allow deductions for a multipurpose space. Check with a tax consultant or attorney.

3. See that computers, fax machines, printers, and similar electronic components have electrical surge protection.

4. Try to store seldom-used materials in a place other than the office. Individuals are typically far more productive if they work in clean, uncluttered surroundings.

5. One drawback to many computer hutches, desks, and combination office units is that they lack clear desk space. Sure, there are all kinds of nooks, shelves, and drawers, and a pullout keyboard drawer. But there's hardly enough room to place an open reference book, or even enough desk space to make out checks to pay bills. Plan open desk space for any office, and you'll be glad you did.

6. Plan as much window space as possible for an office—with appropriate window treatments.

7. Make sure the flooring matches the work or activities. For instance, artists may favor wood or vinyl that resists paint, glue, and ink spills.

8. Plan noise control for an office.

9. Set up a television/video player, for business and relaxation uses.

10. Combine some sort of exercise equipment or small exercise area in the office (if it's not overwhelming, it won't encroach on the overall office use).

Where to Build It

Where you decide to live is largely a combination of personal and practical choice. City, suburbia, and country all have their good points and bad. Plus, within each of those areas you'll find potential building sites that should each be evaluated according to the lay of the land in relation to the sun's orientation, the prevailing winds, and the natural or engineered features of the surrounding territory.

City, Suburbia, or Country?

Wtih some people it's like asking them if they prefer blondes, brunettes, or redheads. A person attached to a particular blonde might imagine that a brunette would be better. Or a redhead. Others are satisfied with the partner they've got, and never even think of approaching another. It's the same idea with city, suburbia, and country building sites.

Some city dwellers, it seems, have always longed to move to the country, or at least to a wide-open suburb where they can stretch out from the small, crowded lot they've grown up on. Other city residents shudder at the very thought of such isolation and opt to remain where they are. The determination boils down to a combination of work and social activities, practical and financial aspects, and personal preference. A country dweller can long to shed the drafty old farmhouse and 40 acres for a tiny ranch full of modern conveniences on an easy-to-maintain 60- by 120-foot lot. Or maybe not.

THE CITY

Before nations came into existence, there were cities. Living in cities is nothing new. At first they were places where primitive men and women congregated for convenience's sake—places they could farm at, or gather from. During medieval times, the cities had walls around them to provide protection for the inhabitants. Then cities developed into much more sophisticated settlements, and before long, the city existed as a central unifying influence on large groups of people.

Cities and towns are still the most important gathering places for people. The term for city in Latin is "civitas," from which the English words "citizen" and "civilization" derive. In cities, we manufacture, receive, and provide goods and services. We do research, teach, and learn. We encounter slums and crime and corruption. We wrestle with inadequate public services and enjoy the efficiently run ones.

A city is really a community in which everything is drawn together in hopes of creating a desirable way of life for its inhabitants. In a city, you have—or should have—rapid and inexpensive transit systems, effective law enforcement, proper disposal of sewage and garbage, fire protection, provisions for good housing, jobs for the people, education for children and adults, plenty of libraries and museums, theaters, and places for concerts, plays, and public events. There should be recreational sport facilities, adequate care for the sick and poor, and a government that's not overly corrupt.

We avoid isolation in cities, we take in a full range of enriching cultural activities, and we enter a vibrant nightlife. To some extent, it's a "fast" existence, where the action is and where the greatest number of opportunities in the business world are. It's where big-time radio and television stations are based and where major newspapers and other publications keep track of society's pulse.

All of this highlights the main advantage of city life—convenience. Everything is close, including schools, churches, medical services, supermarkets, restaurants, and corner bars. Plus, within a city it's even possible to find a location that *seems* like a piece of country—an isolated lot bordered by rows of mature pines, for instance.

Why then do people move out of cities, or elect to build elsewhere? One reason is because city land, with its high real estate taxes, is scarce and expensive, especially in major metropolitan areas. Another reason is that cities tend to have physical atmospheres more polluted by vehicle exhaust and industrial emissions than other locations do. Some say cities are too fast-paced, and too noisy. Other people shy away from city life because of high crime rates. Some make a deliberate choice to live somewhere else to be near people who are closer to their own social status or income level.

Cities have changed substantially since pre-World War II days when the rich, the poor, and the developing middle class all lived relatively close together in the same or adjacent neighborhoods. Back then there was a sense of social strength in cities that has been largely lost since the masses of middle and upper classes migrated to suburbia.

SUBURBIA

Suburbia is a relatively recent phenomenon that has been studied from every angle by planners, sociologists, and psychologists. In fact, entire books have been written about the suburbanite and his or her environment.

It's true that suburbs were created by a wide variety of technological advances. Automobiles, delivery trucks, rapid transit systems, miles and miles of concrete and asphalt paving, plus sundry inventions such as septic tanks, sewer mains, telephone lines, and miscellaneous energy delivery systems have all contributed toward the establishment of satellite neighborhoods located "so many minutes or hours away" from the nearest city.

And what's more, suburbanites have developed certain characteristics that tend to bind them together, and particular habits that distinguish them from city and country dwellers. The main difference is their mobility: suburbanites are primarily commuters who tend to own their homes in areas that are on or near open spaces, away from crowded urban locations.

When you think of suburbia, you're likely to think of large yards, modern houses, swimming pools, two-car garages, incoming and outgoing transferred executives, couples jogging along the streets in color-coordinated jogging outfits, and long drives to work.

On the surface, suburbs sound like fine, clean places to live, and many of them are. On the other hand, quite a few suburbs consist of subdivisions having residents of roughly the same age group, social strata, and even income level. At one time, neighborhoods were differentiated from each other by race or national origin, and within those neighborhoods you had a healthy cross section of the classes—from rich to poor. Suburbia changed all that. Suburbanites have demanded zoning controls that now completely rule the modern economics of suburban land development and make it impossible for the less affluent to join them. Whenever such middle- to upper-class members of the same age group and income level band together, the healthy diversity found in a neighborhood of large and small houses, young and old residents, and rich and poor families cannot flourish.

In some ways, contemporary subdivisions lack the kind of all-aroundness that's characteristic of older communities, and in doing so perhaps sacrifice the good of the overall community in order to guarantee that the subdivision itself consists of essentially the same type of occupants, all with similar ages, incomes, and interests.

In subdivisions in the suburbs you're likely to have people more interested in maintaining their own property values, at times through political and zoning maneuvers, than being overly concerned about problems of the entire community or the success of community-wide programs developed for charitable causes, cultural enrichment, or the public good. While the older communities could be described as possessing a beneficial diversity within an overall unity, modern subdivisions are much more homogenous and self-centered. Ironically, all of this tends to reflect on the bottom line of suburban housing values in a positive way. Well-planned subdivisions have been a financial boon for the homeowners who live in them. They have been and continue to be places where housing appreciates considerably, unlike the many changing neighborhoods that feature nothing but housing units that are steadily depreciating and losing their owners' life savings at the same time.

Suburbia has also been called "instant living environments," so named after the people who simultaneously move into a newly developed area. When this happens, the area has no tradition to rely upon, no familiar patterns of living for the residents to follow.

Now that the drawbacks of many suburban subdivisions have been touched upon, it's still safe to say that many *other* suburban subdivisions are exceptionally well-rounded places to live, and don't fit into the sociologist's definition of suburbia. It's just another case of many exceptions to a rule.

THE COUNTRY

Country living means many things to many people. To some it means wide-open acreage. It means fields and forests, ponds, meandering streams, corn and wheat and alfalfa, odors of sweet-smelling hay and manure, red barns sporting advertisements for chewing tobacco, snakelike tar and chip roads, dug or drilled water wells, spectacular thunderstorms and full moons, tractors, farm machinery and animals, plenty of fair-weather weekend visitors (especially when vegetable and fruit crops mature), and long drives to practically anywhere—to shopping, to school, to church, to work, to visit relatives. It means children do not have many playmates nearby. Although there's peace and quiet most of the time, there are also hunters in the fall and winter, and maybe in parts of spring and summer as well.

To others, the country offers little but boredom. Some people feel comfortable cohabiting with nature, while others need the fast pace of city life. To novice country dwellers, weeding a garden or feeding a flock of chickens can quickly become tiresome, and routine chores inevitably lose the novelty they at first possessed.

In the country, people generally have time to think, to contemplate. They're likely to have more leisure hours than they would elsewhere, because for some reason, country people tend to get up earlier, despite going to bed with a healthy kind of tiredness.

There's freedom in the country for pets to run loose, and there are plenty of birds and other wildlife for naturalists to feed, study, and even manage. There's room to blast a stereo without aggravating neighbors, and there are places to ride horses and to gather wild mushrooms and blackberries.

AREA CHECKLISTS

City living

- Benefits of community life
- Feelings of security from living close to neighbors
- Fast-moving environment

- A center of media attention
- Nightlife and entertainment
- Less feelings of isolation
- It's where the jobs are
- Provisions for all types of housing
- Heterogeneous neighborhoods
- Good fire protection
- Good police protection
- Hospitals nearby
- Close to schools and churches
- Close to shopping
- Convenient utilities and public services
- Rapid and inexpensive transit systems
- Libraries and museums
- Noisy environments
- Slums and crime
- Polluted air
- Pockets of declining property values
- Occupants range from very poor to very rich, all ages and income levels
- Children will have friends to play with

Suburban living

- Security of neighbors with less crowding
- A quieter place than a city
- Stable and appreciating property values
- Less crime and fewer slums
- Cleaner air
- More privacy

- Larger lots

- Modern houses similar in size and types

- Open playgrounds and parks

- Modern utility systems

- Mostly middle-class and upper-class occupants of similar age and income level

- High property taxes

- A preoccupation with houses and household items

- Not much nightlife nearby nor cultural activities

- Farther away from jobs, shopping, medical services, fire and police protection

- Friends for children to play with

Country living

- Lots of isolation and quiet

- Good for pets and communing with nature

- Good for farming and raising gardens

- Good for thinking and contemplating

- Low real estate taxes

- Clean air

- Outdoors activities: hiking, horseback riding, hunting, fishing, gathering berries

- Not much crime

- Opportunities to study and manage wildlife and land

- Freedom from prying eyes of neighbors

- More time required for grounds maintenance chores

- More equipment needed for grounds maintenance

- Long drives to practically anything: school, church, libraries, hospitals, shopping, recreation, and work

- Private water and septic systems
- Lack of stringent zoning regulations
- Not many children nearby for youngsters to play with
- Possibility of unwanted lengthy visits (often unannounced) from friends and relatives

>>>>>> POINTS TO PONDER

1. Before making a "radical" or major lifestyle change such as moving from city to country, or country to city, or even to or from suburbia, research the change thoroughly. Determine home location features most important to your lifestyle and pocketbook before choosing a rural, suburban, or urban site.

2. City living can mean very close neighbors; friends for children to play with; good transportation systems; convenience to shopping and services; heterogenous populations; good police, fire, and emergency response capabilities; nightlife and entertainment; and educational and career opportunities.

3. Because so many people have been moving out of cities during the previous few decades, there are some real bargains—and often direct financial incentives such as real estate tax exemptions, home energy grants, and low-cost loans—for individuals building new homes within city limits.

4. City living can also mean traffic, pollution, slums, high crime levels, noisy environments, declining property values, and small, cramped building lots.

5. Suburban living can mean not-too-far-away neighbors, some public transportation, mostly middle- and upper-class occupants of similar age and income levels, open parks and playgrounds, and nearby friends for children.

6. Suburban living can also mean a lack of nightlife or cultural activity; high property taxes; distance from jobs, shopping, medical services, fire, police, and emergency response; and a preoccupation with homes and household items.

7. Country or rural living can mean lots of isolation and quiet; a haven for nature, pets, and gardening; low real estate taxes; clean air; privacy; and outdoor activities.

8. If you're considering a move to the country, and you're still skeptical about being isolated in your new surroundings, see if anyone else is interested in building at the same time (a close friend or relative), then research the possibility of subdividing a larger parcel into two neighboring sites—each of which can be built upon.

9. Country or rural living can also mean septic tanks; water wells; feelings of isolation and loneliness; long drives to almost every sort of need, including shopping, services, medical facilities, schools, and jobs; more time required for grounds maintenance chores; and not many friends for children to play with.

10. If you insist on making a major lifestyle/home change and build a dwelling someplace where it eventually does not work out for your family, you can always sell it and move. But that possibility is another reason that, when planning your new home, it pays to preview your building ideas with a real estate broker who one day may have to put the place on the open market. He or she will tell you why to include that third or fourth bedroom, that extra-large garage, that bathroom in the basement, or fireplace in the family room, so the home will be easier to sell if need be.

Selecting a Building Site

If you know the general kind of area you want to live in—country, suburbia, or city—then you've already made several of the most important decisions along the way toward selecting a suitable building site. Now it's time to narrow things down further. A number of considerations should weigh heavily in your search for the best individual site available for your house.

ZONING

Zoning is one of the most elementary considerations to be made when viewing a potential homesite. Local zoning codes are ordinances that divide all the property in a city, town, or county into a number of land-use classifications such as single-family residential, multifamily residential, agricultural, business, commercial, and industrial. In other words, zoning codes state what can and can't be done with all the property within the code's boundaries.

How would you like to invest your life savings into a dream house only to have neighbors move a trailer in across the street, start raising chickens and minks out back, erect big "Eggs for Sale" signs along the road, plus have their four sons run a small engine repair shop in summer and hold snowmobile races during winter? Zoning helps prevent unhealthy mixes of properties and owners having conflicting interests.

Of course, you can take a chance that even though the property across the street is zoned to permit a trailer park, Old Man Peters has owned the land for years, and he'll probably never move. Suppose when he dies, his daughter sells out to someone who would leap at the chance of putting in a 200-unit mobile home park.

One way to guarantee that nearby land won't be used for something that bothers you is to purchase enough of it behind, in front, and to the side of your location. That can be costly, however, and there probably won't be that much property available anyway. Even if you do protect your location, you can't be sure that a few hundred yards down the road—if it's a wide-open zoned area—a trailer court won't still be started up. Those are the chances you take when settling in a loosely regulated location.

When considering such a site, you can, of course, use your best judgment and the opinions of real estate professionals. For instance, if nice houses—the kind you're planning—already dominate such a loosely zoned area, chances are they'll have a positive, inflationary effect on the remaining parcels, and consequently only nice houses will likely be added to the area because that's the highest and most practical use for the land.

Pay particular attention when considering property that's on the borderline of a residential area, or is zoned "transitional." Transitional areas are often dominated by residential dwellings, but they permit some business or commercial uses as well. It's a simple task to check any property by consulting the latest version of the zoning code. Just call the applicable city, town, or county zoning officer. By reviewing a zoning map, the zoning officer can tell what classification the parcel falls under, and the classifications of the surrounding properties.

THE NEIGHBORHOOD

Ask any realtor what the three most important components of real estate value are and he or she will likely counter with "Location, location, location." In a very real sense, the location of a house can set the dollar range of its market value, both the minimum and maximum. This means that you should seek a neighborhood that lends itself to the kind of house you are planning if you want to ensure the highest possible market value for your home. To attain this maximum value and resale potential, your house should not be the largest and most expensive dwelling on the block. If it is, you will be doing your neighbors a good deed, and yourself a disservice. Your house will tend to buoy up the resale value of the less-expensive dwellings that surround it, while those less-expensive, smaller houses will pull the market value of your house down closer to their levels.

On the other hand, if you're willing to totally ignore the ideas of market value and resale potential—say you're planning to live in the house forever, and your children and theirs will one day take it over—and if you genuinely like the neighborhood and know it's not in a declining area, it could be a different story. In that case, by "over building," by matching a larger-than-average, more expensive house to a lot in a less expensive area, you could probably obtain a relatively low-cost building site compared with other lots where larger, more-expensive houses are being built. Also, if you'll consider lots with odd locations, near busy streets, perhaps even next to a ramshackle Tobacco-Road house that sticks out in the neighborhood like a sore thumb and looks ready to fall over in the slightest breeze, you're likely to find bargain building sites.

Regarding the Tobacco-Road house (and there are many of them out there), you *hope* that it falls to the ground because as soon as it does, the value of your house and lot would immediately skyrocket, especially if something nice is erected in the old shack's place.

The location of the entire neighborhood in relation to modern necessities and conveniences is also important. You'll have to carefully consider the pros and cons. An advantage to a newly married couple might be to be very close to grade schools. To a couple not planning to have children, or having children long grown up and gone, that same point could well be a disadvantage.

Is the neighborhood reached by a hilly road that will be difficult to negotiate in winter? Is the potential site far west of town, while your workplace is to the east? If so, remember that you'll not only have to drive twice through the entire city everyday, but you'll have to head into the blinding sun each morning—and then into it again at the end of each day on the return trip. Will you be close to a favorite golf course, tennis club, library, or other high-frequency activity location? Will you be uncomfortably far away from good friends and relatives you like to visit frequently?

Is the location in a high-crime area? Be careful when new to an entire city or area. A brief phone call to a local law enforcement agency will be to your advantage. Realtors can be helpful, too, for revealing neighborhood information and for estimating resale potential.

LOT CONFIGURATION

While shopping for a building site, keep in mind the type of house you're planning. As discussed in chapter 2, building sites with certain configurations naturally lend themselves to specific house types and are impractical for others. Of course, in some situations you can alter the lot contours to suit your house, but usually at substantial cost. In many cases, due to the lay of the land, it's not possible to successfully change the site's topography.

In a nutshell, here again are the matches and mismatches between lots and house types:

- Single-story ranches are ideally suited to flat building sites, or lots that slope gently to the sides or rear, particularly if the plans call for a walkout from a basement or lower living area.

- One-and-one-half-stories are best matched with relatively flat lots or sites sloping slightly to the rear.

- Two-stories can be efficiently situated on small, flat lots, and sites having slight grades.

- Split-foyers are good on sites with front-to-back or back-to-front medium to steep slopes. They're totally incompatible with flat lots.

- Multilevels are ideally suited to side-sloping lots on hilly terrain where the bottom level of the house faces and opens toward the downhill side and the upstairs level opens toward the uphill side. A flat lot won't work for a multilevel.

LOT SIZE

You begin to establish your building site's order of magnitude when selecting either country property (large building site), suburbia (medium building site), or city (relatively small lot), and then you further limit the possibilities by choosing one or several neighborhoods or areas to make your decision from. Finally, it's a combination of what's available, what's suitable, what's affordable, and your personal preference.

Do you like to garden or grow fruit trees? Will you be putting in elaborate swing sets and play areas for children? What about an in- or above-ground swimming pool? Will you be doing a lot of outdoor entertaining, with parties and picnics? Do you prefer to maintain your own landscaping in a big way? Or you could hate the idea of cutting grass and tending bushes, shrubs, and trees. You might want the privacy afforded by a large lot, or you might be nervous not having a neighbor within calling distance. Maybe you don't want to be bothered with a long driveway that has to be shoveled or plowed during winter. Or you might want to be set back from the road to distance yourself from traffic noise.

Some people like to spread out on a roomy parcel, or acreage. Others who spend most of their time away from the house on work or recreational activities might find a large lot superfluous and a bother to maintain. A larger lot can also mean higher real estate taxes.

HOUSE ORIENTATION

The orientation or positioning of your house on any particular lot depends on how the lot is situated along the street, what the topography of the lot and surrounding land is, which direction it faces (north, south, east, or west), local building property line setbacks and regulations, and the house's floor plan.

When a choice of lots exists, orientation potential can become a major factor in the decision of which site to purchase. Window selection and positioning are closely related to orientation theories.

Remember too that a well-planned house can be constructed with any orientation, as long as the dwelling fits the lot. It might mean you will want to use more or less glass than you would have otherwise, or you'll beef up the insulation, or plan extra-wide overhangs. You must weigh the pros and cons of each particular site to come up with the best orientation possible.

Your plans for such a house positioning should address which rooms you want to receive maximum exposure to the sun, and protection from the cold winter winds and driving rains. In some cases, it might be bet-ter to use the mirror copy of your original plans. By flip-flopping the floor plan in certain situations, you can place the garage on the side of the house that shields the living areas from winter storms and subzero chill factors.

SPECIAL LOCATIONS

Some people dream of living on a scenic ocean or lake bluff, or out on their own island in a picturesque bay. Trouble is, once they try such locations they might not like them. The weather can be brutal, house maintenance frequent, and even the views—intense as they are—can become tiresome. Be careful of locations frequented by sightseers, sports enthusiasts, photography buffs, or any special-interest groups. Houses close to steep cliffs or ridges can be hazardous to children. Be aware of long-distance travel time required to reach many special out-of-the-way locations.

BUYING THE LOT

If the zoning is correct, the lot configuration fits your house plan, the orientation is satisfactory, the area meets all your personal qualifica-tions, plus you like the site more than anything else you've seen, then go ahead and buy it. But when you do, take care of the following points:

1. Get a clear title. If you're purchasing the house with a mortgage, the lending institution will require you to have the property's deed searched. An attorney (or someone representing an attor-ney or title company) will go to the county clerk's office and look through the records, checking for any possible claims, liens, judgments, or clouds on the deed that would prevent you from receiving a free and clear title. You should have the records searched even if you pay cash for the property, and there's no mortgage involved, to protect your own interests. Attorneys, or title guarantee companies that perform the same services, are insured in the unlikely event that they make a mistake.

2. If necessary, obtain a septic permit. The ability to secure a septic permit if there is no public or private sanitary system is a must.

The site will be worthless if you can't have a septic system on it. If there's any doubt at all, you should specify in the property's purchase agreement that the transaction be contingent upon the ability to obtain a permit for the type of septic system that you want—perhaps a below-ground system instead of a more expensive and unwieldy above-ground "mound" arrangement.

A percolation test will be made when you apply for a permit. It determines how fast sewage liquids can seep into the ground. If the soil is primarily clay, a septic system might not be approved for below ground because the sewage liquids will not readily pass through the impermeable clay for proper disposal. Even when building on a large site, the size of which (10 acres, for example) exempts you from the necessity of securing a septic permit, you should still test the soil permeability to determine which type of septic system will be the most efficient and safest for you.

3. If needed, procure a water well. If no public or private water supply systems are available, you'll need to provide your own well. If there's any doubt about the prospect of digging or drilling an adequate well, you can include such a contingency in the property's purchase agreement. The well should provide good, drinkable water, in quantities (expressed in gallons per minute) that satisfy local and Federal Housing Administration standards. The well must be dug or drilled a safe distance away from any septic system leaching field.

4. Find out about any subdivision restrictions. If you select a building site in a new or established subdivision, make sure you find out if any building restrictions are in effect. Building restrictions are rules of a subdivision governing various construction and maintenance aspects to make certain that the houses in the subdivision will all be of relatively equal size, condition, and value. They regulate such things as how soon construction must begin and be completed after the lot's deed is transferred to the buyer, how the dwellings must be positioned on each site, what can be stored on the properties and what can't, how the yards must be maintained, and what will happen if those rules and others are disregarded.

In essence, building restrictions are designed to protect the integrity and value of each individual dwelling in a subdivision by prohibiting any house's improper or unusual construction or lack of maintenance that could have derogatory effects on the rest. The theory is, with strict building restrictions you won't end up with Tobacco-Road type houses ruining the neighborhood.

What follows are sample subdivision restrictions that are representative (written in the same kind of jargon) of what you'll find in thousands of similar sets of restrictions throughout the country. They address most of the major concerns you'll encounter anywhere. Keep in mind, though, that each set of subdivision restrictions is slightly different, custom-tailored by the people who began and later live in the subdivision in question.

Declaration of Restrictions for Oakland Hills Subdivision

(A plat of which is recorded in Smith County Map Book 8, page 21)

The following restrictions on property in subdivision to be known as Oakland Hills Subdivision, which is a part of Index No. 202-490-23, located in Crosscreek Township, Smith County, Pennsylvania, and part of Index 7344-700 and 7346-700, located in the City of Dalemont, Pennsylvania, shall govern all lots in said subdivision and they are covenants running with the land and binding upon all owners and their grantees, heirs, legal representatives, successors, and assigns:

1. The property shall be used for private residence purposes only and shall be used only for single one-family residences, together with customary garage with space for not less than two or more than three cars, for sole use of owner or occupant of lot upon which said building is located.

2. No buildings shall be erected nearer to the front line nor nearer to the side street line than the building setback lines of 30 feet shown on the recorded plot, except that where topographical features make it desirable an attached garage on Lots 22 through 37 may, with the approval of the designated Architectural Consultants designated by Realto Corporation, be located no closer than 20 feet from the front property line.

3. Homes built on lots fronting on Ash Street shall have at least the following areas: one-story—shall have at least 2,000 square feet; one and one-half-story—shall have at least 2,000 square feet at ground

level and at least 700 square feet upstairs; two-story—shall have at least 2000 square feet at ground level and at least 1,200 square feet upstairs; split-level—shall have at least 2,000 square feet at ground level and at least 600 square feet total on other levels. Homes built on lots fronting on Douglas Street shall have at least the following areas: one-story—shall have at least 1,800 square feet; one and one-half-story—shall have at least 1,800 square feet at ground level and at least 600 square feet upstairs; two-story—shall have at least 1,800 square feet at ground level and at least 1,000 square feet upstairs; split-level—shall have at least 1,800 square feet at ground level and at least 500 square feet total on other levels.

4. No building, wall, fence, hedge, or other structure shall be erected or maintained unless plans including all floor plans, elevation, plot plan showing proposed grading, location of buildings, fences, hedges, lampposts, outdoor fireplaces or major planting, such plans and elevations to show clearly the design, height, materials, color scheme, shall be submitted to, and approved by the Consulting Architectural Firm designated, at the time of lot purchase, by Realto Corporation. The fee for this consulting service, established at the time of purchase, shall be paid by the Purchaser.

5. No weeds, underbrush, or other unsightly growth shall be permitted to grow or remain anywhere upon this property nor upon adjoining right of way between property and street. Until property is actually occupied through construction of a building, permission is given to Realto Corporation to mow the grass and remove the weeds or unsightly growth.

6. Property is subject to an annual charge or assessment of 60¢ per front foot adjusted annually to reflect cost-of-living change, to be paid by the owner of the property into a fund administered by Realto Corporation, its successors or assigns, such charges or assessments to be applied toward payment of the cost of maintaining right-of-ways, planting, or beautifying and caring for parks, plots, and other open spaces owned by the Corporation and maintained for the general use of owners of the property, caring for vacant and improved lots, removing grass and weeds therefrom and other things necessary or desirable to keep the property neat and in good order.

7. No billboards or advertising signs of any character whatever shall be erected, placed, permitted, or maintained on such property. This shall not be construed, however, to prevent Realto Corporation from

maintaining upon the property, at such locations as it may choose, billboards, signs, or sales office on an unsold lot during the initial sale of lots, nor from maintaining attractive signs of moderate size at the entrances to the subdivision identifying it.

8. Any building started on any lot in the subdivision shall be completed within six months.

9. The keeping of any animals or poultry other than ordinary domestic pet animals is prohibited.

10. A house and garage shall be commenced on a lot within one year after the delivery of the Deed to the lot. If the purchaser shall fail to construct the house and garage within this time, Realto Corporation shall have the option of extending the period for construction for six months *or* repurchasing the lot at the same price it was sold to the purchaser, and the purchaser shall give a good and merchantable deed free and clear of all encumbrances to Realto Corporation or its nominee. Resale of the lot by the purchaser shall not change the requirements for construction expressed herein in any way, and such resale must be made subject to the initial or optionally extended date.

11. Areas designated as Private Parks in the subdivision plan are the property of Realto Corporation, and use of such park areas by the residents of Oakland Hills or its extension is a privilege extended by the corporation, subject to its reasonable and proper regulations to maintain the character of the subdivision, and subject to withdrawal of the right of access and use by any individual(s), at any time for violation of said regulations.

12. No noxious or offensive activity shall be carried on upon any lot, nor shall anything be done, placed or stored thereon which may be or become an annoyance or nuisance to the neighborhood, or occasion any noise or order which will or might disturb the peace, comfort or serenity of the occupants of neighboring properties. Nothing shall be permitted or maintained on the premises or adjoining street or streets unless specifically approved by Realto Corporation, or its successors or assigns. During construction trucks shall use Old State Road exclusively for access in Crosscreek Township.

13. All provisions, conditions, restrictions, and covenants herein shall be binding on all lots and parcels or real estate and the owners thereof, regardless of the source of title of such owners, and any breach thereof, if continued for a period of 30 days from and after

the date that the owner or other property owner shall have notified in writing the owner or lessee in possession of the lot upon which such breach has been committed to refrain from a continuance of such action and to correct such breach, shall warrant the undersigned or other lot owner to apply to any court of law or equity having jurisdiction thereof for an injunction or other proper relief, and if such relief be granted, the plaintiff in such action shall be entitled to receive his reasonable expenses in prosecuting such suit, including attorney's fees, as part of the Decree, Order of Court, or Judgment.

Provided, that any violation of the foregoing provisions, conditions, restrictions, or covenants shall not defeat or render invalid the lien of any mortgage or deed of trust made in good faith for value as to any portion of said property, but such provisions, conditions, restrictions, and covenants shall be enforceable, against any portion of said property acquired by any person through foreclosure or by deed in lieu of foreclosure, for any violation of the provisions, conditions, restrictions, and covenants herein contained occurring after the acquisition of said property through foreclosure or deed in lieu of foreclosure.

14. In the event that any one or more of the provisions, conditions, restrictions, and covenants herein set forth shall be held by any court of competent jurisdiction to be null and void, all remaining provisions, conditions, restrictions, and covenants herein set forth shall continue unimpaired and in full force and effect.

15. Any and all of the rights and powers herein of Oakland Corporation may be assigned to any Corporation, Authority, or Association, and such Corporation, Authority, or Association shall to the extent of such assignment have the same rights and powers assumed and retained by the owner herein.

16. The aforesaid provisions, conditions, restrictions, and covenants and each and all thereof, shall run with the land and continue and remain in full force and effect at all times and against all persons until the following January 1, at which time they shall be automatically extended for a period of 10 years and thereafter for successive 10-year periods unless on or before the end of one of such extension periods the owners of 70 percent of the lots in said subdivision shall by written instrument, duly recorded, declare a termination or modification of the same. The aforesaid provisions, conditions, restrictions, and covenants and each and all thereof

may at any time be amended or modified by the owners of 70 percent of the lots in said subdivision by written instrument duly recorded.

17. No delay or omission on the part of the owner or the owners of any lot or lots in said property in exercising any right, power, or remedy herein provided for in the event of any breach of any of the provisions, conditions, restrictions, and covenants herein contained shall be construed as a waiver thereof or acquiescence therein; and no right of action shall accrue nor shall any action be brought or maintained by anyone whomsoever against the undersigned owner or an account of the failure or neglect of the undersigned owner to exercise any right, power, or remedy herein provided for in the event of any such breach of any said provisions, conditions, restrictions, or covenants which may be unenforceable.

18. The "Owner" herein referred to shall include the present owner of the land in Oakland Hills Subdivision and any extensions thereof, their successors in interest and authorized agents. "Oakland Hills Subdivision" as referred to shall include its successors and assigns.

✔✔✔✔✔ BUILDING SITE CHECKLIST

___ Is the site properly zoned? How are the properties surrounding the site zoned?

___ Is it close enough to
- ■ Work
- ■ Schools
- ■ Shopping
- ■ Neighbors
- ■ Friends
- ■ Family
- ■ Church
- ■ Entertainment centers
- ■ Medical services

___ What's the reputation of the school system?

___ Are there any parks or playgrounds for children?

___ How do the real estate taxes compare with those in other areas?

BUILDING SITE CHECKLIST *(Continued)*

___ Are there any home association dues?

___ Are there other houses similar to yours in size and type and value in the neighborhood?

___ Have you inquired about the crime rate compared with crime rates in other locations?

___ Is the site in an area that is declining, remaining stable, or improving?

___ Are there any potentially irritating factories, dragstrips, or seasonal attractions nearby?

___ Is the location private enough for you? Is there rear and side privacy?

___ Is the site on a hill? Are there loud sounds of trucks and buses shifting gears as they pass by? In winter, could you have trouble making the incline from your driveway?

___ Is the lot at a road intersection where stop signs have the traffic constantly stopping and starting?

___ Is the lot steep where lawn mowing will be required? What about snow removal?

___ Where must the mailbox be placed?

___ Are there any ditches, swampy terrain, right-of-ways, or easements that restrict certain parts of the site from a desired use? Is there a creek or gully that cuts through near the center?

___ Is there an open ditch or culvert across the front, parallel to the road, that will need special attention for driveway access and lawn maintenance?

___ Which utilities, such as natural gas, electricity, water, sewer/septic, phone, and cable TV, are available? Does a utility company have any utility boxes set up or easements for eventual setups?

___ Is the soil sandy—which could require special foundation work?

___ How are the garbage collection services?

___ What kind of fire protection is there?

___ What kind of police protection?

___ What kind of emergency transport systems?

(Continued)

✓✓✓✓✓ BUILDING SITE CHECKLIST *(Continued)*

___ Does the lot suit the type of house you are planning?

___ Does any portion of the site consist of fill dirt?

___ Is there or will there be good drainage on the site? Is the lot in a floodplain?

___ Is the lot large enough for your house and your activities?

___ Is the lot small enough for your house and your activities?

___ Did you see a plot plan of the site?

___ Has a recent property survey been completed? Are the lot's boundaries staked out so you can see them?

___ Do you know at what level or height the sewer line will connect the house plumbing?

___ Will the site provide your house with a good orientation? Any special views available?

___ Are the views available from the location good or bad?

___ Can you get a free and clear title to the land?

___ Will you need a septic permit? Can you get one?

___ Do you need a water well? Can you obtain one?

___ How are the water wells nearby?

___ Do any subdivision or other restrictions apply? And if so, do you understand them?

___ Have you inquired into the probable resale value of your house and property in case you must unexpectedly move in the near future?

___ Where's the nearest fire protection? Police protection? Emergency medical service?

___ Is there good access to major highways?

___ Is the lot close to an airport (noise), set of railroad tracks (noise and crossing hazards), landfill (traffic, dust, trucking and tailgate slamming noise, possible water contamination), exposed power facility (noise), cliff, swamp (mosquitoes), or commercial or industrial property?

___ Will your completed home be the most expensive dwelling in the neighborhood (least desirable), or average, or least expensive (more desirable)?

POINTS TO PONDER

1. Unless you're building in an established residential subdivision, make sure you know the zoning of your site, and those sites around you—on the sides of, across the street from, and behind your property. A call to the local zoning officer can usually be a big help toward understanding zoning patterns that exist around the site in question.

2. Any real estate broker, when asked what the most important components of real estate value are, will invariably answer "Location, location, location."

3. If you're new to an area, secure assistance from individuals you trust (and who have no stake in what or where you buy) such as coworkers, relatives, members of the local police department, and municipal zoning officials or planners.

4. Keep in mind the type of house you want as you look at building sites. For example, if your heart is set on a split-level home, you can pretty much eliminate very flat building sites. If you're thinking of an L-shaped sprawling ranch, that back-to-front sloped ravine site overlooking Higgly Creek probably won't work either.

5. Single-story ranches are ideally suited to flat building sites or lots that slope gently to the sides or rear, particularly if the plans call for a walkout from a basement or lower living area. One-and-one-half-stories and two-stories are also best matched with relatively flat lots or sites sloping slightly to the rear.

6. Split-foyers are good on building sites with front-to-back or back-to-front medium to steep slopes. They're totally incompatible with flat lots.

7. Multilevels are ideally suited to side-sloping lots or hilly terrain where the bottom level of the house faces and opens toward the downhill side, and upstairs levels open toward the uphill side. A flat site won't work for multilevel construction.

8. Does any portion of the site—especially where you plan to excavate—consist of filled material that could interfere with the construction of solid footers and foundations?

9. Don't automatically figure that the "front" of your new home *must* face the street that the house is on. Sure, in a traditional

subdivision, it doesn't make sense to buck the "front-faces-the-street" rule, but on sites away from close neighbors, you can orient the front of the house to take advantage of interesting views toward the back or sides.

10. Before purchasing a building site, make sure you will end up with a clear title, utility hookups, a septic permit if required, a successful water well if applicable, and a complete copy of all easements and building restrictions applicable to your site.

Orientation, Positioning, and Landscaping

The way you orient and position your home on a building site and how you landscape its surroundings will greatly affect the benefits or drawbacks your home will receive from local weather conditions, will affect the home's market value and saleability, and will even affect the liveability of the dwelling in many subtle ways.

ORIENTATION

Four factors play important roles in determining the best orientation for your house:

- The location of the building site in relation to surrounding typographical features, other houses, and the street

- The sun

- The wind

- The available views

Location

If you purchase a building site that's the last one available in a subdivision, or is positioned between two existing dwellings, or anywhere within a subdivision having strict building restrictions, there's nothing dramatic you can do with the orientation; you already know where the house has to sit, which way it has to face, and even where it must be positioned at the front and sides on any one particular lot.

But if you have a wide choice of building sites with several different orientations possible, or if you're planning to build in the country, where few restrictions are in force, it's another story. If so, consider how the following three factors might influence your selection.

The Sun

There's nothing in life quite as regular and dependable as the rising and setting of the sun (clouds are the capricious variables of weather). You can take advantage of our sun's free heat and light by planning and facing the side of your house with the most glass toward the south. That way, low-angled sunrays will penetrate into the rooms during winter, bringing warmth and illumination. Then, in summer, your roof overhangs will block out high-angled rays that will otherwise make your air-conditioning work overtime.

In general, south-facing areas will be warm, north-facing areas will be cold, east-facing areas will get the pleasant early morning sun, and west-facing rooms will bear the brunt of hot afternoon rays.

The Wind

Depending on the circumstances, wind can be a help or hindrance. It can rob you of heat during the winter, with its icy chill factors. Or it can just as easily get rid of unwanted heat during stifling hot summer days.

In North America, the prevailing winds blow from west to east, although seasonal and regional variations frequently find warm, moist breezes lofting up from the south, and cold, dry winds howling out of the north.

Because of the predictable nature of large weather patterns, whenever possible you should minimize the number of windows you place on the north and northwest sections of your house, since they'll be the hardest hit by the most unfavorable winds. Try to locate your garage there instead, to absorb most of the wind's punch before it reaches the rest of your home.

The View

To some people, available views will take precedence over anything else. If your lot is on the south side of a lake and you want to face the water, you can't help but face some of your living quarters toward the north. If so, compensate for such a handicapped orientation by paying more attention to selective landscaping, privacy walls, thermal glass, and similar features.

Be aware of the land or water that surrounds you, and how a nice view can be changed overnight by neighbors who cut down or plant trees, pile up garbage cans, or park a junk car in their backyard.

POSITIONING

Again, the house that's matched to a regular subdivision lot has few options as to its positioning—the only choice might be to construct the house either the actual way the plans are drawn versus the way a mirror image of those plans would appear. For example, a two-story house might have the garage on the left-hand side of the original set of plans. The same house could be "mirrored" so the garage would be positioned to the right.

Keep in mind that any mistake or poor choice on your part could create a house that's obviously mismatched with its lot. Ideally, your home will blend into the site as if it "grew" in place. Several factors determining the best positioning potential follows.

Vehicle Access

You want a practical exit/entrance to your garage from the street. This is especially important in cold-climate locations where snow and ice make driving and walking a chore. Be careful of how steep the driveway's fall will be because it could add to the difficulty of getting in and out. At the same time, watch out for driveways that slope toward their garage. Rainwater could run into the garage, and ice coatings will make such a sloped driveway a definite safety hazard.

The amount of space to allow on the two sides of the house should be considered. Most homes are simply situated at the center of regular city and subdivision lots—sometimes to satisfy subdivision restrictions or to provide minimum clearances from the property lines as dictated by township or other applicable municipalities. If there is an option, it might be best for you to put the house toward one or the other side of the lot. What if someday a large dump truck or backhoe needs to drive into your backyard? What if you decide that your backyard is sloped too much, and you want to level it off with clean fill dirt?

Remember to leave ample space on the side that is most passable for trucks—preferably the garage side of the house. That way heavy equipment will also be able to reach your backyard, in case you someday decide to install an in-ground swimming pool or put up an addition there.

Pedestrian Use

A second point to remember is one that if ignored, can become detrimental to the house's value and saleability. Depending on how your house is oriented, try to minimize the difficulty of having to climb numerous steps when entering or exiting the home.

Utility Connections

The third point to consider when positioning your house is utility connections. A dwelling's corner or side where the utilities need to be connected should be accommodating. A lengthy concrete patio in this area would add difficulty to the hookups and would mean extra length and costs for making those connections.

Outdoor Functions

Some exclusive subdivisions feature houses that have practically no backyards. Instead the homes and their front yards are situated to give visitors a showcase effect—beautiful front lawns, stunning flowers, and well-cared-for trees, all surrounding homes that look architecturally designed for each individual building site.

Other houses and lots are planned to permit a variety of practical outdoor activities. Review your interests and those of your family and friends. Do you like to:

- Grow your own food? Then what about small "kitchen" gardens or large family gardens? What about fruit trees and berry bushes? Do you want to grow your own Christmas trees?

- Keep pets or farm animals? Is there enough room somewhere for a dog to run and a cat to prowl? If permitted, do you plan to provide spaces and buildings for farm animals?

- Participate in recreational activities? Do you have the space to accommodate badminton, croquet, tennis, horseshoes, swimming, basketball, swing sets for children, canoe storage shed, rope swings and hammocks, sandboxes, raising roses and tulips or other interests?

- Plan large outdoor parties and picnics?

- Work at your main business or a part-time business? What about home workshops behind the garage, or those white boxes for beekeeping?

Setback from the Street

If there are already houses on both sides of your lot, you don't have much room to maneuver here. The same applies if your building site is part of a strictly regulated subdivision.

On the other hand, if you're building where there's no one else around, consider keeping the house a reasonable distance away from the road to reduce the amount of dust and noise generated from passing traffic. If you drive through the country you'll notice that some people build very close to the road, while others build quite far from it. In cold-climate areas, if you elect to go way back from the road, be prepared to handle the snow removal in some fashion. The larger and longer the driveway, the more snow you'll have to contend with.

When a choice exists, weigh the advantages and disadvantages of privacy versus convenience, and arrive at a happy medium.

LANDSCAPING

Any realtor will tell you: take two identical houses, put one on a nicely landscaped lot and the other on a landscape that has weeds erupting everywhere, dying trees, overgrown shrubs, and ankle-length grass. Can you guess which property would be easier to sell? And which one would bring a higher market price? And also, which one would be more pleasant to live in?

Landscaping is important, no doubt. It can help you to reduce energy costs. It can make your home a more comfortable place to live. It can eliminate the need for manufactured fences or privacy screens. It can help reduce your grocery bills. It can attract interesting wild birds and animals within sight. It can define a play area for children or a picnic area for adults. It can block off an unsightly view or frame a pleasant pastoral scene. Landscaping is certainly one of the finishing touches required to make a new house an attractive property.

Clearing the Lot

If you're lucky enough to have a wooded or partly wooded building site, remove only those trees necessary to permit construction—unless you already have definite landscaping plans for the entire parcel. It takes only a short time to remove a full-grown tree, but years and years to replace it. Before even a single tree is removed, you should determine the boundaries needed for construction of the house, driveway, and septic system if one must be installed. Then you can selectively remove and save trees in a calculated manner.

Soil

The quality of the site's soil should be checked before the lot is excavated and bulldozed. If there's a layer of good topsoil, have it pushed into a pile on the side to be saved until after the house is up and ready for landscaping. To be sure your grass will be healthy, request a minimum of 3 inches of topsoil. Have at least that much in flower, shrubbery, and garden beds as well.

Plantings

Your lot's final grade should be established and stabilized as soon as possible through the planting of grass or other ground covers to protect the soil from water and wind erosion. A thin layer of straw spread over the seeded areas will minimize harmful water and wind action until the ground cover has grown enough to do the job.

Try to arrange for overall, well-balanced plantings that will alternately bloom or turn throughout the growing seasons, and not burst into magnificent "peacock" displays for two weeks and then disappear.

Remember that landscaping, and especially plantings, can be a gradual process. There's no need to rush things. Don't let professional landscapers pressure you into an all-or-nothing strategy. You can first put in a lawn and a few shrubs. Next year you can add a hardwood tree and some ground cover. And the next year a row of flowering hedges . . . .

Evergreen trees retain their leaves during winter. They can block wind and provide shade year-round. When laying out a wind break, evergreens should ideally be placed between the house and the prevailing northern winds to minimize wind-chill factors. (Fig. 30.1).

Deciduous trees drop their leaves for the winter. They'll let sunlight filter through in the coldest months when it's sorely needed. They're most advantageously placed to the south and west, where they'll also—because their leaves are full during summer and fall—

FIGURE 30.1

Landscaping with evergreens.

block out the sun during the warmest part of the year. A small gap, however, should be arranged to the southwest to allow for refreshing breezes during summer.

By shading the house, the walls, shingles, and curtains will all stay cooler, keeping overall temperatures down and enabling those same components to last longer from reduced exposure levels to harmful ultraviolet rays. Occupants will also feel more comfortable sitting indoors near a shaded wall.

Shading the walls is particularly important if they are brick or other masonry materials. Masonry slowly absorbs the sun's heat in the afternoon and radiates it indoors all evening, forcing air conditioning to run deep into the night. And most ordinary insulation is not so effective at blocking radiant heat. In addition, deciduous trees should be used to help shade outside air-conditioning units. Shade from trees also makes it more comfortable on an outdoor deck or patio, allowing a family to spend less time operating the kitchen range and more time cooking and grilling outdoors in comfort.

With deciduous trees, you may think of shading as the primary means of cooling. While they do provide an excellent source of shade, they also function as natural air conditioners. As leaves on the tree give off moisture, that moisture changes from a liquid phase to a gas, pulling heat from the surrounding air. With properly placed deciduous trees, air temperatures near a house can be nearly 10 degrees Fahrenheit cooler than temperatures near a treeless dwelling. This can reduce home air conditioning costs by as much as 25 percent. Trees with high canopies will effectively cool and shade roof and walls, while lower plantings near the house will help cool through respiration and evaporation processes.

In general, trees offer beauty and provide homes for songbirds. Large trees lend the property that "established community" appearance. Be aware that some of the landscape suppliers might not guarantee their products if you plant the items yourself. On the other hand, many of them will, and it's not very difficult to do the plantings yourself. Just follow the nursery's instructions to the letter.

If there's not much topsoil to start out with, you might want to consider grass sod. The advantage with sod is that you'll have an instant lawn that comes with some of its own topsoil. Naturally, sod costs more than a seeded lawn.

Reducing Siding, Sidewalk, Driveway, and Patio Heat

Foliage plantings can help divert or reduce the amount of heat absorbed by and radiated by sidings, driveways, sidewalks, and patios.

- Tall trees and plants can prevent direct sunlight from striking siding, a sidewalk, driveway or patio, which reduces heat buildup during the warmest part of the day.

- Medium-height plants can block heat that's re-radiating from a warm or hot driveway toward your home's walls and windows. A solar-heated driveway continues to radiate heat well into the evening. The medium-height plants cool off surrounding air at the same time.

- Ground cover can create a cool buffer zone immediately next to the house, in pleasantly planned beds. This is where the plant respiration-evaporation process is very effective. At the same time, ground cover will help prevent sunlight from reflecting against the home's exterior walls, thus keeping the siding materials cooler (Fig. 30.2). Often, the most effective plantings may include a multipurpose combination of different-height species (Fig. 30.3).

When selecting ground cover, consider what grows best in your location as well as the eventual adult plant height, spread, texture and whether a particular species is deciduous or evergreen. In winter you'll likely welcome any extra radiant heat, so try to choose ground cover that will not block it from your dwelling. Depending on what level of landscaping your contractor is responsible for, be aware that for him (or for you, at some later date) to establish dense, healthy ground cover, a thorough preparation of the planting bed is necessary before actual plants are set.

That means consider insisting on arranging for at least 2 inches of extra organic matter such as peat moss to lighten

FIGURE 30.2

Cooling effect of ground cover.

FIGURE 30.3

A multipurpose planting.

clay soils and increase the water holding capacity of light sandy soils. The soil should then be worked to a depth of at least 6 or 8 inches. Weed seeds and weed plants should be cleaned out so they won't compete with the new plants during stress-filled weeks and months when the ground cover is trying to establish itself. Then carefully follow instructions provided by the nursery experts who have supplied the plants.

Remember, when choosing the tall, medium and low plants, keep in mind that deciduous plants accomplish quite a lot the year round. Their leaves provide summertime heat protection, but when they shrivel and drop from their branches in late fall, the sun's rays can reach through and warm that concrete driveway and allow the heat to reflect up toward the home for heat gain, and even on cold winter nights, some of this stored heat will slowly radiate upwards to create a warm thermal buffer area against the home, which ultimately reduces the rate of indoor heat loss through the walls and windows.

Drainage

The landscaping should slope away from the home's foundation and drain all the water from the gutters, downspouts, and sump pump out to the street or to some other harmless place. Make sure the first 10 feet surrounding the house perimeter tapers away from the foundation with at least a 6-inch drop all the way around. Overall there should be a minimum of 1 to 2 feet of fall from the house to the street, and this includes the driveway.

Some lots need a culvert pipe beneath the end of the driveway for proper drainage along the street. Check with the appropriate government office for the right size and method of installation. In some communities the highway department will install the culvert pipe at no cost to the owner. If not, see that its installation is included in the site work contract.

Erosion

To control minor problems with surface erosion on a bank, plant earth-holding shrubbery or ground cover. If an embankment is going to be steep due to the lay of the land, consider building a retaining wall out of railroad ties, rocks, or solid masonry. This will control erosion and simplify your lawn maintenance. If you employ solid masonry retaining walls, make sure they have weep holes to drain groundwater and release hydrostatic pressure that builds up on the earthen side of the wall.

Earthen Berms

Building a landscaping berm or mound of soil, often by using a masonry or treated-wood retaining wall into the northwestern corner of the lot, adjacent to the dwelling in colder-climate locations, or into the southwestern corner for hot-climate areas, can save a lot of energy. Essentially a raised area of ground against the home, it can cut energy bills and increase comfort levels by providing an insulating barrier, by reducing air leakage into the home, and by providing a thermal mass to moderate rapid temperature changes.

The comfort improvement from the heavy thermal mass of the ground and retaining wall will be most noticeable in the summer, with the moderation of typical afternoon temperature rises.

Then, during cold months of winter, the berm helps shelter part of the home from freezing temperatures and strong winds.

Landscape Irrigation

Some individuals take a lot of pride in their well-landscaped property. Others don't really worry about their trees, shrubs, and lawns being maintained in peak condition. One thing for sure, though, is that plants need water to thrive. If your location is in an area where extended periods of drought can occur, or if you want to maintain your living landscape in top condition, consider the purchase and installation of high-quality irrigation sprinklers and sprinkler systems. Top quality sprinkling equipment lasts a long time and will provide excellent watering patterns, while operating at desirable lower pressures and flows.

You can also research automatic watering components featured in drip or sprinkler versions. The heart of either type of system is the automatic electronic controller. It can be pre-set to control several zones to water different areas at various intervals, with varying amounts of water. Some units even have automatic rain sensors to skip a watering cycle when it rains. Electronic water timers are great for getting the most out of the watering that takes place. At least one manufacturer offers a unit that works on a 9-volt battery with low-pressure drip and soaker hoses, as well with standard garden hoses.

Decorative and Finishing Touches

Browse through any of the numerous mail-order catalogs for an idea of how many unusual, exotic, practical, and frivolous plants and trees are available. See if any decorative items such as fountains, bird baths, trellises, pots, garden fences, ornaments, and automatic sprinklers catch your fancy (Figs. 30.4 and 30.5). The selection of landscaping options practically defies description.

Final Landscaping Payment

If you happen to move into your newly constructed house before the grading is done and the lawn is planted (perhaps due to inclement weather, or the season in which the house was completed), make sure that some of the builder's funds are held back in escrow to be released to the builder after what was promised in the contract is completed.

The contract should clearly state whose responsibility it is to provide a final grading with topsoil and a lawn.

>>>>>> **POINTS TO PONDER**

1. Consider how the sun, wind, lay of the land, positions of surrounding homes, and available views could affect the home you plan to build.
2. Try to plan and face the side of the house with the most window and door glass toward the south.
3. When possible, minimize the number of windows you place on the north and northwest sides of the home; locate the garage there instead.

FIGURE 30.4

A decorative landscaping accent.

4. If pleasant or dramatic views are possible, consider going for the views, and compensate for less-than-ideal orientation with

FIGURE 30.5

Landscaping decorations.

heavier thermal glass, privacy walls, selective landscaping, and similar features.

5. If you have a choice, carefully consider the home's setback distance from the street. The further back you go, the more privacy you'll have, along with less dust and noise from passing traffic. On the other hand, the longer your driveway (and your walk to the mailbox) will have to be. Plus, be prepared to handle snow removal in cold-climate areas.

6. Remove only those mature trees necessary to permit construction, unless you already have definite landscaping plans for the entire parcel. You may have to forcefully express yourself on this point, because builders often belong to slash-and-burn, bulldoze-the-whole-lot-clean schools. Consider asking a local agronomist or nursery owner to advise you on which trees should and could be saved, and how to protect them during the construction process. Some individuals have integrated their home/deck plans with existing, majestic trees with great success.

7. Landscaping, and especially plantings, can be a gradual process. Don't rush things. Adding a little at a time will help avoid a frequent problem of overloading a landscape with small plants that—surprise—eventually will encroach upon each other and create a tangle of foliage resembling a jungle.

8. Remember to keep the valuable nutrient-rich topsoil from the initial foundation excavation segregated for reuse as final landscaping cover.

9. The landscaping should slope away from the home's foundation and drain all the water from the gutters, downspouts, and sump pump out to the street or to some other harmless place.

10. Solid masonry retaining walls, in the absence of a comprehensive drainage system, at least need weep holes to drain groundwater and release hydrostatic pressure that can build up on the earthen side of the wall.

Driveways, Sidewalks, and Patios

uts and muddy spots will develop, and weeds can sprout through the gravel's edges. From time to time, the stone will need refreshing with another full or partial truckload.

Had enough? Gravel driveways should be your last resort.

DRIVEWAYS

ASPHALT DRIVEWAYS

Asphalt driveways are much, much better than driveways made of simply gravel. Asphalt driveways are fairly durable. They can look attractive and they're generally less expensive than concrete versions. Drawbacks are that they need periodic resealing or they'll deteriorate substantially faster than concrete will. Asphalt also softens up during hot temperatures and can be pressed out of shape or indented by heavy vehicles or objects such as the legs of a camper/trailer. Although the black color of asphalt can look very attractive with certain homes, it generally clashes with concrete sidewalks when sidewalks are specified at the front of the property by local building codes.

CONCRETE DRIVEWAYS

A concrete drive is the best, most permanent, and trouble-free driveway you can have. It's durable and strong and can be poured in any configuration desired. It matches concrete sidewalks, steps, and patios nicely.

Driveway Configuration and Location

To a certain extent, these characteristics are determined by the house type, orientation, and position on the building site. Hopefully you're reading this material *before* you've completed your house and garage, so you can still make any adjustments that are appropriate. Consider the following points when planning your driveway:

1. Make sure the driveway will be wide enough. Measure driveways at other houses to get an idea of what you want. A single-car drive should be a minimum of 11 feet wide, with its width at the street (the curb entrance) not less than 17 feet to permit cars to easily turn into and back out of it (Fig. 31.1). If you elect to go with a narrower drive, it might be sufficient to drive a car on, but when visitors have to park on the driveway, they'll have to step out of their vehicles into grass or a planting area. A double driveway should be at least 22 feet wide with an entrance at the street of 28 feet. Where any curvature is involved, a few extra feet of width is desirable to prevent drivers, especially visitors, from driving onto the lawn.

2. Your driveway's length will be determined by your house's setback from the street and by the shape of your driveway's approach: straight, curved, or half-circle. In cold-climate areas, consider that long driveways will have to be plowed out by someone: by you or by a hired plow jockey. Whoever plows will need somewhere to put the snow, too.

3. If your lot is large enough, consider having an automobile turnaround (Fig. 31.2). It takes extra surfacing but offers real convenience. It's difficult to realize how often you come and go by car until you have to back out of a driveway onto a busy street every time. When properly laid out, turnarounds can also serve as handy parking areas for visitors and provide a good spot for car washing and maintenance. With multiple-car families, the turnaround can ease the inevitable and irritating shuffle of cars to get the right one out of the rotation.

SINGLE CAR
DRIVE

17'

11'

FIGURE 31.1

A single-car driveway.

4. A step further than the turnaround driveway is the semicircular drive having two accesses to the same street (Fig. 31.3). If you have enough space, and you have a front-entrance garage, this in-one-way and out-the-other pattern can also work to avoid people having to back out of the driveway.

5. Garages that open toward a side of a lot are best served by a wide driveway that extends beyond the garage entrance to furnish turnaround and parking space to the rear.

6. Don't accept a driveway that forces you to back out onto a blind curve or hill. It's far too dangerous for yourself, your family, and unsuspecting visitors.

7. Should you plan a straight or curved approach to your garage? If you have the option, a curved approach often results in a better appearance. It adds flavor and character to a property.

8. Make sure the driveway isn't too steep to negotiate safely. This is important in all climates. It's dangerous to constantly keep cars parked on a steep grade—especially when children are in the neighborhood. Plus, it's inconvenient. People can slip on wet or icy sloped pavement. At the same time, don't plan a driveway that slopes down into a garage. It'll provide a runway for rainwater and snow melt and will be tough to drive up during the winter. If need be, adjust the garage up or down a few blocks.

FIGURE 31.2

A driveway with a turnaround.

Driveway Construction Specifications

1. Driveways shouldn't be dug, graveled, then poured or paved overnight. Rather, it's a two-stage process. First comes the excavation of the ground to permit placement of a base layer of 6 to 10

FIGURE 31.3

A semicircular driveway.

inches of crushed stone. Next comes the pouring of concrete or laying of blacktop (asphalt) surface layers *after* the base stage has had 8 to 12 months to settle and compact. This waiting period while cars and trucks are compacting the gravel base will result in a more stable concrete or asphalt surface that will show considerably less minor cracking and almost no pavement break-off areas where base settling would otherwise be the cause. The waiting period also provides enough time for trouble spots to appear in the base so they can be repaired before the paving occurs.

2. Have the crushed stone or fill material placed about a foot wider on each side of the driveway than the pavement's eventual width. This prevents undercutting of the slab and subsequent breakage by surface water draining off the drive.

3. To ensure proper drainage the driveway must slope away from the garage toward the street about 2 or 3 inches downhill for

FIGURE 31.4

Driveway slope.

every 10 linear feet of driveway (Fig. 31.4). Of course, this applies to only a typical driveway; the long winding drive applies only where it nears the house. If you can't arrange for that much slope on a regular driveway, before the driveway is surfaced have some fine stone added to the base so the gravel layer is crowned in the center. An 11-foot-wide drive should have a crowned or raised center 2 to 2½ inches high, and a 22-foot-wide drive should have a crown reaching 4 to 5 inches in the center, so water will drain off to the sides.

4. Check out any unusual street problems such as a fireplug, utility pole, or tree that might be in the way of your driveway. Consider that there could be a city ordinance covering the number, size, and placement of driveway approaches.

5. Where water causes problems around driveways, a length of plastic pipe might help improve drainage at low spots or water collection points. For instance, if rainwater tends to collect along one side of a driveway, it might cause trouble in the form of surface ice and frost heaval during winter. A length of pipe installed underground, running from a small rock basin at the lowest collection point on one side of the driveway to a screen-covered outlet on the other side, will alleviate the situation (Fig. 31.5).

6. A driveway should be at least 5 inches thick. The builder typically will use 2 by 6s or 1 by 6s to obtain the 5-inch depth, keeping the bottom edges slightly below grade (Fig. 31.6). Specify that the concrete mix should be a minimum of five and one-half bags of cement per cubic yard of concrete.

7. The concrete should have either steel rod or wire mesh running

FIGURE 31.5

Driveway drainage.

FIGURE 31.6

Concrete driveway construction.

through it for strength. Approximately every 11 feet, a groove should be cut into the concrete to allow the pads room to react to temperature changes and other stressful conditions. Spacer felt—thin strips of felt—should be placed between the individual concrete pads or blocks to allow for contraction and expansion due to temperature changes.

8. The finish on a concrete drive can be either a swirl or a broomed effect. It's a matter of personal preference.

9. Freshly poured concrete driveways should be barricaded until they cure and have a chance to be coated with a good concrete sealer. As mentioned in the chapter on garages, concrete sealer will prevent the penetration of any oil or grease into the concrete and will make the surface easier to clean.

10. Asphalt should ideally be applied in two layers over the stone base. Roughly two-thirds (or 3½ inches) of the total thickness

should be laid down as a binder course containing larger stone or aggregate, then the other third (1½ inches) can be laid on top. The wearing course contains finer material so it can be tamped and rolled into a smooth, watertight surface.

SIDEWALKS

Sidewalks are another necessity. You have to get from the driveway to the front, side, and rear entrances somehow. Sidewalks are the accepted, civilized way so you and your visitors won't have to walk through wet grass or dusty ground.

CONCRETE INSTALLATION

The following considerations should be reviewed for pouring concrete diveways, sidewalks, patio, mailbox bases, and similar components.

- There should be no presence of groundwater, mud, or soft spots where the pour is being made.
- Half-inch-wide expansion joints must be placed level with the top of the concrete surface. They should be installed between driveway and sidewalk, foundation and driveway/sidewalk, garage and driveway/sidewalk, and between individual sections of driveway and sidewalk.
- Unless special precautions are understood and taken by the masonry contractor, try to avoid having concrete poured when temperatures are below 40 degrees Fahrenheit.
- Hot-weather concrete pouring must be carefully managed for rapid drying to prevent cracking that will lessen the strength of the completed job. It makes sense to arrange for pourings in the early morning or very late afternoon, when shade and cooler temperatures are available.
- Concrete can be tinted with a variety of colors and shades such as gray, black, brown, or red, to blend in or harmonize with the home's natural surroundings. Ask the contractor to review your options. Numerous textures and patterns can also be achieved with concrete pours—lending the impression of tile or stone, without the accompanying installation or maintenance costs of either. Rough-pattern surfaces also help give driveways and walkways additional slip resistance.

Sidewalk Planning

Here are some considerations to help you plan your sidewalks:

1. Make the lead sidewalk from your driveway to the front entrance steps at least 4 feet wide. Traditional 36-inch-wide sidewalks are fine for side or rear doors, where only one person at a time must be accommodated. Front entrances should be able to be approached by two visitors walking side-by-side instead of single file.

2. Following the rationale used with driveways, a curved sidewalk adds a certain character and flavor to the appearance of a home (Fig. 31.7).

3. Have adequate lighting along sidewalks, especially where steps are located.

4. Many people are tempted to opt for sidewalks, entrance steps, and patios made of brick, flagstone, masonry, or patio blocks. These materials might sound like a good idea, but they're often more trouble than they're worth. If you go with anything other

FIGURE 31.7

A curved sidewalk.

than concrete, be prepared to do a considerable amount of maintenance work every two or three years to correct surface deterioration that may occur. If you desire something that looks more unique than concrete, consider some of the results available through concrete finishers—contractors who specialize in staining, etching, scoring, and sealing concrete so it resembles stone such as marble or slate, tile, or even burnished leather. Also consider, in the long run, how such an unusual finish could influence potential buyers if and when you decide to sell. It's also possible to construct sidewalks out of asphalt, but it's not advisable unless the walk is extremely long and winding, such as a bike path through a wooded area.

Sidewalk Construction

The first step in sidewalk construction (Fig. 31.8) is to excavate the walkway and spread 4 or 5 inches of crushed stone in the excavation, which is to be used as a base layer. The stone base should then be either compacted with a handheld tamping machine or left alone for 6 to 8 months for the ground and gravel to settle naturally. If the ground and stone base are not allowed enough time or compacting effort to settle, the base beneath the sidewalk will sink and move, causing

FIGURE 31.8

Sidewalk construction.

voids that will no longer support the sidewalk in those areas, and cracks or heaved concrete will result. Follow these guidelines:

1. At least 2- by 4-foot lumber should be used to form the sidewalks to provide a 3-inch-thick walk.

2. The sidewalk forms should give walks a slight side slope or length slope that falls away from the house for proper rainwater and snow melt surface drainage (Fig. 31.9).

3. The finish on concrete sidewalks can be either the swirl or the broomed type.

4. As with the garage floor and driveway, make sure that a clear protective sealer is applied over the freshly dried concrete sidewalks.

5. Keep sidewalks above ground level. Don't let weeds and grass sod encroach over sidewalk edges. The surrounding lawn roots

FIGURE 31.9

Sidewalk slope.

should be several inches below the sidewalk surface for easy lawn mowing and a neat appearance.

PATIOS

There are few strict rules when it comes to the size, type, and location of patios. Some people will find a small concrete patio or wood deck to their liking, positioned off the dining room. Others plan huge, sprawling wood decks that completely encircle their dwelling. Some people like to have roofed-over patios, or prefer to close the sides in, too. Certain individuals count on using covered patios year-round and will heat them in cold-climate locations.

Patio Planning

Here are some points to consider when planning patios:

1. The patio is similar to the garage in that it's one of the least expensive parts of a house per square foot of usable area. If you're going to have one, it might as well be a nice roomy one.

2. It's best to construct patios with below-ground footers and foundations, so if you decide to cover it someday you're sure to have sufficient support and you won't have to worry about it heaving in response to freezing temperatures.

3. Whatever your outdoor patio construction materials are, provide some height to the patio by keeping the patio floor surface at least 4 to 6 inches above the surrounding ground. This will make cleaning much simpler.

4. Consider building in some above-the-floor, raised planter areas, walls, dividers, or other permanent features that will provide horizontal or flat surfaces wide enough for people to comfortably sit on (Fig. 31.10).

5. If a patio is more than a few steps above the ground level, it's advisable that step handrails be installed for safety (Fig. 31.11).

6. Make sure your patio is properly positioned for privacy and easy access to the living areas of the house, especially the kitchen.

7. Arrange adequate lighting for patio evening use and enjoyment.

FIGURE 31.10

An outdoor patio deck.

8. Unless you plan a year-round enclosed patio, consider what storage facilities you'll be able to use for storing patio furniture, planters, and other seasonal items. If you have the space, one alternative is to construct an outdoor weatherproof closet or storage enclosure adjacent to the patio or near the garage or rear of the house.

Patio Construction

There are two primary types of patio foundation constructions: concrete and wood. The concrete patio employs the idea of a concrete footer below the frost line with a concrete block foundation built up from there. The inside is backfilled and brought up to the top of the foundation with a 12-inch-thick layer of bank gravel. Then a concrete pad reinforced with wire mesh or rod is poured over the top. Once

FIGURE 31.11

A patio deck with steps and handrails.

cured, the concrete patio floor should be coated with a good concrete sealer. As with sidewalks, unique finishes are available for patios by concrete staining, etching, scoring and sealing.

Wood patios or decks have certain attractions to people who like the warm, soft feel and rustic look of wood. Wood can also be stained or painted to match existing color schemes. All wood decks should be constructed with lumber that can withstand the rigors of constant exposure to the weather. Redwood, cypress, and cedar are all excellent choices, but they're expensive. Salt-treated southern yellow pine is an alternative. It's a durable type of wood at a bargain price. Order grades of salt-treated lumber labeled .25CCA for lumber that will be used above ground level, and .40CCA if it will be used on grade or below.

If your patio will be enclosed with treated wood, follow the suggestions given in the previous paragraph. If it's going to be enclosed as part of the house and covered the same way, then follow the specifications outlined in earlier chapters on interior framing and exterior coverings.

If you plan to go with a treated lumber deck or enclosure, check into the hardware and fastening devices on the market that are manufactured with rust-resistant metals. They include both galvanized steel and aluminum nails.

The probability of warping will be reduced if spans of railing are kept at or less than 8 feet in length. Built-in benches will also add to the stability.

Wood Deck Considerations

- To avoid poor matches of deck to ground, wait until the grading and landscaping is complete before wood decks are framed and installed.

- Use premium, top-grade lumber. Redwood is strong, with natural oils that help keep the wood moist so it doesn't decay quickly. Cedar is also strong and has similar natural oils that maintain moisture, retarding decay. Pressure-treated pine, fir, and Douglas fir are less expensive, and if protected against water, will last many years. Many of the pressurized woods contain arsenic, so they should not be used in areas where they could come into contact with food, or where children or pets are left unsupervised to chew on them. There are some pressurized wood products available that do not use arsenic, yet still resist mold, fungi, and insects. The color is saturated throughout the wood, so periodic staining is not required.

- Galvanized deck screws should be used instead of nails. Screws have greater gripping power; they can pull warped boards into alignment. Screws can easily be removed in the event that individual boards warp or split and need to be replaced.

- Deck boards should have a narrow (⅛-inch) space between each board to allow for ventilation and drainage.

- Posts that support wood decks should not come in contact with saturated soil or standing water. The connections between the posts and deck beams should be covered with flashing to prevent rain or snow melt from soaking into the end grain of the posts. The tops of concrete support piers should be about 6 inches above ground level to keep the base of posts dry. Embed post anchors into the piers before the pier concrete dries. The footings for the support posts need to extend below the frost line so the deck won't heave or move during freezing weather.

- Strap anchors should be used to fasten the deck beam to the deck's foundation to keep the beam from shifting or sliding, and to keep the beam from contacting moist ground. Joist hangers should be the exterior type, galvanized to prevent rusting. Use lag bolts screwed directly into the foundation or floor frame to secure the deck to the house.

- The seam between the deck and house should be covered with flashing to prevent water from settling into the crack and rotting the side of the home.

- Rain, melting snow, and other moisture can penetrate untreated wood fibers so the wood expands and warps, and mold, mildew, and algae can grow. Then some of the wood can start rotting, and as moisture evaporates, some of the wood can dry out, contract or shrink, and may develop long splits and cracks. To prevent this from happening, wood should be treated with preservatives to penetrate the wood and help make it resistant to biological damage. Good water repellants will also help keep wood sound by keeping water contraction and expansion cycles at bay. For best results, the wood should be completely dry before preservatives and penetrating water repellant treatments are applied, so those materials will soak into the wood. Once the boards air dry, they should be further coated with two treatments of a water-resistant coatings, the second treatment to be applied after the first dries.

- After the initial waterproofing and preserving treatments are applied, waterproofing stains or sealers with ultraviolet light absorbers can be reapplied yearly.

- If a permanent gas grill will be installed near the finished deck, arrange for a gas grill line in advance.

> > > > > > | **POINTS TO PONDER**

1. Avoid planning a driveway that forces you to back out on a highway, blind curve, or hill.
2. Whenever possible, have a gradual slope on a driveway—not a steep slope.
3. Wait 8 to 12 months after a driveway has been stoned, used, and compacted before laying down the permanent driveway construction material, be it stone, gravel, brick, asphalt, or concrete.
4. Keep driveway and sidewalk surfaces above ground level; make sure there is a slight runoff slope (away from the home) to rid drives and walks of water.
5. Make sure ½-inch expansion joints are strategically located in concrete drives, walks, and patios.
6. Front lead sidewalks should be at least 4 feet wide, and side or rear walks, 3 feet wide.
7. Generally, curved driveways and sidewalks tend to be more interesting and attractive than straight accesses.
8. If you're going to have a patio or deck, consider making it even larger than you first thought it should be.
9. Patios and decks need to be supported below the frost line to remain level and solid and so freeze/thaw cycles won't cause them to heave.
10. Use only the best grades of deck lumber, fasteners (galvanized or other nonrusting deck screws), and hardware.

Who Should Build It?

Once you know which house you want, and you have a fair idea of how it should be put together, and you think you know where you want it built, it's time to find a contractor.

Finding the right contractor is a task to be taken seriously. To make the entire housebuilding process a pleasant and rewarding experience, it's paramount to select only an established, skilled, reliable builder who knows what he's doing and who's satisfied many a previous client.

Once found, there are ways to work along with a builder that will virtually ensure that a helpful and trusting give-and-take relationship develops.

Selecting a Contractor

By now you should relax and pat yourself on the back. Surely, you are miles ahead of most people who will, regretfully, *begin* by selecting a contractor as their initial step toward acquiring a new house. Consider that these trusting souls choose a contractor without really knowing which house would be best, without understanding building jargon, without realizing the degree to which they can and should participate in the planning of their new home. Too, they have little knowledge of which questions to ask the builder, and often spend time and energy worrying about practically meaningless—at least to the overall worth and enjoyment of the house—details. Rather, they are likely to be led by the nose into purchasing a house that is merely convenient and cost-efficient for the contractor to build, instead of a customized compatible house that will provide the owners with more living enjoyment and value for their money.

But you, by now, understand what houses are all about. You have the knowledge to be able to make the correct choices between the various types of homes that will best suit your needs. You know their advantages and disadvantages, and how each will affect your own situation. Such information is clearly required in order to arrive at an intelligent decision. It's a personal thing, the planning and erecting of a house, and to do it right, you needed to consider the pros and cons of traffic patterns, floor plans, and even of certain building materials. You needed to understand, at least in a fun, general way, how and even why a house is constructed the way it is. You needed to know the importance of the drawings and prints, and about low-grade or minimum-spec materials and construction methods that are being pushed at the unwary by a certain percentage of contractors. And you needed to understand why quality materials and methods should be insisted upon at contract time.

So, in a sense, you've already completed your most critical homework. You know what you want to build. Now you have to determine *who* you want to build it. Select a minimum of four potential contractors from whom you will solicit competitive bids, and then narrow those builders down to one. Of course, at this point you still might not have located a suitable building site, but that can come later.

Be aware that you are on the verge of entering into a unique relationship that should be mutually rewarding with an individual or a large company or corporation in business to build houses.

The contractor will thus be a pivotal figure around which the success or failure of a housebuilding project can occur. Anyone who thinks about the possible consequences—good or bad—will agree that it's a relationship that must be carefully entered into, not formed on the basis of skimpy information or a casual referral. Ask any real estate agent, housing inspector, or mortgage lending officer what are the overriding reasons for bad houses, and you'll likely as not receive an answer blaming inept or dishonest builders.

Naturally, builders vary in quality, just like individuals in any profession. You have good doctors and bad, capable attorneys as well as incompetent ones; and you have skilled, sincere builders and shysters. Be aware that, although the proportion of good, skillful, reliable builders is high—just as in the rest of the professions—there seems to be a disproportionally large number of shoddy houses or marginal-quality homes being built by a relatively few inept or dishonest builders who lend their calling a bad name and draw a lot of harmful publicity to their field.

BUILDER TYPES

Because it's so important to make a correct choice when selecting a builder—you certainly don't want to change builders in midstream—

here are the major types of builders you're likely to encounter while searching through the marketplace.

Established, Skilled, Reputable Builders

First and foremost are the established, skilled, reputable builders. This can mean a large company, a middle-size company, a small company, or a partnership. It can also mean a one-person operation. The larger established, reputable builders are "old faithful" contractors who are often associated with prestigious, well-planned subdivisions and might also have built rental complexes along the way. These contractors have been building houses for years and they tend to specialize in certain types, styles, and price ranges leaning toward mid- to most-expensive houses in an area. These builders are so well respected that real estate agents even use the contractors' names in advertising, as a "Bebell Ranch" or a "Luciano Two-Story."

Other highly respected builders specialize in low- to mid-priced houses. They've learned how to build as much quality as possible into their dwellings for the lowest possible cost. They purchase large quantities of similar materials at a discount and use the same items in all of their homes. They build on less-expensive lots. Their floor plans tend to be smaller and simpler. These builders are exceptionally good at the range of homes they're working in, and the need for their product is great. Builders of inexpensive houses frequently work with customers who cannot afford much, but who can take advantage of government assistance and financing programs; consequently, these contractors become very good at creative financing.

All of these builders are proven pros. They have the building skills, the business acumen, and the people skills needed to survive in their cutthroat, vicious, tumultuous trade. The established builders have seen it all. They're aware of mortgage financing options, of decorating styles, of landscaping solutions, of energy-saving ideas. And if they don't build a good, solid house and back it up with professional service, the word will get around. It spreads through the business community like wildfire. Real estate agents will "talk up" for resale the houses built by reputable contractors, boasting so much that they will even raise the market value of such houses in the same way that name brand recognition will bring more for a supermarket product.

This established, skilled, reputable builder category also includes those "semiretired" individuals who build only a few quality houses per year, methodically walking around with burnished cherry pipes, slowly and surely, with few wasted motions, constructing most of the house themselves, stick by stick, often with the home buyer helping as a laborer to reduce costs. This type of builder can take a long time to complete a house, but it's worth it if the home buyer can wait. The most specialized parts such as the foundation, roof, plumbing, and electrical systems are often subcontracted out. The rest of the house is frequently charged in a cost-plus arrangement, with the builder receiving an hourly wage and the cost of all materials used. It's a good alternative for people who like a lot of individual attention and contact with their builder, and who most definitely aren't in a big hurry.

New Skilled Builders

Next come the relatively new skilled builders with good intentions who have recently begun building houses on their own. These are individuals trying to make a name for themselves who have probably "paid their dues" while working for the builders previously described—the ones who already have become established and reputable. In fact, these newer skilled contractors are where the established and reputable builders come from.

At first, the new skilled builders are happy to build a handful of dwellings per year, and might well build them as soundly as their previous employer. But what many of the new skilled builders lack, in addition to a proven, solid reputation, are the financial reserves to weather bad times and costly errors, plus the ability to run the business end of construction as the artistic science it is. They can be likened to flamboyant rookies coming up through the farm system. Some of them who might be initially productive will fail to weather the distance. These builders often construct their own houses and those of relatives and close friends to get a start and to have finished houses to show potential clients.

Marginal New Builders

The third major type of contractor is the marginal new builder. Note that you won't find any marginal *established* builders around, because the very definition defies longevity. These are builders who begin by remodeling their own kitchens or helping someone else do theirs. They might have worked a summer or two on a framing crew or putting up roofs for a good builder before one day deciding to paint their name on a truck, get an answering machine, and run an ad in the classifieds. They could enlist the support of a relative who happens to work for a real estate agency.

These are the "contractors" who aren't all that concerned with erecting a quality house. They keep a disheveled building site and hire the kind of workers who drink beer on the job and casually toss empty cans and bottles into the foundation excavation. They'd never dream of parting with the dues to join a local builder's organization or chapter of the National Home Building Association. They can afford to keep their prices competitive though, because they tend to build on inexpensive lots, purchase marginal quality materials, employ construction method shortcuts, and build simple, no-frill floor plans. These are builders who are more interested in making a profit than ensuring customer satisfaction. They might not be dishonest (or they don't mean to be) but they don't have the necessary skills, business sense, and reputation as the first or even the second type of builder. A new company formed specifically to develop a large piece of raw land into a subdivision could fall into this category. These individuals, although they might believe they are skilled builders, and can talk a good game, should not be relied upon to come through with a quality house.

Inept, Dishonest Builders

The fourth and last major builder category is that of the inept, dishonest builders. A. M. Watkins, author of a number of fine volumes on house buying, house planning, and home maintenance, refers to these, the worst kind of contractors, as "vanishing builders." "Vanishing" is an appropriate monicker because even shortly after these builders erect a house, no matter if small or large problems arise, the vanishing builders simply disappear from the scene.

The vanishing builders are the ones you *must* guard against. They might seem completely trustworthy when first approached, and even when a house is completed, everything might look in order—but just try to get them back to take care of a downspout that comes loose from a gutter, or heaven forbid, a major problem such as a leaky roof or basement.

The vanishing builders live up to their names and allow their customers no recourse, no means of exacting repair or retribution.

The reasons for these builders' disappearances are legion, and their excuses many. They might have simply pulled up stakes and departed for a more favorable climate. They might have disbanded and gone back to work for someone else because they couldn't take the headaches that come with self-employment. Their phone numbers are likely to be disconnected or changed and unlisted. Or they might declare bankruptcy.

In any event, these builders have neither the skills nor the intentions needed to become established, reputable contractors. They chase the fast dollar. Even the best scenarios will find the vanishing builders starting out as subcontractor helpers who understand the basics of how houses are constructed, observe that successful builders earn a good living, and long for a piece of the action. Several form a partnership and paint their names on their trucks and boom-build a house or two for unsuspecting friends (who don't remain friends for long) and later for gullible relatives. At first, the vanishing builders take care in their initial few houses so they have something they think is nice to show potential customers, and then, when competitively quoting, give low bids, get several jobs, and begin building the houses. They select subcontractors they have been friends with, and aren't firm enough to make them do a good job so the subcontractors make mistakes that don't show up until later—such as a cellar wall that collapses inward because it isn't properly supported. Meanwhile, the vanishing contractors, after running into irate customers, zoning problems, unreliable subcontractors, slow building periods due to the economy, weather delays, and expert competition from the skilled established and new contractors, cannot last.

In fact, few vanishing contractors even know how much money they will make on a particular house. They might actually bid—without fully realizing their expenses—less than it costs them to construct the dwelling. No company, no matter how skilled at building houses, can last or exist unless it generates a fair profit.

Sometimes vanishing builders find backers who put up front money for land they hope to develop. Together the vanishing builders and their representatives can be flashy individuals with persuasive sales skills and wildly inaccurate promises. These people don't care about the satisfaction and security gained by developing a good reputation in the community. Chances are they won't be around long. This can be exceptionally irritating to the home buyers who invest in the first few houses in a promised subdivision that never quite gets off the ground and is saddled with unfinished roads, inadequate utilities, and surroundings scarred by bulldozers—all from poor overall planning.

Now that you know what kinds of contractors are out there, you should be able to decide on which ones you'll consider. If possible, discount the latter two: the new marginal builder and the inept dishonest builder. That leaves the established, skilled, reputable builder and the skilled new builder. The first one is a sure thing. Go with one of them and you'll be guaranteed (or just about) of a satisfying, well-constructed dwelling that the builder will stand behind. Go with the newer builder and you're running a risk, however calculated, that something *could* happen to put that builder out of business in the near future.

Certain factors could influence you to go with a newer builder despite the increased risk. Perhaps you know one personally. Or you prefer to work with someone closer to your own age. Maybe the builder has bid substantially lower than the established builders, on the exact same specifications. All good builders were new contractors when they started, and if you believe one such builder is a rising star on the local scene, fine.

On the other hand, consider that relatively few builders starting out will have the staying power to make a long-range success in the business. Competition is tough, and the home marketplace is not very forgiving. It certainly takes a while to develop the depth of resources, the tricks of the trade, the knowledge of how to handle customers, the required contacts with subcontractors and housing inspectors, and the convenient credit lines at building-material supply houses.

On yet another hand, if you happen to hear that any builder you are considering is being sued for something, it doesn't necessarily mean that the builder is dishonest or incompetent. At one point or another, even the best, most trustworthy, most reliable builders are likely to become involved with some kind of legal actions brought on by unreasonable customers or conditions beyond their control.

SELECTING YOUR BIDDING CONTRACTORS

When approaching contractors for bids on your house, four is a good number of builders to insist upon. If you would choose only two, they *could* be two of the highest bidders available. With four, at least one of them is likely to be significantly lower. And builders, no matter what they say, are influenced by particulars such as the amount of work they already have waiting for them, if they're familiar with and prefer to build the floor plan in question, the time of year, and a host of idiosyncratic reasons too varied to list. In any event, let at least four contractors submit bids: the four you feel are the cream of the crop. That doesn't mean you can't go to more than four. Go ahead if you have the inclination, time, and energy. But on the whole, four will give you a good representation.

While deciding which contractors to select as your bidders, find out what you can about the likely candidates by investigating them in the following manner:

1. Ask real estate brokers and associates. However, be careful to ask only established real estate people. They know who builds the best houses and who gives the best service. They'll give you excellent leads that you can follow up on later. Mention beforehand what type of house you're looking to build, with a price range and, if possible, a setting (rural or city).

2. Ask bankers and lending officers. They know which contractors to avoid and can also refer you to reputable builders. Financial people tend to be slightly more objective than real estate agents, but they can also have slightly less knowledge about current construction particulars in the community.

3. Ask building-material suppliers and subcontractors, especially plumbers, electricians, roofers, and siding contractors. If they hedge, tell them you'll keep the information confidential. These individuals know which builders are erecting a lot of homes and which builders are floundering (not paying or unable to pay their bills). They know which builders go with quality materials and which keep coming back for marginal or poor-quality supplies.

4. Inquire at local chapters of the National Home Builder's Association, the Chamber of Commerce, and the Better Business Bureau. The Home Builder's Association is a good place to start. It's a sharp organization that encourages builders to keep up with the latest designs and technology. More often than not, if

you describe the type of house you're planning and the approximate cost, the representative (probably a local builder) will shuffle his feet and in a low voice suggest a few possibilities— but not officially, of course. The representative will probably give you a membership listing and speak "off the record" in order not to ignore and slight other members by making a publicized referral. For a builder, being a member of an organization such as the Home Builder's Association is a plus, but it needn't be mandatory for your purposes.

5. Follow up your leads and meet the builders. Select the first candidate, call him at his place of business, and identify yourself as a potential customer who would like to meet him for a *few* minutes (it's important to stress a few minutes, because as you'll quickly find out, builders are extremely busy people). Preferably, meet him at his office so you can see firsthand how he takes care of the business end of his work. Find out how long he's been a contractor, how he prefers to work with his customers, and what warranties and guarantees does he make. What responsibility does he assume for subcontractors he will hire? Ask for a list of previous houses he built from five years ago to the present. Naturally, he's not going to steer you to any trouble spots, but any example will be helpful to gauge the quality of his work.

At this point, don't supply a lot of detailed information about the house you want to build. Tell him the type, the size, and perhaps a general idea of the floor plan.

It's a bad sign if a builder has jumped in and out of several construction companies during the past year or two, or if he's changed his company's name several times, or if he went from a one-person operation to a partnership to a corporation, and then back to a one-person show again. A frequent indicator of pride in workmanship (but not 100 percent accurate) is that most good, reputable builders use their names in their company's title.

Ask him to tell you what makes his houses unique. How are they well constructed? What are their selling features? Is it attention to detail? The quality of workmanship? Is it energy efficiency using the latest technological advances? Let him prove to you why you should consider his organization. If he's close-mouthed, irritated, and short of patience with you, it could mean one of two things: that's just his basic personality, or he's not thrilled about receiving the work. If it's the former, remember that if your personality doesn't mesh with his, the relationship will probably be an uncomfortable one. If the latter, maybe he's got all the work he can handle already, and if so, his bid will likely be high anyway. You're usually better off considering only those contractors with whom you can develop an open, friendly rapport, and who also seem to really want the work.

6. Now it's time to start looking at some of the houses the builders have recently erected. Attend any of their open houses you can find and tour some of the examples you've been given as references. It's also a good idea to visit a few open houses constructed by builders you've been told to steer clear of, in order to get a first-hand look at marginal or poor construction. Using the information you've learned so far, you can rate the houses you visit and see how they stack up against one another.

7. Contact some of each contractor's past customers. Building a house is a big deal. You want to select someone who will listen to any problems that crop up later, *after* the house is finished and the builder has been paid. Ask the owners of several of his houses how the builder followed up on problems that might have occurred. Did he act promptly and courteously on anything that needed to be replaced or repaired? Were the owners satisfied with his construction results and after-sale services? Even total strangers like to talk about their houses when approached in a low-key kind of way. From them, you can receive lengthy outpourings of information.

   Don't discuss the houses with the owners while a contractor is present or you'll get clouded information. Owners won't speak freely for fear of insulting or making the contractor angry. If you have to, go back at another time, alone.

8. Have the contractor take you through one of his brand-new or under-construction houses. This is only after scoring him high on the referrals, the personal interview, and the quality of his construction. If possible, have him take you through a house

similar to the one you are planning. Let him do most of the talking. Let him demonstrate why you would be better off going with his services instead of those from somebody else.

Visiting the contractor's job site will also tell you much about his construction habits. If the place is messy and disorganized, it's reasonable to wonder whether he should be trusted to handle your house.

9. Find out if any of the potential contractors possess traits that would give them advantages over other builders. Do any of them own lumber supply stores, or any other building-supply companies? If that's the case, you might be able to obtain lumber, windows, insulation, fixtures, siding, and roofing at or very close to cost. Do any of the builders own land that you'd consider ideal for your building site? Or will any of them provide their own financing, at below-open-market rates and terms?

SOLICITING THE BIDS

Now it's time to take the four or more contractors you select and go to them with your drawings, sketches, specifications, and ideas, and ask them to figure out prices for you. Don't go to your bid meetings unprepared. Instead, make up a copy of what specifications you'd like and have one for yourself and one for each builder. Give a copy to each of the four or more builders who are in the bidding process for your house, so they're all bidding on the same job.

At the end of the chapter is a fairly complete listing of individual specifications for a 2,400-square-foot two-story house with an attached two-car garage. It contains references to most of the specifications you should be concerned with. You can make up a similar set of your own before you approach your builders for bids.

Now all you do is wait for the bids to come back for evaluation. Chances are that at least two of them will be significantly lower than the other and will warrant your closest inspection. Are they talking apples to apples? Review their quotes with the contractors in person to clarify any points that are confusing or too general.

When your evaluations are through, just pick one, the contractor you think you should go with based on his bid, his reputation, his construction examples, and any other factors you're considering. If you've done your homework already, any of the builders you asked to bid would be a safe choice.

Choosing a good contractor will save you money, make you money, and ensure peace of mind and a comfortable, well-built home. It will make the entire house-building experience fun. Selecting a wrong contractor will definitely cost you more money and could even destroy your sanity and faith in humankind.

Before we're off the subject, here are a few additional dos and don'ts to remember when dealing with the selection of your contractor:

1. Don't hire someone who is based out of town.

2. Don't hire a contractor based on price alone.

3. Do be suspicious of extremely low bids. A bid that is miles away from the rest could mean that the builder doesn't know the business costs or that a fraudulent builder is counting on breaking the contract midway through construction by enticing you to change some small detail—consequently rendering the agreement null and void. Once that happens, the builder will renegotiate, charging you additional costs and blackmailing you into accepting either more house or more costs than you originally bargained for.

4. Don't accept oral agreements. Get the specifications in writing.

5. Don't believe that you're going to get excellent construction at discount prices. The best you should hope for is sound value at a fair price.

6. Do avoid the marginal and vanishing builders like the plague.

AFTER YOU'VE SELECTED YOUR CONTRACTOR

After you've selected your contractor it's smart to call the unsuccessful bidders and tell them they didn't get the job. Not many people have the courage or consideration to do so, and the contractors will appreciate your honesty and straightforwardness.

On the following pages, you'll find a sample checklist of frequently chosen specifications. Your final specification checklist should cover as many details as possible. Giving a detailed specification sheet to the contractor will allow for a more complete and accurate bid.

SPECIFICATION CHECKLIST

Foundation

a. **Footers:**
— 12" × 24" footer
concrete mix specification
strength of 3500 psi

b. **Foundation Wall:**
— 10" concrete blocks
11 course high
reinforced with ⅝" steel rods and
cement filled in holes every
other block
specify number of pilasters

c. **Basement Floor:**
— Concrete slab
— 8" of gravel under slab
— 4" thick concrete slab

d. **Footer Drains:**
— 4" plastic pipe in gravel

e. **Supports:**
— Specify size of steel I-beam
— Specify size of steel columns

f. **Windows:**
— Steel, (2), specify size

g. **Sills:**
— 2" × 10"
— ¼" foam under sill plate
— Specify size of bolts for anchors

Flooring

a. **Floor Framing:**
— SPF 2" × 10"
— Bridging 1" × 3"

b. **Subflooring:**
— Plywood 4' × 8' × ½" CDX
first and second floor
right angles
glued and screwed to floor joists

c. **Finish Flooring:**

First Floor:
— ⅝" particleboard, (screwed) all
rooms
15-lb. felt between layers

Second Floor:
— ½" particleboard, (screwed) all
rooms
15-lb. felt between layers

(Continued)

✔✔✔✔✔ SPECIFICATION CHECKLIST (*Continued*)

d. Ceiling Framing:
— SPF 2" × 10" second floor bridging 1" × 3"

Exterior Walls

a. Wood Frame:
— No. 2 BTR SPF 2" × 6" (16″ o.c.) plywood (½" thick) house wrap covering
— Vinyl or aluminum siding (color), grade A, bevel type, double 4 (8"), woodgrain-finish aluminum nails
— 6" fiberglass insulation
— Outside cellwood shutters, front only
color: smoke
— 12" overhangs

Inside Walls:
— SPF 2" × 4" (16" o.c.) ⅝" drywall walls
— Oak trim throughout (stain, sealer, varnish)

Roof Framing:
— Engineered wood I-beam roof rafter, joists (16" o.c.)

Roofing:
— Solid plywood 4' × 8' × ¾" CDX asphalt shingles, 250-lb.
15-lb. waterproof felt under shingles
tin flashing
ridge vent and soffit vents

Gutters and Downspouts

a. Gutters:
— Aluminum
.025 gauge
4" size
shape style 'k

SPECIFICATION CHECKLIST *(Continued)*

b. Downspouts:	— **Aluminum** **.025 gauge** **4" size** **shape—square corrugated** **rectangular** **4 drops total**
Insulation:	
	— **Ceilings 10" fiberglass** **walls 6" fiberglass**
Miscellaneous:	
a. Closets:	— **2 rods/2 shelves per closet**
b. Other on-site improvements:	— **Rough grading only**
c. Landscaping and finish grading:	— **By owner**
d. Walks and driveway:	— **Quote separate price for this** **6" thick with mesh and rod** **reinforcement**
e. Hardware (doors):	— **Brass**
Interior Doors and Trim	
a. Doors:	— **Flush** **oak** **1⅜" thick with 3 hinges**
b. Door Trim:	— **Modern** **oak**
c. Base:	— **Modern** **oak** **3" size**
d. Finish:	— **Doors and trim, stain, sealer,** **varnish**
e. Dining Room:	— **Chair rail**
Windows	
a. Double-hung and casement	— **Vinyl** — **Sash thickness 1⅜"**

(Continued)

✓✓✓✓✓ SPECIFICATION CHECKLIST (*Continued*)

— Insulated grade with glazed low-e glass
— Head flashing (vinyl)
— Weather stripping (vinyl)
— Triple-track storm windows on the outside
— Oak trim (stain, sealer, varnish)

Entrances and Exterior Detail

a. **Main entrance door:**

— Steel
— 36" wide
— 1¾" thick with 3 hinges
— White pine for frame

b. **Garage overhead doors:**

— Steel insulated, two 9' × 7' doors with weather stripping

c. **Garage entrance door:**

— Steel
— 36" wide
— 1¾" thick with 3 hinges
— White pine for frame
— Head flashing (aluminum)
— Weather stripping (vinyl)

d. **Family room door:**

— Double French door
— Center hinged door with screen

Exterior Millwork

— Aluminum (vented) roof louvers

Electric Wiring

a. **General:**

— Circuit breaker
— Specify amp capacity
— 20 circuits
— All copper cable
— Air-conditioning connection
— Washer and dryer hookup in laundry room
— Provisions for a sump pump hookup
— Provisions for garage door openers

SPECIFICATION CHECKLIST (*Continued*)

— Provisions for an overhead fan in the family room
— Doorbell (front door and side garage door)
— 3 exterior outlets (2 front and 1 back)
— Dimmer switch for dining room, family room, and eating area
— Humidifier hookup on furnace
— Freezer outlet in basement

b. Bathroom no. 1:
— Light over vanity
— Exhaust fan
— Ground-fault circuit interrupter outlet

c. Bathroom no. 2:
— Lights over vanity
— Light/exhaust/heat fan
— Ground-fault circuit interrupter outlet

d. Bathroom no. 3:
— Light over vanity
— Light/exhaust fan
— Ground-fault circuit interrupter outlet

e. Outside Lighting:
— 1 at side garage door
— 2 at sides of large garage door
— 2 at front door
— 2 at back sliding doors

f. Inside Lighting:
— 3 recessed lights over fireplace
— 1 in eating area
— 1 in kitchen
— 1 over kitchen sink
— 1 in entrace foyer
— 2 inside garage
— 2 in second floor hallway
— 3 (one in each bedroom)
— 1 in dining room
— 1 over countertop
— 1 inside each clothes closet

(Continued)

✔✔✔✔✔ SPECIFICATION CHECKLIST (*Continued*)

g. Kitchen: — Exhaust fan and light (hood over range)

Plumbing

a. General:
— All copper water pipes
— PVC drain pipes
— Cast-iron piping below cellar
— Washer hookup with sink in laundry room
— 3 exterior faucets (back of house, front of house, and in garage)
— Provisions for a complete bath in basement (sink, shower, toilet)
— Gas line and electric power for laundry room dryer
— Glass-lined, gas water heater (50 gal.)
— Gas hookup for stove in kitchen
— Gas starter in fireplace
— Gas line for furnace
— Dishwasher hookup in kitchen
— Water hookup for humidifier on furnace

b. Kitchen:
— Stainless steel double sink
— Single-lever faucet with spray

c. Bathroom no. 1:
— Sink and toilet with insuliner (first-floor half bath) (specify color of sink and toilet)
faucet

d. Bathroom no. 2:
— Sink and toilet with insuliner (second-floor full bath) (specify color of sink and toilet)
fiberglass tub-shower combo (5') (color)
faucet
showerhead to have pressure-balancing safety valve

SPECIFICATION CHECKLIST (*Continued*)

e. Bathroom no. 3:
— Sink and toilet with insuliner
 (master bedroom full bath)
 (specify color of sink and toilet)
— Fiberglass shower stall with door
 (4') (color)
— Faucet
 showerhead to have pressure-
 balancing safety valve

Heating

— Natural gas
— Fan-forced, two-stage, variable-
 speed blower
— Perimeter system
— Galvanized steel ducts, supply
 and return furnace supply ducts
 to have 2" thick insulation
— Minimum of 2,400 square feet
 heating capacity
— Electric start with pilotless
 ignition

Cooling

— Multilevel cooling, variable-
 speed indoor blower

Porches

— Concrete front porch
 1 pillar

Garage

— Framed as house
 4" concrete floor, with slope to
 floor drain

Floor Covering:

— Carpet to be responsibility of
 buyer
 kitchen and eating area, foyer,
 baths 1, 2, 3 inlaid
 linoleum

(*Continued*)

✔✔✔✔✔ **SPECIFICATION CHECKLIST** (*Continued*)

Bathroom Accessories

— Recessed/chrome
— Attached/chrome

Cabinets and Interior Detail

— Cabinets (oak)
— Countertops
— Medicine cabinets (2)
— Vanity (all baths)
— Mirrors (2)

Stairs

— Oak handrail
— Oak balustrade

Fireplace

— Ash dump and cleanout
— Brick facing
— Firebrick lining
— Brick hearth
— Wood mantel (solid)
— Gas starter

Chimney

— Brick facing
— Block construction
— Tile flue lining
— Heater flue size
— Gas furnace vent size
— Water heater vent size

▶▶▶▶▶ **POINTS TO PONDER**

1. Inquire. Ask real estate brokers, lending officers, building-material suppliers, and subcontractors, especially plumbers, electricians, roofers, and siding contractors, to point out the most reputable home builders they know.

2. Continue asking. Inquire at local chapters of the Home Builder's Association, the Chamber of Commerce, and the Better Business Bureau. You may not get "official" specific recommendations, but you'll likely come away with a number of builder names, based on the size and type of home you're planning to build.

3. Decide on a "field" of builders, then make a point to meet them, if only briefly. Take a look at homes constructed by the builders you are considering: tour their open houses and/or ask them to show you one of their brand-new or under-construction houses.

4. With the builders high on your potential list, contact several of each's past customers, and find out if any of the builders have distinct advantages over the others (i.e., perhaps one owns a builder's supply company, too).

5. Select the top three or four builders and supply them with your home specifications. Tell them exactly what you want.

6. Don't be afraid to entertain suggestions from any of the bidding contractors. Just make allowances for those suggestions when comparing the submitted bids.

7. Chances are that at least two of the contractors will be significantly lower than the other(s), and will warrant your closest inspection. Be suspicious, however, of any extremely low bids. Don't expect excellent construction at a discount price. Instead, be happy with a sound value at a fair price.

8. When your evaluations are through, make your best pick, the contractor you think you should go with based on his bid, his reputation, his construction examples, and any other factors you're considering.

9. Don't accept an oral agreement. Put everything that's agreeable to both you and the contractor in writing.

10. After your decision is made, inform all of the contractors—not just the one you selected.

Working with Your Contractor

After selecting the contractor you want, the next step is to draw up an agreement or contract. This agreement, along with the final plans, drawings, and specifications, will act as a guideline for your relationship with the builder. It has to be signed by all parties before the first shovelful of earth is turned. Most builders will have such an agreement already prepared, with specification blanks to be filled in.

On page 738 is a sample contract agreement between a general contractor and a party who is arranging the construction of a new house. It's a good example, and covers most of the concerns either party could have, yet it can still be amended, its sections changed, added to, or deleted with the approval of both parties.

As another example of how the building materials are described, page 740 shows a sample specifications form filled out for the same two-story house: called a Description of Materials list.

The sample contract addresses the scope of work involved, expected time for completion, and lists reasons for legitimate delays. It also states the inability of the builder to assign his responsibilities to others, describes the contract documents, explains insurance particulars, presents procedures for making alterations or extra work, and discusses housekeeping and trash removal from the building site. It covers compliance with ordinances and statutes, arbitration in the event of

CONTRACT AGREEMENT
By and Between

Mr.   Richard C. Jones

Mrs.   Jennifer H. Jones

Address   2014 Warsaw Avenue

Erie, Pennsylvania

AND

Realto Construction Company
1435 East 12th Street
Erie, Pennsylvania

Building Site   Lot #35, Oakland Hills

THIS AGREEMENT MADE THIS _____ day of _____,
19_____ by and between Richard C. Jones and Jennifer H. Jones of the City of Erie, County
of Erie, and State of Pennsylvania, hereinafter called "Owners"

AND

Realto Construction Company, a corporation with principle offices in the City of Erie, County of
Erie, and State of Pennsylvania, hereinafter called "Contractor."

<u>WITNESSETH</u> The Owners and Contractor for and in consideration of the mutual covenants of
each other, and for and in consideration of the work to be done by the Contractor and the money
to be paid by the Owners, as hereinafter set forth, it is agreed between the parties as follows:

1. <u>SCOPE OF WORK</u> The Contractor covenants and agrees to furnish all the labor, perform all
the work that shall be required for the erection of a 2 story frame dwelling which is more fully
set forth in plans, attached hereto and marked Exhibit "A", and specifications attached hereto and
marked Exhibit "B", both of which documents have been initialed by the parties. Said dwelling
house to be built on the property of the Owners, Lot #35 Oakland Hills Subdivision.

The Contractor covenants and agrees to do and complete all the work set forth in said plans
and specifications for the erection of said dwelling house, in a good and workmanlike manner, and
within a reasonable time after the construction job has been started. The Contractor specifically
covenants and agrees to pursue the work diligently without delay after the construction of said dwelling
house has been started by them. All work shall be new and all workmanship done and performed
under this Contract, by the Contractor, shall be of good quality and shall be performed in a good
and workmanlike manner. The Contractor shall protect all the parts of the work from damage by
cold or other elements. The Contractor shall also be responsible for temporary electrical service.
All the work and materials furnished by the Contractor shall meet or exceed the minimum FHA
requirements. The Contractor shall be responsible for the building permit, gas permit, and sewer
permit and for the expense entailed in obtaining said permits. The Contractor further covenants
and agrees to sign a Release of Mechanic's Lien before any work is started.

2. <u>TIME OF COMPLETION</u> The work shall be started as soon as possible, weather permitting,
and shall be completed as soon as possible, Acts of God, strikes, material shortages, government
regulations, or catastrophes excepted. The Contractor covenants and agrees to pursue the work of
erecting said dwelling house in a diligent manner after the same has been started.

3. <u>DELAY OF COMPLETION</u> If after the dwelling house has been substantially completed and
livable, full completion thereof is materially delayed through no fault of the Contractor, the Owners
shall, and without terminating the Contract, make payment for the balance due the Contractor for
that part of the work fully completed and accepted by the Owners.

4. <u>ASSIGNMENTS</u> The Contractor shall not assign this Contract to others. However, this shall
not prohibit the sub-contracting of parts of the work to others by the Contractor.

5. <u>CONTRACT DOCUMENTS</u> The Contract documents shall consist of the Contract Agreement,
the Specifications, and the Plans and they are all as fully a part of the Contract Agreement as if
attached hereto and herein repeated. The Parties herewith covenant and agree that upon execution
of this agreement they shall, each of them, initial the specifications and the plans.

6. <u>INSURANCE</u> The Contractor shall insure himself against all claims under Workman's Compensation Acts and all other claims for damage for personal injuries, including death, which may arise from operations under this Contract, whether such operations be by themselves, or by anyone directly or indirectly employed by him. The Contractor shall save the Owners of this protection. The Owners shall maintain fire insurance and vandalism insurance on the structure as soon as the sub-floor is completed, and the Contractor shall be reimbursed from said insurance from any and all loss due to fire.

7. <u>EXTRA WORK OR ALTERATIONS</u> The Owners shall have the right to make changes or alterations, but any order for change or alterations shall be in writing and signed by the Owners and the Contractor; said amount shall be stated in the written order, and to be paid to the Contractor (or Owner if it shall be a saving) before final payment is made. The extra charges, if any, shall be considered a part of the contract cost.

8. <u>CLEANING UP</u> The Contractor shall, at all times, keep the premises free from all unnecessary accumulation of waste material or rubbish caused by his employees or the work and at the completion of the work he shall remove all rubbish from and about the building, and all tools, scaffolding, surplus material, and shall leave the work "broom clean."

9. <u>ORDINANCE AND STATUTES COMPLIANCE</u> The Contractor shall conform in all respects to the provisions and regulations of any general or local building acts or ordinances, or any authority pertinent to the area. The Contractor covenants and agrees that he has examined the land, plans and specifications, and understands any and all difficulties that may arise in the execution of this Contract. The Contractor specifically covenants and agrees that in laying out the house, he shall observe the building line required in the sub-division. The Owners, however, shall be responsible for providing an exact survey of the building site.

10. <u>ARBITRATION CLAUSE</u> In the event any dispute arises between the parties hereto which cannot be amicably settled between the parties, it is hereby agreed that each party shall appoint an arbitrator within three days after receipt of written request from the other, that the two arbitrators so appointed shall select a third arbitrator within three days after notice of their appointment, and that the arbitrators shall hear the dispute and, by majority decision, make a decision or award. It is agreed that any compensation required by the arbitrators shall be shared equally by the parties thereto regardless of the decision or award made.

11. <u>ACCEPTANCE BY OWNERS AND OCCUPANCY</u> It is agreed that upon completion, said dwelling shall be inspected by the Owners and the Contractor, and that any repairs or adjustments which are necessary shall be made by the Contractor. It is further agreed that the Owners shall not be permitted to occupy said dwelling until the Contractor is paid the full amount of the Contract. Occupancy of said dwelling by the Owners in violation of the foregoing provisions shall constitute unconditional acceptance of the dwelling house and a waiver of any defects or uncompleted work.

12. <u>TIME OF PAYMENTS</u>
    1st Stage—Platform: 10%
    2nd Stage—Under roof: 35%
    3rd Stage—Plastered: 25%
    4th Stage—Trim completed: 20%
    5th Stage—Completion: 10%
    (Or according to bank regulations that closely resemble the above schedule.)

13. <u>WARRANTY</u> The final payment shall not relieve the Contractor of responsibility for faulty materials or workmanship; and he shall remedy any defects due thereto within a period of one year, material free with minimum service charge. This warranty is only valid when the Contractor is paid contract cost in full.

    This contract shall be binding upon parties, their heirs, executors and assigns. And by this agreement, the parties intend to be legally bound in witness whereof, the parties have hereunto set their hands and seals the day and year first written above.

VETERANS ADMINISTRATION, U.S.D.A. FARMERS HOME ADMINISTRATION, AND
U.S. DEPARTMENT OF HOUSING AND URBAN DEVELOPMENT
HOUSING – FEDERAL HOUSING COMMISSIONER

Form Approved
OMB No. 2502-0192

*(For accurate register of carbon copies, form may be separated along above fold.
Staple completed sheets together in original order.)*

☐ **Proposed Construction**

☐ **Under Construction**

DESCRIPTION OF MATERIALS

No. _____
(To be inserted by FHA, VA or FmHA)

Property address _____ City _____ State _____

Mortgagor or Sponsor _____ _____
                                    (Name)   (Address)

Contractor or Builder _____ _____
                                    (Name)   (Address)

INSTRUCTIONS

1. For additional information on how this form is to be submitted, number of copies, etc., see the instructions applicable to the HUD Application for Mortgage Insurance, VA Request for Determination of Reasonable Value, or FmHA Property Information and Appraisal Report, as the case may be.

2. Describe all materials and equipment to be used, whether or not shown on the drawings, by marking an X in each appropriate check-box and entering the information called for each space. If space is inadequate, enter "See misc." and describe under Item 27 or on an attached sheet. THE USE OF PAINT CONTAINING MORE THAN THE PERCENTAGE OF LEAD BY WEIGHT PERMITTED BY LAW IS PROHIBITED.

3. Work not specifically described or shown will not be considered unless required, then the minimum acceptable will be assumed. Work exceeding minimum requirements cannot be considered unless specifically described.

4. Include no alternates, "or equal" phrases, or contradictory items. (Consideration of a request for acceptance of substitute materials or equipment is not thereby precluded.)

5. Include signatures required at the end of this form.

6. The construction shall be completed in compliance with the related drawings and specifications, as amended during processing. The specifications include this Description of Materials and the applicable Minimum Property Standards.

1. EXCAVATION:
Bearing soil, type ___Gravel, Clay___

2. FOUNDATIONS:
Footings: concrete mix ___Specify Mix___ ; strength psi ___3500#___ Reinforcing _____
Foundation wall: material ___10" Concrete Block___ Reinforcing ___Rods & Cement in Core___
Interior foundation wall: material _____
Columns: material and sizes ___Steel, Specify Size___ Piers: material and reinforcing _____
Girders: material and sizes ___Steel, Specify Size___ Sills: material ___2×10___
Basement entrance areaway _____ Window areaways ___Galvanized Steel___
Waterproofing ___Sprayed Asphalt Coating___ Footing drains ___4" Plastic Pipe in Gravel___
Termite protection _____
Basementless space: ground cover _____ ; insulation _____ ; foundation vents _____
Special foundations _____
Additional information: ___Sill Sealer Insulation___

3. CHIMNEYS:
Material ___Stone & Block___ Prefabricated *(make and size)* _____
Flue lining: material ___Tile___ Heater flue size ___Specify Size___ Fireplace flue size ___Specify Size___
Vents *(material and size)*: gas or oil heater ___Specify Size___ ; water heater ___Specify Size___
Additional information _____

4. FIREPLACES:
Type: ☒ solid fuel; ☐ gas-burning; ☐ circulator *(make and size)* _____ Ash dump and clean-out ___1 Each___
Fireplace: facing ___Stone___ ; lining ___Firebrick___ ; hearth ___Brick___ ; mantel _____
Additional information: ___Include Gas Starter___

5. EXTERIOR WALLS:
Wood frame: wood grade, and species ___#2 BTR SPF (2×6)___ ☐ Corner bracing. Building paper or felt ___Building Paper Covering___
Sheathing ___Plywood___ ; thickness ___1/2"___ ; width ___4'×8'___ ; ☒ solid; ☐ spaced _____ " o. c.; ☐ diagonal; _____
Siding ___Aluminum___ ; grade ___A___ ; type ___Bevel___ ; size ___DBL-4___ ; exposure ___8___ "; fastening ___Alum. Nails___
Shingles _____ ; grade _____ ; type _____ size _____ ; exposure _____ "; fastening _____
Stucco _____ ; thickness _____ "; Lath _____ _____ ; weight _____ lb.

Masonry veneer **Stone** Sills **Stone** Lintels _____ Base flashing _____

Masonry: ☐ solid ☐ faced ☐ stuccoed; total wall thickness _____ "; facing thickness _____ "; facing material _____

Backup material _____; thickness _____ "; bonding _____

Door sills _____ Window sills _____ Lintels _____ Base flashing _____

Interior surfaces dampproofing, _____ coats of _____; furring _____

Additional information: _____

Exterior painting: material **Specify brand** ; number of coats **2**

Gable wall construction ☒ same as main walls, ☐ other construction _____

6. FLOOR FRAMING:

Joists: wood, grade, and species **SPF 2x10** other _____; bridging **1x3** ; anchors **Specify**

Concrete slab: ☒ basement floor, ☐ first floor, ☒ ground supported; ☐ self-supporting; mix **Specify Mix** thickness **4** ";

reinforcing _____; insulation _____; membrane _____

Fill under slab: material **Gravel** ; thickness **8** ". Additional information: _____

7. SUBFLOORING: (Describe underflooring for special floors under item 21.)

Material: grade and species **Plywood** ; size **4x8-½**, type **CDX**

Laid ☒ first floor, ☒ second floor; ☐ attic _____ sq. ft.; ☐ diagonal; ☒ right angles. Additional information: _____

8. FINISH FLOORING: (Wood only. Describe other finish flooring under item 21.)

Location	Rooms	Grade	Species	Thickness	Width	Bldg. Paper	Finish
First floor	All Rooms	5/8"	Particle Board			#15 Felt	
Second floor	All Rooms	½"	Particle Board			#15 Felt	
Attic floor		sq ft					

Additional information: _____

9. PARTITION FRAMING:

Studs: wood, grade, and species **SPF 2x6-outside / 2x4-inside** size and spacing **2x4 - 16" o.c.** Other _____

Additional information: _____

10. CEILING FRAMING:

Joists: wood, grade, and species **2x10 - 2nd Floor** Other _____ Bridging **1x3**

Additional information: _____

11. ROOF FRAMING:

Rafters: wood, grade, and species **Engineered Wood I-Beam Roof Rafters** Roof trusses (see detail): grade and species **16" o.c.**

Additional information: _____

12. ROOFING:

Sheathing: wood, grade, and species **Plywood** ; ☒ solid; ☐ spaced _____ " o.c.

Roofing **Asphalt Shingles** ; grade **C** ; size **4x8-½**; type **CDX**

Underlay **#15 Felt** ; weight or thickness _____; size _____; fastening _____

Built-up roofing _____; number of plies _____; surfacing material _____

Flashing: material **Tin** ; gage or weight _____; ☐ gravel stops; ☐ snow guards

Additional information: _____

13. GUTTERS AND DOWNSPOUTS:

Gutters: material **Aluminum** ; gage or weight **.025** ; size **4"** ; shape **Style K**

Downspouts: material **Aluminum** ; gage or weight **.025** ; size **4"** ; shape **Rectangular**; number **4**

Downspouts connected to: ☐ Storm sewer; ☐ sanitary sewer; ☐ dry-well. ☐ Splash blocks: material and size _____

Additional information: _____

14. LATH AND PLASTER

Lath ☒ walls, ☒ ceilings: material _____; weight or thickness **5/8"** Plaster: coats **1** ; finish _____;

Dry-wall ☐ walls, ☐ ceilings: material _____; thickness _____; finish _____;

Joint treatment _____

15. DECORATING: (Paint, wallpaper, etc.)

Rooms	Wall Finish Material and Application	Ceiling Finish Material and Application
Kitchen		
Bath	By Owner	
Other		

Additional information: _____

16. INTERIOR DOORS AND TRIM:

Doors: type **Flush** ; material **Oak** ; thickness **1-3/8"**

Door trim: type **Modern** ; material **Oak** ; Base: type **Modern** ; material **Oak** ; size **3"**

Finish: doors **Stain - Sealer - Varnish** ; trim **Stain - Sealer - Varnish**

Other trim (item, type and location) _____

Additional information: **3 Hinges Per Door**

17. WINDOWS:
Windows: type _DBL-Hung + Cas._; make _____; material _Vinyl_; sash thickness _1-3/8"_
Glass: grade _Insulated_; ☐ sash weights; ☒ balances, type _____; head flashing _Vinyl_
Trim: type _Modern_; material _Oak_ Paint _Stain-Sealer-Varnish_ number coats _____
Weatherstripping: type _____; material _Vinyl_ Storm sash, number _____
Screens ☒ full; ☐ half; type _____; number _13_; screen cloth material _Aluminum_
Basement windows: type _Hopper_; material _Steel_; screens, number _____ Storm sash, number _____
Special windows _____
Additional information _6' Aluminum Glass Sliding Door_

18. ENTRANCES AND EXTERIOR DETAIL:
Main entrance door: material _Steel_; width _36"_; thickness _1-3/4"_ Frame: material _W. Pine_, thickness _5/4"_
Other entrance doors: material _Steel_; width _36"_; thickness _1-3/4"_ Frame: material _W. Pine_, thickness _5/4"_
Head flashing _Aluminum_ Weatherstripping: type _Vinyl_; saddles _____
Screen doors: thickness _____"; number _____; screen cloth material _____ Storm doors: thickness _____"; number _____
Combination storm and screen doors: thickness _____"; number _____; screen cloth material _____
Shutters: ☐ hinged; ☒ fixed. Railings _____; Attic louvers _____
Exterior millwork: grade and species _Aluminum (vented)_ Paint _____; number coats _____
Additional information: _Roof Louvers_

19. CABINETS AND INTERIOR DETAIL:
Kitchen cabinets, wall units: material _____; lineal feet of shelves _70_; shelf width _12_
Base units: material _____; counter top _____; edging _____
Back and end splash _Formica_ Finish of cabinets _Factory_; number coats _____
Medicine cabinets: make _14 x 18 Bath 2_; model _Mirror - Bath 1 + Lav 1 + 2_
Other cabinets and built-in furniture _Vanity - Bath 1 + Lav 1 + 2_
Additional information _____

20. STAIRS:

Stair	Tread		Riser		Stringer		Handrail		Balusters	
	Material	Thickness	Material	Thickness	Material	Size	Material	Size	Material	Size
Basement	SPF	1-1/2	W. Pine	3/4	SPF	2 x 10	W. Pine	2"		
Main	Oak	1-1/2	W. Pine	3/4	W. Pine	2 x 12	W. Iron			
Attic										

Disappearing: make and model number _____
Additional information: _____

21. SPECIAL FLOORS AND WAINSCOT: *(Describe Carpet as listed in Certified Products Directory)*

	Location	Material, Color, Border, Sizes, Gage, Etc.	Threshold Material	Wall Base Material	Underfloor Material
FLOORS	Kitchen + Eating Area	Inlaid Lino (#___ Sq yd Allowance)		Oak	Particle Brd.
	Bath 1 + 2	" " " " "		"	"
	Lav 1 + 2	" " " " " "		"	"
	Foyer	" " " " " " "		"	"

	Location	Material, Color, Border, Cap. Sizes, Gage, Etc.	Height	Height Over Tub	Height in Showers (From Floor)
WAINSCOT	Bath				

Bathroom accessories: ☒ Recessed; material _Chrome_; number _5_; ☒ Attached; material _Chrome_; number _5_
Additional information: _____

22. PLUMBING:

Fixture	Number	Location	Make	Mfr's Fixture Identification No.	Size	Color
Sink	1	Kitchen	or Equal		32 x 21	St. Steel
Lavatory	4	Baths + Lavs	or Equal		18"	White
Water closet	4	" "	" "		Cadet	White
Bathtub	1	Bath 1	Fiberglass		5'	White
Shower over tub ▲	1	Bath 1				
Stall shower △	1	Bath 2	Fiberglass		4'	White
Laundry trays						

▲☒ Curtain rod △☒ Door ☐ Shower pan: material _Fiberglass_
Water supply ☒ public; ☐ community system; ☐ individual (private) system. ★
Sewage disposal ☒ public; ☐ community system; ☐ individual (private) system. ★

★ *Show and describe individual system in complete detail in separate drawings and specifications according to requirements.*

House drain (inside): ☒ cast iron; ☐ tile; ☐ other ____ House sewer (outside): ☒ cast iron; ☐ tile; ☐ other ____

Water piping ☐ galvanized steel; ☒ copper tubing; ☐ other ____ Sill cocks, number __3__

Domestic water heater: type __Gas__ ; make and model ____ ; heating capacity __40__ ____ gph. 100° rise. Storage tank: material __Glass Lined__ ; capacity __40__ gallons.

Gas service ☐ utility company, ☐ liq. pet. gas, ☐ other ____ Gas piping ☐ cooking; ☐ house heating.

Footing drains connected to ☐ storm sewer; ☒ sanitary sewer; ☐ dry well. Sump pump; make and model ____ ____ ; capacity ____ ; discharges into ____

23. HEATING:

☐ Hot water ☐ Steam. ☐ Vapor. ☐ One-pipe system. ☐ Two-pipe system.

☐ Radiators. ☐ Convectors. ☐ Baseboard radiation. Make and model ____

Radiant panel ☐ floor; ☐ wall; ☐ ceiling. Panel coil: material ____

☐ Circulator. ☐ Return pump. Make and model ____ ; capacity ____ gpm.

Boiler: make and model ____ Output ____ Btuh.; net rating ____ Btuh.

Additional information ____

Warm air: ☐ Gravity ☒ Forced. Type of system __Natural Gas, 2-Stage, Variable Speed__

Duct material: supply __Galv. steel__ ; return __Galv. Steel__ Insulation __Fiberglass__, thickness ____ ☐ Outside air intake.

Furnace: make and model __Brand, Model__ Input __130,000__ Btuh.; output ____ Btuh.

Additional information: ____

☐ Space heater; ☐ floor furnace; ☐ wall heater. Input ____ Btuh.; output ____ Btuh.; number units ____

Make, model ____ Additional information: ____

Controls: make and types ____

Additional information ____

Fuel: ☐ Coal; ☐ oil; ☒ gas; ☐ liq. pet. gas; ☐ electric; ☐ other ____ ; storage capacity ____

Additional information ____

Firing equipment furnished separately: ☐ Gas burner, conversion type. ☐ Stoker: hopper feed ☐; bin feed ☐

Oil burner: ☐ pressure atomizing; ☐ vaporizing ____

Make and model ____ Control ____

Additional information: ____

Electric heating system: type ____ Input ____ watts; @ ____ volts; output ____ Btuh.

Additional information: ____

Ventilating equipment: attic fan, make and model ____ ; capacity ____ cfm.

kitchen exhaust fan, make and model ____

Other heating, ventilating or cooling equipment __Vent Fan Lev 1 + 2__

24. ELECTRIC WIRING:

Service ☒ overhead; ☐ underground. Panel: ☐ fuse box; ☒ circuit-breaker; make __GLS__ AMP's **Specify** __Amps__ No. circuits __20__

Wiring ☐ conduit; ☐ armored cable; ☒ nonmetallic cable; ☐ knob and tube; ☐ other ____

Special outlets ☒ range; ☐ water heater; ☐ other __Dryer__

☐ Doorbell. ☒ Chimes. Push-button locations __Front Door__ Additional information: ____

25. LIGHTING FIXTURES:

Total number of fixtures __22__ Total allowance for fixtures, typical installation, $ ____ __Retail__

Nontypical installation ____

Additional information: ____

26. INSULATION:

Location	Thickness	Material, Type, and Method of Installation	Vapor Barrier
Roof			
Ceiling	10"	Fiberglass	Included
Wall	6"	Fiberglass	Included
Floor			

27. MISCELLANEOUS: (Describe any main dwelling materials, equipment, or construction items not shown elsewhere; or use to provide additional information where the space provided was inadequate. Always reference by item number to correspond to numbering used on this form.)

__Shelf + Rod in closet__

HARDWARE: *(make, material, and finish.)* _____ Brass (Quickset or Equal) _____

SPECIAL EQUIPMENT: *(State material or make, model and quantity.   Include only equipment and appliances which are acceptable by local law, custom and applicable FHA standards.   Do not include items which, by established custom, are supplied by occupant and removed when he vacates premises or chattles prohibited by law from becoming realty.)* _____

JKP27   Double Oven

GSD551W Dishwasher

GFC310   Disposal

C221 Range

PORCHES: Concrete Front Porch _____

TERRACES: By Owner _____

GARAGES: Framed as house, 4" concrete floor, 2-9'x7' overhead Doors

WALKS AND DRIVEWAYS: By Owner
Driveway: width _____ ; base material _____ ; thickness _____ "; surfacing material _____ ; thickness _____ "
Front walk: width _____ ; material _____ ; thickness _____ ". Service walk: width _____ ; material _____ ; thickness _____ "
Steps: material _____ ; treads _____ "; risers _____ ". Cheek walls _____

OTHER ONSITE IMPROVEMENTS:
(Specify all exterior onsite improvements not described elsewhere, including items such as unusual grading, drainage structures, retaining walls, fence, railings, and accessory structures.)

Rough Grading Only

LANDSCAPING, PLANTING, AND FINISH GRADING: By Owner
Topsoil _____ " thick: ☐ front yard; ☐ side yards; ☐ rear yard to _____ feet behind main building.
Lawns *(seeded, sodded, or sprigged)*: ☐ front yard _____ ; ☐ side yards _____ ; ☐ rear yard _____
Planting: ☐ as specified and shown on drawings; ☐ as follows:
_____ Shade trees, deciduous, _____ " caliper.   _____ Evergreen trees. _____ ' to _____ ', B & B.
_____ Low flowering trees, deciduous, _____ ' to _____ '   _____ Evergreen shrubs. _____ ' to _____ ', B & B.
_____ High-growing shrubs, deciduous, _____ ' to _____ '   _____ Vines, 2-year _____
_____ Medium-growing shrubs, deciduous, _____ ' to _____ '   _____
_____ Low-growing shrubs, deciduous, _____ ' to _____ '   _____

IDENTIFICATION.—This exhibit shall be identified by the signature of the builder, or sponsor, and/or the proposed mortgagor if the latter is known at the time of application.

Date_____   Signature _____

                                           Signature _____

DESCRIPTION OF MATERIALS
HUD-92005 (6-79)
VA Form 26-1852, Form FmHA 424-2

any disputes, plus what constitutes the acceptance and occupancy by the owners. It further provides a schedule by which the builder is paid, and describes contractor warranties.

When it comes to your contract, you should slowly review each section with the builder and question anything that isn't crystal clear.

INSURANCE AND WARRANTIES

The contractor probably carries general liability and completed operations insurance. Certainly, if you're working with a relatively new contractor, ask to see his insurance certificates to be safe.

Your contractor might also claim that he'll take care of the insurance—all of it—during the early stages of construction. Even if he means well, consider that the contractor's insurance is purchased specifically with the contractor's best interest in mind, not that of the homeowner's.

It's a good idea to obtain your own homeowners policy before the ground is broken. That will make for an overall combination of the contractor's insurance, and yours. His policy might only cover mistakes that he or his subcontractors might make, plus general liability—but not accidental damage that could occur to the house at any stage of construction. Conversely, your homeowners policy will probably not cover any contractor errors. His insurance will enable him to make repairs if they're needed because his workers, or a subcontractor he hires, make errors resulting in a sunken footer, a collapsed basement wall, or a faulty roof. Your homeowners policy will likely cover only hazards and accidents.

For the relatively inexpensive cost of protection, it's best to watch out for your own interests from the very start.

Warranties are another important consideration. Few houses are constructed perfectly. No matter how good or conscientious the builder is, small problems will inevitably occur, such as sticking doors, a defective appliance, a crack in the basement floor or driveway, or even a minor settling of a wall. Many builders will fix practically anything, no questions asked, some within time periods far beyond that outlined in the original warranty. Others will make the owners work (from repeated phone calls to begging) for the repairs, yet still do them begrudgingly. Some contractors turn around and blame the owners for any problems and refuse to honor the warranty on those

INSURANCE

Insurance is something people hate to buy, but can't do without. Ideally, you want as much as you need, but as little as possible. How do you determine which coverage, and how much coverage, is best?

Many people go for years and years paying for homeowners insurance they know practically nothing about. Plus, they rarely, if ever, collect on it.

The best way to inspect a potential homeowner policy is to simply read the entire proposal, including the fine print. In this day and age, it's foolish not to protect yourself against a major loss. The amount of protection you have on your homeowners policy in addition to the basics—theft, fire, and liability—depends on the type of policy you elect. Some policies are more comprehensive than others. Some may cover items such as damage from frozen pipes, electric surges, lightning, and wind-blown trees. Keep in mind that the higher the deductibles— the amounts you have to pay on each claim or accident before the insurance company begins payment—the lower the cost of the premiums.

■ **Homeowner's Policy.** A homeowners policy is a package of theft, fire, and liability coverages. It should be reviewed annually because inflation, rising property values, and additional possessions you may have purchased will gradually add to your property's total value. Unless your policy has a built-in factor for inflation, you should consider raising your coverage to keep pace with the value of your property and possessions.

Here are a number of ways you can cut homeowner insurance expenses:

— If your home is protected by approved fire or burglar alarm systems you may be eligible for a 5 to 10 percent discount, depending on whether the system automatically notifies the fire or police department.

— Newer homes sometimes qualify for discounts up to 16 percent of the total homeowners insurance cost. Make sure your agent gives you the company's new-home rate.

— Using the same insurance company for auto, life, and homeowners may save between 2 and 15 percent of the total cost.

— Consider going with higher deductibles. Again, as a rule of thumb, the higher the deductible, the lower the premium.

- **Fire Insurance.** Fire insurance is just that. But besides covering full damages from fire and lightning, it should also cover miscellaneous related hazards such as water damage and vandalism.

- **Liability Insurance.** The ice-cream vendor slips on a patch of ice on your porch, and decides to sue you. Under personal liability insurance, you are insured for up to a set amount of dollars if a visitor such as the ice-cream vendor falls down your front steps, slips on your sidewalk, or is bitten by your dog. It also covers certain medical expenses if you or a member of your family accidentally injure someone or damages someone else's property.

- **Property Insurance.** Property insurance is generally extended coverage against loss or damage to your property. It doesn't include personal liability. Property insurance can cover some of a home's contents, including furniture, clothing, appliances, books, electronics, and appliances. Additional supplements, floaters, or riders can be purchased to cover artwork, cameras, furs, jewelry, musical instruments, silverware, sports equipment, stamp and coin collections, and other valuable possessions. Keep in mind when applying for a floater policy to establish how much it would cost to replace the items you are having insured, not simply how much you originally paid for them.

It's a good idea to make a list of possessions. Take an inventory of all appliances, pieces of furniture, and other items of value. Photographs are an excellent way to catalog your home's contents. Once you've made an inventory, put it in a safe place such as a bank deposit box or a fireproof container. Revise the inventory whenever you make significant changes. Most insurance companies have checklists or booklets to help prepare your inventory.

- **Burglary and Theft Insurance.** This insures property against theft. Some policies include an off-premises clause that's active against theft of your possessions that may occur anywhere in the world.

grounds—when they can get away with it. Of course, the vanishing builder is nowhere to be found to be made aware of his mistakes.

All new houses carry an "implied warranty of habitability," which forces builders to repair major construction defects such as a caved-in basement. But smaller problems, especially after the standard warranty period of one year, can leave homeowners with no alternative but to make repairs themselves and eat the costs. Although an owner has little recourse for the small problems after the first year is up, there is an alternative for major defects.

See if your builder can subscribe to any home warranty programs initiated by a Home Builders Association in your area. If so, new home warranties can be extended to up to 10 years of protection. The builder typically pays a single one-time premium that's passed along to the home buyer in the dwelling's cost. But the major house structure, the potentially dehabilitating plumbing, heating, cooling, and electrical systems, plus the general workmanship and materials are protected.

If for some reason the builder can't or doesn't follow through on repairs, the home warranty will cover their expenses after a relatively small deductible is paid by the owners. Warranties available from your builder or other individuals and institutions should be thoroughly researched and considered before the contract is completed.

AFTER THE CONTRACT IS SIGNED

After the contract is signed, it's time for the house construction to begin. Between that time and the date of completion, you'll be locked into a unique and, you hope, satisfying relationship with the general contractor, or if it's a large construction company, with whichever individual is responsible for supervising the construction.

Naturally, in this relationship, like any, there are things you should do and things you shouldn't. While you want to become involved enough to let the contractor know that you understand the building process and are aware of the progress he is making, you don't want to become an impedance to that progress. You don't want to irritate him by making unreasonable demands or by asking too much of his time. Certainly, you don't want to make him angry with you.

To keep the relationship on the up and up, here are a few suggestions that have worked for other home buyers in the past and are likely to work for you as well.

Keep Communications Honest, Open, and Current

The most critical part of your relationship is to keep the lines of communication honest, open, and current. Yes, the builder should return your calls . . . eventually. To say "promptly" is probably asking too much. On the other hand, you shouldn't have to trap him to get his attention. Builders, however, are notoriously hard to pin down. They *are* busy, especially during times when construction is booming, and especially if they're any good. In fact, if they call you right back, something's probably amiss. Maybe it's written somewhere, in secret oath, that one irritating characteristic of a master builder is his delinquency in getting back to you. But, and here is how he differs from the vanishing or marginal builder who never calls back, once the good builder does return your call, he gives you his full attention (undoubtedly irritating some other customer who is waiting for a call back) and will usually go way beyond what could be expected as a normal response to your concerns, or he'll explain to you in depth just why it is that you're wrong.

You want the builder to treat you honestly and fairly. If he makes a mistake, he should tell you about it, then stand by his work until the error is corrected. And he expects the same from you. Sure, it's kind of a biblical attitude: treat others as you would have them treat you . . . but it works. So, be honest and above board. Don't sandbag. If something looks wrong, don't wait until the entire house is completed before bringing it to the builder's attention. If you do, more complications will invariably result because the builder didn't repair the error shortly after it occurred. In fact, bring up concerns as soon as you have them. This also shows the builder that you've prepared yourself to intelligently discuss the ongoing construction with him. You don't want to relinquish all control.

Try not to be at the site just anytime. Instead, time your visits to coincide with important steps of the building process that you'd like to watch to make sure that no skimping is done, and so you'll understand fully what was done, for future reference. For example, good times to be there are when the foundation is being poured over the reinforcement rods, or when some of the wall insulation is going up, or when the first layer of roofing is being laid.

If you have a complaint, don't stand on the job site and argue with the builder in front of his crews. Motion him off to the side or call him by phone later and explain why you have misgivings and then give him a reasonable amount of time to correct the situation if he was wrong.

Contractors almost always take care of minor, irritating problems, at the very least because they'd rather have a satisfied customer than a person bad-mouthing them throughout the neighborhood. Satisfied homeowners can be used as references to develop more business.

Don't Try to Get Extras from the Contractor

You should decide exactly what you want *before* the contractor begins construction. But if you must make a change along the way—and a *few* minor changes are often made with little fuss by the contractor—tell him as soon as possible. For some people, the temptation to make one change after another becomes an obsession. Could the builder make the family room a few feet longer? Maybe. Maybe not. Perhaps there isn't enough room at the side of the house to extend any closer to an adjacent lot. Perhaps the house would then require different roof trusses than the ones already delivered. Could the builder install a bay window in the living room, now that you've just received a surprise income tax refund? Or, since the contract, you have decided not to have any more children and would the builder make the original four bedrooms into three? Can a shower stall be put in the basement? It would only take a few more lengths of pipe and a floor drain . . . .

Those kinds of changes, when insisted upon, especially when requested at a middle or last stage of construction, and especially when one change is piled atop one another, have ruined many a healthy relationship between builder and owner. To avoid such conflicts of interest, try to make all of your changes before the construction starts, or at least keep the changes to a bare minimum and make them as early as possible after the construction begins—plus be prepared to reimburse the contractor for any additional costs incurred because of those changes.

Empathize with the Builder

He has his problems: people not showing up for work, the weather, suppliers running out of materials or sending the wrong things, subcontractors making mistakes that the builder takes the blame for. Try to see things from his point of view, too.

Keep a Friendly Eye on the Work

Don't do it in a hypercritical way. While on the site, jot down questions or concerns for later discussion with the builder. The construction of a house is an interesting process, and you should watch a good deal of it simply to understand how it's put together in case you ever want to modify any part of it or effect major repairs. If you know what went into the house, no one can buffalo you later on as to what's there, and where.

Your main reason for keeping tabs on the construction shouldn't be as watchdog—although you can't help appearing a little like one—but as a student, because you've already guaranteed yourself a good builder and good workmanship by virtue of your initial contractor selection.

Be Friendly and Tactful, Yet Firm

You want to foster an amiable relationship so you wouldn't be afraid to use the same contractor to build another house, should you ever want one. To that effect, you should treat him with the same courtesy you'd treat a good friend or relative. However, do remember that you're picking up the tab; you're paying for everything—the supplies, the labor, the contractor's overhead, and a fair profit all come out of your pocket. Be friendly and tactful, yet firm, and the contractor will respect you for it.

These pointers should help you develop a solid working relationship with your builder. But remember, your builder has seen a lot of customers, a lot of problems, and a lot of crazy situations while in the business. As a group, builders know customer psychology, having seen many more customers than you've seen builders. Many contractors who probably follow a list of their *own* pointers (i.e., listen to whatever the customer says, then build it your own way) are experts at convincing you to see things their way.

An example of this occurred when one particularly taciturn builder, a man of few words yet a master at his craft, was called upon by an owner who was considering knocking out a bedroom wall to expand the sleeping space into an adjacent living room. The builder knew from past dealings with the owners that the husband would be continuously wondering if such a modification would be the right thing to do.

After listening to what the couple wanted done, and agreeing it was a smart move to make, the builder slowly got up and sidled over to the plaster wall in question. He leaned against the wall near a framed oil painting and asked the seated owners if they were sure they wanted the job done. The owner looked at his wife and uttered a tenuous yes. Then the builder, in fluid motion, lifted his steel claw hammer from his belt and smashed a hole in the wall the size of his fist, right then and there, in front of the startled owners.

After the shock wore off, the owners realized why he had done it. The builder's action left little room for them to change their minds overnight, and also took some of the worry out of the very decision itself.

They *had* to do something to fix the hole.

>>>>> **POINTS TO PONDER**

1. Have a written agreement, contract, or "blueprint" for the expected work agreed upon by you and your contractor, before any actual work takes place.
2. Read and understand all sections and items in the agreement before signing it.
3. Make sure your contractor's insurance covers mistakes the contractor and his or her subcontractors might make.
4. Obtain your own homeowners policy to cover accidental damages that could occur to the house at any stage of construction.
5. Keep lines of communications with the contractor honest, open, and current.
6. Don't expect or try to get extras or freebies from the contractor.
7. Empathize with your builder. Don't jump to conclusions if there are problems; get the whole story before making judgment calls. Be reasonable. Recognize problems that may not be within the contractor's control, and participate in a positive manner, with their resolution.
8. Keep a friendly eye on the work; don't smother the contractor with your presence, and refrain from nagging.
9. On the other hand, be friendly and tactful, yet firm. Insist that you get what was agreed upon. Nothing less.
10. Once the home is completed, don't be a stranger. If you're satisfied, let the builder know that you appreciate his efforts. It pays to keep in touch.

Moving In

This is where the results of all your preparations pay off. This is where you set up your maintenance program, you go through the final inspection, and at long last...you move in!

Setting Up Your Maintenance Program

It's best to set up a maintenance program before the contractors leave and before the final inspection. After all, why wait until all of the contractors are gone? This way the house and its components are still fresh in the builders' and subcontractors' minds, and you can readily get all the information you need to customize a schedule and checklists for your particular house and equipment.

What better time to record the serial numbers, to file away the instruction manuals, purchase receipts, and pertinent information such as the installers' phone numbers and manufacturers' spare parts lists? And after you plan your maintenance program, while in the first part of the final inspection with your builder, pretend it's your first maintenance inspection and draw what feedback you can from him about what you're inspecting for.

FOCUS

RECORD KEEPING

Part of any good maintenance program is accurate record keeping. Keeping records will tell when inspections were last done and when they're due again. Records include pertinent backup such as appliance operating manuals, parts lists, servicing and repair histories, warranty and cost information, plus vendor names, phone numbers, and addresses.

Some problems will occur so infrequently that you'll need to jog your memory as to a solution. What did you do the last time the flame in your clothes dryer went out? Was that three years ago when you installed that new water heater, or five? Is it still covered by the warranty? And where is the warranty? Did you throw it out with your old high school papers? Or was it in with the boxful of papers you kept in the garage—the boxful of papers the field mice chewed to smithereens when they constructed their nest in it last winter.

Reasons to develop good record-keeping habits are many. The most important are as follows:

1. For your convenience. It's much more convenient to keep everything together in a house file: with your new home, that means all the documents you obtain from the builder, plus all of the written information you accumulate after taking over. Exactly how you organize the material is nowhere near as important as the fact that all house-construction/ownership/maintenance-related materials can be found in the same place.

2. For your income taxes. You never know when your home could turn into investment property. What if you decide to sell, but nobody wants to buy? So you rent your home for a summer, and make other living arrangements for yourself. A year passes. The renters renew their lease and suddenly you drop the idea of selling and plan instead to handle it as a long-term rental income property. Once that happens, you need to track capital or long-range improvements you make in the property. And maintenance expenditures become tax deductible. Even if you never rent your home, it's still a sound idea to keep track of all home-related costs. It will help you budget for future expenses, and you can better plan repair jobs when needed.

4. To save money. If your builder or contractor needs to be approached about warranty work, it's important to have organized information to fall back on. Most problems are usually taken care of by reputable construction or repair companies. If a nonroutine situation comes up, you should follow certain procedures to have something corrected:

   ■ Check if the problem is covered under the builder or contractor warranty.

■ Identify the exact nature of the problem in a letter to the builder or contractor. Include your name, address, and work phone number. Type the letter if possible. Typed letters are considered to be more official. They get faster and more serious results. Make the letter brief and to the point, but include all relevant details. State exactly what you want done, and how soon you expect the problem to be resolved. Be reasonable. Don't ask for anything beyond what's in the warranty. Include copies of all documents regarding the problem. Keep a copy of the letter for your records. If you have an insured warranty, send a copy of your letter to the warranty company as well as to the builder or contractor.

Having readily accessible home documents and records can make life much easier. If you already have a house file, a cold February day is the time to update it.

Years ago, there wasn't the common expectation of maintenance-free houses as there is today. Sure, it has a lot to do with modern materials and improved manufacturing processes, but also, people today want to spend less time being caretakers to their belongings, houses included, and more time pursuing career and leisure activities. People no longer want to spend a month of their summer scraping and painting a house from foundation to weathervane. They don't want to varnish a porch every year. Or to reseal and caulk windows every fall. Instead, everyone wants trouble-free houses, and for the most part we have them. In fact, compare a drive down a new subdivision street with another ride down a block of older dwellings. There, many of the 60- and 70-year-old houses stand, grouped together on narrow lots, with narrow driveways, tiny front yards, and big porches that are chipped and peeling.

Nowadays, aluminum, vinyl, and a host of other weather- and time-beating materials are standard fare.

However, even though you go to great lengths to obtain the most advanced, efficient, maintenance-free components available for your new home, it doesn't mean you can just live there trouble-free without caring for the place. While there aren't as many ways for a house to deteriorate as there were in previous years, some maintenance inspections and fine-tuning are in order to prevent long-range problems from developing.

Several valid reasons for preventive maintenance exist. Just as people should schedule themselves a physical examination every so often to detect and take care of potential health problems before they can turn into serious conditions with catastrophic results, so should the major components of a house be inspected, to identify and take care of conditions that could lead to serious failures. More specifically, here are the main reasons for preventive maintenance:

1. To prevent failures at inopportune times that could result in safety hazards, such as improper wiring, a malfunctioning furnace or water heater, or a plugged fireplace flue.

2. To allow you to make repairs at your convenience, instead of on an emergency basis.

3. To prevent minor failures that are inexpensive and simple to correct from becoming complex, expensive repairs.

4. To make sure your house is a safe and comfortable place to live in.

5. To maintain your house's value and ensure your pride of ownership.

6. To avoid the expense of a breakdown and repair on a holiday or weekend.

Components in a house seldom fail suddenly. There are usually warning signs. If you know what to watch for and act when you see danger, life on the home front will be easier and much less expensive. The smart homeowner is the one who knows his or her house intimately and who routinely follows a checklist of inspections to make sure no problems are developing. To do this, you should understand the construction and the operation of all appliances and major pieces of equipment. You should know where things are, even hidden items such as septic tanks, wells, sewer lines, and other underground utilities. You should know what the builder and manufacturer guarantees and warranties cover, and what your homeowners insurance is all about.

Preventive maintenance is the idea that you lessen the likelihood of major damages by repairing minor problems. But to repair or even prevent the minor problems, you need to be aware of what they are and where to look for them.

It's a known fact that most breakdowns you're going to encounter will be small ones—many of which you can probably repair or learn to repair yourself. You won't have to worry about replacing washers in a washerless faucet, but you still must contend with items such as plugged drains, cracking asphalt or concrete driveways, sticky windows, and worn-out blower belts on furnaces. Preventive maintenance can't guarantee that breakdowns will never occur, and it won't even prevent surprise failures; but it *will* minimize the time, effort, and money you'll spend on major repairs.

Yes, there's something nice about knowing that your house is in top shape. It instills a feeling of confidence. The proof is reflected in a house's condition. Find a rundown, shoddy-looking house that's not too old, and chances are it got that way through a lack of maintenance—a cumulative deterioration that starts out slowly, almost imperceptibly, but gains momentum once it negotiates past the "maintenance-free" characteristics of new materials as the seasons roll by and each tiny problem mushrooms into others.

SAVING MONEY ON SERVICE CALLS

Planning preventive maintenance in advance gives you time to anticipate what's needed to perform the tasks, and lets you make the best schedule possible for your time and pocketbook. Many homeowners will do this hit or miss, counting that their everyday movements throughout the house will reveal anything that's obviously failing or failed, without having to go out of their way to perform specific inspections.

When something does need attention there's always the question "Who should do the work?" The days of old-fashioned handymen who could fix anything for a song are disappearing. Instead we have armies of specialists: plumbers for plumbing, roofers for roofs, electricians for electrical repairs, and septic people for sewage systems. Naturally, homeowners must not only pay for their time, but for their training and expertise as well; the same person who comes to your house to fix a leaking pipe can easily be an individual qualified to lay out the plumbing for an entire high-rise apartment building. There's no doubt about it: service calls are expensive.

Whenever possible, you can save money by learning how to do the most basic maintenance and repairs. Even if you never want to lay a finger on a furnace or hot water tank, it's worth it just to learn about their operations. Then, when you must call a professional, you can

FINDING A GOOD HANDYPERSON

Notice the difference in terminology here? In previous chapters, we *selected* contractors from individuals and companies known to the open market. In this case we're *looking* for someone special, someone who most likely is already part of an underground network of "informal" or unofficial contractors. We're trying to find a jack-of-many-trades who can tackle a wide variety of jobs around the house: replacing a screen door, painting and caulking the bathrooms, painting the inside of your garage, and so on.

Such a person should be

■ Even-tempered.

■ Reliable.

■ Qualified for what he or she does, and will accept only work that he or she can safely and correctly complete.

■ Able to do or arrange for the entire job.

■ Able to get help when needed.

■ Doing it not only for additional or supplemental income, but also for the love of the work. Be wary of "informal" contractors or handypersons who are trying to support a family solely through their moonlighting efforts.

Where can such a person be found? You've got to ask around. Inquire of friends, coworkers, and casual acquaintances. Who do they use? Finding a good handyperson is part luck and part persistence. It's not easy, but the effort will pay off if successful.

You'll save a great deal of money, time, and aggravation over the years if you find a good handyperson that will help you with routine and emergency jobs. Often he or she, though not able to tackle a particular task, will come up with options and provide help deciding which avenue is best.

Unfortunately, good handypersons are a dying breed. Most maintenance people these days are specialists. Plumbing. Electrical. Concrete. Roofs. Framing.

If you find a good general, all-seasons handyperson, a person who's available at practically any time, who does quality work at reasonable cost, who cleans up after every job, who has a way of suggesting the best of all possible solutions, and who has a wealth of household repair knowledge, treat him or her well. In return, you'll get peace of mind, slimmer repair outlays, and an ongoing friendship that's frequently lacking with many homeowner-contractor relationships.

When more specialized help is needed—for putting in a new driveway or a patio, for example—an alternative to hiring a large concrete or paving contractor is to ask a person who works in a plant or organization that frequently uses the services of paving contractors if any paving contractor employees do driveways or patios on the side. Often the same skilled labor available through higher-priced companies can be obtained at considerably less cost on weekends and during evening hours for anyone who learns how to make the contacts and arrangements.

Are there disadvantages to having "unofficial" contractors and handypersons do work for you? There could be. Handypersons are typically not insured as legitimate contractor businesses, so if damages or injuries occur as a result of their work, major problems could result. Will your homeowners insurance policy be adequate if an injury occurs? Like anything, you've got to weigh the risks. There are excellent handypersons who have been moonlighting their services for years—with nary a problem. But that's why homework on finding a safe, reliable, knowledgeable, and skilled handyperson is so important. As a general guideline, avoid "handyperson contracting" for electrical, plumbing, roofing, and structural work.

Also, make sure you work within the maintenance and repair guidelines given by manufacturers' warranties. If you have a handyperson perform "unauthorized" services, even if the services are correct, they could void the remaining portion of a warranty.

accurately describe the problem so the serviceperson can bring the right tools and materials and won't waste any time once arriving at your house. In fact, a serviceperson might even be able to tell you what to do over the phone.

The largest part of the typical service call bill usually consists of labor. And in most cases, the time spent just getting to and from your house makes up the lion's share of that. The trick is to get as much efficiency out of a call as possible. Do that by finding several other jobs that can be done by the same serviceperson on the same service call. That's why it's important for you to know what kind of shape your equipment is in, and what can be inspected, adjusted, and serviced. Then, when you call a plumber to fix a leaky pipe, he can also service the sump pump and inspect the hot water tank.

If your preventive maintenance is good enough, you should be able to keep the servicepersons away from weekends, late-evening hours, and holidays—all time for which you must pay premiums.

Line up qualified servicepersons *before* you need them, so you'll know who to call without blindly paging through the phone book. Keep away from repairmen who have the same characteristics as vanishing builders.

POTENTIAL TROUBLE SPOTS

For the record, here are most of the items in a typical house that need preventive maintenance inspections and attention.

Heating and Cooling Systems

Poorly maintained, defective heating and cooling units produce less warmth and coolness for the money and cost substantially more to operate. A more important consideration for the heating unit is that one not working properly can be extremely hazardous, with fire and asphyxiation two possibilities.

Many homeowners take both heating and cooling systems for granted until the systems quit working, the former most likely at the front end of a New Year three-day holiday weekend, and the latter in the middle of a Death-Valley-like heatwave.

FUEL BURNERS

Have pilot lights and burners cleaned and adjusted for safety and efficiency by qualified servicepersons. This is the stage at which fuel is consumed. A small or yellow flame at the pilot indicates that either the pressure regulator needs adjustment or that the pilot burner is dirty. Oil burners need more frequent attention than gas burners because oil does not burn as cleanly, but even the most modern gas models can still benefit from yearly inspections and adjustments.

FURNACES

Forced-air furnaces are reliable workhorses that need to have their filters cleaned or changed at least once per month when in use.

Otherwise, a dirty, clogged filter can reduce the efficiency of heat output by as much as 70 percent and will cause the entire heating unit to overexert itself trying to reach a 68-degree thermostat setting when outside temperatures plummet below freezing. The air that passes through the filter is cool air drawn from the inside of the house. After being filtered clean, it gets warmed by the fuel burner flame, then blown back into the house through ducts and registers. Naturally, if you live in a dusty environment or own a long-haired pet, you'll have to clean or replace air filters more frequently than if you lived in a cleaner area and didn't own a pet.

Most furnaces now are direct drive. If your furnace is belt driven, check the condition of the belt (adjust/replace if needed).

A qualified serviceperson should inspect the furnace yearly.

Some of the blower motor and fan assemblies have permanently lubricated bearings, while other bearings should be oiled before each heating season begins and periodically throughout the fall and winter months.

HUMIDIFIERS

If your furnace has a humidifier, it should be checked annually. Change the water panel; make sure the unit is receiving water through its system and discharging excess water out the drain line.

BOILERS

Boilers are expensive and somewhat temperamental heating units, especially if their operating conditions are allowed to vary from those suggested by the manufacturer. Read the instructions and maintenance literature carefully and have boilers inspected by a professional before each heating season, then do it by yourself at least once per month during the rest of the cold months while the boiler is in use. There should be a low-water emergency cutoff that will prevent the boiler from operating in case not enough water gets into the boiler for it to run safely. The low-water cutoff should have water drained through it—to expel any rust or corrosion that might settle there and plug the line (follow the manufacturers' instructions).

If pockets of air form in the pipes, radiators, and baseboards of hot water systems, they must be bled or released so the hot water can freely circulate.

OTHERS

Although electric heating systems have traditionally been some of the most expensive to operate because of the cost of "heating" electricity when compared to the cost of heating with natural gas or oil, they're practically maintenance-free. About all that's needed is to periodically vacuum dust and dirt from the heater and heating coils.

Solar and other alternative heating sources should be inspected and maintained as recommended by the manufacturers. With all equipment, be aware of where emergency shutoff valves and switches are, and how to restart a system if needed. Ask the serviceperson what maintenance you should be doing between service calls, and how you can confirm that everything is working safely and efficiently.

Plumbing

Naturally, the most obvious conditions to inspect plumbing for are leaky pipes and fixtures. You should know quickly if a leak develops by observing a puddle nearby or water dripping from ceilings or stained walls. For the most part, plumbing systems are reliable, with only a few points to keep in mind.

If outside temperatures approach freezing, shut off valves to outside connections and faucets. These shutoff valves should be located inside the house, close to where the pipe goes through an outside wall. When the inside shutoffs are closed, then open the outside fixtures to let any standing water drain from those outside pipes and fixtures.

Every few months remove a gallon or so of water from the drain valve at the bottom of your hot water tank. Along with this expelled water will be any rust, sediments, and mineral deposits that settle on the tank bottom and hinder the efficiency of heat transfer.

Septic tanks should be examined professionally once a year to determine if pumping and cleaning is needed. If services are in order, you won't want to undertake them yourself. They're for specialists with equipment designed to handle such unpleasant tasks.

Sump pumps and well pumps should also be serviced as noted in their instruction manuals. If they're rarely used, put them into service several times per year to make sure they'll work when needed.

Floor drains in the garage and basement should be tested at least twice per year to make sure they'll work in case needed during an emergency. Just lift their covers and stick a running hose down them.

If mud or debris has accumulated beneath the grate cover, shovel it out first.

Fireplaces and Stoves

In this modern age it isn't surprising that most people who use woodburning equipment have had little, if any, practical experience heating with wood. Consequently, a sizeable number of fires occur each year due to faulty installation, misuse, and lack of proper maintenance of fireplaces and stoves. Most fires are caused by one or more of heat radiation from the stove, stovepipe, or chimney igniting adjacent combustible materials; sparks escaping into the house; sparks from the chimney top; flames catching on creosote accumulation in the chimney flue. (Creosote is a dark, sticky, resin-like material formed by unburned chemicals that are borne by smoke up the chimney flue. They coat the inside of the flue and create the danger of chimney or flue fires.)

Before each heating season make sure that the chimney flue is not partially obstructed with bird or squirrel nests, beehives, a fallen branch, or a child's softball. And see that the dampers are in good working order. Remove any ashes and debris from the ash pit, and if the flue is thick with creosote and ash, have it cleaned.

Central Air-Conditioning

With air-conditioning it's filters, filters, filters. Dirty filters can really block the output of cool air and will greatly increase the effort and length of time needed to cool a house. If air-conditioning filters are too dirty or clogged to see the beam from a flashlight through, it's time to clean or replace them.

It's also necessary to check the air conditioner's outside condenser. Keep condenser vents free of vines, leaves, mud, grass, and any other encroaching materials that hinder air circulation. Keep drainage tubes clear.

When it's time to stop using air-conditioning for the year, remove dust and dirt from each unit with a vacuum cleaner and securely cover the exterior housings until the next cooling season begins.

Electrical Systems

The wiring installed in most modern homes is largely trouble-free. Circuit-breaker boxes are included as safety valves. If a circuit breaker trips because too much demand is placed on that part of the wiring from too many appliances plugged in at once, or from operating a defective appliance, just follow the resetting instructions on the panel—usually you flip the circuit-breaker switch back on. Of course, the cause of a tripped circuit should be identified and corrected.

Even if your breakers never trip for any reason, it's a good idea to manually trip them a few times per year to make sure they're operable and the contacts are in working order.

Also, whenever power is lost to the entire house, as during a lightning or ice storm, there can be high-voltage surges that burst through the house wiring that can damage plugged-in appliances and equipment such as stereos and personal computers. During violent storms, it's best to unplug as many appliances as possible.

Roofs

As mentioned earlier, roofs take a beating—from rain, sleet, hail, wind, sun, and alternate freezing and thawing temperatures.

Even if no inside water marks or leaks are noticed, you should still periodically take a pair of binoculars, and depending on the roof's pitch, inspect the entire surface from either the ground nearby or from the second-story windows of neighbors' homes. Look for bent, ripped, or missing shingles, and for metal flashing that's warped, torn loose by the wind, or rusting and corroding.

If a leak does develop, consider that the actual damage might be a substantial distance away from where the water is dripping. If you decide to take care of your own minor repairs, fine. But be careful. Never venture out on a roof when it's wet, or during winter when the shingles are frozen and ice-laden. If ice dams occur on the roof due to constant melting snow running to the roof edges where it keeps freezing and accumulating, and water eventually backs up under the shingles and seeps through the roof into the house, it's a sign that too much heat is escaping near the roof's peak. The outer surface of the roof, even near the peak, should be kept cold during winter by the use of proper insulation above ceilings and by the installation of adequate roof ventilation.

Gutters and Downspouts

Gutters and downspouts absorb much of the same abuse as roofs do, mostly from the elements. Periodically remove collected debris such as twigs, leaves, acorns, and dirt from gutters and downspouts, then flush clean with water. Observe the gutter system while it's raining and check for blockages, leaks, and places where it might be coming loose from the house. Check to see that the water running through the downspouts is flowing away from the house foundation. During winter, don't let large icicles build up and hang on the gutters and downspouts.

Siding and Trim

Few people are aware of just how dirty their siding and trim can get in a year. Weather, dust, soil, and corrosion all conspire to destroy that "new house look" and insidiously damage outer surfaces, causing these materials to wear out far sooner than expected. It's hard to tell, however, because everything gets dirty at the same rate.

To keep your siding and trim in good shape, choose a nice summer day, hop into your bathing suit, get your garden hose and a soft brush attached to an extension handle, fill a pail with mild detergent water (as specified by the siding manufacturer), and go to town. Depending on your house type, you might also need a long ladder.

Doors and Windows

Here, as with many parts of a modern house, maintenance has radically changed for the better from what it was years ago—an unending scenario of scraping, painting, varnishing, de-warping, unsticking wooden doors and window sashes, sills, and frames, and playing with rotten ropes and pulleys from heavy window weights. Today's doors and windows barely need wiping with a damp cloth.

Basement windows are the most notable exceptions. You still have to keep their outside wells or excavations free of leaves, weeds, and rotting grass, and make sure water doesn't collect and rise above the window bottoms. In areas where heavy snowfalls occur, consider using plastic covers designed for protecting basement window wells. Periodically inspect these window frames and sills for rust if metal, and decay if wood.

Wood Porches and Decks

If you used high-quality, pressure-treated wood, you're practically home free. It's a good idea to reseal it once per year, and beyond that, just watch out for and correct cracked boards, or boards that have come loose from walls, foundations, or steps. If you haven't used pressure-treated wood, stock up on paintbrushes and lots of paint or varnish. And keep some funds available to replace rotting boards as needed.

Mildew

Mildew is simply a mold, and mold is a fungus of some type. Mold spores are practically everywhere, borne in the air, and need only a cool or warm, moist environment to flourish. Mildew is not only irritating, it's harmful. It can ruin furniture, furnishings, walls, ceilings, and can even present a health problem to the occupants. It's especially persistent in leaky, damp basements, but will readily occur during periods of high humidity, when water vapor present in warm air condenses on the cool surfaces of walls, floors, pipes, and other items that can provide perfect breeding grounds for fungi.

To combat mildew, merely increase the air circulation. Don't place rubber-backed carpets on basement floors. Keep furniture away from walls where air circulation could be blocked, and operate dehumidifiers around the clock during humid summer months. Small fans will help in cramped locations. Mildew in an attic is a sure sign that ventilation there should be improved.

Asphalt

This material might seem tough, and it is . . . kind of. It'll support your car nicely, and even a large boat and trailer, but it can gradually be ruined by a combination of frost damage, oil and gasoline residues, and road salt drippings.

Whenever asphalt loses its original dark black sheen and begins drying out, developing small cracks and fissures, and starts absorbing oil and gasoline that spills onto its surface, it's time for maintenance. To be safe, inspect blacktop every year, during warm weather. Any cracks, holes, or broken edges should be repaired with blacktop patching compound. This will prevent water from running beneath the pavement and undermining the asphalt. It's particularly critical in cold-climate areas where freezing water can "frost wedge," lift, and crack blacktop to bits.

After the patching is complete a coat of blacktop sealer should be brushed or broomed over the surface to form a protective coating that will repel water, oil, and gasoline. The sealer also fills cracks that are too small to be repaired with the patching material.

Concrete and Masonry

Concrete and masonry surfaces are substantially more durable than asphalt *if* cracks are repaired when they occur and are not allowed to go untouched through periods of freezing and thawing temperatures. With concrete driveways and walks, to prevent water penetration and frost wedging, large cracks should be filled with concrete patching material that you can mix yourself. Small cracks can be caulked.

If a flaking problem exists, it may be due to poor-quality concrete or the harsh effects of rock salt or other chemical snow and ice melters. Brush and clean the surface, preferably with a solution of muriatic acid (be sure to read the directions and safety precautions), then apply a plastic cement surface material available at hardware and builders supply stores.

Oil and grease stains on concrete can be removed with a degreaser. A variety of spray degreasers can be found in auto supply stores. Simply spray the material on the stains, wait 15 minutes or so, then hose it off. If you're wondering why all the fuss over a black stain here and there—it's for safety, because an oil stain can cause slips and falls, especially when it gets wet. And it's also for aesthetics, for looks. The nicer the appearance, the greater the value, and the easier it is to keep concrete clean and well maintained.

To prepare for the finishing touch, after all the stains are taken out and the cracks and flaking areas are fixed, the concrete can be cleaned with another diluted solution of muriatic acid. Once this is completed you can put down a protective coating of clear cure-and-seal to get your concrete safely through winter.

Mortar joints in brickwork are likewise susceptible to the elements, and they should be inspected closely, especially any bricks in direct contact with the ground.

Mortar joints between foundation concrete blocks are the weakest part of foundation walls. These joints should be firm and should not crumble when poked with a sharp tool. If the mortar does crumble easily, or if some has cracked and fallen out, the damage should be repaired to prevent water or termite intrusion. If the foundation is made of solid poured concrete, all cracks should be patched or caulked for the same reasons.

FLUE

CHIMNEY CAP

MORTAR JOINTS

FLASHING

FIGURE 34.1

A chimney cap.

Chimney maintenance usually comes under concrete and masonry. The chimney cap is the part of the chimney that extends above the roof. It takes a terrible beating from the elements and deserves annual inspections. The concrete cap at the very top protects the inside of the chimney from water and downdrafts. If this cap cracks (Fig. 34.1), water can seep into the mortar joints along and between the bricks. All cracks should be patched or caulked.

The mortar between the chimney bricks or stones below the concrete top cap should also be inspected and caulked if necessary. The same goes for the flashing where the roof meets the base of the chimney cap.

After all areas are patched or caulked as needed, a coat of clear chimney water-repellent sealer should be brushed over the chimney to protect the whole works from water penetration.

A MAINTENANCE CHECKLIST

Remember that a well-maintained house does not come naturally to most of us. It might be a pain, but it's the best defense against the toll otherwise taken by the elements, nature, and time. Prepare a year-long maintenance schedule based on where you live, the type of house you have, and the equipment that is in it; then try to follow it. Concentrate on exterior repairs and maintenance during the nice weather, then go inside during the colder months. Naturally, a new house won't require much attention, especially at first. And you can keep it that way with regular preventive maintenance schedules and by following through with repairs.

The Final Inspection

A completed house is the complex result of thousands of separate pieces and parts put together by many craftsmen—craftsmen who have their good days and bad. The materials, too, are not always perfect. Consequently, with this or any effort resulting from sundry components and multiple construction steps (an automobile is another example), there are likely to be errors and imperfections in the final product—"bugs" that must be discovered and taken care of. In addition, a house will go through an initial settling and shrinking period, and as it does, plaster can crack, windows can stick, wood steps could start squeaking, or the plumbing could spring a leak.

Before everyone gets together at your closing—when the attorneys, the contractor, and you all sign the final papers so you can receive the deed and house keys, and the contractor any remaining payments— it's a good idea that you schedule what will be the first step of the final inspection of the property. The first step is a meeting at the site between you and the contractor or crew chief in charge of the construction. Schedule the meeting at least a week in advance (and don't forget to *remind* the builder a day or two in advance) and ask him to bring along any warranties for major appliances or materials such as a water heater, refrigerator, range, or garage door opener. You should bring any warranties you've already received, and the maintenance file you've been putting together.

At this meeting, resolve any questions you have already jotted down on previous visits, and determine as best you can that what was specified in the contract was actually performed. At the same time, inspect the property for obvious flaws. Ask the contractor what imperfections you can reasonably expect, and get his advice on what to do about them if they actually occur. Who do you report the problems to? How would the most likely problems be solved?

The initial and continuing parts of the final inspection are important because *you* are expected to be the moving force to finding and reporting and making sure steps are taken to correct any imperfections that develop. The lender won't be worried about minor, irritating defects. All they expect is to receive your monthly mortgage check—usually by mail. And even if something major goes wrong, your payments can't be stopped. Rather, they continue like clockwork. The builder, too, can't fix what he doesn't know about. And you can't tell him about problems you don't recognize.

Fortunately, if you've followed the advice presented in the chapters on selecting and working with your contractor, problems that arise will likely be handled quickly and professionally. This is not so likely if you have elected or have been unsuspectedly duped into going with an inept or vanishing builder.

Before the meeting is over, review the warranties that were supplied at the time the building contract was signed, and check to make sure you have copies of all the other applicable warranties. Be certain you know who all of the subcontractors were and exactly who you should call for maintenance and repairs at a later date. Go through your maintenance file with the contractor. Ask him if there's anything else he would add to it, or if he sees any part of it that doesn't look quite right. Find out if there's anything special you should do to "break in" certain components of the house.

Maybe during the initial inspection you'll discover that the builder has forgotten to include something promised. It happens. Or maybe the builder is planning to finish a few items that were not completed in time because of scheduling or weather delays. You want to make sure you'll receive what you contracted for—nothing less. If anything has not been completed, find out what the completion schedule is, and for all but the most minor detail, have the attorneys keep a portion of the builder's final payment in escrow—to be released when the remaining work has been completed.

Make sure you know how to operate all of the appliances, including heating and cooling units, sump pumps, and well pumps. Know also where a septic tank is located, or where the sewer connects to the house.

So, you take an hour or two to go through the house with the builder. That's the first step of the final inspection. The rest of the steps are inspections that you'll be making alone, especially during the first year that you live in the place, or until the builder's warranty period is up, whether it's a single year or longer.

During that year, keep a sharp eye and ear out for the development of small flaws that could become serious problems if not taken care of. Don't be afraid to contact the builder later on, either. Remember, he wants you to be satisfied. It's in his best interest to have you say nice things about him so you can be counted on as a future business reference.

But really, if you've followed a good portion of the proven specifications and ideas in this book, there shouldn't be much need for the builder to come back and redo things. You're likely to have a high-quality home, one that will suit your needs, will hold its value, will require a minimum of upkeep, and will provide you with maximum living comfort, convenience, safety, and privacy.

It's more likely that, after the final checkout period of one year, you can spend most of your free time enjoying your home, knowing you've received the most value for your dollars and efforts, and that you're far ahead of the average person who will just take what's available, or what marginal or vanishing builders offer in floor plan, construction quality, and value (Fig. 35.1).

As a parting note, after your home is checked out fully, about a year after the day you move in, send to the builder—as long as he has taken care of you—a brief note, letter, or call, expressing your appreciation and telling him how much you are enjoying the house, if that's the case.

You might even want to send him a case of beer, a fruit basket, a dinner for two at a classy restaurant, or something you know would be appropriate and safe. You'd be surprised at how few people will *ever*

FIGURE 35.1

Enjoying the home.

call a builder with something nice to say. Instead, builders, even the best builders, hear mostly brickbats and complaints.

Surprise your contractor with a token of appreciation. People in the service industries don't usually get them, no matter how good their services are (especially after the services have been transacted). Such a gesture will keep you in that builder's mind for a long, long time, will likely cement a friendship, and anyway, if he's done a good job for you, it's the right thing to do.

It's just another way for you to lift up the entire housebuilding process from the routine and cap off the entire experience with style.

Note: Boldface numbers indicate illustrations; *t* indicates a table.

ABOUT THE AUTHORS

RICHARD M. SCUTELLA has written several books on new construction, home buying, home maintenance, and safety, including *Homebuyer's Checklist*, Second Edition, and the first three editions of this book. He has designed and supervised the construction of many new homes and is a member of the Handyman Club of America.

DAVE HEBERLE is the author of McGraw-Hill's *Construction Safety Manual,* coauthor of the first three editions of this book, and writer of numerous articles on home-building. A former realtor who has also designed and built homes, he currently consults on environmental safety and health issues.